STATUTORY SUPPL

CASES AND MATERIALS ON EMPLOYMENT DISCRIMINATION AND EMPLOYMENT LAW

Fourth Edition

and

CASES AND MATERIALS ON EMPLOYMENT DISCRIMINATION LAW

Fourth Edition

By

Samuel Estreicher
Dwight D. Opperman Professor of Law
New York University

Michael C. Harper
Barreca Labor Relations Scholar and Professor of Law
Boston University

AMERICAN CASEBOOK SERIES®

THOMSON
━━━★━━━ ™
WEST

Mat #41250015

© West, a Thomson business, 2000, 2004

© 2008 Thomson/West

© 2012 Thomson Reuters
        610 Opperman Drive
        St. Paul, MN 55123
        1–800–313–9378

Printed in the United States of America

ISBN: 978–0–314–28039–8

TEXT IS PRINTED ON 10% POST CONSUMER RECYCLED PAPER

Table of Contents

PART B.   PROTECTING SOCIALLY VALUED ACTIVITY

PART C.   PROTECTING EMPLOYEES FROM ARBITRARY OR INTRUSIVE DECISIONMAKING

PART D. MINIMUM–TERMS LAWS: "FILLING OUT" THE EMPLOYMENT CONTRACT

PART E. ISSUES OF PROCEDURAL DESIGN

STATUTORY SUPPLEMENT TO

CASES AND MATERIALS ON EMPLOYMENT DISCRIMINATION AND EMPLOYMENT LAW

Fourth Edition

and

CASES AND MATERIALS ON EMPLOYMENT DISCRIMINATION LAW

Fourth Edition

Part A

PROTECTING EMPLOYEES FROM STATUS DISCRIMINATION

CONSTITUTION OF THE UNITED STATES

AMENDMENT XI

The Judicial power of the United States shall not be construed to extend to any suit in law or equity, commenced or prosecuted against one of the United States by Citizens of another State, or by Citizens or Subjects of any Foreign State.

AMENDMENT XIII

§ 1. Neither slavery nor involuntary servitude, except as a punishment for crime whereof the party shall have been duly convicted, shall exist within the United States, or any place subject to their jurisdiction.

§ 2. Congress shall have power to enforce this article by appropriate legislation.

AMENDMENT XIV

§ 1. All persons born or naturalized in the United States, and subject to the jurisdiction thereof, are citizens of the United States and of the State wherein they reside. No State shall make or enforce any law which shall abridge the privileges or immunities of citizens of the United States; nor shall any State deprive any person of life, liberty, or property, without due process of law; nor deny to any person within its jurisdiction the equal protection of the laws.

§ 2. Representatives shall be apportioned among the several States according to their respective numbers, counting the whole number of persons in each State, excluding Indians not taxed. But when the right to vote at any election for the choice of electors for President and Vice President of the United States, Representatives in Congress, the Executive and Judicial officers of a State, or the members of the Legislature thereof, is denied to any of the male inhabitants of such State, being twenty-one years of age, and citizens of the United States, or in any way abridged, except for participation in rebellion, or other crime, the basis of representation therein shall be reduced in the proportion which the number of such male citizens shall bear to the whole number of male citizens twenty-one years of age in such State.

§ 3. No person shall be a Senator or Representative in Congress, or elector for President and Vice President, or hold any office, civil or military, under the United States, or under any State, who, having previously taken an oath, as a member of Congress, or as an officer of the United States, or as a member of any State legislature, or as an executive or judicial officer of any State, to support the Constitution of the United States, shall have engaged in insurrection or rebellion against the same, or given aid or comfort to the enemies thereof. But Congress may by a vote of two-thirds of each House, remove such disability.

§ 4.   The validity of the public debt of the United States, authorized by law, including debts incurred for payment of pensions and bounties for services in suppressing insurrection or rebellion, shall not be questioned. But neither the United States nor any State shall assume or pay any debt or obligation incurred in aid of insurrection or rebellion against the United States, or any claim for the loss or emancipation of any slave; but all such debts, obligations and claims shall be held illegal and void.

§ 5.   The Congress shall have power to enforce, by appropriate legislation, the provisions of this article.

POST–CIVIL WAR CIVIL RIGHTS ACTS
42 U.S.C. §§ 1981–83, 1985, 1988*

§ 1981. Equal rights under the law

(a) All persons within the jurisdiction of the United States shall have the same right in every State and Territory to make and enforce contracts, to sue, be parties, give evidence, and to the full and equal benefit of all laws and proceedings for the security of persons and property as is enjoyed by white citizens, and shall be subject to like punishment, pains, penalties, taxes, licenses, and exactions of every kind, and to no other.

(b) *For purposes of this section, the term "make and enforce contracts" includes the making, performance, modification, and termination of contracts, and the enjoyment of all benefits, privileges, terms and conditions of the contractual relationship.*

(c) *The rights protected by this section are protected against impairment by nongovernmental discrimination and impairment under color of State law.*

(R.S. § 1977; Pub.L. 102–166, § 101, Nov. 21, 1991, 105 Stat. 1071.)

§ 1981A. Damages in cases of intentional discrimination in employment

(a) Right of Recovery.

(1) Civil rights. In an action brought by a complaining party under section 706 or 717 of the Civil Rights Act of 1964 (42 U.S.C. 2000e–5) against a respondent who engaged in unlawful intentional discrimination (not an employment practice that is unlawful because of its disparate impact) prohibited under section 703, 704, or 717 of the Act (42 U.S.C. 2000e–2 or 2000e–3), and provided that the complaining party cannot recover under section 1977 of the Revised Statutes (42 U.S.C. 1981), the complaining party may recover compensatory and punitive damages as allowed in subsection (b), in addition to any relief authorized by section 706(g) of the Civil Rights Act of 1964, from the respondent.

(2) Disability. In action brought by a complaining party under the powers, remedies, and procedures set forth in section 706 or 717 of the Civil Rights Act of 1964 (as provided in section 107(a) of the Americans with Disabilities Act of 1990 (42 U.S.C. 12117(a)), and section 505(a)(1) of the Rehabilitation Act of 1973 (29 U.S.C. 794a(a) (1)), respectively) against a respondent who engaged in unlawful intentional discrimination (not an employment practice that is un-

---

* Includes amendments made by the Civil Rights Act of 1991 in italics.

lawful because of its disparate impact) under section 501 of the Rehabilitation Act of 1973 (29 U.S.C. 791) and the regulations implementing section 501, or who violated the requirements of section 501 of the Act or the regulations implementing section 501 concerning the provision of a reasonable accommodation, or section 102 of the Americans with Disabilities Act of 1990 (42 U.S.C. 12112), or committed a violation of section 102(b)(5) of the Act, against an individual, the complaining party may recover compensatory and punitive damages as allowed in subsection (b), in addition to any relief authorized by section 706(g) of the Civil Rights Act of 1964, from the respondent.

(3) Reasonable accommodation and good faith effort. In cases where a discriminatory practice involves the provision of a reasonable accommodation pursuant to section 102(b)(5) of the Americans with Disabilities Act of 1990 or regulations implementing section 501 of the Rehabilitation Act of 1973, damages may not be awarded under this section where the covered entity demonstrates good faith efforts, in consultation with the person with the disability who has informed the covered entity that accommodation is needed, to identify and make a reasonable accommodation that would provide such individual with an equally effective opportunity and would not cause an undue hardship on the operation of the business.

(b) Compensatory and Punitive Damages.

(1) Determination of punitive damages. A complaining party may recover punitive damages under this section against a respondent (other than a government, government agency or political subdivision) if the complaining party demonstrates that the respondent engaged in a discriminatory practice or discriminatory practices with malice or with reckless indifference to the federally protected rights of an aggrieved individual.

(2) Exclusions from compensatory damages. Compensatory damages awarded under this section shall not include backpay, interest on backpay, or any other type of relief authorized under section 706(g) of the Civil Rights Act of 1964.

(3) Limitations. The sum of the amount of compensatory damages awarded under this section for future pecuniary losses, emotional pain, suffering, inconvenience, mental anguish, loss of enjoyment of life, and other nonpecuniary losses, and the amount of punitive damages awarded under this section, shall not exceed, for each complaining party—

(A) in the case of a respondent who has more than 14 and fewer than 101 employees in each of 20 or more calendar weeks in the current or preceding calendar year, $50,000;

(B) in the case of a respondent who has more than 100 and fewer than 201 employees in each of 20 or more calendar weeks in the current or preceding calendar year, $100,000;

(C) in the case of a respondent who has more than 200 and fewer than 501 employees in each of 20 or more calendar weeks in the current or preceding calendar year, $200,000; and

(D) in the case of a respondent who has more than 500 employees in each of 20 or more calendar weeks in the current or preceding calendar year, $300,000.

(4) Construction. Nothing in this section shall be construed to limit the scope of, or the relief available under, section 1977 of the Revised Statutes (42 U.S.C. 1981).

(c) Jury Trial. *If a complaining party seeks compensatory or punitive damages under this section—*

(1) any party may demand a trial by jury; and

(2) the court shall not inform the jury of the limitations described in subsection (b)(3).

(d) Definitions. *As used in this section:*

(1) Complaining party. The term "complaining party" means

(A) in the case of a person seeking to bring an action under subsection (a)(1), the Equal Employment Opportunity Commission, the Attorney General, or a person who may bring an action or proceeding under title VII of the Civil Rights Act of 1964 (42 U.S.C. 2000e et seq.); or

(B) in the case of a person seeking to bring an action under subsection (a)(2), the Equal Employment Opportunity Commission, the Attorney General, a person who may bring an action or proceeding under section 505(a)(1) of the Rehabilitation Act of 1973 (29 U.S.C. 794a(a)(1)), or a person who may bring an action or proceeding under title I of the Americans with Disabilities Act of 1990 (42 U.S.C. 12101 et seq.).

(2) Discriminatory practice. The term "discriminatory practice" means the discrimination described in paragraph (1), or the discrimination or the violation described in paragraph (2), of subsection (a).

(Pub.L. 102–166, § 102, Nov. 21, 1991, 105 Stat. 1071.)

§ 1982. Property rights of citizens

All citizens of the United States shall have the same right, in every State and Territory, as is enjoyed by white citizens thereof to inherit, purchase, lease, sell, hold, and convey real and personal property.

(R.S. § 1978.)

§ 1983. Civil action for deprivation of rights

Every person who, under color of any statute, ordinance, regulation, custom, or usage, of any State or Territory or the District of Columbia, subjects, or causes to be subjected, any citizen of the United States or other person within the jurisdiction thereof to the deprivation of any rights, privileges, or immunities secured by the Constitution and laws, shall be liable to the party injured in an action at law, suit in equity, or other proper proceeding for redress. For the purposes of this section, any Act of Congress applicable exclusively to the District of Columbia shall be considered to be a statute of the District of Columbia.

(R.S. § 1979; Pub.L. 96–170, § 1, Dec. 29, 1979, 93 Stat. 1284.)

§ 1985. Conspiracy to interfere with civil rights

(1) If two or more persons in any State or Territory conspire to prevent, by force, intimidation, or threat, any person from accepting or holding any office, trust, or place of confidence under the United States, or from discharging any duties thereof; or to induce by like means any officer of the United States to leave any State, district, or place, where his duties as an officer are required to be performed, or to injure him in his person or property on account of his lawful discharge of the duties of his office, or while engaged in the lawful discharge thereof, or to injure his property so as to molest, interrupt, hinder, or impede him in the discharge of his official duties;

(2) If two or more persons in any State or Territory conspire to deter, by force, intimidation, or threat, any party or witness in any court of the United States from attending such court, or from testifying to any matter pending therein, freely, fully, and truthfully, or to injure such party or witness in his person or property on account of his having so attended or testified, or to influence the verdict, presentment, or indictment of any grand or petit juror in any such court, or to injure such juror in his person or property on account of any verdict, presentment, or indictment lawfully assented to by him, or of his being or having been such juror; or if two or more persons conspire for the purpose of impeding, hindering, obstructing, or defeating, in any manner, the due course of justice in any State or Territory, with intent to deny to any citizen the equal protection of the laws, or to injure him or his property for lawfully enforcing, or attempting to enforce, the right of any person, or class of persons, to the equal protection of the laws;

(3) If two or more persons in any State or Territory conspire or go in disguise on the highway or on the premises of another, for the purpose of depriving, either directly or indirectly, any person or class of persons of the equal protection of the laws, or of equal privileges and immunities under the laws; or for the purpose of preventing or hindering the constituted authorities of any State or Territory from giving or securing to all persons within such State or Territory the equal protection of the laws; or if two or more persons conspire to prevent by force, intimidation, or threat, any citizen who is lawfully entitled to vote, from giving his support or advocacy in a legal manner, toward or in favor of the election of any lawfully qualified person as an elector for President or Vice President, or as a Member of Congress of the United States; or to injure any citizen in person or property on account of such support or advocacy.

In any case of conspiracy set forth in this section, if one or more persons engaged therein do, or cause to be done, any act in furtherance of the object of such conspiracy, whereby another is injured in his person or property, or deprived of having and exercising any right or privilege of a citizen of the United States, the party so injured or deprived may have an action for the recovery of damages occasioned by such injury or deprivation, against any one or more of the conspirators.

(R.S. § 1980.)

§ 1988. Proceedings in vindication of civil rights; attorney's fees

(a) The jurisdiction in civil and criminal matters conferred on the district courts by the provisions of titles 13, 24, and 70 of the Revised Statutes for the protection of all persons in the United States in their civil rights, and for their vindication, shall be exercised and enforced in conformity with the laws of the United States, so far as such laws are suitable to carry the same into effect; but in all cases where they are not adapted to the object, or are deficient in the provisions necessary to furnish suitable remedies and punish offenses against law, the common law, as modified and changed by the constitution and statutes of the State wherein the court having jurisdiction of such civil or criminal cause is held, so far as the same is not inconsistent with the Constitution and laws of the United States, shall be extended to and govern the said courts in the trial and disposition of the cause, and, if it is of a criminal nature, in the infliction of punishment on the party found guilty.

(b) In any action or proceeding to enforce a provision of sections 1981, 1981a, 1982, 1983, 1985, and 1986 of this title, title IX of Public Law 92–318 [20 U.S.C. § 1681 et seq.], the Religious Freedom Restoration Act of 1993 [42 U.S.C. § 2000bb et seq.], the Religious Land Use and Institutionalized Persons Act of 2000 [42 U.S.C. § 2000cc et seq.], title VI of the Civil Rights Act of 1964 [42 U.S.C. § 2000d et seq.], or section 13981 of this title, the court, in its discretion, may allow the prevailing party, other than the United States, a reasonable attorney's fee as part of the costs, except that in any action brought against a judicial officer for an act or omission taken in such officer's judicial capacity such officer shall not be held liable for any costs, including attorney's fees, unless such action was clearly in excess of such officer's jurisdiction.

(c) In awarding an attorney's fee under subsection (b) of this section in any action or proceeding to enforce a provision of section 1981 or 1981a of this title, the court, in its discretion, may include expert fees as part of the attorney's fee.

(R.S. § 722; Pub.L. 94–559, § 2, Oct. 19, 1976, 90 Stat. 2641; Pub.L. 96–481, Title II, § 205(c), Oct. 21, 1980, 94 Stat. 2330; Pub.L. 102–166, Title I, §§ 103, 113(a), Nov. 21, 1991, 105 Stat. 1074, 1079; Pub.L. 103–141, § 4(a), Nov. 16, 1993, 107 Stat. 1489; Pub.L. 103–322, Title IV, § 40303, Sept. 13, 1994, 108 Stat. 1942; Pub.L. 104–317, Title III, § 309(b), Oct. 19, 1996, 110 Stat. 3853; Pub.L. 106–274, § 4(d), Sept. 22, 2000, 114 Stat. 804.)

TITLE VII OF THE CIVIL RIGHTS ACT OF 1964, 42 U.S.C. §§ 2000e–2000e–17*

§ 2000e. (§ 701) Definitions

For the purposes of this subchapter—

(a) The term "person" includes one or more individuals, governments, governmental agencies, political subdivisions, labor unions, partnerships, associations, corporations, legal representatives, mutual companies, joint-stock companies, trusts, unincorporated organizations, trustees, trustees in cases under Title 11, or receivers.

(b) The term "employer" means a person engaged in an industry affecting commerce who has fifteen or more employees for each working day in each of twenty or more calendar weeks in the current or preceding calendar year, and any agent of such a person, but such term does not include (1) the United States, a corporation wholly owned by the Government of the United States, an Indian tribe, or any department or agency of the District of Columbia subject by statute to procedures of the competitive service (as defined in section 2102 of Title 5), or (2) a bona fide private membership club (other than a labor organization) which is exempt from taxation under section 501(c) of Title 26, except that during the first year after March 24, 1972, persons having fewer than twenty-five employees (and their agents) shall not be considered employers.

(c) The term "employment agency" means any person regularly undertaking with or without compensation to procure employees for an employer or to procure for employees opportunities to work for an employer and includes an agent of such a person.

(d) The term "labor organization" means a labor organization engaged in an industry affecting commerce, and any agent of such an organization, and includes any organization of any kind, any agency, or employee representation committee, group, association, or plan so engaged in which employees participate and which exists for the purpose, in whole or in part, of dealing with employers concerning grievances, labor disputes, wages, rates of pay, hours, or other terms or conditions of employment, and any conference, general committee, joint or system board, or joint council so engaged which is subordinate to a national or international labor organization.

(e) A labor organization shall be deemed to be engaged in an industry affecting commerce if (1) it maintains or operates a hiring hall

---

* Includes amendments made by the Civil Rights Act of 1991 in italics. Deletions made by this Act are in brackets. Amendments made by the Lilly Ledbetter Fair Play Act of 2009, Pub.L. 111–2, Jan. 29, 2009, 123 Stat. 5–7, are underscored.

or hiring office which procures employees for an employer or procures for employees opportunities to work for an employer, or (2) the number of its members (or, where it is a labor organization composed of other labor organizations or their representatives, if the aggregate number of the members of such other labor organization) is (A) twenty-five or more during the first year after March 24, 1972, or (B) fifteen or more thereafter, and such labor organization—

(1) is the certified representative of employees under the provisions of the National Labor Relations Act, as amended, or the Railway Labor Act, as amended;

(2) although not certified, is a national or international labor organization or a local labor organization recognized or acting as the representative of employees of an employer or employers engaged in an industry affecting commerce; or

(3) has chartered a local labor organization or subsidiary body which is representing or actively seeking to represent employees of employers within the meaning of paragraph (1) or (2); or

(4) has been chartered by a labor organization representing or actively seeking to represent employees within the meaning of paragraph (1) or (2) as the local or subordinate body through which such employees may enjoy membership or become affiliated with such labor organization; or

(5) is a conference, general committee, joint or system board, or joint council subordinate to a national or international labor organization, which includes a labor organization engaged in an industry affecting commerce within the meaning of any of the preceding paragraphs of this subsection.

(f) The term "employee" means an individual employed by an employer, except that the term "employee" shall not include any person elected to public office in any State or political subdivision of any State by the qualified voters thereof, or any person chosen by such officer to be on such officer's personal staff, or an appointee on the policy making level or an immediate adviser with respect to the exercise of the constitutional or legal powers of the office. The exemption set forth in the preceding sentence shall not include employees subject to the civil service laws of a State government, governmental agency or political subdivision. *With respect to employment in a foreign country, such term includes an individual who is a citizen of the United States.*

(g) The term "commerce" means trade, traffic, commerce, transportation, transmission, or communication among the several States; or between a State and any place outside thereof; or within the District of Columbia, or a possession of the United States; or between points in the same State but through a point outside thereof.

(h) The term "industry affecting commerce" means any activity, business, or industry in commerce or in which a labor dispute would hinder or obstruct commerce or the free flow of commerce and includes any activity or industry "affecting commerce" within the meaning of the Labor–Management Reporting and Disclosure Act of 1959, and further includes any governmental industry, business, or activity.

(i) The term "State" includes a State of the United States, the District of Columbia, Puerto Rico, the Virgin Islands, American Samoa, Guam, Wake Island, the Canal Zone, and Outer Continental Shelf lands defined in the Outer Continental Shelf Lands Act.

(j) The term "religion" includes all aspects of religious observance and practice, as well as belief, unless an employer demonstrates that he is unable to reasonably accommodate to an employee's or prospective employee's religious observance or practice without undue hardship on the conduct of the employer's business.

(k) The terms "because of sex" or "on the basis of sex" include, but are not limited to, because of or on the basis of pregnancy, childbirth, or related medical conditions; and women affected by pregnancy, childbirth, or related medical conditions shall be treated the same for all employment-related purposes, including receipt of benefits under fringe benefit programs, as other persons not so affected but similar in their ability or inability to work, and nothing in section 2000e–2(h) of this title shall be interpreted to permit otherwise. This subsection shall not require an employer to pay for health insurance benefits for abortion, except where the life of the mother would be endangered if the fetus were carried to term, or except where medical complications have arisen from an abortion: *Provided,* That nothing herein shall preclude an employer from providing abortion benefits or otherwise affect bargaining agreements in regard to abortion.

(l) The term "complaining party" means the Commission, the Attorney General, or a person who may bring an action or proceeding under this title.

(m) *The term "demonstrates" means meets the burden of production and persuasion.*

(n) *The term "respondent" means an employer, employment agency, labor organization, joint labor-management committee controlling apprenticeship or other training or retraining program, including an on-the-job training program, or Federal entity subject to section 717.*

(Pub.L. 88–352, Title VII, § 701, July 2, 1964, 78 Stat. 253; Pub.L. 89–554, § 8(a), Sept. 6, 1966, 80 Stat. 662; Pub.L. 92–261, § 2, Mar. 24, 1972, 86 Stat. 103; Pub.L. 95–555, § 1, Oct. 31, 1978, 92 Stat. 2076; Pub.L. 95–598, Title III, § 330, Nov. 6, 1978, 92 Stat. 2679; Pub.L. 102–166, §§ 104, 109, Nov. 21, 1991, 105 Stat. 1071.)

§ 2000e–1.   (§ 702) Subchapter not applicable to employment of aliens outside State and individuals for performance of activities of religious corporations, associations, educational institutions, or societies

(a) This subchapter shall not apply to an employer with respect to the employment of aliens outside any State, or to a religious corporation, association, educational institution, or society with respect to the employment of individuals of a particular religion to perform work connected with the carrying on by such corporation, association, educational institution, or society of its activities.

(b) *It shall not be unlawful under section 703 or 704 for an employer (or a corporation controlled by an employer), labor organization, employment agency, or joint labor-management committee controlling apprenticeship or other training or retraining (including on-the-job training programs) to take any action otherwise prohibited by such section, with respect to an employee in a workplace in a foreign country if compliance with such section would cause such employer (or such corporation), such organization, such agency, or such committee to violate the law of the foreign country in which such workplace is located.*

(c)(1) *If an employer controls a corporation whose place of incorporation is a foreign country, any practice prohibited by section 703 or 704 engaged in by such corporation shall be presumed to be engaged in by such employer.*

(2) Sections 703 and 704 shall not apply with respect to the foreign operations of an employer that is a foreign person not controlled by an American employer.

(3) For purposes of this subsection, the determination of whether an employer controls a corporation shall be based on—

(A) the interrelation of operations;

(B) the common management;

(C) the centralized control of labor relations; and

(D) the common ownership or financial control of the employer and the corporation.

(Pub.L. 88–352, Title VII, § 702, July 2, 1964, 78 Stat. 255; Pub.L. 92–261, § 3, Mar. 24, 1972, 86 Stat. 103; Pub.L. 102–166, § 109, Nov. 21, 1991, 105 Stat. 1071.)

§ 2000e–2. (§ 703) Unlawful employment practices

(a) It shall be an unlawful employment practice for an employer—

(1) to fail or refuse to hire or to discharge any individual, or otherwise to discriminate against any individual with respect to his compensation, terms, conditions, or privileges of employment, because of such individual's race, color, religion, sex, or national origin; or

(2) to limit, segregate, or classify his employees or applicants for employment in any way which would deprive or tend to deprive any individual of employment opportunities or otherwise adversely affect his status as an employee, because of such individual's race, color, religion, sex, or national origin.

(b) It shall be an unlawful employment practice for an employment agency to fail or refuse to refer for employment, or otherwise to discriminate against, any individual because of his race, color, religion, sex, or national origin, or to classify or refer for employment any individual on the basis of his race, color, religion, sex, or national origin.

(c) It shall be an unlawful employment practice for a labor organization—

    (1) to exclude or to expel from its membership, or otherwise to discriminate against, any individual because of his race, color, religion, sex, or national origin;

    (2) to limit, segregate, or classify its membership or applicants for membership, or to classify or fail or refuse to refer for employment any individual, in any way which would deprive or tend to deprive any individual of employment opportunities, or would limit such employment opportunities or otherwise adversely affect his status as an employee or as an applicant for employment, because of such individual's race, color, religion, sex, or national origin; or

    (3) to cause or attempt to cause an employer to discriminate against an individual in violation of this section.

(d) It shall be an unlawful employment practice for any employer, labor organization, or joint labor-management committee controlling apprenticeship or other training or retraining, including on-the-job training programs to [sic] discriminate against any individual because of his race, color, religion, sex, or national origin in admission to, or employment in, any program established to provide apprenticeship or other training.

(e) Notwithstanding any other provision of this subchapter, (1) it shall not be an unlawful employment practice for an employer to hire and employ employees, for an employment agency to classify, or refer for employment any individual, for a labor organization to classify its membership or to classify or refer for employment any individual, or for an employer, labor organization, or joint labor-management committee controlling apprenticeship or other training or retraining programs to admit or employ any individual in any such program, on the basis of his religion, sex, or national origin in those certain instances where religion, sex, or national origin is a bona fide occupational qualification reasonably necessary to the normal operation of that particular business or enterprise, and (2) it shall not be an unlawful employment practice for a school, college, university, or other educational institution or institution of learning to hire and employ employees of a particular religion if such school, college, university, or other educational institution or institution of learning is, in whole or in substantial part, owned, supported, controlled, or managed by a particular religion or by a particular religious corporation, association, or society, or if the curriculum of such school, college, university, or other educational institution or institution of learning is directed toward the propagation of a particular religion.

(f) As used in this subchapter, the phrase "unlawful employment practice" shall not be deemed to include any action or measure taken by an employer, labor organization, joint labor-management committee, or employment agency with respect to an individual who is a member of the Communist Party of the United States or of any other organization required to register as a Communist-action or Communist-front organization by final order of the Subversive Activities Control Board pursuant to the Subversive Activities Control Act of 1950.

(g) Notwithstanding any other provision of this subchapter, it shall not be an unlawful employment practice for an employer to fail or refuse to hire and employ any individual for any position, for an employer to discharge any individual from any position, or for an employment agency to fail or refuse to refer any individual for employment in any position, or for a labor organization to fail or refuse to refer any individual for employment in any position, if—

(1) the occupancy of such position, or access to the premises in or upon which any part of the duties of such position is performed or is to be performed, is subject to any requirement imposed in the interest of the national security of the United States under any security program in effect pursuant to or administered under any statute of the United States or any Executive order of the President; and

(2) such individual has not fulfilled or has ceased to fulfill that requirement.

(h) Notwithstanding any other provision of this subchapter, it shall not be an unlawful employment practice for an employer to apply different standards of compensation, or different terms, conditions, or privileges of employment pursuant to a bona fide seniority or merit system, or a system which measures earnings by quantity or quality of production or to employees who work in different locations, provided that such differences are not the result of an intention to discriminate because of race, color, religion, sex, or national origin, nor shall it be an unlawful employment practice for an employer to give and to act upon the results of any professionally developed ability test provided that such test, its administration or action upon the results is not designed, intended or used to discriminate because of race, color, religion, sex or national origin. It shall not be an unlawful employment practice under this subchapter for any employer to differentiate upon the basis of sex in determining the amount of the wages or compensation paid or to be paid to employees of such employer if such differentiation is authorized by the provisions of section 206(d) of Title 29.

(i) Nothing contained in this subchapter shall apply to any business or enterprise on or near an Indian reservation with respect to any publicly announced employment practice of such business or enterprise under which a preferential treatment is given to any individual because he is an Indian living on or near a reservation.

(j) Nothing contained in this subchapter shall be interpreted to require any employer, employment agency, labor organization, or joint labor-management committee subject to this subchapter to grant preferential treatment to any individual or to any group because of the race, color, religion, sex, or national origin of such individual or group on account of an imbalance which may exist with respect to the total number or percentage of persons of any race, color, religion, sex, or national origin employed by any employer, referred or classified for employment by any employment agency or labor organization, admitted to membership or classified by any labor organization, or admitted to, or employed in, any apprenticeship or other training program, in comparison with the total number or percentage of persons of such race, color, religion, sex, or national origin in any community, State, section, or other area, or in the available work force in any community, State, section, or other area.

(handwritten margin note: No preferential treatment required because of an imbalance)

(k)(1)(A) *An unlawful employment practice based on disparate impact is established under this title only if—*

(handwritten margin note: Disparate Impact)

> *(i) a complaining party demonstrates that a respondent uses a particular employment practice that causes a disparate impact on the basis of race, color, religion, sex, or national origin and the respondent fails to demonstrate that the challenged practice is job related for the position in question and consistent with business necessity; or*

(handwritten margin note: π = show disparate impact ↳ burden of persuasion. Δ = 1) Business necessity, ↳ burden of persuasion.)

> *(ii) the complaining party makes the demonstration described in subparagraph (C) with respect to an alternative employment practice and the respondent refuses to adopt such alternative employment practice.*

(handwritten margin note: π - shows alternative employment practice.)

(handwritten margin note: or - ee shows alternative employment practice...)

(B)(i) With respect to demonstrating that a particular employment practice causes a disparate impact as described in subparagraph (A)(i), the complaining party shall demonstrate that each particular challenged employment practice causes a disparate impact, except that if the complaining party can demonstrate to the court that the elements of a respondent's decisionmaking process are not capable of separation for analysis, the decisionmaking process may be analyzed as one employment practice.

> *(ii) If the respondent demonstrates that a specific employment practice does not cause the disparate impact, the respondent shall not be required to demonstrate that such practice is required by business necessity.*

(handwritten margin note: if no disparate impact; No presumption...)

(C) The demonstration referred to by subparagraph (A)(ii) shall be in accordance with law as it existed on June 4, 1989, with respect to the concept of "alternative employment practice".

(2) A demonstration that an employment practice is required by business necessity may not be used as a defense against a claim of intentional discrimination under this title.

(3) Notwithstanding any other provision of this title, a rule barring the employment of an individual who currently and knowingly uses or possesses a controlled substance, as defined in schedules I and II of section 102(6) of the Controlled Substances Act (21 U.S.C. 802(6)), other than the use or possession of a drug taken under the supervision of a licensed health care professional, or any other use or possession authorized by the Controlled Substances Act or any other provision of Federal law, shall be considered an unlawful employment practice under this title only if such rule is adopted or applied with an intent to discriminate because of race, color, religion, sex, or national origin.

(l) It shall be an unlawful employment practice for a respondent, in connection with the selection or referral of applicants or candidates for employment or promotion, to adjust the scores of, use different cutoff scores for, or otherwise alter the results of, employment related tests on the basis of race, color, religion, sex, or national origin.

(m) Except as otherwise provided in this title, an unlawful employment practice is established when the complaining party demonstrates that race, color, religion, sex, or national origin was a motivating factor for any employment practice, even though other factors also motivated the practice.

Mixed motive—

(n)(1)(A) Notwithstanding any other provision of law, and except as provided in paragraph (2), an employment practice that implements and is within the scope of a litigated or consent judgment or order that resolves a claim of employment discrimination under the Constitution or Federal civil rights laws may not be challenged under the circumstances described in subparagraph (B).

(B) A practice described in subparagraph (A) may not be challenged in a claim under the Constitution or Federal civil rights laws—

(i) by a person who, prior to the entry of the judgment or order described in subparagraph (A), had—

(I) actual notice of the proposed judgment or order sufficient to apprise such person that such judgment or order might adversely affect the interests and legal rights of such person and that an opportunity was available to present objections to such judgment or order by a future date certain; and

(II) a reasonable opportunity to present objections to such judgment or order; or

(ii) by a person whose interests were adequately represented by another person who had previously challenged the judgment or order on the same legal grounds and with a similar factual situation, unless there has been an intervening change in law or fact.

(2) Nothing in this subsection shall be construed to—

(A) *alter the standards for intervention under rule 24 of the Federal Rules of Civil Procedure or apply to the rights of parties who have successfully intervened pursuant to such rule in the proceeding in which the parties intervened;*

(B) *apply to the rights of parties to the action in which a litigated or consent judgment or order was entered, or of members of a class represented or sought to be represented in such action, or of members of a group on whose behalf relief was sought in such action by the Federal Government;*

(C) *prevent challenges to a litigated or consent judgment or order on the ground that such judgment or order was obtained through collusion or fraud, or is transparently invalid or was entered by a court lacking subject matter jurisdiction; or*

(D) *authorize or permit the denial to any person of the due process of law required by the Constitution.*

(3) *Any action not precluded under this subsection that challenges an employment consent judgment or order described in paragraph (1) shall be brought in the court, and if possible before the judge, that entered such judgment or order. Nothing in this subsection shall preclude a transfer of such action pursuant to section 1404 of title 28, United States Code.*

(Pub.L. 88–352, Title VII, § 703, July 2, 1964, 78 Stat. 255; Pub.L. 92–261, § 8(a), (b), Mar. 24, 1972, 86 Stat. 109; Pub.L. 102–166, §§ 105, 106, 107, 108, Nov. 21, 1991, 105 Stat. 1071.)

§ 2000e–3.   (§ 704) Other unlawful employment practices

(a) It shall be an unlawful employment practice for an employer to discriminate against any of his employees or applicants for employment, for an employment agency, or joint labor-management committee controlling apprenticeship or other training or retraining, including on-the-job training programs, to discriminate against any individual, or for a labor organization to discriminate against any member thereof or applicant for membership, because he has opposed any practice made an unlawful employment practice by this subchapter, or because he has made a charge, testified, assisted, or participated in any manner in an investigation, proceeding, or hearing under this subchapter.

(b) It shall be an unlawful employment practice for an employer, labor organization, employment agency, or joint labor-management committee controlling apprenticeship or other training or retraining, including on-the-job training programs, to print or publish or cause to be printed or published any notice or advertisement relating to employment by such an employer or membership in or any classification or referral for employment by such a labor organization, or relating to any classification or referral for employment by such an employment agency, or relating to admission to, or employment in, any program established to provide apprenticeship or other training by such a joint labor-management committee, indicating any preference, limitation, specification, or discrimination, based on race, color, religion, sex, or national origin, except that such a notice or advertisement may indicate a preference, limitation, specification, or discrimination based on religion, sex, or national origin when religion, sex, or national origin is a bona fide occupational qualification for employment.

(Pub.L. 88–352, Title VII, § 704, July 2, 1964, 78 Stat. 257; Pub.L. 92–261, § 8(c), Mar. 24, 1972, 86 Stat. 109.)

§ 2000e–4.   (§ 705) Equal Employment Opportunity Commission

(a) There is hereby created a Commission to be known as the Equal Employment Opportunity Commission, which shall be composed of five members, not more than three of whom shall be members of the same political party. Members of the Commission shall be appointed by the President by and with the advice and consent of the Senate for a term of five years. Any individual chosen to fill a vacancy shall be appointed only for the unexpired term of the member whom he shall succeed, and all members of the Commission shall continue to serve until their successors are appointed and qualified, except that no such member of the Commission shall continue to serve (1) for more than sixty days when the Congress is in session unless a nomination to fill such vacancy shall have been submitted to the Senate, or (2) after the adjournment sine die of the session of the Senate in which such nomination was submitted. The President shall designate one member to serve as Chairman of the Commission, and one member to serve as Vice Chairman. The Chairman shall be responsible on behalf of the Commission for the administrative operations of the Commission, and, except as provided in subsection (b) of this section, shall appoint, in accordance with the provisions of Title 5 governing appointments in the competitive service, such officers, agents, attorneys, administrative law judges, and employees as he deems necessary to assist it in the performance of its functions and to fix their compensation in accordance with the provisions of chapter 51 and subchapter III of chapter 53 of Title 5, relating to classification and General Schedule pay rates: *Provided,* That assignment, removal, and compensation of administrative law judges shall be in accordance with sections 3105, 3344, 5372, and 7521 of Title 5.

(b)(1) There shall be a General Counsel of the Commission appointed by the President, by and with the advice and consent of the Senate, for a term of four years. The General Counsel shall have responsibility for the conduct of litigation as provided in sections 2000e–5 and 2000e–6 of this title. The General Counsel shall have such other duties as the Commission may prescribe or as may be provided by law and shall concur with the Chairman of the Commission on the appointment and supervision of regional attorneys. The General Counsel of the Commission on the effective date of this Act shall continue in such position and perform the functions specified in this subsection until a successor is appointed and qualified.

(2) Attorneys appointed under this section may, at the direction of the Commission, appear for and represent the Commission in any case in court, provided that the Attorney General shall conduct all litigation to which the Commission is a party in the Supreme Court pursuant to this subchapter.

(c) A vacancy in the Commission shall not impair the right of the remaining members to exercise all the powers of the Commission and three members thereof shall constitute a quorum.

(d) The Commission shall have an official seal which shall be judicially noticed.

(e) The Commission shall at the close of each fiscal year report to the Congress and to the President concerning the action it has taken and the moneys it has disbursed. It shall make such further reports on the cause of and means of eliminating discrimination and such recommendations for further legislation as may appear desirable.

(f) The principal office of the Commission shall be in or near the District of Columbia, but it may meet or exercise any or all its powers at any other place. The Commission may establish such regional or State offices as it deems necessary to accomplish the purpose of this subchapter.

(g) The Commission shall have power—

(1) to cooperate with and, with their consent, utilize regional, State, local, and other agencies, both public and private, and individuals;

(2) to pay to witnesses whose depositions are taken or who are summoned before the Commission or any of its agents the same witness and mileage fees as are paid to witnesses in the courts of the United States;

(3) to furnish to persons subject to this subchapter such technical assistance as they may request to further their compliance with this subchapter or an order issued thereunder;

(4) upon the request of (i) any employer, whose employees or some of them, or (ii) any labor organization, whose members or some of them, refuse or threaten to refuse to cooperate in effectuating the provisions of this subchapter, to assist in such effectuation by conciliation or such other remedial action as is provided by this subchapter;

(5) to make such technical studies as are appropriate to effectuate the purposes and policies of this subchapter and to make the results of such studies available to the public;

(6) to intervene in a civil action brought under section 2000e-5 of this title by an aggrieved party against a respondent other than a government, governmental agency or political subdivision.

(h)*(1)* The Commission shall, in any of its educational or promotional activities, cooperate with other departments and agencies in the performance of such educational and promotional activities.

(2) In exercising its powers under this title, the Commission shall carry out educational and outreach activities (including dissemination of information in languages other than English) targeted to—

(A) individuals who historically have been victims of employment discrimination and have not been equitably served by the Commission; and

(B) individuals on whose behalf the Commission has authority to enforce any other law prohibiting employment discrimination, concerning rights and obligations under this title or such law, as the case may be.

(i) All officers, agents, attorneys, and employees of the Commission shall be subject to the provisions of section 7324 of Title 5, notwithstanding any exemption contained in such section.

(j)*(1) The Commission shall establish a Technical Assistance Training Institute, through which the Commission shall provide technical assistance and training regarding the laws and regulations enforced by the Commission.*

(2) An employer or other entity covered under this title shall not be excused from compliance with the requirements of this title because of any failure to receive technical assistance under this subsection.

(3) There are authorized to be appropriated to carry out this subsection such sums as may be necessary for fiscal year 1992.

(Pub.L. 88–352, Title VII, § 705(a)–(d), (f)–(j), July 2, 1964, 78 Stat. 258, 259; Pub.L. 92–261, § 8(d)–(f), Mar. 24, 1972, 86 Stat. 109, 110; Pub.L. 93–608, § 3(1), Jan. 2, 1975, 88 Stat. 1972; Pub.L. 95–251, § 2(a)(11), Mar. 27, 1978, 92 Stat. 183; Pub.L. 102–166, §§ 110, 111, Nov. 21, 1991, 105 Stat. 1071.)

§ 2000e–5.   (§ 706) Enforcement provisions

(a) The Commission is empowered, as hereinafter provided, to prevent any person from engaging in any unlawful employment practice as set forth in section 2000e–2 or 2000e–3 of this title.

(b) Whenever a charge is filed by or on behalf of a person claiming to be aggrieved, or by a member of the Commission, alleging that an employer, employment agency, labor organization, or joint labor-management committee controlling apprenticeship or other training or retraining, including on-the-job training programs, has engaged in an unlawful employment practice, the Commission shall serve a notice of the charge (including the date, place and circumstances of the alleged unlawful employment practice) on such employer, employment agency, labor organization, or joint labor-management committee (hereinafter referred to as the "respondent") within ten days, and shall make an investigation thereof. Charges shall be in writing under oath or affirmation and shall contain such information and be in such form as the Commission requires. Charges shall not be made public by the Commission. If the Commission determines after such investigation that there is not reasonable cause to believe that the charge is true, it shall dismiss the charge and promptly notify the person claiming to be aggrieved and the respondent of its action. In determining whether reasonable cause exists, the Commission shall accord substantial weight to final findings and orders made by State or local authorities in proceedings commenced under State or local law pursuant to the requirements of subsections (c) and (d) of this section. If the Commission determines after such investigation that there is reasonable cause to believe that the charge is true, the Commission shall endeavor to eliminate any such alleged unlawful employment practice by informal methods of conference, conciliation, and persuasion. Nothing said or done during and as a part of such informal endeavors may be made public by the Commission, its officers or employees, or used as evidence in a subsequent proceeding without the written consent of the persons concerned. Any person who makes public information in violation of this subsection shall be fined not more than $1,000 or imprisoned for not more than one year, or both. The Commission shall make its determination on reasonable cause as promptly as possible and, so far as practicable, not later than one hundred and twenty days from the filing of the charge or, where applicable under subsection (c) or (d) of this section, from the date upon which the Commission is authorized to take action with respect to the charge.

(c) In the case of an alleged unlawful employment practice occurring in a State, or political subdivision of a State, which has a State or local law prohibiting the unlawful employment practice alleged and establishing or authorizing a State or local authority to grant or seek relief from such practice or to institute criminal proceedings with respect thereto upon receiving notice thereof, no charge may be filed under subsection (b) of this section by the person aggrieved before the expiration of sixty days after proceedings have been commenced under the State or local law, unless such proceedings have been earlier terminated, provided that such sixty-day period shall be extended to one hundred and twenty days during the first year after the effective date of such State or local law. If any requirement for the commencement of such proceedings is imposed by a State or local authority other than a requirement of the filing of a written and signed statement of the facts upon which the proceeding is based, the proceeding shall be deemed to have been commenced for the purposes of this subsection at the time such statement is sent by registered mail to the appropriate State or local authority.

(d) In the case of any charge filed by a member of the Commission alleging an unlawful employment practice occurring in a State or political subdivision of a State which has a State or local law prohibiting the practice alleged and establishing or authorizing a State or local authority to grant or seek relief from such practice or to institute criminal proceedings with respect thereto upon receiving notice thereof, the Commission shall, before taking any action with respect to such charge, notify the appropriate State or local officials and, upon request, afford them a reasonable time, but not less than sixty days (provided that such sixty-day period shall be extended to one hundred and twenty days during the first year after the effective day of such State or local law), unless a shorter period is requested, to act under such State or local law to remedy the practice alleged.

(**e**)(*1*) A charge under this section shall be filed within one hundred and eighty days after the alleged unlawful employment practice occurred and notice of the charge (including the date, place and circumstances of the alleged unlawful employment practice) shall be served upon the person against whom such charge is made within ten days thereafter, except that in a case of an unlawful employment practice with respect to which the person aggrieved has initially instituted proceedings with a State or local agency with authority to grant or seek relief from such practice or to institute criminal proceedings with respect thereto upon receiving notice thereof, such charge shall be filed by or on behalf of the person aggrieved within three hundred days after the alleged unlawful employment practice occurred, or within thirty days after receiving notice that the State or local agency has terminated the proceedings under the State or local law, whichever is earlier, and a copy of such charge shall be filed by the Commission with the State or local agency.

(2) For purposes of this section, an unlawful employment practice occurs, with respect to a seniority system that has been adopted for an intentionally discriminatory purpose in violation of this title (whether or not that discriminatory purpose is apparent on the face of the seniority provision), when the seniority system is adopted, when an individual becomes subject to the seniority system, or when a person aggrieved is injured by the application of the seniority system or provision of the system.

(3) (A) For purposes of this section, an unlawful employment practice occurs, with respect to discrimination in compensation in violation of this title, when a discriminatory compensation decision or other practice is adopted, when an individual becomes subject to a discriminatory compensation decision or other practice, or when an individual is affected by application of a discriminatory compensation decision or other practice, including each time wages, benefits, or other compensation is paid, resulting in whole or in part from such a decision or other practice.

(B) In addition to any relief authorized by section 1977A of the Revised Statutes (42 U.S.C. § 1981a), liability may accrue and an aggrieved person may obtain relief as provided in subsection (g)(1), including recovery of back pay for up to two years

preceding the filing of the charge, where the unlawful employment practices that have occurred during the charge filing
period are similar or related to unlawful employment practices
with regard to discrimination in compensation that occurred
outside the time for filing a charge.

(f)(1) If within thirty days after a charge is filed with the Commission or within thirty days after expiration of any period of reference
under subsection (c) or (d) of this section, the Commission has been
unable to secure from the respondent a conciliation agreement acceptable to the Commission, the Commission may bring a civil action
against any respondent not a government, governmental agency, or
political subdivision named in the charge. In the case of a respondent
which is a government, governmental agency, or political subdivision, if
the Commission has been unable to secure from the respondent a
conciliation agreement acceptable to the Commission, the Commission
shall take no further action and shall refer the case to the Attorney
General who may bring a civil action against such respondent in the
appropriate United States district court. The person or persons aggrieved shall have the right to intervene in a civil action brought by the
Commission or the Attorney General in a case involving a government,
governmental agency, or political subdivision. If a charge filed with the
Commission pursuant to subsection (b) of this section is dismissed by
the Commission, or if within one hundred and eighty days from the
filing of such charge or the expiration of any period of reference under
subsection (c) or (d) of this section, whichever is later, the Commission
has not filed a civil action under this section or the Attorney General
has not filed a civil action in a case involving a government, governmental agency, or political subdivision, or the Commission has not entered
into a conciliation agreement to which the person aggrieved is a party,
the Commission, or the Attorney General in a case involving a government, governmental agency, or political subdivision, shall so notify the
person aggrieved and within ninety days after the giving of such notice
a civil action may be brought against the respondent named in the
charge (A) by the person claiming to be aggrieved or (B) if such charge
was filed by a member of the Commission, by any person whom the
charge alleges was aggrieved by the alleged unlawful employment practice. Upon application by the complainant and in such circumstances as
the court may deem just, the court may appoint an attorney for such
complainant and may authorize the commencement of the action without the payment of fees, costs, or security. Upon timely application, the
court may, in its discretion, permit the Commission, or the Attorney
General in a case involving a government, governmental agency, or
political subdivision, to intervene in such civil action upon certification
that the case is of general public importance. Upon request, the court
may, in its discretion, stay further proceedings for not more than sixty
days pending the termination of State or local proceedings described in
subsection (c) or (d) of this section or further efforts of the Commission
to obtain voluntary compliance.

(2) Whenever a charge is filed with the Commission and the Commission concludes on the basis of a preliminary investigation that prompt judicial action is necessary to carry out the purposes of this Act, the Commission, or the Attorney General in a case involving a government, governmental agency, or political subdivision, may bring an action for appropriate temporary or preliminary relief pending final disposition of such charge. Any temporary restraining order or other order granting preliminary or temporary relief shall be issued in accordance with rule 65 of the Federal Rules of Civil Procedure. It shall be the duty of a court having jurisdiction over proceedings under this section to assign cases for hearing at the earliest practicable date and to cause such cases to be in every way expedited.

(3) Each United States district court and each United States court of a place subject to the jurisdiction of the United States shall have jurisdiction of actions brought under this subchapter. Such an action may be brought in any judicial district in the State in which the unlawful employment practice is alleged to have been committed, in the judicial district in which the employment records relevant to such practice are maintained and administered, or in the judicial district in which the aggrieved person would have worked but for the alleged unlawful employment practice, but if the respondent is not found within any such district, such an action may be brought within the judicial district in which the respondent has his principal office. For purposes of sections 1404 and 1406 of Title 28, the judicial district in which the respondent has his principal office shall in all cases be considered a district in which the action might have been brought.

(4) It shall be the duty of the chief judge of the district (or in his absence, the acting chief judge) in which the case is pending immediately to designate a judge in such district to hear and determine the case. In the event that no judge in the district is available to hear and determine the case, the chief judge of the district, or the acting chief judge, as the case may be, shall certify this fact to the chief judge of the circuit (or in his absence, the acting chief judge) who shall then designate a district or circuit judge of the circuit to hear and determine the case.

(5) It shall be the duty of the judge designated pursuant to this subsection to assign the case for hearing at the earliest practicable date and to cause the case to be in every way expedited. If such judge has not scheduled the case for trial within one hundred and twenty days after issue has been joined, that judge may appoint a master pursuant to rule 53 of the Federal Rules of Civil Procedure.

(g)(*1*) If the court finds that the respondent has intentionally engaged in or is intentionally engaging in an unlawful employment practice charged in the complaint, the court may enjoin the respondent from engaging in such unlawful employment practice, and order such affirmative action as may be appropriate, which may include, but is not limited to, reinstatement or hiring of employees, with or without back

[handwritten margin note: any other equitable relief]

pay (payable by the employer, employment agency, or labor organization, as the case may be, responsible for the unlawful employment practice), or any other equitable relief as the court deems appropriate. Back pay liability shall not accrue from a date more than two years prior to the filing of a charge with the Commission. Interim earnings or amounts earnable with reasonable diligence by the person or persons discriminated against shall operate to reduce the back pay otherwise allowable.

[handwritten margin note: up to 2 yrs of back pay prior to filing date.]

(2)(A) No order of the court shall require the admission or reinstatement of an individual as a member of a union, or the hiring, reinstatement, or promotion of an individual as an employee, or the payment to him of any back pay, if such individual was refused admission, suspended, or expelled, or was refused employment or advancement or was suspended or discharged for any reason other than discrimination on account of race, color, religion, sex, or national origin or in violation of section 2000e–3(a) of this title.

(B) On a claim in which an individual proves a violation under section 703(m) and a respondent demonstrates that the respondent would have taken the same action in the absence of the impermissible motivating factor, the court—

[handwritten margin note: Mixed-motive Remedies for disparate treatment. Dessert Place v. Costa]

[handwritten margin note: ⟹ ER can show adverse action w/o discrim practice... ⤷ then remedies are limited to injunctive relief, attny fees...]

    (i) may grant declaratory relief, injunctive relief (except as provided in clause (ii)), and attorney's fees and costs demonstrated to be directly attributable only to the pursuit of a claim under section 703(m); and

    (ii) shall not award damages or issue an order requiring any admission, reinstatement, hiring, promotion, or payment, described in subparagraph (A).

(h) The provisions of sections 101 to 115 of Title 29 shall not apply with respect to civil actions brought under this section.

(i) In any case in which an employer, employment agency, or labor organization fails to comply with an order of a court issued in a civil action brought under this section, the Commission may commence proceedings to compel compliance with such order.

(j) Any civil action brought under this section and any proceedings brought under subsection (i) of this section shall be subject to appeal as provided in sections 1291 and 1292, Title 28.

(k) In any action or proceeding under this subchapter the court, in its discretion, may allow the prevailing party, other than the Commission or the United States, a reasonable attorney's fee (*including expert fees*) as part of the costs, and the Commission and the United States shall be liable for costs the same as a private person.

(Pub.L. 88–352, Title VII, § 706, July 2, 1964, 78 Stat. 259; Pub.L. 92–261, § 4, Mar. 24, 1972, 86 Stat. 104; Pub.L. 102–166, §§ 107, 112, 113, Nov. 21, 1991, 105 Stat. 1071; Pub. L. 111–2, Jan. 29, 2009, 123 Stat. 5.)

§ 2000e–6.   (§ 707) Civil actions by Attorney General

(a) Whenever the Attorney General has reasonable cause to believe that any person or group of persons is engaged in a pattern or practice of resistance to the full enjoyment of any of the rights secured by this subchapter, and that the pattern or practice is of such a nature and is intended to deny the full exercise of the rights herein described, the Attorney General may bring a civil action in the appropriate district court of the United States by filing with it a complaint (1) signed by him (or in his absence the Acting Attorney General), (2) setting forth facts pertaining to such pattern or practice, and (3) requesting such relief, including an application for a permanent or temporary injunction, restraining order or other order against the person or persons responsible for such pattern or practice, as he deems necessary to insure the full enjoyment of the rights herein described.

(b) The district courts of the United States shall have and shall exercise jurisdiction of proceedings instituted pursuant to this section, and in any such proceeding the Attorney General may file with the clerk of such court a request that a court of three judges be convened to hear and determine the case. Such request by the Attorney General shall be accompanied by a certificate that, in his opinion, the case is of general public importance. A copy of the certificate and request for a three-judge court shall be immediately furnished by such clerk to the chief judge of the circuit (or in his absence, the presiding circuit judge of the circuit) in which the case is pending. Upon receipt of such request it shall be the duty of the chief judge of the circuit or the presiding circuit judge, as the case may be, to designate immediately three judges in such circuit, of whom at least one shall be a circuit judge and another of whom shall be a district judge of the court in which the proceeding was instituted, to hear and determine such case, and it shall be the duty of the judges so designated to assign the case for hearing at the earliest practicable date, to participate in the hearing and determination thereof, and to cause the case to be in every way expedited. An appeal from the final judgment of such court will lie to the Supreme Court.

In the event the Attorney General fails to file such a request in any such proceeding, it shall be the duty of the chief judge of the district (or in his absence, the acting chief judge) in which the case is pending immediately to designate a judge in such district to hear and determine the case. In the event that no judge in the district is available to hear and determine the case, the chief judge of the district, or the acting chief judge, as the case may be, shall certify this fact to the chief judge of the circuit (or in his absence, the acting chief judge) who shall then designate a district or circuit judge of the circuit to hear and determine the case.

It shall be the duty of the judge designated pursuant to this section to assign the case for hearing at the earliest practicable date and to cause the case to be in every way expedited.

(c) Effective two years after March 24, 1972, the functions of the Attorney General under this section shall be transferred to the Commission, together with such personnel, property, records, and unexpended balances of appropriations, allocations, and other funds employed, used, held, available, or to be made available in connection with such functions unless the President submits, and neither House of Congress vetoes, a reorganization plan pursuant to chapter 9 of Title 5, inconsistent with the provisions of this subsection. The Commission shall carry out such functions in accordance with subsections (d) and (e) of this section.

(d) Upon the transfer of functions provided for in subsection (c) of this section, in all suits commenced pursuant to this section prior to the date of such transfer, proceedings shall continue without abatement, all court orders and decrees shall remain in effect, and the Commission shall be substituted as a party for the United States of America, the Attorney General, or the Acting Attorney General, as appropriate.

(e) Subsequent to March 24, 1972, the Commission shall have authority to investigate and act on a charge of a pattern or practice of discrimination, whether filed by or on behalf of a person claiming to be aggrieved or by a member of the Commission. All such actions shall be conducted in accordance with the procedures set forth in section 2000e-5 of this title.

(Pub.L. 88–352, Title VII, § 707, July 2, 1964, 78 Stat. 261; Pub.L. 92–261, § 5, Mar. 24, 1972, 86 Stat. 107.)

§ 2000e–7.   (§ 708) Effect on State laws

Nothing in this subchapter shall be deemed to exempt or relieve any person from any liability, duty, penalty, or punishment provided by any present or future law of any State or political subdivision of a State, other than any such law which purports to require or permit the doing of any act which would be an unlawful employment practice under this subchapter.

(Pub.L. 88–352, Title VII, § 708, July 2, 1964, 78 Stat. 262.)

§ 2000e–8.   (§ 709) Investigations

(a) In connection with any investigation of a charge filed under section 2000e–5 of this title, the Commission or its designated representative shall at all reasonable times have access to, for the purposes of examination, and the right to copy any evidence of any person being investigated or proceeded against that relates to unlawful employment practices covered by this subchapter and is relevant to the charge under investigation.

(b) The Commission may cooperate with State and local agencies charged with the administration of State fair employment practices laws and, with the consent of such agencies, may, for the purpose of carrying out its functions and duties under this subchapter and within the limitation of funds appropriated specifically for such purpose, engage in and contribute to the cost of research and other projects of mutual interest undertaken by such agencies, and utilize the services of such agencies and their employees, and, notwithstanding any other provision of law, pay by advance or reimbursement such agencies and their employees for services rendered to assist the Commission in carrying out this subchapter. In furtherance of such cooperative efforts, the Commission may enter into written agreements with such State or local agencies and such agreements may include provisions under which the Commission shall refrain from processing a charge in any cases or class of cases specified in such agreements or under which the Commission shall relieve any person or class of persons in such State or locality from requirements imposed under this section. The Commission shall rescind any such agreement whenever it determines that the agreement no longer serves the interest of effective enforcement of this subchapter.

(c) Every employer, employment agency, and labor organization subject to this subchapter shall (1) make and keep such records relevant to the determinations of whether unlawful employment practices have been or are being committed, (2) preserve such records for such periods, and (3) make such reports therefrom as the Commission shall prescribe by regulation or order, after public hearing, as reasonable, necessary, or appropriate for the enforcement of this subchapter or the regulations or orders thereunder. The Commission shall, by regulation, require each employer, labor organization, and joint labor-management committee subject to this subchapter which controls an apprenticeship or other training program to maintain such records as are reasonably necessary to carry out the purposes of this subchapter, including, but not limited to, a list of applicants who wish to participate in such program, including the chronological order in which applications were received, and to furnish to the Commission upon request, a detailed description of the manner in which persons are selected to participate in the apprenticeship or other training program. Any employer, employment agency, labor organization, or joint labor-management committee which believes that the application to it of any regulation or order issued under this section would result in undue hardship may apply to the Commission for an exemption from the application of such regulation or order, and, if such application for an exemption is denied, bring a civil action in the United States district court for the district where such records are kept. If the Commission or the court, as the case may be, finds that the application of the regulation or order to the employer, employment agency, or labor organization in question would impose an undue hardship, the Commission or the court, as the case may be, may grant appropriate relief. If any person required to comply with the provisions of this subsection fails or refuses to do so, the United States district court for the district in which such person is found, resides, or transacts business, shall, upon application of the Commission, or the Attorney General in a case involving a government, governmental agency or political subdivision, have jurisdiction to issue to such person an order requiring him to comply.

(d) In prescribing requirements pursuant to subsection (c) of this section, the Commission shall consult with other interested State and Federal agencies and shall endeavor to coordinate its requirements with those adopted by such agencies. The Commission shall furnish upon request and without cost to any State or local agency charged with the administration of a fair employment practice law information obtained pursuant to subsection (c) of this section from any employer, employment agency, labor organization, or joint labor-management committee subject to the jurisdiction of such agency. Such information shall be furnished on condition that it not be made public by the recipient agency prior to the institution of a proceeding under State or local law involving such information. If this condition is violated by a recipient agency, the Commission may decline to honor subsequent requests pursuant to this subsection.

(e) It shall be unlawful for any officer or employee of the Commission to make public in any manner whatever any information obtained by the Commission pursuant to its authority under this section prior to the institution of any proceeding under this subchapter involving such information. Any officer or employee of the Commission who shall make public in any manner whatever any information in violation of this subsection shall be guilty of a misdemeanor and upon conviction thereof, shall be fined not more than $1,000, or imprisoned not more than one year.

(Pub.L. 88–352, Title VII, § 709, July 2, 1964, 78 Stat. 262; Pub.L. 92–261, § 6, Mar. 24, 1972, 86 Stat. 107.)

§ 2000e–9. (§ 710) Conduct of hearings and investigations pursuant to section 161 of Title 29

For the purpose of all hearings and investigations conducted by the Commission or its duly authorized agents or agencies, section 161 of Title 29 shall apply.

(Pub.L. 88–352, Title VII, § 710, July 2, 1964, 78 Stat. 264; Pub.L. 92–261, § 7, Mar. 24, 1972, 86 Stat. 109.)

§ 2000e–10. (§ 711) Posting of notices; penalties

(a) Every employer, employment agency, and labor organization, as the case may be, shall post and keep posted in conspicuous places upon its premises where notices to employees, applicants for employment, and members are customarily posted a notice to be prepared or approved by the Commission setting forth excerpts from or, summaries of, the pertinent provisions of this subchapter and information pertinent to the filing of a complaint.

(b) A willful violation of this section shall be punishable by a fine of not more than $100 for each separate offense.

(Pub.L. 88–352, Title VII, § 711, July 2, 1964, 78 Stat. 265.)

§ 2000e–11. (§ 712) Veterans' special rights or preference

Nothing contained in this subchapter shall be construed to repeal or modify any Federal, State, territorial, or local law creating special rights or preference for veterans.

(Pub.L. 88–352, Title VII, § 712, July 2, 1964, 78 Stat. 265.)

§ 2000e–12.   (§ 713) Regulations; conformity of regulations with administrative procedure provisions; reliance on interpretations and instructions of Commission

(a) The Commission shall have authority from time to time to issue, amend, or rescind suitable procedural regulations to carry out the provisions of this subchapter. Regulations issued under this section shall be in conformity with the standards and limitations of subchapter II of chapter 5 of Title 5.

(b) In any action or proceeding based on any alleged unlawful employment practice, no person shall be subject to any liability or punishment for or on account of (1) the commission by such person of an unlawful employment practice if he pleads and proves that the act or omission complained of was in good faith, in conformity with, and in reliance on any written interpretation or opinion of the Commission, or (2) the failure of such person to publish and file any information required by any provision of this subchapter if he pleads and proves that he failed to publish and file such information in good faith, in conformity with the instructions of the Commission issued under this subchapter regarding the filing of such information. Such a defense, if established, shall be a bar to the action or proceeding, notwithstanding that (A) after such act or omission, such interpretation or opinion is modified or rescinded or is determined by judicial authority to be invalid or of no legal effect, or (B) after publishing or filing the description and annual reports, such publication or filing is determined by judicial authority not to be in conformity with the requirements of this subchapter.

(Pub.L. 88–352, Title VII, § 713, July 2, 1964, 78 Stat. 265.)

§ 2000e–13.   (§ 714) Application to personnel of Commission of sections 111 and 1114 of Title 18; punishment for violation of section 1114 of Title 18

The provisions of sections 111 and 1114, Title 18, shall apply to officers, agents, and employees of the Commission in the performance of their official duties. Notwithstanding the provisions of sections 111 and 1114 of Title 18, whoever in violation of the provisions of section 1114 of such title kills a person while engaged in or on account of the performance of his official functions under this Act shall be punished by imprisonment for any term of years or for life.

(Pub.L. 88–352, Title VII, § 714, July 2, 1964, 78 Stat. 265; Pub.L. 92–261, § 8(g), Mar. 24, 1972, 86 Stat. 110.)

§ 2000e–14.   (§ 715) Coordination of efforts and elimination of competition among Federal departments, agencies, etc. in implementation and enforcement of equal employment opportunity legislation, orders, and policies; report to President and Congress

The Equal Employment Opportunity Commission shall have the responsibility for developing and implementing agreements, policies and practices designed to maximize effort, promote efficiency, and eliminate conflict, competition, duplication and inconsistency among the operations, functions and jurisdictions of the various departments, agencies and branches of the Federal Government responsible for the implementation and enforcement of equal employment opportunity legislation, orders, and policies. On or before October 1 of each year, the Equal Employment Opportunity Commission shall transmit to the President and to the Congress a report of its activities, together with such recommendations for legislative or administrative changes as it concludes are desirable to further promote the purposes of this section.

(Pub.L. 88–352, Title VII, § 715, July 2, 1964, 78 Stat. 265; Pub.L. 92–261, § 10, Mar. 24, 1972, 86 Stat. 111; Pub.L. 94–273, § 3(24), Apr. 21, 1976, 90 Stat. 377; 1978 Reorg. Plan No. 1, § 6, 43 F.R. 19807, 92 Stat. 3782.)

§ 2000e–15. (§ 716) Presidential conferences; acquaintance of leadership with provisions for employment rights and obligations; plans for fair administration; membership

The President shall, as soon as feasible after July 2, 1964, convene one or more conferences for the purpose of enabling the leaders of groups whose members will be affected by this subchapter to become familiar with the rights afforded and obligations imposed by its provisions, and for the purpose of making plans which will result in the fair and effective administration of this subchapter when all of its provisions become effective. The President shall invite the participation in such conference or conferences of (1) the members of the President's Committee on Equal Employment Opportunity, (2) the members of the Commission on Civil Rights, (3) representatives of State and local agencies engaged in furthering equal employment opportunity, (4) representatives of private agencies engaged in furthering equal employment opportunity, and (5) representatives of employers, labor organizations, and employment agencies who will be subject to this subchapter.

(Pub.L. 88–352, Title VII, § 716(c), July 2, 1964, 78 Stat. 266.)

§ 2000e–16. (§ 717) Employment by Federal Government

(a) All personnel actions affecting employees or applicants for employment (except with regard to aliens employed outside the limits of the United States) in military departments as defined in section 102 of Title 5, in executive agencies as defined in section 105 of Title 5 (including employees and applicants for employment who are paid from nonappropriated funds), in the United States Postal Service and the Postal Regulatory Commission, in those units of the Government of the District of Columbia having positions in the competitive service, and in those units of the judicial branch of the Federal Government having positions in the competitive service, in the Smithsonian Institution, and in the Government Printing Office, the Government Accountability Office, and the

Library of Congress shall be made free from any discrimination based on race, color, religion, sex, or national origin.

(b) Except as otherwise provided in this subsection, the Equal Employment Opportunity Commission shall have authority to enforce the provisions of subsection (a) of this section through appropriate remedies, including reinstatement or hiring of employees with or without back pay, as will effectuate the policies of this section, and shall issue such rules, regulations, orders and instructions as it deems necessary and appropriate to carry out its responsibilities under this section. The Equal Employment Opportunity Commission shall—

(1) be responsible for the annual review and approval of a national and regional equal employment opportunity plan which each department and agency and each appropriate unit referred to in subsection (a) of this section shall submit in order to maintain an affirmative program of equal employment opportunity for all such employees and applicants for employment;

(2) be responsible for the review and evaluation of the operation of all agency equal employment opportunity programs, periodically obtaining and publishing (on at least a semiannual basis) progress reports from each such department, agency, or unit; and

(3) consult with and solicit the recommendations of interested individuals, groups, and organizations relating to equal employment opportunity.

The head of each such department, agency, or unit shall comply with such rules, regulations, orders, and instructions which shall include a provision that an employee or applicant for employment shall be notified of any final action taken on any complaint of discrimination filed by him thereunder. The plan submitted by each department, agency, and unit shall include, but not be limited to—

(1) provision for the establishment of training and education programs designed to provide a maximum opportunity for employees to advance so as to perform at their highest potential; and

(2) a description of the qualifications in terms of training and experience relating to equal employment opportunity for the principal and operating officials of each such department, agency, or unit responsible for carrying out the equal employment opportunity program and of the allocation of personnel and resources proposed by such department, agency, or unit to carry out its equal employment opportunity program.

With respect to employment in the Library of Congress, authorities granted in this subsection to the Equal Employment Opportunity Commission shall be exercised by the Librarian of Congress.

(c) Within 90 days of receipt of notice of final action taken by a department, agency, or unit referred to in subsection (a) of this section, or by the Equal Employment Opportunity Commission upon an appeal from a decision or order of such department, agency, or unit on a complaint of discrimination based on race, color, religion, sex or national origin, brought pursuant to subsection (a) of this section, Executive Order 11478 or any succeeding Executive orders, or after one hundred and eighty days from the filing of the initial charge with the department, agency, or unit or with the Equal Employment Opportunity Commission on appeal from a decision or order of such department, agency, or unit until such time as final action may be taken by a department, agency, or unit, an employee or applicant for employment, if aggrieved by the final disposition of his complaint, or by the failure to take final action on his complaint, may file a civil action as provided in section 2000e–5 of this title, in which civil action the head of the department, agency, or unit, as appropriate, shall be the defendant.

(d) The provisions of section 2000e–5(f) through (k) of this title, as applicable, shall govern civil actions brought hereunder, and the same interest to compensate for delay in payment shall be available as in cases involving nonpublic parties.

(e) Nothing contained in this Act shall relieve any Government agency or official of its or his primary responsibility to assure nondiscrimination in employment as required by the Constitution and statutes or of its or his responsibilities under Executive Order 11478 relating to equal employment opportunity in the Federal Government.

(f) Section 706(e)(3) shall apply to complaints of discrimination in compensation under this section.

(Pub.L. 88–352, Title VII, § 717, as added Pub.L. 92–261, § 11, Mar. 24, 1972, 86 Stat. 111, and amended 1978 Reorg. Plan No. 1, § 3, eff. Jan. 1, 1979, 43 F.R. 19807, 92 Stat. 3781; Pub.L. 96–191, § 8(g), Feb. 15, 1980, 94 Stat. 34; Pub.L. 102–166, Title I, § 114, Nov. 21, 1991, 105 Stat. 1079; Pub.L. 104–1, Title II, § 201(c)(1), Jan. 23, 1995, 109 Stat. 8; Pub.L. 105–220, Title III, § 341(a), Aug. 7, 1998, 112 Stat. 1092; Pub.L. 108–271, § 8(b), July 7, 2004, 118 Stat. 814; Pub.L. 109–435, Title VI, § 604(f), Dec. 20, 2006, 120 Stat. 3242; Pub.L. 111–2, Jan. 29, 2009, 123 Stat. 5.)

§ 2000e–17. (§ 718) Procedure for denial, withholding, termination, or suspension of Government contract subsequent to acceptance by Government of affirmative action plan of employer; time of acceptance of plan

No Government contract, or portion thereof, with any employer, shall be denied, withheld, terminated, or suspended, by any agency or officer of the United States under any equal employment opportunity law or order, where such employer has an affirmative action plan which has previously been accepted by the Government for the same facility within the past twelve months without first according such employer full hearing and adjudication under the provisions of section 554 of Title 5, and the following pertinent sections: *Provided,* That if such employer has deviated substantially from such previously agreed to affirmative action plan, this section shall not apply: *Provided further,* That for the purposes of this section an affirmative action plan shall be deemed to have been accepted by the Government at the time the appropriate compliance agency has accepted such plan unless within forty-five days thereafter the Office of Federal Contract Compliance has disapproved such plan.

(Pub.L. 88–352, Title VII, § 718, as added Pub.L. 92–261, § 13, Mar. 24, 1972, 86 Stat. 113.)

CIVIL RIGHTS ACT OF 1991*

§ 1. Short Title

This Act may be cited as the "Civil Rights Act of 1991".

§ 2. Findings

The Congress finds that—

(1) additional remedies under Federal law are needed to deter unlawful harassment and intentional discrimination in the workplace;

(2) the decision of the Supreme Court in Wards Cove Packing Co. v. Atonio, 490 U.S. 642 (1989) has weakened the scope and effectiveness of Federal civil rights protections; and

(3) legislation is necessary to provide additional protections against unlawful discrimination in employment.

§ 3. Purposes

The purposes of this Act are—

(1) to provide appropriate remedies for intentional discrimination and unlawful harassment in the workplace;

(2) to codify the concepts of "business necessity" and "job related" enunciated by the Supreme Court in Griggs v. Duke Power Co., 401 U.S. 424 (1971), and in the other Supreme Court decisions prior to Wards Cove Packing Co. v. Atonio, 490 U.S. 642 (1989);

(3) to confirm statutory authority and provide statutory guidelines for the adjudication of disparate impact suits under title VII of the Civil Rights Act of 1964 (42 U.S.C. 2000e et seq.); and

(4) to respond to recent decisions of the Supreme Court by expanding the scope of relevant civil rights statutes in order to provide adequate protection to victims of discrimination.

TITLE I—FEDERAL CIVIL RIGHTS REMEDIES

§ 101. Prohibition against all racial discrimination in the making and enforcement of contracts

Section 1977 of the Revised Statutes (42 U.S.C. 1981) is amended—

(1) by inserting "(a)" before "All persons within"; and

(2) by adding at the end the following new subsections:

* Pub.L. 102–166, Nov. 21, 1991, 105 Stat. 1071.

"(b) For purposes of this section, the term 'make and enforce contracts' includes the making, performance, modification, and termination of contracts, and the enjoyment of all benefits, privileges, terms, and conditions of the contractual relationship.

"(c) The rights protected by this section are protected against impairment by nongovernmental discrimination and impairment under color of State law.".

§ 102. Damages in cases of intentional discrimination

The Revised Statutes are amended by inserting after section 1977 (42 U.S.C. 1981) the following new section:

"§ 1977A. Damages in cases of intentional discrimination in employment

"(a) Right of Recovery.

    "(1) Civil Rights. In an action brought by a complaining party under section 706 or 717 of the Civil Rights Act of 1964 (42 U.S.C. 2000e–5) against a respondent who engaged in unlawful intentional discrimination (not an employment practice that is unlawful because of its disparate impact) prohibited under section 703, 704, or 717 of the Act (42 U.S.C. 2000e–2 or 2000e–3), and provided that the complaining party cannot recover under section 1977 of the Revised Statutes (42 U.S.C. 1981), the complaining party may recover compensatory and punitive damages as allowed in subsection (b), in addition to any relief authorized by section 706(g) of the Civil Rights Act of 1964, from the respondent.

    "(2) Disability. In an action brought by a complaining party under the powers, remedies, and procedures set forth in section 706 or 717 of the Civil Rights Act of 1964 (as provided in section 107(a) of the Americans with Disabilities Act of 1990 (42 U.S.C. 12117(a)), and section 505(a)(1) of the Rehabilitation Act of 1973 (29 U.S.C. 794a(a)(1)), respectively) against a respondent who engaged in unlawful intentional discrimination (not an employment practice that is unlawful because of its disparate impact) under section 501 of the Rehabilitation Act of 1973 (29 U.S.C. 791) and the regulations implementing section 501, or who violated the requirements of section 501 of the Act or the regulations implementing section 501 concerning the provision of a reasonable accommodation, or section 102 of the Americans with Disabilities Act of 1990 (42 U.S.C. 12112), or committed a violation of section 102(b)(5) of the Act, against an individual, the complaining party may recover compensatory and punitive damages as allowed in subsection (b), in addition to any relief authorized by section 706(g) of the Civil Rights Act of 1964, from the respondent.

    "(3) Reasonable Accommodation and Good Faith Effort. In cases where a discriminatory practice involves the provision of a reasonable accommodation pursuant to section 102(b)(5) of the

Americans with Disabilities Act of 1990 or regulations implementing section 501 of the Rehabilitation Act of 1973, damages may not be awarded under this section where the covered entity demonstrates good faith efforts, in consultation with the person with the disability who has informed the covered entity that accommodation is needed, to identify and make a reasonable accommodation that would provide such individual with an equally effective opportunity and would not cause an undue hardship on the operation of the business.

"(b) Compensatory and Punitive Damages.

"**(1) Determination of Punitive Damages.** A complaining party may recover punitive damages under this section against a respondent (other than a government, government agency or political subdivision) if the complaining party demonstrates that the respondent engaged in a discriminatory practice or discriminatory practices with malice or with reckless indifference to the federally protected rights of an aggrieved individual.

"**(2) Exclusions From Compensatory Damages.** Compensatory damages awarded under this section shall not include backpay, interest on backpay, or any other type of relief authorized under section 706(g) of the Civil Rights Act of 1964.

"**(3) Limitations.** The sum of the amount of compensatory damages awarded under this section for future pecuniary losses, emotional pain, suffering, inconvenience, mental anguish, loss of enjoyment of life, and other nonpecuniary losses, and the amount of punitive damages awarded under this section, shall not exceed, for each complaining party—

"(A) in the case of a respondent who has more than 14 and fewer than 101 employees in each of 20 or more calendar weeks in the current or preceding calendar year, $50,000;

"(B) in the case of a respondent who has more than 100 and fewer than 201 employees in each of 20 or more calendar weeks in the current or preceding calendar year, $100,000; and

"(C) in the case of a respondent who has more than 200 and fewer than 501 employees in each of 20 or more calendar weeks in the current or preceding calendar year, $200,000; and

"(D) in the case of a respondent who has more than 500 employees in each of 20 or more calendar weeks in the current or preceding calendar year, $300,000.

"**(4) Construction.** Nothing in this section shall be construed to limit the scope of, or the relief available under, section 1977 of the Revised Statutes (42 U.S.C. 1981).

"**(c) Jury Trial.** If a complaining party seeks compensatory or punitive damages under this section—

"(1) any party may demand a trial by jury; and

"(2) the court shall not inform the jury of the limitations described in subsection (b)(3).

"(d) Definitions. As used in this section:

"(1) Complaining Party. The term 'complaining party' means—

"(A) in the case of a person seeking to bring an action under subsection (a)(1), the Equal Employment Opportunity Commission, the Attorney General, or a person who may bring an action or proceeding under title VII of the Civil Rights Act of 1964 (42 U.S.C. 2000e et seq.); or

"(B) in the case of a person seeking to bring an action under subsection (a)(2), the Equal Employment Opportunity Commission, the Attorney General, a person who may bring an action or proceeding under section 505(a)(1) of the Rehabilitation Act of 1973 (29 U.S.C. 794a(a)(1)), or a person who may bring an action or proceeding under title I of the Americans with Disabilities Act of 1990 (42 U.S.C. 12101 et seq.).

"(2) Discriminatory Practice. The term 'discriminatory practice' means the discrimination described in paragraph (1), or the discrimination or the violation described in paragraph (2), of subsection (a)."

§ 103. Attorney's Fees

The last sentence of section 722 of the Revised Statutes (42 U.S.C. 1988) is amended by inserting ", 1977A" after "1977".

§ 104. Definitions

Section 701 of the Civil Rights Act of 1964 (42 U.S.C. 2000e) is amended by adding at the end the following new subsections:

"(*l*) The term 'complaining party' means the Commission, the Attorney General, or a person who may bring an action or proceeding under this title.

"(m) The term 'demonstrates' means meets the burdens of production and persuasion.

"(n) The term 'respondent' means an employer, employment agency, labor organization, joint labor-management committee controlling apprenticeship or other training or retraining program, including an on-the-job training program, or Federal entity subject to section 717.".

§ 105. Burden of proof in disparate impact cases

(a) Section 703 of the Civil Rights Act of 1964 (42 U.S.C. 2000e–2) is amended by adding at the end the following new subsection:

"(k)(1)(A) An unlawful employment practice based on disparate impact is established under this title only if—

"(i) a complaining party demonstrates that a respondent uses a particular employment practice that causes a disparate impact on the basis of race, color, religion, sex, or national origin and the respondent fails to demonstrate that the challenged practice is job related for the position in question and consistent with business necessity; or

"(ii) the complaining party makes the demonstration described in subparagraph (C) with respect to an alternative employment practice and the respondent refuses to adopt such alternative employment practice.

"(B)(i) With respect to demonstrating that a particular employment practice causes a disparate impact as described in subparagraph (A)(i), the complaining party shall demonstrate that each particular challenged employment practice causes a disparate impact, except that if the complaining party can demonstrate to the court that the elements of a respondent's decisionmaking process are not capable of separation for analysis, the decisionmaking process may be analyzed as one employment practice.

"(ii) If the respondent demonstrates that a specific employment practice does not cause the disparate impact, the respondent shall not be required to demonstrate that such practice is required by business necessity.

"(C) The demonstration referred to by subparagraph (A)(ii) shall be in accordance with the law as it existed on June 4, 1989, with respect to the concept of 'alternative employment practice'.

"(2) A demonstration that an employment practice is required by business necessity may not be used as a defense against a claim of intentional discrimination under this title.

"(3) Notwithstanding any other provision of this title, a rule barring the employment of an individual who currently and knowingly uses or possesses a controlled substance, as defined in schedules I and II of section 102(6) of the Controlled Substances Act (21 U.S.C. 802(6)), other than the use or possession of a drug taken under the supervision of a licensed health care professional, or any other use or possession authorized by the Controlled Substances Act or any other provision of Federal law, shall be considered an unlawful employment practice under this title only if such rule is adopted or applied with an intent to discriminate because of race, color, religion, sex, or national origin.".

(b) No statements other than the interpretive memorandum appearing at Vol. 137 Congressional Record S 15276 (daily ed. Oct. 25, 1991) shall be considered legislative history of, or relied upon in any way as legislative history in construing or applying, any provision of this Act that relates to Wards Cove—Business necessity/cumulation/alternative business practice.

§ 106. Prohibition against discriminatory use of test scores

Section 703 of the Civil Rights Act of 1964 (42 U.S.C. 2000e–2) (as amended by section 105) is further amended by adding at the end the following new subsection:

"(*l*) It shall be an unlawful employment practice for a respondent, in connection with the selection or referral of applicants or candidates for employment or promotion, to adjust the scores of, use different cutoff scores for, or otherwise alter the results of, employment related tests on the basis of race, color, religion, sex, or national origin.".

§ 107. Clarifying Prohibition against impermissible consideration of race, color, religion, sex, or national origin in employment practices

(a) In General. Section 703 of the Civil Rights Act of 1964 (42 U.S.C. 2000e–2) (as amended by sections 105 and 106) is further amended by adding at the end the following new subsection:

"(m) Except as otherwise provided in this title, an unlawful employment practice is established when the complaining party demonstrates that race, color, religion, sex, or national origin was a motivating factor for any employment practice, even though other factors also motivated the practice.".

(b) Enforcement Provisions. Section 706(g) of such Act (42 U.S.C. 2000e–5(g)) is amended—

(1) by designating the first through third sentences as paragraph (1);

(2) by designating the fourth sentence as paragraph (2)(A) and indenting accordingly; and

(3) by adding at the end the following new subparagraph:

"(B) On a claim in which an individual proves a violation under section 703(m) and a respondent demonstrates that the respondent would have taken the same action in the absence of the impermissible motivating factor, the court—

"(i) may grant declaratory relief, injunctive relief (except as provided in clause (ii)), and attorney's fees and costs demonstrated to be directly attributable only to the pursuit of a claim under section 703(m); and

"(ii) shall not award damages or issue an order requiring any admission, reinstatement, hiring, promotion, or payment, described in subparagraph (A).".

§ 108. Facilitating prompt and orderly resolution of challenges to employment practices implementing litigated or consent judgments or orders

Section 703 of the Civil Rights Act of 1964 (42 U.S.C. 2000e–2) (as amended by sections 105, 106, and 107 of this title) is further amended by adding at the end the following new subsection:

"(n)(1)(A) Notwithstanding any other provision of law, and except as provided in paragraph (2), an employment practice that implements and is within the scope of a litigated or consent judgment or order that resolves a claim of employment discrimination under the Constitution or Federal civil rights laws may not be challenged under the circumstances described in subparagraph (B).

"(B) A practice described in subparagraph (A) may not be challenged in a claim under the Constitution or Federal civil rights laws—

"(i) by a person who, prior to the entry of the judgment or order described in subparagraph (A), had—

"(I) actual notice of the proposed judgment or order sufficient to apprise such person that such judgment or order might adversely affect the interests and legal rights of such person and that an opportunity was available to present objections to such judgment or order by a future date certain; and

"(II) a reasonable opportunity to present objections to such judgment or order; or

"(ii) by a person whose interests were adequately represented by another person who had previously challenged the judgment or order on the same legal grounds and with a similar factual situation, unless there has been an intervening change in law or fact.

"(2) Nothing in this subsection shall be construed to—

"(A) alter the standards for intervention under rule 24 of the Federal Rules of Civil Procedure or apply to the rights of parties who have successfully intervened pursuant to such rule in the proceeding in which the parties intervened;

"(B) apply to the rights of parties to the action in which a litigated or consent judgment or order was entered, or of members of a class represented or sought to be represented in such action, or of members of a group on whose behalf relief was sought in such action by the Federal Government;

"(C) prevent challenges to a litigated or consent judgment or order on the ground that such judgment or order was obtained through collusion or fraud, or is transparently invalid or was entered by a court lacking subject matter jurisdiction; or

"(D) authorize or permit the denial to any person of the due process of law required by the Constitution.

"(3) Any action not precluded under this subsection that challenges an employment consent judgment or order described in paragraph (1) shall be brought in the court, and if possible before the judge, that entered such judgment or order. Nothing in this subsection shall preclude a transfer of such action pursuant to section 1404 of title 28, United States Code.".

§ 109. Protection of extraterritorial employment

(a) Definition of Employee. Section 701(f) of the Civil Rights Act of 1964 (42 U.S.C. 2000e(f)) and section 101(4) of the Americans with Disabilities Act of 1990 (42 U.S.C. 12111(4)) are each amended by adding at the end the following: "With respect to employment in a foreign country, such term includes an individual who is a citizen of the United States.".

(b) Exemption.

(1) Civil Rights Act of 1964. Section 702 of the Civil Rights Act of 1964 (42 U.S.C. 2000e–1) is amended—

(A) by inserting "(a)" after "Sec. 702."; and

(B) by adding at the end the following:

"(b) It shall not be unlawful under section 703 or 704 for an employer (or a corporation controlled by an employer), labor organization, employment agency, or joint labor-management committee controlling apprenticeship or other training or retraining (including on-the-job training programs) to take any action otherwise prohibited by such section, with respect to an employee in a workplace in a foreign country if compliance with such section would cause such employer (or such corporation), such organization, such agency, or such committee to violate the law of the foreign country in which such workplace is located.

"(c)(1) If an employer controls a corporation whose place of incorporation is a foreign country, any practice prohibited by section 703 or 704 engaged in by such corporation shall be presumed to be engaged in by such employer.

"(2) Sections 703 and 704 shall not apply with respect to the foreign operations of an employer that is a foreign person not controlled by an American employer.

"(3) For purposes of this subsection, the determination of whether an employer controls a corporation shall be based on—

"(A) the interrelation of operations;

"(B) the common management;

"(C) the centralized control of labor relations; and

"(D) the common ownership or financial control, of the employer and the corporation.".

(2) Americans With Disabilities Act of 1990. Section 102 of the Americans with Disabilities Act of 1990 (42 U.S.C. 12112) is amended—

(A) by redesignating subsection (c) as subsection (d); and

(B) by inserting after subsection (b) the following new subsection:

"(c) Covered Entities in Foreign Countries.

"**(1) In General.** It shall not be unlawful under this section for a covered entity to take any action that constitutes discrimination under this section with respect to an employee in a workplace in a foreign country if compliance with this section would cause such covered entity to violate the law of the foreign country in which such workplace is located.

"(2) Control of Corporation.

"**(A) Presumption.** If an employer controls a corporation whose place of incorporation is a foreign country, any practice that constitutes discrimination under this section and is engaged in by such corporation shall be presumed to be engaged in by such employer.

"**(B) Exception.** This section shall not apply with respect to the foreign operations of an employer that is a foreign person not controlled by an American employer.

"**(C) Determination.** For purposes of this paragraph, the determination of whether an employer controls a corporation shall be based on—

"(i) the interrelation of operations;

"(ii) the common management;

"(iii) the centralized control of labor relations; and

"(iv) the common ownership or financial control, of the employer and the corporation.".

(c) Application of Amendments. The amendments made by this section shall not apply with respect to conduct occurring before the date of the enactment of this Act.

§ 110. Technical Assistance Training Institute

(a) Technical Assistance. Section 705 of the Civil Rights Act of 1964 (42 U.S.C. 2000e–4) is amended by adding at the end the following new subsection:

"(j)(1) The Commission shall establish a Technical Assistance Training Institute, through which the Commission shall provide technical assistance and training regarding the laws and regulations enforced by the Commission.

"(2) An employer or other entity covered under this title shall not be excused from compliance with the requirements of this title because of any failure to receive technical assistance under this subsection.

"(3) There are authorized to be appropriated to carry out this subsection such sums as may be necessary for fiscal year 1992.".

(b) Effective Date. The amendment made by this section shall take effect on the date of the enactment of this Act.

§ 111.   Education and outreach

Section 705(h) of the Civil Rights Act of 1964 (42 U.S.C. 2000e–4(h)) is amended—

(1) by inserting "(1)" after "(h)"; and

(2) by adding at the end the following new paragraph:

"(2) In exercising its powers under this title, the Commission shall carry out educational and outreach activities (including dissemination of information in languages other than English) targeted to—

"(A) individuals who historically have been victims of employment discrimination and have not been equitably served by the Commission; and

"(B) individuals on whose behalf the Commission has authority to enforce any other law prohibiting employment discrimination,

concerning rights and obligations under this title or such law, as the case may be.".

§ 112.   Expansion of right to challenge discriminatory seniority systems

Section 706(e) of the Civil Rights Act of 1964 (42 U.S.C. 2000e–5(e)) is amended—

(1) by inserting "(1)" before "A charge under this section"; and

(2) by adding at the end the following new paragraph:

"(2) For purposes of this section, an unlawful employment practice occurs, with respect to a seniority system that has been adopted for an intentionally discriminatory purpose in violation of this title (whether or not that discriminatory purpose is apparent on the face of the seniority provision), when the seniority system is adopted, when an individual becomes subject to the seniority system, or when a person aggrieved is injured by the application of the seniority system or provision of the system.".

§ 113.   Authorizing award of expert fees

(a) Revised Statutes. Section 722 of the Revised Statutes is amended—

(1) by designating the first and second sentences as subsections (a) and (b), respectively, and indenting accordingly; and

(2) by adding at the end the following new subsection:

"(c) In awarding an attorney's fee under subsection (b) in any action or proceeding to enforce a provision of section 1977 or 1977A of the Revised Statutes, the court, in its discretion, may include expert fees as part of the attorney's fee.".

(b) Civil Rights Act of 1964. Section 706(k) of the Civil Rights Act of 1964 (42 U.S.C. 2000e–5(k)) is amended by inserting "(including expert fees)" after "attorney's fee".

§ 114. Providing for interest and extending the statute of limitations in actions against the federal government

Section 717 of the Civil Rights Act of 1964 (42 U.S.C. 2000e–16) is amended—

(1) in subsection (c), by striking "thirty days" and inserting "90 days"; and

(2) in subsection (d), by inserting before the period ", and the same interest to compensate for delay in payment shall be available as in cases involving nonpublic parties.".

§ 115. Notice of limitations period under the Age Discrimination in Employment Act of 1967

Section 7(e) of the Age Discrimination in Employment Act of 1967 (29 U.S.C. 626(e)) is amended—

(1) by striking paragraph (2);

(2) by striking the paragraph designation in paragraph (1);

(3) by striking "Sections 6 and" and inserting "Section"; and

(4) by adding at the end the following:

"If a charge filed with the Commission under this Act is dismissed or the proceedings of the Commission are otherwise terminated by the Commission, the Commission shall notify the person aggrieved. A civil action may be brought under this section by a person defined in section 11(a) against the respondent named in the charge within 90 days after the date of the receipt of such notice.".

§ 116. Lawful court–ordered remedies, affirmative action, and conciliation agreements not affected

Nothing in the amendments made by this title shall be construed to affect court-ordered remedies, affirmative action, or conciliation agreements, that are in accordance with the law.

§ 117. Coverage of House of Representatives and the Agencies of the Legislative Branch

(a) Coverage of the House of Representatives.

(1) In General. Notwithstanding any provision of title VII of the Civil Rights Act of 1964 (42 U.S.C. 2000e et seq.) or of other law, the purposes of such title shall, subject to paragraph (2), apply in their entirety to the House of Representatives.

(2) Employment in the House.

(A) Application. The rights and protections under title VII of the Civil Rights Act of 1964 (42 U.S.C. 2000e et seq.) shall, subject to subparagraph (B), apply with respect to any employee in an employment position in the House of Representatives and any employing authority of the House of Representatives.

(B) Administration.

(i) In General. In the administration of this paragraph, the remedies and procedures made applicable pursuant to the resolution described in clause (ii) shall apply exclusively.

(ii) Resolution. The resolution referred to in clause (i) is the Fair Employment Practices Resolution (House Resolution 558 of the One Hundredth Congress, as agreed to October 4, 1988), as incorporated into the Rules of the House of Representatives of the One Hundred Second Congress as Rule LI, or any other provision that continues in effect the provisions of such resolution.

(C) Exercise of Rulemaking Power. The provisions of subparagraph (B) are enacted by the House of Representatives as an exercise of the rulemaking power of the House of Representatives, with full recognition of the right of the House to change its rules, in the same manner, and to the same extent as in the case of any other rule of the House.

(b) Instrumentalities of Congress.

(1) In General. The rights and protections under this title and title VII of the Civil Rights Act of 1964 (42 U.S.C. 2000e et seq.) shall, subject to paragraph (2), apply with respect to the conduct of each instrumentality of the Congress.

(2) Establishment of Remedies and Procedures by Instrumentalities. The chief official of each instrumentality of the Congress shall establish remedies and procedures to be utilized with respect to the rights and protections provided pursuant to paragraph (1). Such remedies and procedures shall apply exclusively, except for the employees who are defined as Senate employees, in section 301(c)(1).

(3) Report to Congress. The chief official of each instrumentality of the Congress shall, after establishing remedies and procedures for purposes of paragraph (2), submit to the Congress a report describing the remedies and procedures.

(4) Definition of Instrumentalities. For purposes of this section, instrumentalities of the Congress include the following: the

Architect of the Capitol, the Congressional Budget Office, the General Accounting Office, the Government Printing Office, the Office of Technology Assessment, and the United States Botanic Garden.

(5) Construction. Nothing in this section shall alter the enforcement procedures for individuals protected under section 717 of title VII for the Civil Rights Act of 1964 (42 U.S.C. 2000e–16).

§ 118. Alternative Means of Dispute Resolution

Where appropriate and to the extent authorized by law, the use of alternative means of dispute resolution, including settlement negotiations, conciliation, facilitation, mediation, factfinding, minitrials, and arbitration, is encouraged to resolve disputes arising under the Acts or provisions of Federal law amended by this title.

TITLE II—GLASS CEILING

§ 201. Short Title

This title may be cited as the "Glass Ceiling Act of 1991".

§ 202. Findings and Purpose

(a) Findings. Congress finds that—

(1) despite a dramatically growing presence in the workplace, women and minorities remain underrepresented in management and decisionmaking positions in business;

(2) artificial barriers exist to the advancement of women and minorities in the workplace;

(3) United States corporations are increasingly relying on women and minorities to meet employment requirements and are increasingly aware of the advantages derived from a diverse work force;

(4) the "Glass Ceiling Initiative" undertaken by the Department of Labor, including the release of the report entitled "Report on the Glass Ceiling Initiative", has been instrumental in raising public awareness of—

(A) the underrepresentation of women and minorities at the management and decisionmaking levels in the United States work force;

(B) the underrepresentation of women and minorities in line functions in the United States work force;

(C) the lack of access for qualified women and minorities to credential-building developmental opportunities; and

(D) the desirability of eliminating artificial barriers to the advancement of women and minorities to such levels;

(5) the establishment of a commission to examine issues raised by the Glass Ceiling Initiative would help—

(A) focus greater attention on the importance of eliminating artificial barriers to the advancement of women and minorities to management and decisionmaking positions in business; and

(B) promote work force diversity;

(6) a comprehensive study that includes analysis of the manner in which management and decisionmaking positions are filled, the developmental and skill-enhancing practices used to foster the necessary qualifications for advancement, and the compensation programs and reward structures utilized in the corporate sector would assist in the establishment of practices and policies promoting opportunities for, and eliminating artificial barriers to, the advancement of women and minorities to management and decisionmaking positions; and

(7) a national award recognizing employers whose practices and policies promote opportunities for, and eliminate artificial barriers to, the advancement of women and minorities will foster the advancement of women and minorities into higher level positions by—

(A) helping to encourage United States companies to modify practices and policies to promote opportunities for, and eliminate artificial barriers to, the upward mobility of women and minorities; and

(B) providing specific guidance for other United States employers that wish to learn how to revise practices and policies to improve the access and employment opportunities of women and minorities.

(b) **Purpose.** The purpose of this title is to establish—

(1) a Glass Ceiling Commission to study—

(A) the manner in which business fills management and decisionmaking positions;

(B) the developmental and skill-enhancing practices used to foster the necessary qualifications for advancement into such positions; and

(C) the compensation programs and reward structures currently utilized in the workplace; and

(2) an annual award for excellence in promoting a more diverse skilled work force at the management and decisionmaking levels in business.

§ 203. Establishment of Glass Ceiling Commission

(a) **In General.** There is established a Glass Ceiling Commission (referred to in this title as the "Commission"), to conduct a study and prepare recommendations concerning—

(1) eliminating artificial barriers to the advancement of women and minorities; and

(2) increasing the opportunities and developmental experiences of women and minorities to foster advancement of women and minorities to management and decisionmaking positions in business.

(b) Membership.

(1) Composition. The Commission shall be composed of 21 members, including—

(A) six individuals appointed by the President;

(B) six individuals appointed jointly by the Speaker of the House of Representatives and the Majority Leader of the Senate;

(C) one individual appointed by the Majority Leader of the House of Representatives;

(D) one individual appointed by the Minority Leader of the House of Representatives;

(E) one individual appointed by the Majority Leader of the Senate;

(F) one individual appointed by the Minority Leader of the Senate;

(G) two Members of the House of Representatives appointed jointly by the Majority Leader and the Minority Leader of the House of Representatives;

(H) two Members of the Senate appointed jointly by the Majority Leader and the Minority Leader of the Senate; and

(I) the Secretary of Labor.

(2) Considerations. In making appointments under subparagraphs (A) and (B) of paragraph (1), the appointing authority shall consider the background of the individuals, including whether the individuals—

(A) are members of organizations representing women and minorities, and other related interest groups;

(B) hold management or decisionmaking positions in corporations or other business entities recognized as leaders on issues relating to equal employment opportunity; and

(C) possess academic expertise or other recognized ability regarding employment issues.

(3) Balance. In making the appointments under subparagraphs (A) and (B) of paragraph (1), each appointing authority shall seek to include an appropriate balance of appointees from among the groups of appointees described in subparagraphs (A), (B), and (C) of paragraph (2).

(c) Chairperson. The Secretary of Labor shall serve as the Chairperson of the Commission.

(d) Term of Office. Members shall be appointed for the life of the Commission.

(e) Vacancies. Any vacancy occurring in the membership of the Commission shall be filled in the same manner as the original appointment for the position being vacated. The vacancy shall not affect the power of the remaining members to execute the duties of the Commission.

(f) Meetings.

(1) Meetings Prior to Completion of Report. The Commission shall meet not fewer than five times in connection with and pending the completion of the report described in section 204(b). The Commission shall hold additional meetings if the Chairperson or a majority of the members of the Commission request the additional meetings in writing.

(2) Meetings After Completion of Report. The Commission shall meet once each year after the completion of the report described in section 204(b). The Commission shall hold additional meetings if the Chairperson or a majority of the members of the Commission request the additional meetings in writing.

(g) Quorum. A majority of the Commission shall constitute a quorum for the transaction of business.

(h) Compensation and Expenses.

(1) Compensation. Each member of the Commission who is not an employee of the Federal Government shall receive compensation at the daily equivalent of the rate specified for level V of the Executive Schedule under section 5316 of title 5, United States Code, for each day the member is engaged in the performance of duties for the Commission, including attendance at meetings and conferences of the Commission, and travel to conduct the duties of the Commission.

(2) Travel Expenses. Each member of the Commission shall receive travel expenses, including per diem in lieu of subsistence, at rates authorized for employees of agencies under subchapter I of chapter 57 of title 5, United States Code, for each day the member is engaged in the performance of duties away from the home or regular place of business of the member.

(3) Employment Status. A member of the Commission, who is not otherwise an employee of the Federal Government, shall not be deemed to be an employee of the Federal Government except for the purposes of—

(A) the tort claims provisions of chapter 171 of title 28, United States Code; and

(B) subchapter I of chapter 81 of title 5, United States Code, relating to compensation for work injuries.

§ 204. Research on Advancement of Women and Minorities to Management and Decisionmaking Positions in Business

(a) Advancement Study. The Commission shall conduct a study of opportunities for, and artificial barriers to, the advancement of women and minorities to management and decisionmaking positions in business. In conducting the study, the Commission shall—

(1) examine the preparedness of women and minorities to advance to management and decisionmaking positions in business;

(2) examine the opportunities for women and minorities to advance to management and decisionmaking positions in business;

(3) conduct basic research into the practices, policies, and manner in which management and decisionmaking positions in business are filled;

(4) conduct comparative research of businesses and industries in which women and minorities are promoted to management and decisionmaking positions, and businesses and industries in which women and minorities are not promoted to management and decisionmaking positions;

(5) compile a synthesis of available research on programs and practices that have successfully led to the advancement of women and minorities to management and decisionmaking positions in business, including training programs, rotational assignments, developmental programs, reward programs, employee benefit structures, and family leave policies; and

(6) examine any other issues and information relating to the advancement of women and minorities to management and decisionmaking positions in business.

(b) Report. Not later than 15 months after the date of the enactment of this Act, the Commission shall prepare and submit to the President and the appropriate committees of Congress a written report containing—

(1) the findings and conclusions of the Commission resulting from the study conducted under subsection (a); and

(2) recommendations based on the findings and conclusions described in paragraph (1) relating to the promotion of opportunities for, and elimination of artificial barriers to, the advancement of women and minorities to management and decisionmaking positions in business, including recommendations for—

(A) policies and practices to fill vacancies at the management and decisionmaking levels;

(B) developmental practices and procedures to ensure that women and minorities have access to opportunities to gain the exposure, skills, and expertise necessary to assume management and decisionmaking positions;

(C) compensation programs and reward structures utilized to reward and retain key employees; and

(D) the use of enforcement (including such enforcement techniques as litigation, complaint investigations, compliance reviews, conciliation, administrative regulations, policy guidance, technical assistance, training, and public education) of Federal equal employment opportunity laws by Federal agencies as a means of eliminating artificial barriers to the advancement of women and minorities in employment.

(c) **Additional Study.** The Commission may conduct such additional study of the advancement of women and minorities to management and decisionmaking positions in business as a majority of the members of the Commission determines to be necessary.

§ 205. Establishment of the National Award for Diversity and Excellence in American Executive Management

(a) **In General.** There is established the National Award for Diversity and Excellence in American Executive Management, which shall be evidenced by a medal bearing the inscription "Frances Perkins–Elizabeth Hanford Dole National Award for Diversity and Excellence in American Executive Management". The medal shall be of such design and materials, and bear such additional inscriptions, as the Commission may prescribe.

(b) **Criteria for Qualification.** To qualify to receive an award under this section a business shall—

(1) submit a written application to the Commission, at such time, in such manner, and containing such information as the Commission may require, including at a minimum information that demonstrates that the business has made substantial effort to promote the opportunities and developmental experiences of women and minorities to foster advancement to management and decisionmaking positions within the business, including the elimination of artificial barriers to the advancement of women and minorities, and deserves special recognition as a consequence; and

(2) meet such additional requirements and specifications as the Commission determines to be appropriate.

(c) **Making and Presentation of Award.**

(1) **Award.** After receiving recommendations from the Commission, the President or the designated representative of the President shall annually present the award described in subsection (a) to businesses that meet the qualifications described in subsection (b).

(2) Presentation. The President or the designated representative of the President shall present the award with such ceremonies as the President or the designated representative of the President may determine to be appropriate.

(3) Publicity. A business that receives an award under this section may publicize the receipt of the award and use the award in its advertising, if the business agrees to help other United States businesses improve with respect to the promotion of opportunities and developmental experiences of women and minorities to foster the advancement of women and minorities to management and decisionmaking positions.

(d) Business. For the purposes of this section, the term "business" includes—

(1)(A) a corporation including nonprofit corporations;

(B) a partnership;

(C) a professional association;

(D) a labor organization; and

(E) a business entity similar to an entity described in subparagraphs (A) through (D);

(2) an education referral program, a training program, such as an apprenticeship or management training program or a similar program; and

(3) a joint program formed by a combination of any entities described in paragraph (1) or (2).

§ 206. Powers of the Commission

(a) In General. The Commission is authorized to—

(1) hold such hearings and sit and act at such times;

(2) take such testimony;

(3) have such printing and binding done;

(4) enter into such contracts and other arrangements;

(5) make such expenditures; and

(6) take such other actions;

as the Commission may determine to be necessary to carry out the duties of the Commission.

(b) Oaths. Any member of the Commission may administer oaths or affirmations to witnesses appearing before the Commission.

(c) Obtaining Information From Federal Agencies. The Commission may secure directly from any Federal agency such information as the Commission may require to carry out its duties.

(d) Voluntary Service. Notwithstanding section 1342 of title 31, United States Code, the Chairperson of the Commission may accept for the Commission voluntary services provided by a member of the Commission.

(e) Gifts and Donations. The Commission may accept, use, and dispose of gifts or donations of property in order to carry out the duties of the Commission.

(f) Use of Mail. The Commission may use the United States mails in the same manner and under the same conditions as Federal agencies.

§ 207. Confidentiality of Information

(a) Individual Business Information.

(1) In General. Except as provided in paragraph (2), and notwithstanding section 552 of title 5, United States Code, in carrying out the duties of the Commission, including the duties described in sections 204 and 205, the Commission shall maintain the confidentiality of all information that concerns—

(A) the employment practices and procedures of individual businesses; or

(B) individual employees of the businesses.

(2) Consent. The content of any information described in paragraph (1) may be disclosed with the prior written consent of the business or employee, as the case may be, with respect to which the information is maintained.

(b) Aggregate Information. In carrying out the duties of the Commission, the Commission may disclose—

(1) information about the aggregate employment practices or procedures of a class or group of businesses; and

(2) information about the aggregate characteristics of employees of the businesses, and related aggregate information about the employees.

§ 208. Staff and Consultants

(a) Staff.

(1) Appointment and Compensation. The Commission may appoint and determine the compensation of such staff as the Commission determines to be necessary to carry out the duties of the Commission.

(2) Limitations. The rate of compensation for each staff member shall not exceed the daily equivalent of the rate specified for level V of the Executive Schedule under section 5316 of title 5, United States Code for each day the staff member is engaged in the performance of duties for the Commission. The Commission may otherwise appoint and determine the compensation of staff without regard to the provisions of title 5, United States Code, that govern appointments in the competitive service, and the provisions of chapter 51 and subchapter III of chapter 53 of title 5, United States Code, that relate to classification and General Schedule pay rates.

(b) Experts and Consultants. The Chairperson of the Commission may obtain such temporary and intermittent services of experts and consultants and compensate the experts and consultants in accordance with section 3109(b) of title 5, United States Code, as the Commission determines to be necessary to carry out the duties of the Commission.

(c) Detail of Federal Employees. On the request of the Chairperson of the Commission, the head of any Federal agency shall detail, without reimbursement, any of the personnel of the agency to the Commission to assist the Commission in carrying out its duties. Any detail shall not interrupt or otherwise affect the civil service status or privileges of the Federal employee.

(d) Technical Assistance. On the request of the Chairperson of the Commission, the head of a Federal agency shall provide such technical assistance to the Commission as the Commission determines to be necessary to carry out its duties.

§ 209. Authorization of Appropriations

There are authorized to be appropriated to the Commission such sums as may be necessary to carry out the provisions of this title. The sums shall remain available until expended, without fiscal year limitation.

§ 210. Termination

(a) Commission. Notwithstanding section 15 of the Federal Advisory Committee Act (5 U.S.C.App.), the Commission shall terminate 4 years after the date of the enactment of this Act.

(b) Award. The authority to make awards under section 205 shall terminate 4 years after the date of the enactment of this Act.

TITLE III—GOVERNMENT EMPLOYEE RIGHTS

§ 301. Government Employee Rights Act of 1991

(a) Short Title. This title may be cited as the "Government Employee Rights Act of 1991".

(b) Purpose. The purpose of this title is to provide procedures to protect the right of Senate and other government employees, with respect to their public employment, to be free of discrimination on the basis of race, color, religion, sex, national origin, age, or disability.

(c) Definitions. For purposes of this title:

(1) **Senate Employee.** The term "Senate employee" or "employee" means—

(A) any employee whose pay is disbursed by the Secretary of the Senate;

(B) any employee of the Architect of the Capitol who is assigned to the Senate Restaurants or to the Superintendent of the Senate Office Buildings;

(C) any applicant for a position that will last 90 days or more and that is to be occupied by an individual described in subparagraph (A) or (B); or

(D) any individual who was formerly an employee described in subparagraph (A) or (B) and whose claim of a violation arises out of the individual's Senate employment.

(2) Head of Employing Office. The term "head of employing office" means the individual who has final authority to appoint, hire, discharge, and set the terms, conditions or privileges of the Senate employment of an employee.

(3) Violation. The term "violation" means a practice that violates section 302 of this title.

§ 302. Discriminatory Practices Prohibited

All personnel actions affecting employees of the Senate shall be made free from any discrimination based on—

(1) race, color, religion, sex, or national origin, within the meaning of section 717 of the Civil Rights Act of 1964 (42 U.S.C. 2000e–16);

(2) age, within the meaning of section 15 of the Age Discrimination in Employment Act of 1967 (29 U.S.C. 633a); or

(3) handicap or disability, within the meaning of section 501 of the Rehabilitation Act of 1973 (29 U.S.C. 791) and sections 102–104 of the Americans with Disabilities Act of 1990 (42 U.S.C. 12112–14).

§ 303. Establishment of Office of Senate Fair Employment Practices

(a) In General. There is established, as an office of the Senate, the Office of Senate Fair Employment Practices (referred to in this title as the "Office"), which shall—

(1) administer the processes set forth in sections 305 through 307;

(2) implement programs for the Senate to heighten awareness of employee rights in order to prevent violations from occurring.

(b) Director.

(1) In General. The Office shall be headed by a Director (referred to in this title as the "Director") who shall be appointed by the President pro tempore, upon the recommendation of the Majority Leader in consultation with the Minority Leader. The appointment shall be made without regard to political affiliation and solely on the basis of fitness to perform the duties of the position. The Director shall be appointed for a term of service which shall expire at the end of the Congress following the Congress during which the Director is appointed. A Director may be reappointed at the termination of any term of service. The President pro tempore, upon the joint recommendation of the Majority Leader in consultation with the Minority Leader, may remove the Director at any time.

(2) Salary. The President pro tempore, upon the recommendation of the Majority Leader in consultation with the Minority Leader, shall establish the rate of pay for the Director. The salary of the Director may not be reduced during the employment of the Director and shall be increased at the same time and in the same manner as fixed statutory salary rates within the Senate are adjusted as a result of annual comparability increases.

(3) Annual Budget. The Director shall submit an annual budget request for the Office to the Committee on Appropriations.

(4) Appointment of Director. The first Director shall be appointed and begin service within 90 days after the date of enactment of this Act, and thereafter the Director shall be appointed and begin service within 30 days after the beginning of the session of the Congress immediately following the termination of a Director's term of service or within 60 days after a vacancy occurs in the position.

(c) Staff of the Office.

(1) Appointment. The Director may appoint and fix the compensation of such additional staff, including hearing officers, as are necessary to carry out the purposes of this title.

(2) Detailees. The Director may, with the prior consent of the Government department or agency concerned and the Committee on Rules and Administration, use on a reimbursable or nonreimbursable basis the services of any such department or agency, including the services of members or personnel of the General Accounting Office Personnel Appeals Board.

(3) Consultants. In carrying out the functions of the Office, the Director may procure the temporary (not to exceed 1 year) or intermittent services of individual consultants, or organizations thereof, in the same manner and under the same conditions as a standing committee of the Senate may procure such services under section 202(i) of the Legislative Reorganization Act of 1946 (2 U.S.C. 72a(i)).

(d) Expenses of the Office. In fiscal year 1992, the expenses of the Office shall be paid out of the Contingent Fund of the Senate from the appropriation account Miscellaneous Items. Beginning in fiscal year 1993, and for each fiscal year thereafter, there is authorized to be appropriated for the expenses of the Office such sums as shall be necessary to carry out its functions. In all cases, expenses shall be paid out of the Contingent Fund of the Senate upon vouchers approved by the Director, except that a voucher shall not be required for—

(1) the disbursement of salaries of employees who are paid at an annual rate;

(2) the payment of expenses for telecommunications services provided by the Telecommunications Department, Sergeant at Arms, United States Senate;

(3) the payment of expenses for stationery supplies purchased through the Keeper of the Stationery, United States Senate;

(4) the payment of expenses for postage to the Postmaster, United States Senate; and

(5) the payment of metered charges on copying equipment provided by the Sergeant at Arms, United States Senate.

The Secretary of the Senate is authorized to advance such sums as may be necessary to defray the expenses incurred in carrying out this title. Expenses of the Office shall include authorized travel for personnel of the Office.

(e) Rules of the Office. The Director shall adopt rules governing the procedures of the Office, including the procedures of hearing boards, which rules shall be submitted to the President pro tempore for publication in the Congressional Record. The rules may be amended in the same manner. The Director may consult with the Chairman of the Administrative Conference of the United States on the adoption of rules.

(f) Representation by the Senate Legal Counsel. For the purpose of representation by the Senate Legal Counsel, the Office shall be deemed a committee, within the meaning of title VII of the Ethics in Government Act of 1978 (2 U.S.C. 288, et seq.).

§ 304. Senate Procedure for Consideration of Alleged Violations

The Senate procedure for consideration of alleged violations consists of 4 steps as follows:

(1) Step I, counseling, as set forth in section 305.

(2) Step II, mediation, as set forth in section 306.

(3) Step III, formal complaint and hearing by a hearing board, as set forth in section 307.

(4) Step IV, review of a hearing board decision, as set forth in section 308 or 309.

§ 305. Step I: Counseling

(a) In General. A Senate employee alleging a violation may request counseling by the Office. The Office shall provide the employee with all relevant information with respect to the rights of the employee. A request for counseling shall be made not later than 180 days after the alleged violation forming the basis of the request for counseling occurred. No request for counseling may be made until 10 days after the first Director begins service pursuant to section 303(b)(4).

(b) Period of Counseling. The period for counseling shall be 30 days unless the employee and the Office agree to reduce the period. The period shall begin on the date the request for counseling is received.

(c) Employees of the Architect of the Capitol and Capitol Police. In the case of an employee of the Architect of the Capitol or an employee who is a member of the Capitol Police, the Director may refer the employee to the Architect of the Capitol or the Capitol Police Board for resolution of the employee's complaint through the internal grievance procedures of the Architect of the Capitol or the Capitol Police Board for a specific period of time, which shall not count against the time available for counseling or mediation under this title.

§ 306. Step II: Mediation

(a) In General. Not later than 15 days after the end of the counseling period, the employee may file a request for mediation with the Office. Mediation may include the Office, the employee, and the employing office in a process involving meetings with the parties separately or jointly for the purpose of resolving the dispute between the employee and the employing office.

(b) Mediation Period. The mediation period shall be 30 days beginning on the date the request for mediation is received and may be extended for an additional 30 days at the discretion of the Office. The Office shall notify the employee and the head of the employing office when the mediation period has ended.

§ 307. Step III: Formal Complaint and Hearing

(a) Formal Complaint and Request for Hearing. Not later than 30 days after receipt by the employee of notice from the Office of the end of the mediation period, the Senate employee may file a formal complaint with the Office. No complaint may be filed unless the employee has made a timely request for counseling and has completed the procedures set forth in sections 305 and 306.

(b) Hearing Board. A board of 3 independent hearing officers (referred to in this title as "hearing board"), who are not Senators or officers or employees of the Senate, chosen by the Director (one of whom shall be designated by the Director as the presiding hearing officer) shall be assigned to consider each complaint filed under this section. The Director shall appoint hearing officers after considering any candidates who are recommended to the Director by the Federal Mediation and Conciliation Service, the Administrative Conference of the United States, or organizations composed primarily of individuals experienced in adjudicating or arbitrating personnel matters. A hearing board shall act by majority vote.

(c) Dismissal of Frivolous Claims. Prior to a hearing under subsection (d), a hearing board may dismiss any claim that it finds to be frivolous.

(d) Hearing. A hearing shall be conducted—

(1) in closed session on the record by a hearing board;

(2) no later than 30 days after filing of the complaint under subsection (a), except that the Office may, for good cause, extend up to an additional 60 days the time for conducting a hearing; and

(3) except as specifically provided in this title and to the greatest extent practicable, in accordance with the principles and procedures set forth in sections 554 through 557 of title 5, United States Code.

(e) Discovery. Reasonable prehearing discovery may be permitted at the discretion of the hearing board.

(f) Subpoena.

(1) Authorization. A hearing board may authorize subpoenas, which shall be issued by the presiding hearing officer on behalf of the hearing board, for the attendance of witnesses at proceedings of the hearing board and for the production of correspondence, books, papers, documents, and other records.

(2) Objections. If a witness refuses, on the basis of relevance, privilege, or other objection, to testify in response to a question or to produce records in connection with the proceedings of a hearing board, the hearing board shall rule on the objection. At the request of the witness, the employee, or employing office, or on its own initiative, the hearing board may refer the objection to the Select Committee on Ethics for a ruling.

(3) Enforcement. The Select Committee on Ethics may make to the Senate any recommendations by report or resolution, including recommendations for criminal or civil enforcement by or on behalf of the Office, which the Select Committee on Ethics may consider appropriate with respect to—

(A) the failure or refusal of any person to appear in proceedings under this section or to produce records in obedience to a subpoena or order of the hearing board; or

(B) the failure or refusal of any person to answer questions during his or her appearance as a witness in a proceeding under this section.

For purposes of section 1365 of title 28, United States Code, the Office shall be deemed to be a committee of the Senate.

(g) Decision. The hearing board shall issue a written decision as expeditiously as possible, but in no case more than 45 days after the conclusion of the hearing. The written decision shall be transmitted by the Office to the employee and the employing office. The decision shall state the issues raised by the complaint, describe the evidence in the record, and contain a determination as to whether a violation has occurred.

(h) Remedies. If the hearing board determines that a violation has occurred, it shall order such remedies as would be appropriate if awarded under section 706(g) and (k) of the Civil Rights Act of 1964 (42 U.S.C. 2000e–5(g) and (k)), and may also order the award of such compensatory damages as would be appropriate if awarded under section 1977 and section 1977A(a) and (b)(2) of the Revised Statutes (42 U.S.C. §§ 1981 and 1981A(a) and (b)(2)). In the case of a determination that a violation based on age has occurred, the hearing board shall order such remedies as would be appropriate if awarded under section 15(c) of the Age Discrimination in Employment Act of 1967 (29 U.S.C. § 633a(c)). Any order requiring the payment of money must be approved by a Senate resolution reported by the Committee on Rules and Administration. The hearing board shall have no authority to award punitive damages.

(i) Precedent and Interpretations. Hearing boards shall be guided by judicial decisions under statutes referred to in section 302 and subsection (h) of this section, as well as the precedents developed by the Select Committee on Ethics under section 308, and other Senate precedents.

§ 308.   Review by the Select Committee on Ethics

(a) In General. An employee or the head of an employing office may request that the Select Committee on Ethics (referred to in this section as the "Committee"), or such other entity as the Senate may designate, review a decision under section 307, including any decision following a remand under subsection (c), by filing a request for review with the Office not later than 10 days after the receipt of the decision of a hearing board. The Office, at the discretion of the Director, on its own initiative and for good cause, may file a request for review by the Committee of a decision of a hearing board not later than 5 days after the time for the employee or employing office to file a request for review has expired. The Office shall transmit a copy of any request for review to the Committee and notify the interested parties of the filing of the request for review.

(b) Review. Review under this section shall be based on the record of the hearing board. The Committee shall adopt and publish in the Congressional Record procedures for requests for review under this section.

(c) Remand. Within the time for a decision under subsection (d), the Committee may remand a decision no more than one time to the hearing board for the purpose of supplementing the record or for further consideration.

(d) Final Decision.

(1) **Hearing Board.** If no timely request for review is filed under subsection (a), the Office shall enter as a final decision, the decision of the hearing board.

(2) **Select Committee on Ethics.**

(A) If the Committee does not remand under subsection (c), it shall transmit a written final decision to the Office for entry in the records of the Office. The Committee shall transmit the decision not later than 60 calendar days during which the Senate is in session after the filing of a request for review under subsection (a). The Committee may extend for 15 calendar days during which the Senate is in session the period for transmission to the Office of a final decision.

(B) The decision of the hearing board shall be deemed to be a final decision, and entered in the records of the Office as a final decision, unless a majority of the Committee votes to reverse or remand the decision of the hearing board within the time for transmission to the Office of a final decision.

(C) The decision of the hearing board shall be deemed to be a final decision, and entered in the records of the Office as a final decision, if the Committee, in its discretion, decides not to review, pursuant to a request for review under subsection (a), a decision of the hearing board, and notifies the interested parties of such decision.

(3) Entry of a Final Decision. The entry of a final decision in the records of the Office shall constitute a final decision for purposes of judicial review under section 309.

(e) Statement of Reasons. Any decision of the Committee under subsection (c) or subsection (d)(2)(A) shall contain a written statement of the reasons for the Committee's decision.

§ 309. Judicial Review

(a) In General. Any Senate employee aggrieved by a final decision under section 308(d), or any Member of the Senate who would be required to reimburse the appropriate Federal account pursuant to the section entitled "Payments by the President or a Member of the Senate" and a final decision entered pursuant to section 308(d)(2)(B), may petition for review by the United States Court of Appeals for the Federal Circuit.

(b) Law Applicable. Chapter 158 of title 28, United States Code, shall apply to a review under this section except that—

(1) with respect to section 2344 of title 28, United States Code, service of the petition shall be on the Senate Legal Counsel rather than on the Attorney General;

(2) the provisions of section 2348 of title 28, United States Code, on the authority of the Attorney General, shall not apply;

(3) the petition for review shall be filed not later than 90 days after the entry in the Office of a final decision under section 308(d);

(4) the Office shall be an "agency" as that term is used in chapter 158 of title 28, United States Code; and

(5) the Office shall be the respondent in any proceeding under this section.

(c) Standard of Review. To the extent necessary to decision and when presented, the court shall decide all relevant questions of law and interpret constitutional and statutory provisions. The court shall set aside a final decision if it is determined that the decision was—

(1) arbitrary, capricious, an abuse of discretion, or otherwise not consistent with law;

(2) not made consistent with required procedures; or

(3) unsupported by substantial evidence.

In making the foregoing determinations, the court shall review the whole record, or those parts of it cited by a party, and due account shall be taken of the rule of prejudicial error. The record on review shall include the record before the hearing board, the decision of the hearing board, and the decision, if any, of the Select Committee on Ethics.

(d) Attorney's Fees. If an employee is the prevailing party in a proceeding under this section, attorney's fees may be allowed by the court in accordance with the standards prescribed under section 706(k) of the Civil Rights Act of 1964 (42 U.S.C. § 2000e–5(k)).

§ 310. Resolution of Complaint

If, after a formal complaint is filed under section 307, the employee and the head of the employing office resolve the issues involved, the employee may dismiss the complaint or the parties may enter into a written agreement, subject to the approval of the Director.

§ 311. Costs of Attending Hearings

Subject to the approval of the Director, an employee with respect to whom a hearing is held under this title may be reimbursed for actual and reasonable costs of attending proceedings under sections 307 and 308, consistent with Senate travel regulations. Senate Resolution 259, agreed to August 5, 1987 (100th Congress, 1st Session), shall apply to witnesses appearing in proceedings before a hearing board.

§ 312. Prohibition of Intimidation

Any intimidation of, or reprisal against, any employee by any Member, officer, or employee of the Senate, or by the Architect of the Capitol, or anyone employed by the Architect of the Capitol, as the case may be, because of the exercise of a right under this title constitutes an unlawful employment practice, which may be remedied in the same manner under this title as is a violation.

§ 313. Confidentiality

(a) Counseling. All counseling shall be strictly confidential except that the Office and the employee may agree to notify the head of the employing office of the allegations.

(b) Mediation. All mediation shall be strictly confidential.

(c) Hearings. Except as provided in subsection (d), the hearings, deliberations, and decisions of the hearing board and the Select Committee on Ethics shall be confidential.

(d) Final Decision of Select Committee on Ethics. The final decision of the Select Committee on Ethics under section 308 shall be made public if the decision is in favor of the complaining Senate employee or if the decision reverses a decision of the hearing board which had been in favor of the employee. The Select Committee on Ethics may decide to release any other decision at its discretion. In the absence of a proceeding under section 308, a decision of the hearing board that is favorable to the employee shall be made public.

(e) Release of Records for Judicial Review. The records and decisions of hearing boards, and the decisions of the Select Committee on Ethics, may be made public if required for the purpose of judicial review under section 309.

§ 314. Exercise of Rulemaking Power

The provisions of this title, except for sections 309, 320, 321, and 322, are enacted by the Senate as an exercise of the rulemaking power of the Senate, with full recognition of the right of the Senate to change its rules, in the same manner, and to the same extent, as in the case of any other rule of the Senate. Notwithstanding any other provision of law, except as provided in section 309, enforcement and adjudication with respect to the discriminatory practices prohibited by section 302, and arising out of Senate employment, shall be within the exclusive jurisdiction of the United States Senate.

§ 315. Technical and Conforming Amendments

Section 509 of the Americans with Disabilities Act of 1990 (42 U.S.C. 12209) is amended—

(1) in subsection (a)—

(A) by striking paragraphs (2) through (5);

(B) by redesignating paragraphs (6) and (7) as paragraphs (2) and (3), respectively; and

(C) in paragraph (3), as redesignated by subparagraph (B) of this paragraph—

(i) by striking "(2) and (6)(A)" and inserting "(2)(A)", as redesignated by subparagraph (B) of this paragraph; and

(ii) by striking "(3), (4), (5), (6)(B), and (6)(C)" and inserting "(2)"; and

(2) in subsection (c)(2), by inserting ", except for the employees who are defined as Senate employees, in section 301(c)(1) of the Civil Rights Act of 1991" after "shall apply exclusively".

§ 316. Political Affiliation and Place of Residence

(a) In General. It shall not be a violation with respect to an employee described in subsection (b) to consider the—

(1) party affiliation;

(2) domicile; or

(3) political compatibility with the employing office, of such an employee with respect to employment decisions.

(b) Definition. For purposes of this section, the term "employee" means—

(1) an employee on the staff of the Senate leadership;

(2) an employee on the staff of a committee or subcommittee;

(3) an employee on the staff of a Member of the Senate;

(4) an officer or employee of the Senate elected by the Senate or appointed by a Member, other than those described in paragraphs (1) through (3); or

(5) an applicant for a position that is to be occupied by an individual described in paragraphs (1) through (4).

§ 317. Other Review

No Senate employee may commence a judicial proceeding to redress discriminatory practices prohibited under section 302 of this title, except as provided in this title.

§ 318. Other Instrumentalities of the Congress

It is the sense of the Senate that legislation should be enacted to provide the same or comparable rights and remedies as are provided under this title to employees of instrumentalities of the Congress not provided with such rights and remedies.

§ 319. Rule XLII of the Standing Rules of the Senate

(a) Reaffirmation. The Senate reaffirms its commitment to Rule XLII of the Standing Rules of the Senate, which provides as follows:

"No Member, officer, or employee of the Senate shall, with respect to employment by the Senate or any office thereof—

"(a) fail or refuse to hire an individual;

"(b) discharge an individual; or

"(c) otherwise discriminate against an individual with respect to promotion, compensation, or terms, conditions, or privileges of employment on the basis of such individual's race, color, religion, sex, national origin, age, or state of physical handicap.".

(b) Authority to Discipline. Notwithstanding any provision of this title, including any provision authorizing orders for remedies to Senate employees to redress employment discrimination, the Select

Committee on Ethics shall retain full power, in accordance with its authority under Senate Resolution 338, 88th Congress, as amended, with respect to disciplinary action against a Member, officer, or employee of the Senate for a violation of Rule XLII.

§ 320.   Coverage of Presidential Appointees

(a) In General.

(1) Application. The rights, protections, and remedies provided pursuant to section 302 and 307(h) of this title shall apply with respect to employment of Presidential appointees.

(2) Enforcement by Administrative Action. Any Presidential appointee may file a complaint alleging a violation, not later than 180 days after the occurrence of the alleged violation, with the Equal Employment Opportunity Commission, or such other entity as is designated by the President by Executive Order, which, in accordance with the principles and procedures set forth in sections 554 through 557 of title 5, United States Code, shall determine whether a violation has occurred and shall set forth its determination in a final order. If the Equal Employment Opportunity Commission, or such other entity as is designated by the President pursuant to this section, determines that a violation has occurred, the final order shall also provide for appropriate relief.

(3) Judicial Review.

(A) In General. Any party aggrieved by a final order under paragraph (2) may petition for review by the United States Court of Appeals for the Federal Circuit.

(B) Law Applicable. Chapter 158 of title 28, United States Code, shall apply to a review under this section except that the Equal Employment Opportunity Commission or such other entity as the President may designate under paragraph (2) shall be an "agency" as that term is used in chapter 158 of title 28, United States Code.

(C) Standard of Review. To the extent necessary to decision and when presented, the reviewing court shall decide all relevant questions of law and interpret constitutional and statutory provisions. The court shall set aside a final order under paragraph (2) if it is determined that the order was—

(i) arbitrary, capricious, an abuse of discretion, or otherwise not consistent with law;

(ii) not made consistent with required procedures; or

(iii) unsupported by substantial evidence.

In making the foregoing determinations, the court shall review the whole record or those parts of it cited by a party, and due account shall be taken of the rule of prejudicial error.

(D) Attorney's fees. If the presidential appointee is the prevailing party in a proceeding under this section, attorney's fees may be allowed by the court in accordance with the standards prescribed under section 706(k) of the Civil Rights Act of 1964 (42 U.S.C. 2000e–5(k)).

(b) Presidential Appointee. For purposes of this section, the term "Presidential appointee" means any officer or employee, or an applicant seeking to become an officer or employee, in any unit of the Executive Branch, including the Executive Office of the President, whether appointed by the President or by any other appointing authority in the Executive Branch, who is not already entitled to bring an action under any of the statutes referred to in section 302 but does not include any individual—

(1) whose appointment is made by and with the advice and consent of the Senate;

(2) who is appointed to an advisory committee, as defined in section 3(2) of the Federal Advisory Committee Act (5 U.S.C.App.); or

(3) who is a member of the uniformed services.

§ 321. Coverage of Previously Exempt State Employees

(a) Application. The rights, protections, and remedies provided pursuant to section 302 and 307(h) of this title shall apply with respect to employment of any individual chosen or appointed, by a person elected to public office in any State or political subdivision of any State by the qualified voters thereof—

(1) to be a member of the elected official's personal staff;

(2) to serve the elected official on the policymaking level; or

(3) to serve the elected official as an immediate advisor with respect to the exercise of the constitutional or legal powers of the office.

(b) Enforcement by Administrative Action.

(1) In General. Any individual referred to in subsection (a) may file a complaint alleging a violation, not later than 180 days after the occurrence of the alleged violation, with the Equal Employment Opportunity Commission, which, in accordance with the principles and procedures set forth in sections 554 through 557 of title 5, United States Code, shall determine whether a violation has occurred and shall set forth its determination in a final order. If the Equal Employment Opportunity Commission determines that a violation has occurred, the final order shall also provide for appropriate relief.

(2) Referral to State and Local Authorities.

(A) Application. Section 706(d) of the Civil Rights Act of 1964 (42 U.S.C. 2000e–5(d)) shall apply with respect to any proceeding under this section.

(B) Definition. For purposes of the application described in subparagraph (A), the term "any charge filed by a member of the Commission alleging an unlawful employment practice" means a complaint filed under this section.

(c) Judicial Review. Any party aggrieved by a final order under subsection (b) may obtain a review of such order under chapter 158 of title 28, United States Code. For the purpose of this review, the Equal Employment Opportunity Commission shall be an "agency" as that term is used in chapter 158 of title 28, United States Code.

(d) Standard of Review. To the extent necessary to decision and when presented, the reviewing court shall decide all relevant questions of law and interpret constitutional and statutory provisions. The court shall set aside a final order under subsection (b) if it is determined that the order was—

(1) arbitrary, capricious, an abuse of discretion, or otherwise not consistent with law;

(2) not made consistent with required procedures; or

(3) unsupported by substantial evidence.

In making the foregoing determinations, the court shall review the whole record or those parts of it cited by a party, and due account shall be taken of the rule of prejudicial error.

(e) Attorney's Fees. If the individual referred to in subsection (a) is the prevailing party in a proceeding under this subsection, attorney's fees may be allowed by the court in accordance with the standards prescribed under section 706(k) of the Civil Rights Act of 1964 (42 U.S.C. 2000e–5(k)).

§ 322. Severability

Notwithstanding section 401 of this Act, if any provision of section 309 or 320(a)(3) is invalidated, both sections 309 and 320(a)(3) shall have no force and effect.

§ 323. Payments by the President or a Member of the Senate

The President or a Member of the Senate shall reimburse the appropriate Federal account for any payment made on his or her behalf out of such account for a violation committed under the provisions of this title by the President or Member of the Senate not later than 60 days after the payment is made.

§ 324. Reports of Senate Committees

(a) Each report accompanying a bill or joint resolution of a public character reported by any committee of the Senate (except the Committee on Appropriations and the Committee on the Budget) shall contain a listing of the provisions of the bill or joint resolution that apply to Congress and an evaluation of the impact of such provisions on Congress.

(b) The provisions of this section are enacted by the Senate as an exercise of the rulemaking power of the Senate, with full recognition of the right of the Senate to change its rules, in the same manner, and to the same extent, as in the case of any other rule of the Senate.

§ 325. Intervention and Expedited Review of Certain Appeals

(a) Intervention. Because of the constitutional issues that may be raised by section 309 and section 320, any Member of the Senate may intervene as a matter of right in any proceeding under section 309 for the sole purpose of determining the constitutionality of such section.

(b) Threshold Matter. In any proceeding under section 309 or section 320, the United States Court of Appeals for the Federal Circuit shall determine any issue presented concerning the constitutionality of such section as a threshold matter.

(c) Appeal.

(1) In General. An appeal may by taken directly to the Supreme Court of the United States from any interlocutory or final judgment, decree, or order issued by the United States Court of Appeals for the Federal Circuit ruling upon the constitutionality of section 309 or 320.

(2) Jurisdiction. The Supreme Court shall, if it has not previously ruled on the question, accept jurisdiction over the appeal referred to in paragraph (1), advance the appeal on the docket and expedite the appeal to the greatest extent possible.

TITLE IV—GENERAL PROVISIONS

§ 401. Severability

If any provision of this Act, or an amendment made by this Act, or the application of such provision to any person or circumstances is held to be invalid, the remainder of this Act and the amendments made by this Act, and the application of such provision to other persons and circumstances, shall not be affected.

§ 402. Effective Date

(a) In General. Except as otherwise specifically provided, this Act and the amendments made by this Act shall take effect upon enactment.

(b) Certain Disparate Impact Cases. Notwithstanding any other provision of this Act, nothing in this Act shall apply to any disparate impact case for which a complaint was filed before March 1, 1975, and for which an initial decision was rendered after October 30, 1983.

TITLE VI OF THE CIVIL RIGHTS ACT OF 1964 (INCLUDING THE CIVIL RIGHTS RESTORATION ACT OF 1967), 42 U.S.C. §§ 2000d, d–1, d–3, d–4a

§ 2000d. (§ 601) Prohibition against exclusion from participation in, denial of benefits of, and discrimination under Federally assisted programs on ground of race, color, or national origin

No person in the United States shall, on the ground of race, color, or national origin, be excluded from participation in, be denied the benefits of, or be subjected to discrimination under any program or activity receiving Federal financial assistance.

(Pub.L. 88–352, Title VI, § 601, July 2, 1964, 78 Stat. 252.)

§ 2000d–1. (§ 602) Federal authority and financial assistance to programs or activities by way of grant, loan, or contract other than contract of insurance or guaranty; rules and regulations, etc.

Each Federal department and agency which is empowered to extend Federal financial assistance to any program or activity, by way of grant, loan, or contract other than a contract of insurance or guaranty, is authorized and directed to effectuate the provisions of section 2000d of this title with respect to such program or activity by issuing rules, regulations, or orders of general applicability which shall be consistent with achievement of the objectives of the statute authorizing the financial assistance in connection with which the action is taken. No such rule, regulation, or order shall become effective unless and until approved by the President. Compliance with any requirement adopted pursuant to this section may be effected (1) by the termination of or refusal to grant or to continue assistance under such program or activity to any recipient as to whom there has been an express finding on the record, after opportunity for hearing, of a failure to comply with such requirement, but such termination or refusal shall be limited to the particular political entity, or party thereof, or other recipient as to whom such a finding has been made and, shall be limited in its effect to the particular program, or part thereof, in which such noncompliance has been so found, or (2) by any other means authorized by law: *Provided, however,* That no such action shall be taken until the department or agency concerned has advised the appropriate person or persons of the failure to comply with the requirement and has determined that compliance cannot be secured by voluntary means. In the case of any action terminating, or refusing to grant or continue, assistance because of failure to comply with a requirement imposed pursuant to this section, the head of the Federal department or agency shall file with the committees of the House and Senate having legislative jurisdiction over the program or activity involved a full written report of the circumstances and the grounds for such action. No such action shall become effective until thirty days have elapsed after the filing of such report.

(Pub.L. 88–352, Title VI, § 602, July 2, 1964, 78 Stat. 252.)

§ 2000d–3.   (§ 604) Construction of provisions not to authorize administrative action with respect to employment practices except where primary objective of Federal financial assistance is to provide employment

Nothing contained in this subchapter shall be construed to authorize action under this subchapter by any department or agency with respect to any employment practice of any employer, employment agency, or labor organization except where a primary objective of the Federal financial assistance is to provide employment.

(Pub.L. 88–352, Title VI, § 604, July 2, 1964, 78 Stat. 253.)

§ 2000d–4a.   (§ 606) "Program or activity" defined

For the purposes of this subchapter, the term "program or activity" and the term "program" mean all of the operations of—

(1)(A) a department, agency, special purpose district, or other instrumentality of a State or of a local government; or

(B) the entity of such State or local government that distributes such assistance and each such department or agency (and each other State or local government entity) to which the assistance is extended, in the case of assistance to a State or local government;

(2)(A) a college, university, or other postsecondary institution, or a public system of higher education; or

(B) a local educational agency (as defined in section 9101 of the Elementary and Secondary Education Act of 1965, system of vocational education), or other school system;

(3)(A) an entire corporation, partnership, or other private organization, or an entire sole proprietorship—

(i) if assistance is extended to such corporation, partnership, private organization, or sole proprietorship as a whole; or

(ii) which is principally engaged in the business of providing education, health care, housing, social services, or parks and recreation; or

(B) the entire plant or other comparable, geographically separate facility to which Federal financial assistance is extended, in the case of any other corporation, partnership, private organization, or sole proprietorship; or

(4) any other entity which is established by two or more of the entities described in paragraph (1), (2), or (3);

any part of which is extended Federal financial assistance.

(Pub.L. 88–352, Title VI, § 606, as added Pub.L. 100–259, § 6, Mar. 22, 1988, 102 Stat. 31.)

EQUAL PAY ACT OF 1963
29 U.S.C. § 206(d)

§ 206.   (§ 6) Minimum wage

Prohibition of sex discrimination

(d)(1) No employer having employees subject to any provisions of this section shall discriminate, within any establishment in which such employees are employed, between employees on the basis of sex by paying wages to employees in such establishment at a rate less than the rate at which he pays wages to employees of the opposite sex in such establishment for equal work on jobs the performance of which requires equal skill, effort, and responsibility, and which are performed under similar working conditions, except where such payment is made pursuant to (i) a seniority system; (ii) a merit system; (iii) a system which measures earnings by quantity or quality of production; or (iv) a differential based on any other factor other than sex: *Provided,* That an employer who is paying a wage rate differential in violation of this subsection shall not, in order to comply with the provisions of this subsection, reduce the wage rate of any employee.

(2) No labor organization, or its agents, representing employees of an employer having employees subject to any provisions of this section shall cause or attempt to cause such an employer to discriminate against an employee in violation of paragraph (1) of this subsection.

(3) For purposes of administration and enforcement, any amounts owing to any employee which have been withheld in violation of this subsection shall be deemed to be unpaid minimum wages or unpaid overtime compensation under this chapter.

(4) As used in this subsection, the term "labor organization" means any organization of any kind, or any agency or employee representation committee or plan, in which employees participate and which exists for the purpose, in whole or in part, of dealing with employers concerning grievances, labor disputes, wages, rates of pay, hours of employment, or conditions of work.

(June 10, 1963, Pub. L. 88–38, § 3, 77 Stat. 56).

FAMILY AND MEDICAL LEAVE ACT
29 U.S.C. §§ 2601, 2611–19

§ 2601. Findings and purposes

(a) Findings.

Congress finds that—

(1) the number of single-parent households and two-parent households in which the single parent or both parents work is increasing significantly;

(2) it is important for the development of children and the family unit that fathers and mothers be able to participate in early childrearing and the care of family members who have serious health conditions;

(3) the lack of employment policies to accommodate working parents can force individuals to choose between job security and parenting;

(4) there is inadequate job security for employees who have serious health conditions that prevent them from working for temporary periods;

(5) due to the nature of the roles of men and women in our society, the primary responsibility for family caretaking often falls on women, and such responsibility affects the working lives of women more than it affects the working lives of men; and

(6) employment standards that apply to one gender only have serious potential for encouraging employers to discriminate against employees and applicants for employment who are of that gender.

(b) Purposes.

It is the purpose of this Act—

(1) to balance the demands of the workplace with the needs of families, to promote the stability and economic security of families, and to promote national interests in preserving family integrity;

(2) to entitle employees to take reasonable leave for medical reasons, for the birth or adoption of a child, and for the care of a child, spouse, or parent who has a serious health condition;

(3) to accomplish the purposes described in paragraphs (1) and (2) in a manner that accommodates the legitimate interests of employers;

(4) to accomplish the purposes described in paragraphs (1) and (2) in a manner that, consistent with the Equal Protection Clause of the Fourteenth Amendment minimizes the potential for employment discrimination on the basis of sex by ensuring generally that leave is available for eligible medical reasons (including maternity-related disability) and for compelling family reasons, on a gender-neutral basis;

(5) to promote the goal of equal employment opportunity for women and men, pursuant to such clause.

(Pub. L. 103–3, Title I, 107 Stat. 6.)

§ 2611. Definitions

As used in this subchapter:

(1) Commerce. The terms "commerce" and "industry or activity affecting commerce" mean any activity, business, or industry in commerce or in which a labor dispute would hinder or obstruct commerce or the free flow of commerce, and include "commerce" and any "industry affecting commerce" as defined in paragraphs (1) and (3) of section 142 of this title.

(2) Eligible employee.

(A) In general. The term "eligible employee" means an employee who has been employed—

(i) for at least 12 months by the employer with respect to whom leave is requested under section 2612 of this title; and

(ii) for at least 1,250 hours of service with such employer during the previous 12–month period.

(B) Exclusions. The term "eligible employee" does not include—

(i) any Federal officer or employee covered under subchapter V of chapter 63 of Title 5; or

(ii) any employee of an employer who is employed at a worksite at which such employer employs less than 50 employees if the total number of employees employed by that employer within 75 miles of that worksite is less than 50.

(C) Determination. For purposes of determining whether an employee meets the hours of service requirement specified in subparagraph (A)(ii), the legal standards established under section 207 of this title shall apply.

(3) Employ; employee; State. The terms "employ", "employee", and "State" shall have the same meanings given such terms in subsections (c), (e), and (g) of section 203 of this title.

(4) Employer.

(A) In general. The term "employer"—

(i) means any person engaged in commerce or in any industry or activity affecting commerce who employs 50 or more employees for each working day during each of 20 or more calendar workweeks in the current or preceding calendar year;

(ii) includes—

(I) any person who acts, directly or indirectly, in the interest of an employer to any of the employees of such employer; and

(II) any successor in interest of an employer;

(iii) includes any "public agency", as defined in section 203(x) of this title; and

(iv) includes the General Accounting Office and the Library of Congress.

(B) Public agency. For purposes of subparagraph (A)(iii), a public agency shall be considered to be a person engaged in commerce or in an industry or activity affecting commerce.

(5) Employment benefits. The term "employment benefits" means all benefits provided or made available to employees by an employer, including group life insurance, health insurance, disability insurance, sick leave, annual leave, educational benefits, and pensions, regardless of whether such benefits are provided by a practice or written policy of an employer or through an "employee benefit plan", as defined in section 1002(3) of this title.

(6) Health care provider. The term "health care provider" means—

(A) a doctor of medicine or osteopathy who is authorized to practice medicine or surgery (as appropriate) by the State in which the doctor practices; or

(B) any other person determined by the Secretary to be capable of providing health care services.

(7) Parent. The term "parent" means the biological parent of an employee or an individual who stood in loco parentis to an employee when the employee was a son or daughter.

(8) Person. The term "person" has the same meaning given such term in section 203(a) of this title.

(9) Reduced leave schedule. The term "reduced leave schedule" means a leave schedule that reduces the usual number of hours per workweek, or hours per workday, of an employee.

(10) Secretary. The term "Secretary" means the Secretary of Labor.

(11) Serious health condition. The term "serious health condition" means an illness, injury, impairment, or physical or mental condition that involves—

(A) inpatient care in a hospital, hospice, or residential medical care facility; or

(B) continuing treatment by a health care provider.

(12) Son or daughter. The term "son or daughter" means a biological, adopted, or foster child, a stepchild, a legal ward, or a child of a person standing in loco parentis, who is—

(A) under 18 years of age; or

(B) 18 years of age or older and incapable of self-care because of a mental or physical disability.

(13) Spouse. The term "spouse" means a husband or wife, as the case may be.

(Pub. L. 103–3, Title I, § 101, 107 Stat. 7; Pub. L. 104–1, Title II, § 202(c)(1)(A), 109 Stat. 9.)

§ 2612.   Leave requirement

(a) In general.

(1) Entitlement to leave. Subject to section 103, an eligible employee shall be entitled to a total of 12 workweeks of leave during any 12–month period for one or more of the following:

(A) Because of the birth of a son or daughter of the employee and in order to care for such son or daughter.

(B) Because of the placement of a son or daughter with the employee for adoption or foster care.

(C) In order to care for the spouse, or a son, daughter, or parent, of the employee, if such spouse, son, daughter, or parent has a serious health condition.

(D) Because of a serious health condition that makes the employee unable to perform the functions of the position of such employee.

(E) Because of any qualifying exigency (as the Secretary shall, by regulation, determine) arising out of the fact that the spouse, or a son, daughter, or parent of the employee is on active duty (or has been notified of an impending call or order to active duty) in the Armed Forces in support of a contingency operation.

(2) Expiration of entitlement. The entitlement to leave under subparagraphs (A) and (B) of paragraph (1) for a birth or placement of a son or daughter shall expire at the end of the 12–month period beginning on the date of such birth or placement.

(3) Servicemember family leave. Subject to section 103, an eligible employee who is the spouse, son, daughter, parent, or next of kin of a covered servicemember shall be entitled to a total of 26 workweeks of leave during a 12–month period to care for the servicemember. The leave described in this paragraph shall only be available during a single 12–month period.

(4) Combined leave total. During the single 12–month period described in paragraph (3), an eligible employee shall be entitled to a combined total of 26 workweeks of leave under paragraphs (1) and (3). Nothing in this paragraph shall be construed to limit the availability of leave under paragraph (1) during any other 12–month period.

(b) Leave taken intermittently or on a reduced leave schedule.

(1) In general. Leave under subparagraph (A) or (B) of subsection (a)(1) shall not be taken by an employee intermittently or on a reduced leave schedule unless the employee and the employer of the employee agree otherwise. Subject to paragraph (2), subsection (e)(2), and subsection (b)(5) or (f) (as appropriate) of section 103, leave under subparagraph (C) or (D) of subsection (a)(1) or under subsection (a)(3) may be taken intermittently or on a reduced leave schedule when medically necessary. Subject to subsection (e)(3) and section 103(f), leave under subsection (a)(1)(E) may be taken intermittently or on a reduced leave schedule. The taking of leave intermittently or on a reduced leave schedule pursuant to this paragraph shall not result in a reduction in the total amount of leave to which the employee is entitled under subsection (a) beyond the amount of leave actually taken.

(2) Alternative position. If an employee requests intermittent leave, or leave on a reduced leave schedule, under subparagraph (C) or (D) of subsection (a)(1) or under subsection (a)(3), that is foreseeable based on planned medical treatment, the employer may require such employee to transfer temporarily to an available alternative position offered by the employer for which the employee is qualified and that—

    (A) has equivalent pay and benefits; and

    (B) better accommodates recurring periods of leave than the regular employment position of the employee.

(c) Unpaid leave permitted. Except as provided in subsection (d), leave granted under subsection (a) may consist of unpaid leave. Where an employee is otherwise exempt under regulations issued by the Secretary pursuant to section 13(a)(1) of the Fair Labor Standards Act of 1938 (29 U.S.C. 213(a)(1)), the compliance of an employer with this title by providing unpaid leave shall not affect the exempt status of the employee under such section.

(d) Relationship to paid leave.

(1) Unpaid leave. If an employer provides paid leave for fewer than 12 workweeks (or 26 workweeks in the case of leave provided under subsection (a)(3)), the additional weeks of leave necessary to attain the 12 workweeks (or 26 workweeks, as appropriate) of leave required under this title may be provided without compensation.

(2) Substitution of paid leave.

    (A) In general. An eligible employee may elect, or an employer may require the employee, to substitute any of the accrued paid vacation leave, personal leave, or family leave of the employee for leave provided under subparagraph (A), (B), (C), or (E) of subsection (a)(1) for any part of the 12-week period of such leave under such subsection.

(B) Serious health condition. An eligible employee may elect, or an employer may require the employee, to substitute any of the accrued paid vacation leave, personal leave, or medical or sick leave of the employee for leave provided under subparagraph (C) or (D) of subsection (a)(1) for any part of the 12–week period of such leave under such subsection, except that nothing in this title shall require an employer to provide paid sick leave or paid medical leave in any situation in which such employer would not normally provide any such paid leave. An eligible employee may elect, or an employer may require the employee, to substitute any of the accrued paid vacation leave, personal leave, family leave, or medical or sick leave of the employee for leave provided under subsection (a)(3) for any part of the 26–week period of such leave under such subsection, except that nothing in this title requires an employer to provide paid sick leave or paid medical leave in any situation in which the employer would not normally provide any such paid leave.

(e) Foreseeable leave.

(1) Requirement of notice. In any case in which the necessity for leave under subparagraph (A) or (B) of subsection (a)(1) is foreseeable based on an expected birth or placement, the employee shall provide the employer with not less than 30 days' notice, before the date the leave is to begin, of the employee's intention to take leave under such subparagraph, except that if the date of the birth or placement requires leave to begin in less than 30 days, the employee shall provide such notice as is practicable.

(2) Duties of employee. In any case in which the necessity for leave under subparagraph (C) or (D) of subsection (a)(1) or under subsection (a)(3) is foreseeable based on planned medical treatment, the employee—

(A) shall make a reasonable effort to schedule the treatment so as not to disrupt unduly the operations of the employer, subject to the approval of the health care provider of the employee or the health care provider of the son, daughter, spouse, or parent of the employee, as appropriate; and

(B) shall provide the employer with not less than 30 days' notice, before the date the leave is to begin, of the employee's intention to take leave under such subparagraph, except that if the date of the treatment requires leave to begin in less than 30 days, the employee shall provide such notice as is practicable.

(3) Notice for leave due to active duty of family member. In any case in which the necessity for leave under subsection (a)(1)(E) is foreseeable, whether because the spouse, or a son, daughter, or parent, of the employee is on active duty, or because of notification of an impending call or order to active duty in support of a contingency operation, the employee shall provide such notice to the employer as is reasonable and practicable.

(f) Spouses employed by the same employer.

(1) In general. In any case in which a husband and wife entitled to leave under subsection (a) are employed by the same employer, the aggregate number of workweeks of leave to which both may be entitled may be limited to 12 workweeks during any 12–month period, if such leave is taken—

    (A) under subparagraph (A) or (B) of subsection (a)(1); or

    (B) to care for a sick parent under subparagraph (C) of such subsection.

(2) Servicemember family leave.

    (A) In general. The aggregate number of workweeks of leave to which both that husband and wife may be entitled under subsection (a) may be limited to 26 workweeks during the single 12–month period described in subsection (a)(3) if the leave is—

        (i) leave under subsection (a)(3); or

        (ii) a combination of leave under subsection (a)(3) and leave described in paragraph (1).

    (B) Both limitations applicable. If the leave taken by the husband and wife includes leave described in paragraph (1), the limitation in paragraph (1) shall apply to the leave described in paragraph (1).

(Feb. 5, 1993, P.L. 103–3, Title I, § 102, 107 Stat. 9; as amended Jan. 28, 2008, P.L. 110–181, Div. A, Title V, Subtitle H, § 585(a)(2)–(3)(D), 122 Stat. 129.)

§ 2613. Certification

(a) In general. An employer may require that a request for leave under subparagraph (C) or (D) of paragraph (1) or paragraph (3) of section 102(a) be supported by a certification issued by the health care provider of the eligible employee or of the son, daughter, spouse, or parent of the employee, or of the next of kin of an individual in the case of leave taken under such paragraph (3), as appropriate. The employee shall provide, in a timely manner, a copy of such certification to the employer.

(b) Sufficient certification. Certification provided under subsection (a) shall be sufficient if it states—

    (1) the date on which the serious health condition commenced;

    (2) the probable duration of the condition;

    (3) the appropriate medical facts within the knowledge of the health care provider regarding the condition;

    (4)(A) for purposes of leave under section 102(a)(1)(C), a statement that the eligible employee is needed to care for the son, daughter, spouse, or parent and an estimate of the amount of time that such employee is needed to care for the son, daughter, spouse, or parent; and

(B) for purposes of leave under section 102(a)(1)(D), a statement that the employee is unable to perform the functions of the position of the employee;

(5) in the case of certification for intermittent leave, or leave on a reduced leave schedule, for planned medical treatment, the dates on which such treatment is expected to be given and the duration of such treatment;

(6) in the case of certification for intermittent leave, or leave on a reduced leave schedule, under section 102(a)(1)(D), a statement of the medical necessity for the intermittent leave or leave on a reduced leave schedule, and the expected duration of the intermittent leave or reduced leave schedule; and

(7) in the case of certification for intermittent leave, or leave on a reduced leave schedule, under section 102(a)(1)(C), a statement that the employee's intermittent leave or leave on a reduced leave schedule is necessary for the care of the son, daughter, parent, or spouse who has a serious health condition, or will assist in their recovery, and the expected duration and schedule of the intermittent leave or reduced leave schedule.

(c) Second opinion.

(1) In general. In any case in which the employer has reason to doubt the validity of the certification provided under subsection (a) for leave under subparagraph (C) or (D) of section 102(a)(1), the employer may require, at the expense of the employer, that the eligible employee obtain the opinion of a second health care provider designated or approved by the employer concerning any information certified under subsection (b) for such leave.

(2) Limitation. A health care provider designated or approved under paragraph (1) shall not be employed on a regular basis by the employer.

(d) Resolution of conflicting opinions.

(1) In general. In any case in which the second opinion described in subsection (c) differs from the opinion in the original certification provided under subsection (a), the employer may require, at the expense of the employer, that the employee obtain the opinion of a third health care provider designated or approved jointly by the employer and the employee concerning the information certified under subsection (b).

(2) Finality. The opinion of the third health care provider concerning the information certified under subsection (b) shall be considered to be final and shall be binding on the employer and the employee.

(e) Subsequent recertification. The employer may require that the eligible employee obtain subsequent recertifications on a reasonable basis.

(f) Certification related to active duty or call to active duty. An employer may require that a request for leave under section 102(a)(1)(E) be supported by a certification issued at such time and in such manner as the Secretary may by regulation prescribe. If the Secretary issues a regulation requiring such certification, the employee shall provide, in a timely manner, a copy of such certification to the employer.

(Feb. 5, 1993, P.L. 103–3, Title I, § 103, 107 Stat. 11; as amended Jan. 28, 2008, P.L. 110–181, Div. A, Title V, Subtitle H, § 585(a)(3)(E), 122 Stat. 130).

§ 2614.   Employment and benefits protection

(a) Restoration to position.

(1) In general. Except as provided in subsection (b), any eligible employee who takes leave under section 2612 for the intended purpose of the leave shall be entitled, on return from such leave—

(A) to be restored by the employer to the position of employment held by the employee when the leave commenced; or

(B) to be restored to an equivalent position with equivalent employment benefits, pay, and other terms and conditions of employment.

(2) Loss of benefits. The taking of leave under section 2612 shall not result in the loss of any employment benefit accrued prior to the date on which the leave commenced.

(3) Limitations. Nothing in this section shall be construed to entitle any restored employee to—

(A) the accrual of any seniority or employment benefits during any period of leave; or

(B) any right, benefit, or position of employment other than any right, benefit, or position to which the employee would have been entitled had the employee not taken the leave.

(4) Certification. As a condition of restoration under paragraph (1) for an employee who has taken leave under section 2612(a)(1)(D), the employer may have a uniformly applied practice or policy that requires each such employee to receive certification from the health care provider of the employee that the employee is able to resume work, except that nothing in this paragraph shall supersede a valid State or local law or a collective bargaining agreement that governs the return to work of such employees.

(5) Construction. Nothing in this subsection shall be construed to prohibit an employer from requiring an employee on leave under section 2612 to report periodically to the employer on the status and intention of the employee to return to work.

(b) Exemption concerning certain highly compensated employees.

(1) Denial of restoration. An employer may deny restoration under subsection (a) to any eligible employee described in paragraph (2) if—

(A) such denial is necessary to prevent substantial and grievous economic injury to the operations of the employer;

(B) the employer notifies the employee of the intent of the employer to deny restoration on such basis at the time the employer determines that such injury would occur; and

(C) in any case in which the leave has commenced, the employee elects not to return to employment after receiving such notice.

(2) Affected employees. An eligible employee described in paragraph (1) is a salaried eligible employee who is among the highest paid 10 percent of the employees employed by the employer within 75 miles of the facility at which the employee is employed.

(c) Maintenance of health benefits.

(1) Coverage. Except as provided in paragraph (2), during any period that an eligible employee takes leave under section 2612, the employer shall maintain coverage under any "group health plan" (as defined in section 5000(b)(1) of the Internal Revenue Code of 1986 [26 U.S.C. § 5000(b)(1)]) for the duration of such leave at the level and under the conditions coverage would have been provided if the employee had continued in employment continuously for the duration of such leave.

(2) Failure to return from leave. The employer may recover the premium that the employer paid for maintaining coverage for the employee under such group health plan during any period of unpaid leave under section 2612 if—

(A) the employee fails to return from leave under section 2612 after the period of leave to which the employee is entitled has expired; and

(B) the employee fails to return to work for a reason other than—

(i) the continuation, recurrence, or onset of a serious health condition that entitles the employee to leave under subparagraph (C) or (D) of section 2612(a)(1) or under section 2612(a)(3); or

(ii) other circumstances beyond the control of the employee.

(3) Certification.

(A) Issuance. An employer may require that a claim that an employee is unable to return to work because of the continuation, recurrence, or onset of the serious health condition described in paragraph (2)(B)(i) be supported by—

(i) a certification issued by the health care provider of the son, daughter, spouse, or parent of the employee, as appropriate, in the case of an employee unable to return to work because of a condition specified in section 2612(a)(1)(C);

(ii) a certification issued by the health care provider of the eligible employee, in the case of an employee unable to return to work because of a condition specified in section 2612(a)(1)(D); or

(iii) a certification issued by the health care provider of the service member being cared for by the employee, in the case of an employee unable to work because of a condition specified in section 2612(a)(3).

(B) Copy. The employee shall provide, in a timely manner, a copy of such certification to the employer.

(C) Sufficiency of certification.

(i) Leave due to serious health condition of employee. The certification described in subparagraph (A)(ii) shall be sufficient if the certification states that a serious health condition prevented the employee from being able to perform the functions of the position of the employee on the date that the leave of the employee expired.

(ii) Leave due to serious health condition of family member. The certification described in subparagraph (A)(i) shall be sufficient if the certification states that the employee is needed to care for the son, daughter, spouse, or parent who has a serious health condition on the date that the leave of the employee expired.

(Pub. L. 103–3, Title I, § 104, 107 Stat. 12, Pub.L. 110–181, 122 Stat. 131.)

§ 2615. Prohibited acts

(a) Interference with rights.

(1) Exercise of rights. It shall be unlawful for any employer to interfere with, restrain, or deny the exercise of or the attempt to exercise, any right provided under this title [29 USC §§ 2611 et seq.].

(2) Discrimination. It shall be unlawful for any employer to discharge or in any other manner discriminate against any individual for opposing any practice made unlawful by this title [29 USC §§ 2611 et seq.].

(b) Interference with proceedings or inquiries.

It shall be unlawful for any person to discharge or in any other manner discriminate against any individual because such individual—

(1) has filed any charge, or has instituted or caused to be instituted any proceeding, under or related to this Act;

(2) has given, or is about to give, any information in connection with any inquiry or proceeding relating to any right provided under this Act; or

(3) has testified, or is about to testify, in any inquiry or proceeding relating to any right provided under this Act.

(Pub. L. 103–3, Title I, § 105, 107 Stat. 14.)

§ 2616. Investigative authority

(a) In general.

To ensure compliance with the provisions of this Act, or any regulation or order issued under this Act, the Secretary shall have, subject to subsection (c), the investigative authority provided under section 211(a) of this title.

(b) Obligation to keep and preserve records.

Any employer shall make, keep, and preserve records pertaining to compliance with this Act in accordance with section 211(c) of this title and in accordance with regulations issued by the Secretary.

(c) Required submissions generally limited to an annual basis.

The Secretary shall not under the authority of this section require any employer or any plan, fund, or program to submit to the Secretary any books or records more than once during any 12–month period, unless the Secretary has reasonable cause to believe there may exist a violation of this Act or any regulation or order issued pursuant to this Act, or is investigating a charge pursuant to section 2617(b).

(d) Subpoena powers.

For the purposes of any investigation provided for in this section, the Secretary shall have the subpoena authority provided for under section 209 of this title.

(Pub. L. 103–3, Title I, § 105, 107 Stat. 15.)

§ 2617. Enforcement

(a) Civil action by employees.

(1) Liability. Any employer who violates section 2615 shall be liable to any eligible employee affected—

(A) for damages equal to—

(i) the amount of—

(I) any wages, salary, employment benefits, or other compensation denied or lost to such employee by reason of the violation; or

(II) in a case in which wages, salary, employment benefits, or other compensation have not been denied or lost to the employee, any actual monetary losses sustained by the employee as a direct result of the violation, such as the cost of providing care, up to a sum equal to 12 weeks (or 26 weeks in a case involving leave under Section 2612(a)(3)) of wages or salary for the employee;

(ii) the interest on the amount described in clause (i) calculated at the prevailing rate; and

(iii) an additional amount as liquidated damages equal to the sum of the amount described in clause (i) and the interest described in clause (ii), except that if an employer who has violated section 2615 proves to the satisfaction of the court that the act or omission which violated section 2615 was in good faith and that the employer had reasonable grounds for believing that the act or omission was not a violation of section 2615, such court may, in the discretion of the court, reduce the amount of the liability to the amount and interest determined under clauses (i) and (ii), respectively; and

(B) for such equitable relief as may be appropriate, including employment, reinstatement, and promotion.

(2) Right of action. An action to recover the damages or equitable relief prescribed in paragraph (1) may be maintained against any employer (including a public agency) in any Federal or State court of competent jurisdiction by any one or more employees for and in behalf of—

(A) the employees; or

(B) the employees and other employees similarly situated.

(3) Fees and costs. The court in such an action shall, in addition to any judgment awarded to the plaintiff, allow a reasonable attorney's fee, reasonable expert witness fees, and other costs of the action to be paid by the defendant.

(4) Limitations. The right provided by paragraph (2) to bring an action by or on behalf of any employee shall terminate—

(A) on the filing of a complaint by the Secretary in an action under subsection (d) in which restraint is sought of any further delay in the payment of the amount described in paragraph (1)(A) to such employee by an employer responsible under paragraph (1) for the payment; or

(B) on the filing of a complaint by the Secretary in an action under subsection (b) in which a recovery is sought of the damages described in paragraph (1)(A) owing to an eligible employee by an employer liable under paragraph (1), unless the action described in subparagraph (A) or (B) is dismissed without prejudice on motion of the Secretary.

(b) Action by the Secretary.

(1) Administrative action. The Secretary shall receive, investigate, and attempt to resolve complaints of violations of section 2615 in the same manner that the Secretary receives, investigates, and attempts to resolve complaints of violations of sections 206 and 207 of this title.

(2) Civil action. The Secretary may bring an action in any court of competent jurisdiction to recover the damages described in subsection (a)(1)(A).

(3) Sums recovered. Any sums recovered by the Secretary pursuant to paragraph (2) shall be held in a special deposit account and shall be paid, on order of the Secretary, directly to each employee affected. Any such sums not paid to an employee because of inability to do so within a period of 3 years shall be deposited into the Treasury of the United States as miscellaneous receipts.

(c) Limitation.

(1) In general. Except as provided in paragraph (2), an action may be brought under this section not later than 2 years after the date of the last event constituting the alleged violation for which the action is brought.

(2) Willful violation. In the case of such action brought for a willful violation of section 2615, such action may be brought within 3 years of the date of the last event constituting the alleged violation for which such action is brought.

(3) Commencement. In determining when an action is commenced by the Secretary under this section for the purposes of this subsection, it shall be considered to be commenced on the date when the complaint is filed.

(d) Action for injunction by Secretary.

The district courts of the United States shall have jurisdiction, for cause shown, in an action brought by the Secretary—

(1) to restrain violations of section 2615, including the restraint of any withholding of payment of wages, salary, employment benefits, or other compensation, plus interest, found by the court to be due to eligible employees; or

(2) to award such other equitable relief as may be appropriate, including employment, reinstatement, and promotion.

(e) Solicitor of Labor.

The Solicitor of Labor may appear for and represent the Secretary on any litigation brought under this section.

(f) General Accounting Office and Library of Congress.

In the case of the General Accounting Office and the Library of Congress, the authority of the Secretary of Labor under this Act shall be exercised respectively by the Comptroller General of the United States and the Librarian of Congress.

(Pub. L. 103–3, Title I, § 107, 107 Stat. 15; Pub. L. 104–1, Title II, Part A, § 202(c)(1)(B), 109 Stat. 9, Pub.L. 110–181, 122 Stat. 131.)

§ 2618.   Special rules concerning employees of local educational agencies

(a) Application.

(1) In general. Except as otherwise provided in this section, the rights (including the rights under section 2614, which shall extend throughout the period of leave of any employee under this section), remedies, and procedures under this Act shall apply to—

(A) any "local educational agency" (as defined in section 14101 of the Elementary and Secondary Education Act of 1965 [20 U.S.C. §§ 8801, 2891(12)]) and an eligible employee of the agency; and

(B) any private elementary or secondary school and an eligible employee of the school.

(2) Definitions. For purposes of the application described in paragraph (1):

(A) **Eligible employee.** The term "eligible employee" means an eligible employee of an agency or school described in paragraph (1).

(B) **Employer.** The term "employer" means an agency or school described in paragraph (1).

(b) Leave does not violate certain other Federal laws.

A local educational agency and a private elementary or secondary school shall not be in violation of the Individuals with Disabilities Education Act (20 U.S.C. §§ 1400 et seq.), section 504 of the Rehabilitation Act of 1973 (29 U.S.C. § 794), or title VI of the Civil Rights Act of 1964 (42 U.S.C. §§ 2000d et seq.), solely as a result of an eligible employee of such agency or school exercising the rights of such employee under this Act.

(c) Intermittent leave or leave on a reduced schedule for instructional employees.

(1) In general. Subject to paragraph (2), in any case in which an eligible employee employed principally in an instructional capacity by any such educational agency or school requests leave under subparagraph (C) or (D) of section 2612(a)(1) or under Section

2612(a)(3) that is foreseeable based on planned medical treatment and the employee would be on leave for greater than 20 percent of the total number of working days in the period during which the leave would extend, the agency or school may require that such employee elect either—

    (A) to take leave for periods of a particular duration, not to exceed the duration of the planned medical treatment; or

    (B) to transfer temporarily to an available alternative position offered by the employer for which the employee is qualified, and that—

        (i) has equivalent pay and benefits; and

        (ii) better accommodates recurring periods of leave than the regular employment position of the employee.

    (2) Application. The elections described in subparagraphs (A) and (B) of paragraph (1) shall apply only with respect to an eligible employee who complies with section 2612(e)(2).

(d) Rules applicable to periods near the conclusion of an academic term.

The following rules shall apply with respect to periods of leave near the conclusion of an academic term in the case of any eligible employee employed principally in an instructional capacity by any such educational agency or school:

    (1) Leave more than 5 weeks prior to end of term. If the eligible employee begins leave under section 2612 more than 5 weeks prior to the end of the academic term, the agency or school may require the employee to continue taking leave until the end of such term, if—

    (A) the leave is of at least 3 weeks duration; and

    (B) the return to employment would occur during the 3–week period before the end of such term.

    (2) Leave less than 5 weeks prior to end of term. If the eligible employee begins leave under subparagraph (A), (B), or (C) of section 2612(a)(1) or under section 2612(a)(3) during the period that commences 5 weeks prior to the end of the academic term, the agency or school may require the employee to continue taking leave until the end of such term, if—

    (A) the leave is of greater than 2 weeks duration; and

    (B) the return to employment would occur during the 2–week period before the end of such term.

    (3) Leave less than 3 weeks prior to end of term. If the eligible employee begins leave under subparagraph (A), (B), or (C) of section 2612(a)(1) or under section 2612(a)(3) during the period that commences 3 weeks prior to the end of the academic term and the duration of the leave is greater than 5 working days, the agency or

school may require the employee to continue to take leave until the end of such term.

(e) Restoration to equivalent employment position.

For purposes of determinations under section 2612(a)(1)(B) (relating to the restoration of an eligible employee to an equivalent position), in the case of a local educational agency or a private elementary or secondary school, such determination shall be made on the basis of established school board policies and practices, private school policies and practices, and collective bargaining agreements.

(f) Reduction of the amount of liability.

If a local educational agency or a private elementary or secondary school that has violated this Act proves to the satisfaction of the court that the agency, school, or department had reasonable grounds for believing that the underlying act or omission was not a violation of this Act, such court may, in the discretion of the court, reduce the amount of the liability provided for under section 2617(a)(1)(A) to the amount and interest determined under clauses (i) and (ii), respectively, of such section.

(Pub. L. 103–3, Title I, § 108, 107 Stat. 17; Pub. L. 103–382, Title III, Part I, § 394(e), 108 Stat. 4027; Pub. L. 110–181, 122 Stat. 131.)

§ 2619. Notice

(a) In general.

Each employer shall post and keep posted, in conspicuous places on the premises of the employer where notices to employees and applicants for employment are customarily posted, a notice, to be prepared or approved by the Secretary, setting forth excerpts from, or summaries of, the pertinent provisions of this Act and information pertaining to the filing of a charge.

(b) Penalty.

Any employer that willfully violates this section may be assessed a civil money penalty not to exceed $100 for each separate offense.

(Pub. L. 103–3, Title I, § 109, 107 Stat. 19.)

LILLY LEDBETTER FAIR PAY ACT OF 2009[†]

§ 1.   Short Title

This Act may be cited as the Lilly Ledbetter Fair Pay Act of 2009.

§ 2.   Findings

Congress finds the following:

(1) The Supreme Court in Ledbetter v. Goodyear Tire & Rubber Co., 550 U.S. 618, 127 S.Ct. 2162, 167 L.Ed.2d 982 (2007), significantly impairs statutory protections against discrimination in compensation that Congress established and that have been bedrock principles of American law for decades. The Ledbetter decision undermines those statutory protections by unduly restricting the time period in which victims of discrimination can challenge and recover for discriminatory compensation decisions or other practices, contrary to the intent of Congress.

(2) The limitation imposed by the Court on the filing of discriminatory compensation claims ignores the reality of wage discrimination and is at odds with the robust application of the civil rights laws that Congress intended.

(3) With regard to any charge of discrimination under any law, nothing in this Act is intended to preclude or limit an aggrieved person's right to introduce evidence of an unlawful employment practice that has occurred outside the time for filing a charge of discrimination.

(4) Nothing in this Act is intended to change current law treatment of when pension distributions are considered paid.

§ 3.   Discrimination in Compensation Because of Race, Color, Religion, Sex, or National Origin

Section 706(e) of the Civil Rights Act of 1964 (42 U.S.C. 2000e–5(e)) is amended by adding at the end the following:

"(3)(A) For purposes of this section, an unlawful employment practice occurs, with respect to discrimination in compensation in violation of this title, when a discriminatory compensation decision or other practice is adopted, when an individual becomes subject to a discriminatory compensation decision or other practice, or when an individual is affected by application of a discriminatory compensation decision or other practice, including each time wages, benefits,

† Pub.L. 111–2, Jan. 29, 2009, 123 Stat. 5–7.

or other compensation is paid, resulting in whole or in part from such a decision or other practice.

(B) In addition to any relief authorized by section 1977A of the Revised Statutes (42 U.S.C. 1981a), liability may accrue and an aggrieved person may obtain relief as provided in subsection (g)(1), including recovery of back pay for up to two years preceding the filing of the charge, where the unlawful employment practices that have occurred during the charge filing period are similar or related to unlawful employment practices with regard to discrimination in compensation that occurred outside the time for filing a charge.''.

§ 4. Discrimination in Compensation Because of Age

Section 7(d) of the Age Discrimination in Employment Act of 1967 (29 U.S.C. 626(d)) is amended—

(1) in the first sentence—

(A) by redesignating paragraphs (1) and (2) as subparagraphs (A) and (B), respectively; and

(B) by striking (d) and inserting ''(d)(1)'';

(2) in the third sentence, by striking ''Upon'' and inserting the following:

''(2) Upon''; and

(3) by adding at the end the following:

''(3) For purposes of this section, an unlawful practice occurs, with respect to discrimination in compensation in violation of this Act, when a discriminatory compensation decision or other practice is adopted, when a person becomes subject to a discriminatory compensation decision or other practice, or when a person is affected by application of a discriminatory compensation decision or other practice, including each time wages, benefits, or other compensation is paid, resulting in whole or in part from such a decision or other practice.''.

§ 5. Application to Other Laws

(a) **Americans With Disabilities Act of 1990**—The amendments made by section 3 shall apply to claims of discrimination in compensation brought under title I and section 503 of the Americans with Disabilities Act of 1990 (42 U.S.C. 12111 et seq., 12203), pursuant to section 107(a) of such Act (42 U.S.C. 12117(a)), which adopts the powers, remedies, and procedures set forth in section 706 of the Civil Rights Act of 1964 (42 U.S.C. 2000e–5).

(b) **Rehabilitation Act of 1973**—The amendments made by section 3 shall apply to claims of discrimination in compensation brought under sections 501 and 504 of the Rehabilitation Act of 1973 (29 U.S.C. 791, 794), pursuant to—

(1) sections 501(g) and 504(d) of such Act (29 U.S.C. 791(g), 794(d)), respectively, which adopt the standards applied under title I of the Americans with Disabilities Act of 1990 for determining whether a violation has occurred in a complaint alleging employment discrimination; and

(2) paragraphs (1) and (2) of section 505(a) of such Act (29 U.S.C. 794a(a)) (as amended by subsection (c)).

(c) Conforming Amendments—

(1) Rehabilitation Act of 1973—Section 505(a) of the Rehabilitation Act of 1973 (29 U.S.C. 794a(a)) is amended—

(A) in paragraph (1), by inserting after "(42 U.S.C. 2000e–5 (f) through (k))" the following:

"(and the application of section 706(e)(3) (42 U.S.C. 2000e–5(e)(3)) to claims of discrimination in compensation)"; and

(B) in paragraph (2), by inserting after "1964" the following:

"(42 U.S.C. 2000d et seq.) (and in subsection (e)(3) of section 706 of such Act (42 U.S.C. 2000e–5), applied to claims of discrimination in compensation)".

(2) Civil Rights Act of 1964—Section 717 of the Civil Rights Act of 1964 (42 U.S.C. 2000e–16) is amended by adding at the end the following:

"(f) Section 706(e)(3) shall apply to complaints of discrimination in compensation under this section."

(3) Age Discrimination in Employment Act of 1967—Section 15(f) of the Age Discrimination in Employment Act of 1967 (29 U.S.C. 633a(f)) is amended by striking "of section" and inserting "of sections 7(d)(3) and".

§ 6. Effective Date

This Act, and the amendments made by this Act, take effect as if enacted on May 28, 2007 and apply to all claims of discrimination in compensation under title VII of the Civil Rights Act of 1964 (42 U.S.C. 2000e et seq.), the Age Discrimination in Employment Act of 1967 (29 U.S.C. 621 et seq.), title I and section 503 of the Americans with Disabilities Act of 1990, and sections 501 and 504 of the Rehabilitation Act of 1973, that are pending on or after that date.

AGE DISCRIMINATION IN EMPLOYMENT ACT OF 1967
29 U.S.C. §§ 621–633a*

§ 621.　(§ 2) Congressional statement of findings and purpose

(a) The Congress hereby finds and declares that—

(1) in the face of rising productivity and affluence, older workers find themselves disadvantaged in their efforts to retain employment, and especially to regain employment when displaced from jobs;

(2) the setting of arbitrary age limits regardless of potential for job performance has become a common practice, and certain otherwise desirable practices may work to the disadvantage of older persons;

(3) the incidence of unemployment, especially long-term unemployment with resultant deterioration of skill, morale, and employer acceptability is, relative to the younger ages, high among older workers; their numbers are great and growing; and their employment problems grave;

(4) the existence in industries affecting commerce, of arbitrary discrimination in employment because of age, burdens commerce and the free flow of goods in commerce.

(b) It is therefore the purpose of this chapter to promote employment of older persons based on their ability rather than age; to prohibit arbitrary age discrimination in employment; to help employers and workers find ways of meeting problems arising from the impact of age on employment.

(Pub.L. 90–202, § 2, Dec. 15, 1967, 81 Stat. 602.)

§ 622.　(§ 3) Education and research program; recommendation to Congress

(a) The Secretary of Labor shall undertake studies and provide information to labor unions, management, and the general public concerning the needs and abilities of older workers, and their potentials [sic] for continued employment and contribution to the economy. In order to achieve the purposes of this chapter, the Secretary of Labor shall carry on a continuing program of education and information, under which he may, among other measures—

* Includes amendments made by Older Workers Benefit Protection Act of 1990 and Civil Rights Act of 1991, and amendments thereto, in italics. Deletions made by these Acts are in brackets.

(1) undertake research, and promote research, with a view to reducing barriers to the employment of older persons, and the promotion of measures for utilizing their skills;

(2) publish and otherwise make available to employers, professional societies, the various media of communication, and other interested persons the findings of studies and other materials for the promotion of employment;

(3) foster through the public employment service system and through cooperative effort the development of facilities of public and private agencies for expanding the opportunities and potentials of older persons;

(4) sponsor and assist State and community informational and educational programs.

(b) Not later than six months after the effective date of this chapter, the Secretary shall recommend to the Congress any measures he may deem desirable to change the lower or upper age limits set forth in section 631 of this title.

(Pub.L. 90–202, § 3, Dec. 15, 1967, 81 Stat. 602.)

§ 623.   (§ 4) Prohibition of age discrimination*

(a) It shall be unlawful for an employer—

(1) to fail or refuse to hire or to discharge any individual or otherwise discriminate against any individual with respect to his compensation, terms, conditions, or privileges of employment, because of such individual's age;

(2) to limit, segregate, or classify his employees in any way which would deprive or tend to deprive any individual of employment opportunities or otherwise adversely affect his status as an employee, because of such individual's age; or

(3) to reduce the wage rate of any employee in order to comply with this chapter.

(b) It shall be unlawful for an employment agency to fail or refuse to refer for employment, or otherwise to discriminate against, any individual because of such individual's age, or to classify or refer for employment any individual on the basis of such individual's age.

(c) It shall be unlawful for a labor organization—

* Sections 104 and 105 of the Older Workers Benefit Protection Act, Pub.L. 101–433, Oct. 16, 1990, 104 Stat. 981, codified as a Note to § 623, state:

"§ 104.   Rules and Regulations.

Notwithstanding section 9 of the Age Discrimination in Employment Act of 1967 (29 U.S.C. 628), the Equal Employment Opportunity Commission may issue such rules and regulations as the Commission may consider necessary or appropriate for carrying out this title, and the amendments made by this title, only after consultation with the Secretary of the Treasury and the Secretary of Labor.

"§ 105.   Effective Date [not included]."

(1) to exclude or to expel from its membership, or otherwise to discriminate against, any individual because of his age;

(2) to limit, segregate, or classify its membership, or to classify or fail or refuse to refer for employment any individual, in any way which would deprive or tend to deprive any individual of employment opportunities, or would limit such employment opportunities or otherwise adversely affect his status as an employee or as an applicant for employment, because of such individual's age;

(3) to cause or attempt to cause an employer to discriminate against an individual in violation of this section.

(d) It shall be unlawful for an employer to discriminate against any of his employees or applicants for employment, for an employment agency to discriminate against any individual, or for a labor organization to discriminate against any member thereof or applicant for membership, because such individual, member or applicant for membership has opposed any practice made unlawful by this section, or because such individual, member or applicant for membership has made a charge, testified, assisted, or participated in any manner in an investigation, proceeding, or litigation under this chapter.

(e) It shall be unlawful for an employer, labor organization, or employment agency to print or publish, or cause to be printed or published, any notice or advertisement relating to employment by such an employer or membership in or any classification or referral for employment by such a labor organization, or relating to any classification or referral for employment by such an employment agency, indicating any preference, limitation, specification, or discrimination, based on age.

(f) It shall not be unlawful for an employer, employment agency, or labor organization—

(1) to take any action otherwise prohibited under subsections (a), (b), (c), or (e) of this section where age is a bona fide occupational qualification reasonably necessary to the normal operation of the particular business, or where the differentiation is based on reasonable factors other than age, or where such practices involve an employee in a workplace in a foreign country, and compliance with such subsections would cause such employer, or a corporation controlled by such employer, to violate the laws of the country in which such workplace is located;

[(2) to observe the terms of a bona fide seniority system or any bona fide employee benefit plan such as a retirement, pension, or insurance plan, which is not a subterfuge to evade the purposes of this chapter, except that no such employee benefit plan shall excuse the failure to hire any individual, and no such seniority system or employee benefit plan shall require or permit the involuntary retirement of any individual specified by section 631(a) of this title because of the age of such individual; or]

(2) to take any action otherwise prohibited under subsections (a), (b), (c), or (e) of this section—

(A) to observe the terms of a bona fide seniority system that is not intended to evade the purposes of this Act, except that no such seniority system shall require or permit the involuntary retirement of any individual specified by section 12(a) because of the age of such individual; or

(B) to observe the terms of a bona fide employee benefit plan—

(i) where, for each benefit or benefit package, the actual amount of payment made or cost incurred on behalf of an older worker is no less than that made or incurred on behalf of a younger worker, as permissible under section 1625.10, title 29, Code of Federal Regulations (as in effect on June 22, 1989); or

(ii) that is a voluntary early retirement incentive plan consistent with the relevant purpose or purposes of this Act.

Notwithstanding clause (i) or (ii) of subparagraph (B), no such employee benefit plan or voluntary early retirement incentive plan shall excuse the failure to hire any individual, and no such employee benefit plan shall require or permit the involuntary retirement of any individual specified by section 12(a), because of the age of such individual. An employer, employment agency, or labor organization acting under subparagraph (A), or under clause (i) or (ii) of subparagraph (B), shall have the burden of proving that such actions are lawful in any civil enforcement proceeding brought under this Act; or

(3) to discharge or otherwise discipline an individual for good cause.

(g) [Deleted]

(h)(1) If an employer controls a corporation whose place of incorporation is in a foreign country, any practice by such corporation prohibited under this section shall be presumed to be such practice by such employer.

(2) The prohibitions of this section shall not apply where the employer is a foreign person not controlled by an American employer.

(3) For the purpose of this subsection the determination of whether an employer controls a corporation shall be based upon the—

(A) interrelation of operations,

(B) common management,

(C) centralized control of labor relations, and

(D) common ownership or financial control,

of the employer and the corporation.

(i)(1) Except as otherwise provided in this subsection, it shall be unlawful for an employer, an employment agency, a labor organization, or any combination thereof to establish or maintain an employee pension benefit plan which requires or permits—

(A) in the case of a defined benefit plan, the cessation of an employee's benefit accrual, or the reduction of the rate of an employee's benefit accrual, because of age, or

(B) in the case of a defined contribution plan, the cessation of allocations to an employee's account, or the reduction of the rate at which amounts are allocated to an employee's account, because of age.

(2) Nothing in this section shall be construed to prohibit an employer, employment agency, or labor organization from observing any provision of an employee pension benefit plan to the extent that such provision imposes (without regard to age) a limitation on the amount of benefits that the plan provides or a limitation on the number of years of service or years or participation which are taken into account for purposes of determining benefit accrual under the plan.

(3) In the case of any employee who, as of the end of any plan year under a defined benefit plan, has attained normal retirement age under such plan—

(A) if distribution of benefits under such plan with respect to such employee has commenced as of the end of such plan year, then any requirement of this subsection for continued accrual of benefits under such plan with respect to such employee during such plan year shall be treated as satisfied to the extent of the actuarial equivalent of in-service distribution of benefits, and

(B) if distribution of benefits under such plan with respect to such employee has not commenced as of the end of such year in accordance with section 206(a)(3) of the Employee Retirement Income Security Act of 1974 and section 401(a)(14)(C) of the Internal Revenue Code of 1986, and the payment of benefits under such plan with respect to such employee is not suspended during such plan year pursuant to section 203(a)(3)(B) of the Employee Retirement Income Security Act of 1974, then any requirement of this subsection for continued accrual of benefits under such plan with respect to such employee during such plan year shall be treated as satisfied to the extent of any adjustment in the benefit payable under the plan during such plan year attributable to the delay in the distribution of benefits after the attainment of normal retirement age.

The provisions of this paragraph shall apply in accordance with regulations of the Secretary of the Treasury. Such regulations shall provide for the application of the preceding provisions of this paragraph to all employee pension benefit plans subject to this subsection and may provide for the application of such provisions, in the case of any such employee, with respect to any period of time within a plan year.

(4) Compliance with the requirements of this subsection with respect to an employee pension benefit plan shall constitute compliance with the requirements of this section relating to benefit accrual under such plan.

(5) Paragraph (1) shall not apply with respect to any employee who is a highly compensated employee (within the meaning of section 414(q) of the Internal Revenue Code of 1986 [26 U.S.C. § 414(q)]) to the extent provided in regulations prescribed by the Secretary of the Treasury for purposes of precluding discrimination in favor of highly compensated employees within the meaning of subchapter D of chapter 1 of the Internal Revenue Code of 1986.

(6) A plan shall not be treated as failing to meet the requirements of paragraph (1) solely because the subsidized portion of any early retirement benefit is disregarded in determining benefit accruals or it is a plan permitted by subsection (m).

(7) Any regulations prescribed by the Secretary of the Treasury pursuant to clause (v) of section 411(b)(1)(h) of the Internal Revenue Code of 1986 and subparagraphs (C) and (D) of section 411(b)(2) of such Code shall apply with respect to the requirements of this subsection in the same manner and to the same extent as such regulations apply with respect to the requirements of such sections 411(b)(1)(H) and 411(b)(2).

(8) A plan shall not be treated as failing to meet the requirements of this section solely because such plan provides a normal retirement age described in section 3(24)(B) of the Employee Retirement Income Security Act of 1974 and section 411(a)(8)(B) of the Internal Revenue Code of 1986.

(9) For purposes of this subsection—

(A) The terms "employee pension benefit plan", "defined benefit plan", "defined contribution plan", and "normal retirement age" have the meanings provided such terms in section 3 of the Employee Retirement Income Security Act of 1974 (29 U.S.C. § 1002).

(B) The term "compensation" has the meaning provided by section 414(s) of the Internal Revenue Code of 1986.

(10) Special rules relating to age.

(A) Comparison to similarly situated younger individual.

(i) In general. A plan shall not be treated as failing to meet the requirements of paragraph (1) if a participant's accrued benefit, as determined as of any date under the terms of the plan, would be equal to or greater than that of any similarly situated, younger individual who is or could be a participant.

(ii) Similarly situated. For purposes of this subparagraph, a participant is similarly situated to any other individual if such participant is identical to such other individual in every respect (including period of service, compensation, position, date of hire, work history, and any other respect) except for age.

(iii) Disregard of subsidized early retirement benefits. In determining the accrued benefit as of any date for purposes of this clause, the subsidized portion of any early retirement benefit or retirement–type subsidy shall be disregarded.

(iv) Accrued benefit. For purposes of this subparagraph, the accrued benefit may, under the terms of the plan, be expressed as an annuity payable at normal retirement age, the balance of a hypothetical account, or the current value of the accumulated percentage of the employee's final average compensation.

(B) Applicable defined benefit plans.

(i) Interest credits.

(I) In general. An applicable defined benefit plan shall be treated as failing to meet the requirements of paragraph (1) unless the terms of the plan provide that any interest credit (or an equivalent amount) for any plan year shall be at a rate which is not greater than a market rate of return. A plan shall not be treated as failing to meet the requirements of this subclause merely because the plan provides for a reasonable minimum guaranteed rate of return or for a rate of return that is equal to the greater of a fixed or variable rate of return.

(II) Preservation of capital. An interest credit (or an equivalent amount) of less than zero shall in no event result in the account balance or similar amount being less than the aggregate amount of contributions credited to the account.

(III) Market rate of return. The Secretary of the Treasury may provide by regulation for rules governing the calculation of a market rate of return for purposes of subclause (I) and for permissible methods of crediting interest to the account (including fixed or variable interest rates) resulting in effective rates of return meeting the requirements of subclause (I).

(ii) Special rule for plan conversions. If, after June 29, 2005, an applicable plan amendment is adopted, the plan shall be treated as failing to meet the requirements of paragraph (1)(H) unless the requirements of clause (iii) are met with respect to each individual who was a participant in the plan immediately before the adoption of the amendment.

(iii) Rate of benefit accrual. Subject to clause (iv), the requirements of this clause are met with respect to any participant if the accrued benefit of the participant under the terms of the plan as in effect after the amendment is not less than the sum of—

(I) the participant's accrued benefit for years of service before the effective date of the amendment, determined under the terms of the plan as in effect before the amendment, plus

(II) the participant's accrued benefit for years of service after the effective date of the amendment, determined under the terms of the plan as in effect after the amendment.

(iv) Special rules for early retirement subsidies. For purposes of clause (iii)(I), the plan shall credit the accumulation account or similar amount with the amount of any early retirement benefit or retirement–type subsidy for the plan year in which the participant retires if, as of such time, the participant has met the age, years of service, and other requirements under the plan for entitlement to such benefit or subsidy.

(v) Applicable plan amendment. For purposes of this subparagraph—

(I) In general. The term "applicable plan amendment" means an amendment to a defined benefit plan which has the effect of converting the plan to an applicable defined benefit plan.

(II) Special rule for coordinated benefits. If the benefits of 2 or more defined benefit plans established or maintained by an employer are coordinated in such a manner as to have the effect of the adoption of an amendment described in subclause (I), the sponsor of the defined benefit plan or plans providing for such coordination shall be treated as having adopted such a plan amendment as of the date such coordination begins.

(III) Multiple amendments. The Secretary of the Treasury shall issue regulations to prevent the avoidance of the purposes of this subparagraph through the use of 2 or more plan amendments rather than a single amendment.

(IV) Applicable defined benefit plan. For purposes of this subparagraph, the term "applicable defined benefit plan" has the meaning given such term by section 203(f)(3) of the Employee Retirement Income Security Act of 1974.

(vi) Termination requirements. An applicable defined benefit plan shall not be treated as meeting the requirements of clause (i) unless the plan provides that, upon the termination of the plan—

(I) if the interest credit rate (or an equivalent amount) under the plan is a variable rate, the rate of interest used to determine accrued benefits under the plan shall be equal to the average of the rates of interest used under the plan during the 5-year period ending on the termination date, and

(II) the interest rate and mortality table used to determine the amount of any benefit under the plan payable in the form of an annuity payable at normal retirement age shall be the rate and table specified under the plan for such purpose as of the termination date, except that if such interest rate is a variable rate, the interest rate shall be determined under the rules of subclause (I).

(C) Certain offsets permitted. A plan shall not be treated as failing to meet the requirements of paragraph (1) solely because the plan provides offsets against benefits under the plan to the extent such offsets are allowable in applying the requirements of *section 401(a) of the Internal Revenue Code of 1986.*

(D) Permitted disparities in plan contributions or benefits. A plan shall not be treated as failing to meet the requirements of paragraph (1) solely because the plan provides a disparity in contributions or benefits with respect to which the requirements of section 401(*l*) of the Internal Revenue Code of 1986 are met.

(E) Indexing permitted.

(i) In general. A plan shall not be treated as failing to meet the requirements of paragraph (1) solely because the plan provides for indexing of accrued benefits under the plan.

(ii) Protection against loss. Except in the case of any benefit provided in the form of a variable annuity, clause (i) shall not apply with respect to any indexing which results in an accrued benefit less than the accrued benefit determined without regard to such indexing.

(iii) Indexing. For purposes of this subparagraph, the term "indexing" means, in connection with an accrued benefit, the periodic adjustment of the accrued benefit by means of the application of a recognized investment index or methodology.

(F) Early retirement benefit or retirement-type subsidy. For purposes of this paragraph, the terms "early retirement benefit" and "retirement-type subsidy" have the meaning given such terms in section 203(g)(2)(A) of the Employee Retirement Income Security Act of 1974.

(G) Benefit accrued to date. For purposes of this paragraph, any reference to the accrued benefit shall be a reference to such benefit accrued to date.

(**j**) It shall not be unlawful for an employer which is a State, a political subdivision of a State, an agency or instrumentality of a State or a political subdivision of a State, or an interstate agency to fail or refuse to hire or to discharge any individual because of such individual's age if such action is taken—

(1) with respect to the employment of an individual as a firefighter or as a law enforcement officer, the employer has complied with section 3(d)(2) of the Age Discrimination in Employment Amendments of 1996 if the individual was discharged after the date described in such section, and the individual has attained—

(A) the age of hiring or retirement, respectively, in effect under applicable State or local law on March 3, 1983; or

(B)(i) if the individual was not hired, the age of hiring in effect on the date of such failure or refusal to hire under applicable State or local law enacted after the date of enactment of the Age Discrimination in Employment Amendments of 1996 [Sept. 30, 1996]; or

(ii) if applicable State or local law was enacted after the date of enactment of the Age Discrimination in Employment Amendments of 1996 [Sept. 30, 1996] and the individual was discharged, the higher of—

(I) the age of retirement in effect on the date of such discharge under such law; and

(II) age 55; and

(2) pursuant to a bona fide hiring or retirement plan that is not a subterfuge to evade the purposes of this Act.

(**k**) *A seniority system or employee benefit plan shall comply with this Act regardless of the date of adoption of such system or plan.*

(***l***) *Notwithstanding clause (i) or (ii) of subsection (f)(2)(B)—*

(1)(A) It shall not be a violation of subsection (a), (b), (c), or (e) solely because—

(i) an employee pension benefit plan (as defined in section 3(2) of the Employee Retirement Income Security

Act of 1974 (*29 U.S.C. 1002(2)*)) provides for the attainment of a minimum age as a condition of eligibility for normal or early retirement benefits; or

(ii) a defined benefit plan (as defined in section 3(35) of such Act) provides for—

(I) payments that constitute the subsidized portion of an early retirement benefit; or

(II) social security supplements for plan participants that commence before the age and terminate at the age (specified by the plan) when participants are eligible to receive reduced or unreduced old-age insurance benefits under title II of the Social Security Act (*42 U.S.C. 401* et seq.), and that do not exceed such old-age insurance benefits.

(B) A voluntary early retirement incentive plan that—

(i) is maintained by—

(I) a local educational agency (as defined in section 9101 of the Elementary and Secondary Education Act of 1965 (*20 U.S.C. 7801*)), or

(II) an education association which principally represents employees of 1 or more agencies described in subclause (I) and which is described in section 501(c)(5) or (6) of the Internal Revenue Code of 1986 and exempt from taxation under section 501(a) of such Code, and

(ii) makes payments or supplements described in subclauses (I) and (II) of subparagraph (A)(ii) in coordination with a defined benefit plan (as so defined) maintained by an eligible employer described in section 457(e)(1)(A) of such Code or by an education association described in clause (i)(II),

shall be treated solely for purposes of subparagraph (A)(ii) as if it were a part of the defined benefit plan with respect to such payments or supplements. Payments or supplements under such a voluntary early retirement incentive plan shall not constitute severance pay for purposes of paragraph (2).

(2)(A) It shall not be a violation of subsection (a), (b), (c), or (e) solely because following a contingent event unrelated to age—

(i) the value of any retiree health benefits received by an individual eligible for an immediate pension;

(ii) the value of any additional pension benefits that are made available solely as a result of the contingent event unrelated to age and following which the individual is

eligible for not less than an immediate and unreduced pension; or

(iii) the values described in both clauses (i) and (ii);

are deducted from severance pay made available as a result of the contingent event unrelated to age.

(B) For an individual who receives immediate pension benefits that are actuarially reduced under subparagraph (A)(i), the amount of the deduction available pursuant to subparagraph (A)(i) shall be reduced by the same percentage as the reduction in the pension benefits.

(C) For purposes of this paragraph, severance pay shall include that portion of supplemental unemployment compensation benefits (as described in section 501(c)(17) of the Internal Revenue Code of 1986) that—

(i) constitutes additional benefits of up to 52 weeks;

(ii) has the primary purpose and effect of continuing benefits until an individual becomes eligible for an immediate and unreduced pension; and

(iii) is discontinued once the individual becomes eligible for an immediate and unreduced pension.

(D) For purposes of this paragraph and solely in order to make the deduction authorized under this paragraph, the term "retiree health benefits" means benefits provided pursuant to a group health plan covering retirees, for which (determined as of the contingent event unrelated to age)—

(i) the package of benefits provided by the employer for the retirees who are below age 65 is at least comparable to benefits provided under title XVIII of the Social Security Act (42 U.S.C. §§ 1395 et seq.);

(ii) the package of benefits provided by the employer for the retirees who are age 65 and above is at least comparable to that offered under a plan that provides a benefit package with one-fourth the value of benefits provided under title XVIII of such Act; or

(iii) the package of benefits provided by the employer is as described in clauses (i) and (ii).

(E)(i) If the obligation of the employer to provide retiree health benefits is of limited duration, the value for each individual shall be calculated at a rate of $3,000 per year for benefit years before age 65, and $750 per year for benefit years beginning at age 65 and above.

(ii) If the obligation of the employer to provide retiree health benefits is of unlimited duration, the value for each individual shall be calculated at a rate of $48,000 for

individuals below age 65, and $24,000 for individuals age 65 and above.

(iii) The values described in clauses (i) and (ii) shall be calculated based on the age of the individual as of the date of the contingent event unrelated to age. The values are effective on the date of enactment of this subsection [Oct. 16, 1990], and shall be adjusted on an annual basis, with respect to a contingent event that occurs subsequent to the first year after the date of enactment of this subsection [Oct. 16, 1990], based on the medical component of the Consumer Price Index for all-urban consumers published by the Department of Labor.

(iv) If an individual is required to pay a premium for retiree health benefits, the value calculated pursuant to this subparagraph shall be reduced by whatever percentage of the overall premium the individual is required to pay.

(F) If an employer that has implemented a deduction pursuant to subparagraph (A) fails to fulfill the obligation described in subparagraph (E), any aggrieved individual may bring an action for specific performance of the obligation described in subparagraph (E). The relief shall be in addition to any other remedies provided under Federal or State law.

(3) It shall not be a violation of subsection (a), (b), (c), or (e) solely because an employer provides a bona fide employee benefit plan or plans under which long-term disability benefits received by an individual are reduced by any pension benefits (other than those attributable to employee contributions)—

(A) paid to the individual that the individual voluntarily elects to receive; or

(B) for which an individual who has attained the later of age 62 or normal retirement age is eligible.

(m) Notwithstanding subsection (f)(2)(B), it shall not be a violation of subsection (a), (b), (c), or (e) solely because a plan of an institution of higher education (as defined in section 101 of the Higher Education Act of 1965) offers employees who are serving under a contract of unlimited tenure (or similar arrangement providing for unlimited tenure) supplemental benefits upon voluntary retirement that are reduced or eliminated on the basis of age, if—

(1) such institution does not implement with respect to such employees any age-based reduction or cessation of benefits that are not such supplemental benefits, except as permitted by *other* provisions of this Act;

(2) such supplemental benefits are in addition to any retirement or severance benefits which have been offered generally to employees serving under a contract of unlimited tenure (or similar arrangement providing for unlimited tenure), independent of any

early retirement or exit-incentive plan, within the preceding 365 days; and

(3) any employee who attains the minimum age and satisfies all non-age-based conditions for receiving a benefit under the plan has an opportunity lasting not less than 180 days to elect to retire and to receive the maximum benefit that could then be elected by a younger but otherwise similarly situated employee, and the plan does not require retirement to occur sooner than 180 days after such election.

(Dec. 15, 1967, P.L. 90–202, § 4, 81 Stat. 603; April 6, 1978, P.L. 95–256, § 2(a), 92 Stat. 189 Sept. 3, 1982, P.L. 97–248, Title I, Subtitle A, Part I, Subpart C, § 116(a), 96 Stat. 353; July 18, 1984, P.L. 98–369, Division B, Title III, Subtitle A, Part I, § 2301(b), 98 Stat. 1063; Oct. 9, 1984, P.L. 98–459, Title VIII, § 802(b), 98 Stat. 1792; April 7, 1986, P.L. 99–272, Title IX, Part 2, Subpart A, § 9201(b)(1), (3), 100 Stat. 171; Oct. 21, 1986, P.L. 99–509, Title IX, Subtitle C, § 9201, 100 Stat. 1973; Oct. 31, 1986, P.L. 99–592, §§ 2(a), (b), 3, 100 Stat. 3342; Dec. 19, 1989, P.L. 101–239, Title VI, Subtitle A, Part 3, Subpart A, § 6202(b)(3)(C)(i), (ii), 103 Stat. 2233; Oct. 16, 1990, P.L. 101–433, Title I, § 103, 104 Stat. 978; Nov. 5, 1990, P.L. 101–521, 104 Stat. 2287; Sept. 30, 1996, P.L. 104–208, Div. A, Title I, § 101(a) [Title I, § 119 (subsec. 1(b))], 110 Stat. 3009–23; Oct. 7, 1998, P.L. 105–244, Title IX, Part D, § 941(a), (b), 112 Stat. 1834.)

(As amended Aug. 17, 2006, P.L. 109–280, Title VII, § 701(c), Title XI, § 1104(a)(2), 120 Stat. 988, 1058.)

§ 624. (§ 5) Study by Secretary of Labor; reports to President and Congress; scope of study; implementation of study; transmittal date of reports

* * *

(1) The Equal Employment Opportunity Commission shall, not later than 12 months after the date of enactment of this Act [Oct. 31, 1986], enter into an agreement with the National Academy of Sciences for the conduct of a study to analyze the potential consequences of the elimination of mandatory retirement on institutions of higher education.

(2) The study required by paragraph (1) of this subsection shall be conducted under the general supervision of the National Academy of Sciences by a study panel composed of 9 members. The study panel shall consist of—

(A) 4 members who shall be administrators at institutions of higher education selected by the National Academy of Sciences after consultation with the American Council of Education, the Association of American Universities, and the National Association of State Universities and Land Grant Colleges;

(B) 4 members who shall be teachers or retired teachers at institutions of higher education (who do not serve in an administrative capacity at such institutions), selected by the National Academy of Sciences after consultation with the American Federation of Teachers, the National Education Association, the American Association of University Professors, and the American Association of Retired Persons; and

(C) one member selected by the National Academy of Sciences.

(3) The results of the study shall be reported, with recommendations, to the President and to the Congress not later than 5 years after the date of enactment of this Act [Oct. 31, 1986].

(4) The expenses of the study required by this subsection shall be paid from funds available to the Equal Employment Opportunity Commission.

(Pub.L. 99–592, § 6(c), Oct. 31, 1986, 100 Stat. 3344.)

21§ 625. (§ 6) Administration

The Secretary shall have the power—

(a) to make delegations, to appoint such agents and employees, and to pay for technical assistance on a fee for service basis, as he deems necessary to assist him in the performance of his functions under this chapter;

(b) to cooperate with regional, State, local, and other agencies, and to cooperate with and furnish technical assistance to employers, labor organizations, and employment agencies to aid in effectuating the purposes of this chapter.

(Pub.L. 90–202, § 6, Dec. 15, 1967, 81 Stat. 604.)

§ 626. (§ 7) Recordkeeping, investigation, and enforcement*

(a) The Equal Employment Opportunity Commission shall have the power to make investigations and require the keeping of records necessary or appropriate for the administration of this chapter in accordance with the powers and procedures provided in sections 209 and 211 of this title.

(b) The provisions of this chapter shall be enforced in accordance with the powers, remedies, and procedures provided in sections 211(b),

* Section 202 of the Older Workers Benefit Protection Act, Pub.L. 101–433, Oct. 16, 1990, 104 Stat. 984, codified as a Note to § 626, states:

"§ 202. Effective Date.

(a) In General.

The amendment made by section 201 [adding § 626(f)] shall not apply with respect to waivers that occur before the date of enactment of this Act.

(b) Rule of Waivers.

Effective on the date of enactment of this Act, the rule on waivers issued by the Equal Employment Opportunity Commission and contained in section 1627.16(c) of title 29, Code of Federal Regulations, shall have no force and effect."

216 (except for subsection (a) thereof), and 217 of this title, and subsection (c) of this section. Any act prohibited under section 623 of this title shall be deemed to be a prohibited act under section 215 of this title. Amounts owing to a person as a result of a violation of this chapter shall be deemed to be unpaid minimum wages or unpaid overtime compensation for purposes of sections 216 and 217 of this title: *Provided,* That liquidated damages shall be payable only in cases of willful violations of this chapter. In any action brought to enforce this chapter the court shall have jurisdiction to grant such legal or equitable relief as may be appropriate to effectuate the purposes of this chapter, including without limitation judgments compelling employment, reinstatement or promotion, or enforcing the liability for amounts deemed to be unpaid minimum wages or unpaid overtime compensation under this section. Before instituting any action under this section, the Equal Employment Opportunity Commission shall attempt to eliminate the discriminatory practice or practices alleged, and to effect voluntary compliance with the requirements of this chapter through informal methods of conciliation, conference, and persuasion.

(c)(1) Any person aggrieved may bring a civil action in any court of competent jurisdiction for such legal or equitable relief as will effectuate the purposes of this chapter: *Provided,* That the right of any person to bring such action shall terminate upon the commencement of an action by the Equal Employment Opportunity Commission to enforce the right of such employee under this chapter.

(2) In an action brought under paragraph (1), a person shall be entitled to a trial by jury of

any issue of fact in any such action for recovery of amounts owing as a result of a violation of this chapter, regardless of whether equitable relief is sought by any party in such action.

(d) (1) No civil action may be commenced by an individual under this section until 60 days after a charge alleging unlawful discrimination has been filed with the Equal Employment Opportunity Commission. Such a charge shall be filed—

(A) within 180 days after the alleged unlawful practice occurred; or

(B) in a case to which section 633(b) of this title applies, within 300 days after the alleged unlawful practice occurred, or within 30 days after receipt by the individual of notice of termination of proceedings under State law, whichever is earlier.

(2) Upon receiving such a charge, the Commission shall promptly notify all persons named in such charge as prospective defendants in the action and shall promptly seek to eliminate any alleged unlawful practice by informal methods of conciliation, conference, and persuasion.

(3) For purposes of this section, an unlawful practice occurs, with respect to discrimination in compensation in violation of this Act, when a discriminatory compensation decision or other practice is adopted, when a person becomes subject to a discriminatory compensation decision or other practice, or when a person is affected by application of a discriminatory compensation decision or other practice, including each time wages, benefits, or other compensation is paid, resulting in whole or in part from such a decision or other practice.

(e)[(1) Sections 255 and] *Section* 259 of this title shall apply to actions under this chapter. If a charge filed with the Commission under this Act is dismissed or the proceedings of the Commission are otherwise terminated by the Commission, the Commission shall notify the person aggrieved. A civil action may be brought under this section by a person defined in section 11(a) against the respondent named in the charge within 90 days after the date of the receipt of such notice.

[(2) For the period during which the Equal Employment Opportunity Commission is attempting to effect voluntary compliance with requirements of this chapter through informal methods of conciliation, conference, and persuasion pursuant to subsection (b) of this section, the statute of limitations as provided in section 255 of this title shall be tolled, but in no event for a period in excess of one year.]

(f)(1) An individual may not waive any right or claim under this Act unless the waiver is knowing and voluntary. Except as provided in paragraph (2), a waiver may not be considered knowing and voluntary unless at a minimum—

(A) the waiver is part of an agreement between the individual and the employer that is written in a manner calculated to be understood by such individual, or by the average individual eligible to participate;

(B) the waiver specifically refers to rights or claims arising under this Act;

(C) the individual does not waive rights or claims that may arise after the date the waiver is executed;

(D) the individual waives rights or claims only in exchange for consideration in addition to anything of value to which the individual already is entitled;

(E) the individual is advised in writing to consult with an attorney prior to executing the agreement;

(F)(i) the individual is given a period of at least 21 days within which to consider the agreement; or

(ii) if a waiver is requested in connection with an exit incentive or other employment termination program offered to a group or class of employees, the individual is given a

period of at least 45 days within which to consider the agreement;

(G) the agreement provides that for a period of at least 7 days following the execution of such agreement, the individual may revoke the agreement, and the agreement shall not become effective or enforceable until the revocation period has expired;

(H) if a waiver is requested in connection with an exit incentive or other employment termination program offered to a group or class of employees, the employer (at the commencement of the period specified in subparagraph (F)) informs the individual in writing in a manner calculated to be understood by the average individual eligible to participate, as to—

(i) any class, unit, or group of individuals covered by such program, any eligibility factors for such program, and any time limits applicable to such program; and

(ii) the job titles and ages of all individuals eligible or selected for the program, and the ages of all individuals in the same job classification or organizational unit who are not eligible or selected for the program.

(2) A waiver in settlement of a charge filed with the Equal Employment Opportunity Commission, or an action filed in court by the individual or the individual's representative, alleging age discrimination of a kind prohibited under section 4 or 15 may not be considered knowing and voluntary unless at a minimum—

(A) subparagraphs (A) through (E) of paragraph (1) have been met; and

(B) the individual is given a reasonable period of time within which to consider the settlement agreement.

(3) In any dispute that may arise over whether any of the requirements, conditions, and circumstances set forth in subparagraph (A), (B), (C), (D), (E), (F), (G), or (H) of paragraph (1), or subparagraph (A) or (B) of paragraph (2), have been met, the party asserting the validity of a waiver shall have the burden of proving in a court of competent jurisdiction that a waiver was knowing and voluntary pursuant to paragraph (1) or (2).

(4) No waiver agreement may affect the Commission's rights and responsibilities to enforce this Act. No waiver may be used to justify interfering with the protected right of an employee to file a charge or participate in an investigation or proceeding conducted by the Commission.

(Pub.L. 90–202, § 7, Dec. 15, 1967, 81 Stat. 604; Pub.L. 95–256, § 4(a), (b)(1), (c)(1), Apr. 6, 1978, 92 Stat. 190, 191; 1978 Reorg. Plan. No. 1, § 2, eff. Jan. 1, 1979, 43 F.R. 19807, 92 Stat. 3781; Pub.L. 101–433, § 201, Oct. 16, 1990, 104 Stat. 978; Pub.L. 102–166, § 115, Nov. 21, 1991, 105 Stat. 1071; Pub.L. 111–2, Jan. 29, 2009, 123 Stat. 6.)

§ 627. (§ 8) Notices to be posted

Every employer, employment agency, and labor organization shall post and keep posted in conspicuous places upon its premises a notice to be prepared or approved by the Equal Employment Opportunity Commission setting forth information as the Commission deems appropriate to effectuate the purposes of this chapter.

(Pub.L. 90–202, § 8, Dec. 15, 1967, 81 Stat. 605; 1978 Reorg. Plan No. 1, § 2, eff. Jan. 1, 1979, 43 F.R. 19807, 92 Stat. 3781.)

§ 628. (§ 9) Rules and regulations; exemptions

In accordance with the provisions of subchapter II of chapter 5 of Title 5, the Equal Employment Opportunity Commission may issue such rules and regulations as it may consider necessary or appropriate for carrying out this chapter, and may establish such reasonable exemptions to and from any or all provisions of this chapter as it may find necessary and proper in the public interest.

(Pub.L. 90–202, § 9, Dec. 15, 1967, 81 Stat. 605; 1978 Reorg. Plan No. 1, § 2, eff. Jan. 1, 1979, 43 F.R. 19807, 92 Stat. 3781.)

§ 629. (§ 10) Criminal penalties

Whoever shall forcibly resist, oppose, impede, intimidate or interfere with a duly authorized representative of the Equal Employment Opportunity Commission while it is engaged in the performance of duties under this chapter shall be punished by a fine of not more than $500 or by imprisonment for not more than one year, or by both: *Provided, however,* That no person shall be imprisoned under this section except when there has been a prior conviction hereunder.

(Pub.L. 90–202, § 10, Dec. 15, 1967, 81 Stat. 605; 1978 Reorg. Plan No. 1, § 2, eff. Jan. 1, 1979, 43 F.R. 19807, 92 Stat. 3781.)

§ 630. (§ 11) Definitions

For the purposes of this chapter—

(a) The term "person" means one or more individuals, partnerships, associations, labor organizations, corporations, business trusts, legal representatives, or any organized groups of persons.

(b) The term "employer" means a person engaged in an industry affecting commerce who has twenty or more employees for each working day in each of twenty or more calendar weeks in the current or preceding calendar year: *Provided,* That prior to June 30, 1968, employers having fewer than fifty employees shall not be considered employers. The term also means (1) any agent of such a person, and (2) a State or political subdivision of a State and any agency or instrumentality of a State or a political subdivision of a State, and any interstate agency, but such term does not include the United States, or a corporation wholly owned by the Government of the United States.

(c) The term "employment agency" means any person regularly undertaking with or without compensation to procure employees for an employer and includes an agent of such a person; but shall not include an agency of the United States.

(d) The term "labor organization" means a labor organization engaged in an industry affecting commerce, and any agent of such an organization, and includes any organization of any kind, any agency, or employee representation committee, group, association, or plan so engaged in which employees participate and which exists for the purpose, in whole or in part, of dealing with employers concerning grievances, labor disputes, wages, rates of pay, hours, or other terms or conditions of employment, and any conference, general committee, joint or system board, or joint council so engaged which is subordinate to a national or international labor organization.

(e) A labor organization shall be deemed to be engaged in an industry affecting commerce if (1) it maintains or operates a hiring hall or hiring office which procures employees for an employer or procures for employees opportunities to work for an employer, or (2) the number of its members (or, where it is a labor organization composed of other labor organizations or their representatives, if the aggregate number of the members of such other labor organization) is fifty or more prior to July 1, 1968, or twenty-five or more on or after July 1, 1968, and such labor organization—

(1) is the certified representative of employees under the provisions of the National Labor Relations Act, as amended [29 U.S.C. §§ 151 et seq.], or the Railway Labor Act, as amended [45 U.S.C. §§ 151 et seq.]; or

(2) although not certified, is a national or international labor organization or a local labor organization recognized or acting as the representative of employees of an employer or employers engaged in an industry affecting commerce; or

(3) has chartered a local labor organization or subsidiary body which is representing or actively seeking to represent employees of employers within the meaning of paragraph (1) or (2); or

(4) has been chartered by a labor organization representing or actively seeking to represent employees within the meaning of paragraph (1) or (2) as the local or subordinate body through which such employees may enjoy membership or become affiliated with such labor organization; or

(5) is a conference, general committee, joint or system board, or joint council subordinate to a national or international labor organization, which includes a labor organization engaged in an industry affecting commerce within the meaning of any of the preceding paragraphs of this subsection.

(f) The term "employee" means an individual employed by any employer except that the term "employee" shall not include any person elected to public office in any State or political subdivision of any State by the qualified voters thereof, or any person chosen by such officer to be on such officer's personal staff, or an appointee on the policymaking level or an immediate adviser with respect to the exercise of the constitutional or legal powers of the office. The exemption set forth in the preceding sentence shall not include employees subject to the civil service laws of a State government, governmental agency, or political subdivision. The term "employee" includes any individual who is a citizen of the United States employed by an employer in a workplace in a foreign country.

(g) The term "commerce" means trade, traffic, commerce, transportation, transmission, or communication among the several States; or between a State and any place outside thereof; or within the District of Columbia, or a possession of the United States; or between points in the same State but through a point outside thereof.

(h) The term "industry affecting commerce" means any activity, business, or industry in commerce or in which a labor dispute would hinder or obstruct commerce or the free flow of commerce and includes any activity or industry "affecting commerce" within the meaning of the Labor–Management Reporting and Disclosure Act of 1959 [29 U.S.C. §§ 401 et seq.].

(i) The term "State" includes a State of the United States, the District of Columbia, Puerto Rico, the Virgin Islands, American Samoa, Guam, Wake Island, the Canal Zone, and Outer Continental Shelf lands defined in the Outer Continental Shelf Lands Act [43 U.S.C. §§ 1331 et seq.].

(j) The term "firefighter" means an employee, the duties of whose position are primarily to perform work directly connected with the control and extinguishment of fires or the maintenance and use of firefighting apparatus and equipment, including an employee engaged in this activity who is transferred to a supervisory or administrative position.

(k) The term "law enforcement officer" means an employee, the duties of whose position are primarily the investigation, apprehension, or detention of individuals suspected or convicted of offenses against the criminal laws of a State, including an employee engaged in this activity who is transferred to a supervisory or administrative position. For the purpose of this subsection, "detention" includes the duties of employees assigned to guard individuals incarcerated in any penal institution.

(*l*) *The term "compensation, terms, conditions, or privileges of employment" encompasses all employee benefits, including such benefits provided pursuant to a bona fide employee benefit plan.*

(Pub.L. 90–202, § 11, Dec. 15, 1967, 81 Stat. 605; Pub.L. 93–259, § 28(a)(1)–(4), Apr. 8, 1974, 88 Stat. 74; Pub.L. 98–459, Title VIII, § 802(a), Oct. 9, 1984, 98 Stat. 1792; Pub.L. 99–592, § 4, Oct. 31, 1986, 100 Stat. 3343; Pub.L. 101–433, § 102, Oct. 16, 1990, 104 Stat. 978.)

§ 631.   (§ 12) Age limits

(a) The prohibitions in this chapter (except the provisions of section 623(g) of this title) shall be limited to individuals who are at least 40 years of age.

(b) In the case of any personnel action affecting employees or applicants for employment which is subject to the provisions of section 633a of this title, the prohibitions established in section 633a of this title shall be limited to individuals who are at least 40 years of age.

(c)(1) Nothing in this chapter shall be construed to prohibit compulsory retirement of any employee who has attained 65 years of age and who, for the 2–year period immediately before retirement, is employed in a bona fide executive or a high policymaking position, if such employee is entitled to an immediate nonforfeitable annual retirement benefit from a pension, profit-sharing, savings, or deferred compensation plan, or any combination of such plans, of the employer of such employee, which equals, in the aggregate, at least $44,000.

(2) In applying the retirement benefit test of paragraph (1) of this subsection, if any such retirement benefit is in a form other than a straight life annuity (with no ancillary benefits), or if employees contribute to any such plan or make rollover contributions, such benefit shall be adjusted in accordance with regulations prescribed by the Equal Employment Opportunity Commission, after consultation with the Secretary of the Treasury, so that the benefit is the equivalent of a straight life annuity (with no ancillary benefits) under a plan to which employees do not contribute and under which no rollover contributions are made.

(Pub.L. 90–202, § 12, Dec. 15, 1967, 81 Stat. 607; Pub.L. 95–256, § 3(a), (b)(3), Apr. 6, 1978, 92 Stat. 189, 190; 1978 Reorg. Plan No. 1, § 2, eff. Jan. 1, 1979, 43 F.R. 19807, 92 Stat. 3781; Pub.L. 98–459, Title VIII, § 802(c)(1), Oct. 9, 1984, 98 Stat. 1792; Pub.L. 99–272, Title IX, § 9201(b)(2), Apr. 7, 1986, 100 Stat. 171; Pub.L. 99–592, § 2(c), § 6(a), Oct. 31, 1986, 100 Stat. 3342, 3344.)

§ 632.   (§ 13) Annual report to Congress

The Equal Employment Opportunity Commission shall submit annually in January a report to the Congress covering its activities for the preceding year and including such information, data, and recommendations for further legislation in connection with the matters covered by this chapter as it may find advisable. Such report shall contain an evaluation and appraisal by the Commission of the effect of the minimum and maximum ages established by this chapter, together with its recommendations to the Congress. In making such evaluation and appraisal, the Commission shall take into consideration any changes which may have occurred in the general age level of the population, the effect of the chapter upon workers not covered by its provisions, and such other factors as it may deem pertinent.

(Pub.L. 90–202, § 13, Dec. 15, 1967, 81 Stat. 607; 1978 Reorg. Plan No. 1, § 2, eff. Jan. 1, 1979, 43 F.R. 19807, 92 Stat. 3781.)

§ 633.   (§ 14) Federal–State relationship

(a) Nothing in this chapter shall affect the jurisdiction of any agency of any State performing like functions with regard to discriminatory employment practices on account of age except that upon commencement of action under this chapter such action shall supersede any State action.

(b) In the case of an alleged unlawful practice occurring in a State which has a law prohibiting discrimination in employment because of age and establishing or authorizing a State authority to grant or seek relief from such discriminatory practice, no suit may be brought under section 626 of this title before the expiration of sixty days after proceedings have been commenced under the State law, unless such proceedings have been earlier terminated: *Provided,* That such sixty-day period shall be extended to one hundred and twenty days during the first year after the effective date of such State law. If any requirement for the commencement of such proceedings is imposed by a State authority other than a requirement of the filing of a written and signed statement of the facts upon which the proceeding is based, the proceeding shall be deemed to have been commenced for the purposes of this subsection at the time such statement is sent by registered mail to the appropriate State authority.

(Pub.L. 90–202, § 14, Dec. 15, 1967, 81 Stat. 607.)

§ 633a.   (§ 15) Nondiscrimination on account of age in Federal Government employment

(a) All personnel actions affecting employees or applicants for employment who are at least 40 years of age (except personnel actions with regard to aliens employed outside the limits of the United States) in military departments as defined in section 102 of Title 5, in executive agencies as defined in section 105 of Title 5 (including employees and applicants for employment who are paid from nonappropriated funds), in the United States Postal Service and the Postal Regulatory Commission, in those units in the government of the District of Columbia having positions in the competitive service, and in those units of the legislative and judicial branches of the Federal Government having positions in the competitive service, and in the Library of Congress shall be made free from any discrimination based on age.

(b) Except as otherwise provided in this subsection, the Equal Employment Opportunity Commission is authorized to enforce the provisions of subsection (a) of this section through appropriate remedies, including reinstatement or hiring of employees with or without backpay, as will effectuate the policies of this section. The Equal Employment Opportunity Commission shall issue such rules, regulations, orders, and instructions as it deems necessary and appropriate to carry out its responsibilities under this section. The Equal Employment Opportunity Commission shall—

    (1) be responsible for the review and evaluation of the operation of all agency programs designed to carry out the policy of this section, periodically obtaining and publishing (on at least a semiannual basis) progress reports from each department, agency, or unit referred to in subsection (a) of this section;

    (2) consult with and solicit the recommendations of interested individuals, groups, and organizations relating to nondiscrimination in employment on account of age; and

    (3) provide for the acceptance and processing of complaints of discrimination in Federal employment on account of age.

The head of each such department, agency, or unit shall comply with such rules, regulations, orders, and instructions of the Equal Employment Opportunity Commission which shall include a provision that an employee or applicant for employment shall be notified of any final action taken on any complaint of discrimination filed by him thereunder. Reasonable exemptions to the provisions of this section may be established by the Commission but only when the Commission has established a maximum age requirement on the basis of a determination that age is a bona fide occupational qualification necessary to the performance of the duties of the position. With respect to employment in the Library of Congress, authorities granted in this subsection to the Equal Employment Opportunity Commission shall be exercised by the Librarian of Congress.

(c) Any person aggrieved may bring a civil action in any Federal district court of competent jurisdiction for such legal or equitable relief as will effectuate the purposes of this chapter.

(d) When the individual has not filed a complaint concerning age discrimination with the Commission, no civil action may be commenced by any individual under this section until the individual has given the Commission not less than thirty days' notice of an intent to file such action. Such notice shall be filed within one hundred and eighty days after the alleged unlawful practice occurred. Upon receiving a notice of intent to sue, the Commission shall promptly notify all persons named therein as prospective defendants in the action and take any appropriate action to assure the elimination of any unlawful practice.

(e) Nothing contained in this section shall relieve any Government agency or official of the responsibility to assure nondiscrimination on account of age in employment as required under any provision of Federal law.

(f) Any personnel action of any department, agency, or other entity referred to in subsection (a) of this section shall not be subject to, or affected by, any provision of this chapter, other than the provisions of sections 7(d)(3) and 12(b) of this Act and the provisions of this section.

(g)(1) The Equal Employment Opportunity Commission shall undertake a study relating to the effects of the amendments made to this section by the Age Discrimination in Employment Act Amendments of 1978, and the effects of section 631(b) of this title.

(2) The Equal Employment Opportunity Commission shall transmit a report to the President and to the Congress containing the findings of the Commission resulting from the study of the Commission under paragraph (1) of this subsection. Such report shall be transmitted no later than January 1, 1980.

(Pub.L. 90–202, § 15, as added Pub.L. 93–259, § 28(b)(2), Apr. 8, 1974, 88 Stat. 74, and amended Pub.L. 95–256, § 5(a), (e), Apr. 6, 1978, 92 Stat. 191; 1978 Reorg. Plan No. 1, eff. Jan. 1, 1979, § 2, 43 F.R. 19807, 92 Stat. 378; Pub. L. 111–2, Jan. 29, 2009, 123 Stat. 5.)

REHABILITATION ACT OF 1973 (INCLUDING THE CIVIL RIGHTS RESTORATION ACT OF 1987)—SELECTED PROVISIONS 29 U.S.C. §§ 705, 791, 793–794a*

§ 705. Definitions

For the purposes of this Act:

* * *

(9) Disability. The term "disability" means—

(A) except as otherwise provided in subparagraph (B), a physical or mental impairment that constitutes or results in a substantial impediment to employment; or

(B) for purposes of sections 2, 14, and 15, and titles II, IV, V, and VII [29 U.SC. 701, 713, 714, 760 et seq., 780 et seq., 791 et seq., 796 et seq.], the meaning given it in section 3 of the Americans with Disabilities Act of 1990 (42 U.S.C. 12102).

(10) Drug and illegal use of drugs.

(A) The term "drug" means a controlled substance, as defined in schedules I through V of section 202 of the Controlled Substances Act (*21 U.S.C. 812*).

(B) The term "illegal use of drugs" means the use of drugs, the possession or distribution of which is unlawful under the Controlled Substances Act [*21 USCS §§ 801* et seq.]. Such term does not include the use of a drug taken under supervision by a licensed health care professional, or other uses authorized by the Controlled Substances Act [*21 USCS §§ 801* et seq.] or other provisions of Federal law.

* * *

(20) Individual with a disability.

(A) Except as otherwise provided in subparagraph (B), the term "individual with a disability" means any individual who—

(i) has a physical or mental impairment which for such individual constitutes or results in a substantial impediment to employment; and

---

* Includes amendments made by Americans with Disabilities Act of 1990 (ADA), Pub.L. 101–336, July 26, 1990, 104 Stat. 327; and ADA Amendment Act of 2008, Pub.L. 110–325, Sept. 25, 2008, 122 Stat. 3353.

(ii) can benefit in terms of an employment outcome from vocational rehabilitation services provided pursuant to title I, III, or VI [*29 U.S.C. §§ 720* et seq., 771 et seq., or 795 et seq.].

(B) Subject to subparagraphs (C), (D), (E), and (F), the term "individual with a disability" means, for purposes of sections 2, 14, and 15, and titles II, IV, V, and VII of this Act [*29 U.S.C. §§ 701*, 714, 715, 760 et seq., 780 et seq., 791 et seq., 796 et seq.], any person who has a disability as defined in section 3 of the Americans with Disabilities Act of 1990 [42 U.S.C. 12102].

(C)(i) For purposes of title V [29 U.S.C. §§ 791 *et seq.], the term "individual with a disability" does not include an individual who is currently engaging in the illegal use of drugs, when a covered entity acts on the basis of such use.*

(ii) Nothing in clause (i) shall be construed to exclude as an individual with a disability an individual who—

(I) has successfully completed a supervised drug rehabilitation program and is no longer engaging in the illegal use of drugs, or has otherwise been rehabilitated successfully and is no longer engaging in such use;

(II) is participating in a supervised rehabilitation program and is no longer engaging in such use; or

(III) is erroneously regarded as engaging in such use, but is not engaging in such use;

except that it shall not be a violation of this Act for a covered entity to adopt or administer reasonable policies or procedures, including but not limited to drug testing, designed to ensure that an individual described in subclause (I) or (II) is no longer engaging in the illegal use of drugs.

(iii) Notwithstanding clause (i), for purposes of programs and activities providing health services and services provided under titles I, II, and III [*29 U.S.C. §§ 720* et seq., 760 et seq., 771 et seq.], an individual shall not be excluded from the benefits of such programs or activities on the basis of his or her current illegal use of drugs if he or she is otherwise entitled to such services.

(iv) For purposes of programs and activities providing educational services, local educational agencies may take disciplinary action pertaining to the use or possession of illegal drugs or alcohol against any student who is an individual with a disability and who currently is engaging in the illegal use of drugs or in the use of alcohol to the same extent that such disciplinary action is taken against students who are not individuals with disabilities. Furthermore, the due process procedures at section 104.36 of title 34, Code of Federal Regulations (or any corresponding similar regulation or ruling) shall not apply to such disciplinary actions.

(v) For purposes of sections 503 and 504 [*29 U.S.C. §§ 793,* 794] as such sections relate to employment, the term "individual with a disability" does not include any individual who is an alcoholic whose current use of alcohol prevents such individual from performing the duties of the job in question or whose employment, by reason of such current alcohol abuse, would constitute a direct threat to property or the safety of others.

(D) For the purposes of sections 503 and 504 [*29 U.S.C. §§ 793,* 794], as such sections relate to employment, such term does not include an individual who has a currently contagious disease or infection and who, by reason of such disease or infection, would constitute a direct threat to the health or safety of other individuals or who, by reason of the currently contagious disease or infection, is unable to perform the duties of the job.

(E) Rights provisions; exclusion of individuals on basis of homosexuality or bisexuality. For the purposes of sections 501, 503, and 504 [*29 U.S.C. §§ 791,* 793, 794]—

(i) for purposes of the application of subparagraph (B) to such sections, the term "impairment" does not include homosexuality or bisexuality; and

(ii) therefore the term "individual with a disability" does not include an individual on the basis of homosexuality or bisexuality.

(F) For the purposes of sections 501, 503, and 504 [*29 U.S.C. §§ 791,* 793, 794], the term "individual with a disability" does not include an individual on the basis of—

(i) transvestism, transsexualism, pedophilia, exhibitionism, voyeurism, gender identity disorders not resulting from physical impairments, or other sexual behavior disorders;

(ii) compulsive gambling, kleptomania, or pyromania; or

(iii) psychoactive substance use disorders resulting from current illegal use of drugs.

(G) Individuals with disabilities. The term "individuals with disabilities" means more than one individual with a disability.

* * *

(Pub.L. 93–112, § 7, Sept. 26, 1973, 87 Stat. 359; as added, Pub. L. 10–220, Title IV, Aug. 7, 1998, 112 Stat. 1097; Pub. L. 105–224, Title I, § 102(a)(9)(A), Oct. 7, 1998, 112 Stat. 1620; Pub. L. 105–277, Div. A, § 101(f), Oct. 21, 1998, 112 Stat. 2681; Pub. L. 105–394, Title IV, § 402(a), Nov. 13, 1998, 112 Stat. 3661.)

§ 791. (§ 501) Employment of individuals with disabilities

(a) There is established within the Federal Government an Interagency Committee on Disabilities (hereinafter in this section referred to as the "Committee"), comprised of such members as the President may select, including the following (or their designees whose positions are Executive Level IV or higher): the Chairman of the Equal Employment Opportunity Commission (hereafter in this section referred to as the "Commission"), the Administrator of Veterans' Affairs, and the Secretary of Labor, the Secretary of Education, and the Secretary of Health and Human Services. The Secretary of Education and the Chairman of the Commission shall serve as co-chairpersons of the Committee. The resources of the President's Committees on Employment of People With Disabilities and on Mental Retardation shall be made fully available to the Committee. It shall be the purpose and function of the Committee (1) to provide a focus for Federal and other employment of individuals with disabilities, and to review, on a periodic basis, in cooperation with the Commission, the adequacy of hiring, placement, and advancement practices with respect to individuals with disabilities, by each department, agency, and instrumentality in the executive branch of Government, and to insure that the special needs of such individuals are being met; and (2) to consult with the Commission to assist the Commission to carry out its responsibilities under subsections (b), (c), and (d) of this section. On the basis of such review and consultation, the Committee shall periodically make to the Commission such recommendations for legislative and administrative changes as it deems necessary or desirable. The Commission shall timely transmit to the appropriate committees of Congress any such recommendations.

(b) Each department, agency, and instrumentality (including the United States Postal Service and the Postal Regulatory Commission) in the executive branch shall, within one hundred and eighty days after September 26, 1973, submit to the Commission and to the Committee an affirmative action program plan for the hiring, placement, and advancement of individuals with disabilities in such department, agency, or instrumentality. Such plan shall include a description of the extent to which and methods whereby the special needs of employees with disabilities are being met. Such plan shall be updated annually, and shall be reviewed annually and approved by the Commission if the Commission determines, after consultation with the Committee, that such plan provides sufficient assurances, procedures and commitments to provide adequate hiring, placement, and advancement opportunities for individuals with disabilities.

(c) The Commission, after consultation with the Committee, shall develop and recommend to the Secretary for referral to the appropriate State agencies, policies and procedures which will facilitate the hiring, placement, and advancement in employment of individuals who have received rehabilitation services under State vocational rehabilitation programs, veterans' programs, or any other program for individuals with disabilities, including the promotion of job opportunities for such individuals. The Secretary shall encourage such State agencies to adopt and implement such policies and procedures.

(d) The Commission, after consultation with the Committee, shall, on June 30, 1974, and at the end of each subsequent fiscal year, make a complete report to the appropriate committees of the Congress with respect to the practices of and achievements in hiring, placement, and advancement of individuals with disabilities by each department, agency, and instrumentality and the effectiveness of the affirmative action programs required by subsection (b) of this section, together with recommendations as to legislation which have been submitted to the Commission under subsection (a) of this section, or other appropriate action to insure the adequacy of such practices. Such report shall also include an evaluation by the Committee of the effectiveness of the activities of the Commission under subsections (b) and (c) of this section.

(e) An individual who, as a part of an individualized written rehabilitation program under a State plan approved under this chapter, participates in a program of unpaid work experience in a Federal agency, shall not, by reason thereof, be considered to be a Federal employee or to be subject to the provisions of law relating to Federal employment, including those relating to hours of work, rates of compensation, leave, unemployment compensation, and Federal employee benefits.

(f)(1) The Secretary of Labor and the Secretary of Education are authorized and directed to cooperate with the President's Committee on Employment of People With Disabilities in carrying out its functions.

(2) In selecting personnel to fill all positions on the President's Committee on Employment of People With Disabilities, special consideration shall be given to qualified individuals with disabilities.

* * *

(Pub.L. 93–112, Title V, § 501, Sept. 26, 1973, 87 Stat. 390; Pub.L. 98–221, Title I, § 104(b)(3), Feb. 22, 1984, 98 Stat. 18; Pub.L. 99–506, Title I, § 103(d)(2)(C), Title X, §§ 1001(f)(1), 1002(e)(1), (2)(A), Oct. 21, 1986, 100 Stat. 1810, 1843, 1844; Pub.L. 100–630, Title II, § 206(a), Nov. 7, 1988, 102 Stat. 3311.)

§ 793.   (§ 503) Employment under Federal contracts

(a) Any contract in excess of $2,500 entered into by any Federal department or agency for the procurement of personal property and nonpersonal services (including construction) for the United States shall contain a provision requiring that, in employing persons to carry out such contract, the party contracting with the United States shall take affirmative action to employ and advance in employment qualified individuals with disabilities as defined in section 706(8) of this title. The provisions of this section shall apply to any subcontract in excess of $2,500 entered into by a prime contractor in carrying out any contract for the procurement of personal property and nonpersonal services (including construction) for the United States. The President shall implement the provisions of this section by promulgating regulations within ninety days after September 26, 1973.

(b) If any individual with disabilities believes any contractor has failed or refused to comply with the provisions of a contract with the United States, relating to employment of individuals with handicaps, such individual may file a complaint with the Department of Labor. The Department shall promptly investigate such complaint and shall take such action thereon as the facts and circumstances warrant, consistent with the terms of such contract and the laws and regulations applicable thereto.

(c) The requirements of this section may be waived, in whole or in part, by the President with respect to a particular contract or subcontract, in accordance with guidelines set forth in regulations which the President shall prescribe, when the President determines that special circumstances in the national interest so require and states in writing the reasons for such determination.

(Pub.L. 93–112, Title V, § 503, Sept. 26, 1973, 87 Stat. 393; Pub.L. 95–602, Title I, § 122(d)(1), Nov. 6, 1978, 92 Stat. 2987; Pub.L. 99–506, Title I, § 103(d)(2)(B), (C), Title X, §§ 1001(f)(2), (3), 1002(e)(3), Oct. 21, 1986, 100 Stat. 1810, 1843, 1844; Pub.L. 100–630, Title II, § 206(c), Nov. 7, 1988, 102 Stat. 3312.)

§ 794.   (§ 504) Nondiscrimination under federal grants and programs; promulgation of rules and regulations

(a) No otherwise qualified individual with a disability in the United States, as defined in section 705(20) of this title, shall, solely by reason of her or his disability, be excluded from the participation in, be denied the benefits of, or be subjected to discrimination under any program or activity receiving Federal financial assistance or under any program or activity conducted by any Executive agency or by the United States Postal Service. The head of each such agency shall promulgate such regulations as may be necessary to carry out the amendments to this section made by the Rehabilitation, Comprehensive Services, and Developmental Disabilities Act of 1978. Copies of any proposed regulation shall be submitted to appropriate authorizing committees of the Congress, and such regulation may take effect no earlier than the thirtieth day after the date on which such regulation is so submitted to such committees.

(b) For the purposes of this section, the term "program or activity" means all of the operations of—

(1)(A) a department, agency, special purpose district, or other instrumentality of a State or of a local government; or

(B) the entity of such State or local government that distributes such assistance and each such department or agency (and each other State or local government entity) to which the assistance is extended, in the case of assistance to a State or local government;

(2)(A) a college, university, or other postsecondary institution, or a public system of higher education; or

(B) a local educational agency (as defined in section 7801 of Title 20) system of vocational education, or other school system;

(3)(A) an entire corporation, partnership, or other private organization, or an entire sole proprietorship—

(i) if assistance is extended to such corporation, partnership, private organization, or sole proprietorship as a whole; or

(ii) which is principally engaged in the business of providing education, health care, housing, social services, or parks and recreation; or

(B) the entire plant or other comparable, geographically separate facility to which Federal financial assistance is extended, in the case of any other corporation, partnership, private organization, or sole proprietorship; or

(4) any other entity which is established by two or more of the entities described in paragraph (1), (2), or (3);

any part of which is extended Federal financial assistance.

(c) Small providers are not required by subsection (a) of this section to make significant structural alterations to their existing facilities for the purpose of assuring program accessibility, if alternative means of providing the services are available. The terms used in this subsection shall be construed with reference to the regulations existing on March 22, 1988.

(Pub.L. 93–112, Title V, § 504, Sept. 26, 1973, 87 Stat. 394; Pub.L. 95–602, Title I, §§ 119, 122(d)(2), Nov. 6, 1978, 92 Stat. 2982, 2987; Pub.L. 99–506, Title I, § 103(d)(2)(B), Title X, § 1002(e)(4), Oct. 21, 1986, 100 Stat. 1810, 1844; Pub.L. 100–259, § 4, Mar. 22, 1988, 102 Stat. 29; Pub.L. 100–630, Title II, § 206(d), Nov. 7, 1988, 102 Stat. 3312.)

§ 794a.   (§ 505) Remedies and attorney fees

(a)(1) The remedies, procedures, and rights set forth in section 717 of the Civil Rights Act of 1964 (42 U.S.C. § 2000e–16), including the application of sections 706(f) through 706(k) (42 U.S.C. §§ 2000e–5(f) through (k)) (and the application of section 706(e)(3) (42 U.S.C. § 2000e–5(e)(3)) to claims of discrimination in compensation) shall be available, with respect to any complaint under section 791 of this title, to any employee or applicant for employment aggrieved by the final disposition of such complaint, or by the failure to take final action on such complaint. In fashioning an equitable or affirmative action remedy under such section, a court may take into account the reasonableness of the cost of any necessary work place accommodation, and the availability of alternatives therefor or other appropriate relief in order to achieve an equitable and appropriate remedy.

(2) The remedies, procedures, and rights set forth in Title VI of the Civil Rights Act of 1964 [42 U.S.C. §§ 2000d et seq.] (and in subsection (e)(3) of section 706 of such Act (42 U.S.C. § 2000e–50), applied to claims of discrimination in compensation) shall be available to any person aggrieved by any act or failure to act by any recipient of Federal assistance or Federal provider of such assistance under section 794 of this title.

(b) In any action or proceeding to enforce or charge a violation of a provision of this subchapter, the court, in its discretion, may allow the prevailing party, other than the United States, a reasonable attorney's fee as part of the costs.

(Pub.L. 93–112, Title V, § 505, as added Pub.L. 95–602, Title I, § 120, Nov. 6, 1978, 92 Stat. 2982. Pub. L. 111–2, Jan. 29, 2009, 123 Stat. 5.)

AMERICANS WITH DISABILITIES ACT OF 1990 (ADA), AS AMENDED BY ADA AMENDMENTS ACT OF 2008— SELECTED PROVISIONS*
42 U.S.C. §§ 12101 et seq.

§ 2. [42 U.S.C. § 12101] Findings and Purposes

(a) Findings.

The Congress finds that—

(1) <u>physical or mental disabilities in no way diminish a person's right to fully participate in all aspects of society, yet many people with physical or mental disabilities have been precluded from doing so because of discrimination; others who have a record of a disability or are regarded as having a disability also have been subjected to discrimination;</u>

(2) historically, society has tended to isolate and segregate individuals with disabilities, and, despite some improvements, such forms of discrimination against individuals with disabilities continue to be a serious and pervasive social problem;

(3) discrimination against individuals with disabilities persists in such critical areas as employment, housing, public accommodations, education, transportation, communication, recreation, institutionalization, health services, voting, and access to public services;

(4) unlike individuals who have experienced discrimination on the basis of race, color, sex, national origin, religion, or age, individuals who have experienced discrimination on the basis of disability have often had no legal recourse to redress such discrimination;

(5) individuals with disabilities continually encounter various forms of discrimination, including outright intentional exclusion, the discriminatory effects of architectural, transportation, and communication barriers, overprotective rules and policies, failure to make modifications to existing facilities and practices, exclusionary qualification standards and criteria, segregation, and relegation to lesser services, programs, activities, benefits, jobs, or other opportunities;

(6) census data, national polls, and other studies have documented that people with disabilities, as a group, occupy an inferior status in our society, and are severely disadvantaged socially, vocationally, economically, and educationally;

(7) ~~individuals with disabilities are a discrete and insular minority who have been faced with restrictions and limitation, subject-~~

---

* Includes amendments made by Civil Rights Act of 1991 in italics; and text added by the ADA Amendments Act of 2008 is underscored; deletions are struck through.

127

ed to a history of purposeful unequal treatment, and relegated to a position of political powerlessness in our society, based on characteristics that are beyond the control of such individuals and resulting from stereotypic assumptions not truly indicate of the individual ability of such individuals to participate in, and contribute to society;

(7) the Nation's proper goals regarding individuals with disabilities are to assure equality of opportunity, full participation, independent living, and economic self-sufficiency for such individuals; and

(8) the continuing existence of unfair and unnecessary discrimination and prejudice denies people with disabilities the opportunity to compete on an equal basis and to pursue those opportunities for which our free society is justifiably famous, and costs the United States billions of dollars in unnecessary expenses resulting from dependency and nonproductivity.

(b) Purpose.

It is the purpose of this Act—

(1) to provide a clear and comprehensive national mandate for the elimination of discrimination against individuals with disabilities;

(2) to provide clear, strong, consistent, enforceable standards addressing discrimination against individuals with disabilities;

(3) to ensure that the Federal Government plays a central role in enforcing the standards established in this Act on behalf of individuals with disabilities; and

(4) to invoke the sweep of congressional authority, including the power to enforce the fourteenth amendment and to regulate commerce, in order to address the major areas of discrimination faced day-to-day by people with disabilities.

§ 3. [42 U.S.C. § 12102] Definition of Disability

As used in this Act:

(1) Disability. The term "disability" means, with respect to an individual—

(A) a physical or mental impairment that substantially limits one or more major life activities of such individual;

(B) a record of such an impairment; or

(C) being regarded as having such an impairment (as described in paragraph (3)).

(2) Major life activities.

(A) In general. For purposes of paragraph (1), major life activities include, but are not limited to, caring for oneself, performing manual tasks, seeing, hearing, eating, sleeping, walking, standing, lifting, bending, speaking, breathing, learning, reading, concentrating, thinking, communicating, and working.

(B) Major bodily functions. For purposes of paragraph (1), a major life activity also includes the operation of a major bodily function, including but not limited to, functions of the immune system, normal cell growth, digestive, bowel, bladder, neurological, brain, respiratory, circulatory, endocrine, and reproductive functions.

(3) Regarded as having such an impairment. For purposes of paragraph (1)(C):

(A) An individual meets the requirement of "being regarded as having such an impairment" if the individual establishes that he or she has been subjected to an action prohibited under this Act because of an actual or perceived physical or mental impairment whether or not the impairment limits or is perceived to limit a major life activity.

(B) Paragraph (1)(C) shall not apply to impairments that are transitory and minor. A transitory impairment is an impairment with an actual or expected duration of 6 months or less.

(4) Rules of construction regarding the definition of disability. The definition of "disability" in paragraph (1) shall be construed in accordance with the following:

(A) The definition of disability in this Act shall be construed in favor of broad coverage of individuals under this Act, to the maximum extent permitted by the terms of this Act.

(B) The term "substantially limits" shall be interpreted consistently with the findings and purposes of the ADA Amendments Act of 2008.

(C) An impairment that substantially limits one major life activity need not limit other major life activities in order to be considered a disability.

(D) An impairment that is episodic or in remission is a disability if it would substantially limit a major life activity when active.

(E) (i) The determination of whether an impairment substantially limits a major life activity shall be made without regard to the ameliorative effects of mitigating measures such as—

(I) medication, medical supplies, equipment, or appliances, low-vision devices (which do not include ordinary eyeglasses or contact lenses), prosthetics including limbs and devices, hearing aids and cochlear implants or other implantable hearing devices, mobility devices, or oxygen therapy equipment and supplies;

(II) use of assistive technology;

(III) reasonable accommodations or auxiliary aids or services; or

(IV) learned behavioral or adaptive neurological modifications.

(ii) The ameliorative effects of the mitigating measures of ordinary eyeglasses or contact lenses shall be considered in determining whether an impairment substantially limits a major life activity.

(iii) As used in this subparagraph—

(I) the term "ordinary eyeglasses or contact lenses" means lenses that are intended to fully correct visual acuity or eliminate refractive error; and

(II) the term "low-vision devices" means devices that magnify, enhance, or otherwise augment a visual image.

(July 26, 1990, P.L. 101–336, § 3, 104 Stat. 329; Sept. 25, 2008, P.L. 110–325, § 4(a), 122 Stat. 3555.)

§ 4. [42 U.S.C. § 12103] Additional Definitions

As used in this Act:

(1) Auxiliary Aids and Services. The term "auxiliary aids and services" includes—

(A) qualified interpreters or other effective methods of making aurally delivered materials available to individuals with hearing impairments;

(B) qualified readers, taped texts, or other effective methods of making visually delivered materials available to individuals with visual impairments;

(C) acquisition or modification of equipment or devices; and

(D) other similar services and actions.

(2) State. The term "State" means each of the several States, the District of Columbia, the Commonwealth of Puerto Rico, Guam, American Samoa, the Virgin Islands, the Trust Territory of the Pacific Islands, and the Commonwealth of the Northern Mariana Islands. * * *

(July 26, 1990, P.L. 101–336, § 3, 104 Stat. 329; Sept. 25, 2008, P.L. 110–325, § 4(a), 122 Stat. 3555.)

TITLE I—EMPLOYMENT

§ 101. [42 U.S.C. § 12111] Definitions

As used in this title:

(1) Commission. The term "Commission" means the Equal Employment Opportunity Commission established by section 705 of the Civil Rights Act of 1964 (42 U.S.C. § 2000e–4).

(2) Covered Entity. The term "covered entity" means an employer, employment agency, labor organization, or joint labor-management committee.

(3) Direct Threat. The term "direct threat" means a significant risk to the health or safety of others that cannot be eliminated by reasonable accommodation.

(4) Employee. The term "employee" means an individual employed by an employer. *With respect to employment in a foreign country, such term includes an individual who is a citizen of the United States.**

(5) Employer.

(A) In General. The term "employer" means a person engaged in an industry affecting commerce who has 15 or more employees for each working day in each of 20 or more calendar weeks in the current or preceding calendar year, and any agent of such person, except that, for two years following the effective date of this title, an employer means a person engaged in an industry affecting commerce who has 25 or more employees for each working day in each of 20 or more calendar weeks in the current or preceding year, and any agent of such person.

(B) Exceptions. The term "employer" does not include—

(i) the United States, a corporation wholly owned by the government of the United States, or an Indian tribe; or

(ii) a bona fide private membership club (other than a labor organization) that is exempt from taxation under section 501(c) of the Internal Revenue Code of 1986.

(6) Illegal Use of Drugs.

(A) In General. The term "illegal use of drugs" means the use of drugs, the possession or distribution of which is unlawful under the Controlled Substances Act (21 U.S.C. § 812). Such term does not include the use of a drug taken under supervision by a licensed health care professional, or other uses authorized by the Controlled Substances Act or other provisions of Federal law.

(B) Drugs. The term "drug" means a controlled substance, as defined in schedules I through V of section 202 of the Controlled Substances Act.

(7) Person, etc. The terms "person", "labor organization", "employment agency", "commerce", and "industry affecting commerce", shall have the same meaning given such terms in section 701 of the Civil Rights Act of 1964 (42 U.S.C. § 2000e).

(8) Qualified Individual with a Disability. The term "qualified individual with a disability" means an individual with a disability who,

---

* The provisions of the last sentence shall not apply to conduct occurring before November 21, 1991, the date of enactment of the Civil Rights Act of 1991. See Pub.L. 102–166, § 109(c), Nov. 21, 1991, 105 Stat. 1071.

with or without reasonable accommodation, can perform the essential functions of the employment position that such individual holds or desires. For the purposes of this title, consideration shall be given to the employer's judgment as to what functions of a job are essential, and if an employer has prepared a written description before advertising or interviewing applicants for the job, this description shall be considered evidence of the essential functions of the job.

(9) Reasonable Accommodation. The term "reasonable accommodation" may include—

(A) making existing facilities used by employees readily accessible to and usable by individuals with disabilities; and

(B) job restructuring, part-time or modified work schedules, reassignment to a vacant position, acquisition or modification of equipment or devices, appropriate adjustment or modifications of examinations, training materials or policies, the provision of qualified readers or interpreters, and with other similar accommodations for individuals with disabilities.

(10) Undue Hardship.

(A) In General. The term "undue hardship" means an action requiring significant difficulty or expense, when considered in light of the factors set forth in subparagraph (B).

(B) Factors to Be Considered. In determining whether an accommodation would impose an undue hardship on a covered entity, factors to be considered include—

(i) the nature and cost of the accommodation needed under this Act;

(ii) the overall financial resources of the facility or facilities involved in the provision of the reasonable accommodation; the number of persons employed at such facility; the effect on expenses and resources, or the impact otherwise of such accommodation upon the operation of the facility;

(iii) the overall financial resources of the covered entity; the overall size of the business of a covered entity with respect to the number of its employees; the number, type, and location of its facilities; and

(iv) the type of operation or operations of the covered entity, including the composition, structure, and functions of the workforce of such entity; the geographic separateness, administrative, or fiscal relationship of the facility or facilities in question to the covered entity.

§ 102.   [42 U.S.C. § 12112] Discrimination

(a) General Rule. No covered entity shall discriminate against a qualified individual <u>on the basis of disability</u> in regard to job application procedures, the hiring, advancement, or discharge of employees, employee compensation, job training, and other terms, conditions, and privileges of employment.

(b) Construction. As used in subsection (a), the term "discriminate against a qualified individual on the basis of disability" includes—

(1) limiting, segregating, or classifying a job applicant or employee in a way that adversely affects the opportunities or status of such applicant or employee because of the disability of such applicant or employee;

(2) participating in a contractual or other arrangement or relationship that has the effect of subjecting a covered entity's qualified applicant or employee with a disability to the discrimination prohibited by this title (such relationship includes a relationship with an employment or referral agency, labor union, an organization providing fringe benefits to an employee of the covered entity, or an organization providing training and apprenticeship programs);

(3) utilizing standards, criteria, or methods of administration— (A) that have the effect of discrimination on the basis of disability; or (B) that perpetuate the discrimination of others who are subject to common administrative control;

(4) excluding or otherwise denying equal jobs or benefits to a qualified individual because of the known disability of an individual with whom the qualified individual is known to have a relationship or association;

(5)(A) not making reasonable accommodations to the known physical or mental limitations of an otherwise qualified individual with a disability who is an applicant or employee, unless such covered entity can demonstrate that the accommodation would impose an undue hardship on the operation of the business of such covered entity; or (B) denying employment opportunities to a job applicant or employee who is an otherwise qualified individual with a disability, if such denial is based on the need of such covered entity to make reasonable accommodation to the physical or mental impairments of the employee or a applicant;

(6) using qualification standards, employment tests or other selection criteria that screen out or tend to screen out an individual with a disability or a class of individuals with disabilities unless the standard, test or other selection criteria, as used by the covered entity, is shown to be job-related for the position in question and is consistent with business necessity; and

(7) failing to select and administer tests concerning employment in the most effective manner to ensure that, when such test is administered to a job applicant or employee who has a disability that impairs sensory, manual, or speaking skills, such test results accurately reflect the skills, aptitude, or whatever other factor of such

applicant or employee that such test purports to measure, rather than reflecting the impaired sensory, manual, or speaking skills of such employee or applicant (except where such skills are the factors that the test purports to measure).

(c) Covered Entities in Foreign Countries.

(1) In General. It shall not be unlawful under this section for a covered entity to take any action that constitutes discrimination under this section with respect to an employee in a workplace in a foreign country if compliance with this section would cause such covered entity to violate the law of the foreign country in which such workplace is located.

(2) Control of Corporation.

(A) Presumption. If an employer controls a corporation whose place of incorporation is a foreign country, any practice that constitutes discrimination under this section and is engaged in by such corporation shall be presumed to be engaged in by such employer.

(B) Exception. This section shall not apply with respect to the foreign operations of an employer that is a foreign person not controlled by an American employer.

(C) Determination. For purposes of this paragraph, the determination of whether an employer controls a corporation shall be based on—

> *(i) the interrelation of operations;*
>
> *(ii) the common management;*
>
> *(iii) the centralized control of labor relations; and*
>
> *(iv) the common ownership or financial control, of the employer and the corporation.*

(d) Medical Examinations and Inquiries.

(1) In General. The prohibition against discrimination as referred to in subsection (a) shall include medical examinations and inquiries.

(2) Preemployment.

(A) Prohibited Examination or Inquiry. Except as provided in paragraph (3), a covered entity shall not conduct a medical examination or make inquiries of a job applicant as to whether such applicant is an individual with a disability or as to the nature or severity of such disability.

(B) Acceptable Inquiry. A covered entity may make preemployment inquiries into the ability of an applicant to perform job-related functions.

(3) Employment Entrance Examination. A covered entity may require a medical examination after an offer of employment has been made to job applicant and prior to the commencement of the employment duties of such applicant, and may condition an offer of employment on the results of such examination, if—

(A) all entering employees are subjected to such an examination regardless of disability;

(B) information obtained regarding the medical condition or history of the applicant is collected and maintained on separate forms and in separate medical files and is treated as a confidential medical record, except that—

(i) supervisors and managers may be informed regarding necessary restrictions on the work or duties of the employee and necessary accommodations;

(ii) first aid and safety personnel may be informed, when appropriate, if the disability might require emergency treatment; and

(iii) government officials investigating compliance with this Act shall be provided relevant information on request; and

(C) the results of such examination are used only in accordance with this title.

(4) Examination and Inquiry.

(A) Prohibited Examinations and Inquiries. A covered entity shall not require a medical examination and shall not make inquiries of an employee as to whether such employee is an individual with a disability or as to the nature or severity of the disability, unless such examination or inquiry is shown to be job-related and consistent with business necessity.

(B) Acceptable Examinations and Inquiries. A covered entity may conduct voluntary medical examinations, including voluntary medical histories, which are part of an employee health program available to employees at that work site. A covered entity may make inquiries into the ability of an employee to perform job-related functions.

(C) Requirement. Information obtained under subparagraph (B) regarding the medical condition or history of any employee are subject to the requirements of subparagraphs (B) and (C) of paragraph (3).

§ 103. [42 U.S.C. § 12113] Defenses

(a) In General. It may be a defense to a charge of discrimination under this Act that an alleged application of qualification standards, tests, or selection criteria that screen out or tend to screen out or otherwise deny a job or benefit to an individual with a disability has been shown to be job-related and consistent with business necessity, and such performance cannot be accomplished by reasonable accommodation, as required under this title.

(b) Qualification Standards. The term "qualification standards" may include a requirement that an individual shall not pose a direct threat to the health or safety of other individuals in the workplace.

(c) Qualification Standards and Tests Related to Uncorrected Vision. Notwithstanding section 3(4)(E)(ii) [42 U.S.C. 12102(4)(E)(ii)], a covered entity shall not use qualification standards, employment tests, or other selection criteria based on an individual's uncorrected vision unless the standard, test, or other selection criteria, as used by the covered entity, is shown to be job-related for the position in question and consistent with business necessity.

(d) Religious Entities.

(1) In General. This title shall not prohibit a religious corporation, association, educational institution, or society from giving preference in employment to individuals of a particular religion to perform work connected with the carrying on by such corporation, association, educational institution, or society of its activities.

(2) Religious Tenets Requirement. Under this title, a religious organization may require that all applicants and employees conform to the religious tenets of such organization.

(e) List of Infectious and Communicable Diseases.

(1) In General. The Secretary of Health and Human Services, not later than 6 months after the date of enactment of this Act, shall—

(A) review all infectious and communicable diseases which may be transmitted through handling the food supply;

(B) publish a list of infectious and communicable diseases which are transmitted through handling the food supply;

(C) publish the methods by which such diseases are transmitted; and

(D) widely disseminate such information regarding the list of diseases and their modes of transmissability to the general public. Such list shall be updated annually.

(2) Applications. In any case in which an individual has an infectious or communicable disease that is transmitted to others through the handling of food, that is included on the list developed by the Secretary of Health and Human Services under paragraph (1), and which cannot be eliminated by reasonable accommodation, a covered entity may refuse to assign or continue to assign such individual to a job involving food handling.

(3) Construction. Nothing in this Act shall be construed to preempt, modify, or amend any State, county, or local law, ordinance, or regulation applicable to food handling which is designed to protect the public health from individuals who pose a significant risk to the health or safety of others, which cannot be eliminated by reasonable accommodation, pursuant to the list of infectious or communicable diseases and the modes of transmissability published by the Secretary of Health and Human Services.

§ 104. [42 U.S.C. § 12114] Illegal Use of Drugs and Alcohol

(a) Qualified Individual With a Disability. For purposes of this title, the term "a qualified individual with a disability" shall not include any employee or applicant who is currently engaging in the illegal use of drugs, when the covered entity acts on the basis of such use.

(b) Rules of Construction. Nothing in subsection (a) shall be construed to exclude as a qualified individual with a disability an individual who—

(1) has successfully completed a supervised drug rehabilitation program and is no longer engaging in the illegal use of drugs, or has otherwise been rehabilitated successfully and is no longer engaging in such use;

(2) is participating in a supervised rehabilitation program and is no longer engaging in such use; or

(3) is erroneously regarded as engaging in such use, but is not engaging in such use;

except that it shall not be a violation of this Act for a covered entity to adopt or administer reasonable policies or procedures, including but not limited to drug testing, designed to ensure that an individual described in paragraph (1) or (2) is no longer engaging in the illegal use of drugs.

(c) Authority of Covered Entity. A covered entity—

(1) may prohibit the illegal use of drugs and the use of alcohol at the workplace by all employees;

(2) may require that employees shall not be under the influence of alcohol or be engaging in the illegal use of drugs at the workplace;

(3) may require that employees behave in conformance with the requirements established under the Drug–Free Workplace Act of 1988 (41 U.S.C. §§ 701 et seq.);

(4) may hold an employee who engages in the illegal use of drugs or who is an alcoholic to the same qualification standards for employment or job performance and behavior that such entity holds other employees, even if any unsatisfactory performance or behavior is related to the drug use or alcoholism of such employee; and

(5) may, with respect to Federal regulations regarding alcohol and the illegal use of drugs, require that—

(A) employees comply with the standards established in such regulations of the Department of Defense, if the employees of the covered entity are employed in an industry subject to such regulations, including complying with regulations (if any) that apply to employment in sensitive positions in such an industry, in the case of employees of the covered entity who are employed in such positions (as defined in the regulations of the Department of Defense);

(B) employees comply with the standards established in such regulations of the Nuclear Regulatory Commission, if the employees of the covered entity are employed in an industry subject to such regulations, including complying with regulations (if any) that apply to employment in sensitive positions in such an industry, in the case of employees of the covered entity who are employed in such positions (as defined in the regulations of the Nuclear Regulatory Commission); and

(C) employees comply with the standards established in such regulations of the Department of Transportation, if the employees of the covered entity are employed in a transportation industry subject to such regulations, including complying with such regulations (if any) that apply to employment in sensitive positions in such an industry, in the case of employees of the covered entity who are employed in such positions (as defined in the regulations of the Department of Transportation).

(d) Drug Testing.

(1) In General. For purposes of this title, a test to determine the illegal use of drugs shall not be considered a medical examination.

(2) Construction. Nothing in this title shall be construed to encourage, prohibit, or authorize the conducting of drug testing for the illegal use of drugs by job applicants or employees or making employment decisions based on such test results.

(e) Transportation Employees. Nothing in this title shall be construed to encourage, prohibit, restrict, or authorize the otherwise lawful exercise by entities subject to the jurisdiction of the Department of Transportation of authority to—

(1) test employees of such entities in, and applicants for, positions involving safety-sensitive duties for the illegal use of drugs and for on-duty impairment by alcohol; and

(2) remove such persons who test positive for illegal use of drugs and on-duty impairment by alcohol pursuant to paragraph (1) from safety-sensitive duties in implementing subsection (c).

§ 105. [42 U.S.C. § 12115] Posting Notices

Every employer, employment agency, labor organization, or joint labor-management committee covered under this title shall post notices in an accessible format to applicants, employees, and members describing the applicable provisions of this Act, in the manner prescribed by section 711 of the Civil Rights Act of 1964 (42 U.S.C. § 2000e–10).

§ 106. [42 U.S.C. § 12116] Regulations

Not later than 1 year after the date of enactment of this Act, the Commission shall issue regulations in an accessible format to carry out this title in accordance with subchapter II of chapter 5 of title 5, United States Code.

§ 107. [42 U.S.C. § 12117] Enforcement

(a) **Powers, Remedies, and Procedures.** The powers, remedies, and procedures set forth in sections 705, 706, 707, 709, and 710 of the Civil Rights Act of 1964 (42 U.S.C. §§ 2000e–4, 2000e–5, 2000e–6, 2000e–8, and 2000e–9) shall be the powers, remedies, and procedures this title provides to the Commission, to the Attorney General, or to any person alleging discrimination on the basis of disability in violation of any provision of this Act, or regulations promulgated under section 106, concerning employment.

(b) **Coordination.** The agencies with enforcement authority for actions which allege employment discrimination under this title and under the Rehabilitation Act of 1973 shall develop procedures to ensure that administrative complaints filed under this title and under the Rehabilitation Act of 1973 are dealt with in a manner that avoids duplication of effort and prevents imposition of inconsistent or conflicting standards for the same requirements under this title and the Rehabilitation Act of 1973. The Commission, the Attorney General, and the Office of Federal Contract Compliance Programs shall establish such coordinating mechanisms (similar to provisions contained in the joint regulations promulgated by the Commission and the Attorney General at part 42 of title 28 and part 1691 of title 29, Code of Federal Regulations, and the Memorandum of Understanding between the Commission and the Office of Federal Contract Compliance Programs dated January 16, 1981 (46 Fed.Reg. 7435, January 23, 1981)) in regulations implementing this title and Rehabilitation Act of 1973 not later than 18 months after the date of enactment of this Act.

§ 108. Effective Date

This title shall become effective 24 months after the date of enactment.

* * *

TITLE V—MISCELLANEOUS PROVISIONS

§ 501. [42 U.S.C. § 12201] Construction

(a) **In General.** Except as otherwise provided in this Act, nothing in this Act shall be construed to apply a lesser standard than the standards applied under title V of the Rehabilitation Act of 1973 (29

U.S.C. §§ 790 et seq.) or the regulations issued by Federal agencies pursuant to such title.

(b) Relationship to Other Laws. Nothing in this Act shall be construed to invalidate or limit the remedies, rights, and procedures of any Federal law or law of an State or political subdivision of any State or jurisdiction that provides greater or equal protection for the rights of individuals with disabilities than are afforded by this Act. Nothing in this Act shall be construed to preclude the prohibition of, or the imposition of restrictions on, smoking in places of employment covered by title I, in transportation covered by title II or III, or in places of public accommodation covered by title III.

(c) Insurance. Titles I through IV of this Act shall not be construed to prohibit or restrict—

(1) an insurer, hospital or medical service company, health maintenance organization, or any agent, or entity that administers benefit plans, or similar organizations from underwriting risks, classifying risks, or administering such risks that are based on or not inconsistent with State law; or

(2) a person or organization covered by this Act from establishing, sponsoring, observing or administering the terms of a bona fide benefit plan that are based on underwriting risks, classifying risks, or administering such risks that are based on or not inconsistent with State law; or

(3) a person or organization covered by this Act from establishing, sponsoring, observing or administering the terms of a bona fide benefit plan that is not subject to State laws that regulate insurance.

Paragraphs (1), (2), and (3) shall not be used as a subterfuge to evade the purposes of title I and III.

(d) Accommodations and Services. Nothing in this Act shall be construed to require an individual with a disability to accept an accommodation, aid, service, opportunity, or benefit which such individual chooses not to accept.

(e) Benefits under State Worker's Compensation Laws. Nothing in this Act alters the standards for determining eligibility for benefits under State worker's compensation laws or under State and Federal disability benefit programs.

(f) Fundamental Alteration. Nothing in this Act alters the provision of section 302(b)(2)(A)(ii) [42 U.S.C. 12182(b)(2)(A)(ii)], specifying that reasonable modifications in policies, practices, or procedures shall be required, unless an entity can demonstrate that making such modifications in policies, practices, or procedures, including academic requirements in postsecondary education, would fundamentally alter the nature of the goods, services, facilities, privileges, advantages, or accommodations involved.

(g) Claims of No Disability. Nothing in this Act shall provide the basis for a claim by an individual without a disability that the individual was subject to discrimination because of the individual's lack of disability.

(h) Reasonable Accommodations and Modifications. A covered entity under title I * * * need not provide a reasonable accommodation or a reasonable modification to policies, practices, or procedures to an individual who meets the definition of disability in section 3(1) [42 U.S.C. 12102(1)] solely under subparagraph (C) of such section.

§ 502. [42 U.S.C. § 12202] State Immunity

A State shall not be immune under the eleventh amendment to the Constitution of the United States from an action in Federal or State court of competent jurisdiction for a violation of this Act. In any action against a State for a violation of the requirements of this Act, remedies (including remedies both at law and in equity) are available for such a violation to the same extent as such remedies are available for such a violation in an action against any public or private entity other than a State.

§ 503. [42 U.S.C. § 12203] Prohibition Against Retaliation and Coercion

(a) Retaliation. No person shall discriminate against any individual because such individual has opposed any act or practice made unlawful by this Act or because such individual made a charge, testified, assisted, or participated in any manner in an investigation, proceeding, or hearing under this Act.

(b) Interference, Coercion, or Intimidation. It shall be unlawful to coerce, intimidate, threaten, or interfere with any individual in the exercise or enjoyment of, or on account of his or her having exercised or enjoyed, or on account of his or her having aided or encouraged any other individual in the exercise or enjoyment of, any right granted or protected by this Act.

(c) Remedies and Procedures. The remedies and procedures available under sections 107, 203, and 308 of this Act shall be available to aggrieved persons for violations of subsections (a) and (b), with respect to title I, title II and title III, respectively.

* * *

§ 505. [42 U.S.C. § 12205] Attorney's Fees

In any action or administrative proceeding commenced pursuant to this Act, the court or agency, in its discretion, may allow the prevailing party, other than the United States, a reasonable attorney's fee, including litigation expenses, and costs, and the United States shall be liable for the foregoing the same as a private individual.

* * *

§ 509.   [42 U.S.C. § 12208] Transvestites

For the purposes of this Act, the term "disabled" or "disability" shall not apply to an individual solely because that individual is a transvestite.

* * *

§ 511.   [42 U.S.C. § 12210] Illegal Use of Drugs

(a) In General. For purposes of this Act, the term "individual with a disability" does not include an individual who is currently engaging in the illegal use of drugs, when the covered entity acts on the basis of such use.

(b) Rules of Construction. Nothing in subsection (a) shall be construed to exclude as an individual with a disability an individual who—

(1) has successfully completed a supervised drug rehabilitation program and is no longer engaging in the illegal use of drugs, or has otherwise been rehabilitated successfully and is no longer engaging in such use;

(2) is participating in a supervised rehabilitation program and is no longer engaging in such use; or

(3) is erroneously regarded as engaging in such use, but is not engaging in such use;

except that it shall not be a violation of this Act for a covered entity to adopt or administer reasonable policies or procedures, including but not limited to drug testing, designed to ensure that an individual described in paragraph (1) or (2) is no longer engaging in the illegal use of drugs; however, nothing in this section shall be construed to encourage, prohibit, restrict, or authorize the conducting of testing for the illegal use of drugs.

(c) Health and Other Services. Notwithstanding subsection (a) and section 512 (b)(3), an individual shall not be denied health services, or services provided in connection with drug rehabilitation, on the basis of the current illegal use of drugs if the individual is otherwise entitled to such services.

(d) Definition of Illegal Use of Drugs.

(1) In General. The term "illegal use of drugs" means the use of drugs, the possession or distribution of which is unlawful under the Controlled Substances Act (21 U.S.C. § 812). Such term does not include the use of a drug taken under supervision by a licensed health care professional, or other uses authorized by the Controlled Substances Act or other provisions of Federal law.

(2) Drugs. The term "drug" means a controlled substance, as defined in schedules I through V of section 202 of the Controlled Substances Act.

§ 512. [42 U.S.C. § 12211] Definitions

(a) Homosexuality and Bisexuality. For purposes of the definition of "disability" in section 3(2), homosexuality and bisexuality are not impairments and as such are not disabilities under this Act.

(b) Certain Conditions. Under this Act, the term "disability" shall not include—

(1) transvestism, transsexualism, pedophilia, exhibitionism, voyeurism, gender identity disorders not resulting from physical impairments, or other sexual behavior disorders;

(2) compulsive gambling, kleptomania, or pyromania; or

(3) psychoactive substance use disorders resulting from current illegal use of drugs.

* * *

§ 514. [42 U.S.C. § 12212] Alternative Means of Dispute Resolution

Where appropriate and to the extent authorized by law, the use of alternative means of dispute resolution, including settlement negotiations, conciliation, and arbitration.

(Pub.L. 101–336, July 26, 1990, 104 Stat. 327; Pub.L. 102–166, § 109, Nov. 21, 1991, 105 Stat. 1071.)

ADA AMENDMENTS ACT OF 2008[†]

§ 1. Short Title

This Act may be cited as the "ADA Amendments Act of 2008".

§ 2. Findings and Purposes

(a) Findings.—Congress finds that—

(1) in enacting the Americans with Disabilities Act of 1990 (ADA), Congress intended that the Act "provide a clear and comprehensive national mandate for the elimination of discrimination against individuals with disabilities" and provide broad coverage;

(2) in enacting the ADA, Congress recognized that physical and mental disabilities in no way diminish a person's right to fully participate in all aspects of society, but that people with physical or mental disabilities are frequently precluded from doing so because of prejudice, antiquated attitudes, or the failure to remove societal and institutional barriers;

(3) while Congress expected that the definition of disability under the ADA would be interpreted consistently with how courts had applied the definition of a handicapped individual under the Rehabilitation Act of 1973, that expectation has not been fulfilled;

(4) the holdings of the Supreme Court in Sutton v. United Air Lines, Inc., 527 U.S. 471, 119 S.Ct. 2139, 144 L.Ed.2d 450 (1999) and its companion cases have narrowed the broad scope of protection intended to be afforded by the ADA, thus eliminating protection for many individuals whom Congress intended to protect;

(5) the holding of the Supreme Court in Toyota Motor Manufacturing, Kentucky, Inc. v. Williams, 534 U.S. 184, 122 S.Ct. 681, 151 L.Ed.2d 615 (2002) further narrowed the broad scope of protection intended to be afforded by the ADA;

(6) as a result of these Supreme Court cases, lower courts have incorrectly found in individual cases that people with a range of substantially limiting impairments are not people with disabilities;

(7) in particular, the Supreme Court, in the case of Toyota Motor Manufacturing, Kentucky, Inc. v. Williams, 534 U.S. 184, 122 S.Ct. 681, 151 L.Ed.2d 615 (2002), interpreted the term "substantially limits" to require a greater degree of limitation than was intended by Congress; and

(8) Congress finds that the current Equal Employment Opportunity Commission ADA regulations defining the term "substantial-

† Pub.L. 110–325, Sept. 25, 2008, 122 Stat. 3553.

ly limits" as "significantly restricted" are inconsistent with congressional intent, by expressing too high a standard.

(b) Purposes.—The purposes of this Act are—

(1) to carry out the ADA's objectives of providing "a clear and comprehensive national mandate for the elimination of discrimination" and "clear, strong, consistent, enforceable standards addressing discrimination" by reinstating a broad scope of protection to be available under the ADA;

(2) to reject the requirement enunciated by the Supreme Court in Sutton v. United Air Lines, Inc., 527 U.S. 471, 119 S.Ct. 2139, 144 L.Ed.2d 450 (1999) and its companion cases that whether an impairment substantially limits a major life activity is to be determined with reference to the ameliorative effects of mitigating measures;

(3) to reject the Supreme Court's reasoning in Sutton v. United Air Lines, Inc., 527 U.S. 471, 119 S.Ct. 2139, 144 L.Ed.2d 450 (1999) with regard to coverage under the third prong of the definition of disability and to reinstate the reasoning of the Supreme Court in School Board of Nassau County v. Arline, 480 U.S. 273, 107 S.Ct. 1123, 94 L.Ed.2d 307 (1987) which set forth a broad view of the third prong of the definition of handicap under the Rehabilitation Act of 1973;

(4) to reject the standards enunciated by the Supreme Court in Toyota Motor Manufacturing, Kentucky, Inc. v. Williams, 534 U.S. 184, 122 S.Ct. 681, 151 L.Ed.2d 615 (2002), that the terms "substantially" and "major" in the definition of disability under the ADA "need to be interpreted strictly to create a demanding standard for qualifying as disabled," and that to be substantially limited in performing a major life activity under the ADA "an individual must have an impairment that prevents or severely restricts the individual from doing activities that are of central importance to most people's daily lives";

(5) to convey congressional intent that the standard created by the Supreme Court in the case of Toyota Motor Manufacturing, Kentucky, Inc. v. Williams, 534 U.S. 184, 122 S.Ct. 681, 151 L.Ed.2d 615 (2002) for "substantially limits", and applied by lower courts in numerous decisions, has created an inappropriately high level of limitation necessary to obtain coverage under the ADA, to convey that it is the intent of Congress that the primary object of attention in cases brought under the ADA should be whether entities covered under the ADA have complied with their obligations, and to convey that the question of whether an individual's impairment is a disability under the ADA should not demand extensive analysis; and

(6) to express Congress' expectation that the Equal Employment Opportunity Commission will revise that portion of its current regulations that defines the term "substantially limits" as "signifi-

cantly restricted" to be consistent with this Act, including the amendments made by this Act.

§ 3. Codified Findings

Section 2(a) of the Americans with Disabilities Act of 1990 (42 U.S.C. 12101) is amended—

(1) by amending paragraph (1) to read as follows:

"(1) physical or mental disabilities in no way diminish a person's right to fully participate in all aspects of society, yet many people with physical or mental disabilities have been precluded from doing so because of discrimination; others who have a record of a disability or are regarded as having a disability also have been subjected to discrimination;";

(2) by striking paragraph (7); and

(3) by redesignating paragraphs (8) and (9) as paragraphs (7) and (8), respectively.

§ 4. Disability Defined and Rules of Construction

(a) Definition of Disability.—Section 3 of the Americans with Disabilities Act of 1990 (42 U.S.C. 12102) is amended to read as follows:

"Sec. 3. DEFINITION OF DISABILITY.

"As used in this Act:

"(1) Disability.—The term 'disability' means, with respect to an individual—

"(A) a physical or mental impairment that substantially limits one or more major life activities of such individual;

"(B) a record of such an impairment; or

"(C) being regarded as having such an impairment (as described in paragraph (3)).

"(2) Major life activities.—

"(A) In general.—For purposes of paragraph (1), major life activities include, but are not limited to, caring for oneself, performing manual tasks, seeing, hearing, eating, sleeping, walking, standing, lifting, bending, speaking, breathing, learning, reading, concentrating, thinking, communicating, and working.

"(B) Major bodily functions.—For purposes of paragraph (1), a major life activity also includes the operation of a major bodily function, including but not limited to, functions of the immune system, normal cell growth, digestive, bowel, bladder, neurological, brain, respiratory, circulatory, endocrine, and reproductive functions.

"(3) Regarded as having such an impairment.—For purposes of paragraph (1)(C):

"(A) An individual meets the requirement of 'being regarded as having such an impairment' if the individual establishes that he or she has been subjected to an action prohibited under this Act because of an actual or perceived physical or mental impairment whether or not the impairment limits or is perceived to limit a major life activity.

"(B) Paragraph (1)(C) shall not apply to impairments that are transitory and minor. A transitory impairment is an impairment with an actual or expected duration of 6 months or less.

"(4) Rules of construction regarding the definition of disability.—The definition of 'disability' in paragraph (1) shall be construed in accordance with the following:

"(A) The definition of disability in this Act shall be construed in favor of broad coverage of individuals under this Act, to the maximum extent permitted by the terms of this Act.

"(B) The term 'substantially limits' shall be interpreted consistently with the findings and purposes of the ADA Amendments Act of 2008.

"(C) An impairment that substantially limits one major life activity need not limit other major life activities in order to be considered a disability.

"(D) An impairment that is episodic or in remission is a disability if it would substantially limit a major life activity when active.

"(E)(i) The determination of whether an impairment substantially limits a major life activity shall be made without regard to the ameliorative effects of mitigating measures such as—

"(I) medication, medical supplies, equipment, or appliances, low-vision devices (which do not include ordinary eyeglasses or contact lenses), prosthetics including limbs and devices, hearing aids and cochlear implants or other implantable hearing devices, mobility devices, or oxygen therapy equipment and supplies;

"(II) use of assistive technology;

"(III) reasonable accommodations or auxiliary aids or services; or

"(IV) learned behavioral or adaptive neurological modifications.

"(ii) The ameliorative effects of the mitigating measures of ordinary eyeglasses or contact lenses shall be considered in determining whether an impairment substantially limits a major life activity.

"(iii) As used in this subparagraph—

"(I) the term 'ordinary eyeglasses or contact lenses' means lenses that are intended to fully correct visual acuity or eliminate refractive error; and

"(II) the term 'low-vision devices' means devices that magnify, enhance, or otherwise augment a visual image.".

(b) Conforming Amendment.—The Americans with Disabilities Act of 1990 (42 U.S.C. 12101 et seq.) is further amended by adding after section 3 the following:

"Sec. 4. Additional Definitions.

"As used in this Act:

"(1) Auxiliary aids and services.—The term 'auxiliary aids and services' includes—

"(A) qualified interpreters or other effective methods of making aurally delivered materials available to individuals with hearing impairments;

"(B) qualified readers, taped texts, or other effective methods of making visually delivered materials available to individuals with visual impairments;

"(C) acquisition or modification of equipment or devices; and

"(D) other similar services and actions.

"(2) State.—The term 'State' means each of the several States, the District of Columbia, the Commonwealth of Puerto Rico, Guam, American Samoa, the Virgin Islands of the United States, the Trust Territory of the Pacific Islands, and the Commonwealth of the Northern Mariana Islands.".

(c) Amendment to the Table of Contents.—The table of contents contained in section 1(b) of the Americans with Disabilities Act of 1990 is amended by striking the item relating to section 3 and inserting the following items:

"Sec. 3. Definition of disability.

"Sec. 4. Additional definitions.".

§ 5. Discrimination on the Basis of Disability

(a) On the Basis of Disability.—Section 102 of the Americans with Disabilities Act of 1990 (42 U.S.C. 12112) is amended—

(1) in subsection (a), by striking "with a disability because of the disability of such individual" and inserting "on the basis of disability"; and

(2) in subsection (b) in the matter preceding paragraph (1), by striking "discriminate" and inserting "discriminate against a qualified individual on the basis of disability".

(b) Qualification Standards and Tests Related to Uncorrected Vision.—Section 103 of the Americans with Disabilities Act of 1990 (42 U.S.C. 12113) is amended by redesignating subsections (c) and (d) as subsections (d) and (e), respectively, and inserting after subsection (b) the following new subsection:

"(c) Qualification Standards and Tests Related to Uncorrected Vision.—Notwithstanding section 3(4)(E)(ii), a covered entity shall not use qualification standards, employment tests, or other selection criteria based on an individual's uncorrected vision unless the standard, test, or other selection criteria, as used by the covered entity, is shown to be job-related for the position in question and consistent with business necessity.".

(c) Conforming Amendments.—

(1) Section 101(8) of the Americans with Disabilities Act of 1990 (42 U.S.C. 12111(8)) is amended—

(A) in the paragraph heading, by striking "with a disability"; and

(B) by striking "with a disability" after "individual" both places it appears.

(2) Section 104(a) of the Americans with Disabilities Act of 1990 (42 U.S.C. 12114(a)) is amended by striking "the term 'qualified individual with a disability' shall" and inserting "a qualified individual with a disability shall".

§ 6. Rules of Construction

(a) Title V of the Americans with Disabilities Act of 1990 (42 U.S.C. 12201 et seq.) is amended—

(1) by adding at the end of section 501 the following:

"(e) Benefits Under State Worker's Compensation Laws.— Nothing in this Act alters the standards for determining eligibility for benefits under State worker's compensation laws or under State and Federal disability benefit programs.

"(f) Fundamental Alteration.—Nothing in this Act alters the provision of section 302(b)(2)(A)(ii), specifying that reasonable modifications in policies, practices, or procedures shall be required, unless an entity can demonstrate that making such modifications in policies, practices, or procedures, including academic requirements in postsecondary education, would fundamentally alter the nature of the goods, services, facilities, privileges, advantages, or accommodations involved.

"(g) Claims of No Disability.—Nothing in this Act shall provide the basis for a claim by an individual without a disability that the individual was subject to discrimination because of the individual's lack of disability.

"(h) Reasonable Accommodations and Modifications.—A covered entity under title I, a public entity under title II, and any person who owns, leases (or leases to), or operates a place of public accommodation under title III, need not provide a reasonable accommodation or a reasonable modification to policies, practices, or procedures to an individual who meets the definition of disability in section 3(1) solely under subparagraph (C) of such section.";

(2) by redesignating section 506 through 514 as sections 507 through 515, respectively, and adding after section 505 the following:

"Sec. 506. Rule of Construction Regarding Regulatory Authority.

"The authority to issue regulations granted to the Equal Employment Opportunity Commission, the Attorney General, and the Secretary of Transportation under this Act includes the authority to issue regulations implementing the definitions of disability in section 3 (including rules of construction) and the definitions in section 4, consistent with the ADA Amendments Act of 2008."; and

(3) in section 511 (as redesignated by paragraph (2)) (42 U.S.C. 12211), in subsection (c), by striking "511(b)(3)" and inserting "512(b)(3)".

(b) The table of contents contained in section 1(b) of the Americans with Disabilities Act of 1990 is amended by redesignating the items relating to sections 506 through 514 as the items relating to sections 507 through 515, respectively, and by inserting after the item relating to section 505 the following new item:

"Sec. 506. Rule of construction regarding regulatory authority.".

§ 7. Conforming Amendments

Section 7 of the Rehabilitation Act of 1973 (29 U.S.C. 705) is amended—

(1) in paragraph (9)(B), by striking "a physical" and all that follows through "major life activities", and inserting "the meaning given it in section 3 of the Americans with Disabilities Act of 1990 (42 U.S.C. 12102)"; and

(2) in paragraph (20)(B), by striking "any person who" and all that follows through the period at the end, and inserting "any person who has a disability as defined in section 3 of the Americans with Disabilities Act of 1990 (42 U.S.C. 12102).".

§ 8. Effective Date

This Act and the amendments made by this Act shall become effective on January 1, 2009.

GENETIC INFORMATION NONDISCRIMINATION ACT OF 2008 (GINA)— SELECTED PROVISIONS 42 U.S.C. § 2000*

TITLE II—PROHIBITING EMPLOYMENT DISCRIMINATION ON THE BASIS OF GENETIC INFORMATION

§ 201. [42 U.S.C. § 2000ff] Definitions

* * *

(3) Family member.—The term "family member" means, with respect to an individual—

(A) a dependent (as such term is used for purposes of section 701(f)(2) of the Employee Retirement Income Security Act of 1974) of such individual, and

(B) any other individual who is a first-degree, second-degree, third-degree, or fourth-degree relative of such individual or of an individual described in subparagraph (A).

(4) Genetic information.—

(A) In general.—The term "genetic information" means, with respect to any individual, information about—

(i) such individual's genetic tests,

(ii) the genetic tests of family members of such individual, and

(iii) the manifestation of a disease or disorder in family members of such individual.

(B) Inclusion of genetic services and participation in genetic research.—Such term includes, with respect to any individual, any request for, or receipt of, genetic services, or participation in clinical research which includes genetic services, by such individual or any family member of such individual.

(C) Exclusions.—The term "genetic information" shall not include information about the sex or age of any individual.

(5) Genetic monitoring.—The term "genetic monitoring" means the periodic examination of employees to evaluate acquired modifications to their genetic material, such as chromosomal damage or evidence of increased occurrence of mutations, that may have developed in the course of employment due to exposure to toxic substances in the workplace, in order to identify, evaluate, and

* Pub.L. 110–233, May 21, 2008, 122 Stat. 881.

respond to the effects of or control adverse environmental exposures in the workplace.

(6) **Genetic services.**—The term "genetic services" means—

(A) a genetic test;

(B) genetic counseling (including obtaining, interpreting, or assessing genetic information); or

(C) genetic education.

(7) **Genetic test.**—

(A) In general.—The term "genetic test" means an analysis of human DNA, RNA, chromosomes, proteins, or metabolites, that detects genotypes, mutations, or chromosomal changes.

(B) Exceptions.—The term "genetic test" does not mean an analysis of proteins or metabolites that does not detect genotypes, mutations, or chromosomal changes.

§ 202. [42 U.S.C. § 2000ff–1] Employer Practices

(a) **Discrimination Based on Genetic Information.**—It shall be an unlawful employment practice for an employer—

(1) to fail or refuse to hire, or to discharge, any employee, or otherwise to discriminate against any employee with respect to the compensation, terms, conditions, or privileges of employment of the employee, because of genetic information with respect to the employee; or

(2) to limit, segregate, or classify the employees of the employer in any way that would deprive or tend to deprive any employee of employment opportunities or otherwise adversely affect the status of the employee as an employee, because of genetic information with respect to the employee.

(b) **Acquisition of Genetic Information.**—It shall be an unlawful employment practice for an employer to request, require, or purchase genetic information with respect to an employee or a family member of the employee except—

(1) where an employer inadvertently requests or requires family medical history of the employee or family member of the employee;

(2) where—

(A) health or genetic services are offered by the employer, including such services offered as part of a wellness program;

(B) the employee provides prior, knowing, voluntary, and written authorization;

(C) only the employee (or family member if the family member is receiving genetic services) and the licensed health care professional or board certified genetic counselor involved in providing such services receive individually identifiable information concerning the results of such services; and

(D) any individually identifiable genetic information provided under subparagraph (C) in connection with the services provided under subparagraph (A) is only available for purposes of such services and shall not be disclosed to the employer except in aggregate terms that do not disclose the identity of specific employees;

(3) where an employer requests or requires family medical history from the employee to comply with the certification provisions of section 103 of the Family and Medical Leave Act of 1993 (*29 U.S.C. 2613*) or such requirements under State family and medical leave laws;

(4) where an employer purchases documents that are commercially and publicly available (including newspapers, magazines, periodicals, and books, but not including medical databases or court records) that include family medical history;

(5) where the information involved is to be used for genetic monitoring of the biological effects of toxic substances in the workplace, but only if—

(A) the employer provides written notice of the genetic monitoring to the employee; (B)

(i) the employee provides prior, knowing, voluntary, and written authorization; or

(ii) the genetic monitoring is required by Federal or State law;

(C) the employee is informed of individual monitoring results;

(D) the monitoring is in compliance with—

(i) any Federal genetic monitoring regulations, including any such regulations that may be promulgated by the Secretary of Labor pursuant to the Occupational Safety and Health Act of 1970 (*29 U.S.C. 651* et seq.), the Federal Mine Safety and Health Act of 1977 (*30 U.S.C. 801* et seq.), or the Atomic Energy Act of 1954 (*42 U.S.C. 2011* et seq.); or

(ii) State genetic monitoring regulations, in the case of a State that is implementing genetic monitoring regulations under the authority of the Occupational Safety and Health Act of 1970 (*29 U.S.C. 651* et seq.); and

(E) the employer, excluding any licensed health care professional or board certified genetic counselor that is involved in the genetic monitoring program, receives the results of the monitoring only in aggregate terms that do not disclose the identity of specific employees; or

(6) where the employer conducts DNA analysis for law enforcement purposes as a forensic laboratory or for purposes of human remains identification, and requests or requires genetic information of such employer's employees, but only to the extent that such genetic information is used for analysis of DNA identification markers for quality control to detect sample contamination.

(c) Preservation of Protections.—In the case of information to which any of paragraphs (1) through (6) of subsection (b) applies, such information may not be used in violation of paragraph (1) or (2) of subsection (a) or treated or disclosed in a manner that violates section 206.

§ 207.   [42 U.S.C. § 2000ff–7] Remedies and Enforcement

(a) Employees Covered by Title VII of the Civil Rights Act of 1964.—

(1) In general.—The powers, procedures, and remedies provided in sections 705, 706, 707, 709, 710, and 711 of the Civil Rights Act of 1964 (*42 U.S.C. 2000e–4* et seq.) to the Commission, the Attorney General, or any person, alleging a violation of title VII of that Act (*42 U.S.C. 2000e* et seq.) shall be the powers, procedures, and remedies this title provides to the Commission, the Attorney General, or any person, respectively, alleging an unlawful employment practice in violation of this title against an employee described in section 201(2)(A)(i), except as provided in paragraphs (2) and (3).

(2) Costs and fees.—The powers, remedies, and procedures provided in subsections (b) and (c) of section 722 of the Revised Statutes of the United States (*42 U.S.C. 1988*), shall be powers, remedies, and procedures this title provides to the Commission, the Attorney General, or any person, alleging such a practice.

(3) Damages.—The powers, remedies, and procedures provided in section 1977A of the Revised Statutes of the United States (*42 U.S.C. 1981a*), including the limitations contained in subsection (b)(3) of such section 1977A, shall be powers, remedies, and procedures this title provides to the Commission, the Attorney General, or any person, alleging such a practice (not an employment practice specifically excluded from coverage under section 1977A(a)(1) of the Revised Statutes of the United States).

* * *

(e) Employees Covered by Section 717 of the Civil Rights Act of 1964.—

(1) In general.—The powers, remedies, and procedures provided in section 717 of the Civil Rights Act of 1964 (*42 U.S.C. 2000e–16*) to the Commission, the Attorney General, the Librarian of Congress, or any person, alleging a violation of that section shall be the powers, remedies, and procedures this title provides to the Commission, the Attorney General, the Librarian of Congress, or any person, respectively, alleging an unlawful employment practice in violation of this title against an employee or applicant described in section 201(2)(A)(v), except as provided in paragraphs (2) and (3).

(2) Costs and fees.—The powers, remedies, and procedures provided in subsections (b) and (c) of section 722 of the Revised Statutes of the United States (*42 U.S.C. 1988*), shall be powers, remedies, and procedures this title provides to the Commission, the Attorney General, the Librarian of Congress, or any person, alleging such a practice.

(3) Damages.—The powers, remedies, and procedures provided in section 1977A of the Revised Statutes of the United States (*42 U.S.C. 1981a*), including the limitations contained in subsection (b)(3) of such section 1977A, shall be powers, remedies, and procedures this title provides to the Commission, the Attorney General, the Librarian of Congress, or any person, alleging such a practice (not an employment practice specifically excluded from coverage under section 1977A(a)(1) of the Revised Statutes of the United States).

(f) Prohibition Against Retaliation.—No person shall discriminate against any individual because such individual has opposed any act or practice made unlawful by this title or because such individual made a charge, testified, assisted, or participated in any manner in an investigation, proceeding, or hearing under this title. The remedies and procedures otherwise provided for under this section shall be available to aggrieved individuals with respect to violations of this subsection.

(g) Definition.—In this section, the term "Commission" means the Equal Employment Opportunity Commission.

§ 208. [42 U.S.C. § 2000ff–8] Disparate Impact

(a) General Rule.—Notwithstanding any other provision of this Act, "disparate impact", as that term is used in section 703(k) of the Civil Rights Act of 1964 (*42 U.S.C. 2000e–2(k)*), on the basis of genetic information does not establish a cause of action under this Act.

(b) Commission.—On the date that is 6 years after the date of enactment of this Act, there shall be established a commission, to be known as the Genetic Nondiscrimination Study Commission (referred to in this section as the "Commission") to review the developing science of genetics and to make recommendations to Congress regarding whether to provide a disparate impact cause of action under this Act.

* * *

§ 210. [42 U.S.C. § 2000ff–10] Medical Information That Is Not Genetic Information

An employer, employment agency, labor organization, or joint labor-management committee shall not be considered to be in violation of this title based on the use, acquisition, or disclosure of medical information that is not genetic information about a manifested disease, disorder, or pathological condition of an employee or member, including a manifested disease, disorder, or pathological condition that has or may have a genetic basis.

EXECUTIVE ORDER 11246 SEPTEMBER 28, 1965, 30 F.R. 12319

Equal Employment Opportunity

Under and by virtue of the authority vested in me as President of the United States by the Constitution and statutes of the United States, it is ordered as follows:

PART I—NONDISCRIMINATION IN GOVERNMENT EMPLOYMENT

§ **101.** It is the policy of the Government of the United States to provide equal opportunity in Federal employment for all qualified persons, to prohibit discrimination in employment because of race, creed, color, or national origin, and to promote the full realization of equal employment opportunity through a positive, continuing program in each executive department and agency. The policy of equal opportunity applies to every aspect of Federal employment policy and practice.

§ **102.** The head of each executive department and agency shall establish and maintain a positive program of equal employment opportunity for all civilian employees and applicants for employment within his jurisdiction in accordance with the policy set forth in Section 101.

§ **103.** The Civil Service Commission shall supervise and provide leadership and guidance in the conduct of equal employment opportunity programs for the civilian employees of and applications for employment within the executive departments and agencies and shall review agency program accomplishments periodically. In order to facilitate the achievement of a model program for equal employment opportunity in the Federal service, the Commission may consult from time to time with such individuals, groups, or organizations as may be of assistance in improving the Federal program and realizing the objectives of this Part.

§ **104.** The Civil Service Commission shall provide for the prompt, fair, and impartial consideration of all complaints of discrimination in Federal employment on the basis of race, creed, color, or national origin. Procedures for the consideration of complaints shall include at least one impartial review within the executive department or agency and shall provide for appeal to the Civil Service Commission.

§ **105.** The Civil Service Commission shall issue such regulations, orders, and instructions as it deems necessary and appropriate to carry out its responsibilities under this Part, and the head of each executive department and agency shall comply with the regulations, orders, and instructions issued by the Commission under this Part.

PART II—NONDISCRIMINATION IN EMPLOYMENT BY GOVERNMENT CONTRACTORS AND SUBCONTRACTORS

SUBPART A—DUTIES OF THE SECRETARY OF LABOR

§ 201. The Secretary of Labor shall be responsible for the administration of Parts II and III of this Order and shall adopt such rules and regulations and issue such orders as he deems necessary and appropriate to achieve the purposes thereof.

SUBPART B—CONTRACTORS' AGREEMENTS

§ 202. Except in contracts exempted in accordance with Section 204 of this Order, all Government contracting agencies shall include in every Government contract hereafter entered into the following provisions:

"During the performance of this contract, the contractor agrees as follows:

"(1) The contractor will not discriminate against any employee or applicant for employment because of race, creed, color, or national origin. The contractor will take affirmative action to ensure that applicants are employed, and that employees are treated during employment, without regard to their race, creed, color, or national origin. Such action shall include, but not be limited to the following: employment, upgrading, demotion, or transfer; recruitment or recruitment advertising; layoff or termination; rates of pay or other forms of compensation; and selection for training, including apprenticeship. The contractor agrees to post in conspicuous places, available to employees and applicants for employment, notices to be provided by the contracting officer setting forth the provisions of this nondiscrimination clause.

"(2) The contractor will, in all solicitations or advertisements for employees placed by or on behalf of the contractor, state that all qualified applicants will receive consideration for employment without regard to race, creed, color, or national origin.

"(3) The contractor will send to each labor union or representative of workers with which he has a collective bargaining agreement or other contract or understanding, a notice, to be provided by the agency contracting officer, advising the labor union or workers' representative of the contractor's commitments under Section 202 of Executive Order No. 11246 of September 24, 1965, and shall post copies of the notice in conspicuous places available to employees and applicants for employment.

"(4) The contractor will comply with all provisions of Executive Order No. 11246 of Sept. 24, 1965, and of the rules, regulations, and relevant orders of the Secretary of Labor.

"(5) The contractor will furnish all information and reports required by Executive Order No. 11246 of September 24, 1965, and by the rules, regulations, and orders of the Secretary of Labor, or pursuant thereto, and will permit access to his books, records, and accounts by the contracting agency and the Secretary of Labor for purposes of investigation to ascertain compliance with such rules, regulations, and orders.

"(6) In the event of the contractor's noncompliance with the nondiscrimination clauses of this contract or with any of such rules, regulations, or orders, this contract may be cancelled, terminated or suspended in whole or in part and the contractor may be declared ineligible for further Government contracts in accordance with procedures authorized in Executive Order No. 11246 of Sept. 24, 1965, and such other sanctions may be imposed and remedies invoked as provided in Executive Order No. 11246 of September 24, 1965, or by rule, regulation, or order of the Secretary of Labor, or as otherwise provided by law.

"(7) The contractor will include the provisions of Paragraphs (1) through (7) in every subcontract or purchase order unless exempted by rules, regulations, or orders of the Secretary of Labor issued pursuant to Section 204 of Executive Order No. 11246 of Sept. 24, 1965, so that such provisions will be binding upon each subcontractor or vendor. The contractor will take such action with respect to any subcontract or purchase order as the contracting agency may direct as a means of enforcing such provisions including sanctions for noncompliance: *Provided, however,* That in the event the contractor becomes involved in, or is threatened with, litigation with a subcontractor or vendor as a result of such direction by the contracting agency, the contractor may request the United States to enter into such litigation to protect the interests of the United States."

§ 203. (a) Each contractor having a contract containing the provisions prescribed in Section 202 shall file, and shall cause each of his subcontractors to file, Compliance Reports with the contracting agency or the Secretary of Labor as may be directed. Compliance Reports shall be filed within such times and shall contain such information as to the practices, policies, programs, and employment policies, programs, and employment statistics of the contractor and each subcontractor, and shall be in such form, as the Secretary of Labor may prescribe.

(b) Bidders or prospective contractors or subcontractors may be required to state whether they have participated in any previous contract subject to the provisions of this Order, or any preceding similar Executive order, and in that event to submit, on behalf of themselves and their proposed subcontractors, Compliance Reports prior to or as an initial part of their bid or negotiation of a contract.

(c) Whenever the contractor or subcontractor has a collective bargaining agreement or other contract or understanding with a labor union or an agency referring workers or providing or supervising apprenticeship or training for such workers, the Compliance Report shall include such information as to such labor union's or agency's practices and policies affecting compliance as the Secretary of Labor may prescribe: *Provided*, That to the extent such information is within the exclusive possession of a labor union or an agency referring workers or providing or supervising apprenticeship or training and such labor union or agency shall refuse to furnish such information to the contractor, the contractor shall so certify to the contracting agency as part of its Compliance Report and shall set forth what efforts he has made to obtain such information.

(d) The contracting agency or the Secretary of Labor may direct that any bidder or prospective contractor or subcontractor shall submit, as part of his Compliance Report, a statement in writing, signed by an authorized officer or agent on behalf of any labor union or any agency referring workers or providing or supervising apprenticeship or other training, with which the bidder or prospective contractor deals, with supporting information, to the effect that the signer's practices and policies do not discriminate on the grounds of race, color, creed, or national origin, and that the signer either will affirmatively cooperate in the implementation of the policy and provisions of this Order or that it consents and agrees that recruitment, employment, and the terms and conditions of employment under the proposed contract shall be in accordance with the purposes and provisions of the Order. In the event that the union or the agency shall refuse to execute such a statement, the Compliance Report shall so certify and set forth what efforts have been made to secure such a statement and such additional factual material as the contracting agency or the Secretary of Labor may require.

§ 204.   The Secretary of Labor may, when he deems that special circumstances in the national interest so require, exempt a contracting agency from the requirement of including any or all of the provisions of Section 202 of this Order in any specific contract, subcontract, or purchase order. The Secretary of Labor may, by rule or regulation, also exempt certain classes of contracts, subcontracts, or purchase orders (1) whenever work is to be or has been performed outside the United States and no recruitment of workers within the limits of the United States is involved; (2) for standard commercial supplies or raw materials; (3) involving less than specified amounts of money or specified numbers of workers; or (4) to the extent that they involve subcontracts below a specified tier. The Secretary of Labor may also provide, by rule, regulation, or order, for the exemption of facilities of a contractor which are in all respects separate and distinct from activities of the contractor related to the performance of the contract: *Provided*, That such an exemption will not interfere with or impede the effectuation of the purposes of this Order: *And provided further*, That in the absence of such an exemption all facilities shall be covered by the provisions of this Order.

SUBPART C—POWERS AND DUTIES OF THE SECRETARY OF LABOR AND THE CONTRACTING AGENCIES

§ 205.   Each contracting agency shall be primarily responsible for obtaining compliance with the rules, regulations, and orders of the

Secretary of Labor with respect to contracts entered into by such agency or its contractors. All contracting agencies shall comply with the rules of the Secretary of Labor in discharging their primary responsibility for securing compliance with the provisions of contracts and otherwise with the terms of this Order and of the rules, regulations, and orders of the Secretary of Labor issued pursuant to this Order. They are directed to cooperate with the Secretary of Labor and to furnish the Secretary of Labor such information and assistance as he may require in the performance of his functions under this Order. They are further directed to appoint or designate, from among the agency's personnel, compliance officers. It shall be the duty of such officers to seek compliance with the objectives of this Order by conference, conciliation, mediation, or persuasion.

§ 206. (a) The Secretary of Labor may investigate the employment practices of any Government contractor or subcontractor, or initiate such investigation by the appropriate contracting agency, to determine whether or not the contractual provisions specified in Section 202 of this Order have been violated. Such investigation shall be conducted in accordance with the procedures established by the Secretary of Labor and the investigating agency shall report to the Secretary of Labor any action taken or recommended.

(b) The Secretary of Labor may receive and investigate or cause to be investigated complaints by employees or prospective employees of a Government contractor or subcontractor which allege discrimination contrary to the contractual provisions specified in Section 202 of this Order. If this investigation is conducted for the Secretary of Labor by a contracting agency, that agency shall report to the Secretary what action has been taken or is recommended with regard to such complaints.

§ 207. The Secretary of Labor shall use his best efforts, directly and through contracting agencies, other interested Federal, State, and local agencies, contractors, and all other available instrumentalities to cause any labor union engaged in work under Government contracts or any agency referring workers or providing or supervising apprenticeship or training for or in the course of such work to cooperate in the implementation of the purposes of this Order. The Secretary of Labor shall, in appropriate cases, notify the Equal Employment Opportunity Commission, the Department of Justice, or other appropriate Federal agencies whenever it has reason to believe that the practices of any such labor organization or agency violate Title VI or Title VII of the Civil Rights Act of 1964 or other provision of Federal law.

§ 208. (a) The Secretary of Labor, or any agency, officer, or employee in the executive branch of the Government designated by rule, regulation, or order of the Secretary, may hold such hearings, public or private, as the Secretary may deem advisable for compliance, enforcement, or educational purposes.

(b) The Secretary of Labor may hold, or cause to be held, hearings in accordance with Subsection (a) of this Section prior to imposing, ordering, or recommending the imposition of penalties and sanctions under this Order. No order for debarment of any contractor from further Government contracts under Section 209(a)(6) shall be made without affording the contractor an opportunity for a hearing.

SUBPART D—SANCTIONS AND PENALTIES

§ 209. (a) In accordance with such rules, regulations, or orders as the Secretary of Labor may issue or adopt, the Secretary or the appropriate contracting agency may:

(1) Publish, or cause to be published, the names of contractors or unions which it has concluded have complied or have failed to comply with the provisions of this Order or of the rules, regulations, and orders of the Secretary of Labor.

(2) Recommend to the Department of Justice that, in cases in which there is substantial or material violation or the threat of substantial or material violation of the contractual provisions set forth in Section 202 of this Order, appropriate proceedings be brought to enforce those provisions, including the enjoining, within the limitations of applicable law, of organizations, individuals, or groups who prevent directly or indirectly, or seek to prevent directly or indirectly, compliance with the provisions of this Order.

(3) Recommend to the Equal Employment Opportunity Commission or the Department of Justice that appropriate proceedings be instituted under Title VII of the Civil Rights Act of 1964.

(4) Recommend to the Department of Justice that criminal proceedings be brought for the furnishing of false information to any contracting agency or to the Secretary of Labor as the case may be.

(5) Cancel, terminate, suspend, or cause to be cancelled, terminated, or suspended, any contract, or any portion or portions thereof, for failure of the contractor or subcontractor to comply with the nondiscrimination provisions of the contract. Contracts may be cancelled, terminated, or suspended absolutely or continuance of contracts may be conditioned upon a program for future compliance approved by the contracting agency.

(6) Provide that any contracting agency shall refrain from entering into further contracts, or extensions or other modifications of existing contracts, with any noncomplying contractor, until such contractor has satisfied the Secretary of Labor that such contractor has established and will carry out personnel and employment policies in compliance with the provisions of this Order.

(b) Under rules and regulations prescribed by the Secretary of Labor, each contracting agency shall make reasonable efforts within a reasonable time limitation to secure compliance with the contract provisions of this Order by methods of conference, conciliation, mediation, and persuasion before proceedings shall be instituted under Subsection (a)(2) of this Section, or before a contract shall be cancelled or terminated in whole or in part under Subsection (a)(5) of this Section for failure of a contractor or subcontractor to comply with the contract provisions of this Order.

§ **210.** Any contracting agency taking any action authorized by this Subpart, whether on its own motion, or as directed by the Secretary of Labor, or under the rules and regulations of the Secretary, shall promptly notify the Secretary of such action. Whenever the Secretary of Labor makes a determination under this Section, he shall promptly notify the appropriate contracting agency of the action recommended. The agency shall take such action and shall report the results thereof to the Secretary of Labor within such time as the Secretary shall specify.

§ **211.** If the Secretary shall so direct, contracting agencies shall not enter into contracts with any bidder or prospective contractor unless the bidder or prospective contractor has satisfactorily complied with the provisions of this Order or submits a program for compliance acceptable to the Secretary of Labor or, if the Secretary so authorizes, to the contracting agency.

§ **212.** Whenever a contracting agency cancels or terminates a contract, or whenever a contractor has been debarred from further Government contracts, under Section 209(a)(6) because of noncompliance with the contract provisions with regard to nondiscrimination, the Secretary of Labor, or the contracting agency involved, shall promptly notify the Comptroller General of the United States. Any such debarment may be rescinded by the Secretary of Labor or by the contracting agency which imposed the sanction.

SUBPART E—CERTIFICATES OF MERIT

§ **213.** The Secretary of Labor may provide for issuance of a United States Government Certificate of Merit to employers or labor unions, or other agencies which are or may hereafter be engaged in work under Government contracts, if the Secretary is satisfied that the personnel and employment practices of the employer, or that the personnel, training, apprenticeship, membership, grievance and representation, upgrading, and other practices and policies of the labor union or other agency conform to the purposes and provisions of this Order.

§ **214.** Any Certificate of Merit may at any time be suspended or revoked by the Secretary of Labor if the holder thereof, in the judgment of the Secretary, has failed to comply with the provisions of this Order.

§ **215.** The Secretary of Labor may provide for the exemption of any employer, labor union, or other agency from any reporting requirements imposed under or pursuant to this Order if such employer, labor union, or other agency has been awarded a Certificate of Merit which has not been suspended or revoked.

PART III—NONDISCRIMINATION PROVISIONS IN FEDERALLY ASSISTED CONSTRUCTION CONTRACTS

§ 301. Each executive department and agency which administers a program involving Federal financial assistance shall require as a condition for the approval of any grant, contract, loan, insurance, or guarantee thereunder, which may involve a construction contract, that the applicant for Federal assistance undertake and agree to incorporate, or cause to be incorporated, into all construction contracts paid for in whole or in part with funds obtained from the Federal Government or borrowed on the credit of the Federal Government pursuant to such grant, contract, loan, insurance, or guarantee, or undertaken pursuant to any Federal program involving such grant, contract, loan, insurance, or guarantee, the provisions prescribed for Government contracts by Section 202 of this Order or such modification thereof, preserving in substance the contractor's obligations thereunder, as may be approved by the Secretary of Labor, together with such additional provisions as the Secretary deems appropriate to establish and protect the interest of the United States in the enforcement of those obligations. Each such applicant shall also undertake and agree (1) to assist and cooperate actively with the administering department or agency and the Secretary of Labor in obtaining the compliance of contractors and subcontractors with those contract provisions and with the rules, regulations, and relevant orders of the Secretary, (2) to obtain and to furnish to the administering department or agency and to the Secretary of Labor such information as they may require for the supervision of such compliance, (3) to carry out sanctions and penalties for violation of such obligations imposed upon contractors and subcontractors by the Secretary of Labor or the administering department or agency pursuant to Part II, Subpart D, of this Order, and (4) to refrain from entering into any contract subject to this Order, or extension or other modification of such a contract with a contractor debarred from Government contracts under Part II, Subpart D, of this Order.

§ 302. **(a)** "Construction contract" as used in this Order means any contract for the construction, rehabilitation, alteration, conversion, extension, or repair of buildings, highways, or other improvements to real property.

(b) The provisions of Part II of this Order shall apply to such construction contracts, and for purposes of such application the administering department or agency shall be considered the contracting agency referred to therein.

(c) The term "applicant" as used in this Order means an applicant for Federal assistance or, as determined by agency regulation, other program participant, with respect to whom an application for any grant, contract, loan, insurance, or guarantee is not finally acted upon prior to the effective date of this Part, and it includes such an applicant after he becomes a recipient of such Federal assistance.

§ 303. (a) Each administering department and agency shall be responsible for obtaining the compliance of such applicants with their undertakings under this Order. Each administering department and agency is directed to cooperate with the Secretary of Labor, and to furnish the Secretary such information and assistance as he may require in the performance of his functions under this Order.

(b) In the event an applicant fails and refuses to comply with his undertakings, the administering department or agency may take any or all of the following actions: (1) cancel, terminate, or suspend in whole or in part the agreement, contract, or other arrangement with such applicant with respect to which the failure and refusal occurred; (2) refrain from extending any further assistance to the applicant under the program with respect to which the failure or refusal occurred until satisfactory assurance of future compliance has been received from such applicant; and (3) refer the case to the Department of Justice for appropriate legal proceedings.

(c) Any action with respect to an applicant pursuant to Subsection (b) shall be taken in conformity with Section 602 of the Civil Rights Act of 1964 (and the regulations of the administering department or agency issued thereunder), to the extent applicable. In no case shall action be taken with respect to an applicant pursuant to Clause (1) or (2) of Subsection (b) without notice and opportunity for hearing before the administering department or agency.

§ 304. Any executive department or agency which imposes by rule, regulation, or order requirements of nondiscrimination in employment, other than requirements imposed pursuant to this Order, may delegate to the Secretary of Labor by agreement such responsibilities with respect to compliance standards, reports, and procedures as would tend to bring the administration of such requirements into conformity with the administration of requirements imposed under this Order: *Provided,* That actions to effect compliance by recipients of Federal financial assistance with requirements imposed pursuant to Title VI of the Civil Rights Act of 1964 shall be taken in conformity with the procedures and limitations prescribed in Section 602 thereof and the regulations of the administering department or agency issued thereunder.

PART IV—MISCELLANEOUS

§ 401. The Secretary of Labor may delegate to any officer, agency, or employee in the Executive branch of the Government, any function or duty of the Secretary under Parts II and III of this Order, except authority to promulgate rules and regulations of a general nature.

§ 402. The Secretary of Labor shall provide administrative support for the execution of the program known as the "Plans for Progress."

§ **403.** **(a)** Executive Orders Nos. 10590 (January 19, 1955), 10722 (August 5, 1957), 10925 (March 6, 1961), 11114 (June 22, 1963), and 11162 (July 28, 1964), are hereby superseded and the President's Committee on Equal Employment Opportunity established by Executive Order No. 10925 is hereby abolished. All records and property in the custody of the Committee shall be transferred to the Civil Service Commission and the Secretary of Labor, as appropriate.

(b) Nothing in this Order shall be deemed to relieve any person of any obligation assumed or imposed under or pursuant to any Executive Order superseded by this Order. All rules, regulations, orders, instructions, designations, and other directives issued by the President's Committee on Equal Employment Opportunity and those issued by the heads of various departments or agencies under or pursuant to any of the Executive orders superseded by this Order, shall, to the extent that they are not inconsistent with this Order, remain in full force and effect unless and until revoked or superseded by appropriate authority. References in such directives to provisions of the superseded orders shall be deemed to be references to the comparable provisions of this Order.

§ **404.** The General Services Administration shall take appropriate action to revise the standard Government contract forms to accord with the provisions of this Order and of the rules and regulations of the Secretary of Labor.

§ **405.** This Order shall become effective thirty days after the date of this Order.

LYNDON B. JOHNSON
THE WHITE HOUSE,
September 24, 1965.

UNIFORM GUIDELINES ON EMPLOYEE SELECTION PROCEDURES—SELECTED PROVISIONS (1978) 29 C.F.R. §§ 1607.1–1607.7

Authority: Secs. 709 and 713, Civil Rights Act of 1964 (78 Stat. 265) as amended by the Equal Employment Opportunity Act of 1972 (Pub.L. 92–261); 42 U.S.C. §§ 2000e–8, 2000e–12.

General Principles

§ 1607.1 Statement of purpose

A. *Need for uniformity—Issuing agencies.* The Federal government's need for a uniform set of principles on the question of the use of tests and other selection procedures has long been recognized. The Equal Employment Opportunity Commission, the Civil Service Commission, the Department of Labor, and the Department of Justice jointly have adopted these uniform guidelines to meet that need, and to apply the same principles to the Federal Government as are applied to other employers.

B. *Purpose of guidelines.* These guidelines incorporate a single set of principles which are designed to assist employers, labor organizations, employment agencies, and licensing and certification boards to comply with requirements of Federal law prohibiting employment practices which discriminate on grounds of race, color, religion, sex, and national origin. They are designed to provide a framework for determining the proper use of tests and other selection procedures. These guidelines do not require a user to conduct validity studies of selection procedures where no adverse impact results. However, all users are encouraged to use selection procedures which are valid, especially users operating under merit principles.

C. *Relation to prior guidelines.* These guidelines are based upon and supersede previously issued guidelines on employee selection procedures. These guidelines have been built upon court decisions, the previously issued guidelines of the agencies, and the practical experience of the agencies, as well as the standards of the psychological profession. These guidelines are intended to be consistent with existing law.

§ 1607.2 Scope

A. *Application of guidelines.* These guidelines will be applied by the Equal Employment Opportunity Commission in the enforcement of title VII of the Civil Rights Act of 1964, as amended by the Equal Employment Opportunity Act of 1972 (hereinafter "Title VII"); by the Department of Labor, and the contract compliance agencies until the transfer of authority contemplated by the President's Reorganization Plan No. 1 of 1978, in the administration and enforcement of Executive Order 11246, as amended by Executive Order 11375 (hereinafter "Executive Order 11246"); by the Civil Service Commission and other Federal agencies subject to section 717 of Title VII; by the Civil Service Commission in exercising its responsibilities toward State and local governments under section 208(b)(1) of the Intergovernmental–Personnel Act; by the Department of Justice in exercising its responsibilities under Federal law; by the Office of Revenue Sharing of the Department of the Treasury under the State and Local Fiscal Assistance Act of 1972, as amended; and by any other Federal agency which adopts them.

B.   *Employment decisions.* These guidelines apply to tests and other selection procedures which are used as a basis for any employment decision. Employment decisions include but are not limited to hiring, promotion, demotion, membership (for example, in a labor organization), referral, retention, and licensing and certification, to the extent that licensing and certification may be covered by Federal equal employment opportunity law. Other selection decisions, such as selection for training or transfer, may also be considered employment decisions if they lead to any of the decisions listed above.

C.   *Selection procedures.* These guidelines apply only to selection procedures which are used as a basis for making employment decisions. For example, the use of recruiting procedures designed to attract members of a particular race, sex, or ethnic group, which were previously denied employment opportunities or which are currently underutilized, may be necessary to bring an employer into compliance with Federal law, and is frequently an essential element of any effective affirmative action program; but recruitment practices are not considered by these guidelines to be selection procedures. Similarly, these guidelines do not pertain to the question of the lawfulness of a seniority system within the meaning of section 703(h), Executive Order 11246 or other provisions of Federal law or regulation, except to the extent that such systems utilize selection procedures to determine qualifications or abilities to perform the job. Nothing in these guidelines is intended or should be interpreted as discouraging the use of a selection procedure for the purpose of determining qualifications or for the purpose of selection on the basis of relative qualifications, if the selection procedure had been validated in accord with these guidelines for each such purpose for which it is to be used.

D.   *Limitations.* These guidelines apply only to persons subject to Title VII, Executive Order 11246, or other equal employment opportunity requirements of Federal law. These guidelines do not apply to responsibilities under the Age Discrimination in Employment Act of 1967, as amended, not to discriminate on the basis of age, or under sections 501, 503, and 504 of the Rehabilitation Act of 1973, not to discriminate on the basis of handicap.

E. *Indian preference not affected.* These guidelines do not restrict any obligation imposed or right granted by Federal law to users to extend a preference in employment to Indians living on or near an Indian reservation in connection with employment opportunities on or near an Indian reservation.

§ 1607.3   Discrimination defined: Relationship between use of selection procedures and discrimination

A. *Procedure having adverse impact constitutes discrimination unless justified.* The use of any selection procedure which has an adverse impact on the hiring, promotion, or other employment or membership opportunities of members of any race, sex, or ethnic group will be considered to be discriminatory and inconsistent with these guidelines, unless the procedure has been validated in accordance with these guidelines, or the provisions of section 6 below are satisfied.

B. *Consideration of suitable alternative selection procedures.* Where two or more selection procedures are available which serve the user's legitimate interest in efficient and trustworthy workmanship, and which are substantially equally valid for a given purpose, the user should use the procedure which has been demonstrated to have the lesser adverse impact. Accordingly, whenever a validity study is called for by these guidelines, the user should include, as a part of the validity study, an investigation of suitable alternative selection procedures and suitable alternative methods of using the selection procedure which have as little adverse impact as possible, to determine the appropriateness of using or validating them in accord with these guidelines. If a user has made a reasonable effort to become aware of such alternative procedures and validity has been demonstrated in accord with these guidelines, the use of the test or other selection procedure may continue until such time as it should reasonably be reviewed for currency. Whenever the user is shown an alternative selection procedure with evidence of less adverse impact and substantial evidence of validity for the same job in similar circumstances, the user should investigate it to determine the appropriateness of using or validating it in accord with these guidelines. This subsection is not intended to preclude the combination of procedures into a significantly more valid procedure, if the use of such a combination has been shown to be in compliance with the guidelines.

§ 1607.4   Information on impact

A. *Records concerning impact.* Each user should maintain and have available for inspection records or other information which will disclose the impact which its tests and other selection procedures have upon employment opportunities of persons by identifiable race, sex, or ethnic group as set forth in subparagraph B below in order to determine compliance with these guidelines. Where there are large numbers of applicants and procedures are administered frequently, such information may be retained on a sample basis, provided that the sample is appropriate in terms of the applicant population and adequate in size.

B. *Applicable race, sex, and ethnic groups for recordkeeping.* The records called for by this section are to be maintained by sex, and the following races and ethnic groups: Blacks (Negroes), American Indians (including Alaskan Natives), Asians (including Pacific Islanders), Hispanic (including persons of Mexican, Puerto Rican, Cuban, Central or South American, or other Spanish origin or culture regardless of race), whites (Caucasians) other than Hispanic, and totals. The race, sex, and ethnic classifications called for by this section are consistent with the Equal Employment Opportunity Standard Form 100, Employer Information Report EEO-1 series of reports. The user should adopt safeguards to insure that the records required by this paragraph are used for appropriate purposes such as determining adverse impact, or (where required) for developing and monitoring affirmative action programs, and that such records are not used improperly. See sections 4E and 17(4), below.

C. *Evaluation of selection rates. The "bottom line."* If the information called for by sections 4A and B above shows that the total selection process for a job has an adverse impact, the individual components of the selection process should be evaluated for adverse impact. If this information shows that the total selection process does not have an adverse impact, the Federal enforcement agencies, in the exercise of their administrative and prosecutorial discretion, in usual circumstances, will not expect a user to evaluate the individual components for adverse impact, or to validate such individual components, and will not take enforcement action based upon adverse impact of any component of that process, including the separate parts of a multipart selection procedure or any separate procedure that is used as an alternative method of selection. However, in the following circumstances the Federal enforcement agencies will expect a user to evaluate the individual components for adverse impact and may, where appropriate, take enforcement action with respect to the individual components: (1) Where the selection procedure is a significant factor in the continuation of patterns of assignments of incumbent employees caused by prior discriminatory employment practices, (2) where the weight of court decisions or administrative interpretations hold that a specific procedure (such as height or weight requirements or no-arrest records) is not job related in the same or similar circumstances. In unusual circumstances, other than those listed in (1) and (2) above, the Federal enforcement agencies may request a user to evaluate the individual components for adverse impact and may, where appropriate, take enforcement action with respect to the individual component.

D. *Adverse impact and the "four-fifths rule."* A selection rate for any race, sex, or ethnic group which is less than four-fifths (or eighty percent) of the rate for the group with the highest rate will generally be regarded by the Federal enforcement agencies as evidence of adverse impact, while a greater than four-fifths rate will generally not be regarded by Federal enforcement agencies as evidence of adverse impact. Smaller differences in selection rate may nevertheless constitute adverse impact, where they are significant in both statistical and practical terms or where a user's actions have discouraged applicants disproportionately on grounds of race, sex, or ethnic group. Greater differences in selection rate may not constitute adverse impact where the differences are based on small numbers and are not statistically significant, or where special recruiting or other programs cause the pool of minority or female candidates to be atypical of the normal pool of applicants from that group. Where the user's evidence concerning the impact of a selection procedure indicates adverse impact but is based upon numbers which are too small to be reliable, evidence concerning the impact of the procedure over a longer period of time and/or evidence concerning the impact which the selection procedure had when used in the same manner in similar circumstances elsewhere may be considered in determining adverse impact. Where the user has not maintained data on adverse impact as required by the documentation section of applicable guidelines, the Federal enforcement agencies may draw an inference of adverse impact of the selection process from the failure of the user to maintain such data, if the user has an underutilization of a group in the job category, as compared to the group's representation in the relevant labor market or, in the case of jobs filled from within, the applicable work force.

E. *Consideration of user's equal employment opportunity posture.* In carrying out their obligations, the Federal enforcement agencies will consider the general posture of the user with respect to equal employment opportunity for the job or group of jobs in question. Where a user has adopted an affirmative action program, the Federal enforcement agencies will consider the provisions of that program, including the goals and timetables which the user has adopted and the progress which the user has made in carrying out that program and in meeting the goals and timetables. While such affirmative action programs may in design and execution be race, color, sex, or ethnic conscious, selection procedures under such programs should be based upon the ability or relative ability to do the work.

§ 1607.5   General standards for validity studies

A. *Acceptable types of validity studies.* For the purposes of satisfying these guidelines, users may rely upon criterion-related validity studies, content validity studies or construct validity studies, in accordance with the standards set forth in the technical standards of these guidelines, section 14 below. New strategies for showing the validity of selection procedures will be evaluated as they become accepted by the psychological profession.

B. *Criterion-related, content, and construct validity.* Evidence of the validity of a test or other selection procedure by a criterion-related validity study should consist of empirical data demonstrating that the selection procedure is predictive of or significantly correlated with important elements of job performance. See section 14B below. Evidence of the validity of a test or other selection procedure by a content validity study should consist of data showing that the content of the selection procedure is representative of important aspects of performance on the job for which the candidates are to be evaluated. See 14C below. Evidence of the validity of a test or other selection procedure through a construct validity study should consist of data showing that the procedure measures the degree to which candidates have identifiable characteristics which have been determined to be important in successful performance in the job for which the candidates are to be evaluated. See section 14D below.

C. *Guidelines are consistent with professional standards.* The provisions of these guidelines relating to validation of selection procedures are intended to be consistent with generally accepted professional standards for evaluating standardized tests and other selection procedures, such as those described in the Standards for Educational and Psychological Tests prepared by a joint committee of the American Psychological Association, the American Educational Research Association, and the National Council on Measurement in Education (American Psychological Association, Washington, D.C., 1974) (hereinafter "A.P.A. Standards") and standard textbooks and journals in the field of personnel selection.

D. *Need for documentation of validity.* For any selection procedure which is part of a selection process which has an adverse impact and which selection procedure has an adverse impact, each user should maintain and have available such documentation as is described in section 15 below.

E. *Accuracy and standardization.* Validity studies should be carried out under conditions which assure insofar as possible the adequacy and accuracy of the research and the report. Selection procedures should be administered and scored under standardized conditions.

F. *Caution against selection on basis of knowledge, skills, or ability learned in brief orientation period.* In general, users should avoid making employment decisions on the basis of measures of knowledge, skills, or abilities which are normally learned in a brief orientation period, and which have an adverse impact.

G. *Method of use of selection procedures.* The evidence of both the validity and utility of a selection procedure should support the method the user chooses for operational use of the procedure, if that method of use has a greater adverse impact than another method of use. Evidence which may be sufficient to support the use of a selection procedure on a pass/fail (screening) basis may be insufficient to support the use of the same procedure on a ranking basis under these guidelines. Thus, if a user decides to use a selection procedure on a ranking basis, and that method of use has a greater adverse impact than use on an appropriate pass/fail basis (see section 5H below), the user should have sufficient evidence of validity and utility to support the use on a ranking basis. See sections 3B, 14B(5) and (6), and 14C(8) and (9).

use the least adverse impact or justify why...

H. *Cutoff scores.* Where cutoff scores are used, they should normally be set so as to be reasonable and consistent with normal expectations of acceptable proficiency within the work force. Where applicants are ranked on the basis of properly validated selection procedures and those applicants scoring below a higher cutoff score than appropriate in light of such expectations have little or no chance of being selected for employment, the higher cutoff score may be appropriate, but the degree of adverse impact should be considered.

I. *Use of selection procedures for higher level jobs.* If job progression structures are so established that employees will probably, within a reasonable period of time and in a majority of cases, progress to a higher level, it may be considered that the applicants are being evaluated for a job or jobs at the higher level. However, where job progression is not so nearly automatic, or the time span is such that higher level jobs or employees' potential may be expected to change in significant ways, it should be considered that applicants are being evaluated for a job at or near the entry level. A "reasonable period of time" will vary for different jobs and employment situations but will seldom be more than 5 years. Use of selection procedures to evaluate applicants for a higher level job would not be appropriate:

(1) If the majority of those remaining employed do not progress to the higher level job;

(2) If there is a reason to doubt that the higher level job will continue to require essentially similar skills during the progression period; or

(3) If the selection procedures measure knowledge, skills, or abilities required for advancement which would be expected to develop principally from the training or experience on the job.

J. *Interim use of selection procedures.* Users may continue the use of a selection procedure which is not at the moment fully supported by the required evidence of validity, provided: (1) The user has available substantial evidence of validity, and (2) the user has in progress, when technically feasible, a study which is designed to produce the additional evidence required by these guidelines within a reasonable time. If such a study is not technically feasible, see section 6B. If the study does not demonstrate validity, this provision of these guidelines for interim use shall not constitute a defense in any action, nor shall it relieve the user of any obligations arising under Federal law.

K. *Review of validity studies for currency.* Whenever validity has been shown in accord with these guidelines for the use of a particular selection procedure for a job or group of jobs, additional studies need not be performed until such time as the validity study is subject to review as provided in section 3B above. There are no absolutes in the area of determining the currency of a validity study. All circumstances concerning the study, including the validation strategy used, and changes in the relevant labor market and the job should be considered in the determination of when a validity study is outdated.

§ 1607.6   Use of selection procedures which have not been validated

A. *Use of alternate selection procedures to eliminate adverse impact.* A user may choose to utilize alternative selection procedures in order to eliminate adverse impact or as part of an affirmative action program. See section 13 below. Such alternative procedures should eliminate the adverse impact in the total selection process, should be lawful and should be as job related as possible.

B. *Where validity studies cannot or need not be performed.* There are circumstances in which a user cannot or need not utilize the validation techniques contemplated by these guidelines. In such circumstances, the user should utilize selection procedures which are as job related as possible and which will minimize or eliminate adverse impact, as set forth below.

(1) *Where informal or unscored procedures are used.* When an informal or unscored selection procedure which has an adverse impact is utilized, the user should eliminate the adverse impact, or modify the procedure to one which is a formal, scored or quantified measure or combination of measures and then validate the procedure in accord with these guidelines, or otherwise justify continued use of the procedure in accord with Federal law.

(2) *Where formal and scored procedures are used.* When a formal and scored selection procedure is used which has an adverse impact, the validation techniques contemplated by these guidelines usually should be followed if technically feasible. Where the user cannot or need not follow the validation techniques anticipated by these guidelines, the user should either modify the procedure to eliminate adverse impact or otherwise justify continued use of the procedure in accord with Federal law.

§ 1607.7 Use of other validity studies

A. *Validity studies not conducted by the user.* Users may, under certain circumstances, support the use of selection procedures by validity studies conducted by other users or conducted by test publishers or distributors and described in test manuals. While publishers of selection procedures have a professional obligation to provide evidence of validity which meets generally accepted professional standards (see section 5C above), users are cautioned that they are responsible for compliance with these guidelines. Accordingly, users seeking to obtain selection procedures from publishers and distributors should be careful to determine that, in the event the user becomes subject to the validity requirements of these guidelines, the necessary information to support validity has been determined and will be made available to the user.

B. *Use of criterion-related validity evidence from other sources.* Criterion-related validity studies conducted by one test user, or described in test manuals and the professional literature, will be considered acceptable for use by another user when the following requirements are met:

(1) *Validity evidence.* Evidence from the available studies meeting the standards of section 14B below clearly demonstrates that the selection procedure is valid;

(2) *Job similarity.* The incumbents in the user's job and the incumbents in the job or group of jobs on which the validity study was conducted perform substantially the same major work behaviors, as shown by appropriate job analyses both on the job or group of jobs on which the validity study was performed and on the job for which the selection procedure is to be used; and

(3) *Fairness evidence.* The studies include a study of test fairness for each race, sex, and ethnic group which constitutes a significant factor in the borrowing user's relevant labor market for the job or jobs in question. If the studies under consideration satisfy (1) and (2) above but do not contain an investigation of test fairness, and it is not technically feasible for the borrowing user to conduct an internal study of test fairness, the borrowing user may utilize the study until studies conducted elsewhere meeting the requirements of these guidelines show test unfairness, or until such time as it becomes technically feasible to conduct an internal study of test fairness and the results of that study can be acted upon. Users obtaining selection procedures from publishers should consider, as one factor in the decision to purchase a particular selection procedure, the availability of evidence concerning test fairness.

C. *Validity evidence from multiunit study.* If validity evidence from a study covering more than one unit within an organization satisfies the requirements of section 14B below, evidence of validity specific to each unit will not be required unless there are variables which are likely to affect validity significantly.

D. *Other significant variables.* If there are variables in the other studies which are likely to affect validity significantly, the user may not rely upon such studies, but will be expected either to conduct an internal validity study or to comply with section 6 above.

OFFCP REGULATIONS ON AFFIRMATIVE ACTION PROGRAMS—SELECTED PROVISIONS
41 C.F.R. §§ 60–2.10–2.17

SUBPART B—PURPOSE AND CONTENTS OF AFFIRMATIVE ACTION PROGRAMS

§ 60–2.10 General purpose and contents of affirmative action programs.

(a) Purpose. (1) An affirmative action program is a management tool designed to ensure equal employment opportunity. A central premise underlying affirmative action is that, absent discrimination, over time a contractor's workforce, generally, will reflect the gender, racial and ethnic profile of the labor pools from which the contractor recruits and selects. Affirmative action programs contain a diagnostic component which includes a number of quantitative analyses designed to evaluate the composition of the workforce of the contractor and compare it to the composition of the relevant labor pools. Affirmative action programs also include action-oriented programs. If women and minorities are not being employed at a rate to be expected given their availability in the relevant labor pool, the contractor's affirmative action program includes specific practical steps designed to address this underutilization. Effective affirmative action programs also include internal auditing and reporting systems as a means of measuring the contractor's progress toward achieving the workforce that would be expected in the absence of discrimination.

(2) An affirmative action program also ensures equal employment opportunity by institutionalizing the contractor's commitment to equality in every aspect of the employment process. Therefore, as part of its affirmative action program, a contractor monitors and examines its employment decisions and compensation systems to evaluate the impact of those systems on women and minorities.

(3) An affirmative action program is, thus, more than a paperwork exercise. An affirmative action program includes those policies, practices, and procedures that the contractor implements to ensure that all qualified applicants and employees are receiving an equal opportunity for recruitment, selection, advancement, and every other term and privilege associated with employment. Affirmative action, ideally, is a part of the way the contractor regularly conducts its business. OFCCP has found that when an affirmative action program is approached from this perspective, as a powerful management tool, there is a positive correlation between the presence of affirmative action and the absence of discrimination.

(b) Contents of affirmative action programs. (1) An affirmative action program must include the following quantitative analyses:

(i) Organizational profile—§ 60–2.11;

(ii) Job group analysis—§ 60–2.12;

(iii) Placement of incumbents in job groups—§ 60–2.13;

(iv) Determining availability—§ 60–2.14;

(v) Comparing incumbency to availability—§ 60–2.15; and

(vi) Placement goals—§ 60–2.16.

(2) In addition, an affirmative action program must include the following components specified in the § 60–2.17 of this part:

(i) Designation of responsibility for implementation;

(ii) Identification of problem areas;

(iii) Action-oriented programs; and

(iv) Periodic internal audits.

(c) Documentation. Contractors must maintain and make available to OFCCP documentation of their compliance with §§ 60–2.11 through 60–2.17.

§ 60–2.11   Organizational profile.

(a) Purpose. An organizational profile is a depiction of the staffing pattern within an establishment. It is one method contractors use to determine whether barriers to equal employment opportunity exist in their organizations. The profile provides an overview of the workforce at the establishment that may assist in identifying organizational units where women or minorities are underrepresented or concentrated. The contractor must use either the organizational display or the workforce analysis as its organizational profile:

(b) Organizational display. (1) An organizational display is a detailed graphical or tabular chart, text, spreadsheet or similar presentation of the contractor's organizational structure. The organizational display must identify each organizational unit in the establishment, and show the relationship of each organizational unit to the other organizational units in the establishment.

(2) An organizational unit is any component that is part of the contractor's corporate structure. In a more traditional organization, an organizational unit might be a department, division, section, branch, group or similar component. In a less traditional organization, an organizational unit might be a project team, job family, or similar component. The term includes an umbrella unit (such as a department) that contains a number of subordinate units, and it separately includes each of the subordinate units (such as sections or branches).

(3) For each organizational unit, the organizational display must indicate the following:

(i) The name of the unit;

(ii) The job title, gender, race, and ethnicity of the unit supervisor (if the unit has a supervisor);

(iii) The total number of male and female incumbents; and

(iv) the total number of male and female incumbents in each of the following groups: Blacks, Hispanics, Asians/Pacific Islanders, and American Indians/Alaskan Natives.

(c) Workforce analysis. (1) A workforce analysis is a listing of each job title as appears in applicable collective bargaining agreements or payroll records ranked from the lowest paid to the highest paid within each department or other similar organizational unit including departmental or unit supervision.

(2) If there are separate work units or lines of progression within a department, a separate list must be provided for each such work unit, or line, including unit supervisors. For lines of progression there must be indicated the order of jobs in the line through which an employee could move to the top of the line.

(3) Where there are no formal progression lines or usual promotional sequences, job titles should be listed by department, job families, or disciplines, in order of wage rates or salary ranges.

(4) For each job title, the total number of incumbents, the total number of male and female incumbents, and the total number of male and female incumbents in each of the following groups must be given: Blacks, Hispanics, Asians/Pacific Islanders, and American Indians/Alaskan Natives. The wage rate or salary range for each job title must be given. All job titles, including all managerial job titles, must be listed.

§ 60–2.12   Job group analysis.

(a) Purpose: A job group analysis is a method of combining job titles within the contractor's establishment. This is the first step in the contractor's comparison of the representation of minorities and women in its workforce with the estimated availability of minorities and women qualified to be employed.

(b) In the job group analysis, jobs at the establishment with similar content, wage rates, and opportunities must be combined to form job groups. Similarity of content refers to the duties and responsibilities of the job titles which make up the job group. Similarity of opportunities refers to training, transfers, promotions, pay, mobility, and other career enhancement opportunities offered by the jobs within the job group.

(c) The job group analysis must include a list of the job titles that comprise each job group. If, pursuant to § 60–2.1(d) and (e) the job group analysis contains jobs that are located at another establishment, the job group analysis must be annotated to identify the actual location of those jobs. If the establishment at which the jobs actually are located maintains an affirmative action program, the job group analysis of that program must be annotated to identify the program in which the jobs are included.

(d) Except as provided in § 60–2.1(d), all jobs located at an establishment must be reported in the job group analysis of that establishment.

(e) Smaller employers: If a contractor has a total workforce of fewer than 150 employees, the contractor may prepare a job group analysis that utilizes EEO–1 categories as job groups. EEO–1 categories refers to the nine occupational groups used in the Standard Form 100, the Employer Information EEO–1 Survey: Officials and managers, professionals, technicians, sales, office and clerical, craft workers (skilled), operatives (semiskilled), laborers (unskilled), and service workers.

§ 60–2.13   Placement of incumbents in job groups.

The contractor must separately state the percentage of minorities and the percentage of women it employs in each job group established pursuant to § 60–2.12.

§ 60–2.14   Determining availability.

(a) Purpose: Availability is an estimate of the number of qualified minorities or women available for employment in a given job group, expressed as a percentage of all qualified persons available for employment in the job group. The purpose of the availability determination is to establish a benchmark against which the demographic composition of the contractor's incumbent workforce can be compared in order to determine whether barriers to equal employment opportunity may exist within particular job groups.

(b) The contractor must separately determine the availability of minorities and women for each job group.

(c) In determining availability, the contractor must consider at least the following factors:

(1) The percentage of minorities or women with requisite skills in the reasonable recruitment area. The reasonable recruitment area is defined as the geographical area from which the contractor usually seeks or reasonably could seek workers to fill the positions in question.

(2) The percentage of minorities or women among those promotable, transferable, and trainable within the contractor's organization. Trainable refers to those employees within the contractor's organization who could, with appropriate training which the contractor is reasonably able to provide, become promotable or transferable during the AAP year.

(d) The contractor must use the most current and discrete statistical information available to derive availability figures. Examples of such information include census data, data from local job service offices, and data from colleges or other training institutions.

(e) The contractor may not draw its reasonable recruitment area in such a way as to have the effect of excluding minorities or women. For each job group, the reasonable recruitment area must be identified, with a brief explanation of the rationale for selection of that recruitment area.

(f) The contractor may not define the pool of promotable, transferable, and trainable employees in such a way as to have the effect of excluding minorities or women. For each job group, the pool of promotable, transferable, and trainable employees must be identified with a brief explanation of the rationale for the selection of that pool.

(g) Where a job group is composed of job titles with different availability rates, a composite availability figure for the job group must be calculated. The contractor must separately determine the availability for each job title within the job group and must determine the proportion of job group incumbents employed in each job title. The contractor must weight the availability for each job title by the proportion of job group incumbents employed in that job group. The sum of the weighted availability estimates for all job titles in the job group must be the composite availability for the job group.

§ 60–2.15 Comparing incumbency to availability.

(a) The contractor must compare the percentage of minorities and women in each job group determined pursuant to § 60–2.13 with the availability for those job groups determined pursuant to § 60–2.14.

(b) When the percentage of minorities or women employed in a particular job group is less than would reasonably be expected given their availability percentage in that particular job group, the contractor must establish a placement goal in accordance with § 60–2.16.

§ 60–2.16 Placement goals.

(a) Purpose: Placement goals serve as objectives or targets reasonably attainable by means of applying every good faith effort to make all aspects of the entire affirmative action program work. Placement goals also are used to measure progress toward achieving equal employment opportunity.

(b) A contractor's determination under § 60–2.15 that a placement goal is required constitutes neither a finding nor an admission of discrimination.

(c) Where, pursuant to § 60–2.15, a contractor is required to establish a placement goal for a particular job group, the contractor must establish a percentage annual placement goal at least equal to the availability figure derived for women or minorities, as appropriate, for that job group.

(d) The placement goal-setting process described above contemplates that contractors will, where required, establish a single goal for all minorities. In the event of a substantial disparity in the utilization of a particular minority group or in the utilization of men or women of a particular minority group, a contractor may be required to establish separate goals for those groups.

(e) In establishing placement goals, the following principles also apply:

(1) Placement goals may not be rigid and inflexible quotas, which must be met, nor are they to be considered as either a ceiling or a floor for the employment of particular groups. Quotas are expressly forbidden.

(2) In all employment decisions, the contractor must make selections in a nondiscriminatory manner. Placement goals do not provide the contractor with a justification to extend a preference to any individual, select an individual, or adversely affect an individual's employment status, on the basis of that person's race, color, religion, sex, or national origin.

(3) Placement goals do not create set-asides for specific groups, nor are they intended to achieve proportional representation or equal results.

(4) Placement goals may not be used to supersede merit selection principles. Affirmative action programs prescribed by the regulations in this part do not require a contractor to hire a person who lacks qualifications to perform the job successfully, or hire a less qualified person in preference to a more qualified one.

(f) A contractor extending a publicly announced preference for American Indians as is authorized in 41 CFR 60–1.5(a)(6) may reflect in its placement goals the permissive employment preference for American Indians living on or near an Indian reservation.

§ 60–2.17 Additional required elements of affirmative action programs.

In addition to the elements required by § 60–2.10 through § 60–2.16, an acceptable affirmative action program must include the following:

(a) Designation of responsibility. The contractor must provide for the implementation of equal employment opportunity and the affirmative action program by assigning responsibility and accountability to an official of the organization. Depending upon the size of the contractor, this may be the official's sole responsibility. He or she must have the authority, resources, support of and access to top management to ensure the effective implementation of the affirmative action program.

(b) Identification of problem areas. The contractor must perform in-depth analyses of its total employment process to determine whether and where impediments to equal employment opportunity exist. At a minimum the contractor must evaluate:

(1) The workforce by organizational unit and job group to determine whether there are problems of minority or female utilization (i.e., employment in the unit or group), or of minority or female distribution (i.e., placement in the different jobs within the unit or group);

(2) personnel activity (applicant flow, hires, terminations, promotions, and other personnel actions) to determine whether there are selection disparities;

(3) compensation system(s) to determine whether there are gender-, race-, or ethnicity-based disparities;

(4) selection, recruitment, referral, and other personnel procedures to determine whether they result in disparities in the employment or advancement of minorities or women; and

(5) any other areas that might impact the success of the affirmative action program.

(c) Action-oriented programs. The contractor must develop and execute action-oriented programs designed to correct any problem areas identified pursuant to § 60–2.17(b) and to attain established goals and objectives. In order for these action-oriented programs to be effective, the contractor must ensure that they consist of more than following the same procedures which have previously produced inadequate results. Furthermore, a contractor must demonstrate that it has made good faith efforts to remove identified barriers, expand employment opportunities, and produce measurable results.

(d) Internal audit and reporting system. The contractor must develop and implement an auditing system that periodically measures the effectiveness of its total affirmative action program. The actions listed below are key to a successful affirmative action program:

(1) Monitor records of all personnel activity, including referrals, placements, transfers, promotions, terminations, and compensation, at all levels to ensure the nondiscriminatory policy is carried out;

(2) Require internal reporting on a scheduled basis as to the degree to which equal employment opportunity and organizational objectives are attained;

(3) Review report results with all levels of management; and

(4) Advise top management of program effectiveness and submit recommendations to improve unsatisfactory performance.

(*65 Fed. Reg. 68022, 68046,* Nov. 13, 2000).

EEOC GUIDELINES ON AGE DISCRIMINATION IN EMPLOYMENT ACT— SELECTED PROVISIONS
29 C.F.R. §§ 1625.2, 1625.6, 1625.7, 1625.10, 1625.22, 1625.23, 1625.32

§ 1625.2 Discrimination Prohibited by the Act

It is unlawful for an employer to discriminate against an individual in any aspect of employment because that individual is 40 years old or older, unless one of the statutory exceptions applies. Favoring an older individual over a younger individual because of age is not unlawful discrimination under the ADEA, even if the younger individual is at least 40 years old. However, the ADEA does not require employers to prefer older individuals and does not affect applicable state, municipal, or local laws that prohibit such preferences.

§ 1625.6 Bona fide occupational qualifications

(a) Whether occupational qualifications will be deemed to be "bona fide" to a specific job and "reasonably necessary to the normal operation of the particular business," will be determined on the basis of all the pertinent facts surrounding each particular situation. It is anticipated that this concept of a bona fide occupational qualification will have limited scope and application. Further, as this is an exception to the Act it must be narrowly construed.

(b) An employer asserting a BFOQ defense has the burden of proving that (1) the age limit is reasonably necessary to the essence of the business, and either (2) that all or substantially all individuals excluded from the job involved are in fact disqualified, or (3) that some of the individuals so excluded possess a disqualifying trait that cannot be ascertained except by reference to age. If the employer's objective in asserting a BFOQ is the goal of public safety, the employer must prove that the challenged practice does indeed effectuate that goal and that there is no acceptable alternative which would better advance it or equally advance it with less discriminatory impact.

(c) Many State and local governments have enacted laws or administrative regulations which limit employment opportunities based on age. Unless these laws meet the standards for the establishment of a valid bona fide occupational qualification under section 4(f)(1) of the Act, they will be considered in conflict with and effectively superseded by the ADEA.

§ 1625.7 Differentiations based on reasonable factors other than age

RFOA.

(a) Section 4(f)(1) of the Act provides that

* * * it shall not be unlawful for an employer, employment agency, or labor organization * * * to take any action otherwise prohibited under paragraphs (a), (b), (c), or (e) of this section * * * where the differentiation is based on reasonable factors other than age * * *.

§ 1625.7 Differentiations based on reasonable factors other than age.

(a) Section 4(f)(1) of the Act provides that

* * * it shall not be unlawful for an employer, employment agency, or labor organization * * * to take any action otherwise prohibited under paragraphs (a), (b), (c), or (e) of this section * * * where the differentiation is based on reasonable factors other than age * * *.

(b) When an employment practice uses age as a limiting criterion, the defense that the practice is justified by a reasonable factor other than age is unavailable.

(c) Any employment practice that adversely affects individuals within the protected age group on the basis of older age is discriminatory unless the practice is justified by a "reasonable factor other than age." An individual challenging the allegedly unlawful practice is responsible for isolating and identifying the specific employment practice that allegedly causes any observed statistical disparities.

DI

(d) Whenever the "reasonable factors other than age" defense is raised, the employer bears the burdens of production and persuasion to demonstrate the defense. The "reasonable factors other than age" provision is not available as a defense to a claim of disparate treatment.

(e)(1) A reasonable factor other than age is a non-age factor that is objectively reasonable when viewed from the position of a prudent employer mindful of its responsibilities under the ADEA under like circumstances. Whether a differentiation is based on reasonable factors other than age must be decided on the basis of all the particular facts and circumstances surrounding each individual situation. To establish the RFOA defense, an employer must show that the employment practice was both reasonably designed to further or achieve a legitimate business purpose and administered in a way that reasonably achieves that purpose in light of the particular facts and circumstances that were known, or should have been known, to the employer.

(2) Considerations that are relevant to whether a practice is based on a reasonable factor other than age include, but are not limited to:

(i) The extent to which the factor is related to the employer's stated business purpose;

(ii) The extent to which the employer defined the factor accurately and applied the factor fairly and accurately, including the extent to which managers and supervisors were given guidance or training about how to apply the factor and avoid discrimination;

(iii) The extent to which the employer limited supervisors' discretion to assess employees subjectively, particularly where the criteria that the supervisors were asked to evaluate are known to be subject to negative age-based stereotypes;

(iv) The extent to which the employer assessed the adverse impact of its employment practice on older workers; and

(v) The degree of the harm to individuals within the protected age group, in terms of both the extent of injury and the numbers of persons adversely affected, and the extent to which the employer took steps to reduce the harm, in light of the burden of undertaking such steps.

(3) No specific consideration or combination of considerations need be present for a differentiation to be based on reasonable factors other than age. Nor does the presence of one of these considerations automatically establish the defense.

(f) A differentiation based on the average cost of employing older employees as a group is unlawful except with respect to employee benefit plans which qualify for the section 4(f)(2) exception to the Act.

[46 FR 47726, Sept. 29, 1981; 77 FR 19080, 19095, Mar. 30, 2012]

§ 1625.10   Costs and benefits under employee benefit plans

(a)(1) *General.* Section 4(f)(2) of the Act provides that it is not unlawful for an employer, employment agency, or labor organization "to observe the terms of * * * any bona fide employee benefit plan such as a retirement, pension, or insurance plan, which is not a subterfuge to evade the purposes of this Act, except that no such employee benefit plan shall excuse the failure to hire any individual, and no such * * * employee benefit plan shall require or permit the involuntary retirement of any individual specified by section 12(a) of this Act because of the age of such individuals." The legislative history of this provision indicates that its purpose is to permit age-based reductions in employee benefit plans where such reductions are justified by significant cost considerations. Accordingly, section 4(f)(2) does not apply, for example, to paid vacations and uninsured paid sick leave, since reductions in these benefits would not be justified by significant cost considerations. Where employee benefit plans do meet the criteria in section 4(f)(2), benefit levels for older workers may be reduced to the extent necessary to achieve approximate equivalency in cost for older and younger workers. A benefit plan will be considered in compliance with the statute where the actual amount of payment made, or cost incurred, in behalf of an older worker is equal to that made or incurred in behalf of a younger worker, even though the older worker may thereby receive a lesser amount of benefits or insurance coverage. Since section 4(f)(2) is an exception from the general non-discrimination provisions of the Act, the burden is on the one seeking to invoke the exception to show that every element has been clearly and unmistakably met. The exception must be narrowly construed. The following sections explain three key elements of the exception: (i) What a "bona fide employee benefit plan" is; (ii) what it means to "observe the terms" of such a plan; and (iii) what kind of plan, or plan provision, would be considered "a subterfuge to evade the purposes of [the] Act." There is also a discussion of the application of the general rules governing all plans with respect to specific kinds of employee benefit plans.

(2) *Relation of section 4(f)(2) to sections 4(a), 4(b) and 4(c).* Sections 4(a), 4(b) and 4(c) prohibit specified acts of discrimination on the basis of age. Section 4(a) in particular makes it unlawful for an employer to "discriminate against any individual with respect to his compensation, terms, conditions, or privileges of employment, because of such individual's age * * *." Section 4(f)(2) is an exception to this general prohibition. Where an employer under an employee benefit plan provides the same level of benefits to older workers as to younger workers, there is no violation of section 4(a), and accordingly the practice does not have to be justified under section 4(f)(2).

(b) *"Bona fide employee benefit plan."* Section 4(f)(2) applies only to bona fide employee benefit plans. A plan is considered "bona fide" if its terms (including cessation of contributions or accruals in the case of retirement income plans) have been accurately described in writing to all employees and if it actually provides the benefits in accordance with the terms of the plan. Notifying employees promptly of the provisions and changes in an employee benefit plan is essential if they are to know how the plan affects them. For these purposes, it would be sufficient under the ADEA for employers to follow the disclosure requirements of ERISA and the regulations thereunder. The plan must actually provide the benefits its provisions describe, since otherwise the notification of the provisions to employees is misleading and inaccurate. An "employee benefit plan" is a plan, such as a retirement, pension, or insurance plan, which provides employees with what are frequently referred to as "fringe benefits." The term does not refer to wages or salary in cash; neither section 4(f)(2) nor any other section of the Act excuses the payment of lower wages or salary to older employees on account of age. Whether or not any particular employee benefit plan may lawfully provide lower benefits to older employees on account of age depends on whether all of the elements of the exception have been met. An "employee-pay-all" employee benefit plan is one of the "terms, conditions, or privileges of employment" with respect to which discrimination on the basis of age is forbidden under section 4(a)(1). In such a plan, benefits for older workers may be reduced only to the extent and according to the same principles as apply to other plans under section 4(f)(2).

(c) *"To observe the terms"* *of a plan.* In order for a bona fide employee benefit plan which provides lower benefits to older employees on account of age to be within the section 4(f)(2) exception, the lower benefits must be provided in "observ[ance of] the terms of" the plan. As this statutory text makes clear, the section 4(f)(2) exception is limited to otherwise discriminatory actions which are actually prescribed by the terms of a bona fide employee benefit plan. Where the employer, employment agency, or labor organization is not required by the express provisions of the plan to provide lesser benefits to older workers, section 4(f)(2) does not apply. Important purposes are served by this requirement. Where a discriminatory policy is an express term of a benefit plan, employees presumably have some opportunity to know of the policy and to plan (or protest) accordingly. Moreover, the requirement that the discrimination actually be prescribed by a plan assures that the particular plan provision will be equally applied to all employees of the same age. Where a discriminatory provision is an optional term of the plan, it permits individual, discretionary acts of discrimination, which do not fall within the section 4(f)(2) exception.

(d) *"Subterfuge."* In order for a bona fide employee benefit plan which prescribes lower benefits for older employees on account of age to be within the section 4(f)(2) exception, it must not be "a subterfuge to evade the purposes of [the] Act." In general, a plan or plan provision which prescribes lower benefits for older employees on account of age is not a "subterfuge" within the meaning of section 4(f)(2), provided that the lower level of benefits is justified by age-related cost considerations. (The only exception to this general rule is with respect to certain retirement plans. See paragraph (f)(4) of this section.) There are certain other requirements that must be met in order for a plan not to be a subterfuge. These requirements are set forth below.

(1) *Cost data—general.* Cost data used in justification of a benefit plan which provides lower benefits to older employees on account of age must be valid and reasonable. This standard is met where an employer has cost data which show the actual cost to it of providing the particular benefit (or benefits) in question over a representative period of years. An employer may rely in cost data for its own employees over such a period, or on cost data for a larger group of similarly situated employees. Sometimes, as a result of experience rating or other causes, an employer incurs costs that differ significantly from costs for a group of similarly situated employees. Such an employer may not rely on cost data for the similarly situated employees where such reliance would result in significantly lower benefits for its own older employees. Where reliable cost information is not available, reasonable projections made from existing cost data meeting the standards set forth above will be considered acceptable.

(2) *Cost data—Individual benefit basis and "benefit package" basis.* Cost comparisons and adjustments under section 4(f)(2) must be made on a benefit-by-benefit basis or on a "benefit package" basis, as described below.

(i) *Benefit-by-benefit basis.* Adjustments made on a benefit-by-benefit basis must be made in the amount or level of a specific form of benefit for a specific event or contingency. For example, higher group term life insurance costs for older workers would justify a corresponding reduction in the amount of group term life insurance coverage for older workers, on the basis of age. However, a benefit-by-benefit approach would not justify the substitution of one form of benefit for another, even though both forms of benefit are designed for the same contingency, such as death. See paragraph (f)(1) of this section.

(ii) *"Benefit package" basis.* As an alternative to the benefit-by-benefit basis, cost comparisons and adjustments under section 4(f)(2) may be made on a limited "benefit package" basis. Under this approach, subject to the limitations described below, cost comparisons and adjustments can be made with respect to section 4(f)(2) plans in the aggregate. This alternative basis provides greater flexibility than a benefit-by-benefit basis in order to carry out the declared statutory purpose "to help employers and workers find ways of meeting problems arising from the impact of age on employment." A "benefit package" approach is an alternative approach consistent with this purpose and with the general purpose of section 4(f)(2) only if it is not used to reduce the cost to the employer or the favorability to the employees of overall employee benefits for older employees. A "benefit package" approach used for either of these purposes would be a subterfuge to evade the purposes of the Act. In order to assure that such a "benefit package" approach is not abused and is consistent with the legislative intent, it is subject to the limitations described in paragraph (f), which also includes a general example.

(3) *Cost data—five year maximum basis.* Cost comparisons and adjustments under section 4(f)(2) may be made on the basis of age brackets of up to 5 years. Thus a particular benefit may be reduced for employees of any age within the protected age group by an amount no greater than that which could be justified by the additional cost to provide them with the same level of the benefit as younger employees within a specified five-year age group immediately preceding theirs. For example, where an employer chooses to provide unreduced group term life insurance benefits until age 60, benefits for employees who are between 60 and 65 years of age may be reduced only to the extent necessary to achieve approximate equivalency in costs with employees who are 55 to 60 years old. Similarly, any reductions in benefit levels for 65 to 70 year old

employees cannot exceed an amount which is proportional to the additional costs for their coverage over 60 to 65 year old employees.

(4) *Employee contributions in support of employee benefit plans*—(i) *As a condition of employment.* An older employee within the protected age group may not be required as a condition of employment to make greater contributions than a younger employee in support of an employee benefit plan. Such a requirement would be in effect a mandatory reduction in take-home pay, which is never authorized by section 4(f)(2), and would impose an impediment to employment in violation of the specific restrictions in section 4(f)(2).

(ii) *As a condition of participation in a voluntary employee benefit plan.* An older employee within the protected age group may be required as a condition of participation in a voluntary employee benefit plan to make a greater contribution than a younger employee only if the older employee is not thereby required to bear a greater proportion of the total premium cost (employer-paid and employee-paid) than the younger employee. Otherwise the requirement would discriminate against the older employee by making compensation in the form of an employer contribution available on less favorable terms than for the younger employee and denying that compensation altogether to an older employee unwilling or unable to meet the less favorable terms. Such discrimination is not authorized by section 4(f)(2). This principle applies to three different contribution arrangements as follows:

(A) *Employee-pay-all plans.* Older employees, like younger employees, may be required to contribute as a condition of participation up to the full premium cost for their age.

(B) *Non-contributory ("employer-pay-all") plans.* Where younger employees are not required to contribute any portion of the total premium cost, older employees may not be required to contribute any portion.

(C) *Contributory plans.* In these plans employers and participating employees share the premium cost. The required contributions of participants may increase with age so long as the *proportion* of the total premium required to be paid by the participants does not increase with age.

(iii) *As an option in order to receive an unreduced benefit.* An older employee may be given the option, as an individual, to make the additional contribution necessary to receive the same level of benefits as a younger employee (provided that the contemplated reduction in benefits is otherwise justified by section 4(f)(2)).

(5) *Forfeiture clauses.* Clauses in employee benefit plans which state that litigation or participation in any manner in a formal

proceeding by an employee will result in the forfeiture of his rights are unlawful insofar as they may be applied to those who seek redress under the Act. This is by reason of section 4(d) which provides that it is unlawful for an employer, employment agency, or labor organization to discriminate against any individual because such individual "has made a charge, testified, assisted, or participated in any manner in an investigation, proceeding, or litigation under this Act."

(6) *Refusal to hire clauses.* Any provision of an employee benefit plan which requires or permits the refusal to hire an individual specified in section 12(a) of the Act on the basis of age is a subterfuge to evade the purposes of the Act and cannot be excused under section 4(f)(2).

(7) *Involuntary retirement clauses.* Any provision of an employee benefit plan which requires or permits the involuntary retirement of any individual specified in section 12(a) of the Act on the basis of age is a subterfuge to evade the purpose of the Act and cannot be excused under section 4(f)(2).

(e) *Benefits provided by the Government.* An employer does not violate the Act by permitting certain benefits to be provided by the Government, even though the availability of such benefits may be based on age. For example, it is not necessary for an employer to provide health benefits which are otherwise provided to certain employees by Medicare. However, the availability of benefits from the Government will not justify a reduction in employer-provided benefits if the result is that, taking the employer-provided and Government-provided benefits together, an older employee is entitled to a lesser benefit of any type (including coverage for family and/or dependents) than a similarly situated younger employee. For example, the availability of certain benefits to an older employee under Medicare will not justify denying an older employee a benefit which is provided to younger employees and is not provided to the older employee by Medicare.

(f) *Application of section 4(f)(2) to various employee benefit plans—* (1) *Benefit-by-benefit approach.* This portion of the interpretation discusses how a benefit-by-benefit approach would apply to four of the most common types of employee benefit plans.

(i) *Life insurance.* It is not uncommon for life insurance coverage to remain constant until a specified age, frequently 65, and then be reduced. This practice will not violate the Act (even if reductions start before age 65), provided that the reduction for an employee of a particular age is no greater than is justified by the increased cost of coverage for that employee's specific age bracket encompassing no more than five years. It should be noted that a total denial of life insurance, on the basis of age, would not be justified under a benefit-by-benefit analysis. However, it is not unlawful for life insurance coverage to cease upon separation from service.

(ii) *Long-term disability*. Under a benefit-by-benefit approach, where employees who are disabled at younger ages are entitled to long-term disability benefits, there is no cost-based justification for denying such benefits altogether, on the basis of age, to employees who are disabled at older ages. It is not unlawful to cut off long-term disability benefits and coverage on the basis of some non-age factor, such as recovery from disability. Reductions on the basis of age in the level or duration of benefits available for disability are justifiable only on the basis of age-related cost considerations as set forth elsewhere in this section. An employer which provides long-term disability coverage to all employees may avoid any increases in the cost to it that such coverage for older employees would entail by reducing the level of benefits available to older employees. An employer may also avoid such cost increases by reducing the duration of benefits available to employees who become disabled at older ages, without reducing the level of benefits. In this connection, the Department would not assert a violation where the level of benefits is not reduced and the duration of benefits is reduced in the following manner:

(A) With respect to disabilities which occur at age 60 or less, benefits cease at age 65.

(B) With respect to disabilities which occur after age 60, benefits cease 5 years after disablement. Cost data may be produced to support other patterns of reduction as well.

(iii) *Retirement plans*—(A) *Participation*. No employee hired prior to normal retirement age may be excluded from a defined contribution plan. With respect to defined benefit plans not subject to the Employee Retirement Income Security Act (ERISA), Pub.L. 93–406, 29 U.S.C. 1001, 1003(a) and (b), an employee hired at an age more than 5 years prior to normal retirement age may not be excluded from such a plan unless the exclusion is justifiable on the basis of cost considerations as set forth elsewhere in this section. With respect to defined benefit plans subject to ERISA, such an exclusion would be unlawful in any case. An employee hired less than 5 years prior to normal retirement age may be excluded from a defined benefit plan, regardless of whether or not the plan is covered by ERISA. Similarly, any employee hired after normal retirement age may be excluded from a defined benefit plan.

(2) *"Benefit package" approach*. A "benefit package" approach to compliance under section 4(f)(2) offers greater flexibility than a benefit-by-benefit approach by permitting deviations from a benefit-by-benefit approach so long as the overall result is no lesser cost to the employer *and* no less favorable benefits for employees. As previously noted, in order to assure that such an approach is used for the benefit of older workers and not to their detriment, and is

otherwise consistent with the legislative intent, it is subject to limitations as set forth below:

(i) *A benefit package approach shall apply only to employee benefit plans which fall within section 4(f)(2).*

(ii) *A benefit package approach shall not apply to a retirement or pension plan.* The 1978 legislative history sets forth specific and comprehensive rules governing such plans, which have been adopted above. These rules are not tied to actuarially significant cost considerations but are intended to deal with the special funding arrangements of retirement or pension plans. Variations from these special rules are therefore not justified by variations from the cost-based benefit-by-benefit approach in other benefit plans, nor may variations from the special rules governing pension and retirement plans justify variations from the benefit-by-benefit approach in other benefit plans.

(iii) *A benefit package approach shall not be used to justify reductions in health benefits greater than would be justified under a benefit-by-benefit approach.* Such benefits appear to be of particular importance to older workers in meeting "problems arising from the impact of age" and were of particular concern to Congress. Therefore, the "benefit package" approach may not be used to reduce health insurance benefits by more than is warranted by the increase in the cost to the employer of those benefits alone. Any greater reduction would be a subterfuge to evade the purpose of the Act.

(iv) *A benefit reduction greater than would be justified under a benefit-by-benefit approach must be offset by another benefit available to the same employees.* No employees may be deprived because of age of one benefit without an offsetting benefit being made available to them.

(v) *Employers who wish to justify benefit reductions under a benefit package approach must be prepared to produce data to show that those reductions are fully justified.* Thus employers must be able to show that deviations from a benefit-by-benefit approach do not result in lesser cost to them or less favorable benefits to their employees. A general example consistent with these limitations may be given. Assume two employee benefit plans, providing Benefit "A" and Benefit "B." Both plans fall within section 4(f)(2), and neither is a retirement or pension plan subject to special rules. Both benefits are available to all employees. Age-based cost increases would justify a 10% decrease in both benefits on a benefit-by-benefit basis. The affected employees would, however, find it more favorable—that is, more consistent with meeting their needs—for no reduction to be made in Benefit "A" and a greater reduction to be made in Benefit "B." This "trade-off" would not result in a reduction in health benefits. The "trade-off" may therefore be made. The details of the "trade-off" depend on data on the relative cost to the employer of the two benefits. If the data show that Benefit "A" and Benefit "B" cost the same, Benefit "B" may be reduced up to 20% if Benefit "A" is unreduced. If the data show that Benefit "A" costs only half as much as Benefit "B", however, Benefit "B" may be reduced up to only 15% if Benefit "A" is unreduced, since a greater reduction in Benefit "B" would result in an impermissible reduction in total benefit costs.

(g) *Relation of ADEA to State laws.* The ADEA does not preempt State age discrimination in employment laws. However, the failure of the ADEA to preempt such laws does not affect the issue of whether section 514 of the Employee Retirement Income Security Act (ERISA) preempts State laws which relate[ ] to employee benefit plans.

§ 1625.22   Waivers of Rights and Claims Under the ADEA

(a) *Introduction.* (1) Congress amended the ADEA in 1990 to clarify the prohibitions against discrimination on the basis of age. In Title II of OWBPA, Congress addressed waivers of rights and claims under the ADEA, amending section 7 of the ADEA by adding a new subsection (f).

(2) Section 7(f)(1) of the ADEA expressly provides that waivers may be valid and enforceable under the ADEA only if the waiver is "knowing and voluntary". Sections 7(f)(1) and 7(f)(2) of the ADEA set out the minimum requirements for determining whether a waiver is knowing and voluntary.

(3) Other facts and circumstances may bear on the question of whether the waiver is knowing and voluntary, as, for example, if there is a material mistake, omission, or misstatement in the information furnished by the employer to an employee in connection with the waiver.

(4) The rules in this section apply to all waivers of ADEA rights and claims, regardless of whether the employee is employed in the private or public sector, including employment by the United States Government.

(b) *Wording of Waiver Agreements.* (1) Section 7(f)(1)(A) of the ADEA provides, as part of the minimum requirements for a knowing and voluntary waiver, that:

The waiver is part of an agreement between the individual and the employer that is written in a manner calculated to be understood by such individual, or by the average individual eligible to participate.

(2) The entire waiver agreement must be in writing.

(3) Waiver agreements must be drafted in plain language geared to the level of understanding of the individual party to the agreement or individuals eligible to participate. Employers should take into account such factors as the level of comprehension and

education of typical participants. Consideration of these factors usually will require the limitation or elimination of technical jargon and of long, complex sentences.

(4) The waiver agreement must not have the effect of misleading, misinforming, or failing to inform participants and affected individuals. Any advantages or disadvantages described shall be presented without either exaggerating the benefits or minimizing the limitations.

(5) Section 7(f)(1)(H) of the ADEA, relating to exit incentive or other employment termination programs offered to a group or class of employees, also contains a requirement that information be conveyed "in writing in a manner calculated to be understood by the average participant." The same standards applicable to the similar language in section 7(f)(1)(A) of the ADEA apply here as well.

(6) Section 7(f)(1)(B) of the ADEA provides, as part of the minimum requirements for a knowing and voluntary waiver, that "the waiver specifically refers to rights or claims under this Act." Pursuant to this subsection, the waiver agreement must refer to the Age Discrimination in Employment Act (ADEA) by name in connection with the waiver.

(7) Section 7(f)(1)(E) of the ADEA requires that an individual must be "advised in writing to consult with an attorney prior to executing the agreement."

(c) *Waiver of future rights.* (1) Section 7(f)(1)(C) of the ADEA provides that:

A waiver may not be considered knowing and voluntary unless at a minimum ... the individual does not waive rights or claims that may arise after the date the waiver is executed.

(2) The waiver of rights or claims that arise following the execution of a waiver is prohibited. However, section 7(f)(1)(C) of the ADEA does not bar, in a waiver that otherwise is consistent with statutory requirements, the enforcement of agreements to perform future employment-related actions such as the employee's agreement to retire or otherwise terminate employment at a future date.

(d) *Consideration.* (1) Section 7(f)(1)(D) of the ADEA states that:

A waiver may not be considered knowing and voluntary unless at a minimum * * * the individual waives rights or claims only in exchange for consideration in addition to anything of value to which the individual already is entitled.

(2) "Consideration in addition" means anything of value in addition to that to which the individual is already entitled in the absence of a waiver.

(3) If a benefit or other thing of value was eliminated in contravention of law or contract, express or implied, the subsequent offer of such benefit or thing of value in connection with a waiver

will not constitute "consideration" for purposes of section 7(f)(1) of the ADEA. Whether such elimination as to one employee or group of employees is in contravention of law or contract as to other employees, or to that individual employee at some later time, may vary depending on the facts and circumstances of each case.

(4) An employer is not required to give a person age 40 or older a greater amount of consideration than is given to a person under the age of 40, solely because of that person's membership in the protected class under the ADEA.

(e) *Time periods.* (1) Section 7(f)(1)(F) of the ADEA states that:

A waiver may not be considered knowing and voluntary unless at a minimum * * *

(i) The individual is given a period of at least 21 days within which to consider the agreement: or

(ii) If a waiver is requested in connection with an exit incentive or other employment termination program offered to a group or class of employees, the individual is given a period of at least 45 days within which to consider the agreement.

(2) Section 7(f)(1)(G) of the ADEA states:

A waiver may not be considered knowing and voluntary unless at a minimum ... the agreement provides that for a period of at least 7 days following the execution of such agreement, the individual may revoke the agreement, and the agreement shall not become effective or enforceable until the revocation period has expired.

(3) The term "exit incentive or other employment termination program" includes both voluntary and involuntary programs.

(4) The 21 or 45 day period runs from the date of the employer's final offer. Material changes to the final offer restart the running of the 21 or 45 day period; changes made to the final offer that are not material do not restart the running of the 21 or 45 day period. The parties may agree that changes, whether material or immaterial, do not restart the running of the 21 or 45 day period.

(5) The 7 day revocation period cannot be shortened by the parties, by agreement or otherwise.

(6) An employee may sign a release prior to the end of the 21 or 45 day time period, thereby commencing the mandatory 7 day revocation period. This is permissible as long as the employee's decision to accept such shortening of time is knowing and voluntary and is not induced by the employer through fraud, misrepresentation, a threat to withdraw or alter the offer prior to the expiration of the 21 or 45 day time period, or by providing different terms to employees who sign the release prior to the expiration of such time period. However, if an employee signs a release before the expiration

of the 21 or 45 day time period, the employer may expedite the processing of the consideration provided in exchange for the waiver.

(f) *Informational requirements.* (1) Introduction. (i) Section 7(f)(1)(H) of the ADEA provides that:

A waiver may not be considered knowing and voluntary unless at a minimum . . . if a waiver is requested in connection with an exit incentive or other employment termination program offered to a group or class of employees, the employer (at the commencement of the period specified in subparagraph (F)) [which provides time periods for employees to consider the waiver] informs the individual in writing in a manner calculated to be understood by the average individual eligible to participate, as to—

(i) Any class, unit, or group of individuals covered by such program, any eligibility factors for such program, and any time limits applicable to such program; and

(ii) The job titles and ages of all individuals eligible or selected for the program, and the ages of all individuals in the same job classification or organizational unit who are not eligible or selected for the program.

(ii) Section 7(f)(1)(H) of the ADEA addresses two principal issues: to whom information must be provided, and what information must be disclosed to such individuals.

(iii)(A) Section 7(f)(1)(H) of the ADEA references two types of "programs" under which employers seeking waivers must make written disclosures: "exit incentive programs" and "other employment termination programs." Usually an "exit incentive program" is a voluntary program offered to a group or class of employees where such employees are offered consideration in addition to anything of value to which the individuals are already entitled (hereinafter in this section, "additional consideration") in exchange for their decision to resign voluntarily and sign a waiver. Usually "other employment termination program" refers to a group or class of employees who were involuntarily terminated and who are offered additional consideration in return for their decision to sign a waiver.

(B) The question of the existence of a "program" will be decided based upon the facts and circumstances of each case. A "program" exists when an employer offers additional consideration for the signing of a waiver pursuant to an exit incentive or other employment termination (e.g., a reduction in force) to two or more employees. Typically, an involuntary termination program is a standardized formula or package of benefits that is available to two or more employees, while an exit incentive program typically is a standardized formula or package of benefits designed to induce employees to sever their employment voluntarily. In both cases, the terms of the programs generally are not subject to negotiation between the parties.

(C) Regardless of the type of program, the scope of the terms "class," "unit," "group," "job classification," and "organizational unit" is determined by examining the "decisional unit" at issue. (*See* paragraph (f)(3) of this section, "The Decisional Unit.")

(D) A "program" for purposes of the ADEA need not constitute an "employee benefit plan" for purposes of the Employee Retirement Income Security Act of 1974 (ERISA). An employer may or may not have an ERISA severance plan in connection with its OWBPA program.

(iv) The purpose of the informational requirements is to provide an employee with enough information regarding the program to allow the employee to make an informed choice whether or not to sign a waiver agreement.

(2) To whom must the information be given. The required information must be given to each person in the decisional unit who is asked to sign a waiver agreement.

(3) The decisional unit. (i)(A) The terms "class," "unit," or "group" in section 7(f)(1)(H)(i) of the ADEA and "job classification or organizational unit" in section 7(f)(1)(H)(ii) of the ADEA refer to examples of categories or groupings of employees affected by a program within an employer's particular organizational structure. The terms are not meant to be an exclusive list of characterizations of an employer's organization.

(B) When identifying the scope of the "class, unit, or group," and "job classification or organizational unit," an employer should consider its organizational structure and decision-making process. A "decisional unit" is that portion of the employer's organizational structure from which the employer chose the persons who would be offered consideration for the signing of a waiver and those who would not be offered consideration for the signing of a waiver. The term "decisional unit" has been developed to reflect the process by which an employer chose certain employees for a program and ruled out others from that program.

(ii)(A) The variety of terms used in section 7(f)(1)(H) of the ADEA demonstrates that employers often use differing terminology to describe their organizational structures. When identifying the population of the decisional unit, the employer acts on a case-by-case basis, and thus the determination of the appropriate class, unit, or group, and job classification or organizational unit for purposes of section 7(f)(1)(H) of the ADEA also must be made on a case-by-case basis.

(B) The examples in paragraph (f)(3)(iii), of this section demonstrate that in appropriate cases some subgroup of a facility's work force may be the decisional unit. In other situations, it may be appropriate for the decisional unit to comprise several facilities. However, as the decisional unit is typically no broader than the facility, in general the disclosure need be no broader than the facility. "Facility" as it is used throughout this section generally refers to place or location. However, in some circumstances terms such as "school," "plant," or "complex" may be more appropriate.

(C) Often, when utilizing a program an employer is attempting to reduce its workforce at a particular facility in an effort to eliminate what it deems to be excessive overhead, expenses, or costs from its organization at that facility. If the employer's goal is the reduction of its workforce at a particular facility and that employer undertakes a decision-making process by which certain employees of the facility are selected for a program, and others are not selected for a program, then that facility generally will be the decisional unit for purposes of section 7(f)(1)(H) of the ADEA.

(D) However, if an employer seeks to terminate employees by exclusively considering a particular portion or subgroup of its operations at a specific facility, then that subgroup or portion of the workforce at that facility will be considered the decisional unit.

(E) Likewise, if the employer analyzes its operations at several facilities, specifically considers and compares ages, seniority rosters, or similar factors at differing facilities, and determines to focus its workforce reduction at a particular facility, then by the nature of that employer's decision-making process the decisional unit would include all considered facilities and not just the facility selected for the reductions.

(iii) The following examples are not all-inclusive and are meant only to assist employers and employees in determining the appropriate decisional unit. Involuntary reductions in force typically are structured along one or more of the following lines:

(A) *Facility-wide:* Ten percent of the employees in the Springfield facility will be terminated within the next ten days;

(B) *Division-wide:* Fifteen of the employees in the Computer Division will be terminated in December;

(C) *Department-wide:* One-half of the workers in the Keyboard Department of the Computer Division will be terminated in December;

(D) *Reporting:* Ten percent of the employees who report to the Vice President for Sales, wherever the employees are located, will be terminated immediately;

(E) *Job Category:* Ten percent of all accountants, wherever the employees are located, will be terminated next week.

(iv) In the examples in paragraph (f)(3)(iii) of this section, the decisional units are, respectively:

(A) The Springfield facility;

(B) The Computer Division;

(C) The Keyboard Department;

(D) All employees reporting to the Vice President for Sales; and

(E) All accountants.

(v) While the particular circumstances of each termination program will determine the decisional unit, the following examples also may assist in determining when the decisional unit is other than the entire facility:

(A) A number of small facilities with interrelated functions and employees in a specific geographic area may comprise a single decisional unit;

(B) If a company utilizes personnel for a common function at more than one facility, the decisional unit for that function (i.e., accounting) may be broader than the one facility;

(C) A large facility with several distinct functions may comprise a number of decisional units; for example, if a single facility has distinct internal functions with no employee overlap (i.e., manufacturing, accounting, human resources), and the program is confined to a distinct function, a smaller decisional unit may be appropriate.

(vi)(A) For purposes of this section, higher level review of termination decisions generally will not change the size of the decisional unit unless the reviewing process alters its scope. For example, review by the Human Resources Department to monitor compliance with discrimination laws does not affect the decisional unit. Similarly, when a regional manager in charge of more than one facility reviews the termination decisions regarding one of those facilities, the review does not alter the decisional unit, which remains the one facility under consideration.

(B) However, if the regional manager in the course of review determines that persons in other facilities should also be considered for termination, the decisional unit becomes the population of all facilities considered. Further, if, for example, the regional manager and his three immediate subordinates jointly review the termination decisions, taking into account more than one facility, the decisional unit becomes the populations of all facilities considered.

(vii) This regulatory section is limited to the requirements of section 7(f)(1)(H) and is not intended to affect the scope of discovery or of substantive proceedings in the processing of charges of violation of the ADEA or in litigation involving such charges.

(4) Presentation of information. (i) The information provided must be in writing and must be written in a manner calculated to be understood by the average individual eligible to participate.

(ii) Information regarding ages should be broken down according to the age of each person eligible or selected for the program and each person not eligible or selected for the program. The use of age bands broader than one year (such as ''age 20–30'') does not satisfy this requirement.

(iii) In a termination of persons in several established grade levels and/or other established subcategories within a job category or job title, the information shall be broken down by grade level or other subcategory.

(iv) If an employer in its disclosure combines information concerning both voluntary and involuntary terminations, the employer shall present the information in a manner that distinguishes between voluntary and involuntary terminations.

(v) If the terminees are selected from a subset of a decisional unit, the employer must still disclose information for the entire population of the decisional unit. For example, if the employer decides that a 10% RIF in the Accounting Department will come from the accountants whose performance is in the bottom one-third of the Division, the employer still must disclose information for all employees in the Accounting Department, even those who are the highest rated.

(vi) An involuntary termination program in a decisional unit may take place in successive increments over a period of time. Special rules apply to this situation. Specifically, information supplied with regard to the involuntary termination program should be cumulative, so that later terminees are provided ages and job titles or job categories, as appropriate, for all persons in the decisional unit at the beginning of the program and all persons terminated to date. There is no duty to supplement the information given to earlier terminees so long as the disclosure, at the time it is given, conforms to the requirements of this section.

(vii) The following example demonstrates one way in which the required information could be presented to the employees. (This example is not presented as a prototype notification agreement that automatically will comply with the ADEA. Each information disclosure must be structured based upon the individual case, taking into account the corporate structure, the population of the decisional unit, and the requirements of section 7(f)(1)(H) of the ADEA): Example: Y Corporation lost a major construction contract and determined that it must terminate 10% of the employees in the Construction Division. Y decided to offer all terminees $20,000 in severance pay in exchange for a waiver of all rights. The waiver provides the section 7(f)(1)(H) of the ADEA information as follows:

(A) The decisional unit is the Construction Division.

(B) All persons in the Construction Division are eligible for the program. All persons who are being terminated in our November RIF are selected for the program.

(C) All persons who are being offered consideration under a waiver agreement must sign the agreement and return it to the Personnel Office within 45 days after receiving the waiver. Once the signed waiver is returned to the Personnel Office, the employee has 7 days to revoke the waiver agreement.

(D) The following is a listing of the ages and job titles of persons in the Construction Division who were and were not selected for termination and the offer of consideration for signing a waiver:

Job Title	Age	No. Selected	No. not selected
(1) Mechanical Engineers, I	25	21	48
	26	11	73
	63	4	18
	64	3	11
(2) Mechanical Engineers, II	28	3	10
	29	11	17
	Etc., for all ages		
(3) Structural Engineers, I	21	5	8
	Etc., for all ages		
(4) Structural Engineers, II	23	2	4
	Etc., for all ages		
(5) Purchasing Agents	26	10	11
	Etc., for all ages		

(g) *Waivers settling charges and lawsuits.* (1) Section 7(f)(2) of the ADEA provides that:

A waiver in settlement of a charge filed with the Equal Employment Opportunity Commission, or an action filed in court by the individual or the individual's representative, alleging age discrimination of a kind prohibited under section 4 or 15 may not be considered knowing and voluntary unless at a minimum—

(A) Subparagraphs (A) through (E) of paragraph (1) have been met; and

(B) The individual is given a reasonable period of time within which to consider the settlement agreement.

(2) The language in section 7(f)(2) of the ADEA, "discrimination of a kind prohibited under section 4 or 15" refers to allegations of age discrimination of the type prohibited by the ADEA.

(3) The standards set out in paragraph (f) of this section for complying with the provisions of section 7(f)(1) (A)–(E) of the ADEA also will apply for purposes of complying with the provisions of section 7(f)(2)(A) of the ADEA.

(4) The term "reasonable time within which to consider the settlement agreement" means reasonable under all the circumstances, including whether the individual is represented by counsel or has the assistance of counsel.

(5) However, while the time periods under section 7(f)(1) of the ADEA do not apply to subsection 7(f)(2) of the ADEA, a waiver agreement under this subsection that provides an employee the time periods specified in section 7(f)(1) of the ADEA will be considered "reasonable" for purposes of section 7(f)(2)(B) of the ADEA.

(6) A waiver agreement in compliance with this section that is in settlement of an EEOC charge does not require the participation or supervision of EEOC.

(h) *Burden of proof.* In any dispute that may arise over whether any of the requirements, conditions, and circumstances set forth in section 7(f) of the ADEA, subparagraph (A), (B), (C), (D), (E), (F), (G), or (H) of paragraph (1), or subparagraph (A) or (B) of paragraph (2), have been met, the party asserting the validity of a waiver shall have the burden of proving in a court of competent jurisdiction that a waiver was knowing and voluntary pursuant to paragraph (1) or (2) of section 7(f) of the ADEA.

(i) *EEOC's enforcement powers.* (1) Section 7(f)(4) of the ADEA states:

No waiver agreement may affect the Commission's rights and responsibilities to enforce [the ADEA]. No waiver may be used to justify interfering with the protected right of an employee to file a charge or participate in an investigation or proceeding conducted by the Commission.

(2) No waiver agreement may include any provision prohibiting any individual from:

(i) Filing a charge or complaint, including a challenge to the validity of the waiver agreement, with EEOC, or

(ii) Participating in any investigation or proceeding conducted by EEOC.

(3) No waiver agreement may include any provision imposing any condition precedent, any penalty, or any other limitation adversely affecting any individual's right to:

(i) File a charge or complaint, including a challenge to the validity of the waiver agreement, with EEOC, or

(ii) Participate in any investigation or proceeding conducted by EEOC.

(j) *Effective date of this section.* (1) This section is effective July 6, 1998.

(2) This section applies to waivers offered by employers on or after the effective date specified in paragraph (j)(1) of this section.

(3) No inference is to be drawn from this section regarding the validity of waivers offered prior to the effective date.

(k) *Statutory authority.* The regulations in this section are legislative regulations issued pursuant to section 9 of the ADEA and Title II of OWBPA.

§ 1625.23   Waivers of rights and claims: Tender back of consideration.

(a) An individual alleging that a waiver agreement, covenant not to sue, or other equivalent arrangement was not knowing and voluntary under the ADEA is not required to tender back the consideration given for that agreement before filing either a lawsuit or a charge of discrimination with EEOC or any state or local fair employment practices agency acting as an EEOC referral agency for purposes of filing the charge with EEOC. Retention of consideration does not foreclose a challenge to any waiver agreement, covenant not to sue, or other equivalent arrangement; nor does the retention constitute the ratification of any waiver agreement, covenant not to sue, or other equivalent arrangement.

(b) No ADEA waiver agreement, covenant not to sue, or other equivalent arrangement may impose any condition precedent, any penalty, or any other limitation adversely affecting any individual's right to challenge the agreement. This prohibition includes, but is not limited to, provisions requiring employees to tender back consideration received, and provisions allowing employers to recover attorneys' fees and/or damages because of the filing of an ADEA suit. This rule is not intended to preclude employers from recovering attorneys' fees or costs specifically authorized under federal law.

(c) *Restitution, recoupment, or setoff.* (1) Where an employee successfully challenges a waiver agreement, covenant not to sue, or other equivalent arrangement, and prevails on the merits of an ADEA claim, courts have the discretion to determine whether an employer is entitled to restitution, recoupment or setoff (hereinafter, "reduction") against the employee's monetary award. A reduction never can exceed the amount recovered by the employee, or the consideration the employee received for signing the waiver agreement, covenant not to sue, or other equivalent arrangement, whichever is less.

(2) In a case involving more than one plaintiff, any reduction must be applied on a plaintiff-by-plaintiff basis. No individual's award can be reduced based on the consideration received by any other person.

(d) No employer may abrogate its duties to any signatory under a waiver agreement, covenant not to sue, or other equivalent arrangement, even if one or more of the signatories or the EEOC successfully challenges the validity of that agreement under the ADEA.

§ 1625.32 Coordination of retiree health benefits with Medicare and State health benefits

(a) *Definitions.*

(1) Employee benefit plan means an employee benefit plan as defined in 29 U.S.C. 1002(3).

(2) Medicare means the health insurance program available pursuant to Title XVIII of the Social Security Act, 42 U.S.C. 1395 et seq.

(3) Comparable State health benefit plan means a State-sponsored health benefit plan that, like Medicare, provides retired participants who have attained a minimum age with health benefits, whether or not the type, amount or value of those benefits is equivalent to the type, amount or value of the health benefits provided under Medicare.

(b) *Exemption.* Some employee benefit plans provide health benefits for retired participants that are altered, reduced or eliminated when the participant is eligible for Medicare health benefits or for health benefits under a comparable State health benefit plan, whether or not the participant actually enrolls in the other benefit program. Pursuant to the authority contained in section 9 of the Act, and in accordance with the procedures provided therein and in Sec. 1625.30(b) of this part, it is hereby found necessary and proper in the public interest to exempt from all prohibitions of the Act such coordination of retiree health benefits with Medicare or a comparable State health benefit plan.

(c) *Scope of Exemption.* This exemption shall be narrowly construed. No other aspects of ADEA coverage or employment benefits other than those specified in paragraph (b) of this section are affected by the exemption. Thus, for example, the exemption does not apply to the use of eligibility for Medicare or a comparable State health benefit plan in connection with any act, practice or benefit of employment not specified in paragraph (b) of this section. Nor does it apply to the use of the age of eligibility for Medicare or a comparable State health benefit plan in connection with any act, practice or benefit of employment not specified in paragraph (b) of this section.

REGULATIONS TO IMPLEMENT THE EQUAL EMPLOYMENT PROVISIONS OF THE AMERICANS WITH DISABILITIES ACT (INCLUDING THE ADA AMENDMENTS ACT)—SELECTED PROVISIONS

29 C.F.R. Part 1630, 76 F.R. 16999, March 25, 2011

§ 1630.2 Definitions.

(g) *Definition of "disability."* (1) *In general. Disability* means, with respect to an individual—(i) A physical or mental impairment that substantially limits one or more of the major life activities of such individual; (ii) A record of such an impairment; or (iii) Being regarded as having such an impairment as described in paragraph (*l*) of this section. This means that the individual has been subjected to an action prohibited by the ADA as amended because of an actual or perceived impairment that is not both "transitory and minor." (2) An individual may establish coverage under any one or more of these three prongs of the definition of disability, i.e., paragraphs (g)(1)(i) (the "actual disability" prong), (g)(1)(ii) (the "record of" prong), and/or (g)(1)(iii) (the "regarded as" prong) of this section. (3) Where an individual is not challenging a covered entity's failure to make reasonable accommodations and does not require a reasonable accommodation, it is generally unnecessary to proceed under the "actual disability" or "record of" prongs, which require a showing of an impairment that substantially limits a major life activity or a record of such an impairment. In these cases, the evaluation of coverage can be made solely under the "regarded as" prong of the definition of disability, which does not require a showing of an impairment that substantially limits a major life activity or a record of such an impairment. An individual may choose, however, to proceed under the "actual disability" and/or "record of" prong regardless of whether the individual is challenging a covered entity's failure to make reasonable accommodations or requires a reasonable accommodation. Note to paragraph (g): See § 1630.3 for exceptions to this definition.

(h) *Physical or mental impairment* means—(1) Any physiological disorder or condition, cosmetic disfigurement, or anatomical loss affecting one or more body systems, such as neurological, musculoskeletal, special sense organs, respiratory (including speech organs), cardiovascular, reproductive, digestive, genitourinary, immune, circulatory, hemic, lymphatic, skin, and endocrine; or (2) Any mental or psychological disorder, such as an intellectual disability (formerly termed "mental retardation"), organic brain syndrome, emotional or mental illness, and specific learning disabilities.

(i) *Major life activities*—(1) *In general.* Major life activities include, but are not limited to: (i) Caring for oneself, performing manual tasks, seeing, hearing, eating, sleeping, walking, standing, sitting, reaching, lifting, bending, speaking, breathing, learning, reading, concentrating, thinking, communicating, interacting with others, and working; and (ii) The operation of a major bodily function, including functions of the immune system, special sense organs and skin; normal cell growth; and digestive, genitourinary, bowel, bladder, neurological, brain, respiratory, circulatory, cardiovascular, endocrine, hemic, lymphatic, musculoskeletal, and reproductive functions. The operation of a major bodily function includes the operation of an individual organ within a body system. (2) In determining other examples of major life activities, the term "major" shall not be interpreted strictly to create a demanding standard for disability. ADAAA section 2(b)(4) (Findings and Purposes). Whether an activity is a "major life activity" is not determined by reference to whether it is of "central importance to daily life."

(j) *Substantially limits*—(1) *Rules of construction.* The following rules of construction apply when determining whether an impairment substantially limits an individual in a major life activity: (i) The term "substantially limits" shall be construed broadly in favor of expansive coverage, to the maximum extent permitted by the terms of the ADA. "Substantially limits" is not meant to be a demanding standard. (ii) An impairment is a disability within the meaning of this section if it substantially limits the ability of an individual to perform a major life activity as compared to most people in the general population. An impairment need not prevent, or significantly or severely restrict, the individual from performing a major life activity in order to be considered substantially limiting. Nonetheless, not every impairment will constitute a disability within the meaning of this section. (iii) The primary object of attention in cases brought under the ADA should be whether covered entities have complied with their obligations and whether discrimination has occurred, not whether an individual's impairment "substantially limits" a major life activity. Accordingly, the threshold issue of whether an impairment substantially limits a major life activity should not demand extensive analysis. (iv) The determination of whether an impairment "substantially limits" a major life activity requires an individualized assessment. However, in making this assessment, the term "substantially limits" shall be interpreted and applied to require a degree of functional limitation that is lower than the standard for "substantially limits" applied prior to the ADAAA. (v) The comparison of an individual's performance of a major life activity to the performance of the same major life activity by most people in the general population usually will not require scientific, medical, or statistical analysis. Nothing in this paragraph is intended, however, to prohibit the presentation of scientific, medical, or statistical evidence to make such a comparison where appropriate. (vi) The determination of whether an impairment substantially limits a major life activity shall be made without regard to the ameliorative effects of mitigating measures. However, the ameliorative effects of ordinary eyeglasses or contact lenses shall be considered in determining whether an impairment substantially limits a major life activity. (vii) An impairment that is episodic or in remission is a disability if it would substantially limit a major life activity when active. (viii) An impairment that substantially limits one major life activity need not substantially limit other major life activities in order to be considered a substantially limiting impairment. (ix) The six-month "transitory" part of the "transitory and minor" exception to "regarded as" coverage in § 1630.15(f) does not apply to the definition of "disability" under paragraphs (g)(1)(i) (the "actual disability" prong) or (g)(1)(ii) (the "record of" prong) of this section. The effects of an impairment lasting or expected to last fewer than six months can be substantially limiting within the meaning of this section. (2) *Non-applicability to the "regarded as" prong.* Whether an individual's impairment "substantially limits" a major life activity is not relevant to coverage under paragraph (g)(1)(iii) (the "regarded as" prong) of this section. * * *

(**m**) The term *"qualified,"* with respect to an individual with a disability, means that the individual satisfies the requisite skill, experience, education and other job-related requirements of the employment position such individual holds or desires and, with or without reasonable accommodation, can perform the essential functions of such position. See § 1630.3 for exceptions to this definition.

(**n**) *Essential functions*—(1) *In general.* The term *essential functions* means the fundamental job duties of the employment position the individual with a disability holds or desires. The term "essential functions" does not include the marginal functions of the position. (2) A job function may be considered essential for any of several reasons, including but not limited to the following: (i) The function may be essential because the reason the position exists is to perform that function; (ii) The function may be essential because of the limited number of employees available among whom the performance of that job function can be distributed; and/or (iii) The function may be highly specialized so that the incumbent in the position is hired for his or her expertise or ability to perform the particular function. (3) Evidence of whether a particular function is essential includes, but is not limited to: (i) The employer's judgment as to which functions are essential; (ii) Written job descriptions prepared before advertising or interviewing applicants for the job; (iii) The amount of time spent on the job performing the function; (iv) The consequences of not requiring the incumbent to perform the function; (v) The terms of a collective bargaining agreement; (vi) The work experience of past incumbents in the job; and/or (vii) The current work experience of incumbents in similar jobs.

(**o**) *Reasonable accommodation.* (1) The term *reasonable accommodation* means: (i) Modifications or adjustments to a job application process that enable a qualified applicant with a disability to be considered for the position such qualified applicant desires; or (ii) Modifications or adjustments to the work environment, or to the manner or circumstances under which the position held or desired is customarily performed, that enable a qualified individual with a disability to perform the essential functions of that position; or (iii) Modifications or adjustments that enable a covered entity's employee with a disability to enjoy equal benefits and privileges of employment as are enjoyed by its other similarly situated employees without disabilities. (2) *Reasonable accommodation* may include but is not limited to: (i) Making existing facilities used by employees readily accessible to and usable by individuals with disabilities; and (ii) Job restructuring; part-time or modified work schedules; reassignment to a vacant position; acquisition or modifications of equipment or devices; appropriate adjustment or modifications of examinations, training materials, or policies; the provision of qualified readers or interpreters; and other similar accommodations for individuals with disabilities. (3) To determine the appropriate reasonable accommodation it may be necessary for the covered entity to initiate an informal, interactive process with the individual with a disability in need of the accommodation. This process should identify the precise limitations resulting from the disability and potential reasonable accommodations that could overcome those limitations. (4) A covered entity is required, absent undue hardship, to provide a reasonable accommodation to an otherwise qualified individual who meets the definition of disability under the "actual disability" prong (paragraph (g)(1)(i) of this section), or "record of" prong (paragraph (g)(1)(ii) of this section), but is not required to provide a reasonable accommodation to an individual who meets the definition of disability solely under the "regarded as" prong (paragraph (g)(1)(iii) of this section).

(p) *Undue hardship*—(1) *In general. Undue hardship* means, with respect to the provision of an accommodation, significant difficulty or expense incurred by a covered entity, when considered in light of the factors set forth in paragraph (p)(2) of this section.

(2) *Factors to be considered.* In determining whether an accommodation would impose an undue hardship on a covered entity, factors to be considered include: (i) The nature and net cost of the accommodation needed under this part, taking into consideration the availability of tax credits and deductions, and/or outside funding; (ii) The overall financial resources of the facility or facilities involved in the provision of the reasonable accommodation, the number of persons employed at such facility, and the effect on expenses and resources; (iii) The overall financial resources of the covered entity, the overall size of the business of the covered entity with respect to the number of its employees, and the number, type and location of its facilities; (iv) The type of operation or operations of the covered entity, including the composition, structure and functions of the workforce of such entity, and the geographic separateness and administrative or fiscal relationship of the facility or facilities in question to the covered entity; and(v) The impact of the accommodation upon the operation of the facility, including the impact on the ability of other employees to perform their duties and the impact on the facility's ability to conduct business.

(q) *Qualification standards* means the personal and professional attributes including the skill, experience, education, physical, medical, safety and other requirements established by a covered entity as requirements which an individual must meet in order to be eligible for the position held or desired.

(r) *Direct Threat* means a significant risk of substantial harm to the health or safety of the individual or others that cannot be eliminated or reduced by reasonable accommodation. The determination that an individual poses a "direct threat" shall be based on an individualized assessment of the individual's present ability to safely perform the essential functions of the job. This assessment shall be based on a reasonable medical judgment that relies on the most current medical knowledge and/or on the best available objective evidence. In determining whether an individual would pose a direct threat, the factors to be considered include: (1) The duration of the risk; (2) The nature and severity of the potential harm; (3) The likelihood that the potential harm will occur; and (4) The imminence of the potential harm.

[56 FR 35734, July 26, 1991, as amended at 76 FR 16999, Mar. 25, 2011]

§ 1630.10 Qualification standards, tests, and other selection criteria.

(a) *In general.* It is unlawful for a covered entity to use qualification standards, employment tests or other selection criteria that screen out or tend to screen out an individual with a disability or a class of individuals with disabilities, on the basis of disability, unless the standard, test, or other selection criteria, as used by the covered entity, is shown to be job related for the position in question and is consistent with business necessity. (b) *Qualification standards and tests related to uncorrected vision.* Notwithstanding § 1630.2(j)(1)(vi) of this part, a covered entity shall not use qualification standards, employment tests, or other selection criteria based on an individual's uncorrected vision unless the standard, test, or other selection criterion, as used by the covered entity, is shown to be job related for the position in question and is consistent with business necessity. An individual challenging a covered entity's application of a qualification standard, test, or other criterion based on uncorrected vision need not be a person with a disability, but must be adversely affected by the application of the standard, test, or other criterion.

[76 FR 17002, Mar. 25 , 2011]

1630.11 Administration of tests.

It is unlawful for a covered entity to fail to select and administer tests concerning employment in the most effective manner to ensure that, when a test is administered to a job applicant or employee who has a disability that impairs sensory, manual or speaking skills, the test results accurately reflect the skills, aptitude, or whatever other factor of the applicant or employee that the test purports to measure, rather than reflecting the impaired sensory, manual, or speaking skills of such employee or applicant (except where such skills are the factors that the test purports to measure).

§ 1630.12   Retaliation and coercion.

(a) *Retaliation.* It is unlawful to discriminate against any individual because that individual has opposed any act or practice made unlawful by this part or because that individual made a charge, testified, assisted, or participated in any manner in an investigation, proceeding, or hearing to enforce any provision contained in this part. (b) *Coercion, interference or intimidation.* It is unlawful to coerce, intimidate, threaten, harass or interfere with any individual in the exercise or enjoyment of, or because that individual aided or encouraged any other individual in the exercise of, any right granted or protected by this part.

§ 1630.13   Prohibited medical examinations and inquiries.

(a) *Pre-employment examination or inquiry.* Except as permitted by § 1630.14, it is unlawful for a covered entity to conduct a medical examination of an applicant or to make inquiries as to whether an applicant is an individual with a disability or as to the nature or severity of such disability. (b) *Examination or inquiry of employees.* Except as permitted by § 1630.14, it is unlawful for a covered entity to require a medical examination of an employee or to make inquiries as to whether an employee is an individual with a disability or as to the nature or severity of such disability.

§ 1630.14   Medical examinations and inquiries specifically permitted.

(a) *Acceptable pre-employment inquiry.* A covered entity may make pre-employment inquiries into the ability of an applicant to perform job-related functions, and/or may ask an applicant to describe or to demonstrate how, with or without reasonable accommodation, the applicant will be able to perform job-related functions. (b) *Employment entrance examination.* A covered entity may require a medical examination (and/or inquiry) after making an offer of employment to a job applicant and before the applicant begins his or her employment duties, and may condition an offer of employment on the results of such examination (and/or inquiry), if all entering employees in the same job category are subjected to such an examination (and/or inquiry) regardless of disability. (1) Information obtained under paragraph (b) of this section regarding the medical condition or history of the applicant shall be collected and maintained on separate forms and in separate medical files and be treated as a confidential medical record, except that: (i) Supervisors and managers may be informed regarding necessary restrictions on the work or duties of the employee and necessary accommodations; (ii) First aid and safety personnel may be informed, when appropriate, if the disability might require emergency treatment; and (iii) Government officials investigating compliance with this part shall be provided relevant information on request. (2) The results of such examination shall not be used for any purpose inconsistent with this part. (3) Medical examinations conducted in accordance with this section do not have to be job-related and consistent with business necessity. However, if certain criteria are used to screen out an employee or employees with disabilities as a result of such an examination or inquiry, the exclusionary criteria must be job-related and consistent with business necessity, and performance of the essential job functions cannot be accomplished with reasonable accommodation as required in this part. (See § 1630.15(b) Defenses to charges of discriminatory application of selection criteria.) (c) *Examination of employees.* A covered entity may require a medical examination (and/or inquiry) of an employee that is job-related and consistent with business necessity. A covered entity may make inquiries into the ability of an employee to perform job-related functions. Information obtained under paragraph (c) of this section regarding the medical condition or history of any employee shall be collected and maintained on separate forms and in separate medical files and be treated as a confidential medical record, except that: (i) Supervisors and managers may be informed regarding necessary restrictions on the work or duties of the employee and necessary accommodations; (ii) First aid and safety personnel may be informed, when appropriate, if the disability might require emergency treatment; and (iii) Government officials investigating compliance with this part shall be provided relevant information on request. (2) Information obtained under paragraph (c) of this section regarding the medical condition or history of any employee shall not be used for any purpose inconsistent with this part. (d) *Other acceptable examinations and inquiries.* A covered entity may conduct voluntary medical examinations and activities, including voluntary medical histories, which are part of an employee health program available to employees at the work site. (1) Information obtained under paragraph (d) of this section regarding the medical condition or history of any employee shall be collected and maintained on separate forms and in separate medical files and be treated as a confidential medical record, except that: (i) Supervisors and managers may be informed regarding necessary restrictions on the work or duties of the employee and necessary accommodations; (ii) First aid and safety personnel may be informed, when appropriate, if the disability might require emergency treatment; and (iii) Government officials investigating compliance with this part shall be provided relevant information on request. (2) Information obtained under paragraph (d) of this section regarding the medical condition or history of any employee shall not be used for any purpose inconsistent with this part. * * *

§ 1630.15 Defenses.

Defenses to an allegation of discrimination under this part may include, but are not limited to, the following: (a) *Disparate treatment charges.* It may be a defense to a charge of disparate treatment brought under §§ 1630.4 through 1630.8 and 1630.11 through 1630.12 that the challenged action is justified by a legitimate, nondiscriminatory reason.

(b) *Charges of discriminatory application of selection criteria*—(1) *In general.* It may be a defense to a charge of discrimination, as described in § 1630.10, that an alleged application of qualification standards, tests, or selection criteria that screens out or tends to screen out or otherwise denies a job or benefit to an individual with a disability has been shown to be job-related and consistent with business necessity, and such performance cannot be accomplished with reasonable accommodation, as required in this part. (2) *Direct threat as a qualification standard.* The term "qualification standard" may include a requirement that an individual shall not pose a direct threat to the health or safety of the individual or others in the workplace. (See § 1630.2(r) defining direct threat.) (c) *Other disparate impact charges.* It may be a defense to a charge of discrimination brought under this part that a uniformly applied standard, criterion, or policy has a disparate impact on an individual with a disability or a class of individuals with disabilities that the challenged standard, criterion or policy has been shown to be job-related and consistent with business necessity, and such performance cannot be accomplished with reasonable accommodation, as required in this part. (d) *Charges of not making reasonable accommodation.* It may be a defense to a charge of discrimination, as described in § 1630.9, that a requested or necessary accommodation would impose an undue hardship on the operation of the covered entity's business. (e) *Conflict with other Federal laws.* It may be a defense to a charge of discrimination under this part that a challenged action is required or necessitated by another Federal law or regulation, or that another Federal law or regulation prohibits an action (including the provision of a particular reasonable accommodation) that would otherwise be required by this part.

(f) *Claims based on transitory and minor impairments under the "regarded as" prong.* It may be a defense to a charge of discrimination by an individual claiming coverage under the regarded as prong of the definition of disability that the impairment is (in the case of an actual impairment) or would be (in the case of a perceived impairment) "transitory and minor." To establish this defense, a covered entity must demonstrate that the impairment is both "transitory" and "minor." Whether the impairment at issue is or would be "transitory and minor" is to be determined objectively. A covered entity may not defeat "regarded as" coverage of an individual simply by demonstrating that it subjectively believed the impairment was transitory and minor; rather, the covered entity must demonstrate that the impairment is (in the case of an actual impairment) or would be (in the case of a perceived impairment) both transitory and minor. For purposes of this section, "transitory" is defined as lasting or expected to last six months or less. (g) *Additional defenses.* It may be a defense to a charge of discrimination under this part that the alleged discriminatory action is specifically permitted by § 1630.14 or § 1630.16.

[56 FR 35734, July 26, 1991, as amended at 76 FR 17003, Mar. 25, 2011]

§ 1630.16   Specific activities permitted.

(a) *Religious entities.* A religious corporation, association, educational institution, or society is permitted to give preference in employment to individuals of a particular religion to perform work connected with the carrying on by that corporation, association, educational institution, or society of its activities. A religious entity may require that all applicants and employees conform to the religious tenets of such organization. However, a religious entity may not discriminate against a qualified individual, who satisfies the permitted religious criteria, on the basis of his or her disability.

(b) *Regulation of alcohol and drugs.* A covered entity: (1) May prohibit the illegal use of drugs and the use of alcohol at the workplace by all employees; (2) May require that employees not be under the influence of alcohol or be engaging in the illegal use of drugs at the workplace; (3) May require that all employees behave in conformance with the requirements established under the Drug–Free Workplace Act of 1988 (41 U.S.C. 701 *et seq.*); (4) May hold an employee who engages in the illegal use of drugs or who is an alcoholic to the same qualification standards for employment or job performance and behavior to which the entity holds its other employees, even if any unsatisfactory performance or behavior is related to the employee's drug use or alcoholism; (5) May require that its employees employed in an industry subject to such regulations comply with the standards established in the regulations (if any) of the Departments of Defense and Transportation, and of the Nuclear Regulatory Commission, regarding alcohol and the illegal use of drugs; and (6) May require that employees employed in sensitive positions comply with the regulations (if any) of the Departments of Defense and Transportation and of the Nuclear Regulatory Commission that apply to employment in sensitive positions subject to such regulations.

(c) *Drug testing*—(1) *General policy.* For purposes of this part, a test to determine the illegal use of drugs is not considered a medical examination. Thus, the administration of such drug tests by a covered entity to its job applicants or employees is not a violation of § 1630.13 of this part. However, this part does not encourage, prohibit, or authorize a covered entity to conduct drug tests of job applicants or employees to determine the illegal use of drugs or to make employment decisions based on such test results. (2) *Transportation employees.* This part does not encourage, prohibit, or authorize the otherwise lawful exercise by entities subject to the jurisdiction of the Department of Transportation of authority to:

(i) Test employees of entities in, and applicants for, positions involving safety sensitive duties for the illegal use of drugs or for on-duty impairment by alcohol; and (ii) Remove from safety-sensitive positions persons who test positive for illegal use of drugs or on-duty impairment by alcohol pursuant to paragraph (c)(2)(i) of this section. (3) *Confidentiality.* Any information regarding the medical condition or history of any employee or applicant obtained from a test to determine the illegal use of drugs, except information regarding the illegal use of drugs, is subject to the requirements of § 1630.14(b) (2) and (3) of this part.

(d) *Regulation of smoking.* A covered entity may prohibit or impose restrictions on smoking in places of employment. Such restrictions do not violate any provision of this part.

(e) *Infectious and communicable diseases; food handling jobs*—(1) *In general.* Under title I of the ADA, section 103(d)(1), the Secretary of Health and Human Services is to prepare a list, to be updated annually, of infectious and communicable diseases which are transmitted through the handling of food. (Copies may be obtained from Center for Infectious Diseases, Centers for Disease Control, 1600 Clifton Road, NE., Mailstop C09, Atlanta, GA 30333.) If an individual with a disability is disabled by one of the infectious or communicable diseases included on this list, and if the risk of transmitting the disease associated with the handling of food cannot be eliminated by reasonable accommodation, a covered entity may refuse to assign or continue to assign such individual to a job involving food handling. However, if the individual with a disability is a current employee, the employer must consider whether he or she can be accommodated by reassignment to a vacant position not involving food handling. (2) *Effect on State or other laws.* This part does not preempt, modify, or amend any State, county, or local law, ordinance or regulation applicable to food handling which: (i) Is in accordance with the list, referred to in paragraph (e)(1) of this section, of infectious or communicable diseases and the modes of transmissibility published by the Secretary of Health and Human Services; and (ii) Is designed to protect the public health from individuals who pose a significant risk to the health or safety of others, where that risk cannot be eliminated by reasonable accommodation.

(f) *Health insurance, life insurance, and other benefit plans*—(1) An insurer, hospital, or medical service company, health maintenance organization, or any agent or entity that administers benefit plans, or similar organizations may underwrite risks, classify risks, or administer such risks that are based on or not inconsistent with State law. (2) A covered entity may establish, sponsor, observe or administer the terms of a bona fide benefit plan that are based on underwriting risks, classifying risks, or administering such risks that are based on or not inconsistent with State law. (3) A covered entity may establish, sponsor, observe, or administer the terms of a bona fide benefit plan that is not subject to State laws that regulate insurance. (4) The activities described in paragraphs (f)(1), (2), and (3) of this section are permitted unless these activities are being used as a subterfuge to evade the purposes of this part.

[56 FR 35734, July 26, 1991, 76 FR 17003, Mar. 25, 2011]

APPENDIX A TO PART 16300—INTERPRETIVE GUIDANCE TO TITLE I OF THE AMERICANS WITH DISABILITIES ACT— SELECTED PROVISIONS

§ 1630.2   Definitions * * *

§ 1630.2(g)   Disability

In addition to the term "covered entity," there are several other terms that are unique to the ADA as amended. The first of these is the term "disability." "This definition is of critical importance because as a threshold issue it determines whether an individual is covered by the ADA." 2008 Senate Statement of Managers at 6. In the original ADA, "Congress sought to protect anyone who experiences discrimination because of a current, past, or perceived disability." 2008 Senate Statement of Managers at 6. Accordingly, the definition of the term "disability" is divided into three prongs: An individual is considered to have a "disability" if that individual (1) has a physical or mental impairment that substantially limits one or more of that person's major life activities (the "actual disability" prong); (2) has a record of such an impairment (the "record of" prong); or (3) is regarded by the covered entity as an individual with a disability as defined in § 1630.2(*l*) (the "regarded as" prong). The ADAAA retained the basic structure and terms of the original definition of disability. However, the Amendments Act altered the interpretation and application of this critical statutory term in fundamental ways. See 2008 Senate Statement of Managers at 1 ("The bill maintains the ADA's inherently functional definition of disability" but "clarifies and expands the definition's meaning and application."). As noted above, the primary purpose of the ADAAA is to make it easier for people with disabilities to obtain protection under the ADA. See Joint Hoyer–Sensenbrenner Statement at 2. Accordingly, the ADAAA provides rules of construction regarding the definition of disability. Consistent with the congressional intent to reinstate a broad scope of protection under the ADA, the ADAAA's rules of construction require that the definition of "disability" "shall be construed in favor of broad coverage of individuals under [the ADA], to the maximum extent permitted by the terms of [the ADA]." 42 U.S.C. 12102(4)(A). The legislative history of the ADAAA is replete with references emphasizing this principle. See Joint Hoyer–Sensenbrenner Statement at 2 ("[The bill] establishes that the definition of disability must be interpreted broadly to achieve the remedial purposes of the ADA"); 2008 Senate Statement of Managers at 1 (the ADAAA's purpose is to "enhance the protections of the [ADA]" by "expanding the definition, and by rejecting several opinions of the United States Supreme Court that have had the effect of restricting the meaning and application of the definition of disability"); id. (stressing

214

the importance of removing barriers "to construing and applying the definition of disability more generously"); id. at 4 ("The managers have introduced the [ADAAA] to restore the proper balance and application of the ADA by clarifying and broadening the definition of disability, and to increase eligibility for the protections of the ADA."); id. ("It is our expectation that because the bill makes the definition of disability more generous, some people who were not covered before will now be covered."); id. (warning that "the definition of disability should not be unduly used as a tool for excluding individuals from the ADA's protections"); id. (this principle "sends a clear signal of our intent that the courts must interpret the definition of disability broadly rather than stringently"); 2008 House Judiciary Committee Report at 5 ("The purpose of the bill is to restore protection for the broad range of individuals with disabilities as originally envisioned by Congress by responding to the Supreme Court's narrow interpretation of the definition of disability."). Further, as the purposes section of the ADAAA explicitly cautions, the "primary object of attention" in cases brought under the ADA should be whether entities covered under the ADA have complied with their obligations. As noted above, this means, for example, examining whether an employer has discriminated against an employee, including whether an employer has fulfilled its obligations with respect to providing a "reasonable accommodation" to an individual with a disability; or whether an employee has met his or her responsibilities under the ADA with respect to engaging in the reasonable accommodation "interactive process." ADAAA section 2(b)(5); See also 2008 Senate Statement of Managers at 4 ("[L]ower court cases have too often turned solely on the question of whether the plaintiff is an individual with a disability rather than the merits of discrimination claims, such as whether adverse decisions were impermissibly made by the employer on the basis of disability, reasonable accommodations were denied, or qualification standards were unlawfully discriminatory."); 2008 House Judiciary Committee Report (criticizing pre-ADAAA court decisions which "prevented individuals that Congress unquestionably intended to cover from ever getting a chance to prove their case"). Accordingly, the threshold coverage question of whether an individual's impairment is a disability under the ADA "should not demand extensive analysis." ADAAA section 2(b)(5).

Section 1630.2(g)(2) provides that an individual may establish coverage under any one or more (or all three) of the prongs in the definition of disability. However, to be an individual with a disability, an individual is only required to satisfy one prong. As § 1630.2(g)(3) indicates, in many cases it may be unnecessary for an individual to resort to coverage under the "actual disability" or "record of" prongs. Where the need for a reasonable accommodation is not at issue—for example, where there is no question that the individual is "qualified" without a reasonable accommodation and is not seeking or has not sought a reasonable accommodation—it would not be necessary to determine whether the individual is substantially limited in a major life activity (under the actual disability prong) or has a record of a substantially limiting impairment (under the record of prong). Such claims could be evaluated solely under the "regarded as" prong of the definition. In fact, Congress expected the first and second prongs of the definition of disability "to be used only by people who are affirmatively seeking reasonable accommodations * * *" and that "[a]ny individual who has been discriminated against because of an impairment—short of being granted a reasonable accommodation * * *—should be bringing a claim under the third prong of the definition which will require no showing with regard to the severity of his or her impairment." Joint Hoyer–Sensenbrenner Statement at 4. An individual may choose, however, to proceed under the "actual disability" and/or "record of" prong regardless of whether the individual is challenging a covered entity's failure to make reasonable accommodation or requires a reasonable accommodation. To fully understand the meaning of the term "disability," it is also necessary to understand what is meant by the terms "physical or mental impairment," "major life activity," "substantially limits," "record of," and "regarded as." Each of these terms is discussed below.

§ 1630.2(h)   Physical or Mental Impairment

Neither the original ADA nor the ADAAA provides a definition for the terms "physical or mental impairment." However, the legislative history of the Amendments Act notes that Congress "expect[s] that the current regulatory definition of these terms, as promulgated by agencies such as the U.S. Equal Employment Opportunity Commission (EEOC), the Department of Justice (DOJ) and the Department of Education Office of Civil Rights (DOE OCR) will not change." 2008 Senate Statement of Managers at 6. The definition of "physical or mental impairment" in the EEOC's regulations remains based on the definition of the term "physical or mental impairment" found in the regulations implementing section 504 of the Rehabilitation Act at 34 CFR part 104. However, the definition in EEOC's regulations adds additional body systems to those provided in the section 504 regulations and makes clear that the list is non-exhaustive. It is important to distinguish between conditions that are impairments and physical, psychological, environmental, cultural, and economic characteristics that are not impairments. The definition of the term "impairment" does not include physical characteristics such as eye color, hair color, left-handedness, or height, weight, or muscle tone that are within "normal" range and are not the result of a physiological disorder. The definition, likewise, does not include characteristic predisposition to illness or disease. Other conditions, such as pregnancy, that are not the result of a physiological disorder are also not impairments. However, a pregnancy-related impairment that substantially limits a major life activity is a disability under the first prong of the definition. Alternatively, a pregnancy-related impairment may constitute a "record of" a substantially "limiting impairment," or may be covered under the "regarded as" prong if it is the basis for a prohibited employment action and is not "transitory and minor." The definition of an impairment also does not include common personality traits such as poor judgment or a quick temper where these are not symptoms of a mental or psychological disorder. Environmental, cultural, or economic disadvantages such as poverty, lack of education, or a prison record are not impairments. Advanced age, in and of itself, is also not an impairment. However, various medical conditions commonly associated with age, such as hearing loss, osteoporosis, or arthritis would constitute impairments within the meaning of this part. See 1989 Senate Report at 22–23; 1990 House Labor Report at 51–52; 1990 House Judiciary Report at 28–29.

§ 1630.2(i) Major Life Activities

The ADAAA provided significant new guidance and clarification on the subject of "major life activities." As the legislative history of the Amendments Act explains, Congress anticipated that protection under the ADA would now extend to a wider range of cases, in part as a result of the expansion of the category of major life activities. See 2008 Senate Statement of Managers at 8 n.17. For purposes of clarity, the Amendments Act provides an illustrative list of major life activities, including caring for oneself, performing manual tasks, seeing, hearing, eating, sleeping, walking, standing, lifting, bending, speaking, breathing, learning, reading, concentrating, thinking, communicating, and working. The ADA Amendments expressly made this statutory list of examples of major life activities non-exhaustive, and the regulations include sitting, reaching, and interacting with others as additional examples. Many of these major life activities listed in the ADA Amendments Act and the regulations already had been included in the EEOC's 1991 now-superseded regulations implementing title I of the ADA and in sub-regulatory documents, and already were recognized by the courts. The ADA as amended also explicitly defines "major life activities" to include the operation of "major bodily functions." This was an important addition to the statute. This clarification was needed to ensure that the impact of an impairment on the operation of a major bodily function would not be overlooked or wrongly dismissed as falling outside the definition of "major life activities" under the ADA. 2008 House Judiciary Committee Report at 16; See also 2008 Senate Statement of Managers at 8 ("for the first time [in the ADAAA], the category of "major life activities" is defined to include the operation of major bodily functions, thus better addressing chronic impairments that can be substantially limiting"). The regulations include all of those major bodily functions identified in the ADA Amendments Act's non-exhaustive list of examples and add a number of others that are consistent with the body systems listed in the regulations' definition of "impairment" (at § 1630.2(h)) and with the U.S. Department of Labor's nondiscrimination and equal employment opportunity regulations implementing section 188 of the Workforce Investment Act of 1998, 29 U.S.C. 2801, *et seq.* Thus, special sense organs, skin, genitourinary, cardiovascular, hemic, lymphatic, and musculoskeletal functions are major bodily functions not included in the statutory list of examples but included in § 1630.2(i)(1)(ii). The Commission has added these examples to further illustrate the non-exhaustive list of major life activities, including major bodily functions, and to emphasize that the concept of major life activities is to be interpreted broadly consistent with the Amendments Act. The regulations also provide that the operation of a major bodily function may include the operation of an individual organ within a body system. This would include, for example, the operation of the kidney, liver, pancreas, or other organs. The link between particular impairments and various major bodily functions should not be difficult to identify. Because impairments, by definition, affect the functioning of body systems, they will generally affect major bodily functions. For example, cancer affects an individual's normal cell growth; diabetes affects the operation of the pancreas and also the function of the endocrine system; and Human Immunodeficiency Virus (HIV) infection affects the immune system. Likewise, sickle cell disease affects the functions of the hemic system, lymphedema affects lymphatic functions, and rheumatoid arthritis affects musculoskeletal functions. In the legislative history of the ADAAA, Congress expressed its expectation that the statutory expansion of "major life activities" to include major bodily functions (along with other statutory changes) would lead to more expansive coverage. See 2008 Senate Statement of Managers at 8 n.17 (indicating that these changes will make it easier for individuals to show that they are eligible for the ADA's protections under the first prong of the definition of disability). The House Education and Labor Committee explained that the inclusion of major bodily functions would "affect cases such as *U.S.* v. *Happy Time Day Care Ctr.* in which the courts struggled to analyze whether the impact of HIV infection substantially limits various major life activities of a five-year-old child, and recognizing, among other things, that 'there is something inherently illogical about inquiring whether' a five-year-old's ability to procreate is substantially limited by his HIV infection; *Furnish* v. *SVI Sys., Inc,* in which the court found that an individual with cirrhosis of the liver caused by Hepatitis B is not disabled because liver function—unlike eating, working, or reproducing—'is not integral to one's daily existence;' and *Pimental* v. *Dartmouth-Hitchcock Clinic,* in which the court concluded that the plaintiff's stage three breast cancer did not substantially limit her ability to care for herself, sleep, or concentrate. The Committee expects that the plaintiffs in each of these cases could establish a [substantial limitation] on major bodily functions that would qualify them for protection under the ADA." 2008 House Education and Labor Committee Report at 12.

The examples of major life activities (including major bodily functions) in the ADAAA and the EEOC's regulations are illustrative and non-exhaustive, and the absence of a particular life activity or bodily function from the examples does not create a negative implication as to whether an omitted activity or function constitutes a major life activity under the statute. See 2008 Senate Statement of Managers at 8; See also 2008 House Committee on Educ. and Labor Report at 11; 2008 House

Judiciary Committee Report at 17. The Commission anticipates that courts will recognize other major life activities, consistent with the ADA Amendments Act's mandate to construe the definition of disability broadly. As a result of the ADA Amendments Act's rejection of the holding in *Toyota Motor Mfg., Ky., Inc.* v. *Williams,* 534 U.S. 184 (2002), whether an activity is a "major life activity" is not determined by reference to whether it is of "central importance to daily life." See *Toyota,* 534 U.S. at 197 (defining "major life activities" as activities that are of "central importance to most people's daily lives"). Indeed, this holding was at odds with the earlier Supreme Court decision of *Bragdon* v. *Abbott,* 524 U.S. 624 (1998), which held that a major life activity (in that case, reproduction) does not have to have a "public, economic or daily aspect." Id. at 639. Accordingly, the regulations provide that in determining other examples of major life activities, the term "major" shall not be interpreted strictly to create a demanding standard for disability. Cf. 2008 Senate Statement of Managers at 7 (indicating that a person is considered an individual with a disability for purposes of the first prong when one or more of the individual's "important life activities" are restricted) (citing 1989 Senate Report at 23). The regulations also reject the notion that to be substantially limited in performing a major life activity, an individual must have an impairment that prevents or severely restricts the individual from doing "activities that are of central importance to most people's daily lives." Id.; see also 2008 Senate Statement of Managers at 5 n.12. Thus, for example, lifting is a major life activity regardless of whether an individual who claims to be substantially limited in lifting actually performs activities of central importance to daily life that require lifting. Similarly, the Commission anticipates that the major life activity of performing manual tasks (which was at issue in *Toyota*) could have many different manifestations, such as performing tasks involving fine motor coordination, or performing tasks involving grasping, hand strength, or pressure. Such tasks need not constitute activities of central importance to most people's daily lives, nor must an individual show that he or she is substantially limited in performing all manual tasks.

§ 1630.2(j)   Substantially Limits

In any case involving coverage solely under the "regarded as" prong of the definition of "disability" (e.g., cases where reasonable accommodation is not at issue), it is not necessary to determine whether an individual is "substantially limited" in any major life activity. See 2008 Senate Statement of Managers at 10; id. at 13 ("The functional limitation imposed by an impairment is irrelevant to the third 'regarded as' prong."). Indeed, Congress anticipated that the first and second prongs of the definition of disability would "be used only by people who are affirmatively seeking reasonable accommodations * * *" and that "[a]ny individual who has been discriminated against because of an impairment—short of being granted a reasonable accommodation * * *— should be bringing a claim under the third prong of the definition which will require no showing with regard to the severity of his or her impairment." Joint Hoyer–Sensenbrenner Statement at 4. Of course, an individual may choose, however, to proceed under the "actual disability" and/or "record of" prong regardless of whether the individual is challenging a covered entity's failure to make reasonable accommodations or requires a reasonable accommodation. The concept of "substantially limits" is only relevant in cases involving coverage under the "actual disability" or "record of" prong of the definition of disability. Thus, the information below pertains to these cases only. Section 1630.2(j)(1) Rules of Construction. It is clear in the text and legislative history of the ADAAA that Congress concluded the courts had incorrectly construed "substantially limits," and disapproved of the EEOC's now-superseded 1991 regulation defining the term to mean "significantly restricts." See 2008 Senate Statement of Managers at 6 ("We do not believe that the courts have correctly instituted the level of coverage we intended to establish with the term 'substantially limits' in the ADA" and "we believe that the level of limitation, and the intensity of focus, applied by the Supreme Court in *Toyota* goes beyond what we believe is the appropriate standard to create coverage under this law."). Congress extensively deliberated over whether a new term other than "substantially limits" should be adopted to denote the appropriate functional limitation necessary under the first and second prongs of the definition of disability. See 2008 Senate Statement of Managers at 6–7. Ultimately, Congress affirmatively opted to retain this term in the Amendments Act, rather than replace it. It concluded that "adopting a new, undefined term that is subject to widely disparate meanings is not the best way to achieve the goal of ensuring consistent and appropriately broad coverage under this Act." Id. Instead, Congress determined "a better way * * * to express [its] disapproval of *Sutton* and *Toyota* (along with the current EEOC regulation) is to retain the words 'substantially limits,' but clarify that it is not meant to be a demanding standard." Id. at 7. To achieve that goal, Congress set forth detailed findings and purposes and "rules of construction" to govern the interpretation and application of this concept going forward. See ADAAA Sections 2–4; 42 U.S.C. 12102(4).

The Commission similarly considered whether to provide a new definition of "substantially limits" in the regulation. Following Congress's lead, however, the Commission ultimately concluded that a new definition would inexorably lead to greater focus and intensity of attention on the threshold issue of coverage than intended by Congress. Therefore, the regulations simply provide rules of construction that must be applied in determining whether an impairment substantially limits (or substantially limited) a major life activity. These are each discussed in greater detail below.

§ 1630.2(j)(1)(i) Broad Construction; not a Demanding Standard

Section 1630.2(j)(1)(i) states: "The term 'substantially limits' shall be construed broadly in favor of expansive coverage, to the maximum extent permitted by the terms of the ADA. 'Substantially limits' is not meant to be a demanding standard." Congress stated in the ADA Amendments Act that the definition of disability "shall be construed in favor of broad coverage," and that "the term 'substantially limits' shall be interpreted consistently with the findings and purposes of the ADA Amendments Act of 2008." 42 U.S.C. 12101(4)(A)–(B), as amended. "This is a textual provision that will legally guide the agencies and courts in properly interpreting the term 'substantially limits.'" Hoyer–Sensenbrenner Congressional Record Statement at H8295. As Congress noted in the legislative history of the ADAAA, "[t]o be clear, the purposes section conveys our intent to clarify not only that 'substantially limits' should be measured by a lower standard than that used in *Toyota,* but also that the definition of disability should not be unduly used as a tool for excluding individuals from the ADA's protections." 2008 Senate Statement of Managers at 5 (also stating that "[t]his rule of construction, together with the rule of construction providing that the definition of disability shall be construed in favor of broad coverage of individuals sends a clear signal of our intent that the courts must interpret the definition of disability broadly rather than stringently"). Put most succinctly, "substantially limits" "is not meant to be a demanding standard." 2008 Senate Statement of Managers at 7. Section 1630.2(j)(1)(ii): Significant or Severe Restriction Not Required; Nonetheless, Not Every Impairment Is Substantially Limiting. Section 1630.2(j)(1)(ii) states: "An impairment is a disability within the meaning of this section if it substantially limits the ability of an individual to perform a major life activity as compared to most people in the general population. An impairment need not prevent, or significantly or severely restrict, the individual from performing a major life activity in order to be considered substantially limiting. Nonetheless, not every impairment will constitute a 'disability' within the meaning of this section." In keeping with the instruction that the term "substantially limits" is not meant to be a demanding standard, the regulations provide that an impairment is a disability if it substantially limits the ability of an individual to perform a major life activity as compared to most people in the general population. However, to be substantially limited in performing a major life activity an individual need not have an impairment that prevents or significantly or severely restricts the individual from performing a major life activity. See 2008 Senate Statement of Managers at 2, 6–8 & n.14; 2008 House Committee on Educ. and Labor Report at 9–10 ("While the limitation imposed by an impairment must be important, it need not rise to the level of severely restricting or significantly restricting the ability to perform a major life activity to qualify as a disability."); 2008 House Judiciary Committee Report at 16 (similarly requiring an "important" limitation). The level of limitation required is "substantial" as compared to most people in the general population, which does not require a significant or severe restriction. Multiple impairments that combine to substantially limit one or more of an individual's major life activities also constitute a disability. Nonetheless, not every impairment will constitute a "disability" within the meaning of this section. See 2008 Senate Statement of Managers at 4 ("We reaffirm that not every individual with a physical or mental impairment is covered by the first prong of the definition of disability in the ADA.") Section 1630.2(j)(1)(iii): Substantial Limitation Should Not Be Primary Object of Attention; Extensive Analysis Not Needed. Section 1630.2(j)(1)(iii) states: The primary object of attention in cases brought under the ADA should be whether covered entities have complied with their obligations, not whether an individual's impairment substantially limits a major life activity. Accordingly, the threshold issue of whether an impairment 'substantially limits' a major life activity should not demand extensive analysis.

Congress retained the term substantially limits in part because it was concerned that adoption of a new phrase—and the resulting need for further judicial scrutiny and construction—would not help move the focus from the threshold issue of disability to the primary issue of discrimination. 2008 Senate Statement of Managers at 7. This was the primary problem Congress sought to solve in enacting the ADAAA. It recognized that clearing the initial [disability] threshold is critical, as individuals who are excluded from the definition 'never have the opportunity to have their condition evaluated in light of medical evidence and a determination made as to whether they [are] 'otherwise qualified.'' 2008 House Judiciary Committee Report at 7; See also id. (expressing concern that "[a]n individual who does not qualify as disabled does not meet th[e] threshold question of coverage in the protected class and is therefore not permitted to attempt to prove his or her claim of discriminatory treatment); 2008 Senate Statement of Managers at 4 (criticizing pre-ADAAA lower court cases that "too often turned solely on the question of whether the plaintiff is an individual with a disability rather than the merits of discrimination claims, such as whether adverse decisions were impermissibly made by the employer on the basis of disability, reasonable accommodations were denied, or qualification standards were unlawfully discriminatory"). Accordingly, the Amendments Act and the amended regulations make plain that the emphasis in ADA cases now should be squarely on the merits and not on the initial coverage question. The revised regulations therefore provide that an impairment is a disability if it substantially limits the ability of an individual to perform a major life activity as compared to most people in the general population and deletes the language to which Congress objected. The Commission believes that this provides a useful framework in which to analyze whether an impairment satisfies the definition of disability. Further, this framework better reflects Congress's expressed intent in the ADA Amendments Act that the definition of the term "disability" shall be construed broadly, and is consistent with statements in the Amendments Act's legislative history. See 2008 Senate Statement of Managers at 7 (stating that "adopting a new, undefined term" and the "resulting need for further judicial scrutiny and construction will not help move the focus from the threshold issue of disability to the primary issue of discrimination," and finding that " 'substantially limits' as construed consistently with the findings and purposes of this legislation establishes an appropriate functionality test of determining whether an individual has a disability" and that "using the correct standard—one that is lower than the strict or demanding standard created by the Supreme Court in *Toyota*—will make the disability determination an appropriate threshold issue but not an onerous burden for those seeking accommodations or modifications"). Consequently, this rule of construction makes clear that the question of whether an impairment substantially limits a major life activity should not demand extensive analysis. As the legislative history explains, "[w]e expect that courts interpreting [the ADA] will not demand such an extensive analysis over whether a person's physical or mental impairment constitutes a disability." Hoyer–Sensenbrenner Congressional Record Statement at H8295; see id. ("Our goal throughout this process has been to simplify that analysis.")

§ 1630.2(j)(1)(iv) Individualized Assessment Required, But With Lower Standard Than Previously Applied

Section 1630.2(j)(1)(iv) states: "The determination of whether an impairment substantially limits a major life activity requires an individualized assessment. However, in making this assessment, the term 'substantially limits' shall be interpreted and applied to require a degree of functional limitation that is lower than the standard for 'substantially limits' applied prior to the ADAAA. By retaining the essential elements of the definition of disability including the key term "substantially limits," Congress reaffirmed that not every individual with a physical or mental impairment is covered by the first prong of the definition of disability in the ADA. See 2008 Senate Statement of Managers at 4. To be covered under the first prong of the definition, an individual must establish that an impairment substantially limits a major life activity. That has not changed—nor will the necessity of making this determination on an individual basis. Id. However, what the ADAAA changed is the standard required for making this determination. Id. at 4–5. The Amendments Act and the EEOC's regulations explicitly reject the standard enunciated by the Supreme Court in *Toyota Motor Mfg., Ky., Inc.* v. *Williams*, 534 U.S. 184 (2002), and applied in the lower courts in numerous cases. See ADAAA section 2(b)(4). That previous standard created "an inappropriately high level of limitation necessary to obtain coverage under the ADA." Id. at section 2(b)(5). The Amendments Act and the EEOC's regulations reject the notion that "substantially limits" should be interpreted strictly to create a demanding standard for qualifying as disabled. Id. at section 2(b)(4). Instead, the ADAAA and these regulations establish a degree of functional limitation required for an impairment to constitute a disability that is consistent with what Congress originally intended. 2008 Senate Statement of Managers at 7. This will make the disability determination an appropriate threshold issue but not an onerous burden for those seeking to prove discrimination under the ADA. Id.

§ 1630.2(j)(1)(v) Scientific, Medical, or Statistical Analysis Not Required, But Permissible When Appropriate

Section 1630.2(j)(1)(v) states: "The comparison of an individual's performance of a major life activity to the performance of the same major life activity by most people in the general population usually will not require scientific, medical, or statistical analysis. Nothing in this paragraph is intended, however, to prohibit the presentation of scientific, medical, or statistical evidence to make such a comparison where appropriate." The term "average person in the general population," as the basis of comparison for determining whether an individual's impairment substantially limits a major life activity, has been changed to "most people in the general population." This revision is not a substantive change in the concept, but rather is intended to conform the language to the simpler and more straightforward terminology used in the legislative history to the Amendments Act. The comparison between the individual and "most people" need not be exacting, and usually will not require scientific, medical, or statistical analysis. Nothing in this subparagraph is intended, however, to prohibit the presentation of scientific, medical, or statistical evidence to make such a comparison where appropriate. The comparison to most people in the general population continues to mean a comparison to other people in the general population, not a comparison to those similarly situated. For example, the ability of an individual with an amputated limb to perform a major life activity is compared to other people in the general population, not to other amputees. This does not mean that disability cannot be shown where an impairment, such as a learning disability, is clinically diagnosed based in part on a disparity between an individual's aptitude and that individual's actual versus expected achievement, taking into account the person's chronological age, measured intelligence, and age-appropriate education. Individuals diagnosed with dyslexia or other learning disabilities will typically be substantially limited in performing activities such as learning, reading, and thinking when compared to most people in the general population, particularly when the ameliorative effects of mitigating measures, including therapies, learned behavioral or adaptive neurological modifications, assistive devices (e.g., audio recordings, screen reading devices, voice activated software), studying longer, or receiving more time to take a test, are disregarded as required under the ADA Amendments Act.

§ 1630.2(j)(1)(vi) Mitigating Measures

Section 1630.2(j)(1)(vi) states: "The determination of whether an impairment substantially limits a major life activity shall be made without regard to the ameliorative effects of mitigating measures. However, the ameliorative effects of ordinary eyeglasses or contact lenses shall be considered in determining whether an impairment substantially limits a major life activity." The ameliorative effects of mitigating measures shall not be considered in determining whether an impairment substantially limits a major life activity. Thus, "[w]ith the exception of ordinary eyeglasses and contact lenses, impairments must be examined in their unmitigated state." See 2008 Senate Statement of Managers at 5. This provision in the ADAAA and the EEOC's regulations "is intended to eliminate the catch–22 that exist[ed] * * * where individuals who are subjected to discrimination on the basis of their disabilities [we]re frequently unable to invoke the ADA's protections because they [we]re not considered people with disabilities when the effects of their medication, medical supplies, behavioral adaptations, or other interventions [we]re considered." Joint Hoyer–Sensenbrenner Statement at 2; See also 2008 Senate Statement of Managers at 9 ("This provision is intended to eliminate the situation created under [prior] law in which impairments that are mitigated [did] not constitute disabilities but [were the basis for discrimination]."). To the extent cases pre-dating the 2008 Amendments Act reasoned otherwise, they are contrary to the law as amended. See 2008 House Judiciary Committee Report at 9 & nn.25, 20–21 (citing, e.g., *McClure* v. *General Motors Corp.*, 75 F. App'x 983 (5th Cir. 2003) (court held that individual with muscular dystrophy who, with the mitigating measure of "adapting" how he performed manual tasks, had successfully learned to live and work with his disability was therefore not an individual with a disability); *Orr* v. *Wal-Mart Stores, Inc.*, 297 F.3d 720 (8th Cir. 2002) (court held that *Sutton* v. *United Air Lines, Inc.*, 527 U.S. 471 (1999), required consideration of the ameliorative effects of plaintiff's careful regimen of medicine, exercise and diet, and declined to consider impact of uncontrolled diabetes on plaintiff's ability to see, speak, read, and walk); *Gonzales* v. *National Bd. of Med. Examiners*, 225 F.3d 620 (6th Cir. 2000) (where the court found that an individual with a diagnosed learning disability was not substantially limited after considering the impact of self-accommodations that allowed him to read and achieve academic success); *McMullin* v. *Ashcroft*, 337 F. Supp. 2d 1281 (D. Wyo. 2004) (individual fired because of clinical depression not protected because of the successful management of the condition with medication for fifteen years); *Eckhaus* v. *Consol. Rail Corp.*, 2003 WL 23205042 (D.N.J. Dec. 24, 2003) (individual fired because of a hearing impairment was not protected because a hearing aid helped correct that impairment); *Todd* v. *Academy Corp.*, 57 F. Supp. 2d 448, 452 (S.D. Tex. 1999) (court held that because medication reduced the frequency and intensity of plaintiff's seizures, he was not disabled)).

An individual who, because of the use of a mitigating measure, has experienced no limitations, or only minor limitations, related to the impairment may still be an individual with a disability, where there is evidence that in the absence of an effective mitigating measure the individual's impairment would be substantially limiting. For example, someone who began taking medication for hypertension before experiencing substantial limitations related to the impairment would still be an individual with a disability if, without the medication, he or she would now be substantially limited in functions of the cardiovascular or circulatory system. Evidence showing that an impairment would be substantially limiting in the absence of the ameliorative effects of mitigating measures could include evidence of limitations that a person experienced prior to using a mitigating measure, evidence concerning the expected course of a particular disorder absent mitigating measures, or readily available and reliable information of other types. However, we expect that consistent with the Amendments Act's command (and the related rules of construction in the regulations) that the definition of disability "should not demand extensive analysis," covered entities and courts will in many instances be able to conclude that a substantial limitation has been shown without resort to such evidence. The Amendments Act provides an "illustrative but non-comprehensive list of the types of mitigating measures that are not to be considered." See 2008 Senate Statement of Managers at 9. Section 1630.2(j)(5) of the regulations includes all of those mitigating measures listed in the ADA Amendments Act's illustrative list of mitigating measures, including reasonable accommodations (as applied under title I) or "auxiliary aids or services" (as defined by 42 U.S.C. 12103(1) and applied under titles II and III). Since it would be impossible to guarantee comprehensiveness in a finite list, the list of examples of mitigating measures provided in the ADA and the regulations is non-exhaustive. See 2008 House Judiciary Committee Report at 20. The absence of any particular mitigating measure from the list in the regulations should not convey a negative implication as to whether the measure is a mitigating measure under the ADA. See 2008 Senate Statement of Managers at 9. For example, the fact that mitigating measures include "reasonable accommodations" generally makes it unnecessary to mention specific kinds of accommodations. Nevertheless, the use of a service animal, job coach, or personal assistant on the job would certainly be considered types of mitigating measures, as would the use of any device that could be considered assistive technology, and whether individuals who use these measures have disabilities would be determined without reference to their ameliorative effects. See 2008 House Judiciary Committee Report at 20; 2008 House Educ. & Labor Rep. at 15. Similarly, adaptive strategies that might mitigate, or even allow an individual to otherwise avoid performing particular major life activities, are mitigating measures and also would not be considered in determining whether an impairment is substantially limiting. Id. The determination of whether or not an individual's impairment substantially limits a major life activity is unaffected by whether the individual chooses to forgo mitigating measures. For individuals who do not use a mitigating measure (including for example medication or reasonable accommodation that could alleviate the effects of an impairment), the availability of such measures has no bearing on whether the impairment substantially limits a major life activity. The limitations posed by the impairment on the individual and any negative (non-ameliorative) effects of mitigating measures used determine whether an impairment is substantially limiting. The origin of the impairment, whether its effects can be mitigated, and any ameliorative effects of mitigating measures in fact used may not be considered in determining if the impairment is substantially limiting. However, the use or non-use of mitigating measures, and any consequences thereof, including any ameliorative and non-ameliorative effects, may be relevant in determining whether the individual is qualified or poses a direct threat to safety. The ADA Amendments Act and the regulations state that "ordinary eyeglasses or contact lenses" *shall* be considered in determining whether someone has a disability. This is an exception to the rule that the ameliorative effects of mitigating measures are not to be taken into account. "The rationale behind this exclusion is that the use of ordinary eyeglasses or contact lenses, without more, is not significant enough to warrant protection under the ADA." Joint Hoyer–Sensenbrenner Statement at 2. Nevertheless, as discussed in greater detail below at § 1630.10(b), if an applicant or employee is faced with a qualification standard that requires uncorrected vision (as the plaintiffs in the *Sutton* case were), and the applicant or employee who is adversely affected by the standard brings a challenge under the ADA, an employer will be required to demonstrate that the qualification standard is job related and consistent with business necessity. 2008 Senate Statement of Managers at 9.

The ADAAA and the EEOC's regulations both define the term "ordinary eyeglasses or contact lenses" as lenses that are "intended to fully correct visual acuity or eliminate refractive error." So, if an individual with severe myopia uses eyeglasses or contact lenses that are intended to fully correct visual acuity or eliminate refractive error, they are ordinary eyeglasses or contact lenses, and therefore any inquiry into whether such individual is substantially limited in seeing or reading would be based on how the individual sees or reads with the benefit of the eyeglasses or contact lenses. Likewise, if the only visual loss an individual experiences affects the ability to see well enough to read, and the individual's ordinary reading glasses are intended to completely correct for this visual loss, the ameliorative effects of using the reading glasses must be considered in determining whether the individual is substantially limited in seeing. Additionally, eyeglasses or contact lenses that are the wrong prescription or an outdated prescription may nevertheless be "ordinary" eyeglasses or contact lenses, if a proper prescription would fully correct visual acuity or eliminate refractive error. Both the statute and the regulations distinguish "ordinary eyeglasses or contact lenses" from "low vision devices," which function by magnifying, enhancing, or otherwise augmenting a visual image, and which are not considered when determining whether someone has a disability. The regulations do not establish a specific level of visual acuity (e.g., 20/20) as the basis for determining whether eyeglasses or contact lenses should be considered "ordinary" eyeglasses or contact lenses. Whether lenses fully correct visual acuity or eliminate refractive error is best determined on a case-by-case basis, in light of current and objective medical evidence. Moreover, someone who uses ordinary eyeglasses or contact lenses is not automatically considered to be outside the ADA's protection. Such an individual may demonstrate that, even with the use of ordinary eyeglasses or contact lenses, his vision is still substantially limited when compared to most people.

§ 1630.2(j)(1)(vii) Impairments That Are Episodic or in Remission

Section 1630.2(j)(1)(vii) states: "An impairment that is episodic or in remission is a disability if it would substantially limit a major life activity when active." An impairment that is episodic or in remission is a disability if it would substantially limit a major life activity in its active state. "This provision is intended to reject the reasoning of court decisions concluding that certain individuals with certain conditions—such as epilepsy or post traumatic stress disorder—were not protected by the ADA because their conditions were episodic or intermittent." Joint Hoyer–Sensenbrenner Statement at 2–3. The legislative history provides: "This * * * rule of construction thus rejects the reasoning of the courts in cases like *Todd* v. *Academy Corp.* [57 F. Supp. 2d 448, 453 (S.D. Tex. 1999)] where the court found that the plaintiff's epilepsy, which resulted in short seizures during which the plaintiff was unable to speak and experienced tremors, was not sufficiently limiting, at least in part because those seizures occurred episodically. It similarly rejects the results reached in cases [such as *Pimental* v. *Dartmouth-Hitchock Clinic*, 236 F. Supp. 2d 177, 182–83 (D.N.H. 2002)] where the courts have discounted the impact of an impairment [such as cancer] that may be in remission as too short-lived to be substantially limiting. It is thus expected that individuals with impairments that are episodic or in remission (e.g., epilepsy, multiple sclerosis, cancer) will be able to establish coverage if, when active, the impairment or the manner in which it manifests (e.g., seizures) substantially limits a major life activity." 2008 House Judiciary Committee Report at 19–20. Other examples of impairments that may be episodic include, but are not limited to, hypertension, diabetes, asthma, major depressive disorder, bipolar disorder, and schizophrenia. See 2008 House Judiciary Committee Report at 19–20. The fact that the periods during which an episodic impairment is active and substantially limits a major life activity may be brief or occur infrequently is no longer relevant to determining whether the impairment substantially limits a major life activity. For example, a person with posttraumatic stress disorder who experiences intermittent flashbacks to traumatic events is substantially limited in brain function and thinking.

§ 1630.2(j)(1)(viii) Substantial Limitation in Only One Major Life Activity Required

Section 1630.2(j)(1)(viii) states: "An impairment that substantially limits one major life activity need not substantially limit other major life activities in order to be considered a substantially limiting impairment."

The ADAAA explicitly states that an impairment need only substantially limit one major life activity to be considered a disability under the ADA. See ADAAA Section 4(a); 42 U.S.C. 12102(4)(C). "This responds to and corrects those courts that have required individuals to show that an impairment substantially limits more than one life activity.'' 2008 Senate Statement of Managers at 8. In addition, this rule of construction is ''intended to clarify that the ability to perform one or more particular tasks within a broad category of activities does not preclude coverage under the ADA.'' Id. To the extent cases pre-dating the applicability of the 2008 Amendments Act reasoned otherwise, they are contrary to the law as amended. Id. (citing *Holt* v. *Grand Lake Mental Health Ctr., Inc.,* 443 F. 3d 762 (10th Cir. 2006) (holding an individual with cerebral palsy who could not independently perform certain specified manual tasks was not substantially limited in her ability to perform a ''broad range'' of manual tasks)); See also 2008 House Judiciary Committee Report at 19 & n.52 (this legislatively corrects court decisions that, with regard to the major life activity of performing manual tasks, ''have offset substantial limitation in the performance of some tasks with the ability to perform others'' (citing *Holt*)). For example, an individual with diabetes is substantially limited in endocrine function and thus an individual with a disability under the first prong of the definition. He need not also show that he is substantially limited in eating to qualify for coverage under the first prong. An individual whose normal cell growth is substantially limited due to lung cancer need not also show that she is substantially limited in breathing or respiratory function. And an individual with HIV infection is substantially limited in the function of the immune system, and therefore is an individual with a disability without regard to whether his or her HIV infection substantially limits him or her in reproduction. In addition, an individual whose impairment substantially limits a major life activity need not additionally demonstrate a resulting limitation in the ability to perform activities of central importance to daily life in order to be considered an individual with a disability under § 1630.2(g)(1)(i) or § 1630.2(g)(1)(ii), as cases relying on the Supreme Court's decision in *Toyota Motor Mfg., Ky., Inc.* v. *Williams,* 534 U.S. 184 (2002), had held prior to the ADA Amendments Act. Thus, for example, someone with an impairment resulting in a 20–pound lifting restriction that lasts or is expected to last for several months is substantially limited in the major life activity of lifting, and need not also show that he is unable to perform activities of daily living that require lifting in order to be considered substantially limited in lifting. Similarly, someone with monocular vision whose depth perception or field of vision would be substantially limited, with or without any compensatory strategies the individual may have developed, need not also show that he is unable to perform activities of central importance to daily life that require seeing in order to be substantially limited in seeing.

§ 1630.2(j)(1)(ix)   Effects of an Impairment Lasting Fewer Than Six Months Can Be Substantially Limiting

Section 1630.2(j)(1)(ix) states: ''The six-month 'transitory' part of the 'transitory and minor' exception to 'regarded as' coverage in

§ 1630.2(*l*) does not apply to the definition of 'disability' under § 1630.2(g)(1)(i) or § 1630.2(g)(1)(ii). The effects of an impairment lasting or expected to last fewer than six months can be substantially limiting within the meaning of this section." The regulations include a clear statement that the definition of an impairment as transitory, that is, "lasting or expected to last for six months or less," only applies to the "regarded as" (third) prong of the definition of "disability" as part of the "transitory and minor" defense to "regarded as" coverage. It does not apply to the first or second prong of the definition of disability. See Joint Hoyer–Sensenbrenner Statement at 3 ("[T]here is no need for the transitory and minor exception under the first two prongs because it is clear from the statute and the legislative history that a person can only bring a claim if the impairment substantially limits one or more major life activities or the individual has a record of an impairment that substantially limits one or more major life activities."). Therefore, an impairment does not have to last for more than six months in order to be considered substantially limiting under the first or the second prong of the definition of disability. For example, as noted above, if an individual has a back impairment that results in a 20–pound lifting restriction that lasts for several months, he is substantially limited in the major life activity of lifting, and therefore covered under the first prong of the definition of disability. At the same time, "[t]he duration of an impairment is one factor that is relevant in determining whether the impairment substantially limits a major life activity. Impairments that last only for a short period of time are typically not covered, although they may be covered if sufficiently severe." Joint Hoyer–Sensenbrenner Statement at 5. Section 1630.2(j)(3) Predictable Assessments. As the regulations point out, disability is determined based on an individualized assessment. There is no "per se" disability. However, as recognized in the regulations, the individualized assessment of some kinds of impairments will virtually always result in a determination of disability. The inherent nature of these types of medical conditions will in virtually all cases give rise to a substantial limitation of a major life activity. Cf. *Heiko* v. *Columbo Savings Bank, F.S.B.,* 434 F.3d 249, 256 (4th Cir. 2006) (stating, even pre-ADAAA, that "certain impairments are by their very nature substantially limiting: the major life activity of seeing, for example, is always substantially limited by blindness"). Therefore, with respect to these types of impairments, the necessary individualized assessment should be particularly simple and straightforward.

This result is the consequence of the combined effect of the statutory changes to the definition of disability contained in the Amendments Act and flows from application of the rules of construction set forth in §§ 1630.2(j)(1)(i)–(ix) (including the lower standard for "substantially limits"; the rule that major life activities include major bodily functions; the principle that impairments that are episodic or in remission are disabilities if they would be substantially limiting when active; and the requirement that the ameliorative effects of mitigating measures (other than ordinary eyeglasses or contact lenses) must be disregarded in assessing whether an individual has a disability). The regulations at § 1630.2(j)(3)(iii) provide examples of the types of impairments that should easily be found to substantially limit a major life activity. The legislative history states that Congress modeled the ADA definition of disability on the definition contained in the Rehabilitation Act, and said it wished to return courts to the way they had construed that definition. See 2008 House Judiciary Committee Report at 6. Describing this goal, the legislative history states that courts had interpreted the Rehabilitation Act definition "broadly to include persons with a wide range of physical and mental impairments such as epilepsy, diabetes, multiple sclerosis, and intellectual and developmental disabilities * * * even where a mitigating measure—like medication or a hearing aid—might lessen their impact on the individual." Id.; See also id. at 9 (referring to individuals with disabilities that had been covered under the Rehabilitation Act and that Congress intended to include under the ADA—"people with serious health conditions like epilepsy, diabetes, cancer, cerebral palsy, multiple sclerosis, intellectual and developmental disabilities"); id. at n.6 (citing cases also finding that cerebral palsy, hearing impairments, mental retardation, heart disease, and vision in only one eye were disabilities under the Rehabilitation Act); id. at 10 (citing testimony from Rep. Steny H. Hoyer, one of the original lead sponsors of the ADA in 1990, stating that "we could not have fathomed that people with diabetes, epilepsy, heart conditions, cancer, mental illnesses and other disabilities would have their ADA claims denied because they would be considered too functional to meet the definition of disability"); 2008 Senate Statement of Managers at 3 (explaining that "we [we]re faced with a situation in which physical or mental impairments that would previously [under the Rehabilitation Act] have been found to constitute disabilities [we]re not considered disabilities" and citing individuals with impairments such as amputation, intellectual disabilities, epilepsy, multiple sclerosis, diabetes, muscular dystrophy, and cancer as examples). Of course, the impairments listed in subparagraph 1630.2(j)(3)(iii) may substantially limit a variety of other major life activities in addition to those listed in the regulation. For example, mobility impairments requiring the use of a wheelchair substantially limit the major life activity of walking. Diabetes may substantially limit major life activities such as eating, sleeping, and thinking. Major depressive disorder may substantially limit major life activities such as thinking, concentrating, sleeping, and interacting with others. Multiple sclerosis may substantially limit major life activities such as walking, bending, and lifting. By using the term "brain function" to describe the system affected by various mental impairments, the Commission is expressing no view on the debate concerning whether mental illnesses are caused by environmental or biological factors, but rather intends the term to capture functions such as the ability of the brain to regulate thought processes and emotions.

§ 1630.2(j)(4) Condition, Manner, or Duration

The regulations provide that facts such as the "condition, manner, or duration" of an individual's performance of a major life activity may be useful in determining whether an impairment results in a substantial limitation. In the legislative history of the ADAAA, Congress reiterated what it had said at the time of the original ADA: "A person is considered an individual with a disability for purposes of the first prong of the definition when [one or more of] the individual's important life activities are restricted as to the conditions, manner, or duration under which they can be performed in comparison to most people." 2008 Senate Statement of Managers at 7 (citing 1989 Senate Report at 23). According to Congress: "We particularly believe that this test, which articulated an analysis that considered whether a person's activities are limited in condition, duration and manner, is a useful one. We reiterate that using the correct standard—one that is lower than the strict or demanding standard created by the Supreme Court in *Toyota*—will make the disability determination an appropriate threshold issue but not an onerous burden for those seeking accommodations * * *. At the same time, plaintiffs should not be constrained from offering evidence needed to establish that their impairment is substantially limiting." 2008 Senate Statement of Managers at 7.

Consistent with the legislative history, an impairment may substantially limit the "condition" or "manner" under which a major life activity can be performed in a number of ways. For example, the condition or manner under which a major life activity can be performed may refer to the way an individual performs a major life activity. Thus, the condition or manner under which a person with an amputated hand performs manual tasks will likely be more cumbersome than the way that someone with two hands would perform the same tasks. Condition or manner may also describe how performance of a major life activity affects the individual with an impairment. For example, an individual whose impairment causes pain or fatigue that most people would not experience when performing that major life activity may be substantially limited. Thus, the condition or manner under which someone with coronary artery disease performs the major life activity of walking would be substantially limiting if the individual experiences shortness of breath and fatigue when walking distances that most people could walk without experiencing such effects. Similarly, condition or manner may refer to the extent to which a major life activity, including a major bodily function, can be performed. For example, the condition or manner under which a major bodily function can be performed may be substantially limited when the impairment "causes the operation [of the bodily function] to over-produce or under-produce in some harmful fashion." See 2008 House Judiciary Committee Report at 17. "Duration" refers to the length of time an individual can perform a major life activity or the length of time it takes an individual to perform a major life activity, as compared to most people in the general population. For example, a person whose back or leg impairment precludes him or her from standing for more than two hours without significant pain would be substantially limited in standing, since most people can stand for more than two hours without significant pain. However, a person who can walk for ten miles continuously is not substantially limited in walking merely because on the eleventh mile, he or she begins to experience pain because most people would not be able to walk eleven miles without experiencing some discomfort. See 2008 Senate Statement of Managers at 7 (citing 1989 Senate Report at 23). The regulations provide that in assessing substantial limitation and considering facts such as condition, manner, or duration, the non-ameliorative effects of mitigating measures may be considered. Such "non-ameliorative effects" could include negative side effects of medicine, burdens associated with following a particular treatment regimen, and complications that arise from surgery, among others. Of course, in many instances, it will not be necessary to assess the negative impact of a mitigating measure in determining that a particular impairment substantially limits a major life activity. For example, someone with end-stage renal disease is substantially limited in kidney function, and it thus is not necessary to consider the burdens that dialysis treatment imposes.

Condition, manner, or duration may also suggest the amount of time or effort an individual has to expend when performing a major life activity because of the effects of an impairment, even if the individual is able to achieve the same or similar result as someone without the impairment. For this reason, the regulations include language which says that the outcome an individual with a disability is able to achieve is not determinative of whether he or she is substantially limited in a major life activity. Thus, someone with a learning disability may achieve a high level of academic success, but may nevertheless be substantially limited in the major life activity of learning because of the additional time or effort he or she must spend to read, write, or learn compared to most people in the general population. As Congress emphasized in passing the Amendments Act, "[w]hen considering the condition, manner, or duration in which an individual with a specific learning disability performs a major life activity, it is critical to reject the assumption that an individual who has performed well academically cannot be substantially limited in activities such as learning, reading, writing, thinking, or speaking." 2008 Senate Statement of Managers at 8. Congress noted that: "In particular, some courts have found that students who have reached a high level of academic achievement are not to be considered individuals with disabilities under the ADA, as such individuals may have difficulty demonstrating substantial limitation in the major life activities of learning or reading relative to 'most people.' When considering the condition, manner or duration in which an individual with a specific learning disability performs a major life activity, it is critical to reject the assumption that an individual who performs well academically or otherwise cannot be substantially limited in activities such as learning, reading, writing, thinking, or speaking. As such, the Committee rejects the findings in *Price* v. *National Board of Medical Examiners, Gonzales* v. *National Board of Medical Examiners,* and *Wong* v. *Regents of University of California.* The Committee believes that the comparison of individuals with specific learning disabilities to 'most people' is not problematic unto itself, but requires a careful analysis of the method and manner in which an individual's impairment limits a major life activity. For the majority of the population, the basic mechanics of reading and writing do not pose extraordinary lifelong challenges; rather, recognizing and forming letters and words are effortless, unconscious, automatic processes. Because specific learning disabilities are neurologically-based impairments, the process of reading for an individual with a reading disability (e.g. dyslexia) is word-by-word, and otherwise cumbersome, painful, deliberate and slow—throughout life. The Committee expects that individuals with specific learning disabilities that substantially limit a major life activity will be better protected under the amended Act." 2008 House Educ. & Labor Rep. at 10–11.

* * * Finally, "condition, manner, or duration" are not intended to be used as a rigid three-part standard that must be met to establish a substantial limitation. "Condition, manner, or duration" are not required "factors" that must be considered as a talismanic test. Rather, in referring to "condition, manner, *or* duration," the regulations make clear that these are merely the types of facts that may be considered in appropriate cases. To the extent such aspects of limitation may be useful or relevant to show a substantial limitation in a particular fact pattern, some or all of them (and related facts) may be considered, but evidence relating to each of these facts may not be necessary to establish coverage. At the same time, individuals seeking coverage under the first or second prong of the definition of disability should not be constrained from offering evidence needed to establish that their impairment is substantially limiting. See 2008 Senate Statement of Managers at 7. Of course, covered entities may defeat a showing of "substantial limitation" by refuting whatever evidence the individual seeking coverage has offered, or by offering evidence that shows an impairment does not impose a substantial limitation on a major life activity. However, a showing of substantial limitation is not defeated by facts related to "condition, manner, or duration" that are not pertinent to the substantial limitation the individual has proffered.

§§ 1630.2(j)(5) and (6)   Examples of Mitigating Measures; Ordinary Eyeglasses or Contact Lenses

These provisions of the regulations provide numerous examples of mitigating measures and the definition of "ordinary eyeglasses or contact lenses." These definitions have been more fully discussed in the portions of this interpretive guidance concerning the rules of construction in § 1630.2(j)(1). Substantially Limited in Working. The Commission has removed from the text of the regulations a discussion of the major life activity of working. This is consistent with the fact that no other major life activity receives special attention in the regulation, and with the fact that, in light of the expanded definition of disability established by the Amendments Act, this major life activity will be used in only very targeted situations. In most instances, an individual with a disability will be able to establish coverage by showing substantial limitation of a major life activity other than working; impairments that substantially limit a person's ability to work usually substantially limit one or more other major life activities. This will be particularly true in light of the changes made by the ADA Amendments Act. See, e.g., *Corley* v. *Dep't of Veterans Affairs ex rel Principi,* 218 F. App'x. 727, 738 (10th Cir. 2007) (employee with seizure disorder was not substantially limited in working because he was not foreclosed from jobs involving driving, operating machinery, childcare, military service, and other jobs; employee would now be substantially limited in neurological function); *Olds* v. *United Parcel Serv., Inc.,* 127 F. App'x. 779, 782 (6th Cir. 2005) (employee with bone marrow cancer was not substantially limited in working due to lifting restrictions caused by his cancer; employee would now be substantially limited in normal cell growth); *Williams* v. *Philadelphia Hous. Auth. Police Dep't,* 380 F.3d 751, 763–64 (3d Cir. 2004) (issue of material fact concerning whether police officer's major depression substantially limited him in performing a class of jobs due to restrictions on his ability to carry a firearm; officer would now be substantially limited in brain function).[2]

Demonstrating a substantial limitation in performing the unique aspects of a single specific job is not sufficient to establish that a person is substantially limited in the major life activity of working. A class of jobs may be determined by reference to the nature of the work that an individual is limited in performing (such as commercial truck driving, assembly line jobs, food service jobs, clerical jobs, or law enforcement

---

2. In addition, many cases previously analyzed in terms of whether the plaintiff was "substantially limited in working" will now be analyzed under the "regarded as" prong of the definition of disability as revised by the Amendments Act. See, e.g., *Cannon* v. *Levi Strauss & Co.,* 29 F. App'x. 331 (6th Cir. 2002) (factory worker laid off due to her carpal tunnel syndrome not regarded as substantially limited in working because her job of sewing machine operator was not a "broad class of jobs"; she would now be protected under the third prong because she was fired because of her impairment, carpal tunnel syndrome); *Bridges* v. *City of Bossier,* 92 F.3d 329 (5th Cir. 1996) (applicant not hired for firefighting job because of his mild hemophilia not regarded as substantially limited in working; applicant would now be protected under the third prong because he was not hired because of his impairment, hemophilia).

In the rare cases where an individual has a need to demonstrate that an impairment substantially limits him or her in working, the individual can do so by showing that the impairment substantially limits his or her ability to perform a class of jobs or broad range of jobs in various classes as compared to most people having comparable training, skills, and abilities. In keeping with the findings and purposes of the Amendments Act, the determination of coverage under the law should not require extensive and elaborate assessment, and the EEOC and the courts are to apply a lower standard in determining when an impairment substantially limits a major life activity, including the major life activity of working, than they applied prior to the Amendments Act. The Commission believes that the courts, in applying an overly strict standard with regard to "substantially limits" generally, have reached conclusions with regard to what is necessary to demonstrate a substantial limitation in the major life activity of working that would be inconsistent with the changes now made by the Amendments Act. Accordingly, as used in this section the terms "class of jobs" and "broad range of jobs in various classes" will be applied in a more straightforward and simple manner than they were applied by the courts prior to the Amendments Act. * * *

jobs) or by reference to job-related requirements that an individual is limited in meeting (for example, jobs requiring repetitive bending, reaching, or manual tasks, jobs requiring repetitive or heavy lifting, prolonged sitting or standing, extensive walking, driving, or working under conditions such as high temperatures or noise levels). For example, if a person whose job requires heavy lifting develops a disability that prevents him or her from lifting more than fifty pounds and, consequently, from performing not only his or her existing job but also other jobs that would similarly require heavy lifting, that person would be substantially limited in working because he or she is substantially limited in performing the class of jobs that require heavy lifting.

§ 1630.2(k)   Record of a Substantially Limiting Impairment

The second prong of the definition of "disability" provides that an individual with a record of an impairment that substantially limits or limited a major life activity is an individual with a disability. The intent of this provision, in part, is to ensure that people are not discriminated against because of a history of disability. For example, the "record of" provision would protect an individual who was treated for cancer ten years ago but who is now deemed by a doctor to be free of cancer, from discrimination based on that prior medical history. This provision also ensures that individuals are not discriminated against because they have been misclassified as disabled. For example, individuals misclassified as having learning disabilities or intellectual disabilities (formerly termed "mental retardation") are protected from discrimination on the basis of that erroneous classification. Senate Report at 23; House Labor Report at 52–53; House Judiciary Report at 29; 2008 House Judiciary Report at 7–8 & n.14. Similarly, an employee who in the past was misdiagnosed with bipolar disorder and hospitalized as the result of a temporary reaction to medication she was taking has a record of a substantially limiting impairment, even though she did not actually have bipolar disorder.

This part of the definition is satisfied where evidence establishes that an individual has had a substantially limiting impairment. The impairment indicated in the record must be an impairment that would substantially limit one or more of the individual's major life activities. There are many types of records that could potentially contain this information, including but not limited to, education, medical, or employment records.Such evidence that an individual has a past history of an impairment that substantially limited a major life activity is all that is necessary to establish coverage under the second prong. An individual may have a "record of" a substantially limiting impairment—and thus be protected under the "record of" prong of the statute—even if a covered entity does not specifically know about the relevant record. Of course, for the covered entity to be liable for discrimination under title I of the ADA, the individual with a "record of" a substantially limiting impairment must prove that the covered entity discriminated on the basis of the record of the disability. The terms "substantially limits" and "major life activity" under the second prong of the definition of "disability" are to be construed in accordance with the same principles applicable under the "actual disability" prong, as set forth in § 1630.2(j). Individuals who are covered under the "record of" prong will often be covered under the first prong of the definition of disability as well. This is a consequence of the rule of construction in the ADAAA and the regulations providing that an individual with an impairment that is episodic or in remission can be protected under the first prong if the impairment would be substantially limiting when active. See 42 U.S.C. 12102(4)(D); § 1630.2(j)(1)(vii). Thus, an individual who has cancer that is currently in remission is an individual with a disability under the "actual disability" prong because he has an impairment that would substantially limit normal cell growth when active. He is also covered by the "record of" prong based on his history of having had an impairment that substantially limited normal cell growth. Finally, this section of the EEOC's regulations makes it clear that an individual with a record of a disability is entitled to a reasonable accommodation currently needed for limitations resulting from or relating to the past substantially limiting impairment. This conclusion, which has been the Commission's long-standing position, is confirmed by language in the ADA Amendments Act stating that individuals covered only under the "regarded as" prong of the definition of disability are not entitled to reasonable accommodation. See 42 U.S.C. 12201(h). By implication, this means that individuals covered under the first or second prongs are otherwise eligible for reasonable accommodations. See 2008 House Judiciary Committee Report at 22 ("This makes clear that the duty to accommodate . . . arises only when an individual establishes coverage under the first or second prong of the definition."). Thus, as the regulations explain, an employee with an impairment that previously substantially limited but no longer substantially limits, a major life activity may need leave or a schedule change to permit him or her to attend follow-up or "monitoring" appointments from a health care provider.

§ 1630.2(*l*) Regarded as Substantially Limited in a Major Life Activity

Coverage under the "regarded as" prong of the definition of disability should not be difficult to establish. See 2008 House Judiciary Committee Report at 17 (explaining that Congress never expected or intended it would be a difficult standard to meet). Under the third prong of the definition of disability, an individual is "regarded as having such an impairment" if the individual is subjected to an action prohibited by the ADA because of an actual or perceived impairment that is not "transitory and minor." This third prong of the definition of disability was originally intended to express Congress's understanding that "unfounded concerns, mistaken beliefs, fears, myths, or prejudice about disabilities are often just as disabling as actual impairments, and [its] corresponding desire to prohibit discrimination founded on such perceptions."

2008 Senate Statement of Managers at 9; 2008 House Judiciary Committee Report at 17 (same). In passing the original ADA, Congress relied extensively on the reasoning of *School Board of Nassau County* v. *Arline* [480 U.S. at 282–83] "that the negative reactions of others are just as disabling as the actual impact of an impairment." 2008 Senate Statement of Managers at 9. The ADAAA reiterates Congress's reliance on the broad views enunciated in that decision, and Congress "believe[s] that courts should continue to rely on this standard." Id.

Accordingly, the ADA Amendments Act broadened the application of the "regarded as" prong of the definition of disability. 2008 Senate Statement of Managers at 9–10. In doing so, Congress rejected court decisions that had required an individual to establish that a covered entity perceived him or her to have an impairment that substantially limited a major life activity. This provision is designed to restore Congress's intent to allow individuals to establish coverage under the "regarded as" prong by showing that they were treated adversely because of an impairment, without having to establish the covered entity's beliefs concerning the severity of the impairment. Joint Hoyer–Sensenbrenner Statement at 3.

Thus it is not necessary, as it was prior to the ADA Amendments Act, for an individual to demonstrate that a covered entity perceived him as substantially limited in the ability to perform a major life activity in order for the individual to establish that he or she is covered under the "regarded as" prong. Nor is it necessary to demonstrate that the impairment relied on by a covered entity is (in the case of an actual impairment) or would be (in the case of a perceived impairment) substantially limiting for an individual to be "regarded as having such an impairment." In short, to qualify for coverage under the "regarded as" prong, an individual is not subject to any functional test. See 2008 Senate Statement of Managers at 13 ("The functional limitation imposed by an impairment is irrelevant to the third 'regarded as' prong."); 2008 House Judiciary Committee Report at 17 (that is, "the individual is not required to show that the perceived impairment limits performance of a major life activity"). The concepts of "major life activities" and "substantial limitation" simply are not relevant in evaluating whether an individual is "regarded as having such an impairment." To illustrate how straightforward application of the "regarded as" prong is, if an employer refused to hire an applicant because of skin graft scars, the employer has regarded the applicant as an individual with a disability. Similarly, if an employer terminates an employee because he has cancer, the employer has regarded the employee as an individual with a disability. A "prohibited action" under the "regarded as" prong refers to an action of the type that would be unlawful under the ADA (but for any defenses to liability). Such prohibited actions include, but are not limited to, refusal to hire, demotion, placement on involuntary leave, termination, exclusion for failure to meet a qualification standard, harassment, or denial of any other term, condition, or privilege of employment.

Where an employer bases a prohibited employment action on an actual or perceived impairment that is not "transitory and minor," the employer regards the individual as disabled, whether or not myths, fears, or stereotypes about disability motivated the employer's decision. Establishing that an individual is "regarded as having such an impairment" does not, by itself, establish liability. Liability is established only if an individual meets the burden of proving that the covered entity discriminated unlawfully within the meaning of section 102 of the ADA, 42 U.S.C. 12112.

Whether a covered entity can ultimately establish a defense to liability is an inquiry separate from, and follows after, a determination that an individual was regarded as having a disability. Thus, for example, an employer who terminates an employee with angina from a manufacturing job that requires the employee to work around machinery, believing that the employee will pose a safety risk to himself or others if he were suddenly to lose consciousness, has regarded the individual as disabled. Whether the employer has a defense (e.g., that the employee posed a direct threat to himself or coworkers) is a separate inquiry. The fact that the "regarded as" prong requires proof of causation in order to show that a person is covered does not mean that proving a "regarded as" claim is complex. While a person must show, for both coverage under the "regarded as" prong and for ultimate liability, that he or she was subjected to a prohibited action because of an actual or perceived impairment, this showing need only be made once. Thus, evidence that a covered entity took a prohibited action because of an impairment will establish coverage and will be relevant in establishing liability, although liability may ultimately turn on whether the covered entity can establish a defense. As prescribed in the ADA Amendments Act, the regulations provide an exception to coverage under the "regarded as" prong where the impairment on which a prohibited action is based is both transitory (having an actual or expected duration of six months or less) and minor. The regulations make clear (at § 1630.2(l)(2) and § 1630.15(f)) that this exception is a defense to a claim of discrimination. "Providing this exception responds to concerns raised by employer organizations and is reasonable under the 'regarded as' prong of the definition because individuals seeking coverage under this prong need not meet the functional limitation requirement contained in the first two prongs of the definition." 2008 Senate Statement of Managers at 10; See also 2008 House Judiciary Committee Report at 18 (explaining that "absent this exception, the third prong of the definition would have covered individuals who are regarded as having common ailments like the cold or flu, and this exception responds to concerns raised by members of the business community regarding potential abuse of this provision and misapplication of resources on individuals with minor ailments that last only a short period of time"). However, as an exception to the general rule for broad coverage under the "regarded as" prong, this limitation on coverage should be construed narrowly. 2008 House Judiciary Committee Report at 18.

The relevant inquiry is whether the actual or perceived impairment on which the employer's action was based is objectively "transitory and minor," not whether the employer claims it subjectively believed the impairment was transitory and minor. For example, an employer who terminates an employee whom it believes has bipolar disorder cannot take advantage of this exception by asserting that it believed the employee's impairment was transitory and minor, since bipolar disorder is not objectively "transitory and minor." At the same time, an employer that terminated an employee with an objectively transitory and minor hand wound, mistakenly believing it to be symptomatic of HIV infection, will nevertheless have "regarded" the employee as an individual with a disability, since the covered entity took a prohibited employment action based on a perceived impairment (HIV infection) that is not "transitory and minor." An individual covered only under the "regarded as" prong is not entitled to reasonable accommodation. 42 U.S.C. 12201(h). Thus, in cases where reasonable accommodation is not at issue, the third prong provides a more straightforward framework for analyzing whether discrimination occurred. As Congress observed in enacting the ADAAA: "[W]e expect [the first] prong of the definition to be used only by people who are affirmatively seeking reasonable accommodations or modifications. Any individual who has been discriminated against because of an impairment—short of being granted a reasonable accommodation or modification—should be bringing a claim under the third prong of the definition which will require no showing with regard to the severity of his or her impairment." Joint Hoyer–Sensenbrenner Statement at 6.

§ 1630.2(m)   Qualified Individual

The ADA prohibits discrimination on the basis of disability against a qualified individual. The determination of whether an individual with a disability is "qualified" should be made in two steps. The first step is to determine if the individual satisfies the prerequisites for the position, such as possessing the appropriate educational background, employment experience, skills, licenses, etc. For example, the first step in determining whether an accountant who is paraplegic is qualified for a certified public accountant (CPA) position is to examine the individual's credentials to determine whether the individual is a licensed CPA. This is sometimes referred to in the Rehabilitation Act caselaw as determining whether the individual is "otherwise qualified" for the position. See Senate Report at 33; House Labor Report at 64–65. (See § 1630.9 Not Making Reasonable Accommodation). The second step is to determine whether or not the individual can perform the essential functions of the position held or desired, with or without reasonable accommodation. The purpose of this second step is to ensure that individuals with disabilities who can perform the essential functions of the position held or desired are not denied employment opportunities because they are not able to perform marginal functions of the position. House Labor Report at 55. The determination of whether an individual with a disability is qualified is to be made at the time of the employment decision. This determination should be based on the capabilities of the individual with a disability at the time of the employment decision, and should not be based on speculation that the employee may become unable in the future or may cause increased health insurance premiums or workers compensation costs

§ 1630.2(n)   Essential Functions

The determination of which functions are essential may be critical to the determination of whether or not the individual with a disability is qualified. The essential functions are those functions that the individual who holds the position must be able to perform unaided or with the assistance of a reasonable accommodation. The inquiry into whether a particular function is essential initially focuses on whether the employer actually requires employees in the position to perform the functions that the employer asserts are essential. For example, an employer may state that typing is an essential function of a position. If, in fact, the employer has never required any employee in that particular position to type, this will be evidence that typing is not actually an essential function of the position. If the individual who holds the position is actually required to perform the function the employer asserts is an essential function, the inquiry will then center around whether removing the function would fundamentally alter that position. This determination of whether or not a particular function is essential will generally include one or more of the following factors listed in part 1630. The first factor is whether the position exists to perform a particular function. For example, an individual may be hired to proofread documents. The ability to proofread the documents would then be an essential function, since this is the only reason the position exists. The second factor in determining whether a function is essential is the number of other employees available to perform that job function or among whom the performance of that job function can be distributed. This may be a factor either because the total number of available employees is low, or because of the fluctuating demands of the business operation. For example, if an employer has a relatively small number of available employees for the volume of work to be performed, it may be necessary that each employee perform a multitude of different functions. Therefore, the performance of those functions by each employee becomes more critical and the options for reorganizing the work become more limited. In such a situation, functions that might not be essential if there were a larger staff may become essential because the staff size is small compared to the volume of work that has to be done. See *Treadwell* v. *Alexander,* 707 F.2d 473 (11th Cir. 1983).

A similar situation might occur in a larger work force if the workflow follows a cycle of heavy demand for labor intensive work followed by low demand periods. This type of workflow might also make the performance of each function during the peak periods more critical and might limit the employer's flexibility in reorganizing operating procedures. See *Dexler* v. *Tisch,* 660 F. Supp. 1418 (D. Conn. 1987). The third factor is the degree of expertise or skill required to perform the function. In certain professions and highly skilled positions the employee is hired for his or her expertise or ability to perform the particular function. In such a situation, the performance of that specialized task would be an essential function. Whether a particular function is essential is a factual determination that must be made on a case by case basis. In determining whether or not a particular function is essential, all relevant evidence should be considered. Part 1630 lists various types of evidence, such as an established job description, that should be considered in determining whether a particular function is essential. Since the list is not exhaustive, other relevant evidence may also be presented. Greater weight will not be granted to the types of evidence included on the list than to the types of evidence not listed. Although part 1630 does not require employers to develop or maintain job descriptions, written job descriptions prepared before advertising or interviewing applicants for the job, as well as the employer's judgment as to what functions are essential are among the relevant evidence to be considered in determining whether a particular function is essential. The terms of a collective bargaining agreement are also relevant to the determination of whether a particular function is essential. The work experience of past employees in the job or of current employees in similar jobs is likewise relevant to the determination of whether a particular function is essential. See H.R. Conf. Rep. No. 101–596, 101st Cong., 2d Sess. 58 (1990) [hereinafter Conference Report]; House Judiciary Report at 33–34. See also *Hall* v. *U.S. Postal Service,* 857 F.2d 1073 (6th Cir. 1988). The time spent performing the particular function may also be an indicator of whether that function is essential. For example, if an employee spends the vast majority of his or her time working at a cash register, this would be evidence that operating the cash register is an essential function. The consequences of failing to require the employee to perform the function may be another indicator of whether a particular function is essential. For example, although a firefighter may not regularly have to carry an unconscious adult out of a burning building, the consequence of failing to require the firefighter to be able to perform this function would be serious. It is important to note that the inquiry into essential functions is not intended to second guess an employer's business judgment with regard to production standards, whether qualitative or quantitative, nor to require employers to lower such standards. (See § 1630.10 Qualification Standards, Tests and Other Selection Criteria). If an employer requires its typists to be able to accurately type 75 words per minute, it will not be called upon to explain why an inaccurate work product, or a typing speed of 65 words per minute, would not be adequate. Similarly, if a hotel requires its service workers to thoroughly clean 16 rooms per day, it will not have to explain why it requires thorough cleaning, or why it chose a 16 room rather than a 10 room requirement. However, if an employer does require accurate 75 word per minute typing or the thorough cleaning of 16 rooms, it will have to show that it actually imposes such requirements on its employees in fact, and not simply on paper. It should also be noted that, if it is alleged that the employer intentionally selected the particular level of production to exclude individuals with disabilities, the employer may have to offer a legitimate, nondiscriminatory reason for its selection.

§ 1630.2(*o*) Reasonable Accommodation

An individual with a disability is considered "qualified" if the individual can perform the essential functions of the position held or desired with or without reasonable accommodation. A covered entity is required, absent undue hardship, to provide reasonable accommodation to an otherwise qualified individual with a substantially limiting impairment or a "record of" such an impairment. However, a covered entity is not required to provide an accommodation to an individual who meets the definition of disability solely under the "regarded as" prong. The legislative history of the ADAAA makes clear that Congress included this provision in response to various court decisions that had held (pre-Amendments Act) that individuals who were covered solely under the "regarded as" prong were eligible for reasonable accommodations. In those cases, the plaintiffs had been found not to be covered under the first prong of the definition of disability "because of the overly stringent manner in which the courts had been interpreting that prong." 2008 Senate Statement of Managers at 11. The legislative history goes on to explain that "[b]ecause of [Congress's] strong belief that accommodating individuals with disabilities is a key goal of the ADA, some members [of Congress] continue to have reservations about this provision." Id. However, Congress ultimately concluded that clarifying that individuals covered solely under the "regarded as" prong are not entitled to reasonable accommodations "is an acceptable compromise given our strong expectation that such individuals would now be covered under the first prong of the definition [of disability], properly applied"). Further, individuals covered only under the third prong still may bring discrimination claims (other than failure-to-accommodate claims) under title I of the ADA. 2008 Senate Statement of Managers at 9–10.

In general, an accommodation is any change in the work environment or in the way things are customarily done that enables an individual with a disability to enjoy equal employment opportunities. There are three categories of reasonable accommodation. These are (1) accommodations that are required to ensure equal opportunity in the application process; (2) accommodations that enable the employer's employees with disabilities to perform the essential functions of the position held or desired; and (3) accommodations that enable the employer's employees with disabilities to enjoy equal benefits and privileges of employment as are enjoyed by employees without disabilities. It should be noted that nothing in this part prohibits employers or other covered entities from providing accommodations beyond those required by this part. It may also be a reasonable accommodation to permit an individual with a disability the opportunity to provide and utilize equipment, aids or services that an employer is not required to provide as a reasonable accommodation. For example, it would be a reasonable accommodation for an employer to permit an individual who is blind to use a guide dog at work, even though the employer would not be required to provide a guide dog for the employee.

The accommodations included on the list of reasonable accommodations are generally self explanatory. However, there are a few that require further explanation. One of these is the accommodation of making existing facilities used by employees readily accessible to, and usable by, individuals with disabilities. This accommodation includes both those areas that must be accessible for the employee to perform essential job functions, as well as non-work areas used by the employer's employees for other purposes. For example, accessible break rooms, lunch rooms, training rooms, restrooms etc., may be required as reasonable accommodations. Another of the potential accommodations listed is "job restructuring." An employer or other covered entity may restructure a job by reallocating or redistributing nonessential, marginal job functions. For example, an employer may have two jobs, each of which entails the performance of a number of marginal functions. The employer hires an individual with a disability who is able to perform some of the marginal functions of each job but not all of the marginal functions of either job. As an accommodation, the employer may redistribute the marginal functions so that all of the marginal functions that the individual with a disability can perform are made a part of the position to be filled by the individual with a disability. The remaining marginal functions that the individual with a disability cannot perform would then be transferred to the other position. See Senate Report at 31; House Labor Report at 62. An employer or other covered entity is not required to reallocate essential functions. The essential functions are by definition those that the individual who holds the job would have to perform, with or without reasonable accommodation, in order to be considered qualified for the position. For example, suppose a security guard position requires the individual who holds the job to inspect identification cards. An employer would not have to provide an individual who is legally blind with an assistant to look at the identification cards for the legally blind employee. In this situation the assistant would be performing the job for the individual with a disability rather than assisting the individual to perform the job. See *Coleman* v. *Darden,* 595 F.2d 533 (10th Cir. 1979). An employer or other covered entity may also restructure a job by altering when and/or how an essential function is performed. For example, an essential function customarily performed in the early morning hours may be rescheduled until later in the day as a reasonable accommodation to a disability that precludes performance of the function at the customary hour. Likewise, as a reasonable accommodation, an employee with a disability that inhibits the ability to write, may be permitted to computerize records that were customarily maintained manually.

Reassignment to a vacant position is also listed as a potential reasonable accommodation. In general, reassignment should be considered only when accommodation within the individual's current position would pose an undue hardship. Reassignment is not available to applicants. An applicant for a position must be qualified for, and be able to perform the essential functions of, the position sought with or without reasonable accommodation.

Reassignment may not be used to limit, segregate, or otherwise discriminate against employees with disabilities by forcing reassignments to undesirable positions or to designated offices or facilities. Employers should reassign the individual to an equivalent position, in terms of pay, status, etc., if the individual is qualified, and if the position is vacant within a reasonable amount of time. A "reasonable amount of time" should be determined in light of the totality of the circumstances. As an example, suppose there is no vacant position available at the time that an individual with a disability requests reassignment as a reasonable accommodation. The employer, however, knows that an equivalent position for which the individual is qualified, will become vacant next week. Under these circumstances, the employer should reassign the individual to the position when it becomes available. An employer may reassign an individual to a lower graded position if there are no accommodations that would enable the employee to remain in the current position and there are no vacant equivalent positions for which the individual is qualified with or without reasonable accommodation. An employer, however, is not required to maintain the reassigned individual with a disability at the salary of the higher graded position if it does not so maintain reassigned employees who are not disabled. It should also be noted that an employer is not required to promote an individual with a disability as an accommodation. See Senate Report at 31–32; House Labor Report at 63. The determination of which accommodation is appropriate in a particular situation involves a process in which the employer and employee identify the precise limitations imposed by the disability and explore potential accommodations that would overcome those limitations. This process is discussed more fully in § 1630.9 Not Making Reasonable Accommodation.

§ 1630.2(p)   Undue Hardship

An employer or other covered entity is not required to provide an accommodation that will impose an undue hardship on the operation of the employer's or other covered entity's business. The term "undue hardship" means significant difficulty or expense in, or resulting from, the provision of the accommodation. The "undue hardship" provision takes into account the financial realities of the particular employer or other covered entity. However, the concept of undue hardship is not limited to financial difficulty. "Undue hardship" refers to any accommodation that would be unduly costly, extensive, substantial, or disruptive, or that would fundamentally alter the nature or operation of the business. See Senate Report at 35; House Labor Report at 67. For example, suppose an individual with a disabling visual impairment that makes it extremely difficult to see in dim lighting applies for a position as a waiter in a nightclub and requests that the club be brightly lit as a reasonable accommodation. Although the individual may be able to perform the job in bright lighting, the nightclub will probably be able to demonstrate that that particular accommodation, though inexpensive, would impose an undue hardship if the bright lighting would destroy the ambience of the nightclub and/or make it difficult for the customers to see the stage show. The fact that that particular accommodation poses an undue hardship, however, only means that the employer is not required to provide that accommodation. If there is another accommodation that will not create an undue hardship, the employer would be required to provide the alternative accommodation. An employer's claim that the cost of a particular accommodation will impose an undue hardship will be analyzed in light of the factors outlined in part 1630. In part, this analysis requires a determination of whose financial resources should be considered in deciding whether the accommodation is unduly costly. In some cases the financial resources of the employer or other covered entity in its entirety should be considered in determining whether the cost of an accommodation poses an undue hardship. In other cases, consideration of the financial resources of the employer or other covered entity as a whole may be inappropriate because it may not give an accurate picture of the financial resources available to the particular facility that will actually be required to provide the accommodation. See House Labor Report at 68–69; House Judiciary Report at 40–41; see also Conference Report at 56–57. If the employer or other covered entity asserts that only the financial resources of the facility where the individual will be employed should be considered, part 1630 requires a factual determination of the relationship between the employer or other covered entity and the facility that will provide the accommodation. As an example, suppose that an independently owned fast food franchise that receives no money from the franchisor refuses to hire an individual with a hearing impairment because it asserts that it would be an undue hardship to provide an interpreter to enable the individual to participate in monthly staff meetings. Since the financial relationship between the franchisor and the franchise is limited to payment of an annual franchise fee, only the financial resources of the franchise would be considered in determining whether or not providing the accommodation would be an undue hardship. See House Labor Report at 68; House Judiciary Report at 40.

If the employer or other covered entity can show that the cost of the accommodation would impose an undue hardship, it would still be required to provide the accommodation if the funding is available from another source, *e.g.,* a State vocational rehabilitation agency, or if Federal, State or local tax deductions or tax credits are available to offset the cost of the accommodation. * * *

§ 1630.3 Exceptions to the Definitions of "Disability" and "Qualified Individual with a Disability"

Section 1630.3 (a) through (c) Illegal Use of Drugs Part 1630 provides that an individual currently engaging in the illegal use of drugs is not an individual with a disability for purposes of this part when the employer or other covered entity acts on the basis of such use. Illegal use of drugs refers both to the use of unlawful drugs, such as cocaine, and to the unlawful use of prescription drugs. Employers, for example, may discharge or deny employment to persons who illegally use drugs, on the basis of such use, without fear of being held liable for discrimination. The term "currently engaging" is not intended to be limited to the use of drugs on the day of, or within a matter of days or weeks before, the employment action in question. Rather, the provision is intended to apply to the illegal use of drugs that has occurred recently enough to indicate that the individual is actively engaged in such conduct. See Conference Report at 64. Individuals who are erroneously perceived as engaging in the illegal use of drugs, but are not in fact illegally using drugs are not excluded from the definitions of the terms "disability" and "qualified individual with a disability." Individuals who are no longer illegally using drugs and who have either been rehabilitated successfully or are in the process of completing a rehabilitation program are, likewise, not excluded from the definitions of those terms. The term "rehabilitation program" refers to both in-patient and out-patient programs, as well as to appropriate employee assistance programs, professionally recognized self-help programs, such as Narcotics Anonymous, or other programs that provide professional (not necessarily medical) assistance and counseling for individuals who illegally use drugs. See Conference Report at 64; see also House Labor Report at 77; House Judiciary Report at 47. It should be noted that this provision simply provides that certain individuals are not excluded from the definitions of "disability" and "qualified individual with a disability." Consequently, such individuals are still required to establish that they satisfy the requirements of these definitions in order to be protected by the ADA and this part. An individual erroneously regarded as illegally using drugs, for example, would have to show that he or she was regarded as a drug addict in order to demonstrate that he or she meets the definition of "disability" as defined in this part. Employers are entitled to seek reasonable assurances that no illegal use of drugs is occurring or has occurred recently enough so that continuing use is a real and ongoing problem. The reasonable assurances that employers may ask applicants or employees to provide include evidence that the individual is participating in a drug treatment program and/or evidence, such as drug test results, to show that the individual is not currently engaging in the illegal use of drugs. An employer, such as a law enforcement agency, may also be able to impose a qualification standard that excludes individuals with a history of illegal use of drugs if it can show that the standard is job-related and consistent with business necessity. (See § 1630.10 Qualification Standards, Tests and Other Selection Criteria) See Conference Report at 64.

§ 1630.4 Discrimination Prohibited

Paragraph (a) of this provision prohibits discrimination on the basis of disability against a qualified individual in all aspects of the employment relationship. The range of employment decisions covered by this nondiscrimination mandate is to be construed in a manner consistent with the regulations implementing section 504 of the Rehabilitation Act of 1973. Paragraph (b) makes it clear that the language "on the basis of disability" is not intended to create a cause of action for an individual without a disability who claims that someone with a disability was treated more favorably (disparate treatment), or was provided a reasonable accommodation that an individual without a disability was not provided. See 2008 House Judiciary Committee Report at 21 (this provision "prohibits reverse discrimination claims by disallowing claims based on the lack of disability"). Additionally, the ADA and this part do not affect laws that may require the affirmative recruitment or hiring of individuals with disabilities, or any voluntary affirmative action employers may undertake on behalf of individuals with disabilities. However, part 1630 is not intended to limit the ability of covered entities to choose and maintain a qualified workforce. Employers can continue to use criteria that are job related and consistent with business necessity to select qualified employees, and can continue to hire employees who can perform the essential functions of the job. The Amendments Act modified title I's nondiscrimination provision to replace the prohibition on discrimination "against a qualified individual with a disability because of the disability of such individual" with a prohibition on discrimination "against a qualified individual on the basis of disability." As the legislative history of the ADAAA explains: "[T]he bill modifies the ADA to conform to the structure of Title VII and other civil rights laws by requiring an individual to demonstrate discrimination 'on the basis of disability' rather than discrimination 'against an individual with a disability' because of the individual's disability. We hope this will be an important signal to both lawyers and courts to spend less time and energy on the minutia of an individual's impairment, and more time and energy on the merits of the case—including whether discrimination occurred because of the disability, whether an individual was qualified for a job or eligible for a service, and whether a reasonable accommodation or modification was called for under the law." Joint Hoyer–Sensenbrenner Statement at 4; See also 2008 House Judiciary Report at 21 ("This change harmonizes the ADA with other civil rights laws by focusing on whether a person who has been discriminated against has proven that the discrimination was based on a personal characteristic (disability), not on whether he or she has proven that the characteristic exists.").

§ 1630.5 Limiting, Segregating and Classifying

This provision and the several provisions that follow describe various specific forms of discrimination that are included within the general prohibition of § 1630.4. The capabilities of qualified individuals must be determined on an individualized, case by case basis. Covered entities are also prohibited from segregating qualified employees into separate work areas or into separate lines of advancement on the basis of their disabilities. Thus, for example, it would be a violation of this part for an employer to limit the duties of an employee with a disability based on a presumption of what is best for an individual with such a disability, or on a presumption about the abilities of an individual with such a disability. It would be a violation of this part for an employer to adopt a separate track of job promotion or progression for employees with disabilities based on a presumption that employees with disabilities are uninterested in, or incapable of, performing particular jobs. Similarly, it would be a violation for an employer to assign or reassign (as a reasonable accommodation) employees with disabilities to one particular office or installation, or to require that employees with disabilities only use particular employer provided non-work facilities such as segregated break-rooms, lunch rooms, or lounges. It would also be a violation of this part to deny employment to an applicant or employee with a disability based on generalized fears about the safety of an individual with such a disability, or based on generalized assumptions about the absenteeism rate of an individual with such a disability. In addition, it should also be noted that this part is intended to require that employees with disabilities be accorded equal access to whatever health insurance coverage the employer provides to other employees. This part does not, however, affect pre-existing condition clauses included in health insurance policies offered by employers. Consequently, employers may continue to offer policies that contain such clauses, even if they adversely affect individuals with disabilities, so long as the clauses are not used as a subterfuge to evade the purposes of this part. So, for example, it would be permissible for an employer to offer an insurance policy that limits coverage for certain procedures or treatments to a specified number per year. Thus, if a health insurance plan provided coverage for five blood transfusions a year to all covered employees, it would not be discriminatory to offer this plan simply because a hemophiliac employee may require more than five blood transfusions annually. However, it would not be permissible to limit or deny the hemophiliac employee coverage for other procedures, such as heart surgery or the setting of a broken leg, even though the plan would not have to provide coverage for the additional blood transfusions that may be involved in these procedures. Likewise, limits may be placed on reimbursements for certain procedures or on the types of drugs or procedures covered (e.g. limits on the number of permitted X-rays or non-coverage of experimental drugs or procedures), but that limitation must be applied equally to individuals with and without disabilities. See Senate Report at 28–29; House Labor Report at 58–59; House Judiciary Report at 36.Leave policies or benefit plans that are uniformly applied do not violate this part simply because they do not address the special needs of every individual with a disability. Thus, for example, an employer that reduces the number of paid sick leave days that it will provide to all employees, or reduces the amount of medical insurance coverage that it will provide to all employees, is not in violation of this part, even if the benefits reduction has an impact on employees with disabilities in need of greater sick leave and medical coverage. Benefits reductions adopted for discriminatory reasons are in violation of this part. See *Alexander* v. *Choate*, 469 U.S. 287 (1985). See Senate Report at 85; House Labor Report at 137. (See also, the discussion at § 1630.16(f) Health Insurance, Life Insurance, and Other Benefit Plans).

§ 1630.6   Contractual or Other Arrangements

An employer or other covered entity may not do through a contractual or other relationship what it is prohibited from doing directly. This provision does not affect the determination of whether or not one is a "covered entity" or "employer" as defined in § 1630.2. This provision only applies to situations where an employer or other covered entity has entered into a contractual relationship that has the effect of discriminating against its own employees or applicants with disabilities. Accordingly, it would be a violation for an employer to participate in a contractual relationship that results in discrimination against the employer's employees with disabilities in hiring, training, promotion, or in any other aspect of the employment relationship. This provision applies whether or not the employer or other covered entity intended for the contractual relationship to have the discriminatory effect. Part 1630 notes that this provision applies to parties on either side of the contractual or other relationship. This is intended to highlight that an employer whose employees provide services to others, like an employer whose employees receive services, must ensure that those employees are not discriminated against on the basis of disability. For example, a copier company whose service representative is a dwarf could be required to provide a stepstool, as a reasonable accommodation, to enable him to perform the necessary repairs. However, the employer would not be required, as a reasonable accommodation, to make structural changes to its customer's inaccessible premises. The existence of the contractual relationship adds no new obligations under part 1630. The employer, therefore, is not liable through the contractual arrangement for any discrimination by the contractor against the contractors own employees or applicants, although the contractor, as an employer, may be liable for such discrimination. An employer or other covered entity, on the other hand, cannot evade the obligations imposed by this part by engaging in a contractual or other relationship. For example, an employer cannot avoid its responsibility to make reasonable accommodation subject to the undue hardship limitation through a contractual arrangement. See Conference Report at 59; House Labor Report at 59–61; House Judiciary Report at 36–37. To illustrate, assume that an employer is seeking to contract with a company to provide training for its employees. Any responsibilities of reasonable accommodation applicable to the employer in providing the training remain with that employer even if it contracts with another company for this service. Thus, if the training company were planning to conduct the training at an inaccessible location, thereby making it impossible for an employee who uses a wheelchair to attend, the employer would have a duty to make reasonable accommodation unless to do so would impose an undue hardship. Under these circumstances, appropriate accommodations might include (1) having the training company identify accessible training sites and relocate the training program; (2) having the training company make the training site accessible; (3) directly making the training site accessible or providing the training company with the means by which to make the site accessible; (4) identifying and contracting with another training company that uses accessible sites; or (5) any other accommodation that would result in making the training available to the employee. As another illustration, assume that instead of contracting with a training company, the employer contracts with a hotel to host a conference for its employees. The employer will have a duty to ascertain and ensure the accessibility of the hotel and its conference facilities. To fulfill this obligation the employer could, for example, inspect the hotel first-hand or ask a local disability group to inspect the hotel. Alternatively, the employer could ensure that the contract with the hotel specifies it will provide accessible guest rooms for those who need them and that all rooms to be used for the conference, including exhibit and meeting rooms, are accessible. If the hotel breaches this accessibility provision, the hotel may be liable to the employer, under a non-ADA breach of contract theory, for the cost of any accommodation needed to provide access to the hotel and conference, and for any other costs accrued by the employer. (In addition, the hotel may also be independently liable under title III of the ADA). However, this would not relieve the employer of its responsibility under this part nor shield it from charges of discrimination by its own employees. See House Labor Report at 40; House Judiciary Report at 37.

§ 1630.8 * * * Not Making Reasonable Accommodation

The obligation to make reasonable accommodation is a form of non-discrimination. It applies to all employment decisions and to the job application process. This obligation does not extend to the provision of adjustments or modifications that are primarily for the personal benefit of the individual with a disability. Thus, if an adjustment or modification is job-related, *e.g.,* specifically assists the individual in performing the duties of a particular job, it will be considered a type of reasonable accommodation. On the other hand, if an adjustment or modification assists the individual throughout his or her daily activities, on and off the job, it will be considered a personal item that the employer is not required to provide. Accordingly, an employer would generally not be required to provide an employee with a disability with a prosthetic limb, wheelchair, or eyeglasses. Nor would an employer have to provide as an accommodation any amenity or convenience that is not job-related, such as a private hot plate, hot pot or refrigerator that is not provided to employees without disabilities. See Senate Report at 31; House Labor Report at 62. It should be noted, however, that the provision of such items may be required as a reasonable accommodation where such items are specifically designed or required to meet job-related rather than personal needs. An employer, for example, may have to provide an individual with a disabling visual impairment with eyeglasses specifically designed to enable the individual to use the office computer monitors, but that are not otherwise needed by the individual outside of the office. The term "supported employment," which has been applied to a wide variety of programs to assist individuals with severe disabilities in both competitive and non-competitive employment, is not synonymous with reasonable accommodation. Examples of supported employment include modified training materials, restructuring essential functions to enable an individual to perform a job, or hiring an outside professional ("job coach") to assist in job training. Whether a particular form of assistance would be required as a reasonable accommodation must be determined on an individualized, case by case basis without regard to whether that assistance is referred to as "supported employment." For example, an employer, under certain circumstances, may be required to provide modified training materials or a temporary "job coach" to assist in the training of an individual with a disability as a reasonable accommodation. However, an employer would not be required to restructure the essential functions of a position to fit the skills of an individual with a disability who is not otherwise qualified to perform the position, as is done in certain supported employment programs. See 34 CFR part 363. It should be noted that it would not be a violation of this part for an employer to provide any of these personal modifications or adjustments, or to engage in supported employment or similar rehabilitative programs. The obligation to make reasonable accommodation applies to all services and programs provided in connection with employment, and to all non-work facilities provided or maintained by an employer for use by its employees. Accordingly, the obligation to accommodate is applicable to employer sponsored placement or counseling services, and to employer provided cafeterias, lounges, gymnasiums, auditoriums, transportation and the like. The reasonable accommodation requirement is best understood as a means by which barriers to the equal employment opportunity of an individual with a disability are removed or alleviated. These barriers may, for example, be physical or structural obstacles that inhibit or prevent the access of an individual with a disability to job sites, facilities or equipment. Or they may be rigid work schedules that permit no flexibility as to when work is performed or when breaks may be taken, or inflexible job procedures that unduly limit the modes of communication that are used on the job, or the way in which particular tasks are accomplished.

The term "otherwise qualified" is intended to make clear that the obligation to make reasonable accommodation is owed only to an individual with a disability who is qualified within the meaning of § 1630.2(m) in that he or she satisfies all the skill, experience, education and other job-related selection criteria. An individual with a disability is "otherwise qualified," in other words, if he or she is qualified for a job, except that, because of the disability, he or she needs a reasonable accommodation to be able to perform the job's essential functions. For example, if a law firm requires that all incoming lawyers have graduated from an accredited law school and have passed the bar examination, the law firm need not provide an accommodation to an individual with a visual impairment who has not met these selection criteria. That individual is not entitled to a reasonable accommodation because the individual is not "otherwise qualified" for the position. On the other hand, if the individual has graduated from an accredited law school and passed the bar examination, the individual would be "otherwise qualified." The law firm would thus be required to provide a reasonable accommodation, such as a machine that magnifies print, to enable the individual to perform the essential functions of the attorney position, unless the necessary accommodation would impose an undue hardship on the law firm. See Senate Report at 33–34; House Labor Report at 64–65. The reasonable accommodation that is required by this part should provide the individual with a disability with an equal employment opportunity. Equal employment opportunity means an opportunity to attain the same level of performance, or to enjoy the same level of benefits and privileges of employment as are available to the average similarly situated employee without a disability. Thus, for example, an accommodation made to assist an employee with a disability in the performance of his or her job must be adequate to enable the individual to perform the essential functions of the relevant position. The accommodation, however, does not have to be the "best" accommodation possible, so long as it is sufficient to meet the job-related needs of the individual being accommodated. Accordingly, an employer would not have to provide an employee disabled by a back impairment with a state-of-the art mechanical lifting device if it provided the employee with a less expensive or more readily available device that enabled the employee to perform the essential functions of the job. See Senate Report at 35; House Labor Report at 66; see also *Carter* v. *Bennett,* 840 F.2d 63 (DC Cir. 1988). Employers are obligated to make reasonable accommodation only to the physical or mental limitations resulting from the disability of an individual with a disability that is known to the employer. Thus, an employer would not be expected to accommodate disabilities of which it is unaware. If an employee with a known disability is having difficulty performing his or her job, an employer may inquire whether the employee is in need of a reasonable accommodation. In general, however, it is the responsibility of the individual with a disability to inform the employer that an accommodation is needed. When the need for an accommodation is not obvious, an employer, before providing a reasonable accommodation, may require that the individual with a disability provide documentation of the need for accommodation. See Senate Report at 34; House Labor Report at 65.

Process of Determining the Appropriate Reasonable Accommodation Once an individual with a disability has requested provision of a reasonable accommodation, the employer must make a reasonable effort to determine the appropriate accommodation. The appropriate reasonable accommodation is best determined through a flexible, interactive process that involves both the employer and the individual with a disability. Although this process is described below in terms of accommodations that enable the individual with a disability to perform the essential functions of the position held or desired, it is equally applicable to accommodations involving the job application process, and to accommodations that enable the individual with a disability to enjoy equal benefits and privileges of employment. See Senate Report at 34–35; House Labor Report at 65–67. When an individual with a disability has requested a reasonable accommodation to assist in the performance of a job, the employer, using a problem solving approach, should: (1) Analyze the particular job involved and determine its purpose and essential functions; (2) Consult with the individual with a disability to ascertain the precise job-related limitations imposed by the individual's disability and how those limitations could be overcome with a reasonable accommodation; (3) In consultation with the individual to be accommodated, identify potential accommodations and assess the effectiveness each would have in enabling the individual to perform the essential functions of the position; and (4) Consider the preference of the individual to be accommodated and select and implement the accommodation that is most appropriate for both the employee and the employer.

In many instances, the appropriate reasonable accommodation may be so obvious to either or both the employer and the individual with a disability that it may not be necessary to proceed in this step-by-step fashion. For example, if an employee who uses a wheelchair requests that his or her desk be placed on blocks to elevate the desktop above the arms of the wheelchair and the employer complies, an appropriate accommodation has been requested, identified, and provided without either the employee or employer being aware of having engaged in any sort of "reasonable accommodation process." However, in some instances neither the individual requesting the accommodation nor the employer can readily identify the appropriate accommodation. For example, the individual needing the accommodation may not know enough about the equipment used by the employer or the exact nature of the work site to suggest an appropriate accommodation. Likewise, the employer may not know enough about the individual's disability or the limitations that disability would impose on the performance of the job to suggest an appropriate accommodation. Under such circumstances, it may be necessary for the employer to initiate a more defined problem solving process, such as the step-by-step process described above, as part of its reasonable effort to identify the appropriate reasonable accommodation. This process requires the individual assessment of both the particular job at issue, and the specific physical or mental limitations of the particular individual in need of reasonable accommodation. With regard to assessment of the job, "individual assessment" means analyzing the actual job duties and determining the true purpose or object of the job. Such an assessment is necessary to ascertain which job functions are the essential functions that an accommodation must enable an individual with a disability to perform. After assessing the relevant job, the employer, in consultation with the individual requesting the accommodation, should make an assessment of the specific limitations imposed by the disability on the individual's performance of the job's essential functions. This assessment will make it possible to ascertain the precise barrier to the employment opportunity which, in turn, will make it possible to determine the accommodation(s) that could alleviate or remove that barrier. If consultation with the individual in need of the accommodation still does not reveal potential appropriate accommodations, then the employer, as part of this process, may find that technical assistance is helpful in determining how to accommodate the particular individual in the specific situation. Such assistance could be sought from the Commission, from State or local rehabilitation agencies, or from disability constituent organizations. It should be noted, however, that, as provided in § 1630.9(c) of this part, the failure to obtain or receive technical assistance from the Federal agencies that administer the ADA will not excuse the employer from its reasonable accommodation obligation. Once potential accommodations have been identified, the employer should assess the effectiveness of each potential accommodation in assisting the individual in need of the accommodation in the performance of the essential functions of the position. If more than one of these accommodations will enable the individual to perform the essential functions or if the individual would prefer to provide his or her own accommodation, the preference of the individual with a disability should be given primary consideration. However, the employer providing the accommodation has the ultimate discretion to choose between effective accommodations, and may choose the less expensive accommodation or the accommodation that is easier for it to provide. It should also be noted that the individual's willingness to provide his or her own accommodation does not relieve the employer of the duty to provide the accommodation should the individual for any reason be unable or unwilling to continue to provide the accommodation. * * *

§ 1630.10 Qualification Standards, Tests, and Other Selection Criteria

Section 1630.10(a)—In General The purpose of this provision is to ensure that individuals with disabilities are not excluded from job opportunities unless they are actually unable to do the job. It is to ensure that there is a fit between job criteria and an applicant's (or employee's) actual ability to do the job. Accordingly, job criteria that even unintentionally screen out, or tend to screen out, an individual with a disability or a class of individuals with disabilities because of their disability may not be used unless the employer demonstrates that those criteria, as used by the employer, are job related for the position to which they are being applied and are consistent with business necessity. The concept of "business necessity" has the same meaning as the concept of "business necessity" under section 504 of the Rehabilitation Act of 1973. Selection criteria that exclude, or tend to exclude, an individual with a disability or a class of individuals with disabilities because of their disability but do not concern an essential function of the job would not be consistent with business necessity. The use of selection criteria that are related to an essential function of the job may be consistent with business necessity. However, selection criteria that are related to an essential function of the job may not be used to exclude an individual with a disability if that individual could satisfy the criteria with the provision of a reasonable accommodation. Experience under a similar provision of the regulations implementing section 504 of the Rehabilitation Act indicates that challenges to selection criteria are, in fact, often resolved by reasonable accommodation. This provision is applicable to all types of selection criteria, including safety requirements, vision or hearing requirements, walking requirements, lifting requirements, and employment tests. See 1989 Senate Report at 37–39; House Labor Report at 70–72; House Judiciary Report at 42. As previously noted, however, it is not the intent of this part to second guess an employer's business judgment with regard to production standards. See § 1630.2(n) (Essential Functions). Consequently, production standards will generally not be subject to a challenge under this provision.

The Uniform Guidelines on Employee Selection Procedures (UG-ESP) 29 CFR part 1607 do not apply to the Rehabilitation Act and are similarly inapplicable to this part. * * *

§ 1630.13 Prohibited Medical Examinations and Inquiries

§ 1630.13(a) Pre-employment Examination or Inquiry

This provision makes clear that an employer cannot inquire as to whether an individual has a disability at the pre-offer stage of the selection process. Nor can an employer inquire at the pre-offer stage about an applicant's workers' compensation history. Employers may ask questions that relate to the applicant's ability to perform job-related functions. However, these questions should not be phrased in terms of disability. An employer, for example, may ask whether the applicant has a driver's license, if driving is a job function, but may not ask whether the applicant has a visual disability. Employers may ask about an applicant's ability to perform both essential and marginal job functions. Employers, though, may not refuse to hire an applicant with a disability because the applicant's disability prevents him or her from performing marginal functions. See Senate Report at 39; House Labor Report at 72–73; House Judiciary Report at 42–43. Section 1630.13(b) Examination or Inquiry of Employees. The purpose of this provision is to prevent the administration to employees of medical tests or inquiries that do not serve a legitimate business purpose. For example, if an employee suddenly starts to use increased amounts of sick leave or starts to appear sickly, an employer could not require that employee to be tested for AIDS, HIV infection, or cancer unless the employer can demonstrate that such testing is job-related and consistent with business necessity. See Senate Report at 39; House Labor Report at 75; House Judiciary Report at 44.

§ 1630.14 Medical Examinations and Inquiries Specifically Permitted

§ 1630.14(a) Pre-employment Inquiry

Employers are permitted to make pre-employment inquiries into the ability of an applicant to perform job-related functions. This inquiry must be narrowly tailored. The employer may describe or demonstrate the job function and inquire whether or not the applicant can perform that function with or without reasonable accommodation. For example, an employer may explain that the job requires assembling small parts and ask if the individual will be able to perform that function, with or without reasonable accommodation. See Senate Report at 39; House Labor Report at 73; House Judiciary Report at 43. An employer may also ask an applicant to describe or to demonstrate how, with or without reasonable accommodation, the applicant will be able to perform job-related functions. Such a request may be made of all applicants in the same job category regardless of disability. Such a request may also be made of an applicant whose known disability may interfere with or prevent the performance of a job-related function, whether or not the employer routinely makes such a request of all applicants in the job category. For example, an employer may ask an individual with one leg who applies for a position as a home washing machine repairman to demonstrate or to explain how, with or without reasonable accommodation, he would be able to transport himself and his tools down basement stairs. However, the employer may not inquire as to the nature or severity of the disability. Therefore, for example, the employer cannot ask how the individual lost the leg or whether the loss of the leg is indicative of an underlying impairment. On the other hand, if the known disability of an applicant will not interfere with or prevent the performance of a job-related function, the employer may only request a description or demonstration by the applicant if it routinely makes such a request of all applicants in the same job category. So, for example, it would not be permitted for an employer to request that an applicant with one leg demonstrate his ability to assemble small parts while seated at a table, if the employer does not routinely request that all applicants provide such a demonstration. An employer that requires an applicant with a disability to demonstrate how he or she will perform a job-related function must either provide the reasonable accommodation the applicant needs to perform the function or permit the applicant to explain how, with the accommodation, he or she will perform the function. If the job-related function is not an essential function, the employer may not exclude the applicant with a disability because of the applicant's inability to perform that function. Rather, the employer must, as a reasonable accommodation, either provide an accommodation that will enable the individual to perform the function, transfer the function to another position, or exchange the function for one the applicant is able to perform.

An employer may not use an application form that lists a number of potentially disabling impairments and ask the applicant to check any of the impairments he or she may have. In addition, as noted above, an employer may not ask how a particular individual became disabled or the prognosis of the individual's disability. The employer is also prohibited from asking how often the individual will require leave for treatment or use leave as a result of incapacitation because of the disability. However, the employer may state the attendance requirements of the job and inquire whether the applicant can meet them. An employer is permitted to ask, on a test announcement or application form, that individuals with disabilities who will require a reasonable accommodation in order to take the test so inform the employer within a reasonable established time period prior to the administration of the test. The employer may also request that documentation of the need for the accommodation accompany the request. Requested accommodations may include accessible testing sites, modified testing conditions and accessible test formats. (See § 1630.11 Administration of Tests). Physical agility tests are not medical examinations and so may be given at any point in the application or employment process. Such tests must be given to all similarly situated applicants or employees regardless of disability. If such tests screen out or tend to screen out an individual with a disability or a class of individuals with disabilities, the employer would have to demonstrate that the test is job-related and consistent with business necessity and that performance cannot be achieved with reasonable accommodation. (See § 1630 Not Making Reasonable Accommodation: Process of Determining the Appropriate Reasonable Accommodation). As previously noted, collecting information and inviting individuals to identify themselves as individuals with disabilities as required to satisfy the affirmative action requirements of section 503 of the Rehabilitation Act is not restricted by this part. (See § 1630.1(b) and (c) Applicability and Construction).

§ 1630.14(b)   Employment Entrance Examination

An employer is permitted to require post-offer medical examinations before the employee actually starts working. The employer may condition the offer of employment on the results of the examination, provided that all entering employees in the same job category are subjected to such an examination, regardless of disability, and that the confidentiality requirements specified in this part are met. This provision recognizes that in many industries, such as air transportation or construction, applicants for certain positions are chosen on the basis of many factors including physical and psychological criteria, some of which may be identified as a result of post-offer medical examinations given prior to entry on duty. Only those employees who meet the employer's physical and psychological criteria for the job, with or without reasonable accommodation, will be qualified to receive confirmed offers of employment and begin working. Medical examinations permitted by this section are not required to be job-related and consistent with business necessity. However, if an employer withdraws an offer of employment because the medical examination reveals that the employee does not satisfy certain employment criteria, either the exclusionary criteria must not screen out or tend to screen out an individual with a disability or a class of individuals with disabilities, or they must be job-related and consistent with business necessity. As part of the showing that an exclusionary criteria is job-related and consistent with business necessity, the employer must also demonstrate that there is no reasonable accommodation that will enable the individual with a disability to perform the essential functions of the job. See Conference Report at 59–60; Senate Report at 39; House Labor Report at 73–74; House Judiciary Report at 43. As an example, suppose an employer makes a conditional offer of employment to an applicant, and it is an essential function of the job that the incumbent be available to work every day for the next three months. An employment entrance examination then reveals that the applicant has a disabling impairment that, according to reasonable medical judgment that relies on the most current medical knowledge, will require treatment that will render the applicant unable to work for a portion of the three month period. Under these circumstances, the employer would be able to withdraw the employment offer without violating this part. The information obtained in the course of a permitted entrance examination or inquiry is to be treated as a confidential medical record and may only be used in a manner not inconsistent with this part. State workers' compensation laws are not preempted by the ADA or this part. These laws require the collection of information from individuals for State administrative purposes that do not conflict with the ADA or this part. Consequently, employers or other covered entities may submit information to State workers' compensation offices or second injury funds in accordance with State workers' compensation laws without violating this part.

Consistent with this section and with § 1630.16(f) of this part, information obtained in the course of a permitted entrance examination or inquiry may be used for insurance purposes described in § 1630.16(f).

§ 1630.14(c) Examination of Employees

This provision permits employers to make inquiries or require medical examinations (fitness for duty exams) when there is a need to determine whether an employee is still able to perform the essential functions of his or her job. The provision permits employers or other covered entities to make inquiries or require medical examinations necessary to the reasonable accommodation process described in this part. This provision also permits periodic physicals to determine fitness for duty or other medical monitoring if such physicals or monitoring are required by medical standards or requirements established by Federal, State, or local law that are consistent with the ADA and this part (or in the case of a Federal standard, with section 504 of the Rehabilitation Act) in that they are job-related and consistent with business necessity. Such standards may include Federal safety regulations that regulate bus and truck driver qualifications, as well as laws establishing medical requirements for pilots or other air transportation personnel. These standards also include health standards promulgated pursuant to the Occupational Safety and Health Act of 1970, the Federal Coal Mine Health and Safety Act of 1969, or other similar statutes that require that employees exposed to certain toxic and hazardous substances be medically monitored at specific intervals. See House Labor Report at 74–75. The information obtained in the course of such examination or inquiries is to be treated as a confidential medical record and may only be used in a manner not inconsistent with this part.

Part 1630 permits voluntary medical examinations, including voluntary medical histories, as part of employee health programs. These programs often include, for example, medical screening for high blood pressure, weight control counseling, and cancer detection. Voluntary activities, such as blood pressure monitoring and the administering of prescription drugs, such as insulin, are also permitted. It should be noted, however, that the medical records developed in the course of such activities must be maintained in the confidential manner required by this part and must not be used for any purpose in violation of this part, such as limiting health insurance eligibility. House Labor Report at 75; House Judiciary Report at 43–44.

§ 1630.15   Defenses

The section on defenses in part 1630 is not intended to be exhaustive. However, it is intended to inform employers of some of the potential defenses available to a charge of discrimination under the ADA and this part.

§ 1630.15(a)   Disparate Treatment Defenses

The "traditional" defense to a charge of disparate treatment under title VII, as expressed in *McDonnell Douglas Corp.* v. *Green,* 411 U.S. 792 (1973), *Texas Department of Community Affairs* v. *Burdine,* 450 U.S. 248 (1981), and their progeny, may be applicable to charges of disparate treatment brought under the ADA. See *Prewitt* v. *U.S. Postal Service,* 662 F.2d 292 (5th Cir. 1981). Disparate treatment means, with respect to title I of the ADA, that an individual was treated differently on the basis of his or her disability. For example, disparate treatment has occurred where an employer excludes an employee with a severe facial disfigurement from staff meetings because the employer does not like to look at the employee. The individual is being treated differently because of the employer's attitude towards his or her perceived disability. Disparate treatment has also occurred where an employer has a policy of not hiring individuals with AIDS regardless of the individuals' qualifications. The crux of the defense to this type of charge is that the individual was treated differently not because of his or her disability but for a legitimate nondiscriminatory reason such as poor performance unrelated to the individual's disability. The fact that the individual's disability is not covered by the employer's current insurance plan or would cause the employer's insurance premiums or workers' compensation costs to increase, would not be a legitimate nondiscriminatory reason justifying disparate treatment of an individual with a disability. Senate Report at 85; House Labor Report at 136 and House Judiciary Report at 70. The defense of a legitimate nondiscriminatory reason is rebutted if the alleged nondiscriminatory reason is shown to be pretextual.

§ 1630.15(b) and (c)　　Disparate Impact Defenses

Disparate impact means, with respect to title I of the ADA and this part, that uniformly applied criteria have an adverse impact on an individual with a disability or a disproportionately negative impact on a class of individuals with disabilities. Section 1630.15(b) clarifies that an employer may use selection criteria that have such a disparate impact, *i.e.*, that screen out or tend to screen out an individual with a disability or a class of individuals with disabilities only when they are job-related and consistent with business necessity. For example, an employer interviews two candidates for a position, one of whom is blind. Both are equally qualified. The employer decides that while it is not essential to the job it would be convenient to have an employee who has a driver's license and so could occasionally be asked to run errands by car. The employer hires the individual who is sighted because this individual has a driver's license. This is an example of a uniformly applied criterion, having a driver's permit, that screens out an individual who has a disability that makes it impossible to obtain a driver's permit. The employer would, thus, have to show that this criterion is job-related and consistent with business necessity. See House Labor Report at 55. However, even if the criterion is job-related and consistent with business necessity, an employer could not exclude an individual with a disability if the criterion could be met or job performance accomplished with a reasonable accommodation. For example, suppose an employer requires, as part of its application process, an interview that is job-related and consistent with business necessity. The employer would not be able to refuse to hire a hearing impaired applicant because he or she could not be interviewed. This is so because an interpreter could be provided as a reasonable accommodation that would allow the individual to be interviewed, and thus satisfy the selection criterion. With regard to safety requirements that screen out or tend to screen out an individual with a disability or a class of individuals with disabilities, an employer must demonstrate that the requirement, as applied to the individual, satisfies the "direct threat" standard in § 1630.2(r) in order to show that the requirement is job-related and consistent with business necessity. Section 1630.15(c) clarifies that there may be uniformly applied standards, criteria and policies not relating to selection that may also screen out or tend to screen out an individual with a disability or a class of individuals with disabilities. Like selection criteria that have a disparate impact, non-selection criteria having such an impact may also have to be job-related and consistent with business necessity, subject to consideration of reasonable accommodation. It should be noted, however, that some uniformly applied employment policies or practices, such as leave policies, are not subject to challenge under the adverse impact theory. "No-leave" policies (*e.g.*, no leave during the first six months of employment) are likewise not subject to challenge under the adverse impact theory. However, an employer, in spite of its "no-leave" policy, may, in appropriate circumstances, have to consider the provision of leave to an employee with a disability as a reasonable accommodation, unless the provision of leave would impose an undue hardship. See discussion at § 1630.5 Limiting, Segregating and Classifying, and § 1630.10 Qualification Standards, Tests, and Other Selection Criteria.

§ 1630.15(d) Defense To Not Making Reasonable Accommodation

An employer or other covered entity alleged to have discriminated because it did not make a reasonable accommodation, as required by this part, may offer as a defense that it would have been an undue hardship to make the accommodation. It should be noted, however, that an employer cannot simply assert that a needed accommodation will cause it undue hardship, as defined in § 1630.2(p), and thereupon be relieved of the duty to provide accommodation. Rather, an employer will have to present evidence and demonstrate that the accommodation will, in fact, cause it undue hardship. Whether a particular accommodation will impose an undue hardship for a particular employer is determined on a case by case basis. Consequently, an accommodation that poses an undue hardship for one employer at a particular time may not pose an undue hardship for another employer, or even for the same employer at another time. Likewise, an accommodation that poses an undue hardship for one employer in a particular job setting, such as a temporary construction worksite, may not pose an undue hardship for another employer, or even for the same employer at a permanent worksite. See House Judiciary Report at 42. The concept of undue hardship that has evolved under section 504 of the Rehabilitation Act and is embodied in this part is unlike the "undue hardship" defense associated with the provision of religious accommodation under title VII of the Civil Rights Act of 1964. To demonstrate undue hardship pursuant to the ADA and this part, an employer must show substantially more difficulty or expense than would be needed to satisfy the "de minimis" title VII standard of undue hardship. For example, to demonstrate that the cost of an accommodation poses an undue hardship, an employer would have to show that the cost is undue as compared to the employer's budget. Simply comparing the cost of the accommodation to the salary of the individual with a disability in need of the accommodation will not suffice. Moreover, even if it is determined that the cost of an accommodation would unduly burden an employer, the employer cannot avoid making the accommodation if the individual with a disability can arrange to cover that portion of the cost that rises to the undue hardship level, or can otherwise arrange to provide the accommodation. Under such circumstances, the necessary accommodation would no longer pose an undue hardship. See Senate Report at 36; House Labor Report at 68–69; House Judiciary Report at 40–41.

Excessive cost is only one of several possible bases upon which an employer might be able to demonstrate undue hardship. Alternatively, for example, an employer could demonstrate that the provision of a particular accommodation would be unduly disruptive to its other employees or to the functioning of its business. The terms of a collective bargaining agreement may be relevant to this determination. By way of illustration, an employer would likely be able to show undue hardship if the employer could show that the requested accommodation of the upward adjustment of the business' thermostat would result in it becoming unduly hot for its other employees, or for its patrons or customers. The employer would thus not have to provide this accommodation. However, if there were an alternate accommodation that would not result in undue hardship, the employer would have to provide that accommodation. It should be noted, moreover, that the employer would not be able to show undue hardship if the disruption to its employees were the result of those employees fears or prejudices toward the individual's disability and not the result of the provision of the accommodation. Nor would the employer be able to demonstrate undue hardship by showing that the provision of the accommodation has a negative impact on the morale of its other employees but not on the ability of these employees to perform their jobs.

§ 1630.15(e) Defense—Conflicting Federal Laws and Regulations

There are several Federal laws and regulations that address medical standards and safety requirements. If the alleged discriminatory action was taken in compliance with another Federal law or regulation, the employer may offer its obligation to comply with the conflicting standard as a defense. The employer's defense of a conflicting Federal requirement or regulation may be rebutted by a showing of pretext, or by showing that the Federal standard did not require the discriminatory action, or that there was a nonexclusionary means to comply with the standard that would not conflict with this part. See House Labor Report at 74.

§ 1630.15(f) Claims Based on Transitory and Minor Impairments Under the "Regarded As" Prong

It may be a defense to a charge of discrimination where coverage would be shown solely under the "regarded as" prong of the definition of disability that the impairment is (in the case of an actual impairment) or would be (in the case of a perceived impairment) both transitory and minor. Section 1630.15(f)(1) explains that an individual cannot be "regarded as having such an impairment" if the impairment is both transitory (defined by the ADAAA as lasting or expected to last less than six months) and minor. Section 1630.15(f)(2) explains that the determination of "transitory and minor" is made objectively. For example, an individual who is denied a promotion because he has a minor back injury would be "regarded as" an individual with a disability if the back impairment lasted or was expected to last more than six months. Although minor, the impairment is not transitory. Similarly, if an employer discriminates against an employee based on the employee's bipolar disorder (an impairment that is not transitory and minor), the employee is "regarded as" having a disability even if the employer subjectively believes that the employee's disorder is transitory and minor.

§ 1630.16(c) Drug Testing

This provision reflects title I's neutrality toward testing for the illegal use of drugs. Such drug tests are neither encouraged, authorized nor prohibited. The results of such drug tests may be used as a basis for disciplinary action. Tests for the illegal use of drugs are not considered medical examinations for purposes of this part. If the results reveal information about an individual's medical condition beyond whether the individual is currently engaging in the illegal use of drugs, this additional information is to be treated as a confidential medical record. For example, if a test for the illegal use of drugs reveals the presence of a controlled substance that has been lawfully prescribed for a particular medical condition, this information is to be treated as a confidential medical record. See House Labor Report at 79; House Judiciary Report at 47.

§ 1630.16(e) Infectious and Communicable Diseases; Food Handling Jobs

This provision addressing food handling jobs applies the "direct threat" analysis to the particular situation of accommodating individuals with infectious or communicable diseases that are transmitted through the handling of food. The Department of Health and Human Services is to prepare a list of infectious and communicable diseases that are transmitted through the handling of food. If an individual with a disability has one of the listed diseases and works in or applies for a position in food handling, the employer must determine whether there is a reasonable accommodation that will eliminate the risk of transmitting the disease through the handling of food. If there is an accommodation that will not pose an undue hardship, and that will prevent the transmission of the disease through the handling of food, the employer must provide the accommodation to the individual. The employer, under these circumstances, would not be permitted to discriminate against the individual because of the need to provide the reasonable accommodation and would be required to maintain the individual in the food handling job. If no such reasonable accommodation is possible, the employer may refuse to assign, or to continue to assign the individual to a position involving food handling. This means that if such an individual is an applicant for a food handling position the employer is not required to hire the individual. However, if the individual is a current employee, the employer would be required to consider the accommodation of reassignment to a vacant position not involving food handling for which the individual is qualified. Conference Report at 61–63. (See § 1630.2(r) Direct Threat).

§ 1630.16(f) Health Insurance, Life Insurance, and Other Benefit Plans

This provision is a limited exemption that is only applicable to those who establish, sponsor, observe or administer benefit plans, such as health and life insurance plans. It does not apply to those who establish, sponsor, observe or administer plans not involving benefits, such as liability insurance plans. The purpose of this provision is to permit the development and administration of benefit plans in accordance with accepted principles of risk assessment. This provision is not intended to disrupt the current regulatory structure for self-insured employers. These employers may establish, sponsor, observe, or administer the terms of a bona fide benefit plan not subject to State laws that regulate insurance. This provision is also not intended to disrupt the current nature of insurance underwriting, or current insurance industry practices in sales, underwriting, pricing, administrative and other services, claims and similar insurance related activities based on classification of risks as regulated by the States. The activities permitted by this provision do not violate part 1630 even if they result in limitations on individuals with disabilities, provided that these activities are not used as a subterfuge to evade the purposes of this part. Whether or not these activities are being used as a subterfuge is to be determined without regard to the date the insurance plan or employee benefit plan was adopted. However, an employer or other covered entity cannot deny an individual with a disability who is qualified equal access to insurance or subject an individual with a disability who is qualified to different terms or conditions of insurance based on disability alone, if the disability does not pose increased risks. Part 1630 requires that decisions not based on risk classification be made in conformity with non-discrimination requirements. See Senate Report at 84–86; House Labor Report at 136–138; House Judiciary Report at 70–71. See the discussion of § 1630.5 Limiting, Segregating and Classifying.

[56 FR 35734, July 26, 1991, as amended at 65 FR 36327, June 8, 2000; 76 FR 17003, Mar. 25, 2011]

Part B

PROTECTING SOCIALLY VALUED ACTIVITY

CONSTITUTION OF THE UNITED STATES

AMENDMENT 1

Congress shall make no law respecting an establishment of religion, or prohibiting the free exercise thereof; or abridging the freedom of speech, or of the press; or the right of the people peaceably to assemble, and to petition the Government for a redress of grievances.

OCCUPATIONAL SAFETY AND HEALTH ACT OF 1970—SELECTED PROVISION
29 U.S.C. §§ 660(c)

§ 660. (§ 11) Judicial review

* * *

(c)(1) No person shall discharge or in any manner discriminate against any employee because such employee has filed any complaint or instituted or caused to be instituted any proceeding under or related to this chapter or has testified or is about to testify in any such proceeding or because of the exercise by such employee on behalf of himself or others of any right afforded by this chapter.

(2) Any employee who believes that he has been discharged or otherwise discriminated against by any person in violation of this subsection may, within thirty days after such violation occurs, file a complaint with the Secretary alleging such discrimination. Upon receipt of such complaint, the Secretary shall cause such investigation to be made as he deems appropriate. If upon such investigation, the Secretary determines that the provisions of this subsection have been violated, he shall bring an action in any appropriate United States district court against such person. In any such action the United States district courts shall have jurisdiction, for cause shown to restrain violations of paragraph (1) of this subsection and order all appropriate relief including rehiring or reinstatement of the employee to his former position with back pay.

(3) Within 90 days of the receipt of a complaint filed under this subsection the Secretary shall notify the complainant of his determination under paragraph (2) of this subsection.

(Pub.L. 91–596, § 11, Dec. 29, 1970, 84 Stat. 1602; Pub.L. 98–620, Title IV, § 402(32), Nov. 8, 1984, 98 Stat. 3360.)

ENERGY REORGANIZATION ACT—
SELECTED PROVISIONS
42 U.S.C. § 5851

§ 5851. (§ 201) Employee protection

(a) Discrimination against employee.

(1) No employer may discharge any employee or otherwise discriminate against any employee with respect to his compensation, terms, conditions, or privileges of employment because the employee (or person acting pursuant to a request of the employee)—

(A) notified his employer of an alleged violation of this Act or the Atomic Energy Act of 1954 (42 U.S.C. 2011 et seq.);

(B) refused to engage in any practice made unlawful by this Act or the Atomic Energy Act of 1954, if the employee has identified the alleged illegality to the employer;

(C) testified before Congress or at any Federal or State proceeding regarding any provision (or proposed provision) of this Act or the Atomic Energy Act of 1954;

(D) commenced, caused to be commenced, or is about to commence or cause to be commenced a proceeding under this Act or the Atomic Energy Act of 1954, as amended, or a proceeding for the administration or enforcement of any requirement imposed under this Act or the Atomic Energy Act of 1954, as amended;

(E) testified or is about to testify in any such proceeding or;

(F) assisted or participated or is about to assist or participate in any manner in such a proceeding or in any other manner in such a proceeding or in any other action to carry out the purposes of this Act or the Atomic Energy Act of 1954, as amended.

(2) For purposes of this section, the term "employer" includes—

(A) a licensee of the Commission or of an agreement State under section 274 of the Atomic Energy Act of 1954 (42 U.S.C. 2021);

(B) an applicant for a license from the Commission or such an agreement State;

(C) a contractor or subcontractor of such a licensee or applicant;

(D) a contractor or subcontractor of the Department of Energy that is indemnified by the Department under section 170 d. of the Atomic Energy Act of 1954 (42 U.S.C. 2210(d)), but such term shall not include any contractor or subcontractor covered by Executive Order No. 12344

(E) a contractor or subcontractor of the Commission;

(F) the Commission; and

(G) the Department of Energy.

(b) Complaint, filing and notification.

(1) Any employee who believes that he has been discharged or otherwise discriminated against by any person in violation of subsection (a) may, within 180 days after such violation occurs, file (or have any person file on his behalf) a complaint with the Secretary of Labor (in this section referred to as the "Secretary") alleging such discharge or discrimination. Upon receipt of such a complaint, the Secretary shall notify the person named in the complaint of the filing of the complaint, the Commission, and the Department of Energy.

(2) (A) Upon receipt of a complaint filed under paragraph (1), the Secretary shall conduct an investigation of the violation alleged in the complaint. Within thirty days of the receipt of such complaint, the Secretary shall complete such investigation and shall notify in writing the complainant (and any person acting in his behalf) and the person alleged to have committed such violation of the results of the investigation conducted pursuant to this subparagraph. Within ninety days of the receipt of such complaint the Secretary shall, unless the proceeding on the complaint is terminated by the Secretary on the basis of a settlement entered into by the Secretary and the person alleged to have committed such violation, issue an order either providing the relief prescribed by subparagraph (B) or denying the complaint. An order of the Secretary shall be made on the record after notice and opportunity for public hearing. Upon the conclusion of such hearing and the issuance of a recommended decision that the complaint has merit, the Secretary shall issue a preliminary order providing the relief prescribed in subparagraph (B), but may not order compensatory damages pending a final order. The Secretary may not enter into a settlement terminating a proceeding on a complaint without the participation and consent of the complainant.

(B) If, in response to a complaint filed under paragraph (1), the Secretary determines that a violation of subsection (a) has occurred, the Secretary shall order the person who committed such violation to (i) take affirmative action to abate the violation, and (ii) reinstate the complainant to his former position together with the compensation (including back pay), terms, conditions, and privileges of his employment, and the Secretary may order such person to provide compensatory damages to the complainant. If an order is issued under this paragraph, the Secretary, at the request of the complainant shall assess against the person against whom the order is issued a sum equal to the aggregate amount of all costs and expenses (including attorneys' and expert witness fees) reasonably incurred, as determined by the Secretary, by the complainant for, or in connection with, the bringing of the complaint upon which the order was issued.

(3)(A) The Secretary shall dismiss a complaint filed under paragraph (1), and shall not conduct the investigation required under paragraph (2), unless the complainant has made a prima facie showing that any behavior described in subparagraphs (A) through (F) of subsection (a)(1) was a contributing factor in the unfavorable personnel action alleged in the complaint.

(B) Notwithstanding a finding by the Secretary that the complainant has made the showing required by subparagraph (A), no investigation required under paragraph (2) shall be conducted if the employer demonstrates, by clear and convincing evidence, that it would have taken the same unfavorable personnel action in the absence of such behavior.

(C) The Secretary may determine that a violation of subsection (a) has occurred only if the complainant has demonstrated that any behavior described in subparagraphs (A) through (F) of subsection (a)(1) was a contributing factor in the unfavorable personnel action alleged in the complaint.

(D) Relief may not be ordered under paragraph (2) if the employer demonstrates by clear and convincing evidence that it would have taken the same unfavorable personnel action in the absence of such behavior.

(4) If the Secretary has not issued a final decision within 1 year after the filing of a complaint under paragraph (1), and there is no showing that such delay is due to the bad faith of the person seeking relief under this paragraph, such person may bring an action at law or equity for de novo review in the appropriate district court of the United States, which shall have jurisdiction over such an action without regard to the amount in controversy.

(c) Review.

(1) Any person adversely affected or aggrieved by an order issued under subsection (b) may obtain review of the order in the United States court of appeals for the circuit in which the violation, with respect to which the order was issued, allegedly occurred. The petition for review must be filed within sixty days from the issuance of the Secretary's order. Review shall conform to chapter 7 of title 5 of the United States Code [5 U.S.C. §§ 701 et seq.]. The commencement of proceedings under this subparagraph shall not, unless ordered by the court, operate as a stay of the Secretary's order.

(2) An order of the Secretary with respect to which review could have been obtained under paragraph (1) shall not be subject to judicial review in any criminal or other civil proceeding.

(d) Jurisdiction. Whenever a person has failed to comply with an order issued under subsection (b)(2), the Secretary may file a civil action in the United States district court for the district in which the violation was found to occur to enforce such order. In actions brought under this subsection, the district courts shall have jurisdiction to grant all appropriate relief including, but not limited to, injunctive relief, compensatory, and exemplary damages.

(e) Commencement of action.

(1) Any person on whose behalf an order was issued under paragraph (2) of subsection (b) may commence a civil action against the person to whom such order was issued to require compliance with such order. The appropriate United States district court shall have jurisdiction, without regard to the amount in controversy or the citizenship of the parties, to enforce such order.

(2) The court, in issuing any final order under this subsection, may award costs of litigation (including reasonable attorney and expert witness fees) to any party whenever the court determines such award is appropriate.

(f) Enforcement. Any nondiscretionary duty imposed by this section shall be enforceable in a mandamus proceeding brought under section 1361 of title 28 of the United States Code.

(g) Deliberate violations. Subsection (a) shall not apply with respect to any employee who, acting without direction from his or her employer (or the employer's agent), deliberately causes a violation of any requirement of this Act or of the Atomic Energy Act of 1954, as amended.

(h) Nonpreemption. This section may not be construed to expand, diminish, or otherwise affect any right otherwise available to an employee under Federal or State law to redress the employee's discharge or other discriminatory action taken by the employer against the employee.

(i) Posting requirement. The provisions of this section shall be prominently posted in any place of employment to which this section applies.

(j) Investigation of allegations.

(1) The Commission or the Department of Energy shall not delay taking appropriate action with respect to an allegation of a substantial safety hazard on the basis of—

(A) the filing of a complaint under subsection (b)(1) arising from such allegation; or

(B) any investigation by the Secretary, or other action, under this section in response to such complaint.

(2) A determination by the Secretary under this section that a violation of subsection (a) has not occurred shall not be considered by the Commission or the Department of Energy in its determination of whether a substantial safety hazard exists.

(Oct. 11, 1974, P.L. 93–438, Title II, § 211 [210], as added Nov. 6, 1978, P.L. 95–601, § 10, 92 Stat. 2951; Oct. 24, 1992, P.L. 102–486, Title XXIX, § 2902(a)–(g), (h)(2), (3), 106 Stat. 3123; (as amended Aug. 8, 2005, P.L. 109–58, Title VI, Subtitle B, § 629, 119 Stat. 785.)

FEDERAL JURY SYSTEM IMPROVEMENT ACT
28 U.S.C. § 1875

§ 1875. Protection of jurors' employment

(a) No employer shall discharge, threaten to discharge, intimidate, or coerce any permanent employee by reason of such employee's jury service, or the attendance or scheduled attendance in connection with such service, in any court of the United States.

(b) Any employer who violates the provisions of this section—

(1) shall be liable for damages for any loss of wages or other benefits suffered by an employee by reason of such violation;

(2) may be enjoined from further violations of this section and ordered to provide other appropriate relief, including but not limited to the reinstatement of any employee discharged by reason of his jury service; and

(3) shall be subject to a civil penalty of not more than $5,000 for each violation as to each employee, and may be ordered to perform community service.

(c) Any individual who is reinstated to a position of employment in accordance with the provisions of this section shall be considered as having been on furlough or leave of absence during his period of jury service, shall be reinstated to his position of employment without loss of seniority, and shall be entitled to participate in insurance or other benefits offered by the employer pursuant to established rules and practices relating to employees on furlough or leave of absence in effect with the employer at the time such individual entered upon jury service.

(d) (1) An individual claiming that his employer has violated the provisions of this section may make application to the district court for the district in which such employer maintains a place of business and the court shall, upon finding probable merit in such claim, appoint counsel to represent such individual in any action in the district court necessary to the resolution of such claim. Such counsel shall be compensated and necessary expenses repaid to the extent provided by section 3006A of title 18, United States Code.

(2) In any action or proceeding under this section, the court may award a prevailing employee who brings such action by retained counsel a reasonable attorney's fee as part of the costs. The court may tax a defendant employer, as costs payable to the court, the attorney fees and expenses incurred on behalf of a prevailing employee, where such costs were expended by the court pursuant to paragraph (1) of this subsection. The court may award a prevailing

273

employer a reasonable attorney's fee as part of the costs only if the court finds that the action is frivolous, vexatious, or brought in bad faith.

(Added Nov. 2, 1978, P.L. 95–572, § 6(a)(1), 92 Stat. 2456; Jan. 12, 1983, P.L. 97–463, § 1, 96 Stat. 2531; as amended Oct. 13, 2008, P.L. 110–406, § 19, 122 Stat. 4295.)

CIVIL SERVICE REFORM ACT— SELECTED PROVISIONS
5 U.S.C. §§ 2301–2302

§ 2301.   Merit system principles

(a) This section shall apply to—

(1) an Executive agency; and

(2) the Government Printing Office.

(3) [Redesignated]

(b) Federal personnel management should be implemented consistent with the following merit system principles:

* * *

(8) Employees should be—

(A) protected against arbitrary action, personal favoritism, or coercion for partisan political purposes, and

(B) prohibited from using their official authority or influence for the purpose of interfering with or affecting the result of an election or a nomination for election.

(9) Employees should be protected against reprisal for the lawful disclosure of information which the employees reasonably believe evidences—

(A) a violation of any law, rule, or regulation, or

(B) mismanagement, a gross waste of funds, an abuse of authority, or a substantial and specific danger to public health or safety. * * *

(Added Oct. 13, 1978, P.L. 95–454, Title I, § 101(a), 92 Stat. 1113; Oct. 30, 1990, P.L. 101–474, § 5(c), 104 Stat. 1099.)

§ 2302.   Prohibited personnel practices

(a) (1) For the purpose of this title, "prohibited personnel practice" means any action described in subsection (b).

(2) For the purpose of this section—

(A) "personnel action" means—

(i) an appointment;

(ii) a promotion;

(iii) an action under chapter 75 of this title [5 U.S.C. §§ 7501 et seq.] or other disciplinary or corrective action;

(iv) a detail, transfer, or reassignment;

(v) a reinstatement;

(vi) a restoration;

(vii) a reemployment;

(viii) a performance evaluation under chapter 43 of this title [5 USCS §§ 4301 et seq.];

(ix) a decision concerning pay, benefits, or awards, or concerning education or training if the education or training may reasonably be expected to lead to an appointment, promotion, performance evaluation, or other action described in this subparagraph;

(x) a decision to order psychiatric testing or examination; and

(xi) any other significant change in duties, responsibilities, or working conditions;

with respect to an employee in, or applicant for, a covered position in an agency, and in the case of an alleged prohibited personnel practice described in subsection (b)(8), an employee or applicant for employment in a Government corporation as defined in section 9101 of title 31;

(B) "covered position" means, with respect to any personnel action, any position in the competitive service, a career appointee position in the Senior Executive Service, or a position in the excepted service, but does not include any position which is, prior to the personnel action—

(i) excepted from the competitive service because of its confidential, policy-determining, policy-making, or policy-advocating character; or

(ii) excluded from the coverage of this section by the President based on a determination by the President that it is necessary and warranted by conditions of good administration; * * *

(b) Any employee who has authority to take, direct others to take, recommend, or approve any personnel action, shall not, with respect to such authority—* * *

(3) coerce the political activity of any person (including the providing of any political contribution or service), or take any action against any employee or applicant for employment as a reprisal for the refusal of any person to engage in such political activity; * * *

(8) take or fail to take, or threaten to take or fail to take, a personnel action with respect to any employee or applicant for employment because of—

(A) any disclosure of information by an employee or applicant which the employee or applicant reasonably believes evidences—

(i) a violation of any law, rule, or regulation, or

(ii) gross mismanagement, a gross waste of funds, an abuse of authority, or a substantial and specific danger to public health or safety,

if such disclosure is not specifically prohibited by law and if such information is not specifically required by Executive order to be kept secret in the interest of national defense or the conduct of foreign affairs; or

(B) any disclosure to the Special Counsel, or to the Inspector General of an agency or another employee designated by the head of the agency to receive such disclosures, of information which the employee or applicant reasonably believes evidences—

(i) a violation of any law, rule, or regulation, or

(ii) gross mismanagement, a gross waste of funds, an abuse of authority, or a substantial and specific danger to public health or safety;

(9) take or fail to take, or threaten to take or fail to take, any personnel action against any employee or applicant for employment because of—

(A) the exercise of any appeal, complaint, or grievance right granted by any law, rule, or regulation;

(B) testifying for or otherwise lawfully assisting any individual in the exercise of any right referred to in subparagraph (A);

(C) cooperating with or disclosing information to the Inspector General of an agency, or the Special Counsel, in accordance with applicable provisions of law; or

(D) for refusing to obey an order that would require the individual to violate a law * * *

(Added Oct. 13, 1978, P.L. 95–454, Title I, § 101(a), 92 Stat. 1114; April 10, 1989, P.L. 101–12, § 4, 103 Stat. 32; Oct. 30, 1990, P.L. 101–474, § 5(d), 104 Stat. 1099; Oct. 2, 1992, P.L. 102–378, § 2(5), 106 Stat. 1346; Oct. 6, 1993, P.L. 103–94, § 8(c), 107 Stat. 1007; as amended Oct. 14, 1994, P.L. 103–359, Title V, § 501(c), 108 Stat. 3429; Oct. 29, 1994, P.L. 103–424, § 5, 108 Stat. 4364; Sept. 16, 1996, P.L. 104–197, Title III, § 315(b)(2), 110 Stat. 2416; Sept. 23, 1996, P.L. 104–201, Div. A, Title XI, Subtitle B, § 1122(a)(1), Title XVI, Subtitle A, § 1615(b), 110 Stat. 2687, 2741; Oct. 31, 1998, P.L. 105–339, § 6(a), (b), (c)(2), 112 Stat. 3187, 3188; Oct. 14, 2008, P.L. 110–417, [Div. A,] Title IX, Subtitle D, § 931(a)(1), 122 Stat. 4575.)

FALSE CLAIMS ACT
31 U.S.C. §§ 3729–32

§ 3729. False claims

(a) Liability for certain acts.

(1) In general. Subject to paragraph (2), any person who—

(A) knowingly presents, or causes to be presented, a false or fraudulent claim for payment or approval;

(B) knowingly makes, uses, or causes to be made or used, a false record or statement material to a false or fraudulent claim;

(C) conspires to commit a violation of subparagraph (A), (B), (D), (E), (F), or (G);

(D) has possession, custody, or control of property or money used, or to be used, by the Government and knowingly delivers, or causes to be delivered, less than all of that money or property;

(E) is authorized to make or deliver a document certifying receipt of property used, or to be used, by the Government and, intending to defraud the Government, makes or delivers the receipt without completely knowing that the information on the receipt is true;

(F) knowingly buys, or receives as a pledge of an obligation or debt, public property from an officer or employee of the Government, or a member of the Armed Forces, who lawfully may not sell or pledge property; or

(G) knowingly makes, uses, or causes to be made or used, a false record or statement material to an obligation to pay or transmit money or property to the Government, or knowingly conceals or knowingly and improperly avoids or decreases an obligation to pay or transmit money or property to the Government,

is liable to the United States Government for a civil penalty of not less than $5,000 and not more than $10,000, as adjusted by the Federal Civil Penalties Inflation Adjustment Act of 1990 (28 U.S.C. 2461 note; Public Law 104–410), plus 3 times the amount of damages which the Government sustains because of the act of that person.

(2) Reduced damages. If the court finds that—

(A) the person committing the violation of this subsection furnished officials of the United States responsible for investigating false claims violations with all information known to such person about the violation within 30 days after the date on which the defendant first obtained the information;

(B) such person fully cooperated with any Government investigation of such violation; and

(C) at the time such person furnished the United States with the information about the violation, no criminal prosecution, civil action, or administrative action had commenced under this title with respect to such violation, and the person did not have actual knowledge of the existence of an investigation into such violation,

the court may assess not less than 2 times the amount of damages which the Government sustains because of the act of that person.

(3) Costs of civil actions. A person violating this subsection shall also be liable to the United States Government for the costs of a civil action brought to recover any such penalty or damages.

(b) Definitions. For purposes of this section—

(1) the terms "knowing" and "knowingly"—

(A) mean that a person, with respect to information—

(i) has actual knowledge of the information;

(ii) acts in deliberate ignorance of the truth or falsity of the information; or

(iii) acts in reckless disregard of the truth or falsity of the information; and

(B) require no proof of specific intent to defraud;

(2) the term "claim"—

(A) means any request or demand, whether under a contract or otherwise, for money or property and whether or not the United States has title to the money or property, that—

(i) is presented to an officer, employee, or agent of the United States; or

(ii) is made to a contractor, grantee, or other recipient, if the money or property is to be spent or used on the Government's behalf or to advance a Government program or interest, and if the United States Government—

(I) provides or has provided any portion of the money or property requested or demanded; or

(II) will reimburse such contractor, grantee, or other recipient for any portion of the money or property which is requested or demanded; and

(B) does not include requests or demands for money or property that the Government has paid to an individual as compensation for Federal employment or as an income subsidy with no restrictions on that individual's use of the money or property;

(3) the term "obligation" means an established duty, whether or not fixed, arising from an express or implied contractual, grantor-grantee, or licensor-licensee relationship, from a fee-based or similar relationship, from statute or regulation, or from the retention of any overpayment; and

(4) the term "material" means having a natural tendency to influence, or be capable of influencing, the payment or receipt of money or property.

(c) Exemption from disclosure. Any information furnished pursuant to subsection (a)(2) shall be exempt from disclosure under section 552 of title 5.

(d) Exclusion. This section does not apply to claims, records, or statements made under the Internal Revenue Code of 1986 [26 U.S.C. §§ 1 et seq.].

(e) [Redesignated]

(Sept. 13, 1982, P.L. 97–258, § 1, 96 Stat. 978; Oct. 27, 1986, P.L. 99–562, § 2, 100 Stat. 3153; July 5, 1994, P.L. 103–272, § 4(f)(1)(O), 108 Stat. 1362; as amended May 20, 2009, P.L. 111–21, § 4(a), 123 Stat. 1621.)

§ 3730. Civil actions for false claims

(a) Responsibilities of the Attorney General. The Attorney General diligently shall investigate a violation under section 3729 [31 U.S.C. § 3729]. If the Attorney General finds that a person has violated or is violating section 3729, the Attorney General may bring a civil action under this section against the person.

(b) Actions by private persons.

(1) A person may bring a civil action for a violation of section 3729 for the person and for the United States Government. The action shall be brought in the name of the Government. The action may be dismissed only if the court and the Attorney General give written consent to the dismissal and their reasons for consenting.

(2) A copy of the complaint and written disclosure of substantially all material evidence and information the person possesses shall be served on the Government pursuant to Rule 4(d)(4) of the Federal Rules of Civil Procedure. The complaint shall be filed in camera, shall remain under seal for at least 60 days, and shall not be served on the defendant until the court so orders. The Government may elect to intervene and proceed with the action within 60 days after it receives both the complaint and the material evidence and information.

(3) The Government may, for good cause shown, move the court for extensions of the time during which the complaint remains

under seal under paragraph (2). Any such motions may be supported by affidavits or other submissions in camera. The defendant shall not be required to respond to any complaint filed under this section until 20 days after the complaint is unsealed and served upon the defendant pursuant to Rule 4 of the Federal Rules of Civil Procedure.

(4) Before the expiration of the 60–day period or any extensions obtained under paragraph (3), the Government shall—

(A) proceed with the action, in which case the action shall be conducted by the Government; or

(B) notify the court that it declines to take over the action, in which case the person bringing the action shall have the right to conduct the action.

(5) When a person brings an action under this subsection, no person other than the Government may intervene or bring a related action based on the facts underlying the pending action.

(c) Rights of the parties to qui tam actions.

(1) If the Government proceeds with the action, it shall have the primary responsibility for prosecuting the action, and shall not be bound by an act of the person bringing the action. Such person shall have the right to continue as a party to the action, subject to the limitations set forth in paragraph (2).

(2) (A) The Government may dismiss the action notwithstanding the objections of the person initiating the action if the person has been notified by the Government of the filing of the motion and the court has provided the person with an opportunity for a hearing on the motion.

(B) The Government may settle the action with the defendant notwithstanding the objections of the person initiating the action if the court determines, after a hearing, that the proposed settlement is fair, adequate, and reasonable under all the circumstances. Upon a showing of good cause, such hearing may be held in camera.

(C) Upon a showing by the Government that unrestricted participation during the course of the litigation by the person initiating the action would interfere with or unduly delay the Government's prosecution of the case, or would be repetitious, irrelevant, or for purposes of harassment, the court may, in its discretion, impose limitations on the person's participation, such as—

(i) limiting the number of witnesses the person may call;

(ii) limiting the length of the testimony of such witnesses;

(iii) limiting the person's cross-examination of witnesses; or

(iv) otherwise limiting the participation by the person in the litigation.

(D) Upon a showing by the defendant that unrestricted participation during the course of the litigation by the person initiating the action would be for purposes of harassment or would cause the defendant undue burden or unnecessary expense, the court may limit the participation by the person in the litigation.

(3) If the Government elects not to proceed with the action, the person who initiated the action shall have the right to conduct the action. If the Government so requests, it shall be served with copies of all pleadings filed in the action and shall be supplied with copies of all deposition transcripts (at the Government's expense). When a person proceeds with the action, the court, without limiting the status and rights of the person initiating the action, may nevertheless permit the Government to intervene at a later date upon a showing of good cause.

(4) Whether or not the Government proceeds with the action, upon a showing by the Government that certain actions of discovery by the person initiating the action would interfere with the Government's investigation or prosecution of a criminal or civil matter arising out of the same facts, the court may stay such discovery for a period of not more than 60 days. Such a showing shall be conducted in camera. The court may extend the 60–day period upon a further showing in camera that the Government has pursued the criminal or civil investigation or proceedings with reasonable diligence and any proposed discovery in the civil action will interfere with the ongoing criminal or civil investigation or proceedings.

(5) Notwithstanding subsection (b), the Government may elect to pursue its claim through any alternate remedy available to the Government, including any administrative proceeding to determine a civil money penalty. If any such alternate remedy is pursued in another proceeding, the person initiating the action shall have the same rights in such proceeding as such person would have had if the action had continued under this section. Any finding of fact or conclusion of law made in such other proceeding that has become final shall be conclusive on all parties to an action under this section. For purposes of the preceding sentence, a finding or conclusion is final if it has been finally determined on appeal to the appropriate court of the United States, if all time for filing such an appeal with respect to the finding or conclusion has expired, or if the finding or conclusion is not subject to judicial review.

(d) Award to qui tam plaintiff.

(1) If the Government proceeds with an action brought by a person under subsection (b), such person shall, subject to the second sentence of this paragraph, receive at least 15 percent but not more than 25 percent of the proceeds of the action or settlement of the claim, depending upon the extent to which the person substantially contributed to the prosecution of the action. Where the action is one which the court finds to be based primarily on disclosures of specific information (other than information provided by the person bringing the action) relating to allegations or transactions in a criminal, civil, or administrative hearing, in a congressional, administrative, or Government [General] Accounting Office report, hearing, audit, or investigation, or from the news media, the court may award such sums as it considers appropriate, but in no case more than 10 percent of the proceeds, taking into account the significance of the information and the role of the person bringing the action in advancing the case to litigation. Any payment to a person under the first or second sentence of this paragraph shall be made from the proceeds. Any such person shall also receive an amount for reasonable expenses which the court finds to have been necessarily incurred, plus reasonable attorneys' fees and costs. All such expenses, fees, and costs shall be awarded against the defendant.

(2) If the Government does not proceed with an action under this section, the person bringing the action or settling the claim shall receive an amount which the court decides is reasonable for collecting the civil penalty and damages. The amount shall be not less than 25 percent and not more than 30 percent of the proceeds of the action or settlement and shall be paid out of such proceeds. Such person shall also receive an amount for reasonable expenses which the court finds to have been necessarily incurred, plus reasonable attorneys' fees and costs. All such expenses, fees, and costs shall be awarded against the defendant.

(3) Whether or not the Government proceeds with the action, if the court finds that the action was brought by a person who planned and initiated the violation of section 3729 [31 USCS § 3729] upon which the action was brought, then the court may, to the extent the court considers appropriate, reduce the share of the proceeds of the action which the person would otherwise receive under paragraph (1) or (2) of this subsection, taking into account the role of that person in advancing the case to litigation and any relevant circumstances pertaining to the violation. If the person bringing the action is convicted of criminal conduct arising from his or her role in the violation of section 3729 [31 USCS § 3729], that person shall be dismissed from the civil action and shall not receive any share of the proceeds of the action. Such dismissal shall not prejudice the right of the United States to continue the action, represented by the Department of Justice.

(4) If the Government does not proceed with the action and the person bringing the action conducts the action, the court may award

to the defendant its reasonable attorneys' fees and expenses if the defendant prevails in the action and the court finds that the claim of the person bringing the action was clearly frivolous, clearly vexatious, or brought primarily for purposes of harassment.

(e) Certain actions barred.

(1) No court shall have jurisdiction over an action brought by a former or present member of the armed forces under subsection (b) of this section against a member of the armed forces arising out of such person's service in the armed forces.

(2) (A) No court shall have jurisdiction over an action brought under subsection (b) against a Member of Congress, a member of the judiciary, or a senior executive branch official if the action is based on evidence or information known to the Government when the action was brought.

(B) For purposes of this paragraph, "senior executive branch official" means any officer or employee listed in paragraphs (1) through (8) of section 101(f) of the Ethics in Government Act of 1978 (5 U.S.C. App.).

(3) In no event may a person bring an action under subsection (b) which is based upon allegations or transactions which are the subject of a civil suit or an administrative civil money penalty proceeding in which the Government is already a party.

(4) (A) The court shall dismiss an action or claim under this section, unless opposed by the Government, if substantially the same allegations or transactions as alleged in the action or claim were publicly disclosed—

(i) in a Federal criminal, civil, or administrative hearing in which the Government or its agent is a party;

(ii) in a congressional, Government Accountability Office, or other Federal report, hearing, audit, or investigation; or

(iii) from the news media,

unless the action is brought by the Attorney General or the person bringing the action is an original source of the information.

(B) For purposes of this paragraph, "original source" means an individual who either (i) prior to a public disclosure under subsection (e)(4)(a), has voluntarily disclosed to the Government the information on which allegations or transactions in a claim are based, or (2) who has knowledge that is independent of and materially adds to the publicly disclosed allegations or transactions, and who has voluntarily provided the information to the Government before filing an action under this section.

(f) Government not liable for certain expenses. The Government is not liable for expenses which a person incurs in bringing an action under this section.

(g) Fees and expenses to prevailing defendant. In civil actions brought under this section by the United States, the provisions of section 2412(d) of title 28 shall apply.

(h) Relief from retaliatory actions.

(1) In general. Any employee, contractor, or agent shall be entitled to all relief necessary to make that employee, contractor, or agent whole, if that employee, contractor, or agent is discharged, demoted, suspended, threatened, harassed, or in any other manner discriminated against in the terms and conditions of employment because of lawful acts done by the employee, contractor, agent or associated others in furtherance of an action under this section or other efforts to stop 1 or more violations of this subchapter [31 U.S.C. §§ 3721 et seq.].

(2) Relief. Relief under paragraph (1) shall include reinstatement with the same seniority status that employee, contractor, or agent would have had but for the discrimination, 2 times the amount of back pay, interest on the back pay, and compensation for any special damages sustained as a result of the discrimination, including litigation costs and reasonable attorneys' fees. An action under this subsection may be brought in the appropriate district court of the United States for the relief provided in this subsection.

(3) Limitation on bringing civil action. A civil action under this subsection may not be brought more than 3 years after the date when the retaliation occurred.

(Sept. 13, 1982, P.L. 97–258, § 1, 96 Stat. 978; Oct. 27, 1986, P.L. 99–562, §§ 3, 4, 100 Stat. 3154, 3157; Nov. 19, 1988, P.L. 100–700, § 9, 102 Stat. 4638; May 4, 1990, P.L. 101–280, § 10(a), 104 Stat. 162; July 5, 1994, P.L. 103–272, § 4(f)(1)(P), 108 Stat. 1362; as amended, May 20, 2009, P.L. 111–21, § 4(d), 123 Stat. 1624; March 23, 2010, P.L. 111–148, Title X, Subtitle A, § 10104(j)(2), 124 Stat. 901; July 21, 2010, P.L. 111–203, Title X, Subtitle G, § 1079A(c), 124 Stat. 2079.)

§ 3731. False claims procedure

(a) A subpena [subpoena] requiring the attendance of a witness at a trial or hearing conducted under section 3730 of this title may be served at any place in the United States.

(b) A civil action under section 3730 may not be brought—

(1) more than 6 years after the date on which the violation of section 3729 is committed, or

(2) more than 3 years after the date when facts material to the right of action are known or reasonably should have been known by the official of the United States charged with responsibility to act in

the circumstances, but in no event more than 10 years after the date on which the violation is committed,

whichever occurs last.

(c) If the Government elects to intervene and proceed with an action brought under section 3730(b), the Government may file its own complaint or amend the complaint of a person who has brought an action under section 3730(b) to clarify or add detail to the claims in which the Government is intervening and to add any additional claims with respect to which the Government contends it is entitled to relief. For statute of limitations purposes, any such Government pleading shall relate back to the filing date of the complaint of the person who originally brought the action, to the extent that the claim of the Government arises out of the conduct, transactions, or occurrences set forth, or attempted to be set forth, in the prior complaint of that person.

(d) In any action brought under section 3730, the United States shall be required to prove all essential elements of the cause of action, including damages, by a preponderance of the evidence.

(e) Notwithstanding any other provision of law, the Federal Rules of Criminal Procedure, or the Federal Rules of Evidence, a final judgment rendered in favor of the United States in any criminal proceeding charging fraud or false statements, whether upon a verdict after trial or upon a plea of guilty or nolo contendere, shall estop the defendant from denying the essential elements of the offense in any action which involves the same transaction as in the criminal proceeding and which is brought under subsection (a) or (b) of section 3730.

(Sept. 13, 1982, P.L. 97–258, § 1, 96 Stat. 979; Oct. 27, 1986, P.L. 99–562, § 5, 100 Stat. 3158; as amended May 20, 2009, P.L. 111–21, § 4(b), 123 Stat. 1623.)

§ 3732. False claims jurisdiction

(a) Actions under section 3730. Any action under section 3730 may be brought in any judicial district in which the defendant or, in the case of multiple defendants, any one defendant can be found, resides, transacts business, or in which any act proscribed by section 3729 [31 USCS § 3729] occurred. A summons as required by the Federal Rules of Civil Procedure shall be issued by the appropriate district court and served at any place within or outside the United States.

(b) Claims under State law. The district courts shall have jurisdiction over any action brought under the laws of any State for the recovery of funds paid by a State or local government if the action arises from the same transaction or occurrence as an action brought under section 3730.

(c) Service on State or local authorities. With respect to any State or local government that is named as a co-plaintiff with the United States in an action brought under subsection (b), a seal on the action ordered by the court under section 3730(b) shall not preclude the

Government or the person bringing the action from serving the complaint, any other pleadings, or the written disclosure of substantially all material evidence and information possessed by the person bringing the action on the law enforcement authorities that are authorized under the law of that State or local government to investigate and prosecute such actions on behalf of such governments, except that such seal applies to the law enforcement authorities so served to the same extent as the seal applies to other parties in the action.

(Added Oct. 27, 1986, P.L. 99–562, § 6(a), 100 Stat. 3158; as amended May 20, 2009, P.L. 111–21, § 4(e), 123 Stat. 1625.)

§ 230. Prohibition of discharge, discrimination, or retaliation against employee serving on jury or as witness or seeking relief against domestic violence or sexual assault; Remedies for violation; Misdemeanor; Filing of complaint

(a) An employer may not discharge or in any manner discriminate against an employee for taking time off to serve as required by law on an inquest jury or trial jury, if the employee, prior to taking the time off, gives reasonable notice to the employer that he or she is required to serve.

(b) An employer may not discharge or in any manner discriminate or retaliate against an employee, including, but not limited to, an employee who is a victim of a crime, for taking time off to appear in court to comply with a subpoena or other court order as a witness in any judicial proceeding.

(c) An employer may not discharge or in any manner discriminate or retaliate against an employee who is a victim of domestic violence or a victim of sexual assault for taking time off from work to obtain or attempt to obtain any relief, including, but not limited to, a temporary restraining order, restraining order, or other injunctive relief, to help ensure the health, safety, or welfare of the victim or his or her child.

(d) (1) As a condition of taking time off for a purpose set forth in subdivision (c), the employee shall give the employer reasonable advance notice of the employee's intention to take time off, unless the advance notice is not feasible.

(2) When an unscheduled absence occurs, the employer shall not take any action against the employee if the employee, within a reasonable time after the absence, provides a certification to the employer. Certification shall be sufficient in the form of any of the following:

(A) A police report indicating that the employee was a victim of domestic violence or sexual assault.

(B) A court order protecting or separating the employee from the perpetrator of an act of domestic violence or sexual assault, or other evidence from the court or prosecuting attorney that the employee has appeared in court.

(C) Documentation from a medical professional, domestic violence advocate or advocate for victims of sexual assault, health care provider, or counselor that the employee was undergoing treatment for physical or mental injuries or abuse resulting in victimization from an act of domestic violence or sexual assault.

(3) To the extent allowed by law, the employer shall maintain the confidentiality of any employee requesting leave under subdivision (c).

(e) Any employee who is discharged, threatened with discharge, demoted, suspended, or in any other manner discriminated or retaliated against in the terms and conditions of employment by his or her employer because the employee has taken time off for a purpose set forth in subdivision (a), (b), or (c) shall be entitled to reinstatement and reimbursement for lost wages and work benefits caused by the acts of the employer. Any employer who willfully refuses to rehire, promote, or otherwise restore an employee or former employee who has been determined to be eligible for rehiring or promotion by a grievance procedure or hearing authorized by law is guilty of a misdemeanor.

(f) (1) Any employee who is discharged, threatened with discharge, demoted, suspended, or in any other manner discriminated or retaliated against in the terms and conditions of employment by his or her employer because the employee has exercised his or her rights as set forth in subdivision (a), (b), or (c) may file a complaint with the Division of Labor Standards Enforcement of the Department of Industrial Relations pursuant to Section 98.7.

(2) Notwithstanding any time limitation in Section 98.7, an employee filing a complaint with the division based upon a violation of subdivision (c) shall have one year from the date of occurrence of the violation to file his or her complaint.

(g) An employee may use vacation, personal leave, or compensatory time off that is otherwise available to the employee under the applicable terms of employment, unless otherwise provided by a collective bargaining agreement, for time taken off for a purpose specified in subdivision (a), (b), or (c). The entitlement of any employee under this section shall not be diminished by any collective bargaining agreement term or condition.

(h) For purposes of this section:

(1) "Domestic violence" means any of the types of abuse set forth in Section 6211 of the Family Code, as amended.

(2) "Sexual assault" means any of the crimes set forth in Sections 261, 261.5, 262, 265, 266, 266a, 266b, 266c, 266g, 266j, 267, 269, 273.4, 285, 286, 288, 288a, 288.5, 289, or 311.4 of the Penal Code, as amended.

(Added Stats. 1968 ch. 1270 § 1. Amended Stats. 1978 ch. 161 § 1. Amended Stats. 1999 ch. 340 § 1 (SB 56); Stats. 2000 ch. 487 § 2 (AB 2357); Stats. 2002 ch. 275 § 1 (AB 2195)).

NEVADA REV. STAT. ANN. § 50.070 (2012)

§ 50.070 Termination or threat of termination of employment because of service as witness prohibited; penalty; remedies

1. Any person, corporation, partnership, association or other entity who is:

(a) An employer; or

(b) The employee, agent or officer of an employer, vested with the power to terminate or recommend termination of employment, of a person who is a witness or who has received a summons to appear as a witness in a judicial or administrative proceeding, who deprives the witness or person summoned of his employment, as a consequence of his service as a witness or prospective witness, or who asserts to the witness or person summoned that his service as a witness or prospective witness will result in termination of his employment, is guilty of a misdemeanor.

2. A person discharged from employment in violation of subsection 1 may commence a civil action against his employer and obtain:

(a) Wages and benefits lost as a result of the violation;

(b) An order of reinstatement without loss of position, seniority or benefits;

(c) Damages equal to the amount of the lost wages and benefits; and

(d) Reasonable attorney's fees fixed by the court.

(1981, p. 366; 1995, ch. 141, § 1, p. 209)

CALIFORNIA LABOR CODE §§ 1102–1106 (2012)

§ 1102. Coercing or influencing political activities of employees

No employer shall coerce or influence or attempt to coerce or influence his employees through or by means of threat of discharge or loss of employment to adopt or follow or refrain from adopting or following any particular course or line of political action or political activity.

§ 1103. Violation of chapter as misdemeanor; Punishment

Any employer who violates this chapter is guilty of a misdemeanor punishable, in the case of an individual, by imprisonment in the county jail not to exceed one year or a fine of not to exceed $1000 or both, and, in the case of a corporation, by a fine of not to exceed $5000.

§ 1104. Employer's responsibility for acts of managers, officers, agents and employees

In all prosecutions under this chapter, the employer is responsible for the acts of his managers, officers, agents, and employees.

§ 1105. Recovery of damages by employee

Nothing in this chapter shall prevent the injured employee from recovering damages from his employer for injury suffered through a violation of this chapter.

§ 1106. "Employee"

For purposes of Sections 1102.5, 1102.6, 1102.7, 1102.8, 1104, and 1105, "employee" includes, but is not limited to, any individual employed by the state or any subdivision thereof, any county, city, city and county, including any charter city or county, and any school district, community college district, municipal or public corporation, political subdivision, or the University of California.

(Added Stats. 1992 ch. 1230 § 1 (AB 3486); Amended Stats. 2003 ch. 484 § 7 (SB 777)).

CONNECTICUT GEN. STAT. § 31–51q (2012)

§ 31–51q. Liability of employer for discipline or discharge of employee on account of employee's exercise of certain constitutional rights.

Any employer, including the state and any instrumentality or political subdivision thereof, who subjects any employee to discipline or discharge on account of the exercise by such employee of rights guaranteed by the first amendment to the United States Constitution or section 3, 4 or 14 of article first of the Constitution of the state, provided such activity does not substantially or materially interfere with the employee's bona fide job performance or the working relationship between the employee and the employer, shall be liable to such employee for damages caused by such discipline or discharge, including punitive damages, and for reasonable attorney's fees as part of the costs of any such action for damages. If the court determines that such action for damages was brought without substantial justification, the court may award costs and reasonable attorney's fees to the employer.

NEW JERSEY STAT. §§ 34:19–10 to –11 (2012)

§ 34:19–10. Required participation by employee in meetings, communications prohibited; exception

No employer or employer's agent, representative or designee may, except as provided in [C.34:19–11] of this act, require its employees to attend an employer-sponsored meeting or participate in any communications with the employer or its agents or representatives, the purpose of which is to communicate the employer's opinion about religious or political matters.

This act shall not be construed as prohibiting an employer from permitting its employees to voluntarily attend employer-sponsored meetings or providing other communications to the employees, if the employer notifies the employees that they may refuse to attend the meetings or accept the communications without penalty.

§ 34:19–11. Permitted communication about religious, political matters

a. An employer or its agent, representative or designee may communicate to employees information about religious or political matters that the employer is required by law to communicate, but only to the extent required by law.

b. Nothing in this act shall prohibit:

(1) A religious organization from requiring its employees to attend an employer-sponsored meeting or to participate in any communications with the employer or its agents or representatives, the purpose of which is to communicate the employer's religious beliefs, practices or tenets;

(2) A political organization or party from requiring its employees to attend an employer-sponsored meeting or to participate in any communications with the employer or its agents or representatives, the purpose of which is to communicate the employer's political tenets or purposes; or

(3) An educational institution from requiring a student or instructor to attend lectures on political or religious matters that are part of the regular course work at the institution.

ILLINOIS ANN. STAT. 430/15–10 (2012)

§ 5 ILCS 430/15–10. Protected activity

Sec. 15–10. Protected activity. An officer, a member, a State employee, or a State agency shall not take any retaliatory action against a State employee because the State employee does any of the following:

(1) Discloses or threatens to disclose to a supervisor or to a public body an activity, policy, or practice of any officer, member, State agency, or other State employee that the State employee reasonably believes is in violation of a law, rule, or regulation.

(2) Provides information to or testifies before any public body conducting an investigation, hearing, or inquiry into any violation of a law, rule, or regulation by any officer, member, State agency, or other State employee.

(3) Assists or participates in a proceeding to enforce the provisions of this Act.

63b91. Employees of constitutional officers—Disclosure of prohibited activity—Retaliatory action

§ 1. (a) In any case involving any disclosure of information by an employee of any Constitutional Officer of this State which the employee reasonably believes evidences (1) a violation of any law, rule or regulation or (2) mismanagement, a gross waste of funds, abuse of authority or a substantial and specific danger to public health or safety if the disclosure is not specifically prohibited by law, the identity of the employee may not be disclosed without the consent of the employee during any investigation of the information and any related matters.

(b) No disciplinary action shall be taken against any employee for the disclosure of any alleged prohibited activity under investigation or for any related activity. For the purposes of this Act, disciplinary action means any retaliatory action taken against an employee, including but not limited to reprimand, suspension, discharge, demotion or denial of promotion or transfer.

LOUISIANA REV. STAT. ANN.
§§ 23:961–962 (2012)

§ 961. Political rights and freedom; restrictions forbidden; penalty; employees' right to recover damages

Except as otherwise provided in R.S. 23:962, no employer having regularly in his employ twenty or more employees shall make, adopt, or enforce any rule, regulation, or policy forbidding or preventing any of his employees from engaging or participating in politics, or from becoming a candidate for public office. No such employer shall adopt or enforce any rule, regulation, or policy which will control, direct, or tend to control or direct the political activities or affiliations of his employees, nor coerce or influence, or attempt to coerce or influence any of his employees by means of threats of discharge or of loss of employment in case such employees should support or become affiliated with any particular political faction or organization, or participate in political activities of any nature or character.

Any individual person violating the provisions of this Section shall be fined not less than one hundred dollars nor more than one thousand dollars, or imprisoned for not more than six months, or both; and any firm, corporation or association violating the provisions of this Section shall be fined not less than five hundred dollars nor more than two thousand dollars.

Nothing herein contained shall in any way be construed to prevent the injured employee from recovering damages from the employer as a result of suffering caused by the employer's violations of this Section.

§ 962. Discharge because of political opinions; attempt to control votes; penalty

Any planter, manager, overseer or other employer of laborers who, previous to the expiration of the term of service of any laborer in his employ or under his control, discharges such laborer on account of his political opinions, or attempts to control the suffrage or vote of such laborer by any contract or agreement whatever, shall be fined not less than one hundred dollars, nor more than five hundred dollars and imprisoned for not more than one year.

MICHIGAN COMP. LAWS ANN.
§§ 15.361–15.368 (2012)

§ 15.361 Definitions

Sec. 1. As used in this act:

(a) "Employee" means a person who performs a service for wages or other remuneration under a contract of hire, written or oral, express or implied. Employee includes a person employed by the state or a political subdivision of the state except state classified civil service.

(b) "Employer" means a person who has 1 or more employees. Employer includes an agent of an employer and the state or a political subdivision of the state.

(c) "Person" means an individual, sole proprietorship, partnership, corporation, association, or any other legal entity.

(d) "Public body" means all of the following:

(i) A state officer, employee, agency, department, division, bureau, board, commission, council, authority, or other body in the executive branch of state government.

(ii) An agency, board, commission, council, member, or employee of the legislative branch of state government.

(iii) A county, city, township, village, intercounty, intercity, or regional governing body, a council, school district, special district, or municipal corporation, or a board, department, commission, council, agency, or any member or employee thereof.

(iv) Any other body which is created by state or local authority or which is primarily funded by or through state or local authority, or any member or employee of that body.

(v) A law enforcement agency or any member or employee of a law enforcement agency.

(vi) The judiciary and any member or employee of the judiciary.

§ 15.362 Discharge of, threats to or discrimination against employee for reporting violations of law

Sec. 2. An employer shall not discharge, threaten, or otherwise discriminate against an employee regarding the employee's compensation, terms, conditions, location, or privileges of employment because the employee, or a person acting on behalf of the employee, reports or is about to report, verbally or in writing, a violation or a suspected violation of a law or regulation or rule promulgated pursuant to law of this state, a political subdivision of this state, or the United States to a public body, unless the employee knows that the report is false, or because an employee is requested by a public body to participate in an investigation, hearing, or inquiry held by that public body, or a court action.

§ 15.363   Civil action; alleged violation

Sec. 3. (1) A person who alleges a violation of this act may bring a civil action for appropriate injunctive relief, or actual damages, or both within 90 days after the occurrence of the alleged violation of this act.

(2) An action commenced pursuant to subsection (1) may be brought in the circuit court for the county where the alleged violation occurred, the county where the complainant resides, or the county where the person against whom the civil complaint is filed resides or has his or her principal place of business.

(3) As used in subsection (1), "damages" means damages for injury or loss caused by each violation of this act, including reasonable attorney fees.

(4) An employee shall show by clear and convincing evidence that he or she or a person acting on his or her behalf was about to report, verbally or in writing, a violation or a suspected violation of a law of this state, a political subdivision of this state, or the United States to a public body.

§ 15.364   Judgment order, contents; award

Sec. 4. A court, in rendering a judgment in an action brought pursuant to this act, shall order, as the court considers appropriate, reinstatement of the employee, the payment of back wages, full reinstatement of fringe benefits and seniority rights, actual damages, or any combination of these remedies. A court may also award the complainant all or a portion of the costs of litigation, including reasonable attorney fees and witness fees, if the court determines that the award is appropriate.

§ 15.365   Civil fine, disposition

Sec. 5. (1) A person who violates this act shall be liable for a civil fine of not more than $500.00.

(2) A civil fine which is ordered pursuant to this act shall be submitted to the state treasurer for deposit in the general fund.

§ 15.366   Construction of act, collective bargaining agreement; disclosures affecting confidentiality of communications

Sec. 6. This act shall not be construed to diminish or impair the rights of a person under any collective bargaining agreement, nor to permit disclosures which would diminish or impair the rights of any person to the continued protection of confidentiality of communications where statute or common law provides such protection.

§ 15.367 Construction of act; compensation for participation in investigation

Sec. 7. This act shall not be construed to require an employer to compensate an employee for participation in an investigation, hearing or inquiry held by a public body in accordance with section 2 of this act.

§ 15.368 Posting notices, protections and obligations of act

Sec. 8. An employer shall post notices and use other appropriate means to keep his or her employees informed of their protections and obligations under this act.

NEW JERSEY STAT. §§ 34:19–1 to 19–8

§ 34:19–1. Short title

This act shall be known and may cited as the "Conscientious Employee Protection Act".

§ 34:19–2. Definitions

As used in this act:

a. "Employer" means any individual, partnership, association, corporation or any person or group of persons acting directly or indirectly on behalf of or in the interest of an employer with the employer's consent and shall include all branches of State Government, or the several counties and municipalities thereof, or any other political subdivision of the State, or a school district, or any special district, or any authority, commission, or board or any other agency or instrumentality thereof.

b. "Employee" means any individual who performs services for and under the control and direction of an employer for wages or other remuneration.

c. "Public body" means:

(1) the United States Congress, and State legislature, or any popularly-elected local governmental body, or any member or employee thereof;

(2) any federal, State, or local judiciary, or any member or employee thereof, or any grand or petit jury;

(3) any federal, State, or local regulatory, administrative, or public agency or authority, or instrumentality thereof;

(4) any federal, State, or local law enforcement agency, prosecutorial office, or police or peace officer;

(5) any federal, State or local department of an executive branch of government; or

(6) any division, board, bureau, office, committee or commission of any of the public bodies described in the above paragraphs of this subsection.

d. "Supervisor" means any individual with an employer's organization who has the authority to direct and control the work performance of the affected employee, who has authority to take corrective action regarding the violation of the law, rule or regulation of which the employee complains, or who has been designated by the employer on the notice required under section 7 of this act.

e. "Retaliatory action" means the discharge, suspension or demotion of an employee, or other adverse employment action taken against an employee in the terms and conditions of employment.

f. "Improper quality of patient care" means, with respect to patient care, any practice, procedure, action or failure to act of an employer that is a health care provider which violates any law or any rule, regulation or declaratory ruling adopted pursuant to law, or any professional code of ethics.

§ 34:19–3. Retaliatory action prohibited

An employer shall not take any retaliatory action against an employee because the employee does any of the following:

a. Discloses, or threatens to disclose to a supervisor or to a public body an activity, policy or practice of the employer, or another employer, with whom there is a business relationship, that the employee reasonably believes:

(1) is in violation of a law, or a rule or regulation promulgated pursuant to law, including any violation involving deception of, or misrepresentation to, any shareholder, investor, client, patient, customer, employee, former employee, retiree or pensioner of the employer or any governmental entity, or, in the case of an employee who is a licensed or certified health care professional, reasonably believes constitutes improper quality of patient care; or

(2) is fraudulent or criminal, including any activity, policy or practice of deception or misrepresentation which the employee reasonably believes may defraud any shareholder, investor, client, patient, customer, employee, former employee, retiree or pensioner of the employer or any governmental entity;

b. Provides information to, or testifies before, any public body conducting an investigation, hearing or inquiry into any violation of law, or a rule or regulation promulgated pursuant to law by the employer, or another employer, with whom there is a business relationship, including any violation involving deception of, or misrepresentation to, any shareholder, investor, client, patient, customer, employee, former employee, retiree or pensioner of the employer or any governmental entity, or, in the case of an employee who is a licensed or certified health care professional, provides information to, or testifies before, any public body conducting an investigation, hearing or inquiry into the quality of patient care; or

c. Objects to, or refuses to participate in any activity, policy or practice which the employee reasonably believes:

(1) is in violation of a law, or a rule or regulation promulgated pursuant to law, including any violation involving deception of, or misrepresentation to, any shareholder, investor, client, patient, customer, employee, former employee, retiree or pensioner of the employer or any governmental entity, or, if the employee is a licensed or certified health care professional, constitutes improper quality of patient care;

(2) is fraudulent or criminal, including any activity, policy or practice of deception or misrepresentation which the employee reasonably believes may defraud any shareholder, investor, client, patient, customer, employee, former employee, retiree or pensioner of the employer or any governmental entity; or

(3) is incompatible with a clear mandate of public policy concerning the public health, safety or welfare or protection of the environment.

§ 34:19–4. Written notice required

The protection against retaliatory action provided by this act pertaining to disclosure to a public body shall not apply to an employee who makes a disclosure to a public body unless the employee has brought the activity, policy or practice in violation of a law, or a rule or regulation promulgated pursuant to law to the attention of a supervisor of the employee by written notice and has afforded the employer a reasonable opportunity to correct the activity, policy or practice. Disclosure shall not be required where the employee is reasonably certain that the activity, policy or practice is known to one or more supervisors of the employer or where the employee reasonably fears physical harm as a result of the disclosure provided, however, that the situation is emergency in nature.

§ 34:19–5. Civil action, jury trial; remedies

Upon a violation of any of the provisions of this act, an aggrieved employee or former employee may, within one year, institute a civil action in a court of competent jurisdiction. Upon the application of any party, a jury trial shall be directed to try the validity of any claim under this act specified in the suit. All remedies available in common law tort actions shall be available to prevailing plaintiffs. These remedies are in addition to any legal or equitable relief provided by this act or any other statute. The court shall also order, where appropriate and to the fullest extent possible:

a. An injunction to restrain any violation of this act which is continuing at the time that the court issues its order;

b. The reinstatement of the employee to the same position held before the retaliatory action, or to an equivalent position;

c. The reinstatement of full fringe benefits and seniority rights;

d. The compensation for all lost wages, benefits and other remuneration; and

e. The payment by the employer of reasonable costs, and attorney's fees.

In addition, the court or jury may order: the assessment of a civil fine of not more than $10,000 for the first violation of the act and not more than $20,000 for each subsequent violation, which shall be paid to the State Treasurer for deposit in the General Fund; punitive damages; or both a civil fine and punitive damages. In determining the amount of punitive damages, the court or jury shall consider not only the amount of compensatory damages awarded to the employee, but also the amount of all damages caused to shareholders, investors, clients, patients, customers, employees, former employees, retirees or pensioners of the employer, or to the public or any governmental entity, by the activities, policies or practices of the employer which the employee disclosed, threatened to disclose, provided testimony regarding, objected to, or refused to participate in.

§ 34:19–6. Fees, costs to employer

A court, upon notice of motion in accordance with the Rules Governing the Courts of the State of New Jersey, may also order that reasonable attorneys' fees and court costs be awarded to an employer if the court determines that an action brought by an employee under this act was without basis in law or in fact. However, an employee shall not be assessed attorneys' fees under this section if, after exercising reasonable and diligent efforts after filing a suit, the employee files a voluntary dismissal concerning the employer, within a reasonable time after determining that the employer would not be found to be liable for damages.

§ 34:19–7. Posting of notices

An employer shall conspicuously display, and annually distribute to all employees, written or electronic notices of its employees protections, obligations, rights and procedures under this act, and use other appropriate means to keep its employees so informed. Each notice posted or distributed pursuant to this section shall be in English, Spanish and at the employer's discretion, any other language spoken by the majority of the employer's employees. The notice shall include the name of the person or persons the employer has designated to receive written notifications pursuant to section 4 [C.34:19–4]of this act. The Commissioner of Labor and Workforce Development shall make available to employers a text of a notice fulfilling the requirements of this section and provide copies of the notice suitable for display and distribution to any employers who request the copies, charging them as much as is needed to pay the costs of the department. The commissioner shall also provide notices printed in a language other than English and Spanish, at the request of the employer.

The requirement that an employer annually distribute to all employees written notices of the protections, obligations, rights and procedures provided to the employees by the provisions of P.L. 1986, c. 105 (C. 34:19–1 et seq.) shall not apply to any employer who has less than 10 employees.

§ 34:19–8. Other rights, remedies unaffected

Nothing in this act shall be deemed to diminish the rights, privileges, or remedies of any employee under any other federal or State law or regulation or under any collective bargaining agreement or employment contract; except that the institution of an action in accordance with this act shall be deemed a waiver of the rights and remedies available under any other contract, collective bargaining agreement, State law, rule or regulation or under the common law.

NEW YORK CIVIL SERVICE LAW § 75–b (2012)

§ 75–b. Retaliatory action by public employers

1. For the purposes of this section the term:

(a) "Public employer" or "employer" shall mean (i) the state of New York, (ii) a county, city, town, village or any other political subdivision or civil division of the state, (iii) a school district or any governmental entity operating a public school, college or university, (iv) a public improvement or special district, (v) a public authority, commission or public benefit corporation, or (vi) any other public corporation, agency, instrumentality or unit of government which exercises governmental power under the laws of the state.

(b) "Public employee" or "employee" shall mean any person holding a position by appointment or employment in the service of a public employer except judges or justices of the unified court system and members of the legislature.

(c) "Governmental body" shall mean (i) an officer, employee, agency, department, division, bureau, board, commission, council, authority or other body of a public employer, (ii) employee, committee, member, or commission of the legislative branch of government, (iii) a representative, member or employee of a legislative body of a county, town, village or any other political subdivision or civil division of the state, (iv) a law enforcement agency or any member or employee of law enforcement agency, or (v) the judiciary or any employee of the judiciary.

(d) "Personnel action" shall mean an action affecting compensation, appointment, promotion, transfer, assignment, reassignment, reinstatement or evaluation of performance.

2. **(a)** A public employer shall not dismiss or take other disciplinary or other adverse personnel action against a public employee regarding the employee's employment because the employee discloses to a governmental body information: (i) regarding a violation of a law, rule or regulation which violation creates and presents a substantial and specific danger to the public health or safety; or (ii) which the employee reasonably believes to be true and reasonably believes constitutes an improper governmental action. "Improper governmental action" shall mean any action by a public employer or employee, or an agent of such employer or employee, which is undertaken in the performance of such agent's official duties, whether or not such action is within the scope of his employment, and which is in violation of any federal, state or local law, rule or regulation.

(b) Prior to disclosing information pursuant to paragraph (a) of this subdivision, an employee shall have made a good faith effort to provide the appointing authority or his or her designee the information to be disclosed and shall provide the appointing authority or designee a reasonable time to take appropriate action unless there is imminent and serious danger to public health or safety. For the purposes of this subdivision, an employee who acts pursuant to this paragraph shall be deemed to have disclosed information to a governmental body under paragraph (a) of this subdivision.

3. **(a)** Where an employee is subject to dismissal or other disciplinary action under a final and binding arbitration provision, or other disciplinary procedure contained in a collectively negotiated agreement, or under section seventy-five of this title or any other provision of state or local law and the employee reasonably believes dismissal or other disciplinary action would not have been taken but for the conduct protected under subdivision two of this section, he or she may assert such as a defense before the designated arbitrator or hearing officer. The merits of such defense shall be considered and determined as part of the arbitration award or hearing officer decision of the matter. If there is a finding that the dismissal or other disciplinary action is based solely on a violation by the employer of such subdivision, the arbitrator or hearing officer shall dismiss or recommend dismissal of the disciplinary proceeding, as appropriate, and, if appropriate, reinstate the employee with back pay, and, in the case of an arbitration procedure, may take other appropriate action as is permitted in the collectively negotiated agreement.

(b) Where an employee is subject to a collectively negotiated agreement which contains provisions preventing an employer from taking adverse personnel actions and which contains a final and binding arbitration provision to resolve alleged violations of such provisions of the agreement and the employee reasonably believes that such personnel action would not have been taken but for the conduct protected under subdivision two of this section, he or she may assert such as a claim before the arbitrator. The arbitrator shall consider such claim and determine its merits and shall, if a determination is made that such adverse personnel action is based on a violation by the employer of such subdivision, take such action to remedy the violation as is permitted by the collectively negotiated agreement.

(c) Where an employee is not subject to any of the provisions of paragraph (a) or (b) of this subdivision, the employee may commence an action in a court of competent jurisdiction under the same terms and conditions as set forth in article twenty-C of the labor law.

4. Nothing in this section shall be deemed to diminish or impair the rights of a public employee or employer under any law, rule, regulation or collectively negotiated agreement or to prohibit any personnel action which otherwise would have been taken regardless of any disclosure of information.

NEW YORK LABOR LAW § 740 (2012)

§ 740. Retaliatory personnel action by employers; prohibition

1. Definitions. For purposes of this section, unless the context specifically indicates otherwise:

(a) "Employee" means an individual who performs services for and under the control and direction of an employer for wages or other remuneration.

(b) "Employer" means any person, firm, partnership, institution, corporation, or association that employs one or more employees.

(c) "Law, rule or regulation" includes any duly enacted statute or ordinance or any rule or regulation promulgated pursuant to any federal, state or local statute or ordinance.

(d) "Public body" includes the following:

(i) the United States Congress, any state legislature, or any popularly-elected local governmental body, or any member or employee thereof;

(ii) any federal, state, or local judiciary, or any member or employee thereof, or any grand or petit jury;

(iii) any federal, state, or local regulatory, administrative, or public agency or authority, or instrumentality thereof; or

(iv) any federal, state, or local law enforcement agency, prosecutorial office, or police or peace officer.

(e) "Retaliatory personnel action" means the discharge, suspension or demotion of an employee, or other adverse employment action taken against an employee in the terms and conditions of employment.

(f) "Supervisor" means any individual with an employer's organization who has the authority to direct and control the work performance of the affected employee; or who has managerial authority to take corrective action regarding the violation of the law, rule or regulation of which the employee complains.

(g) "Health care fraud" means health care fraud as defined by article one hundred seventy-seven of the penal law.

2. Prohibitions. An employer shall not take any retaliatory personnel action against an employee because such employee does any of the following:

(a) discloses, or threatens to disclose to a supervisor or to a public body an activity, policy or practice of the employer that is in

305

violation of law, rule or regulation which violation creates and presents a substantial and specific danger to the public health or safety, or which constitutes health care fraud;

(b) provides information to, or testifies before, any public body conducting an investigation, hearing or inquiry into any such violation of a law, rule or regulation by such employer; or

(c) objects to, or refuses to participate in any such activity, policy or practice in violation of a law, rule or regulation.

3. Application. The protection against retaliatory personnel action provided by paragraph (a) of subdivision two of this section pertaining to disclosure to a public body shall not apply to an employee who makes such disclosure to a public body unless the employee has brought the activity, policy or practice in violation of law, rule or regulation to the attention of a supervisor of the employer and has afforded such employer a reasonable opportunity to correct such activity, policy or practice.

4. Violation; remedy.

(a) An employee who has been the subject of a retaliatory personnel action in violation of this section may institute a civil action in a court of competent jurisdiction for relief as set forth in subdivision five of this section within one year after the alleged retaliatory personnel action was taken.

(b) Any action authorized by this section may be brought in the county in which the alleged retaliatory personnel action occurred, in the county in which the complainant resides, or in the county in which the employer has its principal place of business.

(c) It shall be a defense to any action brought pursuant to this section that the personnel action was predicated upon grounds other than the employee's exercise of any rights protected by this section. It shall also be a defense that the individual was an independent contractor.

(d) Notwithstanding the provisions of paragraphs (a) and (c) of this subdivision, a health care employee who has been the subject of a retaliatory action by a health care employer in violation of section seven hundred forty-one of this article may institute a civil action in a court of competent jurisdiction for relief as set forth in subdivision five of this section within two years after the alleged retaliatory personnel action was taken. In addition to the relief set forth in that subdivision, the court, in its discretion, based upon a finding that the employer acted in bad faith in the retaliatory action, may assess the employer a civil penalty of an amount not to exceed ten thousand dollars, to be paid to the improving quality of patient care fund, established pursuant to section ninety-seven-aaaa of the state finance law.

5. Relief. In any action brought pursuant to subdivision four of this section, the court may order relief as follows:

(a) an injunction to restrain continued violation of this section;

(b) the reinstatement of the employee to the same position held before the retaliatory personnel action, or to an equivalent position;

(c) the reinstatement of full fringe benefits and seniority rights;

(d) the compensation for lost wages, benefits and other remuneration; and

(e) the payment by the employer of reasonable costs, disbursements, and attorney's fees.

6. Employer relief. A court, in its discretion, may also order that reasonable attorney's fees and court costs and disbursements be awarded to an employer if the court determines that an action brought by an employee under this section was without basis in law or in fact.

7. Existing rights. Nothing in this section shall be deemed to diminish the rights, privileges, or remedies of any employee under any other law or regulation or under any collective bargaining agreement or employment contract; except that the institution of an action in accordance with this section shall be deemed a waiver of the rights and remedies available under any other contract, collective bargaining agreement, law, rule or regulation or under the common law.

PENNSYLVANIA "WHISTLEBLOWER LAW"
43 PA. STAT. ANN. §§ 1421–28 (2012)

§ 1421. Short title

This act shall be known and may be cited as the Whistleblower Law.

§ 1422. Definitions

The following words and phrases when used in this act shall have the meanings given to them in this section unless the context clearly indicates otherwise:

"APPROPRIATE AUTHORITY." A Federal, State or local government body, agency or organization having jurisdiction over criminal law enforcement, regulatory violations, professional conduct or ethics, or waste; or a member, officer, agent, representative or supervisory employee of the body, agency or organization. The term includes, but is not limited to, the Office of Attorney General, the Department of the Auditor General, the Treasury Department, the General Assembly and committees of the General Assembly having the power and duty to investigate criminal law enforcement, regulatory violations, professional conduct or ethics, or waste.

"EMPLOYEE." A person who performs a service for wages or other remuneration under a contract of hire, written or oral, express or implied, for a public body.

"EMPLOYER." A person supervising one or more employees, including the employee in question; a superior of that supervisor; or an agent of a public body.

"GOOD FAITH REPORT." A report of conduct defined in this act as wrongdoing or waste which is made without malice or consideration of personal benefit and which the person making the report has reasonable cause to believe is true.

"PUBLIC BODY." All of the following:

(1) A State officer, agency, department, division, bureau, board, commission, council, authority or other body in the executive branch of State government.

(2) A county, city, township, regional governing body, council, school district, special district or municipal corporation, or a board, department, commission, council or agency.

(3) Any other body which is created by Commonwealth or political subdivision authority or which is funded in any amount by or through Commonwealth or political subdivision authority or a member or employee of that body.

"WASTE." An employer's conduct or omissions which result in substantial abuse, misuse, destruction or loss of funds or resources belonging to or derived from Commonwealth or political subdivision sources.

"WHISTLEBLOWER." A person who witnesses or has evidence of wrongdoing or waste while employed and who makes a good faith report of the wrongdoing or waste, verbally or in writing, to one of the person's superiors, to an agent of the employer or to an appropriate authority.

"WRONGDOING." A violation which is not of a merely technical or minimal nature of a Federal or State statute or regulation, of a political subdivision ordinance or regulation or of a code of conduct or ethics designed to protect the interest of the public or the employer.

§ 1423. Protection of employees

(A) PERSONS NOT TO BE DISCHARGED.—No employer may discharge, threaten or otherwise discriminate or retaliate against an employee regarding the employee's compensation, terms, conditions, location or privileges of employment because the employee or a person acting on behalf of the employee makes a good faith report or is about to report, verbally or in writing, to the employer or appropriate authority an instance of wrongdoing or waste.

(B) DISCRIMINATION PROHIBITED.—No employer may discharge, threaten or otherwise discriminate or retaliate against an employee regarding the employee's compensation, terms, conditions, location or privileges of employment because the employee is requested by an appropriate authority to participate in an investigation, hearing or inquiry held by an appropriate authority or in a court action.

§ 1424. Remedies

(A) CIVIL ACTION.—A person who alleges a violation of this act may bring a civil action in a court of competent jurisdiction for appropriate injunctive relief or damages, or both, within 180 days after the occurrence of the alleged violation.

(B) NECESSARY SHOWING OF EVIDENCE.—An employee alleging a violation of this act must show by a preponderance of the evidence that, prior to the alleged reprisal, the employee or a person acting on behalf of the employee had reported or was about to report in good faith, verbally or in writing, an instance of wrongdoing or waste to the employer or an appropriate authority.

(C) DEFENSE.—It shall be a defense to an action under this section if the defendant proves by a preponderance of the evidence that the action by the employer occurred for separate and legitimate reasons, which are not merely pretextual.

(D) CIVIL SERVICE EMPLOYEES.—An employee covered by civil service who contests a civil service action, believing it to be motivated by his having made a good faith report, verbally or in writing, of an instance of wrongdoing or waste, may submit as admissible evidence any or all material relating to the action as whistleblower and to the resulting alleged reprisal.

§ 1425. Enforcement

A court, in rendering a judgment in an action brought under this act, shall order, as the court considers appropriate, reinstatement of the employee, the payment of back wages, full reinstatement of fringe benefits and seniority rights, actual damages or any combination of these remedies. A court may also award the complainant all or a portion of the costs of litigation, including reasonable attorney fees and witness fees, if the court determines that the award is appropriate.

§ 1426. Penalties

A person who, under color of an employer's authority, violates this act shall be liable for a civil fine of not more than $500. Additionally, except where the person holds an elected public office, if the court specifically finds that the person, while in the employment of the Commonwealth or a political subdivision, committed a violation of this act with the intent to discourage the disclosure of criminal activity, the court may order the person's suspension from public service for not more than six months. A civil fine which is ordered under this section shall be paid to the State Treasurer for deposit into the General Fund.

§ 1427. Construction

This act shall not be construed to require an employer to compensate an employee for participation in an investigation, hearing or inquiry held by an appropriate authority, or impair the rights of any person under a collective bargaining agreement.

§ 1428. Notice

An employer shall post notices and use other appropriate means to notify employees and keep them informed of protections and obligations under this act.

Part C

PROTECTING EMPLOYEES FROM ARBITRARY OR INTRUSIVE DECISIONMAKING

CONSTITUTION OF THE UNITED STATES

AMENDMENT IV

The right of the people to be secure in their persons, houses, papers, and effects, against unreasonable searches and seizures, shall not be violated, and no Warrants shall issue, but upon probable cause, supported by Oath or affirmation, and particularly describing the place to be searched, and the persons or things to be seized.

AMENDMENT V

No person shall * * * be compelled in any criminal case to be a witness against himself, nor be deprived of life, liberty, or property, without due process of law * * *.

EMPLOYEE POLYGRAPH PROTECTION ACT
OF 1988—SELECTED PROVISIONS
29 U.S.C. §§ 2001–2009

§ 2001. Definitions

As used in this Act:

* * *

(3) The term "lie detector" includes a polygraph, deceptograph, voice stress analyzer, psychological stress evaluator, or any other similar device (whether mechanical or electrical) that is used, or the results of which are used, for the purpose of rendering a diagnostic opinion regarding the honesty or dishonesty of an individual.

(4) The term "polygraph" means an instrument that

(A) records continuously, visually, permanently, and simultaneously changes in cardiovascular, respiratory, and electrodermal patterns as minimum instrumentation standards; and

(B) is used, or the results of which are used, for the purpose of rendering a diagnostic opinion regarding the honesty or dishonesty of an individual.

(June 27, 1998, Pub. L. 100–347, § 2, 102 Stat. 646.)

§ 2002. Prohibitions on lie detector use

Except as provided in sections 7 and 8 [29 U.S.C. §§ 2006, 2007], it shall be unlawful for any employer engaged in or affecting commerce or in the production of goods for commerce—

(1) directly or indirectly, to require, request, suggest, or cause any employee or prospective employee to take or submit to any lie detector test;

(2) to use, accept, refer to, or inquire concerning the results of any lie detector test of any employee or prospective employee;

(3) to discharge, discipline, discriminate against in any manner, or deny employment or promotion to, or threaten to take any such action against—

(A) any employee or prospective employee who refuses, declines, or fails to take or submit to any lie detector test, or

(B) any employee or prospective employee on the basis of the results of any lie detector test; or

(4) to discharge, discipline, discriminate against in any manner, or deny employment or promotion to, or threaten to take any such action against, any employee or prospective employee because—

313

(A) such employee or prospective employee has filed any complaint or instituted or caused to be instituted any proceeding under or related to this Act,

(B) such employee or prospective employee has testified or is about to testify in any such proceeding, or

(C) of the exercise by such employee or prospective employee, on behalf of such employee or another person, of any right afforded by this Act.

(June 27, 1988, Pub. L. 100–347, § 3, 102 Stat. 646.)

§ 2005. Enforcement provisions

(a) Civil penalties.

(1) Subject to paragraph (2), any employer who violates any provision of this Act [29 U.S.C. §§ 2001 et seq.] may be assessed a civil penalty of not more than $10,000.

(2) In determining the amount of any penalty under paragraph (1), the Secretary shall take into account the previous record of the person in terms of compliance with this Act and the gravity of the violation.

* * *

(b) Injunctive actions by the Secretary.

The Secretary may bring an action under this section to restrain violations of this Act. The Solicitor of Labor may appear for and represent the Secretary in any litigation brought under this Act. In any action brought under this section, the district courts of the United States shall have jurisdiction, for cause shown, to issue temporary or permanent restraining orders and injunctions to require compliance with this Act, including such legal or equitable relief incident thereto as may be appropriate, including, but not limited to, employment, reinstatement, promotion, and the payment of lost wages and benefits.

(c) Private civil actions.

(1) An employer who violates this Act shall be liable to the employee or prospective employee affected by such violation. Such employer shall be liable for such legal or equitable relief as may be appropriate, including, but not limited to, employment, reinstatement, promotion, and the payment of lost wages and benefits.

(2) An action to recover the liability prescribed in paragraph (1) may be maintained against the employer in any Federal or State court of competent jurisdiction by an employee or prospective employee for or on behalf of such employee, prospective employee, and other employees or prospective employees similarly situated. No such action may be commenced more than 3 years after the date of the alleged violation.

(3) The court, in its discretion, may allow the prevailing party (other than the United States) reasonable costs, including attorney's fees.

(d) Waiver of rights prohibited.

The rights and procedures provided by this Act may not be waived by contract or otherwise, unless such waiver is part of a written settlement agreed to and signed by the parties to the pending action or complaint under this Act.

(June 27, 1988, Pub. L. 100–347, § 6, 102 Stat. 647.)

§ 2006.   Exemptions

(a) No application to governmental employers. This Act shall not apply with respect to the United States Government, any State or local government, or any political subdivision of a State or local government.

(b) National defense and security exemption. * * *

(c) FBI contractors exemption. Nothing in this Act shall be construed to prohibit the administration, by the Federal Government, in the performance of any counterintelligence function, of any lie detector test to an employee of a contractor of the Federal Bureau of Investigation of the Department of Justice who is engaged in the performance of any work under the contract with such Bureau.

(d) Limited exemption for ongoing investigations. Subject to sections 8 and 10, this Act shall not prohibit an employer from requesting an employee to submit to a polygraph test if—

(1) the test is administered in connection with an ongoing investigation involving economic loss or injury to the employer's business, such as theft, embezzlement, misappropriation, or an act of unlawful industrial espionage or sabotage;

(2) the employee had access to the property that is the subject of the investigation;

(3) the employer has a reasonable suspicion that the employee was involved in the incident or activity under investigation; and

(4) the employer executes a statement, provided to the examinee before the test, that—

(A) sets forth with particularity the specific incident or activity being investigated and the basis for testing particular employees,

(B) is signed by a person (other than a polygraph examiner) authorized to legally bind the employer,

(C) is retained by the employer for at least 3 years, and

(D) contains at a minimum—

(i) an identification of the specific economic loss or injury to the business of the employer,

(ii) a statement indicating that the employee had access to the property that is the subject of the investigation, and

(iii) a statement describing the basis of the employer's reasonable suspicion that the employee was involved in the incident or activity under investigation.

(e) Exemption for security services.

(1) In general. Subject to paragraph (2) and sections 8 and 10, this Act shall not prohibit the use of polygraph tests on prospective employees by any private employer whose primary business purpose consists of providing armored car personnel, personnel engaged in the design, installation, and maintenance of security alarm systems, or other uniformed or plainclothes security personnel and whose function includes protection of—

(A) facilities, materials, or operations having a significant impact on the health or safety of any State or political subdivision thereof, or the national security of the United States, as determined under rules and regulations issued by the Secretary within 90 days after the date of the enactment of this Act [June 27, 1988], including—

(i) facilities engaged in the production, transmission, or distribution of electric or nuclear power,

(ii) public water supply facilities,

(iii) shipments or storage of radioactive or other toxic waste materials, and

(iv) public transportation, or

(B) currency, negotiable securities, precious commodities or instruments, or proprietary information.

(2) Access. The exemption provided under this subsection shall not apply if the test is administered to a prospective employee who would not be employed to protect facilities, materials, operations, or assets referred to in paragraph (1).

(f) Exemption for drug security, drug theft, or drug diversion investigations.

(1) In general. Subject to paragraph (2) and sections 8 and 10, this Act shall not prohibit the use of a polygraph test by any employer authorized to manufacture, distribute, or dispense a controlled substance listed in schedule I, II, III, or IV of section 202 of the Controlled Substances Act (21 U.S.C. 812).

(2) Access. The exemption provided under this subsection shall apply—

(A) if the test is administered to a prospective employee who would have direct access to the manufacture, storage, distribution, or sale of any such controlled substance; or

(B) in the case of a test administered to a current employee, if—

(i) the test is administered in connection with an ongoing investigation of criminal or other misconduct involving, or potentially involving, loss or injury to the manufacture, distribution, or dispensing of any such controlled substance by such employer, and

(ii) the employee had access to the person or property that is the subject of the investigation.

(June 27, 1988, P.L. 100–347, § 7, 102 Stat. 648; Oct. 14, 1994, P.L. 103–359, Title V, § 501(n), 108 Stat. 3430; Sept. 23, 1996, P.L. 104–201, Div. A, Title XI, Subtitle B, § 1122(b)(3), 110 Stat. 2687; as amended Oct. 14, 2008, P.L. 110–417, [Div. A,] Title IX, Subtitle D, § 931(b)(3), 122 Stat. 4575.)

§ 2007. Restrictions on use of exemptions

(a) Test as basis for adverse employment action.

(1) Under ongoing investigations exemption. Except as provided in paragraph (2), the exemption under subsection (d) of section 7 shall not apply if an employee is discharged, disciplined, denied employment or promotion, or otherwise discriminated against in any manner on the basis of the analysis of a polygraph test chart or the refusal to take a polygraph test, without additional supporting evidence. The evidence required by such subsection may serve as additional supporting evidence.

(2) Under other exemptions. In the case of an exemption described in subsection (e) or (f) of such section, the exemption shall not apply if the results of an analysis of a polygraph test chart are used, or the refusal to take a polygraph test is used, as the sole basis upon which an adverse employment action described in paragraph (1) is taken against an employee or prospective employee.

(b) Rights of examinee. The exemptions provided under subsections (d), (e), and (f) of section 7 shall not apply unless the requirements described in the following paragraphs are met:

(1) All phases. Throughout all phases of the test—

(A) the examinee shall be permitted to terminate the test at any time;

(B) the examinee is not asked questions in a manner designed to degrade, or needlessly intrude on, such examinee;

(C) the examinee is not asked any question concerning—

(i) religious beliefs or affiliations,

(ii) beliefs or opinions regarding racial matters,

(iii) political beliefs or affiliations,

(iv) any matter relating to sexual behavior; and

(v) beliefs, affiliations, opinions, or lawful activities regarding unions or labor organizations; and

(D) the examiner does not conduct the test if there is sufficient written evidence by a physician that the examinee is suffering from a medical or psychological condition or undergoing treatment that might cause abnormal responses during the actual testing phase.

(2) Pretest phase. During the pretest phase, the prospective examinee—

(A) is provided with reasonable written notice of the date, time, and location of the test, and of such examinee's right to obtain and consult with legal counsel or an employee representative before each phase of the test;

(B) is informed in writing of the nature and characteristics of the tests and of the instruments involved;

(C) is informed, in writing—

(i) whether the testing area contains a two-way mirror, a camera, or any other device through which the test can be observed,

(ii) whether any other device, including any device for recording or monitoring the test, will be used, or

(iii) that the employer or the examinee may (with mutual knowledge) make a recording of the test;

(D) is read and signs a written notice informing such examinee—

(i) that the examinee cannot be required to take the test as a condition of employment,

(ii) that any statement made during the test may constitute additional supporting evidence for the purposes of an adverse employment action described in subsection (a),

(iii) of the limitations imposed under this section,

(iv) of the legal rights and remedies available to the examinee if the polygraph test is not conducted in accordance with this Act, and

(v) of the legal rights and remedies of the employer under this Act (including the rights of the employer under section 9(c)(2)); and

(E) is provided an opportunity to review all questions to be asked during the test and is informed of the right to terminate the test at any time.

(3) Actual testing phase. During the actual testing phase, the examiner does not ask such examinee any question relevant during the test that was not presented in writing for review to such examinee before the test.

(4) Post-test phase. Before any adverse employment action, the employer shall—

(A) further interview the examinee on the basis of the results of the test; and

(B) provide the examinee with—

(i) a written copy of any opinion or conclusion rendered as a result of the test, and

(ii) a copy of the questions asked during the test along with the corresponding charted responses.

(5) Maximum number and minimum duration of tests. The examiner shall not conduct and complete more than five polygraph tests on a calendar day on which the test is given, and shall not conduct any such test for less than a 90–minute duration.

(c) Qualifications and requirements of examiners. The exemptions provided under subsections (d), (e), and (f) of section 7 shall not apply unless the individual who conducts the polygraph test satisfies the requirements under the following paragraphs:

(1) Qualifications. The examiner—

(A) has a valid and current license granted by licensing and regulatory authorities in the State in which the test is to be conducted, if so required by the State; and

(B) maintains a minimum of a $50,000 bond or an equivalent amount of professional liability coverage.

(2) Requirements. The examiner—

(A) renders any opinion or conclusion regarding the test—

(i) in writing and solely on the basis of an analysis of polygraph test charts,

(ii) that does not contain information other than admissions, information, case facts, and interpretation of the charts relevant to the purpose and stated objectives of the test, and

(iii) that does not include any recommendation concerning the employment of the examinee; and

(B) maintains all opinions, reports, charts, written questions, lists, and other records relating to the test for a minimum period of 3 years after administration of the test.

(June 27, 1988, P.L. 100–347, § 8, 102 Stat. 650.)

§ 2009.   Effect on other law and agreements

Except as provided in subsections (a), (b), and (c) of section 7 [29 U.S.C. § 2006(a)–(c)], this Act shall not preempt any provision of any State or local law or of any negotiated collective bargaining agreement that prohibits lie detector tests or is more restrictive with respect to lie detector tests than any provision of this Act.

(Pub. L. 100–347, § 10, 102 Stat. 653.)

OMNIBUS CRIME CONTROL ACT OF 1968 (INCLUDING ELECTRONIC COMMUNICATIONS ACT OF 1986)—SELECTED PROVISIONS 18 U.S.C. §§ 2510–11, 2515, 2520, 2701–02, 2707–78

§ 2510. Definitions

As used in this chapter [18 U.S.C. §§ 2510 et seq.]—

(1) "wire communication" means any aural transfer made in whole or in part through the use of facilities for the transmission of communications by the aid of wire, cable, or other like connection between the point of origin and the point of reception (including the use of such connection in a switching station) furnished or operated by any person engaged in providing or operating such facilities for the transmission of interstate or foreign communications or communications affecting interstate or foreign commerce;

(2) "oral communication" means any oral communication uttered by a person exhibiting an expectation that such communication is not subject to interception under circumstances justifying such expectation, but such term does not include any electronic communication;

(3) "State" means any State of the United States, the District of Columbia, the Commonwealth of Puerto Rico, and any territory or possession of the United States;

(4) "intercept" means the aural or other acquisition of the contents of any wire, electronic, or oral communication through the use of any electronic, mechanical, or other device.[;]

(5) "electronic, mechanical, or other device" means any device or apparatus which can be used to intercept a wire, oral, or electronic communication other than—

(a) any telephone or telegraph instrument, equipment or facility, or any component thereof, (i) furnished to the subscriber or user by a provider of wire or electronic communication service in the ordinary course of its business and being used by the subscriber or user in the ordinary course of its business or furnished by such subscriber or user for connection to the facilities of such service and used in the ordinary course of its business; or (ii) being used by a provider of wire or electronic communication service in the ordinary course of its business, or by an investigative or law enforcement officer in the ordinary course of his duties;

(b) a hearing aid or similar device being used to correct subnormal hearing to not better than normal;

(6) "person" means any employee, or agent of the United States or any State or political subdivision thereof, and any individual, partnership, association, joint stock company, trust, or corporation;

(7) "Investigative or law enforcement officer" means any officer of the United States or of a State or political subdivision thereof, who is empowered by law to conduct investigations of or to make arrests for offenses enumerated in this chapter, and any attorney authorized by law to prosecute or participate in the prosecution of such offenses;

(8) "contents", when used with respect to any wire, oral, or electronic communication, includes any information concerning the substance, purport, or meaning of that communication;

(9) "Judge of competent jurisdiction" means—

(a) a judge of a United States district court or a United States court of appeals; and

(b) a judge of any court of general criminal jurisdiction of a State who is authorized by a statute of that State to enter orders authorizing interceptions of wire, oral, or electronic communications;

(10) "communication common carrier" has the meaning given that term in section 3 of the Communications Act of 1934 [47 U.S.C. § 153];

(11) "aggrieved person" means a person who was a party to any intercepted wire, oral, or electronic communication or a person against whom the interception was directed;

(12) "electronic communication" means any transfer of signs, signals, writing, images, sounds, data, or intelligence of any nature transmitted in whole or in part by a wire, radio, electromagnetic, photoelectronic or photooptical system that affects interstate or foreign commerce, but does not include—

(A) any wire or oral communication;

(B) any communication made through a tone-only paging device;

(C) any communication from a tracking device (as defined in section 3117 of this title [18 U.S.C. § 3117]); or

(D) electronic funds transfer information stored by a financial institution in a communications system used for the electronic storage and transfer of funds;

(13) "user" means any person or entity who—

(A) uses an electronic communication service; and

(B) is duly authorized by the provider of such service to engage in such use;

(14) "electronic communications system" means any wire, radio, electromagnetic, photooptical or photoelectronic facilities for the transmission of wire or electronic communications, and any computer facili-

ties or related electronic equipment for the electronic storage of such communications;

(15) "electronic communication service" means any service which provides to users thereof the ability to send or receive wire or electronic communications;

(16) "readily accessible to the general public" means, with respect to a radio communication, that such communication is not—[omitted]

(17) "electronic storage" means—

(A) any temporary, intermediate storage of a wire or electronic communication incidental to the electronic transmission thereof; and

(B) any storage of such communication by an electronic communication service for purposes of backup protection of such communication;

(18) "aural transfer" means a transfer containing the human voice at any point between and including the point of origin and the point of reception; * * *

(20) "protected computer" has the meaning set forth in section 1030 [18 U.S.C. § 1030]; and

(21) "computer trespasser"—

(A) means a person who accesses a protected computer without authorization and thus has no reasonable expectation of privacy in any communication transmitted to, through, or from the protected computer; and

(B) does not include a person known by the owner or operator of the protected computer to have an existing contractual relationship with the owner or operator of the protected computer for access to all or part of the protected computer.

(Added June 19, 1968, P.L. 90–351, Title III, § 802, 82 Stat. 212; Oct. 21, 1986, P.L. 99–508, Title I, § 101(a), (c)(1)(A), (4) 100 Stat. 1848, 1851; Oct. 25, 1994, P.L. 103–414, Title II, §§ 202(a), 203, 108 Stat. 4290, 4291; April 24, 1996, P.L. 104–132, Title VII, Subtitle B, § 731, 110 Stat. 1303; Oct. 26, 2001, P.L. 107–56, Title II, §§ 203(b)(2), 209(1), and 217(1), 115 Stat. 280, 283, 291; Dec. 28, 2001, P.L. 107–108, Title III, § 314(b), 115 Stat. 1402; Nov. 2, 2002, P.L. 107–273, Div. B, Title IV, § 4002(e)(10), 116 Stat. 1810.)

§ 2511. Interception and disclosure of wire, oral, or electronic communications prohibited

(1) Except as otherwise specifically provided in this chapter any person who—

(a) intentionally intercepts, endeavors to intercept, or procures any other person to intercept or endeavor to intercept, any wire, oral, or electronic communication;

(b) intentionally uses, endeavors to use, or procures any other person to use or endeavor to use any electronic, mechanical, or other device to intercept any oral communication when—

(i) such device is affixed to, or otherwise transmits a signal through, a wire, cable, or other like connection used in wire communication; or

(ii) such device transmits communications by radio, or interferes with the transmission of such communication; or

(iii) such person knows, or has reason to know, that such device or any component thereof has been sent through the mail or transported in interstate or foreign commerce; or

(iv) such use or endeavor to use (A) takes place on the premises of any business or other commercial establishment the operations of which affect interstate or foreign commerce; or (B) obtains or is for the purpose of obtaining information relating to the operations of any business or other commercial establishment the operations of which affect interstate or foreign commerce; or

(v) such person acts in the District of Columbia, the Commonwealth of Puerto Rico, or any territory or possession of the United States;

(c) intentionally discloses, or endeavors to disclose, to any other person the contents of any wire, oral, or electronic communication, knowing or having reason to know that the information was obtained through the interception of a wire, oral, or electronic communication in violation of this subsection;

(d) intentionally uses, or endeavors to use, the contents of any wire, oral, or electronic communication, knowing or having reason to know that the information was obtained through the interception of a wire, oral, or electronic communication in violation of this subsection; or

* * *

shall be punished as provided in subsection (4) or shall be subject to suit as provided in subsection (5).

(2)(a)(i) It shall not be unlawful under this chapter for an operator of a switchboard, or an officer, employee, or agent of a provider of wire or electronic communication service, whose facilities are used in the transmission of a wire or electronic communication, to intercept, disclose, or use that communication in the normal course of his employment while engaged in any activity which is a necessary incident to the rendition of his service or to the protection of the rights or property of the provider of that service, except that a provider of wire communication service to the public shall not utilize service observing or random monitoring except for mechanical or service quality control checks. * * *

(c) It shall not be unlawful under this chapter for a person acting under color of law to intercept a wire, oral, or electronic communication, where such person is a party to the communication or one of the parties to the communication has given prior consent to such interception.

(d) It shall not be unlawful under this chapter for a person not acting under color of law to intercept a wire, oral, or electronic communication where such person is a party to the communication or where one of the parties to the communication has given prior consent to such interception unless such communication is intercepted for the purpose of committing any criminal or tortious act in violation of the Constitution or laws of the United States or of any State. * * *

(g) It shall not be unlawful under this chapter * * * for any person—

(i) to intercept or access an electronic communication made through an electronic communication system that is configured so that such electronic communication is readily accessible to the general public; * * *

(h) It shall not be unlawful under this chapter— * * *

(ii) for a provider of electronic communication service to record the fact that a wire or electronic communication was initiated or completed in order to protect such provider, another provider furnishing service toward the completion of the wire or electronic communication, or a user of that service, from fraudulent, unlawful or abusive use of such service. * * *

(3)(a) Except as provided in paragraph (b) of this subsection, a person or entity providing an electronic communication service to the public shall not intentionally divulge the contents of any communication (other than one to such person or entity, or an agent thereof) while in transmission on that service to any person or entity other than an addressee or intended recipient of such communication or an agent of such addressee or intended recipient.

(b) A person or entity providing electronic communication service to the public may divulge the contents of any such communication—

(i) as otherwise authorized in sections 2511(2)(a) or 2517 of this title;

(ii) with the lawful consent of the originator or any addressee or intended recipient of such communication;

(iii) to a person employed or authorized, or whose facilities are used, to forward such communication to its destination; or

(iv) which were inadvertently obtained by the service provider and which appear to pertain to the commission of a crime, if such divulgence is made to a law enforcement agency.

(4)(a) Except as provided in paragraph (b) of this subsection or in subsection (5), whoever violates subsection (1) of this section shall be

fined under this title or imprisoned not more than five years, or both.
* * *

(Added June 19, 1968, P.L. 90–351, Title III, § 802, 82 Stat. 213; July 29, 1970, P.L. 91–358, Title II, § 211(a), 84 Stat. 654; Oct. 25, 1978, P.L. 95–511, Title II, § 201(a)–(c), 92 Stat. 1796; Oct. 30, 1984, P.L. 98–549, § 6(b)(2), (3), 98 Stat. 2804; Oct. 21, 1986, P.L. 99–508, Title I, §§ 101(b), (c)(1), (5), (6), (d), (f)(1), 102, 100 Stat. 1848, 1853; Sept. 13, 1994, P.L. 103–322, Title XXXII, Subtitle I, § 320901, Title XXXIII, § 330016(1)(G), 108 Stat. 2123, 2147; Oct. 25, 1994, P.L. 103–414, Title II, §§ 202(b), 204, 205, 108 Stat. 4290, 4291; Oct. 11, 1996, P.L. 104–294, Title VI, § 604(b)(42), 110 Stat. 3509; Oct. 26, 2001, P.L. 107–56, Title II, §§ 204, 217(2), 115 Stat. 281, 291; Nov. 25, 2002, P.L. 107–296, Title II, Subtitle C, § 225(h)(2), (j)(1), 116 Stat. 2158; as amended July 10, 2008, P.L. 110–261, Title I, §§ 101(c)(1), 102(c)(1), Title IV, § 403(b)(2)(C), 122 Stat. 2459, 2474.)

§ 2515. Prohibition of use as evidence of intercepted wire or oral communications

Whenever any wire or oral communication has been intercepted, no part of the contents of such communication and no evidence derived therefrom may be received in evidence in any trial, hearing, or other proceeding in or before any court, grand jury, department, officer, agency, regulatory body, legislative committee, or other authority of the United States, a State, or a political subdivision thereof if the disclosure of that information would be in violation of this chapter.

(June 19, 1968, Pub. L. 90–351, Title III, § 802, 82 Stat. 216.)

* * *

§ 2520. Recovery of civil damages authorized

(a) Except as provided in section 2511(2)(a)(ii), any person whose wire, oral, or electronic communication is intercepted, disclosed, or intentionally used in violation of this chapter may in a civil action recover from the person or entity, other than the United States, which engaged in that violation such relief as may be appropriate.

(b) In an action under this section, appropriate relief includes—

(1) such preliminary and other equitable or declaratory relief as may be appropriate;

(2) damages under subsection (c) and punitive damages in appropriate cases; and

(3) a reasonable attorney's fee and other litigation costs reasonably incurred.

* * *

the violation; or

> (B) statutory damages of whichever is the greater of $100 a day for each day of violation or $10,000.

(d) A good faith reliance on—

> (1) a court warrant or order, a grand jury subpoena, a legislative authorization, or a statutory authorization;

> (2) a request of an investigative or law enforcement officer under section 2518(7) of this title; or

> (3) a good faith determination that sections 2511(3) or 2511(2)(i) of this title permitted the conduct complained of;

is a complete defense against any civil or criminal action brought under this chapter or any other law.

(e) A civil action under this section may not be commenced later than two years after the date upon which the claimant first has a reasonable opportunity to discover the violation.

* * *

(Added June 19, 1968, P.L. 90–351, Title III, § 802, 82 Stat. 223; July 29, 1970, P.L. 91–358, Title II, § 211(c), 84 Stat. 654; Oct. 21, 1986, P.L. 99–508, Title I, § 103, 100 Stat. 1854; as amended, Oct. 26, 2001, P.L. 107–56, Title II, § 223(a), 115 Stat. 293; Nov. 25, 2002, P.L. 107–296, Title II, Subtitle C, § 225(e), 116 Stat. 2157.)

§ 2701. Unlawful access to stored communications

(a) Except as provided in subsection (c) of this section whoever—

> (1) intentionally accesses without authorization a facility through which an electronic communication service is provided; or

> (2) intentionally exceeds an authorization to access that facility;

and thereby obtains, alters, or prevents authorized access to a wire or electronic communication while it is in electronic storage in such system shall be punished as provided in subsection (b) of this section.

(b) The punishment for an offense under subsection (a) of this section is—

> (1) if the offense is committed for purposes of commercial advantage, malicious destruction or damage, or private commercial gain, or in furtherance of any criminal or tortious act in violation of the Constitution or laws of the United States or any State—

>> (A) a fine under this title or imprisonment for not more than 5 years, or both, in the case of a first offense under this subparagraph; and

>> (B) a fine under this title or imprisonment for not more than 10 years, or both, for any subsequent offense under this subparagraph; * * *

(c) Subsection (a) of this section does not apply with respect to conduct authorized—

    (1) by the person or entity providing a wire or electronic communications service;

    (2) by a user of that service with respect to a communication of or intended for that user; or

    (3) in section 2703, 2704 or 2518 of this title.

(Added Oct. 21, 1986, P.L. 99–508, Title II, § 201(a), 100 Stat. 1860; Sept. 13, 1994, P.L. 103–322, Title XXXIII, § 330016(1)(K), (U), 108 Stat. 2147, 2148; Oct. 11, 1996, P.L. 104–294, Title VI, § 601(a)(3), 110 Stat. 3498; Nov. 25, 2002, P.L. 107–296, Title II, Subtitle C, § 225(j)(2), 116 Stat. 2158.)

§ 2702. Voluntary disclosure of customer communications or records

(a) Prohibitions. Except as provided in subsection (b) or (c)—

    (1) a person or entity providing an electronic communication service to the public shall not knowingly divulge to any person or entity the contents of a communication while in electronic storage by that service; and

    (2) a person or entity providing remote computing service to the public shall not knowingly divulge to any person or entity the contents of any communication which is carried or maintained on that service—

        (A) on behalf of, and received by means of electronic transmission from (or created by means of computer processing of communications received by means of electronic transmission from), a subscriber or customer of such service;

        (B) solely for the purpose of providing storage or computer processing services to such subscriber or customer, if the provider is not authorized to access the contents of any such communications for purposes of providing any services other than storage or computer processing; and

    (3) a provider of remote computing service or electronic communication service to the public shall not knowingly divulge a record or other information pertaining to a subscriber to or customer of such service (not including the contents of communications covered by paragraph (1) or (2)) to any governmental entity.

(b) Exceptions for disclosure of communications. A provider described in subsection (a) may divulge the contents of a communication—

    (1) to an addressee or intended recipient of such communication or an agent of such addressee or intended recipient;

(2) as otherwise authorized in sections 2517, 2511(2)(a), or 2703 of this title;

(3) with the lawful consent of the originator or an addressee or intended recipient of such communication, or the subscriber in the case of remote computing service;

(4) to a person employed or authorized or whose facilities are used to forward such communication to its destination;

(5) as may be necessarily incident to the rendition of the service or to the protection of the rights or property of the provider of that service;

(6) to the National Center for Missing and Exploited Children, in connection with a report submitted thereto under section 2258A [18 U.S.C. § 2258A];

(7) to a law enforcement agency—

(A) if the contents—

(i) were inadvertently obtained by the service provider; and

(ii) appear to pertain to the commission of a crime; or

(B) [Deleted]

(8) to a governmental entity, if the provider, in good faith, believes that an emergency involving danger of death or serious physical injury to any person requires disclosure without delay of communications relating to the emergency.

(c) Exceptions for disclosure of customer records. A provider described in subsection (a) may divulge a record or other information pertaining to a subscriber to or customer of such service (not including the contents of communications covered by subsection (a)(1) or (a)(2))—

(1) as otherwise authorized in section 2703;

(2) with the lawful consent of the customer or subscriber;

(3) as may be necessarily incident to the rendition of the service or to the protection of the rights or property of the provider of that service;

(4) to a governmental entity, if the provider, in good faith, believes that an emergency involving danger of death or serious physical injury to any person requires disclosure without delay of information relating to the emergency;

(5) to the National Center for Missing and Exploited Children, in connection with a report submitted thereto under section 2258A [18 U.S.C. § 2258A]; or

(6) to any person other than a governmental entity.

(Added Oct. 21, 1986, P.L. 99–508, Title II, § 201(a), 100 Stat. 1860; Nov. 18, 1988, P.L. 100–690, Title VII, Subtitle B, § 7037, 102 Stat.

4399; Oct. 30, 1998, P.L. 105–314, Title VI, § 604(b), 112 Stat. 2984; Oct. 26, 2001, P.L. 107–56, Title II, § 212(a)(1), 115 Stat. 284; Nov. 25, 2002, P.L. 107–296, Title II, Subtitle C, § 225(d)(1), 116 Stat. 2157; April 30, 2003, P.L. 108–21, Title V, Subtitle A, § 508(b), 117 Stat. 684; March 9, 2006, P.L. 109–177, Title I, § 107(a), (b)(1), (c), 120 Stat. 202, 203; as amended Oct. 13, 2008, P.L. 110–401, Title V, § 501(b)(2), 122 Stat. 4251.)

* * *

§ 2707. Civil action

(a) Except as provided in section 2703(e) any provider of electronic communication service, subscriber, or other person aggrieved by any violation of this chapter in which the conduct constituting the violation is engaged in with a knowing or intentional state of mind may, in a civil action, recover from the person or entity, other than the United States, which engaged in that violation such relief as may be appropriate.

(b) In a civil action under this section, appropriate relief includes—

(1) such preliminary and other equitable or declaratory relief as may be appropriate;

(2) damages under subsection (c); and

(3) a reasonable attorney's fee and other litigation costs reasonably incurred.

(c) The court may assess as damages in a civil action under this section the sum of the actual damages suffered by the plaintiff and any profits made by the violator as a result of the violation, but in no case shall a person entitled to recover receive less than the sum of $1,000. If the violation is willful or intentional, the court may assess punitive damages. In the case of a successful action to enforce liability under this section, the court may assess the costs of the action, together with reasonable attorney fees determined by the court.

(d) If a court or appropriate department or agency determines that the United States or any of its departments or agencies has violated any provision of this chapter, and the court or appropriate department or agency finds that the circumstances surrounding the violation raise serious questions about whether or not an officer or employee of the United States acted willfully or intentionally with respect to the violation, the department or agency shall, upon receipt of a true and correct copy of the decision and findings of the court or appropriate department or agency promptly initiate a proceeding to determine whether disciplinary action against the officer or employee is warranted. If the head of the department or agency involved determines that disciplinary action is not warranted, he or she shall notify the Inspector General with jurisdiction over the department or agency concerned and shall provide the Inspector General with the reasons for such determination.

(e) A good faith reliance on—

(1) a court warrant or order, a grand jury subpoena, a legislative authorization, or a statutory authorization (including a request of a governmental entity under section 2703(f) of this title);

(2) a request of an investigative or law enforcement officer under section 2518(7) of this title; or

(3) a good faith determination that section 2511(3) of this title permitted the conduct complained of; is a complete defense to any civil or criminal action brought under this chapter or any other law.

(f) A civil action under this section may not be commenced later than two years after the date upon which the claimant first discovered or had a reasonable opportunity to discover the violation.

* * *

(Added Oct. 21, 1986, P.L. 99–508, Title II, § 201(a), 100 Stat. 1866; as amended Oct. 11, 1996, P.L. 104–293, Title VI, § 601(c), 110 Stat. 3469; Oct. 26, 2001, P.L. 107–56, Title II, § 223(b), Title VIII, § 815, 115 Stat. 293, 384; Nov. 2, 2002, P.L. 107–273, Div. B, Title IV, 4005(f)(2), 116 Stat. 1813.)

§ 2708. Exclusivity of remedies

The remedies and sanctions described in this chapter [18 U.S.C. §§ 2701 et seq.] are the only judicial remedies and sanctions for nonconstitutional violations of this chapter.

(Oct. 21, 1986, Pub. L. 99–508, Title II, § 201(a), 100 Stat. 1867.)

FAIR CREDIT REPORTING ACT—
SELECTED PROVISIONS
15 U.S.C. §§ 1681a–b, l–t

§ 1681a. Definitions; rules of construction

(d) Consumer report.

(1) In general. The term "consumer report" means any written, oral, or other communication of any information by a consumer reporting agency bearing on a consumer's credit worthiness [credit-worthiness], credit standing, credit capacity, character, general reputation, personal characteristics, or mode of living which is used or expected to be used or collected in whole or in part for the purpose of serving as a factor in establishing the consumer's eligibility for—

(A) credit or insurance to be used primarily for personal, family, or household purposes;

(B) employment purposes; or

(C) any other purpose authorized under section 604 [15 USCS § 1681b].

(2) Exclusions. [omitted].

(3) Restriction on sharing of medical information. [omitted]

(e) The term "investigative consumer report" means a consumer report or portion thereof in which information on a consumer's character, general reputation, personal characteristics, or mode of living is obtained through personal interviews with neighbors, friends, or associates of the consumer reported on or with others with whom he is acquainted or who may have knowledge concerning any such items of information. However, such information shall not include specific factual information on a consumer's credit record obtained directly from a creditor of the consumer or from a consumer reporting agency when such information was obtained directly from a creditor of the consumer or from the consumer.

(f) The term "consumer reporting agency" means any person which, for monetary fees, dues, or on a cooperative nonprofit basis, regularly engages in whole or in part in the practice of assembling or evaluating consumer credit information or other information on consumers for the purpose of furnishing consumer reports to third parties, and which uses any means or facility of interstate commerce for the purpose of preparing or furnishing consumer reports. * * *

(h) The term "employment purposes" when used in connection with a consumer report means a report used for the purpose of evaluating a consumer for employment, promotion, reassignment or retention as an employee. * * *

(k) Adverse action.

(1) Actions included. The term "adverse action"—* * *

(B) means—* * *

(ii) a denial of employment or any other decision for employment purposes that adversely affects any current or prospective employee; * * *

(o) Excluded communications. A communication is described in this subsection if it is a communication—

(1) that, but for subsection (d)(2)(D), would be an investigative consumer report;

(2) that is made to a prospective employer for the purpose of—

(A) procuring an employee for the employer; or

(B) procuring an opportunity for a natural person to work for the employer;

(3) that is made by a person who regularly performs such procurement;

(4) that is not used by any person for any purpose other than a purpose described in subparagraph (A) or (B) of paragraph (2); and

(5) with respect to which—

(A) the consumer who is the subject of the communication—

(i) consents orally or in writing to the nature and scope of the communication, before the collection of any information for the purpose of making the communication;

(ii) consents orally or in writing to the making of the communication to a prospective employer, before the making of the communication; and

(iii) in the case of consent under clause (i) or (ii) given orally, is provided written confirmation of that consent by the person making the communication, not later than 3 business days after the receipt of the consent by that person;

(B) the person who makes the communication does not, for the purpose of making the communication, make any inquiry that if made by a prospective employer of the consumer who is the subject of the communication would violate any applicable Federal or State equal employment opportunity law or regulation; and

(C) the person who makes the communication—

(i) discloses in writing to the consumer who is the subject of the communication, not later than 5 business days after receiving any request from the consumer for such disclosure, the nature and substance of all information in the consumer's file at the time of the request, except that the sources of any information that is acquired solely for use in making the communication and is actually used for no other purpose, need not be disclosed other than under appropriate discovery procedures in any court of competent jurisdiction in which an action is brought; and

(ii) notifies the consumer who is the subject of the communication, in writing, of the consumer's right to request the information described in clause (i).

(y) Exclusion of certain communications for employee investigations.

(1) Communications described in this subsection. A communication is described in this subsection if—

(A) but for subsection (d)(2)(D), the communication would be a consumer report;

(B) the communication is made to an employer in connection with an investigation of—

(i) suspected misconduct relating to employment; or

(ii) compliance with Federal, State, or local laws and regulations, the rules of a self-regulatory organization, or any preexisting written policies of the employer;

(C) the communication is not made for the purpose of investigating a consumer's credit worthiness [creditworthiness], credit standing, or credit capacity; and

(D) the communication is not provided to any person except—

(i) to the employer or an agent of the employer;

(ii) to any Federal or State officer, agency, or department, or any officer, agency, or department of a unit of general local government;

(iii) to any self-regulatory organization with regulatory authority over the activities of the employer or employee;

(iv) as otherwise required by law; or

(v) pursuant to section 608 [15 U.S.C. § 1681f].

(2) Subsequent disclosure. After taking any adverse action based in whole or in part on a communication described in paragraph (1), the employer shall disclose to the consumer a summary containing the nature and substance of the communication upon which the adverse action is based, except that the sources of information acquired solely for use in preparing what would be but for

subsection (d)(2)(D) an investigative consumer report need not be disclosed.

(3) Self-regulatory organization defined. For purposes of this subsection, the term "self-regulatory organization" includes any self-regulatory organization (as defined in section 3(a)(26) of the Securities Exchange Act of 1934 [15 U.S.C. § 78c(a)(26)]), any entity established under title I of the Sarbanes–Oxley Act of 2002 [15 U.S.C. §§ 7211 et seq.], any board of trade designated by the Commodity Futures Trading Commission, and any futures association registered with such Commission.

(May 29, 1968, P.L. 90–321, Title VI, § 603, as added Oct. 26, 1970, P.L. 91–508, Title VI, § 601, 84 Stat. 1128; Oct. 27, 1992, P.L. 102–537, § 2(b), 106 Stat. 3531; Sept. 30, 1996, P.L. 104–208, Div. A, Title II, Subtitle D, Ch. 1, § 2402, 110 Stat. 3009–426; Nov. 2, 1998, P.L. 105–347, § 6(1)–(3), 112 Stat. 3211; Dec. 4, 2003, P.L. 108–159, Title I, Subtitle A, § 111, Title II, § 214(c)(1), Title IV, § 411(b), (c), Title VI, § 611, 117 Stat. 1954, 1983, 2001, 2010; July 21, 2010, P.L. 111–203, Title X, Subtitle H, § 1088(a)(1), (2)(A), (C), (3), 124 Stat. 2086, 2087.)

§ 1681b. Permissible purposes of consumer reports

(b) Conditions for furnishing and using consumer reports for employment purposes.

(1) Certification from user. A consumer reporting agency may furnish a consumer report for employment purposes only if—

(A) the person who obtains such report from the agency certifies to the agency that—

(i) the person has complied with paragraph (2) with respect to the consumer report, and the person will comply with paragraph (3) with respect to the consumer report if paragraph (3) becomes applicable; and

(ii) information from the consumer report will not be used in violation of any applicable Federal or State equal employment opportunity law or regulation; and

(B) the consumer reporting agency provides with the report, or has previously provided, a summary of the consumer's rights under this title, as prescribed by the Bureau under section 609(c)(3) [15 U.S.C. § 1681g(c)(3)].

(2) Disclosure to consumer.

(A) In general. Except as provided in subparagraph (B), a person may not procure a consumer report, or cause a consumer report to be procured, for employment purposes with respect to any consumer, unless—

(i) a clear and conspicuous disclosure has been made in writing to the consumer at any time before the report is procured or caused to be procured, in a document that consists solely of the disclosure, that a consumer report may be obtained for employment purposes; and

(ii) the consumer has authorized in writing (which authorization may be made on the document referred to in clause (i)) the procurement of the report by that person.

(B) Application by mail, telephone, computer, or other similar means. If a consumer described in subparagraph (C) applies for employment by mail, telephone, computer, or other similar means, at any time before a consumer report is procured or caused to be procured in connection with that application—

(i) the person who procures the consumer report on the consumer for employment purposes shall provide to the consumer, by oral, written, or electronic means, notice that a consumer report may be obtained for employment purposes, and a summary of the consumer's rights under section 615(a)(3) [15 U.S.C. § 1681m(a)(3)]; and

(ii) the consumer shall have consented, orally, in writing, or electronically to the procurement of the report by that person.

(C) Scope. Subparagraph (B) shall apply to a person procuring a consumer report on a consumer in connection with the consumer's application for employment only if—

(i) the consumer is applying for a position over which the Secretary of Transportation has the power to establish qualifications and maximum hours of service pursuant to the provisions of section 31502 of title 49, or a position subject to safety regulation by a State transportation agency; and

(ii) as of the time at which the person procures the report or causes the report to be procured the only interaction between the consumer and the person in connection with that employment application has been by mail, telephone, computer, or other similar means.

(3) Conditions on use for adverse actions.

(A) In general. Except as provided in subparagraph (B), in using a consumer report for employment purposes, before taking any adverse action based in whole or in part on the report, the person intending to take such adverse action shall provide to the consumer to whom the report relates—

(i) a copy of the report; and

(ii) a description in writing of the rights of the consumer under this title, as prescribed by the Bureau under section 609(c)(3).

(B) Application by mail, telephone, computer, or other similar means.

(i) If a consumer described in subparagraph (C) applies for employment by mail, telephone, computer, or other similar means, and if a person who has procured a consumer report on the consumer for employment purposes takes adverse action on the employment application based in whole or in part on the report, then the person must provide to the consumer to whom the report relates, in lieu of the notices required under subparagraph (A) of this section and under section 615(a) [15 U.S.C. § 1681m(a)], within 3 business days of taking such action, an oral, written or electronic notification—

(I) that adverse action has been taken based in whole or in part on a consumer report received from a consumer reporting agency;

(II) of the name, address and telephone number of the consumer reporting agency that furnished the consumer report (including a toll-free telephone number established by the agency if the agency compiles and maintains files on consumers on a nationwide basis);

(III) that the consumer reporting agency did not make the decision to take the adverse action and is unable to provide to the consumer the specific reasons why the adverse action was taken; and

(IV) that the consumer may, upon providing proper identification, request a free copy of a report and may dispute with the consumer reporting agency the accuracy or completeness of any information in a report.

(ii) If, under clause (B)(i)(IV), the consumer requests a copy of a consumer report from the person who procured the report, then, within 3 business days of receiving the consumer's request, together with proper identification, the person must send or provide to the consumer a copy of a report and a copy of the consumer's rights as prescribed by the Bureau under section 609(c)(3) [15 USCS § 1681g(c)(3)].

(C) Scope. Subparagraph (B) shall apply to a person procuring a consumer report on a consumer in connection with the consumer's application for employment only if—

(i) the consumer is applying for a position over which the Secretary of Transportation has the power to establish qualifications and maximum hours of service pursuant to the provisions of section 31502 of title 49, or a position subject to safety regulation by a State transportation agency; and

(ii) as of the time at which the person procures the report or causes the report to be procured the only interaction between the consumer and the person in connection with that employment application has been by mail, telephone, computer, or other similar means.

(4) Exception for national security investigations [omitted] * * *

(g) Protection of medical information.

(1) Limitation on consumer reporting agencies. A consumer reporting agency shall not furnish for employment purposes, or in connection with a credit or insurance transaction, a consumer report that contains medical information (other than medical contact information treated in the manner required under section 605(a)(6) [15 U.S.C. § 1681c(a)(6)]) about a consumer, unless—

(A) if furnished in connection with an insurance transaction, the consumer affirmatively consents to the furnishing of the report;

(B) if furnished for employment purposes or in connection with a credit transaction—

(i) the information to be furnished is relevant to process or effect the employment or credit transaction; and

(ii) the consumer provides specific written consent for the furnishing of the report that describes in clear and conspicuous language the use for which the information will be furnished; or

(C) the information to be furnished pertains solely to transactions, accounts, or balances relating to debts arising from the receipt of medical services, products, or devises, where such information, other than account status or amounts, is restricted or reported using codes that do not identify, or do not provide information sufficient to infer, the specific provider or the nature of such services, products, or devices, as provided in section 605(a)(6). * * *

(4) Limitation on redisclosure of medical information. Any person that receives medical information pursuant to paragraph (1) or (3) shall not disclose such information to any other person, except as necessary to carry out the purpose for which the information was initially disclosed, or as otherwise permitted by statute, regulation, or order. * * *

(6) Coordination with other laws. No provision of this subsection shall be construed as altering, affecting, or superseding the applicability of any other provision of Federal law relating to medical confidentiality.

(May 29, 1968, P.L. 90–321, Title VI, § 604, as added, Oct. 26, 1970, P.L. 91–508, Title VI, § 601, 84 Stat. 1129; Aug. 9, 1989, P.L. 101–73, Title

IX, Subtitle F, § 964(c), 103 Stat. 506; Aug. 22, 1996, P.L. 104–193, Title III, Subtitle F, § 352, 110 Stat. 2240; Sept. 30, 1996, P.L. 104–208, Div. A, Title II, Subtitle D, Ch. 1, §§ 2403, 2404(a), (b), 2405, 110 Stat. 3009–430, 3009–434; Nov. 20, 1997, P.L. 105–107, Title III, § 311(a), 111 Stat. 2255; Nov. 2, 1998, P.L. 105–347, §§ 2, 3, 6(4), 112 Stat. 3208, 3211; Nov. 27, 2002, P.L. 107–306, Title VIII, Subtitle B, § 811(b)(8)(A), 116 Stat. 2426; Dec. 4, 2003, P.L. 108–159, Title II, § 213(c), Title IV, §§ 411(a), 412(f), Title VIII, § 811(b), 117 Stat. 1979, 1999, 2003, 2011; Dec. 13, 2003, P.L. 108–177, Title III, Subtitle D, § 361(j), 117 Stat. 2625; Oct. 13, 2006, P.L. 109–351, Title VII, § 719, 120 Stat. 1998; Dec. 26, 2007, P.L. 110–161, Div. D, Title VII, § 743, 121 Stat. 2033; May 22, 2009, P.L. 111–24, Title III, § 302, 123 Stat. 1748; July 21, 2010, P.L. 111–203, Title X, Subtitle H, § 1088(A)(2)(a), (4), 124 Stat. 2087.)

§ 1681l. Restrictions on investigative consumer reports

Whenever a consumer reporting agency prepares an investigative consumer report, no adverse information in the consumer report (other than information which is a matter of public record) may be included in a subsequent consumer report unless such adverse information has been verified in the process of making such subsequent consumer report, or the adverse information was received within the three-month period preceding the date the subsequent report is furnished.

(May 29, 1968, P.L. 90–321, Title VI, § 614, as added Oct. 26, 1970, P.L. 91–508, Title VI, § 601, 84 Stat. 1133.)

§ 1681m. Requirements on users of consumer reports

(a) Duties of users taking adverse actions on the basis of information contained in consumer reports. If any person takes any adverse action with respect to any consumer that is based in whole or in part on any information contained in a consumer report, the person shall—

(1) provide oral, written, or electronic notice of the adverse action to the consumer;

(2) provide to the consumer written or electronic disclosure—

(A) of a numerical credit score as defined in section 609(f)(2)(A) [15 U.S.C. § 1681g(f)(2)(A)] used by such person in taking any adverse action based in whole or in part on any information in a consumer report; and

(B) of the information set forth in subparagraphs (B) through (E) of section 609(f)(1) [15 U.S.C. § 1681g(f)(1)];

(3) provide to the consumer orally, in writing, or electronically—

(A) the name, address, and telephone number of the consumer reporting agency (including a toll-free telephone number established by the agency if the agency compiles and maintains files on consumers on a nationwide basis) that furnished the report to the person; and

(B) a statement that the consumer reporting agency did not make the decision to take the adverse action and is unable to provide the consumer the specific reasons why the adverse action was taken; and

(4) provide to the consumer an oral, written, or electronic notice of the consumer's right—

(A) to obtain, under section 612 [15 U.S.C. § 1681j], a free copy of a consumer report on the consumer from the consumer reporting agency referred to in paragraph (3), which notice shall include an indication of the 60–day period under that section for obtaining such a copy; and

(B) to dispute, under section 611 [15 U.S.C. § 1681i], with a consumer reporting agency the accuracy or completeness of any information in a consumer report furnished by the agency.

(b) Adverse action based on information obtained from third parties other than consumer reporting agencies.

(1) In general. Whenever credit for personal, family, or household purposes involving a consumer is denied or the charge for such credit is increased either wholly or partly because of information obtained from a person other than a consumer reporting agency bearing upon the consumer's credit worthiness, credit standing, credit capacity, character, general reputation, personal characteristics, or mode of living, the user of such information shall, within a reasonable period of time, upon the consumer's written request for the reasons for such adverse action received within sixty days after learning of such adverse action, disclose the nature of the information to the consumer. The user of such information shall clearly and accurately disclose to the consumer his right to make such written request at the time such adverse action is communicated to the consumer. * * *

(c) Reasonable procedures to assure compliance. No person shall be held liable for any violation of this section if he shows by a preponderance of the evidence that at the time of the alleged violation he maintained reasonable procedures to assure compliance with the provisions of this section. * * *

(May 29, 1968, P.L. 90–321, Title VI, § 615, as added Oct. 26, 1970, P.L. 91–508, Title VI, § 601, 84 Stat. 1133; Sept. 30, 1996, P.L. 104–208, Div. A, Title II, Subtitle D, Ch. 1, § 2411, 110 Stat. 3009–443; Dec. 4, 2003, P.L. 108–159, Title I, Subtitle A, § 114, Subtitle B, §§ 154(b), 155, Title II, § 213(a), Title III, § 311(a), Title VIII, § 811(h), 117 Stat. 1960, 1967, 1978, 1988, 2012; July 21, 2010, P.L. 111–203, Title X, Subtitle H, §§ 1088(a)(2)(C), (7)–(9), 1100F, 124 Stat. 2087, 2112; as amended, Dec. 18, 2010, P.L. 111–319, § 2(a), 124 Stat. 3457.)

§ 1681n.   Civil liability for willful noncompliance

(a) In general. Any person who willfully fails to comply with any requirement imposed under this title with respect to any consumer is liable to that consumer in an amount equal to the sum of—

(1) (A) any actual damages sustained by the consumer as a result of the failure or damages of not less than $100 and not more than $1,000; or

(B) in the case of liability of a natural person for obtaining a consumer report under false pretenses or knowingly without a permissible purpose, actual damages sustained by the consumer as a result of the failure or $1,000, whichever is greater;

(2) such amount of punitive damages as the court may allow; and

(3) in the case of any successful action to enforce any liability under this section, the costs of the action together with reasonable attorney's fees as determined by the court.

(b) Civil liability for knowing noncompliance. Any person who obtains a consumer report from a consumer reporting agency under false pretenses or knowingly without a permissible purpose shall be liable to the consumer reporting agency for actual damages sustained by the consumer reporting agency or $1,000, whichever is greater.

(c) Attorney's fees. Upon a finding by the court that an unsuccessful pleading, motion, or other paper filed in connection with an action under this section was filed in bad faith or for purposes of harassment, the court shall award to the prevailing party attorney's fees reasonable in relation to the work expended in responding to the pleading, motion, or other paper. * * *

(May 29, 1968, P.L. 90–321, Title VI, § 616, as added, Oct. 26, 1970, P.L. 91–508, Title VI, § 601, 84 Stat. 1134; Sept. 30, 1996, P.L. 104–208, Div. A, Title II, Subtitle D, Ch. 1, § 2412(a)–(c), (e)(1), 110 Stat. 3009–446, 3009–447; June 3, 2008, P.L. 110–241, § 3(a), 122 Stat. 1566.)

§ 1681o.   Civil liability for negligent noncompliance

(a) Any person who is negligent in failing to comply with any requirement imposed under this title with respect to any consumer is liable to that consumer in an amount equal to the sum of—

(1) any actual damages sustained by the consumer as a result of the failure; and

(2) in the case of any successful action to enforce any liability under this section, the costs of the action together with reasonable attorney's fees as determined by the court.

(b) On a finding by the court that an unsuccessful pleading, motion, or other paper filed in connection with an action under this section was filed in bad faith or for purposes of harassment, the court shall award to the prevailing party attorney's fees reasonable in relation to the work expended in responding to the pleading, motion, or other paper.

(May 29, 1968, P.L. 90–321, Title VI, § 617, as added Oct. 26, 1970, P.L. 91–508, Title VI, § 601, 84 Stat. 1134; Sept. 30, 1996, P.L. 104–208, Div. A, Title II, Subtitle D, Ch. 1, § 2412 (d), (e)(2), 110 Stat. 3009–446, 3009–447; Dec. 4, 2003, P.L. 108–159, Title VIII, § 811(e), 117 Stat. 2012.)

§ 1681p. Jurisdiction of courts; limitation of actions

An action to enforce any liability created under this title may be brought in any appropriate United States district court, without regard to the amount in controversy, or in any other court of competent jurisdiction, not later than the earlier of—

   (1) 2 years after the date of discovery by the plaintiff of the violation that is the basis for such liability; or

   (2) 5 years after the date on which the violation that is the basis for such liability occurs.

(May 29, 1968, P.L. 90–321, Title VI, § 618, as added Oct. 26, 1970, P.L. 91–508, Title VI, § 601, 84 Stat. 1134; Dec. 4, 2003, P.L. 108–159, Title I, Subtitle B, § 156, 117 Stat. 1968.)

§ 1681t. Relation to State laws

   (a) Except as provided in subsections (b) and (c), this title does not annul, alter, affect, or exempt any person subject to the provisions of this title from complying with the laws of any State with respect to the collection, distribution, or use of any information on consumers, or for the prevention of identity theft, except to the extent that those laws are inconsistent with any provision of this title, and then only to the extent of the inconsistency. * * *

(May 29, 1968, P.L. 90–321, Title VI, § 625 [624] [623] [622], as added Oct. 26, 1970, P.L. 91–508, Title VI, § 601, 84 Stat. 1136; Oct. 27, 1992, P.L. 102–537, § 2(a), 106 Stat. 3531; Sept. 30, 1996, P.L. 104–208, Div. A, Title II, Subtitle D, Ch. 1, §§ 2413(a)(1), 2419, 110 Stat. 3009–447, 3009–452; Dec. 4, 2003, P.L. 108–159, Title I, Subtitle B, § 151(a)(2), Title II, §§ 212(e), 214(a)(1), (c)(2), Title III, § 311(b), Title VII, § 711, 117 Stat. 1964, 1977, 1980, 1983, 1989, 2011.)

ECONOMIC ESPIONAGE ACT—
SELECTED PROVISIONS
18 U.S.C. §§ 1831–33, 1836–39

§ 1831. Economic espionage

(a) Whoever, intending or knowing that the offense will benefit any foreign government, foreign instrumentality, or foreign agent, knowingly

(1) steals, or without authorization appropriates, takes, carries away, or conceals, or by fraud, artifice, or deception obtains a trade secret;

(2) without authorization copies, duplicates, sketches, draws, photographs, downloads, uploads, alters, destroys, photocopies, replicates, transmits, delivers, sends, mails, communicates, or conveys a trade secret;

(3) receives, buys, or possesses a trade secret, knowing the same to have been stolen or appropriated, obtained, or converted without authorization;

(4) attempts to commit any offense described in any of paragraphs (1) through (3); or

(5) conspires with one or more other persons to commit any offense described in any of paragraphs (1) through (3), and one or more of such persons do any act to effect the object of the conspiracy,

shall, except as provided in subsection (b), be fined not more than $500,000 or imprisoned not more than 15 years, or both.

(b) Any organization that commits any offense described in subsection (a) shall be fined not more than $10,000,000.

(Oct. 11, 1996, Pub. L. 104–294, Title I, § 101(a), 110 Stat. 3488.)

§ 1832. Theft of trade secrets

(a) Whoever, with intent to convert a trade secret, that is related to or included in a product that is produced for or placed in interstate or foreign commerce, to the economic benefit of anyone other than the owner thereof, and intending or knowing that the offense will, injure any owner of that trade secret, knowingly—

(1) steals, or without authorization appropriates, takes, carries away, or conceals, or by fraud, artifice, or deception obtains such information;

(2) without authorization copies, duplicates, sketches, draws, photographs, downloads, uploads, alters, destroys, photocopies, repli-

cates, transmits, delivers, sends, mails, communicates, or conveys such information;

(3) receives, buys, or possesses such information, knowing the same to have been stolen or appropriated, obtained, or converted without authorization;

(4) attempts to commit any offense described in paragraphs (1) through (3); or

(5) conspires with one or more other persons to commit any offense described in paragraphs (1) through (3), and one or more of such persons do any act to effect the object of the conspiracy,

shall, except as provided in subsection (b), be fined under this title or imprisoned not more than 10 years, or both.

(b) Any organization that commits any offense described in subsection (a) shall be fined not more than $5,000,000.

(Oct. 11, 1996, Pub. L. 104–294, Title I, § 101(a), 110 Stat. 3489.)

§ 1833. Exceptions to prohibitions

This chapter does not prohibit—

(1) any otherwise lawful activity conducted by a governmental entity of the United States, a State, or a political subdivision of a State; or

(2) the reporting of a suspected violation of law to any governmental entity of the United States, a State, or a political subdivision of a State, if such entity has lawful authority with respect to that violation.

(Oct. 11, 1996, Pub. L. 104–294, Title I, § 101(a), 110 Stat. 3489.)

§ 1836. Civil proceedings to enjoin violations

(a) The Attorney General may, in a civil action, obtain appropriate injunctive relief against any violation of this chapter.

(b) The district courts of the United States shall have exclusive original jurisdiction of civil actions under this section.

(Added Oct. 11, 1996, P.L. 104–294, Title I, § 101(a), 110 Stat. 3490; Nov. 2, 2002, P.L. 107–273, Div. B, Title IV, § 4002(e)(9), 116 Stat. 1810.)

§ 1837. Applicability to conduct outside the United States

This chapter also applies to conduct occurring outside the United States if—

(1) the offender is a natural person who is a citizen or permanent resident alien of the United States, or an organization organized under the laws of the United States or a State or political subdivision thereof; or

(2) an act in furtherance of the offense was committed in the United States.

(Oct. 11, 1996, Pub. L. 104–294, Title I, § 101(a), 110 Stat. 3490.)

§ 1838. Construction with other laws

This chapter shall not be construed to preempt or displace any other remedies, whether civil or criminal, provided by United States Federal, State, commonwealth, possession, or territory law for the misappropriation of a trade secret, or to affect the otherwise lawful disclosure of information by any Government employee under section 552 of title 5 (commonly known as the Freedom of Information Act).

(Oct. 11, 1996, Pub. L. 104–294, Title I, § 101(a), 110 Stat. 3490.)

§ 1839. Definitions

As used in this chapter—

(1) the term "foreign instrumentality" means any agency, bureau, ministry, component, institution, association, or any legal, commercial, or business organization, corporation, firm, or entity that is substantially owned, controlled, sponsored, commanded, managed, or dominated by a foreign government;

(2) the term "foreign agent" means any officer, employee, proxy, servant, delegate, or representative of a foreign government;

(3) the term "trade secret" means all forms and types of financial, business, scientific, technical, economic, or engineering information, including patterns, plans, compilations, program devices, formulas, designs, prototypes, methods, techniques, processes, procedures, programs, or codes, whether tangible or intangible, and whether or how stored, compiled, or memorialized physically, electronically, graphically, photographically, or in writing if—

(A) the owner thereof has taken reasonable measures to keep such information secret; and

(B) the information derives independent economic value, actual or potential, from not being generally known to, and not being readily ascertainable through proper means by, the public; and

(4) the term "owner," with respect to a trade secret, means the person or entity in whom or in which rightful legal or equitable title to, or license in, the trade secret is reposed.

(Oct. 11, 1996, Pub. L. 104–294, Title I, § 101(a), 110 Stat. 3490.)

COMPUTER FRAUD AND ABUSE ACT
18 U.S.C. § 1030

§ 1030. Fraud and related activity in connection with computers

(a) Whoever—

(1) having knowingly accessed a computer without authorization or exceeding authorized access, and by means of such conduct having obtained information that has been determined by the United States Government pursuant to an Executive order or statute to require protection against unauthorized disclosure for reasons of national defense or foreign relations, or any restricted data, as defined in paragraph y.[(y)] of section 11 of the Atomic Energy Act of 1954 [42 U.S.C. § 2014(y)], with reason to believe that such information so obtained could be used to the injury of the United States, or to the advantage of any foreign nation willfully communicates, delivers, transmits, or causes to be communicated, delivered, or transmitted, or attempts to communicate, deliver, transmit or cause to be communicated, delivered, or transmitted the same to any person not entitled to receive it, or willfully retains the same and fails to deliver it to the officer or employee of the United States entitled to receive it;

(2) intentionally accesses a computer without authorization or exceeds authorized access, and thereby obtains—

(A) information contained in a financial record of a financial institution, or of a card issuer as defined in section 1602(n) of title 15, or contained in a file of a consumer reporting agency on a consumer, as such terms are defined in the Fair Credit Reporting Act (15 U.S.C. 1681 et seq.);

(B) information from any department or agency of the United States; or

(C) information from any protected computer;

(3) intentionally, without authorization to access any nonpublic computer of a department or agency of the United States, accesses such a computer of that department or agency that is exclusively for the use of the Government of the United States or, in the case of a computer not exclusively for such use, is used by or for the Government of the United States and such conduct affects that use by or for the Government of the United States;

(4) knowingly and with intent to defraud, accesses a protected computer without authorization, or exceeds authorized access, and by means of such conduct furthers the intended fraud and obtains

anything of value, unless the object of the fraud and the thing obtained consists only of the use of the computer and the value of such use is not more than $5,000 in any 1–year period;

(5) (A) knowingly causes the transmission of a program, information, code, or command, and as a result of such conduct, intentionally causes damage without authorization, to a protected computer;

(B) intentionally accesses a protected computer without authorization, and as a result of such conduct, recklessly causes damage; or

(C) intentionally accesses a protected computer without authorization, and as a result of such conduct, causes damage and loss.[;]

(6) knowingly and with intent to defraud traffics (as defined in section 1029 [18 U.S.C. 1029]) in any password or similar information through which a computer may be accessed without authorization, if—

(A) such trafficking affects interstate or foreign commerce; or

(B) such computer is used by or for the Government of the United States; [or]

(7) with intent to extort from any person any money or other thing of value, transmits in interstate or foreign commerce any communication containing any—

(A) threat to cause damage to a protected computer;

(B) threat to obtain information from a protected computer without authorization or in excess of authorization or to impair the confidentiality of information obtained from a protected computer without authorization or by exceeding authorized access; or

(C) demand or request for money or other thing of value in relation to damage to a protected computer, where such damage was caused to facilitate the extortion;

shall be punished as provided in subsection (c) of this section.

(b) Whoever conspires to commit or attempts to commit an offense under subsection (a) of this section shall be punished as provided in subsection (c) of this section.

(c) The punishment for an offense under subsection (a) or (b) of this section is—

[DISCUSSION OF CRIMINAL PENALTIES IS OMITTED.] * * *

(e) As used in this section—

(1) the term "computer" means an electronic, magnetic, optical, electrochemical, or other high speed data processing device perform-

ing logical, arithmetic, or storage functions, and includes any data storage facility or communications facility directly related to or operating in conjunction with such device, but such term does not include an automated typewriter or typesetter, a portable hand held calculator, or other similar device;

(2) the term "protected computer" means a computer—

(A) exclusively for the use of a financial institution or the United States Government, or, in the case of a computer not exclusively for such use, used by or for a financial institution or the United States Government and the conduct constituting the offense affects that use by or for the financial institution or the Government; or

(B) which is used in or affecting interstate or foreign commerce or communication, including a computer located outside the United States that is used in a manner that affects interstate or foreign commerce or communication of the United States;

(3) the term "State" includes the District of Columbia, the Commonwealth of Puerto Rico, and any other commonwealth, possession or territory of the United States;

(4) the term "financial institution" means—[omitted.]

(7) the term "department of the United States" means the legislative or judicial branch of the Government or one of the executive department enumerated in section 101 of title 5;

(8) the term "damage" means any impairment to the integrity or availability of data, a program, a system, or information;

(9) the term "government entity" includes the Government of the United States, any State or political subdivision of the United States, any foreign country, and any state, province, municipality, or other political subdivision of a foreign country;

(10) the term "conviction" shall include a conviction under the law of any State for a crime punishable by imprisonment for more than 1 year, an element of which is unauthorized access, or exceeding authorized access, to a computer;

(11) the term "loss" means any reasonable cost to any victim, including the cost of responding to an offense, conducting a damage assessment, and restoring the data, program, system, or information to its condition prior to the offense, and any revenue lost, cost incurred, or other consequential damages incurred because of interruption of service; and

(12) the term "person" means any individual, firm, corporation, educational institution, financial institution, governmental entity, or legal or other entity.

(f) This section does not prohibit any lawfully authorized investigative, protective, or intelligence activity of a law enforcement agency of the United States, a State, or a political subdivision of a State, or of an intelligence agency of the United States.

(g) Any person who suffers damage or loss by reason of a violation of this section may maintain a civil action against the violator to obtain compensatory damages and injunctive relief or other equitable relief. A civil action for a violation of this section may be brought only if the conduct involves 1 of the factors set forth in subclauses [subclause] (I), (II), (III), (IV), or (V) of subsection (c)(4)(A)(i). Damages for a violation involving only conduct described in subsection (c)(4)(A)(i)(I) are limited to economic damages. No action may be brought under this subsection unless such action is begun within 2 years of the date of the act complained of or the date of the discovery of the damage. No action may be brought under this subsection for the negligent design or manufacture of computer hardware, computer software, or firmware. * * *

[Eds. Subsection (c)(4)(A) provides:

except as provided in subparagraphs (E) and (F), a fine under this title, imprisonment for not more than 5 years, or both, in the case of—

(i) an offense under subsection (a)(5)(B), which does not occur after a conviction for another offense under this section, if the offense caused (or, in the case of an attempted offense, would, if completed, have caused)—

(I) loss to 1 or more persons during any 1–year period (and, for purposes of an investigation, prosecution, or other proceeding brought by the United States only, loss resulting from a related course of conduct affecting 1 or more other protected computers) aggregating at least $5,000 in value;

(II) the modification or impairment, or potential modification or impairment, of the medical examination, diagnosis, treatment, or care of 1 or more individuals;

(III) physical injury to any person;

(IV) a threat to public health or safety;

(V) damage affecting a computer used by or for an entity of the United States Government in furtherance of the administration of justice, national defense, or national security; or

(VI) damage affecting 10 or more protected computers during any 1–year period; or

(ii) an attempt to commit an offense punishable under this subparagraph * * *.]

(Added Oct. 12, 1984, P.L. 98–473, Title II, Ch. XXI, § 2102(a), 98 Stat. 2190; Oct. 16, 1986, P.L. 99–474, § 2, 100 Stat. 1213; Nov. 18, 1988, P.L. 100–690, Title VII, Subtitle B, § 7065, 102 Stat. 4404; Aug. 9, 1989, P.L. 101–73, Title IX, Subtitle F, § 962(a)(5), 103 Stat. 502; Nov. 29, 1990, P.L. 101–647, Title XII, § 1205(e), Title XXV, Subtitle I, § 2597(j), Title XXXV, § 3533, 104 Stat. 4831, 4910, 4925; Sept. 13, 1994, P.L. 103–322, Title XXIX, § 290001(b)–(f), 108 Stat. 2097; Oct. 11, 1996, P.L. 104–294,

Title II, § 201, Title VI, § 604(b)(36), 110 Stat. 3491, 3508; Oct. 26, 2001, P.L. 107–56, Title V, § 506(a), Title VIII, § 814(a)–(e), 115 Stat. 366, 382; Nov. 2, 2002, P.L. 107–273, Div. B, Title IV, §§ 4002(b)(1), (12), 4005(a)(3), (d)(3), 116 Stat. 1807, 1808, 1812, 1813; Nov. 25, 2002, P.L. 107–296, Title II, Subtitle C, § 225(g), 116 Stat. 2158; Sept. 26, 2008, P.L. 110–326, Title II, §§ 203, 204(a), 205–208, 122 Stat. 3561.)

CALIFORNIA LABOR CODE § 2922 (2012)

§ 2922. Employment for unspecified term; Termination; Meaning of employment for specified term

An employment, having no specified term, may be terminated at the will of either party on notice to the other. Employment for a specified term means an employment for a period greater than one month.

GEORGIA O.C.G.A. § 34-7-1

§ 34-7-1. Determination of term of employment; manner of termination of indefinite hiring

If a contract of employment provides that wages are payable at a stipulated period, the presumption shall arise that the hiring is for such period, provided that, if anything else in the contract indicates that the hiring was for a longer term, the mere reservation of wages for a lesser time will not control. An indefinite hiring may be terminated at will by either party.

MONTANA WRONGFUL DISCHARGE
FROM EMPLOYMENT ACT
MONT. CODE ANN. § 39–2–901 TO –915 (2011)

§ 39–2–901. Short title.

This part may be cited as the "Wrongful Discharge From Employment Act".

§ 39–2–902. Purpose.

This part sets forth certain rights and remedies with respect to wrongful discharge. Except as provided in 392912, this part provides the exclusive remedy for a wrongful discharge from employment.

§ 39–2–903. Definitions.

In this part, the following definitions apply:

(1) "Constructive discharge" means the voluntary termination of employment by an employee because of a situation created by an act or omission of the employer which an objective, reasonable person would find so intolerable that voluntary termination is the only reasonable alternative. Constructive discharge does not mean voluntary termination because of an employer's refusal to promote the employee or improve wages, responsibilities, or other terms and conditions of employment.

(2) "Discharge" includes a constructive discharge as defined in subsection (1) and any other termination of employment, including resignation, elimination of the job, layoff for lack of work, failure to recall or rehire, and any other cutback in the number of employees for a legitimate business reason.

(3) "Employee" means a person who works for another for hire. The term does not include a person who is an independent contractor.

(4) "Fringe benefits" means the value of any employer-paid vacation leave, sick leave, medical insurance plan, disability insurance plan, life insurance plan, and pension benefit plan in force on the date of the termination.

(5) "Good cause" means reasonable job-related grounds for dismissal based on a failure to satisfactorily perform job duties, disruption of the employer's operation, or other legitimate business reason. The legal use of a lawful product by an individual off the employer's premises during nonworking hours is not a legitimate business reason, unless the employer acts within the provisions of 39–2–313(3) or (4).

(6) "Lost wages" means the gross amount of wages that would have been reported to the internal revenue service as gross income on Form

W–2 and includes additional compensation deferred at the option of the employee.

(7) "Public policy" means a policy in effect at the time of the discharge concerning the public health, safety, or welfare established by constitutional provision, statute, or administrative rule.

§ 39–2–904. Elements of wrongful discharge—presumptive probationary period.

(1) A discharge is wrongful only if:

(a) it was in retaliation for the employee's refusal to violate public policy or for reporting a violation of public policy;

(b) the discharge was not for good cause and the employee had completed the employer's probationary period of employment; or

(c) the employer violated the express provisions of its own written personnel policy.

(2)(a) During a probationary period of employment, the employment may be terminated at the will of either the employer or the employee on notice to the other for any reason or no reason.

(b) If an employer does not establish a specific probationary period or provide that there is no probationary period prior to or at the time of hire, there is a probationary period of 6 months from the date of hire.

§ 39–2–905. Remedies.

(1) If an employer has committed a wrongful discharge, the employee may be awarded lost wages and fringe benefits for a period not to exceed 4 years from the date of discharge, together with interest on the lost wages and fringe benefits. Interim earnings, including amounts the employee could have earned with reasonable diligence, must be deducted from the amount awarded for lost wages. Before interim earnings are deducted from lost wages, there must be deducted from the interim earnings any reasonable amounts expended by the employee in searching for, obtaining, or relocating to new employment.

(2) The employee may recover punitive damages otherwise allowed by law if it is established by clear and convincing evidence that the employer engaged in actual fraud or actual malice in the discharge of the employee in violation of 39–2–904(1)(a).

(3) There is no right under any legal theory to damages for wrongful discharge under this part for pain and suffering, emotional distress, compensatory damages, punitive damages, or any other form of damages, except as provided for in subsections (1) and (2).

§§ 39–2–906 through 39–2–910 reserved.

§ 39–2–911. Limitation of actions.

(1) An action under this part must be filed within 1 year after the date of discharge.

(2) If an employer maintains written internal procedures, other than those specified in 39–2–912, under which an employee may appeal a discharge within the organizational structure of the employer, the employee shall first exhaust those procedures prior to filing an action under this part. The employee's failure to initiate or exhaust available internal procedures is a defense to an action brought under this part. If the employer's internal procedures are not completed within 90 days from the date the employee initiates the internal procedures, the employee may file an action under this part and for purposes of this subsection the employer's internal procedures are considered exhausted. The limitation period in subsection (1) is tolled until the procedures are exhausted. In no case may the provisions of the employer's internal procedures extend the limitation period in subsection (1) more than 120 days.

(3) If the employer maintains written internal procedures under which an employee may appeal a discharge within the organizational structure of the employer, the employer shall within 7 days of the date of the discharge notify the discharged employee of the existence of such procedures and shall supply the discharged employee with a copy of them. If the employer fails to comply with this subsection, the discharged employee need not comply with subsection (2).

§ 39–2–912. Exemptions.

This part does not apply to a discharge:

(1) that is subject to any other state or federal statute that provides a procedure or remedy for contesting the dispute. The statutes include those that prohibit discharge for filing complaints, charges, or claims with administrative bodies or that prohibit unlawful discrimination based on race, national origin, sex, age, disability, creed, religion, political belief, color, marital status, and other similar grounds.

(2) of an employee covered by a written collective bargaining agreement or a written contract of employment for a specific term.

§ 39–2–913. Preemption of common-law remedies.

Except as provided in this part, no claim for discharge may arise from tort or express or implied contract.

§ 39–2–914. Arbitration.

(1) A party may make a written offer to arbitrate a dispute that otherwise could be adjudicated under this part.

(2) An offer to arbitrate must be in writing and contain the following provisions:

(a) A neutral arbitrator must be selected by mutual agreement or, in the absence of agreement, as provided in 27–5–211.

(b) The arbitration must be governed by the Uniform Arbitration Act, Title 27, chapter 5. If there is a conflict between the Uniform Arbitration Act and this part, this part applies.

(c) The arbitrator is bound by this part.

(3) If a complaint is filed under this part, the offer to arbitrate must be made within 60 days after service of the complaint and must be accepted in writing within 30 days after the date the offer is made.

(4) A discharged employee who makes a valid offer to arbitrate that is accepted by the employer and who prevails in such arbitration is entitled to have the arbitrator's fee and all costs of arbitration paid by the employer.

(5) If a valid offer to arbitrate is made and accepted, arbitration is the exclusive remedy for the wrongful discharge dispute and there is no right to bring or continue a lawsuit under this part. The arbitrator's award is final and binding, subject to review of the arbitrator's decision under the provisions of the Uniform Arbitration Act.

§ 39–2–915. Effect of rejection of offer to arbitrate.

A party who makes a valid offer to arbitrate that is not accepted by the other party and who prevails in an action under this part is entitled as an element of costs to reasonable attorney fees incurred subsequent to the date of the offer.

UNIFORM LAW COMMISSIONERS' MODEL EMPLOYMENT TERMINATION ACT

[*Editors' Note*: The following is the text of a "Model Employment Termination Act," approved and recommended for enactment in all the states by the National Conference of Commissioners on Uniform State Laws at their annual meeting of August 29, 1991 in Naples, Florida. As of this writing, the Model law has not been adopted by any jurisdiction. Material within brackets is found in the original and denotes options.]

MODEL EMPLOYMENT TERMINATION ACT

§ 1. Definitions.—In this [Act]:

(1) "Employee" means an individual who works for hire, including an individual employed in a supervisory, managerial, or confidential position, but not an independent contractor.

(2) "Employer" means a person [, excluding this State, a political subdivision, a municipal corporation, or any other governmental subdivision, agency, or instrumentality,] that has employed [five] or more employees for each working day in each of 20 or more calendar weeks in the two-year period next preceding a termination or an employer's filing of a complaint pursuant to Section 5(c), excluding a parent, spouse, child, or other member of the employer's immediate family or of the immediate family of an individual having a controlling interest in the employer.

(3) "Fringe benefit" means vacation leave, sick leave, medical insurance plan, disability insurance plan, life insurance plan, pension benefit plan, or other benefit of economic value, to the extent the leave, plan, or benefit is paid for by the employer.

(4) "Good cause" means (i) a reasonable basis related to an individual employee for termination of the employee's employment in view of relevant factors and circumstances, which may include the employee's duties, responsibilities, conduct on the job or otherwise, job performance, and employment record, or (ii) the exercise of business judgment in good faith by the employer, including setting its economic or institutional goals and determining methods to achieve those goals, organizing or reorganizing operations, discontinuing, consolidating, or divesting operations or positions or parts of operations or positions, determining the size of its work force and the nature of the positions filled by its work force, and determining and changing standards of performance for positions.

(5) "Good faith" means honesty in fact.

(6) "Pay," as a noun, means hourly wages or periodic salary, including tips, regularly paid and nondiscretionary commissions and bonuses, and regularly paid overtime, but not fringe benefits.

(7) "Person" means an individual, corporation, business trust, estate, trust, partnership, association, joint venture, or any other legal or commercial entity [, excluding government or a governmental subdivision, agency, or instrumentality].

(8) "Termination" means:

(i) a dismissal, including that resulting from the elimination of a position, of an employee by an employer;

(ii) a layoff or suspension of an employee by an employer for more than two consecutive months; or

(iii) a quitting of employment or a retirement by an employee induced by an act or omission of the employer, after notice to the employer of the act or omission without appropriate relief by the employer, so intolerable that under the circumstances a reasonable individual would quit or retire.

Comment

Paragraph (2): The definition of "employer" is based in part on Title VII of the Civil Rights Act of 1964. Since the general view is that state law should apply more broadly than federal law, the suggested minimum number of employees is reduced from 15 to 5, and the 20 qualifying weeks may be spread over a period of 24 months. To enable an early and certain determination of the status of the employer in question, the count should be taken as of the date of the employee's discharge or of the employer's filing for a" declaratory" ruling. Thus, if an employee were terminated on May 31, 1995, the critical period for finding 20 qualifying weeks would run from June 1, 1993, to May 31, 1995. This avoids the problem of the federal approach as reflected in Slack v. Havens, 522 F.2d 1091 (9th Cir.1975). In determining whether a person is an employer, employees of that person are counted even though they are not protected by the Act. The language concerning the exclusion of the employer's immediate family from the count (but not from the protections of the Act if otherwise covered) is drawn from the Fair Labor Standards Act.

Uniformity is less important with regard to public employees because they are not employees of multi-state employers. In addition, many public employees are members of a civil service system that offers protection against termination. Thus, their coverage is left to local option. A state legislature may wish to consider, however, whether it is sound policy to prescribe differential treatment for such institutions as public and private universities.

Paragraph (3): "Benefit of economic value" includes food, lodging, and tuition reimbursement.

Paragraph (4): Examples of "good cause" for a termination under subparagraph (i) include theft, assault, fighting on the job, destruction of property, use or possession of drugs or alcohol on the job, insubordination, excessive absenteeism or tardiness, incompetence, lack of productivity, and inadequate performance or neglect of duty. Off-duty conduct may be good cause if it is relevant to the employee's performance on the job, to the employer's business reputation, or to similar concerns.

In the determination of good cause, principles and considerations generally accepted in arbitration which are to be applied include such factors as the reasonableness of the company rule violated, the employee's knowledge or warning of the rule, the consistency of enforcement of the rule and the penalties assessed, the use of corrective or progressive discipline, the fullness and fairness of the investigation including the opportunity given the employee to present his or her views prior to dismissal, and the appropriateness of the penalty in light of the conduct involved and the employee's employment record. Consideration will also be given to the character of the employee's responsibilities, including the professional, scientific, or technical character of the work, the management level of the employee's position in the enterprise, and its importance to the success of the business. An employer's discrimination in violation of applicable federal, state, or local law, or an employer's violation of established public policy, is inconsistent with the requirement of good cause for termination. Similarly, "whistle-blowers" in various circumstances would be protected against retaliatory discharges.

Under subparagraph (ii), an employer's decision as to the economic goals and methodologies of the enterprise and the size and composition of the work force, as contrasted with decisions as to individual discipline or dismissal, is governed by honest business judgment. In no way is this Act to operate as a plant-closing law; an employer remains entirely free to shut down an operation on economic or institutional grounds. The use of the term "including" in subparagraph (ii) and the listing of illustrative managerial decisions are intended to invoke the principle of *ejusdem generis* in the interpretation of the subparagraph. Although an employer's cutback in the number of employees may be economically justified, an individual employee may still contest his or her selection for layoff on the grounds it was discriminatory under applicable federal, state, or local law, or a violation of established public policy. Examples of valid grounds for selecting a particular employee for layoff include seniority, performance on the job, attendance record, etc. A sham layoff cannot be used as a device to dismiss an employee as to whom there is not good cause for a termination, as it violates the requirement that business judgment be exercised in good faith.

"Standards of performance" for positions will necessarily depend on the nature of the particular position. In fields that are traditionally or inherently highly competitive, such as professional sports, the entertainment industry, most professions, teaching at a university, etc., a performance standard could be "the most proficient performer available for a particular position." An employer is entitled to change the performance standards of any or all of the positions in its operation, as long as those changes are clearly communicated to the employees affected.

With regard to subparagraphs (i) and (ii), allowance is made for the difficulty of evaluating objectively the performance of certain positions.

Paragraph (7): "Person" includes several entities, such as co-employers. Uniformity is less important with regard to public employers and employees for the reasons set forth in the Comments on paragraph (2). Thus, the inclusion of public entities as persons is left to state option.

Paragraph (8)(iii): An act or omission making employment intolerable may consist of several acts or omissions or a course of conduct by an employer. Subparagraph (iii) incorporates the doctrine commonly known as "constructive discharge." It could include a series of suspensions no one of which exceeds the two months necessary to constitute a termination under subparagraph (ii). A "constructive discharge" in and of itself is not a violation of this Act. It is merely a termination, and, like other terminations, it becomes a violation only in the absence of good cause.

§ 2. Scope.

(a) This [Act] applies only to a termination that occurs after the effective date of this [Act].

(b) This [Act] does not apply to a termination at the expiration of an express oral or written agreement of employment for a specified duration, which was valid, subsisting, and in effect on the [effective] date of this [Act].

(c) Except as provided in subsection (e), this [Act] displaces and extinguishes all common-law rights and claims of a terminated employee against the employer, its officers, directors, and employees, which are based on the termination or on acts taken or statements made that are reasonably necessary to initiate or effect the termination if the employee's termination requires good cause under Section 3(a), is subject to an agreement for severance pay under Section 4(c), or is permitted by the expiration of an agreement for a specified duration under Section 4(d).

(d) An employee whose termination is not subject to Section 3(a) or 4(d) and who is not a party to an agreement under Section 4(c) retains all common-law rights and claims.

(e) This [Act] does not displace or extinguish rights or claims of a terminated employee against an employer arising under state or federal statutes or administrative rules or regulations having the force of law [or local ordinances valid under state law], a collective-bargaining agreement between an employer and a labor organization, or an express oral or written agreement relating to employment which does not violate this [Act]. Those rights and claims may not be asserted under this [Act], except as otherwise provided in this [Act]. The existence or adjudication of those rights or claims does not limit the employee's rights or claims under this [Act], except as stated in Section 7(d).

Comment

Subsection (b): The agreement of "specified duration" described here includes a fixed-term agreement of any length, measured in months, years, or some other time period, and is not limited to the type of specified-duration agreement authorized by Section 4(d). Specified-duration agreements permitted under this transitional provision cannot be renewed or extended except by an agreement meeting the requirements of Section 4(d). A state legislature may require that an agreement permitted under this subsection must be in effect on a date other than the effective date of the Act, e.g., on the day the bill was introduced in the legislature.

Subsection (c): In return for statutory protections, tort actions based on the termination of employment as such are abolished. These include defamation, intentional infliction of emotional distress, and the like. There may be independent tort actions for assault, malicious prosecution, false imprisonment, etc., if there are independent facts separate and apart from the termination itself to support such causes of action. The key to the abolition of a tort action is not the nature of the tort, however, but whether its basis is the termination itself or acts taken or statements made that are reasonably necessary to initiate or effect the termination. An employer's report of a termination or the grounds for it, e.g., to another prospective employer, will be governed by the doctrine of qualified privilege. This Act is not intended to expand, contract, or modify in any way a state's common law or statutory law of defamation. Contract actions based on terminations under implied-in-fact employment agreements are also abolished for employees protected by this Act.

Subsection (c) applies only to employee actions against an employer or its representatives, and does not affect employer actions against an employee, e.g., for disloyalty, breach of a covenant not to compete, theft or destruction of property, etc.

Subsections (d) and (e): Employees who get no new statutory protections retain all their common-law rights. At the same time, however, employees who do benefit from the statutory scheme, and thus lose certain common-law rights, retain rights granted them under statutory law, collective-bargaining agreements, and other express employment agreements.

State law, of course, cannot interfere with the rights of "interstate" employees covered by collective-bargaining agreements governed by federal law. Subsection (e) similarly preserves the rights of intrastate employees and public employees under union agreements. Subsection (e) also leaves intact existing law concerning the enforceability of express oral or written agreements having a specified duration—determined either by a fixed time period or by a particular task, e.g., the term agreements of professional athletes and entertainers, business executives, etc.—or agreements providing special benefits upon termination, such as "golden parachutes."

Individuals not otherwise protected by this Act, including employees with less than a year's seniority and part-time workers, may still be protected by express or implied-in-fact agreements of employment, whether written or oral. Furthermore, such "uncovered" individuals retain any other common-law rights to which they may be entitled. Finally, even protected employees retain common-law claims against third parties arising out of a termination.

Unionized employees and employees covered by collective-bargaining agreements subject to federal law are entitled to exercise rights under this Act to the extent permitted by the developing law of federal preemption. See, e.g., Lingle v. Norge Div. of Magic Chef, Inc., 486 U.S. 399 (1988). Unionized employees subject to state law are entitled to exercise rights under this Act to the extent not foreclosed by this or other state statutes. Arbitrators and courts will have to answer the necessary jurisdictional questions on a case-by-case basis.

There is no displacement or extinguishment of rights or claims under state statutes or administrative regulations, such as those relating to "whistle-blowing," workers' compensation, and occupational safety and health. Furthermore, by statutory enactment any state may provide separate, independent remedies for certain classes of terminated employees—for example, whistle-blowers and the victims of egregious violations of public policy—which are broader and more extensive than those prescribed by this Act. It is only common-law rights and claims that this Act displaces. Rights that are preserved from displacement or extinguishment may, at the option of a state, include rights under municipal ordinances that are valid under state law.

Subsection (e): The common-law remedies available to a terminated employee under an agreement include not only any remedies expressly provided by the agreement but also whatever legal or equitable remedies a court would customarily provide for breach of such an agreement.

§ 3. Prohibited Terminations.

(a) Unless otherwise provided in an agreement for severance pay under Section 4(c) or for a specified duration under Section 4(d), an employer may not terminate the employment of an employee without good cause.

(b) Subsection (a) applies only to an employee who has been employed by the same employer for a total period of one year or more and has worked for the employer for at least 520 hours during the 26 weeks next preceding the termination. A layoff or other break in service is not counted in determining whether an employee's period of employment totals one year, but the employee is considered to be employed during paid vacations and other authorized leaves. If an employee is rehired after a break in service exceeding one year, not counting absences due to labor disputes or authorized leaves, the employee is considered to be newly hired. The 26–week period for purposes of this subsection does not include any week during which the employee was absent because of layoffs of one year or less, paid vacations, authorized leaves, or labor disputes.

Comment

Subsection (a): Terminations because of race, sex, religion, or other grounds prohibited by applicable state or federal law are not terminations for "good cause" within the meaning of this Act. Findings and conclusions regarding "good cause" and "public policy" in proceedings under antidiscrimination or similar laws in other forums are entitled to appropriate weight in proceedings under this Act, in accordance with traditional common-law doctrines concerning res judicata, collateral estoppel, and the preclusion of facts, issues, and judgment. See Sections 2(e) and 7(d). A finding in another tribunal that an employer did not practice race or sex discrimination does not, however, preclude a charge that a termination of an employee by the employer was, nonetheless, a termination without good cause under this Act. That an employer has not discriminated does not necessarily mean that it had justifiable grounds for the discharge.

Subsection (b): The Act provides a one-year probationary period before there is a requirement of "good cause" for discharge. Temporary breaks in service (one year or less) do not necessarily destroy the status of a nonprobationary employee and, thus, seasonal workers may be covered. But, in all cases, an average of 20 hours or more per week must be worked during the 26 weeks preceding termination for good cause protections to apply. To that extent, part-time employees are not covered.

A "break in service" includes any time not actually spent on the job except periods, like vacations or sick leaves or "personal days," when an employee is entitled to be away from the job on the basis of the employer's contract, policy, or special permission. Such a break in service or a layoff interrupts the accrual of credit toward meeting the one-year requirement. Thus, seasonal workers would ordinarily need more than one twelve-month calendar period to qualify.

An individual's periods of employment with two separate legal entities may be "tacked" or combined to meet the one-year probationary requirement if both legal entities meet the definition of "employer" (e.g., employing five or more employees) and if the predecessor and the successor are deemed the "same person" because the successor is an "alter ego" of the predecessor, has assumed the legal obligations of the predecessor, etc.

§ 4. Agreements Between Employer and Employee.

(a) A right of an employee under this [Act] may not be waived by agreement except as provided in this section.

(b) By express written agreement, an employer and an employee may provide that the employee's failure to meet specified business-related standards of performance or the employee's commission or omission of specified business-related acts will constitute good cause for termination in proceedings under this [Act]. Those standards or prohibitions are effective only if they have been consistently enforced and they have not been applied to a particular employee in a disparate manner without justification. If the agreement authorizes changes by the employer in the standards or prohibitions, the changes must be clearly communicated to the employee.

(c) By express written agreement, an employer and an employee may mutually waive the requirement of good cause for termination, if the employer agrees that upon the termination of the employee for any reason other than willful misconduct of the employee, the employer will provide severance pay in an amount equal to at least one month's pay for each period of employment totaling one year, up to a maximum total payment equal to 30 months' pay at the employee's rate of pay in effect immediately before the termination. The employer shall make the payment in a lump sum or in a series of monthly installments, none of which may be less than one month's pay plus interest on the principal balance. The lump-sum payment must be made or payment of the monthly installments must begin within 30 days after the employee's termination. An agreement under this subsection constitutes a waiver by the employer and the employee of the right to civil trial, including jury trial, concerning disputes over the nature of the termination and the employee's entitlement to severance pay, and constitutes a stipulation by the parties that those disputes will be subject to the procedures and remedies of this [Act].

(d) The requirement of good cause for termination does not apply to the termination of an employee at the expiration of an express oral or written agreement of employment for a specified duration related to the completion of a specified task, project, undertaking, or assignment. If the employment continues after the expiration of the agreement, Section 3 applies to its termination unless the parties enter into a new express oral or written agreement under this subsection. The period of employment under an agreement described in this subsection counts toward the minimum periods of employment required by Section 3(b).

(e) An employer may provide substantive and procedural rights in addition to those provided by this [Act], either to one or more specific employees by express oral or written agreement, or to employees generally by a written personnel policy or statement, and may provide that those rights are enforceable under the procedures of this [Act].

(f) An employing person and an employee not otherwise subject to this [Act] may become subject to its provisions to the extent provided by express written agreement, in which case the employing person is deemed to be an employer.

(g) An agreement between an employer and an employee subject to this [Act] imposes a duty of good faith in its formation, performance, and enforcement.

(h) By express written agreement, an employer and an employee may settle at any time a claim arising under this [Act].

(i) By express written agreement before or after a dispute or claim arises under this [Act], an employer and an employee may agree to private arbitration or other alternative dispute-resolution procedure for resolving the dispute or claim.

(j) By express written agreement after a dispute or claim arises under this [Act], an employer and an employee may agree to judicial resolution of the dispute or claim.

(k) The substantive provisions of this [Act] apply under an agreement authorized by subsections (i) and (j).

Comment

Section 4 lists ways in which employers and employees may impose significant qualifications on the statutory rights otherwise accorded employees. Subject generally to the requirement of good faith, employers and employees may agree in advance on what will constitute "good cause" for termination, or even dispense with the requirement of good cause altogether as long as a minimum schedule of graduated severance payments is provided. By express agreement, employers may also provide additional substantive and procedural rights for employees. Finally, individuals not covered by the statutory good-cause protections because they are part-time workers, probationers, etc., may "opt in" to the Act with the agreement of their employer. They would, of course, then lose the common-law rights displaced by Section 2(c).

Agreements defining performance standards or specifying conduct that constitutes good cause for termination pursuant to Section 4(b) and agreements for severance pay under Section 4(c), if valid, will be enforced in proceedings under this Act. But employment agreements of a specified duration (Section 4(d)) and other contractual claims preserved under Section 2(e) will be enforceable through the usual processes of law in the courts (or through private arbitration, if so provided) unless the parties expressly agree to use the procedures and remedies provided by this Act.

It is the intent of Section 4 not to allow so-called "contracts of adhesion" to be used to waive or otherwise circumvent employees' rights under the Act.

Section 4 does not affect an employer's right to enter into and enforce covenants not to compete and similar agreements with its employees.

Subsection (b): Great flexibility is accorded employers and employees in agreeing upon performance standards for particular positions, so long as there is no duress or overreaching by either party. If valid, an express written agreement may in effect define what constitutes "good cause" for a termination, a determination that would otherwise have to be made by the arbitrator in the case of an individual employee's dismissal.

Subsection (c): An employer may secure the power to dismiss an employee for any reason at any time, thus making the employment "at will," if the employer gets the employee's agreement in an express writing that provides for a specified minimum graduated severance payment in the event of a termination on any grounds other than the employee's willful misconduct. As a practical matter, the use of such "waiver" agreements is likely to be confined generally to management personnel, key professionals, and other persons not subject to periodic layoff. Otherwise, an employer would be taking the risk that a worker who was laid off for more than two months would opt to treat the layoff as a "termination" under Section 1(8)(ii), thus entitling the employee to severance pay under the Section 4(c) agreement. Of course, such an employee would then forfeit any recall rights with the employer.

Subsection (d): When an employee has been employed only for the completion of a specified task, project, undertaking, or assignment, pursuant to an express oral or written agreement to that effect, a termination upon the expiration of the task, project, etc., does not violate the Act. For example, a skilled craftsperson may be hired to help install the plumbing in a new office building or a university professor may be invited to visit at another school and offer a certain set of courses. Even though each assignment takes over a year of full-time work, neither employee has a claim to continued employment upon the completion of the respective undertakings. Similarly, seasonal employees, even if covered under the Act, would ordinarily be considered as hired for a task or project of specified duration and may lawfully be terminated upon its completion. Such employees, however, are not treated differently from other employees with respect to other sorts of terminations; such employees, if they meet the requirements of Section 3(b), may file complaints under the Act to vindicate their "good cause" rights under Section 3(a) in the event of any other terminations. Like other employees under the Act, such employees also retain, pursuant to Section 2(c) and (d), their full common-law rights until the period of their employment qualifies them for protection under Section 3(a). The execution and application of agreements having a specified duration are subject to the usual principles concerning duress, contracts of adhesion, and the like.

Subsections (h), (i), and (j): Through an express writing parties may either settle substantive claims arising under this Act or agree to resolve them by alternative procedures outside the Act, including court actions. To avoid any pressure on an incumbent employee to agree in advance to what might possibly be costly, complex, and long-delayed judicial proceedings, a resort to the courts may be agreed upon only after a claim has arisen, i.e., ordinarily after a termination has occurred and the employee has little or nothing to lose by insisting on the right to statutory arbitration.

§ 5. Procedure and Limitations.

(a) An employee whose employment is terminated may file a complaint and demand for arbitration under this [Act] with the [Commission; Department; Service] not later than 180 days after the effective date of the termination, the date of the breach of an agreement for severance pay under Section 4(c), or the date the employee learns or should have learned of the facts forming the basis of the claim, whichever is latest. The time for filing is suspended while the employee is pursuing the employer's internal remedies and has not been notified in writing by the employer that the internal procedures have been concluded. Resort to an employer's internal procedures is not a condition for filing a complaint under this [Act].

(b) Except when an employee quits, an employer, within 10 business days after a termination, shall mail or deliver to the terminated employee a written statement of the reasons for the termination and a copy of this [Act] or a summary approved by the [Commission; Department; Service].

(c) An employer may file a complaint and demand for arbitration under this [Act] with the [Commission; Department; Service] to determine whether there is good cause for the termination of a named employee. At least 15 business days before filing, the employer shall mail or deliver to the employee a written statement of the employer's intention to file and the factors alleged to constitute good cause for a termination.

(d) The [Commission; Department; Service] shall promptly mail or deliver to the respondent a copy of the complaint and demand for arbitration. Within 21 days after receipt of a complaint, the respondent must file an answer with the [Commission; Department; Service] and mail a copy of the answer to the complainant. The answer of a respondent employer must include a copy of the statement of the reasons for the termination furnished the employee.

[(e) When a complaint is filed, a complainant employee or employer shall pay a filing fee to the [Commission; Department; Service] in [the amount of $_____] [an amount not exceeding the maximum filing fee for a civil action in the courts of general jurisdiction of this State]. The [Commission; Department; Service] may waive or defer payment of the filing fee upon a showing of the complainant employee's indigency.]

Comment

Subsection (a): No time limit is imposed on the pursuit of an employer's grievance procedures or other internal remedies because the employer can usually terminate them at any time and because the employee can always desist from pursuing them further.

Subsection (e): As a matter of principle, the preferred method for financing the enforcement of a public right like the right not to be discharged without good cause is through the public treasury. Nonetheless, in times of financial stringency, some states may feel it necessary to seek alternative funding rather than assume the full cost of a new administrative procedure. A substantial part of the cost could be placed on the parties themselves, perhaps with a cap in the case of the employee in an amount equal to one or two weeks' pre-termination pay. Or else a state could impose a special "employment termination tax" on businesses covered by the Act, with the use of an experience rating akin to that applied to unemployment insurance.

§ 6. Arbitration; Selection and Powers of Arbitrator; Hearings; Burden of Proof.

(a) Except as otherwise provided in this [Act], the [Uniform Arbitration Act] [_____ arbitration act of this State] applies to proceedings under this [Act] as if the parties had agreed to arbitrate under that statute. The [Commission; Department; Service] shall adopt procedural rules to regulate arbitration under this [Act]. The [Administrative Procedure Act and other] statutes of this State applicable to the procedures of state agencies do not apply to arbitration under this [Act].

(b) The [Commission; Department; Service] shall adopt rules specifying the qualifications, method of selection, and appointment of arbitrators. An arbitrator serving under this [Act] exercises the authority of the state.

(c) Subject to rules adopted by the [Commission; Department; Service], all forms of discovery [provided by applicable state statute, rule, or regulation] are available in the discretion of the arbitrator, who shall ensure there is no undue delay, expense, or inconvenience. Upon request, the employer shall provide the complainant or respondent employee a complete copy of the employee's personnel file.

(d) A party may be represented in arbitration by an attorney or other person authorized under the laws of this State to represent an individual in arbitration.

(e) A complainant employee has the burden of proving that a termination was without good cause or that an employer breached an agreement for severance pay under Section 4(c). A complainant employer has the burden of proving that there is good cause for a termination. In all arbitrations, the employer shall present its case first unless the employee alleges that a quitting or retirement was a termination within the meaning of Section 1(8)(iii).

(f) If an employee establishes that a termination was motivated in part by impermissible grounds, the employer, to avoid liability, must establish by a preponderance of the evidence that it would have terminated the employment even in the absence of the impermissible grounds.

Comment

Subsection (a): As a public right, the right to protection against discharge without good cause should be administered by a public agency, either new or existing. Possibilities include a state department of labor, labor relations commission, mediation service, or unemployment compensation bureau. In many instances, it might be sensible to delegate day-to-day operational functions to an outside private agency like the American Arbitration Association. But to maintain the public character of the proceedings under the Act, the formal appointment of arbitrators should be the responsibility of the public agency.

Although this Act, in the interest of expediting proceedings, does not mandate any sort of agency investigation, screening of complaints, or mediation prior to arbitration, all of these possible intermediate steps are matters that could be considered by the administering agency in preparing its rules and regulations.

Subsection (b): Even though an agency may decide to engage ad hoc arbitrators who devote only a portion of their time to cases under this Act, such arbitrators would be fully invested with the constitutional powers of a public official while operating under this Act. See, e.g., City of Detroit v. Police Officers Ass'n, 408 Mich. 410, 294 N.W.2d 68 (1980), app. dismissed, 450 U.S. 903 (1981); cf. Country–Wide Ins. Co. v. Harnett, 426 F.Supp. 1030 (S.D.N.Y.1977), aff'd, 431 U.S. 934 (1977). Under its authority to prescribe the qualifications of arbitrators, the administering agency may establish a schedule of fees and expenses for arbitrators.

Subsection (c): Arbitration proceedings should generally be informal, speedy, and inexpensive. Discovery ought to be limited to what is reasonably necessary to enable both parties to prepare adequately. Labor arbitration does not ordinarily contemplate that each side will know in advance all the details of the other side's presentation. The arbitrator should take account of these considerations in ruling on a party's request for discovery prior to the hearing. In a given case, it might be appropriate for an arbitrator to hold a prehearing conference with the parties to go over the ground rules on discovery. The arbitrator can deal with genuine, prejudicial surprise to a party at a hearing by calling a recess or granting an adjournment to allow time for rebuttal. Section 7 of the Uniform Arbitration Act contains fairly flexible provisions concerning discovery. In issuing regulations governing discovery under this Act, the administering agency could consider imposing time limits or other restrictions to prevent possible abuse of the discovery process.

Subsection (d): The Act authorizes formal representation in statutory arbitration proceedings by attorneys or by others approved under state law. This may include paralegals acting under the supervision of an attorney. The Act does not intend to prevent an employer or an employee from obtaining the sort of assistance in preparing and presenting a case that is customarily provided in labor arbitrations by personnel managers, labor union officials, and co-workers. Only attorneys, however, may legally represent the parties in judicial proceedings under Section 8, unless the applicable court rules provide otherwise.

Subsection (f): This provision generally incorporates the "dual motive" principles set forth in Price Waterhouse v. Hopkins, 490 U.S. 228 (1989).

§ 7. Awards.

(a) Within 30 days after the close of an arbitration hearing or at a later time agreeable to the parties, the arbitrator shall mail or deliver to the parties a written award sustaining or dismissing the complaint, in whole or in part, and specifying appropriate remedies, if any.

(b) An arbitrator may make one or more of the following awards for a termination in violation of this [Act]:

(1) reinstatement to the position of employment the employee held when employment was terminated or, if that is impractical, to a comparable position;

(2) full or partial backpay and reimbursement for lost fringe benefits, with interest, reduced by interim earnings from employment elsewhere, benefits received, and amounts that could have been received with reasonable diligence;

(3) if reinstatement is not awarded, a lump-sum severance payment at the employee's rate of pay in effect before the termination, for a period not exceeding [36 months] after the date of the award, together with the value of fringe benefits lost during that period, reduced by likely earnings and benefits from employment elsewhere, and taking into account such equitable considerations as the employee's length of service with the employer and the reasons for the termination; and

(4) reasonable attorney's fees and costs.

(c) An arbitrator may make either or both of the following awards for a violation of an agreement for severance pay under Section 4(c):

(1) enforcement of the severance pay and other applicable provisions of the agreement, with interest; and

(2) reasonable attorney's fees and costs.

(d) An arbitrator may not make an award except as provided in subsections (b) and (c). The arbitrator may not award damages for pain and suffering, emotional distress, defamation, fraud, or other injury under the common law; punitive damages; compensatory damages; or any other monetary award. In making a monetary award under this section, the arbitrator shall reduce the award by the amount of any monetary award to the employee in another forum for the same conduct of the employer. In making an award, the arbitrator is subject to the rules of issue, fact, and judgment preclusion applicable in courts of record in this State.

(e) If an arbitrator dismisses an employee's complaint and finds it frivolous, unreasonable, or without foundation, the arbitrator may award reasonable attorney's fees and costs to the prevailing employer.

(f) An arbitrator may sustain an employer's complaint and make an award declaring that there is good cause for the termination of a named employee. If the arbitrator dismisses the employer's complaint, the arbitrator may award reasonable attorney's fees and costs to the prevailing employee.

Comment

Subsection (b): When an employee is terminated without good cause but neither reinstatement, backpay, nor severance pay is warranted or appropriate, an arbitrator may issue an award in the nature of a "declaratory judgment" to vindicate the rights of the employee.

Subsection (b)(2): Backpay may be awarded with or without reinstatement. Thus, if there is no reinstatement but a severance payment is awarded instead, backpay may still be provided. Backpay runs from the termination to the date of the award (or date of reinstatement); severance pay runs from the date of the award. The formulas for calculating backpay and severance pay are also somewhat different.

The objective as to fringe benefits is to make the employee whole for any losses or expenditures related to the wrongful termination. If the employee has exercised COBRA rights and continued health insurance coverage or acquired alternative coverage, all money spent for such coverage should be recouped. In addition, if the substitute coverage did not match the employee's prior protections, whatever additional out-of-pocket expenditures were necessary should also be awarded.

If the employee justifiably did not replace the coverage lost and then incurred medical expenses, the award would include the amount of financial obligation stemming from the wrongful denial of the coverage. All other benefits, including optical, dental, and disability, would be handled in a similar fashion. To balance the obligation of the employer to pay actual expenses when there is no replacement insurance or the subsequent coverage is inferior, the employer should not be responsible for restoring past premiums for unreplaced insurance if the benefit would not have been utilized during the period of unemployment.

With regard to pension rights, if the employee could not be placed in the position of one who had never been terminated, the arbitrator would be charged with placing a dollar value on the vesting time lost.

Deductions are based on the usual common law principles concerning the mitigation of damages by a discharged employee.

In all awards that include the loss of future earnings, pension benefits, etc., the amount of the award should be discounted to reflect present values, and should be reduced where appropriate by the amount of any workers' compensation or other disability payments.

Subsection (b)(3): Reinstatement is the preferred remedy for terminations in violation of this Act. If that is unfeasible because of the personal relations between the employer and the employee, changes in the employer's business, or other appropriate grounds, severance pay may be awarded instead. Whatever maximum period for severance pay is adopted, such an amount should not be awarded as a matter of course even though an arbitrator concludes that a worker will probably not find new employment during that time. Subsection (b)(3) adopts the concept of "proportionality," under which the employer should be held liable on the basis of an assessment of *both* the employee's likely loss and the degree of the employer's responsibility for, or contribution to, that loss. Thus, an employer should be held liable for a much greater portion of the maximum period if it had lured the employee away from another highly paid position, the employee had served long and well, and the reasons for the dismissal were egregious, than if the employee had recently been hired while out of work and the termination was not a flagrant violation of the good cause standard. In fixing the severance payment, the arbitrator should consider any actual earnings received by the employee elsewhere, as well as the likelihood that such reemployment will continue.

Subsections (b)(4), (c)(2), (e), and (f): The language of the Act allowing reasonable attorney's fees and costs to prevailing employees and under certain conditions to prevailing employers deliberately tracks the language of Title VII of the 1964 Civil Rights Act and of Supreme Court decisions interpreting Title VII. See Albemarle Paper Co. v. Moody, 422 U.S. 405 (1975); Christiansburg Garment Co. v. EEOC, 434 U.S. 412 (1978). In calculating the appropriate amount of attorney's fees, federal decisions under Title VII and 42 U.S.C. 1988 may be helpful but are not controlling. The prevailing market rate is a common starting point, and the successful pursuit of a small monetary claim may justify a fee exceeding the amount of the award. See Blum v. Stenson, 465 U.S. 886 (1984); City of Riverside v. Rivera, 477 U.S. 561 (1986). Cf. Hensley v. Eckerhart, 461 U.S. 424 (1983) (extent of success "crucial").

Subsection (d): The last two sentences must be read together. Preclusion covers all claims subject to the usual doctrines of res judicata or collateral estoppel, and the penultimate sentence would not allow a second recovery if the underlying claim had been precluded by a prior judgment or award.

§ 8.   Judicial Review and Enforcement.

(a) Either party to an arbitration may seek vacation, modification, or enforcement of the arbitrator's award in the [court of general jurisdiction] for the [county] in which the termination occurred or in which the employee resides.

(b) An application for vacation or modification must be filed within [90] days after issuance of the arbitrator's award. An application for enforcement may be filed at any time after issuance of the arbitrator's award.

(c) The court may vacate or modify an arbitrator's award only if the court finds that:

(1) the award was procured by corruption, fraud, or other improper means;

(2) there was evident partiality by the arbitrator or misconduct prejudicing the rights of a party;

(3) the arbitrator exceeded the powers of an arbitrator;

(4) the arbitrator committed a prejudicial error of law; or

(5) another ground exists for vacating the award under the [Uniform Arbitration Act] [_____ arbitration act of this State].

(d) In an application for vacation, modification, or enforcement of an arbitrator's award, the court may award a prevailing employee reasonable attorney's fees and costs. In an application by an employee for vacation of an arbitrator's award, the court may award a prevailing employer reasonable attorney's fees and costs if the court finds the employee's application is frivolous, unreasonable, or without foundation.

Comment

Some states have constitutional provisions governing judicial review of administrative decisions that may have to be taken into account.

Subsection (a): The substantive law applicable in either arbitration proceedings or the judicial review of an arbitral award must be determined according to the choice-of-law rules governing transitory rights of action.

Subsection (c)(4): The United States Supreme Court has sharply limited judicial review of the merits of arbitration awards under collective-bargaining agreements subject to federal law. The exceeding of jurisdiction and arbitrator misconduct are about the only recognized grounds for reversal, although of course a court may refuse to enforce an award (like any contract) that is contrary to positive law. Steelworkers v. Enterprise Wheel Car Corp., 363 U.S. 593 (1960); Paperworkers v. Misco, Inc., 484 U.S. 29 (1987). That approach lends great finality to arbitral awards, and it is hoped that courts would similarly accord considerable deference to arbitration awards under this Act. But the basis of the Supreme Court's position is that unions and employers have *agreed* to treat arbitral awards as "final and binding," and that it is the parties' own contract the arbitrator is applying. When individual *statutory* rights are at stake, the Court has declined to give the same weight even to the awards of arbitrators empowered by union-management agreements. Alexander v. Gardner–Denver Co., 415 U.S. 36 (1974); Barrentine v. Arkansas–Best Freight Sys., 450 U.S. 728 (1981). In this Act, individual statutory rights are the issue, and arbitration as the enforcement method has been imposed upon, not agreed to by, the parties. For these reasons the additional ground for judicial review, "prejudicial error of law" by the arbitrator, has been included. But a court should not vacate an award unless the legal error has adversely affected the rights of a party.

Subsection (c)(5): The reference to "another ground" for vacating an arbitral award is meant to be confined to other specific bases spelled out in the Uniform Arbitration Act or cited state arbitration act and is not intended to open up the award for a broadscale judicial review.

§ 9. Posting. An employer shall post a copy of this [Act] or a summary approved by the [Commission; Department; Service] in a prominent place in the work area. An employer who violates this section is subject to a civil penalty not exceeding [$_____]. The [Attorney

General] may bring a civil action, on behalf of this State, to impose and collect any civil penalty arising under this section.

§ 10. Retaliation Prohibited and Civil Action Created. An employer or other employing person may not directly or indirectly take adverse action in retaliation against an individual for filing a complaint, giving testimony, or otherwise lawfully participating in proceedings under this [Act], whether or not the individual is an employee having rights under this [Act]. An employer or other employing person who violates this section is liable to the individual subjected to the adverse action in retaliation for damage caused by the action, punitive damages when appropriate, and reasonable attorney's fees. A separate civil action may be brought to enforce this liability. The employer is also subject to applicable procedures and remedies provided by Sections 5 through 8.

§ 11. Severability Clause. If any provision of this [Act] or its application to any person or circumstance is held invalid, the invalidity does not affect other provisions or applications of this [Act] which can be given effect without the invalid provision or application, and to this end the provisions of this [Act] are severable.

§ 12. Effective Date. This [Act] takes effect _____.

§ 13. Repeals. The following acts and parts of acts are repealed:

(1) . . . .

(2) . . . .

(3) . . . .

§ 14. Savings and Transitional Provisions. This [Act] does not apply to the termination of an employee within six months after the effective date of this [Act] based upon the employee's refusal to enter into an agreement meeting the minimum standards of Section 4(c), which the employer, in the exercise of good faith business judgment, may impose as a condition of continued employment.

APPENDIX

Note: Instead of the arbitration system provided by Sections 5 through 8 of the preceding text, states may select the following Alternative A or Alternative B as the means of enforcement.

ALTERNATIVE A

[Section 5. Administrative Proceedings. [Insert provisions consigning enforcement of the [Act] to a new or existing administrative agency, staffed by civil service or other governmental personnel, operating under applicable state statutes. Delete Sections 5 through 8 of the preceding text and renumber the remaining sections and any cross references accordingly.]

[Section 6. Remedies.

(a) The [Commission; Department; Service] may provide one or more of the following remedies for a termination in violation of this Act]:

(1) reinstatement to the position of employment the employee held when employment was terminated or, if that is impractical, to a comparable position;

(2) full or partial backpay and reimbursement for lost fringe benefits, with interest, reduced by interim earnings from employment elsewhere, benefits received, and amounts that could have been received with reasonable diligence;

(3) if reinstatement is not ordered, a lump-sum severance payment at the employee's rate of pay in effect before the termination, for a period not exceeding [36 months] from the date of the order, together with the value of fringe benefits lost during that period, reduced by likely earnings and benefits from employment elsewhere, and taking into account such equitable considerations as the employee's length of service with the employer and the reasons for the termination; and

(4) reasonable attorney's fees and costs.

(b) The [Commission; Department; Service] may grant either or both of the following remedies for a violation of an agreement for severance pay under Section 4(c):

(1) enforcement of the severance pay and other applicable provisions of the agreement, with interest; and

(2) reasonable attorney's fees and costs.

(c) The [Commission; Department; Service] may not make an award except as provided in subsections (a) and (b). The [Commission; Department; Service] may not award damages for pain and suffering, emotional distress, defamation, fraud, or other injury under the common law; punitive damages; compensatory damages; or any other monetary award under this [Act]. In making a monetary award under this section, the [Commission; Department; Service] shall reduce the award by the amount of any monetary award to the employee in another forum for the same conduct of the employer. In making an award, the [Commission; Department; Service] is subject to the rules of issue, fact, and judgment preclusion applicable in courts of record in this State.

(d) If the [Commission; Department; Service] dismisses an employee's complaint and finds it frivolous, unreasonable, or without foundation, the [Commission; Department; Service] may award reasonable attorney's fees and costs to the prevailing employer.

(e) Upon the complaint of an employer, the [[Commission; Department; Service] may issue an order declaring whether there is good cause for the termination of a named employee. If the [Commission; Department; Service] dismisses the employer's complaint, the [Commission; Department; Service] may award reasonable attorney's fees and costs to the prevailing employee.]

ALTERNATIVE B

[Alternative B would leave the enforcement of the statute to the civil courts. Delete Sections 5 through 8 of the preceding text and renumber the remaining sections and any cross references accordingly.]

[Section 5. Judicial Remedies.—

(a) The court may grant one or more of the following remedies for a termination in violation of this [Act]:

(1) reinstatement to the position of employment the employee held when employment was terminated or, if that is impractical, to a comparable position;

(2) full or partial backpay and reimbursement for lost fringe benefits, with interest, reduced by interim earnings from employment elsewhere, benefits received, and amounts that could have been received with reasonable diligence;

(3) if reinstatement is not awarded, a lump-sum severance payment at the employee's rate of pay in effect before the termination, for a period not exceeding [36 months] from the date of the award, together with the value of fringe benefits lost during that period, reduced by likely earnings and benefits from employment elsewhere, and taking into account such equitable considerations as the employee's length of service with the employer and the reasons for the termination; and

(4) reasonable attorney's fees and costs.

(b) The court may grant either or both of the following remedies for a violation of an agreement for severance pay under Section 4(c):

(1) enforcement of the severance pay and other applicable provisions of the agreement, with interest; and

(2) reasonable attorney's fees and costs.

(c) The court may not make an award except as provided in subsections (a) and (b). The court may not award damages for pain and suffering, emotional distress, defamation, fraud, or other injury under the common law; punitive damages; compensatory damages; or any other monetary award under this [Act]. In making a monetary award under this section, the court shall reduce the award by the amount of any monetary award to the employee in another forum for the same conduct of the employer. In making an award, the court is subject to the rules of issue, fact, and judgment preclusion applicable in courts of record in this State.

(d) If the court dismisses an employee's complaint and finds it frivolous, unreasonable, or without foundation, the court may award reasonable attorney's fees and costs to the prevailing employer.

(e) Upon the complaint of an employer, the court may enter a judgment declaring whether there is good cause for the termination of a named employee. If the court dismisses the employer's complaint, the court may award reasonable attorney's fees and costs to the prevailing employee.]

Comment

The preferred method for enforcing the statutory protection against termination without good cause is through the use of professional arbitrators appointed by an appropriate public agency. Such persons have the requisite skill, training, and experience to understand the special problems of the workplace, and are most likely to be acceptable to the management and employee communities. Their efficiency in resolving disputes over discharge and discipline may also reduce the time and expense of the proceedings.

Some states may believe, however, that it will be less costly to employ full-time civil service or other governmental personnel as hearing officers. For these states, Alternative A is provided.

The third option is Alternative B, which would place enforcement in the hands of the civil courts. This would almost surely be the most complex, expensive, and time-consuming procedure. But a few states may believe that their constitutional provisions on the right to jury trial, access to the courts, etc., preclude the use of other forums.

MASSACHUSETTS GEN. LAWS ANN.
CH. 149, § 52C

§ 52C. Access to Personnel Records; Disagreement With Information Contained Therein; Remedies; Penalty.

As used in this section, the following words shall, unless the context clearly requires otherwise, have the following meanings:—

"Employee", a person currently employed or formerly employed by an employer; provided, however, that for purposes of this section, persons who are employed, or were formerly employed, by a private institution of higher education in positions which may lead to tenure, are tenured, or which involve responsibilities similar to those in tenure-track positions, shall not be considered employees.

"Employer", an individual, corporation, partnership, labor organization, unincorporated association or any other legal business, public or private, or commercial entity including agents of the employer.

"Personnel record", a record kept by an employer that identifies an employee, to the extent that the record is used or has been used, or may affect or be used relative to that employee's qualifications for employment, promotion, transfer, additional compensation or disciplinary action. A personnel record shall include a record in the possession of a person, corporation, partnership or other association that has a contractual agreement with the employer to keep or supply a personnel record as provided in this section. A personnel record shall not include information of a personal nature about a person other than the employee if disclosure of the information would constitute a clearly unwarranted invasion of such other person's privacy. Without limiting the applicability or generality of the foregoing, all of the following written information or documents to the extent prepared by an employer of twenty or more employees regarding an employee shall be included in the personnel record for that employee: the name, address, date of birth, job title and description; rate of pay and any other compensation paid to the employee; starting date of employment; the job application of the employee; resumes or other forms of employment inquiry submitted to the employer in response to his advertisement by the employee; all employee performance evaluations, including but not limited to, employee evaluation documents; written warnings of substandard performance; lists of probationary periods; waivers signed by the employee; copies of dated termination notices; any other documents relating to disciplinary action regarding the employee. A personnel record shall be maintained in typewritten or printed form or may be handwritten in indelible ink.

An employer shall notify an employee within 10 days of the employer placing in the employee's personnel record any information to the extent that the information is, has been used or may be used, to negatively affect the employee's qualification for employment, promotion, transfer, additional compensation or the possibility that the employee will be subject to disciplinary action. An employer receiving a written request from an employee shall provide the employee with an opportunity to review such employee's personnel record within 5 business days of such request. The review shall take place at the place of employment and during normal business hours. An employee shall be given a copy of the employee's personnel record within 5 business days of submission of a written request for such copy to the employer. An employer shall not be required to allow an employee to review the employee's personnel record on more than 2 separate occasions in a calendar year; provided, however, that the notification and review caused by the placing of negative information in the personnel record shall not be deemed to be 1 of the 2 annually permitted reviews.

If there is a disagreement with any information contained in a personnel record, removal or correction of such information may be mutually agreed upon by the employer and the employee. If an agreement is not reached, the employee may submit a written statement explaining the employee's position which shall thereupon be contained therein and shall become a part of such employee's personnel record. The statement shall be included when said information is transmitted to a third party as long as the original information is retained as part of the file. If an employer places in a personnel record any information which such employer knew or should have known to be false, then the employee shall have remedy through the collective bargaining agreement, other personnel procedures or judicial process to have such information expunged. The provisions of this section shall not prohibit the removal of information contained in a personnel record upon mutual agreement of the employer and employee for any reason.

An employer of twenty or more employees shall retain the complete personnel record of an employee as required to be kept under this section without deletions or expungement of information from the date of employment of such employee to a date three years after the termination of employment by the employee with such employer. In any cause of action brought by an employee against such employer of twenty or more employees in any administrative or judicial proceeding, including but not limited to, the Massachusetts Office of Affirmative Action, the Massachusetts Commission Against Discrimination, Massachusetts Civil Service Commission, Massachusetts Labor Relations Commission, attorney general, or a court of appropriate jurisdiction, such employer shall retain any personnel record required to be kept under this section which is relevant to such action until the final disposition thereof.

If an employer of twenty or more employees elects to have a written personnel policy regarding the terms and conditions of employment, such personnel policy, as the same may be amended from time to time, shall be continuously maintained at the office of such employer where personnel matters are administered.

Whoever violates the provisions of this section shall be punished by a fine of not less than five hundred nor more than twenty-five hundred dollars. This section shall be enforced by the attorney general.

MICHIGAN COMP. LAWS ANN.
423.501–11 (2012)

§ 423.501. Short title; definitions

§ 1. (1) This act shall be known and may be cited as the "Bullard–Plawecki employee right to know act."

(2) As used in this act:

(a) "Employee" means a person currently employed or formerly employed by an employer.

(b) "Employer" means an individual, corporation, partnership, labor organization, unincorporated association, the state, or an agency or a political subdivision of the state, or any other legal, business, or commercial entity which has 4 or more employees and includes an agent of the employer.

(c) "Personnel record" means a record kept by the employer that identifies the employee, to the extent that the record is used or has been used, or may affect or be used relative to that employee's qualifications for employment, promotion, transfer, additional compensation, or disciplinary action. A personnel record shall include a record in the possession of a person, corporation, partnership, or other association who has a contractual agreement with the employer to keep or supply a personnel record as provided in this subdivision. A personnel record shall not include:

(i) Employee references supplied to an employer if the identity of the person making the reference would be disclosed.

(ii) Materials relating to the employer's staff planning with respect to more than 1 employee, including salary increases, management bonus plans, promotions, and job assignments.

(iii) Medical reports and records made or obtained by the employer if the records or reports are available to the employee from the doctor or medical facility involved.

(iv) Information of a personal nature about a person other than the employee if disclosure of the information would constitute a clearly unwarranted invasion of the other person's privacy.

(v) Information that is kept separately from other records and that relates to an investigation by the employer pursuant to section 9.

(vi) Records limited to grievance investigations which are kept separately and are not used for the purposes provided in this subdivision.

(vii) Records maintained by an educational institution which are directly related to a student and are considered to be education records under section 513(a) of title 5 of the family educational rights and privacy act of 1974, 20 U.S.C. 1232g.

(viii) Records kept by an executive, administrative, or professional employee that are kept in the sole possession of the maker of the record, and are not accessible or shared with other persons. However, a record concerning an occurrence or fact about an employee kept pursuant to this subparagraph may be entered into a personnel record if entered not more than 6 months after the date of the occurrence or the date the fact becomes known.

§ 423.502. Personnel record information excluded from personnel record, use in judicial or quasi-judicial proceeding, restrictions

§ 2. Personnel record information which was not included in the personnel record but should have been as required by this act shall not be used by an employer in a judicial or quasi-judicial proceeding. However, personnel record information which, in the opinion of the judge in a judicial proceeding or in the opinion of the hearing officer in a quasi-judicial proceeding, was not intentionally excluded in the personnel record, may be used by the employer in the judicial or quasi-judicial proceeding, if the employee agrees or if the employee has been given a reasonable time to review the information. Material which should have been included in the personnel record shall be used at the request of the employee.

§ 423.503. Review of personnel record by employee

§ 3. An employer, upon written request which describes the personnel record, shall provide the employee with an opportunity to periodically review at reasonable intervals, generally not more than 2 times in a calendar year or as otherwise provided by law or a collective bargaining agreement, the employee's personnel record if the employer has a personnel record for that employee. The review shall take place at a location reasonably near the employee's place of employment and during normal office hours. If a review during normal office hours would require an employee to take time off from work with that employer, then the employer shall provide some other reasonable time for the review. The employer may allow the review to take place at another time or location that would be more convenient to the employee.

§ 423.504. Copy of employee's personnel record; fee; mailing

§ 4. After the review provided in section 3, an employee may obtain a copy of the information or part of the information contained in the employee's personnel record. An employer may charge a fee for providing a copy of information contained in the personnel record. The fee shall be limited to the actual incremental cost of duplicating the information. If an employee demonstrates that he or she is unable to review his or her personnel record at the employing unit, then the employer, upon that employee's written request, shall mail a copy of the requested record to the employee.

§ 423.505. Disagreement with personnel record, removal or correction; explanatory statement by employee

§ 5. If there is a disagreement with information contained in a personnel record, removal or correction of that information may be mutually agreed upon by the employer and the employee. If an agreement is not reached, the employee may submit a written statement explaining the employee's position. The statement shall not exceed 5 sheets of 8 1/2 inch by 11-inch paper and shall be included when the information is divulged to a third party and as long as the original information is a part of the file. If either the employer or employee knowingly places in the personnel record information which is false, then the employer or employee, whichever is appropriate, shall have remedy through legal action to have that information expunged.

§ 423.506. Disclosure of disciplinary report, letter of reprimand or other disciplinary action, limitations; written notice to employee; inapplicability of section

§ 6. (1) An employer or former employer shall not divulge a disciplinary report, letter of reprimand, or other disciplinary action to a third party, to a party who is not a part of the employer's organization, or to a party who is not a part of a labor organization representing the employee, without written notice as provided in this section.

(2) The written notice to the employee shall be by first-class mail to the employee's last known address, and shall be mailed on or before the day the information is divulged from the personnel record.

(3) This section shall not apply if any of the following occur:

(a) The employee has specifically waived written notice as part of a written, signed employment application with another employer.

(b) The disclosure is ordered in a legal action or arbitration to a party in that legal action or arbitration.

(c) Information is requested by a government agency as a result of a claim or complaint by an employee.

§ 423.507. Deletion of certain material before release; exception

§ 7. An employer shall review a personnel record before releasing information to a third party and, except when the release is ordered in a legal action or arbitration to a party in that legal action or arbitration, delete disciplinary reports, letters of reprimand, or other records of disciplinary action which are more than 4 years old.

§ 423.508. Prohibition of keeping of certain information, exceptions; inapplicability of prohibition; part of personnel record

§ 8. (1) An employer shall not gather or keep a record of an employee's associations, political activities, publications, or communications of nonemployment activities, except if the information is submitted in writing by or authorized to be kept or gathered, in writing, by the employee to the employer. This prohibition on records shall not apply to the activities that occur on the employer's premises or during the employee's working hours with that employer that interfere with the performance of the employee's duties or duties of other employees.

(2) A record which is kept by the employer as permitted under this section shall be part of the personnel record.

§ 423.509. Criminal activity, reasonable belief; notice to employee, time limitation; destruction of file; criminal justice agency as employer, separate confidential file; employee notification; notation of final disposition of investigation; future use of information

§ 9. (1) If an employer has reasonable cause to believe that an employee is engaged in criminal activity which may result in loss or damage to the employer's property or disruption of the employer's business operation, and the employer is engaged in an investigation, then the employer may keep a separate file of information relating to the investigation. Upon completion of the investigation or after 2 years, whichever comes first, the employee shall be notified that an investigation was or is being conducted of the suspected criminal activity described in this section. Upon completion of the investigation, if disciplinary action is not taken, the investigative file and all copies of the material in it shall be destroyed.

(2) If the employer is a criminal justice agency which is involved in the investigation of an alleged criminal activity or the violation of an agency rule by the employee, the employer shall maintain a separate confidential file of information relating to the investigation. Upon completion of the investigation, if disciplinary action is not taken, the employee shall be notified that an investigation was conducted. If the investigation reveals that the allegations are unfounded, unsubstantiated, or disciplinary action is not taken, the separate file shall contain a notation of the final disposition of the investigation and information in the file shall not be used in any future consideration for promotion, transfer, additional compensation, or disciplinary action.

§ 423.510.   Construction as to Freedom of Information Act

§ **10.**   This act shall not be construed to diminish a right of access to records as provided in Act No. 442 of the Public Acts of 1976, being sections 15.231 to 15.246 of the Michigan Compiled Laws, or as otherwise provided by law.

§ 423.511.   Violation, action to compel compliance; jurisdiction; contempt; damages

§ **11.**   If an employer violates this act, an employee may commence an action in the circuit court to compel compliance with this act. The circuit court for the county in which the complainant resides, the circuit court for the county in which the complainant is employed, or the circuit court for the county in which the personnel record is maintained shall have jurisdiction to issue the order. Failure to comply with an order of the court may be punished as contempt. In addition, the court shall award an employee prevailing in an action pursuant to this act the following damages:

(a) For a violation of this act, actual damages plus costs.

(b) For a wilful and knowing violation of this act, $200.00 plus costs, reasonable attorney's fees, and actual damages.

MONTANA "SERVICE LETTER" LAW
R.S.MO. § 290.140 (2012)

§ 290.140. Letter of dismissal, when—failure to issue, damages—punitive damages, limitations

1. Whenever any employee of any corporation doing business in this state and which employs seven or more employees, who shall have been in the service of said corporation for a period of at least ninety days, shall be discharged or voluntarily quit the service of such corporation and who thereafter within a reasonable period of time, but not later than one year following the date the employee was discharged or voluntarily quit, requests in writing by certified mail to the superintendent, manager or registered agent of said corporation, with specific reference to the statute, it shall be the duty of the superintendent or manager of said corporation to issue to such employee, within forty-five days after the receipt of such request, a letter, duly signed by such superintendent or manager, setting forth the nature and character of service rendered by such employee to such corporation and the duration thereof, and truly stating for what cause, if any, such employee was discharged or voluntarily quit such service.

2. Any corporation which violates the provisions of subsection 1 of this section shall be liable for compensatory but not punitive damages but in the event that the evidence establishes that the employer did not issue the requested letter, said employer may be liable for nominal and punitive damages; but no award of punitive damages under this section shall be based upon the content of any such letter.

CALIFORNIA LABOR CODE § 1050

§ 1050. Misrepresentation preventing former employee from obtaining employment; Misdemeanor

Any person, or agent or officer thereof, who, after having discharged an employee from the service of such person or after an employee has voluntarily left such service, by any misrepresentation prevents or attempts to prevent the former employee from obtaining employment, is guilty of a misdemeanor.

COLORADO C.R.S. § 8–2–114 (2012)

§ 8–2–114. **Immunity from civil liability for employer disclosing information—employer shall not maintain black-list—credit lists excepted**

(1) For purposes of this section, "job performance" means:

(a) The suitability of the employee for reemployment;

(b) The employee's work-related skills, abilities, and habits as they may relate to suitability for future employment; and

(c) In the case of a former employee, the reason for the employee's separation.

(2) It is unlawful for any employer to maintain a blacklist, or to notify any other employer that any current or former employee has been blacklisted by such employer, for the purpose of preventing such employee from receiving employment. * * *

(3) Any employer who provides information about a current or former employee's job history or job performance to a prospective employer of the current or former employee upon request of the prospective employer or the current or former employee is immune from civil liability and is not liable in civil damages for the disclosure or any consequences of the disclosure. This immunity shall not apply when such employee shows by a preponderance of the evidence both of the following:

(a) The information disclosed by the current or former employer was false; and

(b) The employer providing the information knew or reasonably should have known that the information was false.

(4) This section applies to any employee, agent, or other representative of the current or former employer who is authorized to provide and who provides information in accordance with this section.

(5) Any employer that provides written information to a prospective employer about a current or a former employee shall send, upon the request of such current or former employee, a copy of the information provided to the last-known address of the person who is the subject of the reference. Any person who is the subject of such a reference may obtain a copy of the reference information by appearing at the employer's or former employer's place of business during normal business hours. The employer or former employer may charge a fair and reasonable amount for reproduction costs if multiple copies are requested. * * *

NEVADA REV. STAT. ANN. §§ 613.200, 613.210 (2012)

§ 613.200. Prevention of employment of person who has been discharged or who terminates employment unlawful; criminal and administrative penalties; exception

1. Except as otherwise provided in this section, any person, association, company or corporation within this state, or any agent or officer on behalf of the person, association, company or corporation, who willfully does anything intended to prevent any person who for any cause left or was discharged from his or its employ from obtaining employment elsewhere in this state is guilty of a gross misdemeanor and shall be punished by a fine of not more than $5,000.

2. In addition to any other remedy or penalty, the Labor Commissioner may impose against each culpable party an administrative penalty of not more than $5,000 for each such violation.

3. If a fine or an administrative penalty is imposed pursuant to this section, the costs of the proceeding, including investigative costs and attorney's fees, may be recovered by the Labor Commissioner.

4. The provisions of this section do not prohibit a person, association, company, corporation, agent or officer from negotiating, executing and enforcing an agreement with an employee of the person, association, company or corporation which, upon termination of the employment, prohibits the employee from:

(a) Pursuing a similar vocation in competition with or becoming employed by a competitor of the person, association, company or corporation; or

(b) Disclosing any trade secrets, business methods, lists of customers, secret formulas or processes or confidential information learned or obtained during the course of his employment with the person, association, company or corporation,

if the agreement is supported by valuable consideration and is otherwise reasonable in its scope and duration.

§ 613.210. Black lists unlawful; recommendations and statements to be provided employee by employer

1. As used in this section, "employee" means every person who has entered upon service or employment of an employer, and the employment shall be deemed to commence from the date of the entry or performance of any service. Any contract of employment, rule, regulation or device to the contrary is void.

2. A person shall not black-list or cause to be black-listed or publish the name of or cause to be published the name of any employee, mechanic or laborer discharged by that person with the intent to prevent that employee, mechanic or laborer from engaging in or securing similar or other employment from any other person.

3. If any officer or agent of any person black-lists or causes to be black-listed or publishes the name of or causes to be published the name of any employee, mechanic or laborer discharged by that person with the intent to prevent that employee, mechanic or laborer from engaging in or securing similar or other employment from any other person in any manner conspires or contrives, by correspondence or otherwise, to prevent that discharged employee from procuring employment, he is guilty of a misdemeanor.

4. Subsections 2 and 3 do not prohibit any person from giving in writing, at the time the employee leaves or is discharged from the service of the employer, a truthful statement of the reason for such leaving of the service or discharge of that employee, nor do subsections 2 and 3 prevent any employer from giving any employee or former employee any statement with reference to any meritorious services which the employee may have rendered to that employer. The employer shall supply statements as provided in this subsection upon demand from the employee, but no such statement is required unless the employee has been in service for a period of not less than 60 days. Only one such statement may be issued to that employee.

CALIFORNIA LABOR CODE §§ 970–972

§ 970. Influencing, persuading or engaging worker to change from one place to another by false representations

No person, or agent or officer thereof, directly or indirectly, shall influence, persuade, or engage any person to change from one place to another in this State or from any place outside to any place within the State, or from any place within the State to any place outside, for the purpose of working in any branch of labor, through or by means of knowingly false representations, whether spoken, written, or advertised in printed form, concerning either:

(a) The kind, character, or existence of such work;

(b) The length of time such work will last, or the compensation therefor;

(c) The sanitary or housing conditions relating to or surrounding the work;

(d) The existence or nonexistence of any strike, lockout, or other labor dispute affecting it and pending between the proposed employer and the persons then or last engaged in the performance of the labor for which the employee is sought.

§ 971. Influencing worker to change places by false representations as misdemeanor; Punishment

Any person, or agent or officer thereof, who violates Section 970 is guilty of a misdemeanor punishable by a fine of not less than fifty dollars ($50) nor more than one thousand dollars ($1,000) or imprisonment for not more than six months or both.

§ 972. Liability for double damages; Civil action

In addition to such criminal penalty, any person, or agent or officer thereof who violates any provision of section 970 is liable to the party aggrieved, in a civil action, for double damages resulting from such misrepresentations. Such civil action may be brought by an aggrieved person or his assigns or successors in interest, without first establishing any criminal liability.

CALIFORNIA CONSTITUTION

ART. I, § 1.

§ **1.** All people are by nature free and independent and have inalienable rights. Among these are enjoying and defending life and liberty, acquiring, possessing, and protecting property, and pursuing and obtaining safety, happiness, and privacy.

MASSACHUSETTS RIGHT OF PRIVACY LAW
MASS. ANN. GEN. LAWS CH. 214, § 1B

§ 1B. Right of Privacy; Remedy to Enforce

A person shall have a right against unreasonable, substantial or serious interference with his privacy. The superior court shall have jurisdiction in equity to enforce such right and in connection therewith to award damages.

MINNESOTA CODE ANN. §§ 181.950–.957 (2012)

§ 181.950 Definitions

Subdivision 1. For the purposes of sections 181.950 to 181.957, the terms and phrases defined in this section have the meanings given them.

Subd. 2. "Confirmatory test" and "confirmatory retest" mean a drug or alcohol test that uses a method of analysis allowed under one of the programs listed in section 181.953, subdivision 1.

Subd. 3. Repealed, 1991 c 60 s 12

Subd. 4. "Drug" means a controlled substance as defined in section 152.01, subdivision 4.

Subd. 5. "Drug and alcohol testing," "drug or alcohol testing," and "drug or alcohol test" mean analysis of a body component sample according to the standards established under one of the programs listed in section 181.953, subdivision 1, for the purpose of measuring the presence or absence of drugs, alcohol, or their metabolites in the sample tested.

Subd. 6. "Employee" means a person, independent contractor, or person working for an independent contractor who performs services for compensation, in whatever form, for an employer.

Subd. 7. "Employer" means a person or entity located or doing business in this state and having one or more employees, and includes the state and all political or other governmental subdivisions of the state.

Subd. 8. "Initial screening test" means a drug or alcohol test which uses a method of analysis under one of the programs listed in section 181.953, subdivision 1.

Subd. 9. "Job applicant" means a person, independent contractor, or person working for an independent contractor who applies to become an employee of an employer, and includes a person who has received a job offer made contingent on the person passing drug or alcohol testing.

Subd. 10. "Positive test result" means a finding of the presence of drugs, alcohol, or their metabolites in the sample tested in levels at or above the threshold detection levels contained in the standards of one of the programs listed in section 181.953, subdivision 1.

Subd. 11. "Random selection basis" means a mechanism for selection of employees that (1) results in an equal probability that any employee from a group of employees subject to the selection mechanism will be selected and (2) does not give an employer discretion to waive the selection of any employee selected under the mechanism.

Subd. 12. "Reasonable suspicion" means a basis for forming a belief based on specific facts and rational inferences drawn from those facts.

Subd. 13. "Safety-sensitive position" means a job, including any supervisory or management position, in which an impairment caused by drug or alcohol usage would threaten the health or safety of any person.

§ 181.951 Authorized drug and alcohol testing

Subdivision 1. *Limitations on testing.*

(a) An employer may not request or require an employee or job applicant to undergo drug and alcohol testing except as authorized in this section.

(b) An employer may not request or require an employee or job applicant to undergo drug or alcohol testing unless the testing is done pursuant to a written drug and alcohol testing policy that contains the minimum information required in section 181.952; and, is conducted by a testing laboratory which participates in one of the programs listed in section 181.953, subdivision 1.

(c) An employer may not request or require an employee or job applicant to undergo drug and alcohol testing on an arbitrary and capricious basis.

Subd. 2. *Job applicant testing.*—An employer may request or require a job applicant to undergo drug and alcohol testing provided a job offer has been made to the applicant and the same test is requested or required of all job applicants conditionally offered employment for that position. If the job offer is withdrawn, as provided in section 181.953, subdivision 11, the employer shall inform the job applicant of the reason for its action.

Subd. 3. *Routine physical examination testing.*—An employer may request or require an employee to undergo drug and alcohol testing as part of a routine physical examination provided the drug or alcohol test is requested or required no more than once annually and the employee has been given at least two weeks' written notice that a drug or alcohol test may be requested or required as part of the physical examination.

Subd. 4. *Random testing.*—An employer may request or require employees to undergo drug and alcohol testing on a random selection basis only if (1) they are employed in safety-sensitive positions, or (2) they are employed as professional athletes if the professional athlete is subject to a collective bargaining agreement permitting random testing but only to the extent consistent with the collective bargaining agreement.

Subd. 5. *Reasonable suspicion testing.*—An employer may request or require an employee to undergo drug and alcohol testing if the employer has a reasonable suspicion that the employee:

(1) is under the influence of drugs or alcohol;

(2) has violated the employer's written work rules prohibiting the use, possession, sale, or transfer of drugs or alcohol while the employee is working or while the employee is on the employer's

premises or operating the employer's vehicle, machinery, or equipment, provided the work rules are in writing and contained in the employer's written drug and alcohol testing policy;

(3) has sustained a personal injury, as that term is defined in section 176.011, subdivision 16, or has caused another employee to sustain a personal injury; or

(4) has caused a work-related accident or was operating or helping to operate machinery, equipment, or vehicles involved in a work-related accident.

Subd. 6. *Treatment program testing.*—An employer may request or require an employee to undergo drug and alcohol testing if the employee has been referred by the employer for chemical dependency treatment or evaluation or is participating in a chemical dependency treatment program under an employee benefit plan, in which case the employee may be requested or required to undergo drug or alcohol testing without prior notice during the evaluation or treatment period and for a period of up to two years following completion of any prescribed chemical dependency treatment program.

Subd. 7. *No legal duty to test.*—Employers do not have a legal duty to request or require an employee or job applicant to undergo drug or alcohol testing as authorized in this section.

§ 181.952   Policy contents; prior written notice

Subdivision 1. An employer's drug and alcohol testing policy must, at a minimum, set forth the following information:

(1) the employees or job applicants subject to testing under the policy;

(2) the circumstances under which drug or alcohol testing may be requested or required;

(3) the right of an employee or job applicant to refuse to undergo drug and alcohol testing and the consequences of refusal;

(4) any disciplinary or other adverse personnel action that may be taken based on a confirmatory test verifying a positive test result on an initial screening test;

(5) the right of an employee or job applicant to explain a positive test result on a confirmatory test or request and pay for a confirmatory retest; and

(6) any other appeal procedures available.

Subd. 2. An employer shall provide written notice of its drug and alcohol testing policy to all affected employees upon adoption of the policy, to a previously nonaffected employee upon transfer to an affected position under the policy, and to a job applicant upon hire and before any testing of the applicant if the job offer is made contingent on the applicant passing drug and alcohol testing. An employer shall also post notice in an appropriate and conspicuous location on the employer's premises that the employer has adopted a drug and alcohol testing policy and that copies of the policy are available for inspection during regular business hours by its employees or job applicants in the employer's personnel office or other suitable locations.

§ 181.953 Reliability and fairness safeguards

Subdivision 1. *Use of licensed, accredited, or certified laboratory required.*

(a) An employer who requests or requires an employee or job applicant to undergo drug or alcohol testing shall use the services of a testing laboratory that meets one of the following criteria for drug testing:

(1) is certified by the National Institute on Drug Abuse as meeting the mandatory guidelines published at 53 Federal Register 11970 to 11989, April 11, 1988;

(2) is accredited by the College of American Pathologists, 325 Waukegan Road, Northfield, Illinois, 60093–2750, under the forensic urine drug testing laboratory program; or

(3) is licensed to test for drugs by the state of New York, Department of Health, under Public Health Law, article 5, title V, and rules adopted under that law.

(b) For alcohol testing, the laboratory must either be:

(1) licensed to test for drugs and alcohol by the state of New York, Department of Health, under Public Health Law, article 5, title V, and the rules adopted under that law; or

(2) accredited by the College of American Pathologists, 325 Waukegan Road, Northfield, Illinois, 60093–2750, in the laboratory accreditation program.

Subd. 2. [Repealed, 1991 c 60 s 12]

Subd. 3. *Laboratory testing, reporting, and sample retention requirements.*—A testing laboratory that is not certified by the National Institute on Drug Abuse according to subdivision 1 shall follow the chain-of-custody procedures prescribed for employers in subdivision 5. A testing laboratory shall conduct a confirmatory test on all samples that produced a positive test result on an initial screening test. A laboratory shall disclose to the employer a written test result report for each sample tested within three working days after a negative test result on an initial screening test or, when the initial screening test produced a positive test result, within three working days after a confirmatory test. A test report must indicate the drugs, alcohol, or drug or alcohol metabolites tested for and whether the test produced negative or positive test results. A laboratory shall retain and properly store for at least six months all samples that produced a positive test result.

Subd. 4. *Prohibitions on employers.*—An employer may not conduct drug or alcohol testing of its own employees and job applicants using a testing laboratory owned and operated by the employer; except that, one agency of the state may test the employees of another agency of the state. Except as provided in subdivision 9, an employer may not request or require an employee or job applicant to contribute to, or pay the cost of, drug or alcohol testing under sections 181.950 to 181.954.

Subd. 5. *Employer chain-of-custody procedures.*—An employer shall establish its own reliable chain-of-custody procedures to ensure proper record keeping, handling, labeling, and identification of the samples to be tested. The procedures must require the following:

(1) possession of a sample must be traceable to the employee from whom the sample is collected, from the time the sample is collected through the time the sample is delivered to the laboratory;

(2) the sample must always be in the possession of, must always be in view of, or must be placed in a secured area by a person authorized to handle the sample;

(3) a sample must be accompanied by a written chain-of-custody record; and

(4) individuals relinquishing or accepting possession of the sample must record the time the possession of the sample was transferred and must sign and date the chain-of-custody record at the time of transfer.

Subd. 6. *Rights of employees and job applicants.*

(a) Before requesting an employee or job applicant to undergo drug or alcohol testing, an employer shall provide the employee or job applicant with a form, developed by the employer, on which to acknowledge that the employee or job applicant has seen the employer's drug and alcohol testing policy.

(b) If an employee or job applicant tests positive for drug use, the employee must be given written notice of the right to explain the positive test and the employer may request that the employee or job applicant indicate any over-the-counter or prescription medication that the individual is currently taking or has recently taken and any other information relevant to the reliability of, or explanation for, a positive test result.

(c) Within three working days after notice of a positive test result on a confirmatory test, the employee or job applicant may submit information to the employer, in addition to any information already submitted under paragraph (b), to explain that result, or may request a confirmatory retest of the original sample at the employee's or job applicant's own expense as provided under subdivision 9.

Subd. 7. *Notice of test results.*—Within three working days after receipt of a test result report from the testing laboratory, an employer shall inform in writing an employee or job applicant who has undergone drug or alcohol testing of (1) a negative test result on an initial screening test or of a negative or positive test result on a confirmatory test and (2) the right provided in subdivision 8. In the case of a positive test result on a confirmatory test, the employer shall also, at the time of this notice, inform the employee or job applicant in writing of the rights provided in subdivisions 6, paragraph (b), 9, and either subdivision 10 or 11, whichever applies.

Subd. 8. *Right to test result report.*—An employee or job applicant has the right to request and receive from the employer a copy of the test result report on any drug or alcohol test.

Subd. 9. *Confirmatory retests.*—An employee or job applicant may request a confirmatory retest of the original sample at the employee's or job applicant's own expense after notice of a positive test result on a confirmatory test. Within five working days after notice of the confirmatory test result, the employee or job applicant shall notify the employer in writing of the employee's or job applicant's intention to obtain a confirmatory retest. Within three working days after receipt of the notice, the employer shall notify the original testing laboratory that the employee or job applicant has requested the laboratory to conduct the confirmatory retest or transfer the sample to another laboratory licensed under subdivision 1 to conduct the confirmatory retest. The original testing laboratory shall ensure that the chain-of-custody procedures in subdivision 3 are followed during transfer of the sample to the other laboratory. The confirmatory retest must use the same drug or alcohol threshold detection levels as used in the original confirmatory test. If the confirmatory retest does not confirm the original positive test result, no adverse personnel action based on the original confirmatory test may be taken against the employee or job applicant.

Subd. 10. *Limitations on employee discharge, discipline, or discrimination.*

(a) An employer may not discharge, discipline, discriminate against, or request or require rehabilitation of an employee on the basis of a positive test result from an initial screening test that has not been verified by a confirmatory test.

(b) In addition to the limitation under paragraph (a), an employer may not discharge an employee for whom a positive test result on a confirmatory test was the first such result for the employee on a drug or alcohol test requested by the employer unless the following conditions have been met:

(1) the employer has first given the employee an opportunity to participate in, at the employee's own expense or pursuant to coverage under an employee benefit plan, either a drug or alcohol counseling or rehabilitation program, whichever is more appropriate, as determined by the employer after consultation with a certified chemical use counselor or a physician trained in the diagnosis and treatment of chemical dependency; and

(2) the employee has either refused to participate in the counseling or rehabilitation program or has failed to successfully complete the program, as evidenced by withdrawal from the program before its completion or by a positive test result on a confirmatory test after completion of the program.

(c) Notwithstanding paragraph (a), an employer may temporarily suspend the tested employee or transfer that employee to another position at the same rate of pay pending the outcome of the confirmatory test and, if requested, the confirmatory retest, provided the employer believes that it is reasonably necessary to protect the health or safety of the employee, coemployees, or the public. An employee who has been suspended without pay must be reinstated with back pay if the outcome of the confirmatory test or requested confirmatory retest is negative.

(d) An employer may not discharge, discipline, discriminate against, or request or require rehabilitation of an employee on the basis of medical history information revealed to the employer pursuant to subdivision 6 unless the employee was under an affirmative duty to provide the information before, upon, or after hire.

(e) An employee must be given access to information in the employee's personnel file relating to positive test result reports and other information acquired in the drug and alcohol testing process and conclusions drawn from and actions taken based on the reports or other acquired information.

Subd. 11. *Limitation on withdrawal of job offer.*—If a job applicant has received a job offer made contingent on the applicant passing drug and alcohol testing, the employer may not withdraw the offer based on a positive test result from an initial screening test that has not been verified by a confirmatory test.

§ 181.954 Privacy, confidentiality, and privilege safeguards

Subdivision 1. A laboratory may only disclose to the employer test result data regarding the presence or absence of drugs, alcohol, or their metabolites in a sample tested.

Subd. 2. Test result reports and other information acquired in the drug or alcohol testing process are, with respect to private sector employees and job applicants, private and confidential information, and, with respect to public sector employees and job applicants, private data on individuals as that phrase is defined in chapter 13, and may not be disclosed by an employer or laboratory to another employer or to a third-party individual, governmental agency, or private organization without the written consent of the employee or job applicant tested.

Subd. 3. Notwithstanding subdivisions 1 and 2, evidence of a positive test result on a confirmatory test may be: (1) used in an arbitration proceeding pursuant to a collective bargaining agreement, an administrative hearing under chapter 43A or other applicable state or local law, or a judicial proceeding, provided that information is relevant to the hearing or proceeding; (2) disclosed to any federal agency or other unit of the United States government as required under federal law, regulation, or order, or in accordance with compliance requirements of a federal government contract; and (3) disclosed to a substance abuse treatment facility for the purpose of evaluation or treatment of the employee.

Subd. 4. Positive test results from an employer drug or alcohol testing program may not be used as evidence in a criminal action against the employee or job applicant tested.

§ 181.955   Construction

Subdivision 1. Sections 181.950 to 181.954 shall not be construed to limit the parties to a collective bargaining agreement from bargaining and agreeing with respect to a drug and alcohol testing policy that meets or exceeds, and does not otherwise conflict with, the minimum standards and requirements for employee protection provided in those sections.

Subd. 2. Sections 181.950 to 181.954 shall not be construed to interfere with or diminish any employee protections relating to drug and alcohol testing already provided under collective bargaining agreements in effect on the effective date of those sections that exceed the minimum standards and requirements for employee protection provided in those sections.

§ 181.956   Remedies

Subdivision 1. An employee or collective bargaining agent may bring an action under this section only after first exhausting all applicable grievance procedures and arbitration proceeding requirements under a collective bargaining agreement; provided that, an employee's right to bring an action under this section is not affected by a decision of a collective bargaining agent not to pursue a grievance.

Subd. 2. In addition to any other remedies provided by law, an employer or laboratory that violates sections 181.950 to 181.954 is liable to an employee or job applicant injured by the violation in a civil action for any damages allowable at law. If a violation is found and damages awarded, the court may also award reasonable attorney fees for a cause of action based on a violation of sections 181.950 to 181.954 if the court finds that the employer knowingly or recklessly violated sections 181.950 to 181.954.

Subd. 3. An employee or job applicant, a state, county, or city attorney, or a collective bargaining agent who fairly and adequately represents the interests of the protected class has standing to bring an action for injunctive relief requesting the district court to enjoin an employer or laboratory that commits or proposes to commit an act in violation of sections 181.950 to 181.954.

Subd. 4. Upon finding a violation of sections 181.950 to 181.954, or as part of injunctive relief granted under subdivision 3, a court may, in its discretion, grant any other equitable relief it considers appropriate, including ordering the injured employee or job applicant reinstated with back pay.

Subd. 5. An employer may not retaliate against an employee for asserting rights and remedies provided in sections 181.950 to 181.954.

§ 181.957   Federal preemption

Subdivision 1. Except as provided under subdivision 2, the employee and job applicant protections provided under sections 181.950 to 181.956 do not apply to employees and job applicants where the specific work performed requires those employees and job applicants to be subject to drug and alcohol testing pursuant to:

(1) federal regulations that specifically preempt state regulation of drug and alcohol testing with respect to those employees and job applicants;

(2) federal regulations or requirements necessary to operate federally regulated facilities;

(3) federal contracts where the drug and alcohol testing is conducted for security, safety, or protection of sensitive or proprietary data; or

(4) state agency rules that adopt federal regulations applicable to the interstate component of a federally regulated industry, and the adoption of those rules is for the purpose of conforming the nonfederally regulated intrastate component of the industry to identical regulation.

Subd. 2. Employers and testing laboratories must comply with the employee and job applicant protections provided under sections 181.950 to 181.956, with respect to employees or job applicants otherwise excluded under subdivision 1 from those protections, to the extent that the provisions of sections 181.950 to 181.956 are not inconsistent with or specifically preempted by the federal regulations, contract, or requirements applicable to drug and alcohol testing.

UTAH CODE ANN. §§ 34–38–1 TO –15 (2012)

§ 34–38–1. Legislative findings—Purpose and intent of chapter

The Legislature finds that a healthy and productive work force, safe working conditions free from the effects of drugs and alcohol, and maintenance of the quality of products produced and services rendered in this state, are important to employers, employees, and the general public. The Legislature further finds that the abuse of drugs and alcohol creates a variety of workplace problems, including increased injuries on the job, increased absenteeism, increased financial burden on health and benefit programs, increased workplace theft, decreased employee morale, decreased productivity, and a decline in the quality of products and services.

Therefore, in balancing the interests of employers, employees, and the welfare of the general public, the Legislature finds that fair and equitable testing for drugs and alcohol in the workplace, in accordance with this chapter, is in the best interest of all parties.

The Legislature does not intend to prohibit any employee from seeking damages or job reinstatement, if action was taken by his employer based on a false drug or alcohol test result.

§ 34–38–2. Definitions

For purposes of this chapter:

(1) "Alcohol" means ethyl alcohol or ethanol.

(2) "Drugs" means a substance recognized as a drug in the United States Pharmacopoeia, the National Formulary, the Homeopathic Pharmacopoeia, or other drug compendia, or supplement to any of those compendia.

(3) (a) "Employer" means a person, including a public utility or transit district, that has one or more workers or operators employed in the same business, or in or about the same establishment, under any contract of hire, express or implied, oral or written.

(b) "Employer" does not include the federal or state government, or other local political subdivisions.

(4) "Employee" means an individual in the service of an employer for compensation.

(5) "Failed test" means a confirmed drug or alcohol test that indicates that the sample tested is:

(a) positive;

(b) adulterated; or

(c) substituted.

(6) "Inaccurate test result" means a test result that is treated as a positive test result, when the sample should not have resulted in a positive test result.

(7) "Licensed physician" means an individual who is licensed:

(a) as a doctor of medicine under Title 58, Chapter 67, Utah Medical Practice Act, or similar law of another state; or

(b) as an osteopathic physician or surgeon under Title 58, Chapter 68, Utah Osteopathic Medical Practice Act, or similar law of another state.

(8) "Prospective employee" means an individual who applies to an employer, either in writing or orally, to become the employer's employee.

(9) "Sample" means urine, blood, breath, saliva, or hair.

§ 34–38–3. Testing for drugs or alcohol

(1) If an employer tests an employee or prospective employee for the presence of drugs or alcohol as a condition of hiring or continued employment, the employer is protected from liability as provided in this chapter if the employer complies with this chapter. However, employers and management in general shall submit to the testing themselves on a periodic basis.

(2) (a) An organization that operates a storage facility or transfer facility or that is engaged in the transportation of high-level nuclear waste or greater than class C radioactive waste within the exterior boundaries of the state shall establish a mandatory drug testing program regarding drugs and alcohol for prospective and existing employees as a condition of hiring any employee or the continued employment of any employee. As a part of the program, employers and management in general shall submit to the testing themselves on a periodic basis. The program shall implement testing standards and procedures established under Subsection (2)(b).

(b) The executive director of the Department of Environmental Quality, in consultation with the Labor Commission under Section 34A–1–103, shall by rule establish standards for timing of testing and dosage for impairment for the drug and alcohol testing program under this Subsection (2). The standards shall address the protection of the safety, health, and welfare of the public.

§ 34–38–4. Samples—Identification and collection

In order to test reliably for the presence of drugs or alcohol, an employer may require samples from his employees and prospective employees, and may require presentation of reliable identification to the person collecting the samples. Collection of the sample shall be in conformance with the requirements of Section 34–38–6. The employer may designate the type of sample to be used for testing.

§ 34–38–5.   Time of testing, cost of testing and transportation

(1) Any drug or alcohol testing by an employer shall occur during or immediately after the regular work period of current employees and shall be deemed work time for purposes of compensation and benefits for current employees.

(2) An employer shall pay all costs of testing for drugs or alcohol required by the employer, including the cost of transportation if the testing of a current employee is conducted at a place other than the workplace.

§ 34–38–6.   Requirements for collection and testing

(1) The collection and testing of a sample for drugs and alcohol under this chapter shall be performed in accordance with this chapter.

(2) The collection of a sample shall be performed under reasonable and sanitary conditions.

(3) A sample shall be collected and tested:

(a) with due regard to the privacy of the individual being tested; and

(b) in a manner reasonably calculated to prevent substitutions or interference with the collection or testing of a reliable sample.

(4) The sample collection shall be documented. The documentation procedures required by this Subsection (4) include:

(a) labeling of a sample so as reasonably to preclude the probability of erroneous identification of test results; and

(b) an opportunity for the employee or prospective employee to provide notification of any information that the employee or prospective employee considers relevant to the test, including:

(i) identification of currently or recently used prescription or nonprescription drugs; or

(ii) other relevant medical information.

(5) Sample collection, storage, and transportation to the place of testing shall be performed so as reasonably to preclude the probability of sample contamination or adulteration.

(6) (a) Testing of a sample shall conform to scientifically accepted analytical methods and procedures.

(b) Before a test of a sample may be considered a failed test and used as a basis for an action by an employer under Section 34–38–8, testing of the sample shall include a confirmation test:

(i) by gas chromatography, gas chromatography-mass spectroscopy, or other comparably reliable analytical method; and

(ii) if the sample used for a test is a urine sample, by a laboratory that is certified by the United States Department of

Health and Human Services under the National Laboratory Certification Program.

All sample collection and testing for drugs and alcohol under this chapter shall be performed in accordance with the following conditions:

(1) the collection of samples shall be performed under reasonable and sanitary conditions;

(2) samples shall be collected and tested with due regard to the privacy of the individual being tested, and in a manner reasonably calculated to prevent substitutions or interference with the collection or testing of reliable samples;

(3) sample collection shall be documented, and the documentation procedures shall include:

(a) labeling of samples so as reasonably to preclude the probability of erroneous identification of test results; and

(b) an opportunity for the employee or prospective employee to provide notification of any information which he considers relevant to the test, including identification of currently or recently used prescription or nonprescription drugs, or other relevant medical information.

(4) Sample collection, storage, and transportation to the place of testing shall be performed so as reasonably to preclude the probability of sample contamination or adulteration; and

(5) sample testing shall conform to scientifically accepted analytical methods and procedures. Testing shall include verification or confirmation of any positive test result by gas chromatography, gas chromatography-mass spectroscopy, or other comparably reliable analytical method, before the result of any test may be used as a basis for any action by an employer under Section 34–38–8.

§ 34–38–7. Employer's written testing policy—Purposes and requirements for collection and testing—Employer's use of test results

(1) Testing or retesting for the presence of drugs or alcohol by an employer shall be carried out within the terms of a written policy which has been distributed to employees and is available for review by prospective employees.

(2) Within the terms of his written policy, an employer may require the collection and testing of samples for the following purposes:

(a) investigation of possible individual employee impairment;

(b) investigation of accidents in the workplace or incidents of workplace theft;

(c) maintenance of safety for employees or the general public; or

(d) maintenance of productivity, quality of products or services, or security of property or information.

(3) The collection and testing of samples shall be conducted in accordance with Sections 34–38–4, 34–38–5, and 34–38–6, and need not be limited to circumstances where there are indications of individual, job-related impairment of an employee or prospective employee.

(4) The employer's use and disposition of all drug or alcohol test results are subject to the limitations of Sections 34–38–8 and 34–38–13.

§ 34–38–8. Employer's disciplinary or rehabilitative actions

(1) An employer may take an action described in Subsection (2) if:

(a) the employer receives a test result that:

(i) indicates a failed test;

(ii) is confirmed as required by Subsection 34–38–6(6); and

(iii) indicates a violation of the employer's written policy; or

(b) an employee or prospective employee refuses to provide a sample.

(2) An employer may use a test result or a refusal described in Subsection (1) as the basis for disciplinary or rehabilitative actions, which may include the following:

(a) a requirement that the employee enroll in an employer-approved rehabilitation, treatment, or counseling program, which may include additional drug or alcohol testing, as a condition of continued employment;

(b) suspension of the employee with or without pay for a period of time;

(c) termination of employment;

(d) refusal to hire a prospective employee; or

(e) other disciplinary measures in conformance with the employer's usual procedures, including a collective bargaining agreement.

§ 34–38–9. No cause of action for failure to test or detect or for termination of testing program

No cause of action arises in favor of any person against an employer who has established a policy and initiated a testing program in accordance with this chapter, for any of the following:

(1) failure to test for drugs or alcohol, or failure to test for a specific drug or other substance;

(2) failure to test for, or if tested for, failure to detect, any specific drug or other substance, disease, infectious agent, virus, or other physical abnormality, problem, or defect of any kind; or

(3) termination or suspension of any drug or alcohol testing program or policy.

§ 34–38–10.   No cause of action arises against employer unless false test result—Presumption and limitation of damages in claim against employer

(1) A cause of action may not arise in favor of a person against an employer who establishes a program of drug or alcohol testing in accordance with this chapter, and who takes an action under Section 34–38–8, unless the employer takes the action on the basis of an inaccurate test result.

(2) If a person bringing a claim, including a claim under Section 34–38–11, alleges that an employer's action is based on an inaccurate test result:

(a) there is a rebuttable presumption that the test result is valid if the employer complies with Section 34–38–6; and

(b) the employer is not liable for monetary damages if the employer's reliance on an inaccurate test result is reasonable and in good faith.

(3) (a) There is a rebuttable presumption that the employer complies with Section 34–38–6 if as part of the employer's drug and alcohol testing program a licensed physician who is trained in the interpretation of drug and alcohol test results:

(i) provides medical assessment of a result that indicates a failed test;

(ii) requests re-analysis of a test result if necessary; and

(iii) makes a determination whether or not alcohol or other drug use has occurred.

(b) A court may find that an employer complies with Section 34–38–6 notwithstanding that the employer's drug and alcohol testing program does not include an action described in Subsection (3)(a).

§ 34–38–11.   Bases for cause of action for defamation, libel, slander, or damage to reputation

No cause of action for defamation of character, libel, slander, or damage to reputation arises in favor of any person against an employer who has established a program of drug or alcohol testing in accordance with this chapter, unless:

(1) the results of that test were disclosed to any person other than the employer, an authorized employee or agent of the employer, the tested employee, or the tested prospective employee;

(2) the information disclosed is based on an inaccurate test result;

(3) an inaccurate test result is disclosed with malice; and

(4) all elements of an action for defamation of character, libel, slander, or damage to reputation as established by statute or common law, are satisfied.

§ 34–38–12. No cause of action for failure of employer to establish testing program

No cause of action arises in favor of any person based upon the failure of an employer to establish a program or policy of drug or alcohol testing.

CALIFORNIA PUBLIC UTILITIES
CODE § 8251 (2012)

§ 8251. Use of spotter report as basis for disciplinary action; Conduct of hearing

It is unlawful for any public service corporation, or agent, superintendent, or manager thereof, employing any special agent, detective, or person commonly known as a "spotter," for the purpose of investigating, obtaining, and reporting to the employer information concerning its employees, to discipline or discharge any employee, where such act of discipline or the discharge is based upon a report by such special agent, detective, or spotter, which report involves a question of integrity, honesty, or a breach of rules of the employer, unless such employer, its agent, superintendent, or manager, gives notice and accords a hearing to the employee thus accused, when requested by the employee. At such hearing the employer shall state specific charges on which act of discipline or discharge is based, and the accused employee shall have the right to furnish testimony in his defense.

DISTRICT OF COLUMBIA CODE § 32–902 (2012)

§ 32–902. Use prohibited; exceptions

(a) No employer or prospective employer shall administer, accept or use the results of any lie detector test in connection with the employment, application or consideration of an individual, or have administered, inside the District of Columbia, any lie detector test to any employee, or, in or during any hiring procedure, to any person whose employment, as contemplated at the time of administration of the test, would take place in whole or in part in the District of Columbia.

(b) The provisions of this section shall not apply to any criminal or internal disciplinary investigation, or pre-employment investigation conducted by the Metropolitan Police, the Fire Department, and the Department of Corrections; provided that any information received from a lie detector test which renders an applicant ineligible for employment shall be verified through other information and no person may be denied employment based solely on the results of a pre-employment lie detector test.

§ 44808. Unlawful acts of employer.

It shall be unlawful for any employer

(1) To interfere with, restrain, or coerce employees in the exercise of the rights guaranteed in K.S.A. 44803: Provided, however, That no provision of this act shall be so construed as to deprive that employer of his right of "free speech" as guaranteed by both the state and federal constitutions.

(2) To dominate or interfere with the formation or administration of any labor organization or contribute financial or other support to it: Provided, That an employer shall not be prohibited from permitting employees to confer with him during working hours without loss of time or pay.

(3) To refuse to furnish, upon written request of any employee whose services have been terminated, a service letter setting forth the tenure of employment, occupational classification and wage rate paid the employee.

(4) To discharge or otherwise discriminate against an employee because he has brought action or given information or testimony in good faith under the provisions of this act.

(5) To deduct labor organization dues or assessments from an employee's earnings, unless the employer has an individual order therefor, presented and signed by the employee personally, and terminable at the end of any year of its life by the employee giving at least thirty (30) days' written notice of such termination.

(6) To employ any person to spy upon employees or their representatives respecting their exercise of any right created or approved by this act.

MARYLAND CODE ANN., LABOR AND EMPLOYMENT— § 3–712 (2012)

SECTION 1. BE IT ENACTED BY THE GENERAL ASSEMBLY OF MARYLAND, That the Laws of Maryland read as follows:

Article—Labor and Employment 3–712.

(A) (1) IN THIS SECTION THE FOLLOWING WORDS HAVE THE MEANINGS INDICATED.

(2) "APPLICANT" MEANS AN APPLICANT FOR EMPLOYMENT.

(3) (I) "ELECTRONIC COMMUNICATIONS DEVICE" MEANS ANY DEVICE THAT USES ELECTRONIC SIGNALS TO CREATE, TRANSMIT, AND RECEIVE INFORMATION. (II) "ELECTRONIC COMMUNICATIONS DEVICE" INCLUDES COMPUTERS, TELEPHONES, PERSONAL DIGITAL ASSISTANTS, AND OTHER SIMILAR DEVICES.

(4) (I) "EMPLOYER" MEANS:

1. A PERSON ENGAGED IN A BUSINESS, AN INDUSTRY, A PROFESSION, A TRADE, OR OTHER ENTERPRISE IN THE STATE; OR

2. A UNIT OF STATE OR LOCAL GOVERNMENT.

(II) "EMPLOYER" INCLUDES AN AGENT, A REPRESENTATIVE, AND A DESIGNEE OF THE EMPLOYER.

(B) (1) SUBJECT TO PARAGRAPH (2) OF THIS SUBSECTION, AN EMPLOYER MAY NOT REQUEST OR REQUIRE THAT AN EMPLOYEE OR APPLICANT DISCLOSE ANY USER NAME, PASSWORD, OR OTHER MEANS FOR ACCESSING A PERSONAL ACCOUNT OR SERVICE THROUGH AN ELECTRONIC COMMUNICATIONS DEVICE.

(2) AN EMPLOYER MAY REQUIRE AN EMPLOYEE TO DISCLOSE ANY USER NAME, PASSWORD, OR OTHER MEANS FOR ACCESSING NONPERSONAL ACCOUNTS OR SERVICES THAT PROVIDE ACCESS TO THE EMPLOYER'S INTERNAL COMPUTER OR INFORMATION SYSTEMS.

(C) AN EMPLOYER MAY NOT:

(1) DISCHARGE, DISCIPLINE, OR OTHERWISE PENALIZE OR THREATEN TO DISCHARGE, DISCIPLINE, OR OTHERWISE PENALIZE AN EMPLOYEE FOR AN EMPLOYEE'S REFUSAL TO DISCLOSE ANY INFORMATION SPECIFIED IN SUBSECTION (B)(1) OF THIS SECTION; OR

(2) FAIL OR REFUSE TO HIRE ANY APPLICANT AS A RESULT OF THE APPLICANT'S REFUSAL TO DISCLOSE ANY INFORMATION SPECIFIED IN SUBSECTION (B)(1) OF THIS SECTION.

(D) AN EMPLOYEE MAY NOT DOWNLOAD UNAUTHORIZED EMPLOYER PROPRIETARY INFORMATION OR FINANCIAL DATA TO AN EMPLOYEE'S PERSONAL WEB SITE, AN INTERNET WEB SITE, A WEB–BASED ACCOUNT, OR A SIMILAR ACCOUNT.

(E) THIS SECTION DOES NOT PREVENT AN EMPLOYER (1) BASED ON THE RECEIPT OF INFORMATION ABOUT THE USE OF A PERSONAL WEB SITE, INTERNET WEB SITE, WEB–BASED ACCOUNT, OR SIMILAR ACCOUNT BY AN EMPLOYEE FOR BUSINESS PURPOSES, FROM CONDUCTING AN INVESTIGATION FOR THE PURPOSE OF ENSURING COMPLIANCE WITH APPLICABLE SECURITIES OR FINANCIAL LAW, OR REGULATORY REQUIREMENTS; OR

(2) BASED ON THE RECEIPT OF INFORMATION ABOUT THE UNAUTHORIZED DOWNLOADING OF AN EMPLOYER'S PROPRIETARY INFORMATION OR FINANCIAL DATA TO A PERSONAL WEB SITE, INTERNET WEB SITE, WEB–BASED ACCOUNT, OR SIMILAR ACCOUNT BY AN EMPLOYEE, FROM INVESTIGATING AN EMPLOYEE'S ACTIONS UNDER SUBSECTION (D) OF THIS SECTION.

NEVADA REV. STAT. ANN. § 613.160 (2012)

§ 613.160. Spotters: Right of employee to be confronted with accuser; penalty

1. It is unlawful for any person, firm, association or corporation, or agent, superintendent or manager thereof, employing any special agent, detective or person commonly known as a spotter for the purpose of investigating, obtaining and reporting to the employer or his agent, superintendent or manager information concerning his employees, to discipline or discharge any employee in his service, where the act of discipline or the discharge is based upon a report by a special agent, detective or spotter which involves a question of integrity, honesty or a breach of rules of the employer, unless the employer or his agent, superintendent or manager gives notice and a hearing to the employee thus accused, when requested by the employee, at which hearing the accused employee must have the opportunity to confront the person making the report and must have the right to furnish testimony in his defense.

2. Any person, corporation, firm, association or employer who violates any provision of this section is liable to the State of Nevada for a penalty of $5,000 for each offense. The penalty must be recovered and the suit must be brought in the name of the State of Nevada in a court of proper jurisdiction by the attorney general, or under his direction by the district attorney in any county having proper jurisdiction.

3. If a penalty is imposed pursuant to this section, the costs of the proceeding, including investigative costs and attorney's fees, may be recovered by the attorney general or district attorney, as appropriate.

NEW YORK LABOR LAW § 201–a (2012)

§ 201a. Fingerprinting of employees prohibited

Except as otherwise provided by law, no person, as a condition of securing employment or of continuing employment, shall be required to be fingerprinted. This provision shall not apply to employees of the state or any municipal subdivisions or departments thereof, or to the employees of legally incorporated hospitals, supported in whole or in part by public funds or private endowment, or to the employees of medical colleges affiliated with such hospitals or to employees of private proprietary hospitals.

NEW YORK PENAL LAW §§ 250.00, 250.05 (2012)

§ 250.00. Eavesdropping; definitions of terms

The following definitions are applicable to this article:

1. "Wiretapping" means the intentional overhearing or recording of a telephonic or telegraphic communication by a person other than a sender or receiver thereof, without the consent of either the sender or receiver, by means of any instrument, device or equipment. The normal operation of a telephone or telegraph corporation and the normal use of the services and facilities furnished by such corporation pursuant to its tariffs or necessary to protect the rights or property of said corporation shall not be deemed "wiretapping."

2. "Mechanical overhearing of a conversation" means the intentional overhearing or recording of a conversation or discussion, without the consent of at least one party thereto, by a person not present thereat, by means of any instrument, device or equipment.

3. (Added, L 1988) "Telephonic communication" means any aural transfer made in whole or in part through the use of facilities for the transmission of communications by the aid of wire, cable or other like connection between the point of origin and the point of reception (including the use of such connection in a switching station) furnished or operated by any person engaged in providing or operating such facilities for the transmission of communications and such term includes any electronic storage of such communications.

4. (Added, L 1988) "Aural transfer" means a transfer containing the human voice at any point between and including the point of origin and the point of reception.

5. (Added, L 1988) "Electronic communication" means any transfer of signs, signals, writing, images, sounds, data, or intelligence of any nature transmitted in whole or in part by a wire, radio, electromagnetic, photoelectronic or photo-optical system, but does not include:

(a) any telephonic or telegraphic communication; or

(b) any communication made through a tone only paging device; or

(c) any communication made through a tracking device consisting of an electronic or mechanical device which permits the tracking of the movement of a person or object; or

(d) any communication that is disseminated by the sender through a method of transmission that is configured so that such communication is readily accessible to the general public.

6. (Added, L 1988) "Intercepting or accessing of an electronic communication" and "intentionally intercepted or accessed" mean the intentional acquiring, receiving, collecting, overhearing, or recording of an electronic communication, without the consent of the sender or intended receiver thereof, by means of any instrument, device or equipment, except when used by a telephone company in the ordinary course of its business or when necessary to protect the rights or property of such company.

7. (Added, L 1988) "Electronic communication service" means any service which provides to users thereof the ability to send or receive wire or electronic communications.

8. "Unlawfully" means not specifically authorized pursuant to article seven hundred or seven hundred five of the criminal procedure law for the purposes of this section and sections 250.05, 250.10, 250.15, 250.20, 250.25, 250.30 and 250.35 of this article.

§ 250.05. Eavesdropping

A person is guilty of eavesdropping when he unlawfully engages in wiretapping, mechanical overhearing of a conversation, or intercepting or accessing of an electronic communication.

Eavesdropping is a class E felony.

MARYLAND CRIMINAL PROCEDURE
CODE ANN. § 10–109 (2012)

§ 10–109. Prohibited acts

(a) Applications for employment or admission.—

(1) Disclosure of expunged information about criminal charges in an application, interview, or other means may not be required:

    (i) by an employer or educational institution of a person who applies for employment or admission; or

    (ii) by a unit, official, or employee of the State or a political subdivision of the State of a person who applies for a license, permit, registration, or governmental service.

(2) A person need not refer to or give information concerning an expunged charge when answering a question concerning:

    (i) a criminal charge that did not result in a conviction; or

    (ii) a conviction that the Governor pardoned.

(3) Refusal by a person to disclose information about criminal charges that have been expunged may not be the sole reason for:

    (i) an employer to discharge or refuse to hire the person; or

    (ii) a unit, official, or employee of the State or a political subdivision of the State to deny the person's application.

(b) Penalties.—

(1) A person who violates this section is guilty of a misdemeanor and on conviction is subject to a fine not exceeding $1,000 or imprisonment not exceeding 1 year or both for each violation.

(2) In addition to the penalties provided in paragraph (1) of this subsection, an official or employee of the State or a political subdivision of the State who is convicted under this section may be removed or dismissed from public service.

NEW YORK FAIR CREDIT REPORTING ACT
N.Y. GENERAL BUS. LAW § 380–b (2012)

§ 380–b. Permissible dissemination of reports

(a) A consumer reporting agency may furnish a consumer report under the following circumstances and no other:

(1) In response to the order of a court having jurisdiction to issue such an order, or

(2) In accordance with the written instructions of the consumer to whom it relates, or

(3) To a person whom it has reason to believe intends to use the information (i) in connection with a credit transaction involving the consumer on whom the information is to be furnished and involving the extension of credit to, or review or collection of an account of, the consumer, or (ii) for employment purposes, or (iii) in connection with the underwriting of insurance involving the consumer, or (iv) in connection with a determination of the consumer's eligibility for a license or other benefit granted by a governmental instrumentality required by law to consider an applicant's financial responsibility or status, or (v) to a person in connection with a business transaction involving the consumer where the user has a legitimate business need for such information, or (vi) in connection with the rental or lease of a residence.

(b) No person shall request a consumer report, other than an investigative consumer report, in connection with an application made after the effective date of this article, for credit, employment, insurance, or rental or lease of residences, unless the applicant is first informed in writing or in the same manner in which the application is made that (i) a consumer report may be requested in connection with such application, and (ii) the applicant upon request will be informed whether or not a consumer report was requested, and if such report was requested, informed of the name and address of the consumer reporting agency that furnished the report.

(c) Where the notice provided pursuant to subdivision (b) of this section further indicates that subsequent consumer reports, other than investigative consumer reports, may be requested or utilized in connection with an update, renewal, or extension of the credit, employment, insurance, or rental or lease of residences for which application was made, no additional notice to the consumer shall be required at the time such subsequent report is requested.

(d) The notice requirements of this section shall not be applicable to the update, renewal, or extension of credit, employment, insurance, or rental or lease of residences for which initial application was made prior to the effective date of this article.

NEW YORK "LAWFUL ACTIVITIES" LAW
N.Y. LABOR LAW § 201–d (2012)

§ 201–d. Discrimination against the engagement in certain activities

1. Definitions. As used in this section:

a. "Political activities" shall mean (i) running for public office, (ii) campaigning for a candidate for public office, or (iii) participating in fund-raising activities for the benefit of a candidate, political party or political advocacy group;

b. "Recreational activities" shall mean any lawful, leisure-time activity, for which the employee receives no compensation and which is generally engaged in for recreational purposes, including but not limited to sports, games, hobbies, exercise, reading and the viewing of television, movies and similar material;

c. "Work hours" shall mean, for purposes of this section, all time, including paid and unpaid breaks and meal periods, that the employee is suffered, permitted or expected to be engaged in work, and all time the employee is actually engaged in work. This definition shall not be referred to in determining hours worked for which an employee is entitled to compensation under any law including article nineteen of this chapter.

2. Unless otherwise provided by law, it shall be unlawful for any employer or employment agency to refuse to hire, employ or license, or to discharge from employment or otherwise discriminate against an individual in compensation, promotion or terms, conditions or privileges of employment because of:

a. an individual's political activities outside of working hours, off of the employer's premises and without use of the employer's equipment or other property, if such activities are legal, provided, however, that this paragraph shall not apply to persons whose employment is defined in paragraph six of subdivision (a) of section seventy-nine-h of the civil rights law, and provided further that this paragraph shall not apply to persons who would otherwise be prohibited from engaging in political activity pursuant to chapter 15 of title 5 and subchapter III of chapter 73 of title 5 of the U.S.C.;

b. an individual's legal use of consumable products prior to the beginning or after the conclusion of the employee's work hours, and off of the employer's premises and without use of the employer's equipment or other property;

c. an individual's legal recreational activities outside work hours, off of the employer's premises and without use of the employer's equipment or other property; or

d. an individual's membership in a union or any exercise of rights granted under Title 29, U.S.C., Chapter 7 or under article fourteen of the civil service law.

3. The provisions of subdivision two of this section shall not be deemed to protect activity which:

a. creates a material conflict of interest related to the employer's trade secrets, proprietary information or other proprietary or business interest;

b. with respect to employees of a state agency as defined in sections seventy-three and seventy-four of the public officers law respectively, is in knowing violation of subdivision two, three, four, five, seven, eight or twelve of section seventy-three or of section seventy-four of the public officers law, or of any executive order, policy, directive, or other rule which has been issued by the attorney general regulating outside employment or activities that could conflict with employees' performance of their official duties;

c. with respect to employees of any employer as defined in section twenty-seven-a of this chapter, is in knowing violation of a provision of a collective bargaining agreement concerning ethics, conflicts of interest, potential conflicts of interest, or the proper discharge of official duties;

d. with respect to employees of any employer as defined in section twenty-seven-a of this chapter who are not subject to section seventy-three or seventy-four of the public officers law, is in knowing violation of article eighteen of the general municipal law or any local law, administrative code provision, charter provision or rule or directive of the mayor or any agency head of a city having a population of one million or more, where such law, code provision, charter provision, rule or directive concerns ethics, conflicts of interest, potential conflicts of interest, or the proper discharge of official duties and otherwise covers such employees; and

e. with respect to employees other than those of any employer as defined in section twenty-seven-a of this chapter, violates a collective bargaining agreement or a certified or licensed professional's contractual obligation to devote his or her entire compensated working hours to a single employer, provided however that the provisions of this paragraph shall apply only to professionals whose compensation is at least fifty thousand dollars for the year nineteen hundred ninety-two and in subsequent years is an equivalent amount adjusted by the same percentage as the annual increase or decrease in the consumer price index.

4. Notwithstanding the provisions of subdivision three of this section, an employer shall not be in violation of this section where the

employer takes action based on the belief either that: (i) the employer's actions were required by statute, regulation, ordinance or other governmental mandate, (ii) the employer's actions were permissible pursuant to an established substance abuse or alcohol program or workplace policy, professional contract or collective bargaining agreement, or (iii) the individual's actions were deemed by an employer or previous employer to be illegal or to constitute habitually poor performance, incompetency or misconduct.

5. Nothing in this section shall apply to persons who, on an individual basis, have a professional service contract with an employer and the unique nature of the services provided is such that the employer shall be permitted, as part of such professional service contract, to limit the off-duty activities which may be engaged in by such individual.

6. Nothing in this section shall prohibit an organization or employer from offering, imposing or having in effect a health, disability or life insurance policy that makes distinctions between employees for the type of coverage or the price of coverage based upon the employees' recreational activities or use of consumable products, provided that differential premium rates charged employees reflect a differential cost to the employer and that employers provide employees with a statement delineating the differential rates used by the carriers providing insurance for the employer, and provided further that such distinctions in type or price of coverage shall not be utilized to expand, limit or curtail the rights or liabilities of any party with regard to a civil cause of action.

7. a. Where a violation of this section is alleged to have occurred, the attorney general may apply in the name of the people of the state of New York for an order enjoining or restraining the commission or continuance of the alleged unlawful acts. In any such proceeding, the court may impose a civil penalty in the amount of three hundred dollars for the first violation and five hundred dollars for each subsequent violation.

b. In addition to any other penalties or actions otherwise applicable pursuant to this chapter, where a violation of this section is alleged to have occurred, an aggrieved individual may commence an action for equitable relief and damages.

CALIFORNIA BUSINESS & PROFESSIONAL CODE §§ 16600–16602 (2012)

§ 16600.   Unauthorized contracts

Except as provided in this chapter, every contract by which anyone is restrained from engaging in a lawful profession, trade, or business of any kind is to that extent void.

§ 16601.   Sale of goodwill or corporate shares

Any person who sells the goodwill of a business, or any owner of a business entity selling or otherwise disposing of all of his or her ownership interest in the business entity, or any owner of a business entity that sells (a) all or substantially all of its operating assets together with the goodwill of the business entity, (b) all or substantially all of the operating assets of a division or a subsidiary of the business entity together with the goodwill of that division or subsidiary, or (c) all of the ownership interest of any subsidiary, may agree with the buyer to refrain from carrying on a similar business within a specified geographic area in which the business so sold, or that of the business entity, division, or subsidiary has been carried on, so long as the buyer, or any person deriving title to the goodwill or ownership interest from the buyer, carries on a like business therein.

For the purposes of this section, "business entity" means any partnership (including a limited partnership or a limited liability partnership), limited liability company (including a series of a limited liability company formed under the laws of a jurisdiction that recognizes such a series), or corporation.

For the purposes of this section, "owner of a business entity" means any partner, in the case of a business entity that is a partnership (including a limited partnership or a limited liability partnership), or any member, in the case of a business entity that is a limited liability company (including a series of a limited liability company formed under the laws of a jurisdiction that recognizes such a series), or any owner of capital stock, in the case of a business entity that is a corporation.

For the purposes of this section, "ownership interest" means a partnership interest, in the case of a business entity that is a partnership (including a limited partnership a limited liability partnership), a membership interest, in the case of a business entity that is a limited liability company (including a series of a limited liability company formed under the laws of a jurisdiction that recognizes such a series), or a capital stockholder, in the case of a business entity that is a corporation.

For the purposes of this section, "subsidiary" means any business entity over which the selling business entity has voting control or from which the selling business entity has a right to receive a majority share of distributions upon dissolution or other liquidation of the business entity (or has both voting control and a right to receive these distributions.)

§ 16602. Partnership arrangements

(a) Any partner may, upon or in anticipation of any of the circumstances described in subdivision (b), agree that he or she will not carry on a similar business within a specified geographic area where the partnership business has been transacted, so long as any other member of the partnership, or any person deriving title to the business or its goodwill from any such other member of the partnership, carries on a like business therein.

(b) Subdivision (a) applies to either of the following circumstances:

(1) A dissolution of the partnership.

(2) Dissociation of the partner from the partnership.

COLORADO C.R.S. § 8–2–113 (2011)

§ 8–2–113. Unlawful to intimidate worker—agreement not to compete

(1) It shall be unlawful to use force, threats, or other means of intimidation to prevent any person from engaging in any lawful occupation at any place he sees fit.

(2) Any covenant not to compete which restricts the right of any person to receive compensation for performance of skilled or unskilled labor for any employer shall be void, but this subsection (2) shall not apply to:

(a) Any contract for the purchase and sale of a business or the assets of a business;

(b) Any contract for the protection of trade secrets;

(c) Any contractual provision providing for recovery of the expense of educating and training an employee who has served an employer for a period of less than two years;

(d) Executive and management personnel and officers and employees who constitute professional staff to executive and management personnel.

(3) Any covenant not to compete provision of an employment, partnership, or corporate agreement between physicians which restricts the right of a physician to practice medicine, as defined in section 12–36–106, C.R.S., upon termination of such agreement, shall be void; except that all other provisions of such an agreement enforceable at law, including provisions which require the payment of damages in an amount that is reasonably related to the injury suffered by reason of termination of the agreement, shall be enforceable. Provisions which require the payment of damages upon termination of the agreement may include, but not be limited to, damages related to competition.

§ 42. Misappropriation of Trade Secrets; Tort Liability; Extent of Damages Allowable.

Whoever embezzles, steals or unlawfully takes, carries away, conceals, or copies, or by fraud or by deception obtains, from any person or corporation, with intent to convert to his own use, any trade secret, regardless of value, shall be liable in tort to such person or corporation for all damages resulting therefrom. Whether or not the case is tried by a jury, the court, in its discretion, may increase the damages up to double the amount found. The term "trade secret" as used in this section shall have the same meaning as is set forth in section thirty of chapter two hundred and sixty-six.

§ 42A. Injunctive Relief for Misappropriation of Trade Secrets

Any aggrieved person may file a petition in equity in the supreme judicial court or in the superior court for the county in which either the petitioner or the respondent resides or transacts business, or in Suffolk county, to obtain appropriate injunctive relief including orders or decrees restraining and enjoining the respondent from taking, receiving, concealing, assigning, transferring, leasing, pledging, copying or otherwise using or disposing of a trade secret, regardless of value. The term "trade secret" as used in this section shall have the same meaning as set forth in section thirty of chapter two hundred and sixty-six.

In an action by an employer against a former employee under the provisions of this section for the conversion of a trade secret and where such conversion is in violation of the terms of a written employment agreement between said employer and employee, said employer shall, upon petition, be granted a preliminary injunction if it is shown that said employee is working in a directly competitive capacity with his former employer in violation of the terms of such agreement and that in violation of the terms of such agreement said employee has used such trade secret in such competition.

Part D

MINIMUM–TERMS LAWS: "FILLING OUT" THE EMPLOYMENT CONTRACT

FAIR LABOR STANDARDS ACT OF 1938*— SELECTED PROVISIONS (FLSA)— SELECTED PROVISIONS 29 U.S.C. §§ 203, 206–207, 211–13, 215–17, 254–56, 259–60

§ 203. (§ 3) Definitions

As used in this Act—

(a) "Person" means an individual, partnership, association, corporation, business trust, legal representative, or any organized group of persons.

(b) "Commerce" means trade, commerce, transportation, transmission, or communication among the several States or between any State and any place outside thereof.

(c) "State" means any State of the United States or the District of Columbia or any Territory or possession of the United States.

(d) "Employer" includes any person acting directly or indirectly in the interest of an employer in relation to an employee and includes a public agency, but does not include any labor organization (other than when acting as an employer) or anyone acting in the capacity of officer or agent of such labor organization.

(e)(1) Except as provided in paragraphs (2), (3), and (4), the term "employee" means any individual employed by an employer.

(2) In the case of an individual employed by a public agency, such term means—

* * *

(C) any individual employed by a State, political subdivision of a State, or an interstate governmental agency, other than such an individual—

(i) who is not subject to the civil service laws of the State, political subdivision, or agency which employs him; and

(ii) who—

(I) holds a public elective office of that State, political subdivision, or agency,

(II) is selected by the holder of such an office to be a member of his personal staff,

(III) is appointed by such an officeholder to serve on a policymaking level,

---

* Includes Portal-to-Portal Act, 29 U.S.C. §§ 251 et seq.

(IV) is an immediate adviser to such an officeholder with respect to the constitutional or legal powers of his office, or

(V) is an employee in the legislative branch or legislative body of that State, political subdivision, or agency and is not employed by the legislative library of such State, political subdivision, or agency.

* * *

(4)(A) The term "employee" does not include any individual who volunteers to perform services for a public agency which is a State, a political subdivision of a State, or an interstate governmental agency, if—

(i) the individual receives no compensation or is paid expenses, reasonable benefits, or a nominal fee to perform the services for which the individual volunteered; and

(ii) such services are not the same type of services which the individual is employed to perform for such public agency.

(B) An employee of a public agency which is a State, political subdivision of a State, or an interstate governmental agency may volunteer to perform services for any other State, political subdivision, or interstate governmental agency, including a State, political subdivision or agency with which the employing State, political subdivision, or agency has a mutual aid agreement.

(5) The term "employee" does not include individuals who volunteer their services solely for humanitarian purposes to private non-profit food banks and who receive from the food banks groceries.

* * *

(g) "Employ" includes to suffer or permit to work.

* * *

(m) "Wage" paid to any employee includes the reasonable cost, as determined by the Administrator [Secretary], to the employer of furnishing such employee with board, lodging, or other facilities, if such board, lodging, or other facilities are customarily furnished by such employer to his employees: *Provided*, That the cost of board, lodging, or other facilities shall not be included as a part of the wage paid to any employee to the extent it is excluded therefrom under the terms of a bona fide collective-bargaining agreement applicable to the particular employee: *Provided further,* That the Secretary is authorized to determine the fair value of such board, lodging, or other facilities for defined classes of employees and in defined areas, based on average cost to the employer or to groups of employers similarly situated, or average value to groups of employees, or other appropriate measures of fair value. Such evaluations, where applicable and pertinent, shall be used in lieu of actual measure of cost in determining the wage paid to any employee. In determining the wage an employer is required to pay a tipped employee, the amount paid such employee by the employee's employer shall be an amount equal to—

(1) the cash wage paid such employee which for purposes of such determination shall be not less than the cash wage required to be paid such an employee on the date of the enactment of this paragraph; and

(2) an additional amount on account of the tips received by such employee which amount is equal to the difference between the wage specified in paragraph (1) and the wage in effect under section 6(a)(1) [29 U.S.C. § 206(a)(1)].

The additional amount on account of tips may not exceed the value of the tips actually received by an employee. The preceding 2 sentences shall not apply with respect to any tipped employee unless such employee has been informed by the employer of the provisions of this subsection, and all tips received by such employee have been retained by the employee, except that this subsection shall not be construed to prohibit the pooling of tips among employees who customarily and regularly receive tips.

* * *

(*o*) Hours Worked. In determining for the purposes of sections 6 and 7 [29 U.S.C. §§ 206 and 207] the hours for which an employee is employed, there shall be excluded any time spent in changing clothes or washing at the beginning or end of each workday which was excluded from measured working time during the week involved by the express terms of or by custom or practice under a bona fide collective-bargaining agreement applicable to the particular employee.

* * *

(**r**)(1) "Enterprise" means the related activities performed (either through unified operation or common control) by any person or persons for a common business purpose, and includes all such activities whether performed in one or more establishments or by one or more corporate or other organizational units including departments of an establishment operated through leasing arrangements, but shall not include the related activities performed for such enterprise by an independent contractor. Within the meaning of this subsection, a retail or service establishment which is under independent ownership shall not be deemed to be so operated or controlled as to be other than a separate and distinct enterprise by reason of any arrangement, which includes, but is not necessarily limited to, an agreement, (A) that it will sell, or sell only, certain goods specified by a particular manufacturer, distributor, or advertiser, or (B) that it will join with other such establishments in the same industry for the purpose of collective purchasing, or (C) that it will have the exclusive right to sell the goods or use the brand name of a manufacturer, distributor, or advertiser within a specified area, or by reason of the fact that it occupies premises leased to it by a person who also leases premises to other retail or service establishments.

* * *

(t) "Tipped employee" means any employee engaged in an occupation in which he customarily and regularly receives more than $30 a month in tips. * * *

* * *

(June 25, 1938, ch. 676, § 3, 52 Stat. 1060; Oct. 26, 1949, ch. 736, § 3, 63 Stat. 911; May 5, 1961, P.L. 87–30, § 2, 75 Stat. 65; Sept. 23, 1966, P.L. 89–601, Title I, §§ 101–103, Title II, § 215(a), 80 Stat. 830–832, 837; June 23, 1972, P.L. 92–318, Title IX, § 906(b)(2), (3), 86 Stat. 375; April 8, 1974, P.L. 93–259, §§ 6(a), 13(e), 88 Stat. 58, 64; Nov. 1, 1977, P.L. 95–151, §§ 3(a), (b), 9(a)–(c), 91 Stat. 1249, 1251; Nov. 13, 1985, P.L. 99–150, §§ 4(a), 5, 99 Stat. 790; Nov. 17, 1989, P.L. 101–157, §§ 3(a), (d), 5, 103 Stat. 938, 939, 941; as amended Jan. 23, 1995, P.L. 104–1, Title II, Part A, § 203(d), 109 Stat. 10; Aug. 20, 1996, P.L. 104–188, Title II, § 2105(b), 110 Stat. 1929; Aug. 7, 1998, P.L. 105–221, § 2, 112 Stat. 1248; Dec. 9, 1999, P.L. 106–151, § 1, 113 Stat. 1731.)

§ 206. (§ 6) Minimum wages

(a) Employees engaged in commerce; home workers in Puerto Rico and Virgin Islands; employees in American Samoa; seamen on American vessels; agricultural employees. Every employer shall pay to each of his employees who in any workweek is engaged in commerce or in the production of goods for commerce, or is employed in an enterprise engaged in commerce or in the production of goods for commerce, wages at the following rates:

(1) except as otherwise provided in this section, not less than—

(A) $5.85 an hour, beginning on the 60th day after the date of enactment of the Fair Minimum Wage Act of 2007 [enacted May 25, 2007];

(B) $6.55 an hour, beginning 12 months after that 60th day; and

(C) $7.25 an hour, beginning 24 months after that 60th day;

* * *

(d) Prohibition of sex discrimination. [See Stat. Supp., supra, p. 73]

* * *

(June 25, 1938, ch. 676, § 6, 52 Stat. 1062; June 26, 1940, ch. 432, § 3(e), (f), 54 Stat. 616; Oct. 26, 1949, ch. 736, § 6, 63 Stat. 912; Aug. 12,

1955, ch. 867, § 3, 69 Stat. 711; Aug. 8, 1956, ch. 1035, § 2, 70 Stat. 1118; May 5, 1961, P.L. 87–30, § 5, 75 Stat. 67; June 10, 1963, P.L. 88–38, § 3, 77 Stat. 56; Sept. 23, 1966, P.L. 89–601, Title III, §§ 301–305, 80 Stat. 838–841; April 8, 1974, P.L. 93–259, §§ 2–4, 5(b), 7(b)(1), 88 Stat. 55, 56, 62; Nov. 1, 1977, P.L. 95–151, § 2(a)–(c), (d)(1), (2), 91 Stat. 1245; Nov. 17, 1989, P.L. 101–157, §§ 2, 4(b), 103 Stat. 938, 940; Dec. 19, 1989, P.L. 101–239, Title X, Subtitle B, § 10208(d)(2)(B)(i), 103 Stat. 2481; Aug. 20, 1996, P.L. 104–188, Title II, §§ 2104(b), (c), 2105(c), 110 Stat. 1928, 1929; May 25, 2007, P.L. 110–28, Title VIII, Subtitle A, §§ 8102(a), 8103(c)(1)(B), 121 Stat. 188, 189.)

§ 207. (§ 7) Maximum hours

(a) Employees engaged in interstate commerce; additional applicability to employees pursuant to subsequent amendatory provisions.

(1)Except as otherwise provided in this section, no employer shall employ any of his employees who in any workweek is engaged in commerce or in the production of goods for commerce, or is employed in an enterprise engaged in commerce or in the production of goods for commerce, for a workweek longer than forty hours unless such employee receives compensation for his employment in excess of the hours above specified at a rate not less than one and one-half times the regular rate at which he is employed. * * *

(e) "Regular rate" defined. As used in this section the "regular rate" at which an employee is employed shall be deemed to include all remuneration for employment paid to, or on behalf of, the employee, but shall not be deemed to include—

(1) sums paid as gifts; payments in the nature of gifts made at Christmas time or on other special occasions, as a reward for service, the amounts of which are not measured by or dependent on hours worked, production, or efficiency;

(2) payments made for occasional periods when no work is performed due to vacation, holiday, illness, failure of the employer to provide sufficient work, or other similar cause; reasonable payments for traveling expenses, or other expenses, incurred by an employee in the furtherance of his employer's interests and properly reimbursable by the employer; and other similar payments to an employee which are not made as compensation for his hours of employment;

(3) Sums [sums] paid in recognition of services performed during a given period if either, (a) both the fact that payment is to be made and the amount of the payment are determined at the sole discretion of the employer at or near the end of the period and not pursuant to any prior contract, agreement, or promise causing the employee to expect such payments regularly; or (b) the payments are made pursuant to a bona fide profit-sharing plan or trust or bona fide thrift or savings plan, meeting the requirements of the Adminis-

trator [Secretary] set forth in appropriate regulations which he shall issue, having due regard among other relevant factors, to the extent to which the amounts paid to the employee are determined without regard to hours of work, production, or efficiency; or (c) the payments are talent fees (as such talent fees are defined and delimited by regulations of the Administrator [Secretary]) paid to performers, including announcers, on radio and television programs;

(4) contributions irrevocably made by an employer to a trustee or third person pursuant to a bona fide plan for providing old-age, retirement, life, accident, or health insurance or similar benefits for employees;

(5) extra compensation provided by a premium rate paid for certain hours worked by the employee in any day or workweek because such hours are hours worked in excess of eight in a day or in excess of the maximum workweek applicable to such employee under subsection (a) or in excess of the employee's normal working hours or regular working hours, as the case may be;

(6) extra compensation provided by a premium rate paid for work by the employee on Saturdays, Sundays, holidays, or regular days of rest, or on the sixth or seventh day of the workweek, where such premium rate is not less than one and one-half times the rate established in good faith for like work performed in nonovertime hours on other days;

(7) extra compensation provided by a premium rate paid to the employee, in pursuance of an applicable employment contract or collective-bargaining agreement, for work outside of the hours established in good faith by the contract or agreement as the basic, normal, or regular workday (not exceeding eight hours) or workweek (not exceeding the maximum workweek applicable to such employee under subsection (a)[)], where such premium rate is not less than one and one-half times the rate established in good faith by the contract or agreement for like work performed during such workday or workweek; or

(8) any value or income derived from employer-provided grants or rights provided pursuant to a stock option, stock appreciation right, or bona fide employee stock purchase program which is not otherwise excludable under any of paragraphs (1) through (7) if—

(A) grants are made pursuant to a program, the terms and conditions of which are communicated to participating employees either at the beginning of the employee's participation in the program or at the time of the grant;

(B) in the case of stock options and stock appreciation rights, the grant or right cannot be exercisable for a period of at least 6 months after the time of grant (except that grants or rights may become exercisable because of an employee's death, disability, retirement, or a change in corporate ownership, or other circumstances permitted by regulation), and the exercise price is at least 85 percent of the fair market value of the stock at the time of grant;

(C) exercise of any grant or right is voluntary; and

(D) any determinations regarding the award of, and the amount of, employer-provided grants or rights that are based on performance are—

(i) made based upon meeting previously established performance criteria (which may include hours of work, efficiency, or productivity) of any business unit consisting of at least 10 employees or of a facility, except that, any determinations may be based on length of service or minimum schedule of hours or days of work; or

(ii) made based upon the past performance (which may include any criteria) of one or more employees in a given period so long as the determination is in the sole discretion of the employer and not pursuant to any prior contract.

(f) Employment necessitating irregular hours of work. No employer shall be deemed to have violated subsection (a) by employing any employee for a workweek in excess of the maximum workweek applicable to such employee under subsection (a) if such employee is employed pursuant to a bona fide individual contract, or pursuant to an agreement made as a result of collective bargaining by representatives of employees, if the duties of such employee necessitate irregular hours of work, and the contract or agreement (1) specifies a regular rate of pay of not less than the minimum hourly rate provided in subsection (a) or (b) of section 6 [29 USCS § 206(a) or (b)] (whichever may be applicable) and compensation at not less than one and one-half times such rate for all hours worked in excess of such maximum workweek, and (2) provides a weekly guaranty of pay for not more than sixty hours based on the rates so specified.

(g) Employment at piece rates. No employer shall be deemed to have violated subsection (a) by employing any employee for a workweek in excess of the maximum workweek applicable to such employee under such subsection if, pursuant to an agreement or understanding arrived at between the employer and the employee before performance of the work, the amount paid to the employee for the number of hours worked by him in such workweek in excess of the maximum workweek applicable to such employee under such subsection—

(1) in the case of an employee employed at piece rates, is computed at piece rates not less than one and one-half times the bona fide piece rates applicable to the same work when performed during nonovertime hours; or

(2) in the case of an employee performing two or more kinds of work for which different hourly or piece rates have been established, is computed at rates not less than one and one-half times such bona

fide rates applicable to the same work when performed during non-overtime hours; or

(3) is computed at a rate not less than one and one-half times the rate established by such agreement or understanding as the basic rate to be used in computing overtime compensation thereunder: Provided, That the rate so established shall be authorized by regulation by the Administrator [Secretary] as being substantially equivalent to the average hourly earnings of the employee, exclusive of overtime premiums, in the particular work over a representative period of time;

and if (i) the employee's average hourly earnings for the workweek exclusive of payments described in paragraphs (1) through (7) of subsection (e) are not less than the minimum hourly rate required by applicable law, and (ii) extra overtime compensation is properly computed and paid on other forms of additional pay required to be included in computing the regular rate.

(h) Credit toward minimum wage or overtime compensation of amounts excluded from regular rate.

(1) Except as provided in paragraph (2), sums excluded from the regular rate pursuant to subsection (e) shall not be creditable toward wages required under section 6 or overtime compensation required under this section.

(2) Extra compensation paid as described in paragraphs (5), (6), and (7) of subsection (e) shall be creditable toward overtime compensation payable pursuant to this section.

(i) Employment by retail or service establishment. No employer shall be deemed to have violated subsection (a) by employing any employee at a retail or service establishment for a workweek in excess of the applicable workweek specified therein, if (1) the regular rate of pay of such employee is in excess of one and one-half times the minimum hourly rate applicable to him under section 6, and (2) more than half his compensation for a representative period (not less than one month) represents commissions on goods or services. In determining the proportion of compensation representing commissions, all earnings resulting from the application of a bona fide commission rate shall be deemed commissions on goods or services without regard to whether the computed commissions exceed the draw or guarantee.

(j) Employment in hospital or establishment engaged in care of sick, aged, or mentally ill. No employer engaged in the operation of a hospital or an establishment which is an institution primarily engaged in the care of the sick, the aged, or the mentally ill or defective who reside on the premises shall be deemed to have violated subsection (a) if, pursuant to an agreement or understanding arrived at between the employer and the employee before performance of the work, a work period of fourteen consecutive days is accepted in lieu of the workweek of seven consecutive days for purposes of overtime computation and if, for his employment in excess of eight hours in any workday and in excess of eighty hours in such fourteen-day period, the employee receives compensation at a rate not less than one and one-half times the regular rate at which he is employed.

(k) Employment by public agency engaged in fire protection or law enforcement activities. No public agency shall be deemed to have violated subsection (a) with respect to the employment of any employee in fire protection activities or any employee in law enforcement activities (including security personnel in correctional institutions) if—

(1) in a work period of 28 consecutive days the employee receives for tours of duty which in the aggregate exceed the lesser of (A) 216 hours, or (B) the average number of hours (as determined by the Secretary pursuant to section 6(c)(3) of the Fair Labor Standards Amendments of 1974) [29 U.S.C. § 213 note] in tours of duty of employees engaged in such activities in work periods of 28 consecutive days in calendar year 1975; or

(2) in the case of such an employee to whom a work period of at least 7 but less than 28 days applies, in his work period the employee receives for tours of duty which in the aggregate exceed a number of hours which bears the same ratio to the number of consecutive days in his work period as 216 hours (or if lower, the number of hours referred to in clause (B) of paragraph (1)) bears to 28 days, compensation at a rate not less than one and one-half times the regular rate at which he is employed.

* * *

(o) **Compensatory time.**

(1) Employees of a public agency which is a State, a political subdivision of a State, or an interstate governmental agency may receive, in accordance with this subsection and in lieu of overtime compensation, compensatory time off at a rate not less than one and one-half hours for each hour of employment for which overtime compensation is required by this section.

(2) A public agency may provide compensatory time under paragraph (1) only—

(A) pursuant to—

(i) applicable provisions of a collective bargaining agreement, memorandum of understanding, or any other agreement between the public agency and representatives of such employees; or

(ii) in the case of employees not covered by subclause (i), an agreement or understanding arrived at between the employer and employee before the performance of the work; and

(B) if the employee has not accrued compensatory time in excess of the limit applicable to the employee prescribed by paragraph (3). * * *

(3) (A) If the work of an employee for which compensatory time may be provided included work in a public safety activity, an emergency response activity, or a seasonal activity, the employee engaged in such work may accrue not more than 480 hours of compensatory time for hours worked after April 15, 1986. If such work was any other work, the employee engaged in such work may accrue not more than 240 hours of compensatory time for hours worked after April 15, 1986. Any such employee who, after April 15, 1986, has accrued 480 or 240 hours, as the case may be, of compensatory time off shall, for additional overtime hours of work, be paid overtime compensation.

(B) If compensation is paid to an employee for accrued compensatory time off, such compensation shall be paid at the regular rate earned by the employee at the time the employee receives such payment.

(4) An employee who has accrued compensatory time off authorized to be provided under paragraph (1) shall, upon termination of employment, be paid for the unused compensatory time at a rate of compensation not less than—

(A) the average regular rate received by such employee during the last 3 years of the employee's employment, or

(B) the final regular rate received by such employee, whichever is higher[.]

(5) An employee of a public agency which is a State, political subdivision of a State, or an interstate governmental agency—

(A) who has accrued compensatory time off authorized to be provided under paragraph (1), and

(B) who has requested the use of such compensatory time,

shall be permitted by the employee's employer to use such time within a reasonable period after making the request if the use of the compensatory time does not unduly disrupt the operations of the public agency. * * *

(7) For purposes of this subsection—

(A) the term "overtime compensation" means the compensation required by subsection (a), and

(B) the terms "compensatory time" and "compensatory time off" mean hours during which an employee is not working, which are not counted as hours worked during the applicable workweek or other work period for purposes of overtime compensation, and for which the employee is compensated at the employee's regular rate.

(r) Reasonable break time for nursing mothers.

(1) An employer shall provide—

(A) a reasonable break time for an employee to express breast milk for her nursing child for 1 year after the child's birth each time such employee has need to express the milk; and

(B) a place, other than a bathroom, that is shielded from view and free from intrusion from coworkers and the public, which may be used by an employee to express breast milk.

(2) An employer shall not be required to compensate an employee receiving reasonable break time under paragraph (1) for any work time spent for such purpose.

(3) An employer that employs less than 50 employees shall not be subject to the requirements of this subsection, if such requirements would impose an undue hardship by causing the employer significant difficulty or expense when considered in relation to the size, financial resources, nature, or structure of the employer's business.

(4) Nothing in this subsection shall preempt a State law that provides greater protections to employees than the protections provided for under this subsection.

(June 25, 1938, ch. 676, § 7, 52 Stat. 1063; Oct. 29, 1941, ch. 461, 55 Stat. 756; July 20, 1949, ch. 352, § 1, 63 Stat. 446; Oct. 26, 1949, ch. 736, §§ 7, 16(f), 63 Stat. 912, 920; May 5, 1961, P.L. 87-30, § 6, 75 Stat. 69; Sept. 23, 1966, P.L. 89-601, Title II, §§ 204(c), (d), 212(b), Title IV, §§ 401-403, 80 Stat. 835-837, 841, 842; April 8, 1974, P.L. 93-259, §§ 6(c)(1)(A), 7(b)(2), 9(a), 12(b), 19(a)-(c), 21(a), 88 Stat. 60, 62, 64, 66,

68; Nov. 13, 1985, P.L. 99–150, §§ 2(a), 3(a), (b), (c)(1), 99 Stat. 787, 789; Nov. 17, 1989, P.L. 101–157, § 7, 103 Stat. 944; Sept. 6, 1995, P.L. 104–26, § 2, 109 Stat. 264; May 18, 2000, P.L. 106–202, § 2(a), (b), 114 Stat. 308; March 23, 2010, P.L. 111–148, Title IV, Subtitle C, § 4207, 124 Stat. 577.)

§ 211. (§ 11) Collection of data

* * *

(c) Records. Every employer subject to any provision of this Act or of any order issued under this Act shall make, keep, and preserve such records of the persons employed by him and of the wages, hours, and other conditions and practices of employment maintained by him, and shall preserve such records for such periods of time, and shall make such reports therefrom to the Administrator [Secretary] as he shall prescribe by regulation or order as necessary or appropriate for the enforcement of the provisions of this Act or the regulations or orders thereunder. * * *

(d) Homework regulations. The Administrator [Secretary] is authorized to make such regulations and orders regulating, restricting, or prohibiting industrial homework as are necessary or appropriate to prevent the circumvention or evasion of and to safeguard the minimum wage rate prescribed in this Act, and all existing regulations or orders of the Administrator [Secretary] relating to industrial homework are hereby continued in full force and effect.

(June 25, 1938, ch. 676, § 11, 52 Stat. 1066; Oct. 26, 1949, ch. 736, § 9, 63 Stat. 916; Pub.L. 99–150, § 3(c)(2), 99 Stat. 789.)

§ 212. (§ 12) Child labor provisions

(a) Restrictions on shipment of goods; prosecution; conviction. No producer, manufacturer, or dealer shall ship or deliver for shipment in commerce any goods produced in an establishment situated in the United States in or about which within thirty days prior to the removal of such goods therefrom any oppressive child labor has been employed: *Provided,* That any such shipment or delivery for shipment of such goods by a purchaser who acquired them in good faith in reliance on written assurance from the producer, manufacturer, or dealer that the goods were produced in compliance with the requirements of this section, and who acquired such goods for value without notice of any such violation, shall not be deemed prohibited by this subsection: And *provided further,* That a prosecution and conviction of a defendant for the shipment or delivery for shipment of any goods under the conditions herein prohibited shall be a bar to any further prosecution against the same defendant for shipments or deliveries for shipment of any such goods before the beginning of said prosecution.

(June 25, 1938, ch. 676, § 12, 52 Stat. 1067; Oct. 26, 1949, ch. 736, § 10, 63 Stat. 917; Pub. L. 87–30, § 8, 75 Stat. 70; Pub. L. 93–259, § 25(a), 88 Stat. 72.)

§ 213. (§ 13) Exemptions

(a) Minimum wage and maximum hour requirements

The provisions of section 206 (except subsection (d) in the case of paragraph (1) of this subsection) and section 207 shall not apply with respect to—

(1) any employee employed in a bona fide executive, administrative, or professional capacity (including any employee employed in the capacity of academic administrative personnel or teacher in elementary or secondary schools), or in the capacity of outside salesman (as such terms are defined and delimited from time to time by regulations of the Secretary, subject to the provisions of the Administrative Procedure Act [5 U.S.C. 551 et seq.] except than [that] an employee of a retail or service establishment shall not be excluded from the definition of employee employed in a bona fide executive or administrative capacity because of the number of hours in his workweek which he devotes to activities not directly or closely related to the performance of executive or administrative activities, if less than 40 per centum of his hours worked in the workweek are devoted to such activities); * * *

(June 25, 1938, ch. 676, § 13, 52 Stat. 1067; Aug. 9, 1939, ch. 605, 53 Stat. 1266; Oct. 26, 1949, ch. 736, § 11, 63 Stat. 917; Aug. 8, 1956, ch. 1035, § 3, 70 Stat. 1118; Aug. 30, 1957, P.L. 85–231, § 1(1), 71 Stat. 514; July 12, 1960, P.L. 86–624, § 21(b), 74 Stat. 417; May 5, 1961, P.L. 87–30, §§ 9, 10, 75 Stat. 71, 74; Sept. 23, 1966, P.L. 89–601, Title II, §§ 201–204(b), 205–212(a), 213, 214, 215(b), (c), 80 Stat. 833–838; Oct. 15, 1966, P.L. 89–670, § 8(e), 80 Stat. 943; June 23, 1972, P.L. 92–318, Title IX, § 906(b)(1), 86 Stat. 375; April 8, 1974, P.L. 93–259, §§ 6(c)(2), 7(b)(3), (4), 8(a), 9(b), 10(a), (b)(1), 11(a), 12(a), 13(a), 14, 15(a), 16(a), (b), 17, 18, 20(a), (b)(1), (b)(2), (c)(1), (c)(2), 21(b)(1), 22, 23, 25(b), 88 Stat. 61–69, 72; Nov. 1, 1977, P.L. 95–151, §§ 4–8, 9(d), 11, 14(a), (b), 91 Stat. 1249–1252; Sept. 27, 1979, P.L. 96–70, Title I, ch. 2, Subch. II, § 1225(a), 93 Stat. 468; Nov. 17, 1989, P.L. 101–157, § 3(c), 103 Stat. 939; Sept. 30, 1994, P.L. 103–329, Title VI, § 633(d), 108 Stat. 2428; Dec. 29, 1995, P.L. 104–88, Title III, Subtitle B, § 340, 109 Stat. 955; Aug. 6, 1996, P.L. 104–174, § 1, 110 Stat. 1553; Aug. 20, 1996, P.L. 104–188, Title II, § 2105(a), 110 Stat. 1929; Nov. 13, 1997, P.L. 105–78, Title I, § 105, 111 Stat. 1477; Oct. 31, 1998, P.L. 105–334, § 2(a), 112 Stat. 3137; Jan. 23, 2004, P.L. 108–199, Div. E, Title I, § 108, 118 Stat. 236.)

§ 215. (§ 15) Prohibited acts; Prima facie evidence

(a) After the expiration of one hundred and twenty days from the date of enactment of this Act [June 25, 1938], it shall be unlawful for any person—

(1) to transport, offer for transportation, ship, deliver, or sell in commerce, or to ship, deliver, or sell with knowledge that shipment or delivery or sale thereof in commerce is intended, any goods in the production of which any employee was employed in violation of

section 6 or section 7 [29 U.S.C. §§ 206 or 207], or in violation of any regulation or order of the Administrator [Secretary] issued under section 14 [29 U.S.C. § 214]; except that no provisions of this Act shall impose any liability upon any common carrier for the transportation in commerce in the regular course of its business of any goods not produced by such common carrier, and no provision of this Act shall excuse any common carrier from its obligation to accept any goods for transportation; and except that any such transportation, offer, shipment, delivery, or sale of such goods by a purchaser who acquired them in good faith in reliance on written assurance from the producer that the goods were produced in compliance with the requirements of the Act, and who acquired such goods for value without notice of any such violation, shall not be deemed unlawful;

(2) to violate any of the provisions of section 6 or section 7 [29 U.S.C. §§ 206 or 207], or any of the provisions of any regulation or order of the Administrator [Secretary] issued under section 14 [29 U.S.C. § 214];

(3) to discharge or in any other manner discriminate against any employee because such employee has filed any complaint or instituted or caused to be instituted any proceeding under or related to this Act, or has testified or is about to testify in any such proceeding, or has served or is about to serve on an industry committee.[;]

(4) to violate any of the provisions of section 12 [29 U.S.C. § 212];

(5) to violate any of the provisions of section 11(c) [29 U.S.C. § 211(c)] or any regulation or order made or continued in effect under the provisions of section 11(d) [29 U.S.C. § 211(d)], or to make any statement, report, or record filed or kept pursuant to the provisions of such section or of any regulation or order thereunder, knowing such statement, report, or record to be false in a material respect.

(b) For the purposes of subsection (a)(1) proof that any employee was employed in any place of employment where goods shipped or sold in commerce were produced, within ninety days prior to the removal of the goods from such place of employment, shall be prima facie evidence that such employee was engaged in the production of such goods.

(June 25, 1938, ch. 676, § 15, 52 Stat. 1068; Oct. 26, 1949, ch. 736, § 13, 63 Stat. 919.)

§ 216. (§ 16) Penalties

(a) Fines and imprisonment. Any person who willfully violates any of the provisions of section 15 [29 U.S.C. § 215] shall upon conviction thereof be subject to a fine of not more than $10,000, or to imprisonment for not more than six months, or both. No person shall be imprisoned under this subsection except for an offense committed after the conviction of such person for a prior offense under this subsection.

(b) Damages; right of action; attorney's fees and costs; termination of right of action. Any employer who violates the provisions of section 6 or section 7 of this Act [29 U.S.C. §§ 206 or 207] shall be liable to the employee or employees affected in the amount of their unpaid minimum wages, or their unpaid overtime compensation, as the case may be, and in an additional equal amount as liquidated damages. Any employer who violates the provisions of section 15(a)(3) of this Act [29 U.S.C. § 215(a)(3)] shall be liable for such legal or equitable relief as may be appropriate to effectuate the purposes of section 15(a)(3) [29 U.S.C. § 215(a)(3)], including without limitation employment, reinstatement, promotion, and the payment of wages lost and an additional equal amount as liquidated damages. An action to recover the liability prescribed in either of the preceding sentences may be maintained against any employer (including a public agency) in any Federal or State court of competent jurisdiction by any one or more employees for and in behalf of himself or themselves and other employees similarly situated. No employee shall be a party plaintiff to any such action unless he gives his consent in writing to become such a party and such consent is filed in the court in which such action is brought. The court in such action shall, in addition to any judgment awarded to the plaintiff or plaintiffs, allow a reasonable attorney's fee to be paid by the defendant, and costs of the action. The right provided by this subsection to bring an action by or on behalf of any employee, and the right of any employee to become a party plaintiff to any such action, shall terminate upon the filing of a complaint by the Secretary of Labor in an action under section 17 [29 U.S.C. § 217] in which (1) restraint is sought of any further delay in the payment of unpaid minimum wages, or the amount of unpaid overtime compensation, as the case may be, owing to such employee under section 6 or section 7 of this Act [29 U.S.C. §§ 206 or 207] by an employer liable therefor under the provisions of this subsection or (2) legal or equitable relief is sought as a result of alleged violations of section 15(a)(3) [29 U.S.C. § 215(a)(3)].

(c) Payment of wages and compensation; waiver of claims; actions by the Secretary; limitation of actions. The Secretary is authorized to supervise the payment of the unpaid minimum wages or the unpaid overtime compensation owing to any employee or employees under section 6 or 7 of this Act [29 U.S.C. § 206 or 207], and the agreement of any employee to accept such payment shall upon payment in full constitute a waiver by such employee of any right he may have under subsection (b) of this section to such unpaid minimum wages or unpaid overtime compensation and an additional equal amount as liquidated damages. The Secretary may bring an action in any court of competent jurisdiction to recover the amount of the unpaid minimum wages or overtime compensation and an equal amount as liquidated damages. The right provided by subsection (b) to bring to recover the liability specified in the first sentence of such subsection and of any employee to become a party plaintiff to any such action shall terminate upon the filing of a complaint by the Secretary in an action under this subsection in which a recovery is sought of unpaid minimum wages or unpaid overtime compensation under sections 6 and 7 [29 U.S.C. §§ 206 and 207] or liquidated or other damages provided by this subsection owing to such employee by an employer liable under the provisions of subsection (b), unless such action is dismissed without prejudice on motion of the Secretary. Any sums thus recovered by the Administrator [Secretary] on behalf of an employee pursuant to this subsection shall be held in a special deposit account and shall be paid, on order of the Administrator [Secretary], directly to the employee or employees affected. Any such sums not paid to an employee because of inability to do so within a period of three years shall be covered into the Treasury of the United States as miscellaneous receipts. In determining when an action is commenced by the Administrator [Secretary] under this subsection for the purposes of the statutes of limitations provided in section 6(a) of the Portal-to-Portal Act of 1947 [29 U.S.C. § 255(a)], it shall be considered to be commenced in the case of any individual claimant on the date when the complaint is filed if he is specifically named as a party plaintiff in the complaint, or if his name did not so appear, on the subsequent date on which his name is added as a party plaintiff in such action.

* * *

(June 25, 1938, ch. 676, § 16, 52 Stat. 1069; May 14, 1947, ch. 52, Part IV, § 5(a), 61 Stat. 87; Oct. 26, 1949, ch. 736, § 14, 63 Stat. 919; Aug. 8, 1956, ch. 1035, § 4, 70 Stat. 1118; Pub. L. 85–231, § 1(2), 71 Stat. 514; Pub. L. 87–30, § 12(a), 75 Stat. 74; Pub. L. 89–601, Title VI, § 601(a), 80 Stat. 844; April 8, 1974, Pub. L. 93–259, §§ 6(d)(1), 25(c), 26, 88 Stat. 61, 72, 73; Pub.L. 95–151, § 10, 91 Stat. 1252; Pub.L. 101–157, § 9, 103 Stat. 945; Pub.L. 101–508, Title III, Subtitle B, 104 Stat. 1388–29, as amended, Pub .L. 104–174, § 2, 110 Stat. 1554.)

§ 217. (§ 17) Injunction proceedings

The district courts, together with the United States District Court for the District of the Canal Zone, the District Court of the Virgin Islands, and the District Court of Guam shall have jurisdiction, for cause shown, to restrain violations of section 15 [29 U.S.C. § 215], including in the case of violations of section 15(a)(2) [29 U.S.C. § 215(a)(2)] the restraint of any withholding of payment of minimum wages or overtime compensation found by the court to be due to employees under this Act (except sums which employees are barred from recovering, at the time of the commencement of the action to restrain the violations, by virtue of the provisions of section 6 of the Portal-to-Portal Act of 1947 [29 U.S.C. § 255]).

(June 25, 1938, ch. 676, § 17, 52 Stat. 1069; Oct. 26, 1949, ch. 736, § 15, 63 Stat. 919; Pub. L. 85–231, § 1(3), 71 Stat. 514; Pub. L. 86–624, § 21(c), 74 Stat. 417; Pub. L. 87–30, § 12(b), 75 Stat. 74.)

§ **254.   Relief from liability and punishment under the Fair Labor Standards Act of 1938, the Walsh–Healy Act, and the Bacon–Davis Act for failure to pay minimum wage or overtime compensation**

(a) Activities not compensable. Except as provided in subsection (b), no employer shall be subject to any liability or punishment under the Fair Labor Standards Act of 1938, as amended [29 U.S.C. §§ 201 et seq.] the Walsh–Healey Act [41 U.S.C. §§ 35 et seq.], or the Bacon–Davis Act [40 U.S.C. §§ 276a et seq.], on account of the failure of such employer to pay an employee minimum wages, or to pay an employee overtime compensation, for or on account of any of the following activities of such employee engaged in on or after the date of the enactment of this Act [May 14, 1947]—

(1) walking, riding, or traveling to and from the actual place of performance of the principal activity or activities which such employee is employed to perform, and

(2) activities which are preliminary to or postliminary to said principal activity or activities, which occur either prior to the time on any particular workday at which such employee commences, or subsequent to the time on any particular workday at which he ceases, such principal activity or activities. For purposes of this subsection, the use of an employer's vehicle for travel by an employee and activities performed by an employee which are incidental to the use of such vehicle for commuting shall not be considered part of the employee's principal activities if the use of such vehicle for travel is within the normal commuting area for the employer's business or establishment and the use of the employer's vehicle is subject to an agreement on the part of the employer and the employee or representative of such employee.

(b) Compensability by contract or custom. Notwithstanding the provisions of subsection (a) which relieve an employer from liability and punishment with respect to an activity, the employer shall not be so relieved if such activity is compensable by either—

(1) an express provision of a written or nonwritten contract in effect, at the time of such activity, between such employee, his agent, or collective-bargaining representative and his employer; or

(2) a custom or practice in effect, at the time of such activity, at the establishment or other place where such employee is employed, covering such activity, not inconsistent with a written or nonwritten contract, in effect at the time of such activity, between such employee, his agent, or collective-bargaining representative and his employer.

(c) Restriction of time employed with respect to activities. For the purposes of subsection (b), an activity shall be considered as compensable under such contract provision or such custom or practice only when it is engaged in during the portion of the day with respect to which it is so made compensable.

(d) Determination of time employed with respect to activities. In the application of the minimum wage and overtime compensation provisions of the Fair Labor Standards Act of 1938, as amended [29 U.S.C. §§ 201 et seq.], of the Walsh–Healey Act [41 U.S.C. §§ 35 et seq.], or of the Bacon–Davis Act [40 U.S.C. §§ 276a et seq.], in determining the time for which an employer employs an employee with respect to walking, riding, traveling, or other preliminary or postliminary activities described in subsection (a) of this section, there shall be counted all that time, but only that time, during which the employee engages in any such activity which is compensable within the meaning of subsections (b) and (c) of this section.

(May 14, 1947, ch. 52, Part III, § 4, 61 Stat. 86, as amended, Pub. L. 104–188, Title II, § 2102, 110 Stat. 1928.)

§ 255. Statute of limitations

Any action commenced on or after the date of the enactment of this Act [May 14, 1947] to enforce any cause of action for unpaid minimum wages, unpaid overtime compensation, or liquidated damages, under the Fair Labor Standards Act of 1938, as amended [29 U.S.C. §§ 201 et seq.], the Walsh–Healey Act [41 U.S.C. §§ 35 et seq.], or the Bacon–Davis Act [40 U.S.C. §§ 276a et seq.]—

(a) if the cause of action accrues on or after the date of the enactment of this Act [May 14, 1947]—may be commenced within two years after the cause of action accrued, and every such action shall be forever barred unless commenced within two years after the cause of action accrued, except that a cause of action arising out of a willful violation may be commenced within three years after the cause of action accrued;

* * *

(May 14, 1947, ch. 52, Part IV, § 6, 61 Stat. 87; Pub. L. 89–601, Title VI, § 601(b), 80 Stat. 844; Pub. L. 93–259, § 6(d)(2)(A), 88 Stat. 61.)

§ 256. Determination of commencement of future actions

In determining when an action is commenced for the purposes of section 6 [29 U.S.C. § 255], an action commenced on or after the date of the enactment of this Act [May 14, 1947] under the Fair Labor Standards Act of 1938, as amended [29 U.S.C. §§ 201 et seq.], the Walsh–Healey Act [41 U.S.C. §§ 35 et seq.], or the Bacon–Davis Act [40 U.S.C. §§ 276a et seq.], shall be considered to be commenced on the date when the complaint is filed; except that in the case of a collective or class action instituted under the Fair Labor Standards Act of 1938, as amended [29 U.S.C. §§ 201 et seq.], or the Bacon–Davis Act [40 U.S.C. §§ 276a et seq.], it shall be considered to be commenced in the case of any individual claimant—

(a) on the date when the complaint is filed, if he is specifically named as a party plaintiff in the complaint and his written consent to become a party plaintiff is filed on such date in the court in which the action is brought; or

(b) if such written consent was not so filed or if his name did not so appear—on the subsequent date on which such written consent is filed in the court in which the action was commenced.

(May 14, 1947, ch. 52, Part IV, § 7, 61 Stat. 88.)

§ 259. Reliance in future on administrative rulings

(a) In any action or proceeding based on any act or omission on or after the date of the enactment of this Act [May 14, 1947], no employer shall be subject to any liability or punishment for or on account of the failure of the employer to pay minimum wages or overtime compensation under the Fair Labor Standards Act of 1938, as amended [29 U.S.C. §§ 201 et seq.], the Walsh–Healey Act [41 U.S.C. §§ 35 et seq.], or the Bacon–Davis Act [40 U.S.C. §§ 276a et seq.], if he pleads and proves that the act or omission complained of was in good faith in conformity with and in reliance on any written administrative regulation, order, ruling, approval, or interpretation, of the agency of the United States specified in subsection (b) of this section, or any administrative practice or enforcement policy of such agency with respect to the class of employers to which he belonged. Such a defense, if established, shall be a bar to the action or proceeding, notwithstanding that after such act or omission, such administrative regulation, order, ruling, approval, interpretation, practice, or enforcement policy is modified or rescinded or is determined by judicial authority to be invalid or of no legal effect.

* * *

(May 14, 1947, ch. 52, Part IV, § 10, 61 Stat. 89.)

§ 260. Liquidated damages

In any action commenced prior to or on or after the date of the enactment of this Act [May 14, 1947] to recover unpaid minimum wages, unpaid overtime compensation, or liquidated damages, under the Fair Labor Standards Act of 1938, as amended [29 U.S.C. §§ 201 et seq.], if the employer shows to the satisfaction of the court that the act or omission giving rise to such action was in good faith and that he had reasonable grounds for believing that his act or omission was not a violation of the Fair Labor Standards Act of 1938, as amended, the court may, in its sound discretion, award no liquidated damages or award any amount thereof not to exceed the amount specified in section 16 of such Act [29 U.S.C. § 216].

(May 14, 1947, ch. 52, Part IV, § 11, 61 Stat. 89; Pub. L. 93–259, § 6(d)(2)(b), 88 Stat. 62.)

EMPLOYEE RETIREMENT INCOME SECURITY ACT OF 1974* (ERISA)— SELECTED PROVISIONS

29 U.S.C. §§ 1001–02, 1021, 1025, 1052–54, 1056, 1082, 1103–04, 1106–09, 1132–33, 1140, 1144, 1161–13, 1322, 1344

§ 1001. Congressional findings and declaration of policy [omitted]

§ 1002. Definitions

For purposes of this title:

(1) The terms "employee welfare benefit plan" and "welfare plan" mean any plan, fund, or program which was heretofore or is hereafter established or maintained by an employer or by an employee organization, or by both, to the extent that such plan, fund, or program was established or is maintained for the purpose of providing for its participants or their beneficiaries, through the purchase of insurance or otherwise, (A) medical, surgical, or hospital care or benefits, or benefits in the event of sickness, accident, disability, death or unemployment, or vacation benefits, apprenticeship or other training programs, or day care centers, scholarship funds, or prepaid legal services, or (B) any benefit described in section 302(c) of the Labor Management Relations Act, 1947 [29 U.S.C. § 186(c)] (other than pensions on retirement or death, and insurance to provide such pensions).

(2)(A) Except as provided in subparagraph (B), the terms "employee pension benefit plan" and "pension plan" mean any plan, fund, or program which was heretofore or is hereafter established or maintained by an employer or by an employee organization, or by both, to the extent that by its express terms or as a result of surrounding circumstances such plan, fund, or program—

(i) provided retirement income to employees, or

(ii) results in a deferral of income by employees for periods extending to the termination of covered employment or beyond,

regardless of the method of calculating the contributions made to the plan, the method of calculating the benefits under the plan or the method of distributing benefits from the plan. * * *

(B) The Secretary may by regulation prescribe rules consistent with the standards and purposes of this Act providing one or more exempt categories under which—

(i) severance pay arrangements, and

---

* Includes relevant provisions of Consolidated Budget Reconciliation Act of 1986, 29 U.S.C. §§ 1161 et seq.

(ii) supplemental retirement income payments, under which the pension benefits of retirees or their beneficiaries are supplemented to take into account some portion or all of the increases in the cost of living (as determined by the Secretary of Labor) since retirement,

shall, for purposes of this title, be treated as welfare plans rather than pension plans. In the case of any arrangement or payment a principal effect of which is the evasion of the standards or purposes of this Act applicable to pension plans, such arrangement or payment shall be treated as a pension plan. * * *

(3) The term "employee benefit plan" or "plan" means an employee welfare benefit plan or an employee pension benefit plan or a plan which is both an employee welfare benefit plan and an employee pension benefit plan.

* * *

(5) The term "employer" means any person acting directly as an employer, or indirectly in the interest of an employer, in relation to an employee benefit plan; and includes a group or association of employers acting for an employer in such capacity.

(6) The term "employee" means any individual employed by an employer.

(7) The term "participant" means any employee or former employee of an employer, or any member or former member of an employee organization, who is or may become eligible to receive a benefit of any type from an employee benefit plan which covers employees of such employer or members of such organization, or whose beneficiaries may be eligible to receive any such benefit.

(8) The term "beneficiary" means a person designated by a participant, or by the terms of an employee benefit plan, who is or may become entitled to a benefit thereunder.

* * *

(21)(A) Except as otherwise provided in subparagraph (B), a person is a fiduciary with respect to a plan to the extent (i) he exercises any discretionary authority or discretionary control respecting management of such plan or exercises any authority or control respecting management or disposition of its assets, (ii) he renders investment advice for a fee or other compensation, direct or indirect, with respect to any moneys or other property of such plan, or has any authority or responsibility to do so, or (iii) he has any discretionary authority or discretionary responsibility in the administration of such plan. Such term includes any person designated under section 405(c)(1)(B) [29 U.S.C. § 1105(c)(1)(B)].

(B) If any money or other property of an employee benefit plan is invested in securities issued by an investment company registered under the Investment Company Act of 1940, such investment shall not by itself cause such investment company or such investment company's investment adviser or principal underwriter to be deemed to be a fiduciary or a party in interest as those terms are defined in this title, except insofar as such investment company or its investment adviser or principal underwriter acts in connection with an employee benefit plan covering employees of the investment company, the investment adviser, or its principal underwriter. Nothing contained in this subparagraph shall limit the duties imposed on such investment company, investment adviser, or principal underwriter by any other law.

(22) The term "normal retirement benefit" means the greater of the early retirement benefit under the plan, or the benefit under the plan commencing at normal retirement age. The normal retirement benefit shall be determined without regard to—

(A) medical benefits, and

(B) disability benefits not in excess of the qualified disability benefit.

For purposes of this paragraph, a qualified disability benefit is a disability benefit provided by a plan which does not exceed the benefit which would be provided for the participant if he separated from the service at normal retirement age. For purposes of this paragraph, the early retirement benefit under a plan shall be determined without regard to any benefit under the plan which the Secretary of the Treasury finds to be a benefit described in section 204(b)(1)(G) [29 U.S.C. § 1054(b)(1)(G)].

(23) The term "accrued benefit" means—

(A) in the case of a defined benefit plan, the individual's accrued benefit determined under the plan and, except as provided in section 204(c)(3) [29 U.S.C. § 1054(c)(3)], expressed in the form of an annual benefit commencing at normal retirement age, or

(B) in the case of a plan which is an individual account plan, the balance of the individual's account.

The accrued benefit of an employee shall not be less than the amount determined under section 204(c)(2)(B) [29 U.S.C. § 1054(c)(2)(B)] with respect to the employee's accumulated contribution.

(24) The term "normal retirement age" means the earlier of—

(A) the time a plan participant attains normal retirement age under the plan, or

(B) the later of—

(i) the time a plan participant attains age 65, or

(ii) the 5th anniversary of the time a plan participant commenced participation in the plan.

(25) The term "vested liabilities" means the present value of the immediate or deferred benefits available at normal retirement age for participants and their beneficiaries which are nonforfeitable.

(26) The term "current value" means fair market value where available and otherwise the fair value as determined in good faith by a trustee or a named fiduciary (as defined in section 402(a)(2) [29 U.S.C. § 1102(a)(2)]) pursuant to the terms of the plan and in accordance with regulations of the Secretary, assuming an orderly liquidation at the time of such determination.

(27) The term "present value", with respect to a liability, means the value adjusted to reflect anticipated events. Such adjustments shall conform to such regulations as the Secretary of the Treasury may prescribe.

(28) The term "normal service cost" or "normal cost" means the annual cost of future pension benefits and administrative expenses assigned, under an actuarial cost method, to years subsequent to a particular valuation date of a pension plan. The Secretary of the Treasury may prescribe regulations to carry out this paragraph.

(29) The term "accrued liability" means the excess of the present value, as of a particular valuation date of a pension plan, of the projected future benefit costs and administrative expenses for all plan participants and beneficiaries over the present value of future contributions for the normal cost of all applicable plan participants and beneficiaries. The Secretary of the Treasury may prescribe regulations to carry out this paragraph.

(30) The term "unfunded accrued liability" means the excess of the accrued liability, under an actuarial cost method which so provided, over the present value of the assets of a pension plan. The Secretary of the Treasury may prescribe regulations to carry out this paragraph.

(31) The term "advance funding actuarial cost method" or "actuarial cost method" means a recognized actuarial technique utilized for establishing the amount and incidence of the annual actuarial cost of pension plan benefits and expenses. Acceptable actuarial cost methods shall include the accrued benefit cost method (unit credit method), the entry age normal cost method, the individual level premium cost method, the aggregate cost method, the attained age normal cost method, and the frozen initial liability cost method. The terminal funding cost method and the current funding (pay-as-you-go) cost method are not acceptable actuarial cost methods. The Secretary of the Treasury shall issue regulations to further define acceptable actuarial cost methods.

* * *

(37)(A) The term "multiemployer plan" means a plan—

    (i) to which more than one employer is required to contribute,

(ii) which is maintained pursuant to one or more collective bargaining agreements between one or more employee organizations and more than one employer, and

(iii) which satisfies such other requirements as the Secretary may prescribe by regulation.

(B) For purposes of this paragraph, all trades or businesses (whether or not incorporated) which are under common control within the meaning of section 4001(b)(1) [29 U.S.C. § 1301(b)(1)] are considered a single employer.

(C) Notwithstanding subparagraph (A), a plan is a multiemployer plan on and after its termination date if the plan was a multiemployer plan under this paragraph for the plan year preceding its termination date.

(D) For purposes of this title, notwithstanding the preceding provisions of this paragraph, for any plan year which began before the date of the enactment of the Multiemployer Pension Plan Amendments Act of 1980 [Sept. 26, 1980], the term "multiemployer plan" means a plan described in section 3(37) of this Act [para. (37) of this section] as in effect immediately before such date.

* * *

(41) Single-employer plan. The term "single-employer plan" means an employee benefit plan other than a multiemployer plan.

(Sept. 2, 1974, Pub. L. 93–406, Title I, Subtitle A, § 3, 88 Stat. 833; Pub. L. 96–364, Title III, §§ 302, 305, Title IV, §§ 407(a), 409, 94 Stat. 1291, 1294, 1303, 1307; Pub. L. 97–473, Title III, § 302(a), 96 Stat. 2612; Pub. L. 99–272, Title XI, § 11016(c)(1), 100 Stat. 273; Pub. L. 99–509, Title IX, Subtitle C, § 9203(b)(1), 100 Stat. 1979; Pub. L. 99–514, Title XVIII, Subtitle A, ch. 7, § 1879(u)(3), 100 Stat. 2913; Pub. L. 100–202, § 136(a), 101 Stat. 1329–441; Pub. L. 101–239, Title VII, Subtitle G, Part V, Subpart B, § 7871(b)(2), Subpart C, § 7881(m)(2)(D), Subpart D, §§ 7891(a)(1), 7893(a), 7894(a)(1)(A), (2)(A), (3), (4), 103 Stat. 2435, 2444, 2445, 2447, 2448; Pub. L. 101–508, Title XII, Subtitle A, § 12002(b)(2)(C), 104 Stat. 1388–566; Aug. 14, 1991, Pub. L. 102–89, § 2, 105 Stat. 446; Pub. L. 104–290, Title III, § 308(b)(1), 110 Stat. 3440; Pub. L. 105–72, § 1(a), 111 Stat. 1457.)

§ 1021. Duty of disclosure and reporting

(a) Summary plan description and information to be furnished to participants and beneficiaries. The administrator of each employee benefit plan shall cause to be furnished in accordance with section 104(b) [29 U.S.C. § 1024(b)] to each participant covered under the plan and to each beneficiary who is receiving benefits under the plan—

(1) a summary plan description described in section 102(a)(1) [29 U.S.C. § 1022(a)(1)]; and

(2) the information described in sections 104(b)(3) and 105(a) and (c) [29 U.S.C. §§ 1024(b)(3), 1025(a) and (c)].

(b) Plan description, modifications and changes, and reports to be filed with Secretary of Labor. The administrator shall, in accordance with section 104(a) [29 U.S.C. § 1024(a)], file with the Secretary—

(1) the annual report containing the information required by section 103 [29 U.S.C. § 1023]; and

(2) terminal and supplementary reports as required by subsection (c) of this section.

(c) Terminal and supplementary reports.

(1) Each administrator of an employee pension benefit plan which is winding up its affairs (without regard to the number of participants remaining in the plan) shall, in accordance with regulations prescribed by the Secretary, file such terminal reports as the Secretary may consider necessary. A copy of such report shall also be filed with the Pension Benefit Guaranty Corporation.

(2) The Secretary may require terminal reports to be filed with regard to any employee welfare benefit plan which is winding up its affairs in accordance with regulations promulgated by the Secretary.

(3) The Secretary may require that a plan described in paragraph (1) or (2) file a supplementary or terminal report with the annual report in the year such plan is terminated and that a copy of such supplementary or terminal report in the case of a plan described in paragraph (1) be also filed with the Pension Benefit Guaranty Corporation.

(d) Notice of failure to meet minimum funding standards.

(1) If an employer maintaining a plan other than a multiemployer plan fails to make a required installment or other payment required to meet the minimum funding standard under section 302 [29 U.S.C. § 1082] to a plan before the 60th day following the due date for such installment or other payment, the employer shall notify each participant and beneficiary (including an alternate payee as defined in section 206(d)(3)(K) [29 U.S.C. § 1056(d)(3)(K)]) of such plan of such failure. Such notice shall be made at such time and in such manner as the Secretary may prescribe.

(2) This subsection shall not apply to any failure if the employer has filed a waiver request under section 303 [29 U.S.C. § 1083] with respect to the plan year to which the required installment relates, except that if the waiver request is denied, notice under paragraph (1) shall be provided within 60 days after the date of such denial.

(3) For purposes of this subsection, the terms "required installment" and "due date" have the same meanings given such terms by section 302(e) [29 U.S.C. § 1082(e)].

* * *

(h) Simple retirement accounts.

(1) Except as provided in this subsection, no report shall be required under this section by an employer maintaining a qualified salary reduction arrangement under section 408(p) of the Internal Revenue Code of 1986 [26 U.S.C. § 408(p)].

* * *

(Sept. 2, 1974, P.L. 93–406, Title I, Subtitle B, Part 1, § 101, 88 Stat. 840; Dec. 22, 1987, P.L. 100–203, Title IX, Subtitle D, Part II, Subpart A, § 9304(d), 101 Stat. 1330–348; Dec. 19, 1989, P.L. 101–239, Title VII, Subtitle G, Part V, Subpart C, § 7881(b)(5)(A), Subpart D, § 7894(b)(2), 103 Stat. 2438, 2448; Nov. 5, 1990, P.L. 101–508, Title XII, Subtitle B, § 12012(d)(1), 104 Stat. 1388–572; Aug. 10, 1993, P.L. 103–66, Title IV, Subtitle D, § 4301(b), 107 Stat. 375; Dec. 8, 1994, P.L. 103–465, Title VII, Subtitle D, § 731(c)(4)(A), 108 Stat. 5004; Aug. 20, 1996, P.L. 104–188, Title I, Subtitle D, Ch. 2, Subch. A, § 1421(d)(1), 110 Stat. 1799; Aug. 21, 1996, P.L. 104–191, Title I, Subtitle A, Part 1, § 101(e)(1), 110 Stat. 1952; Sept. 26, 1996, P.L. 104–204, Title VI, § 603(b)(3)(B), 110 Stat. 2938; Aug. 5, 1997, P.L. 105–34, Title XV, Subtitle A, § 1503(a), 111 Stat. 1061; July 16, 1998, P.L. 105–200, Title IV, § 401(h)(1)(A), 112 Stat. 668; Dec. 17, 1999, P.L. 106–170, Title V, Subtitle C, Part I, § 535(a)(2)(A), 113 Stat. 1934; July 30, 2002, P.L. 107–204, Title III, § 306(b)(1), 116 Stat. 780; April 10, 2004, P.L. 108–218, Title I, § 103(a), Title II, § 204(b)(1), 118 Stat. 602, 609; Oct. 22, 2004, P.L. 108–357, Title VII, § 709(a)(1), 118 Stat. 1551; Aug. 17, 2006, P.L. 109–280, Title I, Subtitle A, §§ 103(b)(1), 108(a)(1), (11) [107(a)(1), (11)], Title V, §§ 501(a), 502(a)(1), (b)(1), 503(c)(2), 507(a), 509(a), 120 Stat. 815, 818, 819, 939, 940, 944, 936, 948, 952; Dec. 23, 2008, P.L. 110–458, Title I, Subtitle A, §§ 101(c)(1)(A), 105(a), (b)(1), (g), 122 Stat. 5097, 5104, 5105; March 23, 2010, P.L. 111–148, Title VI, Subtitle G, § 6606, 124 Stat. 781; June 25, 2010, P.L. 111–192, Title II, Subtitle A, § 202(a), 124 Stat. 1297.)

§ 1025.   Reporting of participant's benefit rights

(a) Requirements to provide pension benefit statements.

(1) Requirements.

(A) Individual account plan. The administrator of an individual account plan (other than a one-participant retirement plan described in section 101(i)(8)(B)) shall furnish a pension benefit statement—

(i) at least once each calendar quarter to a participant or beneficiary who has the right to direct the investment of assets in his or her account under the plan,

(ii) at least once each calendar year to a participant or beneficiary who has his or her own account under the plan but does not have the right to direct the investment of assets in that account, and

(iii) upon written request to a plan beneficiary not described in clause (i) or (ii).

(B) Defined benefit plan, he administrator of a defined benefit plan (other than a one-participant retirement plan described in section 101(i)(8)(B)) shall furnish a pension benefit statement—

(i) at least once every 3 years to each participant with a nonforfeitable accrued benefit and who is employed by the employer maintaining the plan at the time the statement is to be furnished, and

(ii) to a participant or beneficiary of the plan upon written request.

Information furnished under clause (i) to a participant may be based on reasonable estimates determined under regulations prescribed by the Secretary, in consultation with the Pension Benefit Guaranty Corporation.

(2) Statements.

(A) In general. A pension benefit statement under paragraph (1)—

(i) shall indicate, on the basis of the latest available information—

(I) the total benefits accrued, and

(II) the nonforfeitable pension benefits, if any, which have accrued, or the earliest date on which benefits will become nonforfeitable,

(ii) shall include an explanation of any permitted disparity under section 401(l) of the Internal Revenue Code of 1986 or any floor-offset arrangement that may be applied in determining any accrued benefits described in clause (i),

(iii) shall be written in a manner calculated to be understood by the average plan participant, and

(iv) may be delivered in written, electronic, or other appropriate form to the extent such form is reasonably accessible to the participant or beneficiary.

(B) Additional information. In the case of an individual account plan, any pension benefit statement under clause (i) or (ii) of paragraph (1)(A) shall include—

(i) the value of each investment to which assets in the individual account have been allocated, determined as of the most recent valuation date under the plan, including the value of any assets held in the form of employer securities, without regard to whether such securities were contributed by the plan sponsor or acquired at the direction of the plan or of the participant or beneficiary, and

(ii) in the case of a pension benefit statement under paragraph (1)(A)(i)—

(I) an explanation of any limitations or restrictions on any right of the participant or beneficiary under the plan to direct an investment,

(II) an explanation, written in a manner calculated to be understood by the average plan participant, of the importance, for the long-term retirement security of participants and beneficiaries, of a well-balanced and diversified investment portfolio, including a statement of the risk that holding more than 20 percent of a portfolio in the security of one entity (such as employer securities) may not be adequately diversified, and

(III) a notice directing the participant or beneficiary to the Internet website of the Department of Labor for sources of information on individual investing and diversification.

(C) Alternative notice. The requirements of subparagraph (A)(i)(II) are met if, at least annually and in accordance with requirements of the Secretary, the plan—

(i) updates the information described in such paragraph which is provided in the pension benefit statement, or

(ii) provides in a separate statement such information as is necessary to enable a participant or beneficiary to determine their nonforfeitable vested benefits.

(3) Defined benefit plans.

(A) Alternative notice. In the case of a defined benefit plan, the requirements of paragraph (1)(B)(i) shall be treated as met with respect to a participant if at least once each year the administrator provides to the participant notice of the availability of the pension benefit statement and the ways in which the participant may obtain such statement. Such notice may be delivered in written, electronic, or other appropriate form to the extent such form is reasonably accessible to the participant.

(B) Years in which no benefits accrue. The Secretary may provide that years in which no employee or former employee benefits (within the meaning of section 410(b) of the Internal Revenue Code of 1986) under the plan need not be taken into account in determining the 3–year period under paragraph (1)(B)(i).

* * *

(Sept. 2, 1974, P.L. 93–406, Title I, Subtitle B, Part 1, § 105, 88 Stat. 849; Aug. 23, 1984, P.L. 98–397, Title I, § 106, 98 Stat. 1436; Dec. 19, 1989, P.L. 101–239, Title VII, Subtitle G, Part V, Subpart D,

§§ 7891(a)(1), 7894(b) (5), 103 Stat. 2445, 2448; Aug. 17, 2006, P.L. 109–280, Title V, § 508(a)(1), (2)(A), (B), 120 Stat. 949.)

§ 1052. Minimum participation standards

(a)(1)(A) No pension plan may require, as a condition of participation in the plan, that an employee complete a period of service with the employer or employers maintaining the plan extending beyond the later of the following dates—

(i) the date on which the employee attains the age of 21; or

(ii) the date on which he completes 1 year of service.

(B)(i) In the case of any plan which provides that after not more than 2 years of service each participant has a right to 100 percent of his accrued benefit under the plan which is nonforfeitable at the time such benefit accrues, clause (ii) of subparagraph (A) shall be applied by substituting "2 years of service" for "1 year of service".

* * *

(Sept. 2, 1974, Pub. L. 93–406, Title I, Subtitle B, Part 2, § 202, 88 Stat. 853; Pub.L. 98–397, Title I, § 102(a), (d)(1), (e)(1), 98 Stat. 1426, 1427; Pub. L. 99–509, Title IX, Subtitle C, § 9203(a)(1), 100 Stat. 1979; Pub. L. 99–514, Title XI, Subtitle A, Part II, Subpt. A, § 1113(e)(3), 100 Stat. 2448; Pub. L. 101–239, Title VII, Subtitle G, Part V, Subpart A, § 7861(a)(2), Subpart D, §§ 7891(a)(1), 7892(a), 7894(c)(2), 103 Stat. 2430, 2445, 2447, 2449.)

§ 1053. Minimum vesting standards

(a) **Nonforfeitability requirements.** Each pension plan shall provide that an employee's right to his normal retirement benefit is nonforfeitable upon the attainment of normal retirement age and in addition shall satisfy the requirements of paragraphs (1) and (2) of this subsection.

(1) A plan satisfies the requirements of this paragraph if an employee's rights in his accrued benefit derived from his own contributions are nonforfeitable.

(2)(A)(i) In the case of a defined benefit plan, a plan satisfies the requirements of this paragraph if it satisfies the requirements of clause (ii) or (iii).

(ii) A plan satisfies the requirements of this clause if an employee who has completed at least 5 years of service has a nonforfeitable right to 100 percent of the employee's accrued benefit derived from employer contributions.

(iii) A plan satisfies the requirements of this clause if an employee has a nonforfeitable right to a percentage of the employee's accrued benefit derived from employer contributions determined under the following table:

Years of Service	The nonforfeitable percentage is:
3	20
4	40
5	60
6	80
7 or more	100.

(B)

(i) In the case of an individual account plan, a plan satisfies the requirements of this paragraph if it satisfies the requirements of clause (ii) or (iii).

(ii) A plan satisfies the requirements of this clause if an employee who has completed at least 3 years of service has a nonforfeitable right to 100 percent of the employee's accrued benefit derived from employer contributions.

(iii) A plan satisfies the requirements of this clause if an employee has a nonforfeitable right to a percentage of the employee's accrued benefit derived from employer contributions determined under the following table:

Years of Service	The nonforfeitable percentage is:
2	20
3	40
4	60
5	80
6 or more	100.

(3)(A) A right to an accrued benefit derived from employer contributions shall not be treated as forfeitable solely because the plan provides that it is not payable if the participant dies (except in the case of a survivor annuity which is payable as provided in section 205).

(B) A right to an accrued benefit derived from employer contributions shall not be treated as forfeitable solely because the plan provides that the payment of benefits is suspended for such period as the employee is employed, subsequent to the commencement of payment of such benefits—

(i) in the case of a plan other than a multiemployer plan, by an employer who maintains the plan under which such benefits were being paid; and

(ii) in the case of a multiemployer plan, in the same industry, in the same trade or craft, and the same geographic area covered by the plan, as when such benefits commenced.

The Secretary shall prescribe such regulations as may be necessary to carry out the purposes of this subparagraph, including regulations with respect to the meaning of the term "employed".

(C) A right to an accrued benefit derived from employer contributions shall not be treated as forfeitable solely because plan amendments may be given retroactive application as provided in section 302(d)(2).

(D)(i) A right to an accrued benefit derived from employer contributions shall not be treated as forfeitable solely because the plan provides that, in the case of a participant who does not have a nonforfeitable right to at least 50 percent of his accrued benefit derived from employer contributions, such accrued benefit may be forfeited on account of the withdrawal by the participant of any amount attributable to the benefit derived from mandatory contributions (as defined in the last sentence of section 204(c)(2)(C) made by such participant).

(ii) Clause (i) shall not apply to a plan unless the plan provides that any accrued benefit forfeited under a plan provision described in such clause shall be restored upon repayment by the participant of the full amount of the withdrawal described in such clause plus, in the case of a defined benefit plan, interest. Such interest shall be computed on such amount at the rate determined for purposes of section 204(c)(2)(C) (if such subsection applies) on the date of such repayment (computed annually from the date of such withdrawal). The plan provision required under this clause may provide that such repayment must be made (I) in the case of a withdrawal on account of separation from service, before the earlier of 5 years after the first date on which the participant is subsequently re-employed by the employer, or the close of the first period of 5 consecutive 1-year breaks in service commencing after the withdrawal; or (II) in the case of any other withdrawal, 5 years after the date of the withdrawal.

* * *

(E)(i) A right to an accrued benefit derived from employer contributions under a multiemployer plan shall not be treated as forfeitable solely because the plan provides that benefits accrued as a result of service with the participant's employer before the employer had an obligation to contribute under the plan may not be payable if the employer ceases contributions to the multiemployer plan.

* * *

(Sept. 2, 1974, P.L. 93–406, Title I, Subtitle B, Part 2, § 203, 88 Stat. 854; Sept. 26, 1980, P.L. 96–364, Title III, § 303, 94 Stat. 1292; Aug. 23,

1984, P.L. 98–397, Title I, §§ 102(b), (c), (d)(2), (e)(2), 105(a), 98 Stat. 1426–1428, 1436; Oct. 22, 1986, P.L. 99–514, Title XI, Subtitle A, Part II, Subpart A, § 1113(e)(1), (2), (4)(A), Part IV, § 1139(c)(1), Title XVIII, Subtitle C, Ch. 2, § 1898(a)(1)(B), (4)(B)(i), (d)(1)(B), (2)(B), 100 Stat. 2447, 2448, 2487, 2942, 2944, 2955; Dec. 19, 1989, P.L. 101–239, Title VII, Subtitle G, Part V, Subpart A, §§ 7861(a) (1), (5)(B), (6)(B), 7862(d)(4), (5), (10), Subpart D, §§ 7891(a)(1), (b)(1)(2), 7894(c)(3), 103 Stat. 2430, 2434, 2445, 2449; Dec. 8, 1994, P.L. 103–465, Title VII, Subtitle F, Part I, Subpart C, § 767(c)(1), 108 Stat. 5039; Aug. 20, 1996, P.L. 104–188, Title I, Subtitle D, Ch. 4, § 1442(b), 110 Stat. 1808; Aug. 5, 1997, P.L. 105–34, Title X, Subtitle H, § 1071(b)(1), 111 Stat. 948; June 7, 2001, P.L. 107–16, Title VI, Subtitle C, § 633(b), Subtitle D, § 648 (a)(2), 115 Stat. 116, 127; Oct. 4, 2004, P.L. 108–311, Title IV, § 408(b)(8), 118 Stat. 1193; Aug. 17, 2006, P.L. 109–280, Title I, Subtitle A, § 107(a)(4), Title VII, § 701(a)(2), Title IX, §§ 902(d)(2)(E), 904(b), 120 Stat. 819, 984, 1038, 1049.)

§ 1054. Benefit accrual requirements

(a) Satisfaction of requirements by pension plans. Each pension plan shall satisfy the requirements of subsection (b)(3), and—

(1) in the case of a defined benefit plan, shall satisfy the requirements of subsection (b)(1); and

(2) in the case of a defined contribution plan, shall satisfy the requirements of subsection (b)(2).

(b) Enumeration of plan requirements.

(1)(A) A defined benefit plan satisfies the requirements of this paragraph if the accrued benefit to which each participant is entitled upon his separation from the service is not less than—

(i) 3 percent of the normal retirement benefit to which he would be entitled at the normal retirement age if he commenced participation at the earliest possible entry age under the plan and served continuously until the earlier of age 65 or the normal retirement age specified under the plan, multiplied by

(ii) the number of years (not in excess of 33 1/3) of his participation in the plan.

In the case of a plan providing retirement benefits based on compensation during any period, the normal retirement benefit to which a participant would be entitled shall be determined as if he continued to earn annually the average rate of compensation which he earned during consecutive years of service, not in excess of 10, for which his compensation was the highest. For purposes of this subparagraph, social security benefits and all other relevant factors used to compute benefits shall be treated as remaining constant as of the current year for all years after such current year.

* * *

(2)(A) A defined contribution plan satisfies the requirements of this paragraph if, under the plan, allocations to the employee's account are not ceased, and the rate at which amounts are allocated to the employee's account is not reduced, because of the attainment of any age.

(B) A plan shall not be treated as failing to meet the requirements of subparagraph (A) solely because the subsidized portion of any early retirement benefit is disregarded in determining benefit accruals.

* * *

(Sept. 2, 1974, Pub. L. 93–406, Title I, Subtitle B, Part 2, § 204, 88 Stat. 858; Pub.L. 98–397, Title I, §§ 102(e)(3), (f), 105(b), Title III, § 301(a)(2), 98 Stat. 1429, 1436, 1451; Pub.L. 99–272, Title XI, § 11006(a), 100 Stat. 243; Pub.L. 99–509, Title IX, Subtitle C, § 9202(a), 100 Stat. 1975; Pub.L. 99–514, Title XI, Subtitle A, Part II, Subpart A, § 1113(e)(4)(B), Title XVIII, Subtitle A, ch. 7, § 1879(u)(1), Subtitle C, Ch. 2, § 1898(a)(4)(B)(ii), (f)(1)(B), (2), 100 Stat. 2448, 2913, 2944, 2956; Pub.L. 100–203, Title IX, Subtitle D, Part II, Subpart D, § 9346(a), 101 Stat. 1330–374; Pub.L. 101–239, Title VII, Subtitle G, Part V, Subpart A, § 7862(b)(1)(A), (2), Subpart B, § 7871(a)(1), (3) Subpart C, § 7881(m)(2)(A)–(C), Subpart D, § 7891(a)(1), 7894(c)(4)–(6), 103 Stat. 2432, 2435, 2444, 2445, 2449; Pub. L. 103–465, Title VII, Subtitle F, Part I, Subpart C, § 766(a), 108 Stat. 5036; Pub. L. 105–34, Title X, Subtitle H, § 1071(b)(2), 111 Stat. 948.)

§ 1056. Form and payment of benefits

(a) Commencement date for payment of benefits. Each pension plan shall provide that unless the participant otherwise elects, the payment of benefits under the plan to the participant shall begin not later than the 60th day after the latest of the close of the plan year in which—

(1) occurs the date on which the participant attains the earlier of age 65 or the normal retirement age specified under the plan,

(2) occurs the 10th anniversary of the year in which the participant commenced participation in the plan, or

(3) the participant terminates his service with the employer.

In the case of a plan which provides for the payment of an early retirement benefit, such plan shall provide that a participant who satisfied the service requirements for such early retirement benefit, but separated from the service (with any nonforfeitable right to an accrued benefit) before satisfying the age requirement for such early retirement benefit, is entitled upon satisfaction of such age requirement to receive a benefit not less than the benefit to which he would be entitled at the normal retirement age, actuarially reduced under regulations prescribed by the Secretary of the Treasury.

(b) Decrease in plan benefits by reason of increases in benefit levels under Social Security Act or Railroad Retirement Act of 1937. If—

(1) a participant or beneficiary is receiving benefits under a pension plan, or

(2) a participant is separated from the service and has nonforfeitable rights to benefits,

a plan may not decrease benefits of such a participant by reason of any increase in the benefit levels payable under title II of the Social Security Act [42 U.S.C. §§ 401 et seq.] or the Railroad Retirement Act of 1937, or any increase in the wage base under such title II [42 U.S.C. §§ 401 et seq.], if such increase takes place after the date of the enactment of this Act [enacted Sept. 2, 1974] or (if later) the earlier of the date of first entitlement of such benefits or the date of such separation.

(c) Forfeitures of accrued benefits derived from employer contributions. No pension plan may provide that any part of a participant's accrued benefit derived from employer contributions (whether or not otherwise nonforfeitable) is forfeitable solely because of withdrawal by such participant of any amount attributable to the benefit derived from contributions made by such participant. The preceding sentence shall not apply (1) to the accrued benefit of any participant unless, at the time of such withdrawal, such participant has a nonforfeitable right to at least 50 percent of such accrued benefit, or (2) to the extent that an accrued benefit is permitted to be forfeited in accordance with section 203(a)(3)(D)(iii) [29 U.S.C. § 1053(a)(3)(D)(iii)].

(d) Assignment or alienation of plan benefits.

(1) Each pension plan shall provide that benefits provided under the plan may not be assigned or alienated.

(2) For the purposes of paragraph (1) of this subsection, there shall not be taken into account any voluntary and revocable assignment of not to exceed 10 percent of any benefit payment, or of any irrevocable assignment or alienation of benefits executed before the date of enactment of this Act [Sept. 2, 1974]. The preceding sentence shall not apply to any assignment or alienation made for the purposes of defraying plan administration costs. For purposes of this paragraph a loan made to a participant or beneficiary shall not be treated as an assignment or alienation if such loan is secured by the participant's accrued nonforfeitable benefit and is exempt from the tax imposed by section 4975 of the Internal Revenue Code of 1986 [26 U.S.C. § 4975] (relating to tax on prohibited transactions) by reason of section 4975(d)(1) of such Code [26 U.S.C. § 4975(d)(1)].

(3)(A) Paragraph (1) shall apply to the creation, assignment, or recognition of a right to any benefit payable with respect to a participant pursuant to a domestic relations order, except that paragraph (1) shall not apply if the order is determined to be a qualified domestic relations order. Each pension plan shall provide for the payment of benefits in accordance with the applicable requirements of any qualified domestic relations order.

* * *

(Sept. 2, 1974, Pub. L. 93–406, Title I, Subtitle B, Part 2, § 206, 88 Stat. 864; Pub.L. 98–397, Title I, § 104(a), 98 Stat. 1433; Pub.L. 99–514, Title XVIII, Subtitle C, ch. 2, § 1898(c)(2)(B), (4)(B), (5), (6)(B), (7)(B), 100 Stat. 2952–2954; Pub.L. 101–239, Title VII, Subtitle G, Part V, Subpart D, §§ 7891(a)(1), 7894(c)(8), (9)(A), 103 Stat. 2445, 2449; Pub.L. 103–465, Title VII, Subtitle F, Part I, Subpart B, § 761(a)(9)(B)(i), Part II, § 776(c)(2), 108 Stat. 5033, 5048; Pub.L. 105–34, Title XV, Subtitle A, § 1502(a), 111 Stat. 1058.)

§ 1103. Establishment of trust

(a) Benefit plan assets to be held in trust; authority of trustees. Except as provided in subsection (b), all assets of an employee benefit plan shall be held in trust by one or more trustees. Such trustee or trustees shall be either named in the trust instrument or in the plan instrument described in section 402(a) [29 U.S.C. § 1102(a)] or appointed by a person who is a named fiduciary, and upon acceptance of being named or appointed, the trustee or trustees shall have exclusive authority and discretion to manage and control the assets of the plan, except to the extent that—

(1) the plan expressly provides that the trustee or trustees are subject to the direction of a named fiduciary who is not a trustee, in which case the trustees shall be subject to proper directions of such fiduciary which are made in accordance with the terms of the plan and which are not contrary to this Act, or

(2) authority to manage, acquire, or dispose of assets of the plan is delegated to one or more investment managers pursuant to section 402(c)(3) [28 U.S.C. § 1102(c)(3)].

(b) Exceptions. The requirements of subsection (a) of this section shall not apply—

(1) to any assets of a plan which consist of insurance contracts or policies issued by an insurance company qualified to do business in a State;

(2) to any assets of such an insurance company or any assets of a plan which are held by such an insurance company;

(3) to a plan—

(A) some or all of the participants of which are employees described in section 401(c)(1) of the Internal Revenue Code of 1986 [26 U.S.C. § 401(c)(1)]; or

(B) which consists of one or more individual retirement accounts described in section 408 of the Internal Revenue Code of 1986 [26 U.S.C. § 408];

to the extent that such plan's assets are held in one or more custodial accounts which qualify under section 401(f) or 408(h) of such Code [26 U.S.C. § 401(f) or 408(h)], whichever is applicable.

(4) to a plan which the Secretary exempts from the requirement of subsection (a) and which is not subject to any of the following provisions of this Act—

(A) part 2 of this subtitle [29 U.S.C. §§ 1051 et seq.],

(B) part 3 of this subtitle [29 U.S.C. §§ 1081 et seq.], or

(C) title IV of this Act; or

(5) to a contract established and maintained under section 403(b) of the Internal Revenue Code of 1986 [26 U.S.C. § 403(b)] to the extent that the assets of the contract are held in one or more custodial accounts pursuant to section 403(b)(7) of such Code [26 U.S.C. § 403(b)(7)].

(6) Any plan, fund or program under which an employer, all of whose stock is directly or indirectly owned by employees, former employees or their beneficiaries, proposes through an unfunded arrangement to compensate retired employees for benefits which were forfeited by such employees under a pension plan maintained by a former employer prior to the date such pension plan became subject to this Act.

(c) Assets of plan not to inure to benefit of employer; allowable purposes of holding plan assets.

(1) Except as provided in paragraph (2), (3), or (4) or subsection (d), or under section 4042 and 4044 [29 U.S.C. §§ 1342, 1344] (relating to termination of insured plans), or under section 420 of the Internal Revenue Code of 1986 [26 U.S.C. § 420] (as in effect on the date of the enactment of the Pension Funding Equity Act of 2004), the assets of a plan shall never inure to the benefit of any employer and shall be held for the exclusive purposes of providing benefits to participants in the plan and their beneficiaries and defraying reasonable expenses of administering the plan.

* * *

(d) Termination of plan.

(1) Upon termination of a pension plan to which section 4021 [29 U.S.C. § 1321] does not apply at the time of termination and to which this part [29 U.S.C. §§ 1101 et seq.] applies (other than a plan to which no employer contributions have been made) the assets of the plan shall be allocated in accordance with the provisions of section 4044 of this Act [29 U.S.C. § 1344], except as otherwise provided in regulations of the Secretary.

(2) The assets of a welfare plan which terminates shall be distributed in accordance with the terms of the plan, except as otherwise provided in regulations of the Secretary.

(Sept. 2, 1974, P.L. 93–406, Title I, Subtitle B, Part 4, § 403, 88 Stat. 876; Sept. 26, 1980, P.L. 96–364, Title III, § 310, Title IV, §§ 402(b)(2), 410(a), 411(c), 94 Stat. 1296, 1299, 1308; Dec. 22, 1987, P.L. 100–203, Title IX, Subtitle D, Part II, Subpart D, § 9343(c), 101 Stat. 1330–372; Dec. 19, 1989, P.L. 101–239, Title VII, Subtitle G, Part V, Subpart C, § 7881(k), Subpart D, §§ 7891(a)(1), 7894(e)(1)(A), (3), 103 Stat. 2443, 2445, 2450; Nov. 5, 1990, P.L. 101–508, Title XII, Subtitle B, § 12012(a), 104 Stat. 1388–571; Dec. 8, 1994, P.L. 103–465, Title VII, Subtitle D, § 731(c)(4)(B), 108 Stat. 5004; Dec. 17, 1999, P.L. 106–170, Title V, Subtitle C, Part I, § 535(a)(2)(B), 113 Stat. 1934; April 10, 2004, P.L. 108–218, Title II, § 204(b)(2), 118 Stat. 609; Oct. 22, 2004, P.L. 108–357, Title VII, § 709(a)(2), 118 Stat. 1551; Aug. 17, 2006, P.L. 109–280, Title I, Subtitle A, § 108(a)(11) [107(a)(11)], 120 Stat. 819; June 25, 2010, P.L. 111–192, Title II, Subtitle A, § 202(a), 124 Stat. 1297.)

§ 1104. Fiduciary duties

(a) Prudent man standard of care.

(1) Subject to sections 403(c) and (d), 4042, and 4044, a fiduciary shall discharge his duties with respect to a plan solely in the interest of the participants and beneficiaries and—

(A) for the exclusive purpose of:

(i) providing benefits to participants and their beneficiaries; and

(ii) defraying reasonable expenses of administering the plan;

(B) with the care, skill, prudence, and diligence under the circumstances then prevailing that a prudent man acting in a like capacity and familiar with such matters would use in the conduct of an enterprise of a like character and with like aims;

(C) by diversifying the investments of the plan so as to minimize the risk of large losses, unless under the circumstances it is clearly prudent not to do so; and

(D) in accordance with the documents and instruments governing the plan insofar as such documents and instruments are consistent with the provisions of this title and title IV.

(2) In the case of an eligible individual account plan (as defined in section 407(d)(3)), the diversification requirement of paragraph (1)(C) and the prudence requirement (only to the extent that it requires diversification) of paragraph (1)(B) is not violated by acquisition or holding of qualifying employer real property or qualifying employer securities (as defined in section 407(d)(4) and (5)).

* * *

(c) Control over assets by participant or beneficiary.

(1) (A) In the case of a pension plan which provides for individual accounts and permits a participant or beneficiary to exercise control over assets in his account, if a participant or beneficiary exercises control over the assets in his account (as determined under regulations of the Secretary)—

(i) such participant or beneficiary shall not be deemed to be a fiduciary by reason of such exercise, and

(ii) no person who is otherwise a fiduciary shall be liable under this part [29 USCS 1101 et seq.] for any loss, or by reason of any breach, which results from such participant's or beneficiary's exercise of control, except that this clause shall not apply in connection with such participant or beneficiary for any blackout period during which the ability of such participant or beneficiary to direct the investment of the assets in his or her account is suspended by a plan sponsor or fiduciary.

(B) If a person referred to in subparagraph (A)(ii) meets the requirements of this title in connection with authorizing and implementing the blackout period, any person who is otherwise a fiduciary shall not be liable under this title for any loss occurring during such period.

(C) For purposes of this paragraph, the term "blackout period" has the meaning given such term by section 101(i)(7) [29 U.S.C. 1021(i)(7)]. * * *

(5) Default investment arrangements.

(A) In general. For purposes of paragraph (1), a participant or beneficiary in an individual account plan meeting the notice requirements of subparagraph (B) shall be treated as exercising control over the assets in the account with respect to the amount of contributions and earnings which, in the absence of an investment election by the participant or beneficiary, are invested by the plan in accordance with regulations prescribed by the Secretary. The regulations under this subparagraph shall provide guidance on the appropriateness of designating default investments that include a mix of asset classes consistent with capital preservation or long-term capital appreciation, or a blend of both.

(B) Notice requirements.

(i) In general. The requirements of this subparagraph are met if each participant—

(I) receives, within a reasonable period of time before each plan year, a notice explaining the employee's right under the plan to designate how contributions and earnings will be invested and explaining how, in the absence of any investment election by the participant or beneficiary, such contributions and earnings will be invested, and

(II) has a reasonable period of time after receipt of such notice and before the beginning of the plan year to make such designation. * * *

(Sept. 2, 1974, P.L. 93–406, Title I, Subtitle B, Part 4, § 404, 88 Stat. 877; Sept. 26, 1980, P.L. 96–364, Title III, § 309, 94 Stat. 1296; Nov. 5, 1990, P.L. 101–508, Title XII, Subtitle A, § 12002(b)(1), (2)(A) 104 Stat. 1388–565; Aug. 20, 1996, P.L. 104–188, Title I, Subtitle D, Ch. 2, Subch. A, § 1421(d)(2), 110 Stat. 1799; June 7, 2001, P.L. 107–16, Title VI, Subtitle E, Part I, § 657(c)(1), 115 Stat. 136; March 9, 2002, P.L. 107–147, Title IV, Subtitle B, § 411(t), 116 Stat. 51; Aug. 17, 2006, P.L. 109–280, Title VI, Subtitle C, §§ 621(a), 624(a), 120 Stat. 978, 980; Dec. 23, 2008, P.L. 110–458, Title I, Subtitle A, § 106(d), 122 Stat. 5107.)

§ 1106. Prohibited transactions

(a) Transactions between plan and party in interest. Except as provided in section 408 [29 U.S.C. § 1108]:

(1) A fiduciary with respect to a plan shall not cause the plan to engage in a transaction, if he knows or should know that such transaction constitutes a direct or indirect—

(A) sale or exchange, or leasing, of any property between the plan and a party in interest;

(B) lending of money or other extension of credit between the plan and a party in interest;

(C) furnishing of goods, services, or facilities between the plan and a party in interest;

(D) transfer to, or use by or for the benefit of, a party in interest, of any assets of the plan; or

(E) acquisition, on behalf of the plan, of any employer security or employer real property in violation of section 407(a) [29 U.S.C. § 1107(a)].

(2) No fiduciary who has authority or discretion to control or manage the assets of a plan shall permit the plan to hold any employer security or employer real property if he knows or should know that holding such security or real property violates section 407(a) [29 U.S.C. § 1107(a)].

(b) Transactions between plan and fiduciary. A fiduciary with respect to a plan shall not—

(1) deal with the assets of the plan in his own interest or for his own account,

(2) in his individual or in any other capacity act in any transaction involving the plan on behalf of a party (or represent a party)

whose interests are adverse to the interests of the plan or the interests of its participants or beneficiaries, or

(3) receive any consideration for his own personal account from any party dealing with such plan in connection with a transaction involving the assets of the plan.

* * *

(Sept. 2, 1974, Pub. L. 93–406, Title I, Subtitle B, Part 4, § 406, 88 Stat. 879.)

§ 1107.   Limitation with respect to acquisition and holding of employer securities and employer real property by certain plans

(a) **Percentage limitation.** Except as otherwise provided in this section and section 414 [29 U.S.C. § 1114]:

(1) A plan may not acquire or hold—

(A) any employer security which is not a qualifying employer security, or

(B) any employer real property which is not qualifying employer real property.

(2) A plan may not acquire any qualifying employer security or qualifying employer real property, if immediately after such acquisition the aggregate fair market value of employer securities and employer real property held by the plan exceeds 10 percent of the fair market value of the assets of the plan.

(3)(A) After December 31, 1984, a plan may not hold any qualifying employer securities or qualifying employer real property (or both) to the extent that the aggregate fair market value of such securities and property determined on December 31, 1984, exceeds 10 percent of the greater of—

(i) the fair market value of the assets of the plan, determined on December 31, 1984, or

(ii) the fair market value of the assets of the plan determined on January 1, 1975.

(B) Subparagraph (A) of this paragraph shall not apply to any plan which on any date after December 31, 1974; and before January 1, 1985, did not hold employer securities or employer real property (or both) the aggregate fair market value of which determined on such date exceeded 10 percent of the greater of

(i) the fair market value of the assets of the plan, determined on such date, or

(ii) the fair market value of the assets of the plan determined on January 1, 1975.

(4)(A) After December 31, 1979, a plan may not hold any employer securities or employer real property in excess of the amount specified in regulations under subparagraph (B). This subparagraph shall not apply to a plan after the earliest date after December 31, 1974, on which it complies with such regulations.

(B) Not later than December 31, 1976, the Secretary shall prescribe regulations which shall have the effect of requiring that a plan divest itself of 50 percent of the holdings of employer securities and employer real property which the plan would be required to divest before January 1, 1985, under paragraph (2) or subsection (c) (whichever is applicable).

(b) Exception. [omitted]

(Sept. 2, 1974, Pub. L. 93–406, Title I, Subtitle B, Part 4, § 407, 88 Stat. 880; Pub. L. 100–203, Title IX, Subtitle D, Part II, Subpart D, § 9345(a)(1), (2), (b), 101 Stat. 1330–373; Pub.L. 101–239, Title VII, Subtitle G, Part V, Subpart C, § 7881(*l*)(1)–(4), Subpart D, §§ 7891(a)(1), 7894(e)(2), 103 Stat. 2443, 2445, 2450; Pub.L. 101–540, § 1, 104 Stat. 2379; Pub.L. 105–34, Title XV, Subtitle B, § 1524(a), 111 Stat. 1071.)

§ 1108. Exemptions from prohibited transactions

* * *

(c) Fiduciary benefits and compensation not prohibited by 29 U.S.C. § 1106. Nothing in section 406 [29 U.S.C. § 1106] shall be construed to prohibit any fiduciary from—

(1) receiving any benefit to which he may be entitled as a participant or beneficiary in the plan, so long as the benefit is computed and paid on a basis which is consistent with the terms of the plan as applied to all other participants and beneficiaries;

(2) receiving any reasonable compensation for services rendered, or for the reimbursement of expenses properly and actually incurred, in the performance of his duties with the plan; except that no person so serving who already receives full-time pay from an employer or an association of employers, whose employees are participants in the plan, or from an employee organization whose members are participants in such plan shall receive compensation from such plan, except for reimbursement of expenses properly and actually incurred; or

(3) serving as a fiduciary in addition to being an officer, employee, agent, or other representative of a party in interest.

* * *

(Sept. 2, 1974, Pub. L. 93–406, Title I, Subtitle B, Part 4, § 408, 88 Stat. 883; Pub.L. 96–364, Title III, § 308, 94 Stat. 1295; Pub.L. 97–354, § 5(a)(43), 96 Stat. 1697; Pub.L. 99–514, Title XI, Subtitle A, Part II, Subpart A, § 1114(b)(15)(B), Title XVIII, Subtitle C, ch. 2, § 1898(i)(1),

100 Stat. 2452, 2957; Pub.L. 101–239, Title VII, Subtitle G, Part V, Subpart C, § 7881(*l*)(5), Subpart D, §§ 7891(a), 7894(e)(4)(A), 103 Stat. 2443, 2445, 2450; Pub.L. 101–508, Title XII, Subtitle B, § 12012(b), 104 Stat. 1388–571; Pub.L. 103–465, Title VII, Subtitle D, § 731(c)(4)(C), 108 Stat. 5004; Pub.L. 104–188, Title I, Subtitle G, § 1704(n)(2), 110 Stat. 1886; Pub.L. 105–34, Title XV, Subtitle A, § 1506(b)(2), 111 Stat. 1066, as amended, Pub. L. 106–170, Title V, Subtitle C, Part I, § 535(a)(2)(C), 113 Stat. 1934.)

§ 1109. Liability for breach of fiduciary duty

(a) Any person who is a fiduciary with respect to a plan who breaches any of the responsibilities, obligations, or duties imposed upon fiduciaries by this title shall be personally liable to make good to such plan any losses to the plan resulting from each such breach, and to restore to such plan any profits of such fiduciary which have been made through use of assets of the plan by the fiduciary, and shall be subject to such other equitable or remedial relief as the court may deem appropriate, including removal of such fiduciary. A fiduciary may also be removed for a violation of section 411 of this Act [29 U.S.C. § 1111].

(b) No fiduciary shall be liable with respect to a breach of fiduciary duty under this title if such breach was committed before he became a fiduciary or after he ceased to be a fiduciary.

(Sept. 2, 1974, Pub. L. 93–406, Title I, Subtitle B, Part 4, § 409, 88 Stat. 886.)

§ 1132. Civil enforcement

(a) Persons empowered to bring a civil action. A civil action may be brought—

(1) by a participant or beneficiary—

(A) for the relief provided for in subsection (c) of this section, or

(B) to recover benefits due to him under the terms of his plan, to enforce his rights under the terms of the plan, or to clarify his rights to future benefits under the terms of the plan;

(2) by the Secretary, or by a participant, beneficiary or fiduciary for appropriate relief under section 409 [29 U.S.C. § 1109];

(3) by a participant, beneficiary, or fiduciary (A) to enjoin any act or practice which violates any provision of this title or the terms of the plan, or (B) to obtain other appropriate equitable relief (i) to redress such violations or (ii) to enforce any provisions of this title or the terms of the plan;

(4) by the Secretary, or by a participant, or beneficiary for appropriate relief in the case of a violation of 105(c) [29 U.S.C. § 1025(c)];

(5) except as otherwise provided in subsection (b), by the Secretary (A) to enjoin any act or practice which violates any provision of this title, or (B) to obtain other appropriate equitable relief (i) to redress such violation or (ii) to enforce any provision of this title;

(6) by the Secretary to collect any civil penalty under paragraph (2), (4), (5), (6) , (7), (8), (9) of subsection (c) or under subsection (i) or (l);

* * *

(b) Plans qualified under Internal Revenue Code; maintenance of actions involving delinquent contributions. [omitted]

(c) Administrator's refusal to supply requested information; penalty for failure to provide annual report in complete form.

(1)Any administrator (A) who fails to meet the requirements of paragraph (1) or (4) of section 606, section 101(e)(1), section 101(f), or section 105(a) [29 U.S.C. 1166(a)(1) or (4), 1021(e)(1), 1021(f), or 1025(a)] with respect to a participant or beneficiary, or (B) who fails or refuses to comply with a request for any information which such administrator is required by this title to furnish to a participant or beneficiary (unless such failure or refusal results from matters reasonably beyond the control of the administrator) by mailing the material requested to the last known address of the requesting participant or beneficiary within 30 days after such request may in the court's discretion be personally liable to such participant or beneficiary in the amount of up to $100 a day from the date of such failure or refusal, and the court may in its discretion order such other relief as it deems proper. For purposes of this paragraph, each violation described in subparagraph (A) with respect to any single participant, and each violation described in subparagraph (B) with respect to any single participant or beneficiary, shall be treated as a separate violation.

(2)The Secretary may assess a civil penalty against any plan administrator of up to $1,000 a day from the date of such plan administrator's failure or refusal to file the annual report required to be filed with the Secretary under section 101(b)(1) [29 U.S.C. 1021(b)(1)]. For purposes of this paragraph, an annual report that has been rejected under section 104(a)(4) [29 U.S.C. 1024(a)(4)] for failure to provide material information shall not be treated as having been filed with the Secretary.

(3) Any employer maintaining a plan who fails to meet the notice requirement of section 101(d) [29 U.S.C. 1021(d)] with respect to any participant or beneficiary or who fails to meet the requirements of section 101(e)(2) [29 U.S.C. 1021(e)(2)] with respect to any person or who fails to meet the requirements of section 302(d)(12)(E) with respect to any person may in the court's discretion be liable to such participant or beneficiary or to such person in the amount of up to $100 a day from the date of such failure, and

the court may in its discretion order such other relief as it deems proper.

(d) Status of employee benefit plan as entity.

(1) An employee benefit plan may sue or be sued under this title as an entity. Service of summons, subpena, or other legal process of a court upon a trustee or an administrator of an employee benefit plan in his capacity as such shall constitute service upon the employee benefit plan. In a case where a plan has not designated in the summary plan description of the plan an individual as agent for the service of legal process, service upon the Secretary shall constitute such service. The Secretary, not later than 15 days after receipt of service under the preceding sentence, shall notify the administrator or any trustee of the plan of receipt of such service.

(2) Any money judgment under this title against an employee benefit plan shall be enforceable only against the plan as an entity and shall not be enforceable against any other person unless liability against such person is established in his individual capacity under this title.

(e) Jurisdiction.

(1) Except for actions under subsection (a)(1)(B) of this section, the district courts of the United States shall have exclusive jurisdiction of civil actions under this title brought by the Secretary or by a participant, beneficiary, fiduciary, or any person referred to in section 101(f)(1) [29 U.S.C. § 1021(f)(1)]. State courts of competent jurisdiction and district courts of the United States shall have concurrent jurisdiction of actions under paragraphs (1)(B) and (7) of subsection (a) of this section.

(2) Where an action under this title is brought in a district court of the United States, it may be brought in the district where the plan is administered, where the breach took place, or where a defendant resides or may be found, and process may be served in any other district where a defendant resides or may be found.

(f) Amount in controversy; citizenship of parties. The district courts of the United States shall have jurisdiction, without respect to the amount in controversy or the citizenship of the parties, to grant the relief provided for in subsection (a) of this section in any action.

(g) Attorney's fees and costs; awards in actions involving delinquent contributions. [omitted]

(h) Service upon Secretary of Labor and Secretary of the Treasury. [omitted]

(i) Administrative assessment of civil penalty. In the case of a transaction prohibited by section 406 [29 U.S.C. § 1106] by a party in interest with respect to a plan to which this part applies, the Secretary may assess a civil penalty against such party in interest. The amount of such penalty may not exceed 5 percent of the amount involved in each such transaction (as defined in section 4975(f)(4) of the Internal Revenue Code of 1986 [26 U.S.C. § 4975(f)(4)]) for each year or part thereof during which the prohibited transaction continues, except that, if the transaction is not corrected (in such manner as the Secretary shall prescribe in regulations which shall be consistent with section 4975(f)(5) of such Code [26 U.S.C. § 4975(f)(5)]) within 90 days after notice from the Secretary (or such longer period as the Secretary may permit), such penalty may be in an amount not more than 100 percent of the amount involved. This subsection shall not apply to a transaction with respect to a plan described in section 4975(e)(1) of such Code [26 U.S.C. § 4975(e)(1)].

(j) Direction and control of litigation by Attorney General. [omitted]

(k) Jurisdiction of actions against the Secretary of Labor. Suits by an administrator, fiduciary, participant, or beneficiary of an employee benefit plan to review a final order of the Secretary, to restrain the Secretary from taking any action contrary to the provisions of this Act, or to compel him to take action required under this title, may be brought in the district court of the United States for the district where the plan has its principal office, or in the United States District Court for the District of Columbia.

***(l)* Civil penalties on violations by fiduciaries.**

(1) In the case of—

(A) any breach of fiduciary responsibility under (or other violation of) part 4 [29 U.S.C. §§ 1101 et seq.] by a fiduciary, or

(B) any knowing participation in such a breach or violation by any other person,

the Secretary shall assess a civil penalty against such fiduciary or other person in an amount equal to 20 percent of the applicable recovery amount.

(2) For purposes of paragraph (1), the term "applicable recovery amount" means any amount which is recovered from a fiduciary or other person with respect to a breach or violation described in paragraph (1)—

(A) pursuant to any settlement agreement with the Secretary, or

(B) ordered by a court to be paid by such fiduciary or other person to a plan or its participants and beneficiaries in a judicial proceeding instituted by the Secretary under subsection (a)(2) or (a)(5).

(3) The Secretary may, in the Secretary's sole discretion, waive or reduce the penalty under paragraph (1) if the Secretary determines in writing that—

(A) the fiduciary or other person acted reasonably and in good faith, or

(B) it is reasonable to expect that the fiduciary or other person will not be able to restore all losses to the plan (or to provide the relief ordered pursuant to subsection (a)(9)) without severe financial hardship unless such waiver or reduction is granted.

(4) The penalty imposed on a fiduciary or other person under this subsection with respect to any transaction shall be reduced by the amount of any penalty or tax imposed on such fiduciary or other person with respect to such transaction under subsection (i) of this section and section 4975 of the Internal Revenue Code of 1986 [26 U.S.C. § 4975].

* * *

(Sept. 2, 1974, P.L. 93–406, Title I, Subtitle B, Part 5, § 502, 88 Stat. 891; Sept. 26, 1980, P.L. 96–364, Title III, § 306(b), 94 Stat. 1295; April 7, 1986, P.L. 99–272, Title X, § 10002(b), 100 Stat. 231; Dec. 22, 1987, P.L. 100–203, Title IX, Subtitle D, Part II, Subpart D, §§ 9342(c), 9344, 101 Stat. 1330–372, 1330–373, Dec. 19, 1989, P.L. 101–239, Title II, Subtitle B, § 2101(a), (b), Title VII, Subtitle G, Part V, Subpart C, § 7881(b)(5)(B), (j)(2), (3), Subpart D, §§ 7891(a)(1), 7894(f)(1), 103 Stat. 2123, 2438, 2442, 2445, 2450; Nov. 5, 1990, P.L. 101–508, Title XII, Subtitle B, § 12021(d)(2), 104 Stat. 1388–573; Aug. 10, 1993, P.L. 103–66, Title IV, Subtitle D, § 4301(c)(1)–(3), 107 Stat. 376; Oct. 22, 1994, P.L. 103–401, §§ 2, 3, 108 Stat. 4172; Dec. 8, 1994, P.L. 103–465, Title VII, Subtitle F, Part I, Subpart B, § 761(a)(9)(B)(ii), 108 Stat. 5033; Aug. 21, 1996, P.L. 104–191, Title I, Subtitle A, Part 1, § 101(b), (e)(2), 110 Stat. 1951, 1952; Sept. 26, 1996, P.L. 104–204, Title VI, § 603(b)(3)(E), 110 Stat. 2938; Aug. 5, 1997, P.L. 105–34, Title XV, Subtitle A, § 1503(c)(2)(B), (d)(7), 111 Stat. 1062; July 30, 2002, P.L. 107–204, Title III, § 306(b)(3), 116 Stat. 783; April 10, 2004, P.L. 108–218, Title I, §§ 102(d), 103(b), 104(a)(2), 118 Stat. 602, 603, 606; Aug. 17, 2006, P.L. 109–280, Title I, Subtitle A, § 103(b)(2), Title II, Subtitle A, § 202(b), (c), Title V, §§ 502(a)(2), (b)(2), 507(b), 508(a)(2)(C), Title IX, § 902(f)(2), 120 Stat. 816, 884, 940, 941, 949, 951, 1039; May 21, 2008, P.L. 110–233, Title I, § 101(e), 122 Stat. 886; Dec. 23, 2008, P.L. 110–458, Title I, Subtitle A, §§ 101(c)(1)(H), 102(b)(1)(H), (I), 122 Stat. 5097, 5101; Feb. 4, 2009, P.L. 111–3, Title III, Subtitle B, § 311(b)(1)(E), 123 Stat. 70.)

§ 1133. Claims procedure

In accordance with regulations of the Secretary, every employee benefit plan shall—

(1) provide adequate notice in writing to any participant or beneficiary whose claim for benefits under the plan has been denied, setting forth the specific reasons for such denial, written in a manner calculated to be understood by the participant, and

(2) afford a reasonable opportunity to any participant whose claim for benefits has been denied for a full and fair review by the appropriate named fiduciary of the decision denying the claim.

(Sept. 2, 1974, Pub. L. 93–406, Title I, Subtitle B, Part 5, § 503, 88 Stat. 893.)

§ 1140. Interference with protected rights

It shall be unlawful for any person to discharge, fine, suspend, expel, discipline, or discriminate against a participant or beneficiary for exercising any right to which he is entitled under the provisions of an employee benefit plan, this title, section 3001 [29 U.S.C. § 1201], or the Welfare and Pension Plans Disclosure Act, or for the purpose of interfering with the attainment of any right to which such participant may become entitled under the plan, this title, or the Welfare and Pension Plans Disclosure Act. It shall be unlawful for any person to discharge, fine, suspend, expel, or discriminate against any person because he has given information or has testified or is about to testify in any inquiry or proceeding relating to this Act or the Welfare and Pension Plans Disclosure Act. In the case of a multiemployer plan, it shall be unlawful for the plan sponsor or any other person to discriminate against any contributing employer for exercising rights under this Act or for giving information or testifying in any proceeding relating to this Act before Congress. The provisions of section 502 [29 U.S.C. § 1132] shall be applicable in the enforcement of this section.

(Sept. 2, 1974, Pub. L. 93–406, Title I, Subtitle B, Part 5, § 510, 88 Stat. 895, Pub. l. 109–280, 120 Stat. 889.)

§ 1144. Other laws

(a) Except as provided in subsection (b) of this section, the provisions of this subchapter and subchapter III of this chapter shall supersede any and all State laws insofar as they may now or hereafter relate to any employee benefit plan described in section 1003(a) of this title and not exempt under section 1003(b) of this title. This section shall take effect on January 1, 1975.

(b)(1) This section shall not apply with respect to any cause of action which arose, or any act or omission which occurred, before January 1, 1975.

(2)(A) Except as provided in subparagraph (B), nothing in this subchapter shall be construed to exempt or relieve any person from any law of any State which regulates insurance, banking, or securities.

(B) Neither an employee benefit plan described in section 1003(a) of this title, which is not exempt under section 1003(b) of this title (other than a plan established primarily for the purpose of providing death benefits), nor any trust established under such a plan, shall be deemed to be an insurance company or other insurer, bank, trust company, or investment company or to be engaged in the business of insurance or banking for purposes of any law of any State purporting to regulate insurance companies, insurance contracts, banks, trust companies, or investment companies.

(3) Nothing in this section shall be construed to prohibit use by the Secretary of services or facilities of a State agency as permitted under section 1136 of this title.

(4) Subsection (a) of this section shall not apply to any generally applicable criminal law of a State.

* * *

(6)(A) Notwithstanding any other provision of this section—

(i) in the case of an employee welfare benefit plan which is a multiple employer welfare arrangement and is fully insured (or which is a multiple employer welfare arrangement subject to an exemption under subparagraph (B)), any law of any State which regulates insurance may apply to such arrangement to the extent that such law provides—

(I) standards, requiring the maintenance of specified levels of reserves and specified levels of contributions, which any such plan, or any trust established under such a plan, must meet in order to be considered under such law able to pay benefits in full when due, and

(II) provisions to enforce such standards, and

(ii) in the case of any other employee welfare benefit plan which is a multiple employer welfare arrangement, in addition to this subchapter, any law of any State which regulates insurance may apply to the extent not inconsistent with the preceding sections of this subchapter.

(B) The Secretary may, under regulations which may be prescribed by the Secretary, exempt from subparagraph (A)(ii), individually or by class, multiple employer welfare arrangements which are not fully insured. Any such exemption may be granted with respect to any arrangement or class of arrangements only if such arrangement or each arrangement which is a member of such class meets the requirements of section 1002(1) and section 1003 of this title necessary to be considered an employee welfare benefit plan to which this subchapter applies.

(C) Nothing in subparagraph (A) shall affect the manner or extent to which the provisions of this subchapter apply to an employee welfare benefit plan which is not a multiple employer welfare arrangement and which is a plan, fund, or program participating in, subscribing to, or otherwise using a multiple employer welfare arrangement to fund or administer benefits to such plan's participants and beneficiaries.

(D) For purposes of this paragraph, a multiple employer welfare arrangement shall be considered fully insured only if the terms of the arrangement provide for benefits the amount of all of which the Secretary determines are guaranteed under a contract, or policy of insurance, issued by an insurance company, insurance service, or insurance organization, qualified to conduct business in a State.

(7) Subsection (a) shall not apply to qualified domestic relations orders (within the meaning of section 1056(d)(3)(B)(i) of this title).

(8) Subsection (a) of this section shall not apply to any State law mandating that an employee benefit plan not include any provision which has the effect of limiting or excluding coverage or payment for any health care for an individual who would otherwise be covered or entitled to benefits or services under the terms of the employee benefit plan, because that individual is provided, or is eligible for, benefits or services pursuant to a plan under title XIX of the Social Security Act [42 U.S.C. § 1396 et seq.], to the extent such law is necessary for the State to be eligible to receive reimbursement under title XIX of that Act.

(c) For purposes of this section:

(1) The term "State law" includes all laws, decisions, rules, regulations, or other State action having the effect of law, of any State. A law of the United States applicable only to the District of Columbia shall be treated as a State law rather than a law of the United States.

(2) The term "State" includes a State, any political subdivisions thereof, or any agency or instrumentality of either, which purports to regulate, directly or indirectly, the terms and conditions of employee benefit plans covered by this subchapter.

(d) Nothing in this subchapter shall be construed to alter, amend, modify, invalidate, impair, or supersede any law of the United States (except as provided in sections 1031 and 1137(b) of this title) or any rule or regulation issued under any such law.

* * *

(Pub.L. 93–406, Title I, § 514, Sept. 2, 1974, 88 Stat. 897; Pub.L. 97–473, Title III, §§ 301(a), 302(b), Jan. 14, 1983, 96 Stat. 2611, 2613; Pub.L. 98–397, Title I, § 104(b), 98 Stat. 1436; Apr. 7, 1986, 100 Stat. 207.)

§ 1161. Plans must provide continuation coverage to certain individuals

(a) **In general.** The plan sponsor of each group health plan shall provide, in accordance with this part [29 U.S.C. §§ 1161 et seq.], that each qualified beneficiary who would lose coverage under the plan as a result of a qualifying event is entitled, under the plan, to elect, within the election period, continuation coverage under the plan.

(b) Exception for certain plans. Subsection (a) shall not apply to any group health plan for any calendar year if all employers maintaining such plan normally employed fewer than 20 employees on a typical business day during the preceding calendar year.

(Sept. 2, 1974, Pub. L. 93–406, Title I, Subtitle B, Part 6, § 601, as added, April 7, 1986, Pub. L. 99–272, Title X, § 10002(a), 100 Stat. 227; Pub. L. 101–239, Title VII, Subtitle G, Part V, Subpart A, § 7862(c)(1)(B), 103 Stat. 2432.)

§ 1162.   Continuation coverage [omitted]

§ 1163.   Qualifying event [omitted]

§ 1322.   Single-employer plan benefits guaranteed

(a) Nonforfeitable benefits. Subject to the limitations contained in subsection (b), the corporation shall guarantee in accordance with this section the payment of all nonforfeitable benefits (other than benefits becoming nonforfeitable solely on account of the termination of a plan) under a single-employer plan which terminates at a time when this title applies to it.

* * *

(Sept. 2, 1974, Pub. L. 93–406, Title IV, Subtitle B, § 4022, 88 Stat. 1016; Sept. 26, 1980, Pub. L. 96–364, Title IV, § 403(c), 94 Stat. 1301; Pub. L. 99–272, Title XI, § 11016(c)(8), (9), 100 Stat. 274; Pub. L. 100–203, Title IX, Subtitle D, Part II, Subpart B, § 9312(b)(3)(A), 101 Stat. 1330–362; Pub. L. 101–239, Title VII, Subtitle G, Part V, Subpart C, § 7881(f)(4), (5), (11), Subpart D, §§ 7891(a)(1), 7894(g)(1), (3)(B), 103 Stat. 2440, 2441, 2445, 2451; Pub. L. 103–465, Title VII, Subtitle F, Part I, Subpart C, § 766(c), Part II, § 777(a), 108 Stat. 5037, 5049.)

§ 1344.   Allocation of assets

* * *

(d) Distribution of residual assets; restrictions on reversions pursuant to recently amended plans; assets attributable to employee contributions; calculation of remaining assets.

(1) Subject to paragraph (3), any residual assets of a single-employer plan may be distributed to the employer if—

(A) all liabilities of the plan to participants and their beneficiaries have been satisfied,

(B) the distribution does not contravene any provision of law, and

(C) the plan provides for such a distribution in these circumstances.

(2)(A) In determining the extent to which a plan provides for the distribution of plan assets to the employer for purposes of paragraph (1)(C), any such provision, and any amendment increasing the amount which may be distributed to the employer, shall not be treated as effective before the end of the fifth calendar year following the date of the adoption of such provision or amendment.

(B) A distribution to the employer from a plan shall not be treated as failing to satisfy the requirements of this paragraph if the plan has been in effect for fewer than 5 years and the plan has provided for such a distribution since the effective date of the plan.

(C) Except as otherwise provided in regulations of the Secretary of the Treasury, in any case in which a transaction described in section 208 [29 U.S.C. § 1058] occurs, subparagraph (A) shall continue to apply separately with respect to the amount of any assets transferred in such transaction.

(D) For purposes of this subsection, the term "employer" includes any member of the controlled group of which the employer is a member. For purposes of the preceding sentence, the term "controlled group" means any group treated as a single employer under subsection (b), (c), (m) or (o) of section 414 of the Internal Revenue Code of 1986 [26 U.S.C. § 414(b), (c), (m) or (o)].

(3)(A) Before any distribution from a plan pursuant to paragraph (1), if any assets of the plan attributable to employee contributions remain after satisfaction of all liabilities described in subsection (a), such remaining assets shall be equitably distributed to the participants who made such contributions or their beneficiaries (including alternate payees, within the meaning of section 206(d)(3)(K) [29 U.S.C. § 1056(d)(3)(K)]).

(B) For purposes of subparagraph (A), the portion of the remaining assets which are attributable to employee contributions shall be an amount equal to the product derived by multiplying—

(i) the market value of the total remaining assets, by

(ii) a fraction—

(I) the numerator of which is the present value of all portions of the accrued benefits with respect to participants which are derived from participants' mandatory contributions (referred to in subsection (a)(2)), and

(II) the denominator of which is the present value of all benefits with respect to which assets are allocated under paragraphs (2) through (6) of subsection (a).

(C) For purposes of this paragraph, each person who is, as of the termination date—

(i) a participant under the plan, or

(ii) an individual who has received, during the 3–year period ending with the termination date, a distribution from the plan of such individual's entire nonforfeitable benefit in the form of a single sum distribution in accordance with section 203(e) [29 U.S.C. § 1053(e)] or in the form of irrevocable commitments purchased by the plan from an insurer to provide such nonforfeitable benefit,

shall be treated as a participant with respect to the termination, if all or part of the nonforfeitable benefit with respect to such person is or was attributable to participants' mandatory contributions (referred to in subsection (a)(2)).

* * *

(Sept. 2, 1974, Pub. L. 93–406, Title IV, Subtitle C, § 4044, 88 Stat. 1025.; Sept. 26, 1980, Pub. L. 96–364, Title IV, § 402(a)(7), 94 Stat. 1299; Pub. L. 99–272, Title XI, § 11016(c)(12), (13), 100 Stat. 274; Pub. L. 100–203, Title IX, Subtitle D, Part II, Subpart B, § 9311(a)(1), (b), (c), 101 Stat. 1330–359, 1330–360; Pub. L. 101–239, Title VII, Subtitle G, Part V, Subpart C, § 7881(e)(3), Subpart D, §§ 7891(a)(1), 7894(g)(2), 103 Stat. 2440, 2445, 2451; Pub. L. 101–508, Title XII, Subtitle A, § 12002(b)(2)(B), 104 Stat. 1388–566.)

DEPT. OF LABOR FLSA REGULATIONS— SELECTED PROVISIONS 29 C.F.R. PART 541 (2012)

SUBPART B—EXECUTIVE EMPLOYEES

§ 541.100   General rule for executive employees.

(a) The term "employee employed in a bona fide executive capacity" in section 13(a)(1) of the Act shall mean any employee:

(1) Compensated on a salary basis at a rate of not less than $455 per week (or $380 per week, if employed in American Samoa by employers other than the Federal Government), exclusive of board, lodging or other facilities;

(2) Whose primary duty is management of the enterprise in which the employee is employed or of a customarily recognized department or subdivision thereof;

(3) Who customarily and regularly directs the work of two or more other employees; and

(4) Who has the authority to hire or fire other employees or whose suggestions and recommendations as to the hiring, firing, advancement, promotion or any other change of status of other employees are given particular weight.

(b) The phrase "salary basis" is defined at § 541.602; "board, lodging or other facilities" is defined at § 541.606; "primary duty" is defined at § 541.700; and "customarily and regularly" is defined at § 541.701.

§ 541.101   Business owner.

The term "employee employed in a bona fide executive capacity" in section 13(a)(1) of the Act also includes any employee who owns at least a bona fide 20–percent equity interest in the enterprise in which the employee is employed, regardless of whether the business is a corporate or other type of organization, and who is actively engaged in its management. The term "management" is defined in § 541.102. The requirements of Subpart G (salary requirements) of this part do not apply to the business owners described in this section.

§ 541.102   Management.

Generally, "management" includes, but is not limited to, activities such as interviewing, selecting, and training of employees; setting and adjusting their rates of pay and hours of work; directing the work of employees; maintaining production or sales records for use in supervision or control; appraising employees' productivity and efficiency for the purpose of recommending promotions or other changes in status; handling employee complaints and grievances; disciplining employees; planning the work; determining the techniques to be used; apportioning the work among the employees; determining the type of materials, supplies, machinery, equipment or tools to be used or merchandise to be bought, stocked and sold; controlling the flow and distribution of materials or merchandise and supplies; providing for the safety and security of the employees or the property; planning and controlling the budget; and monitoring or implementing legal compliance measures.

§ 541.103   Department or subdivision.

(a) The phrase "a customarily recognized department or subdivision" is intended to distinguish between a mere collection of employees assigned from time to time to a specific job or series of jobs and a unit with permanent status and function. A customarily recognized department or subdivision must have a permanent status and a continuing function. For example, a large employer's human resources department might have subdivisions for labor relations, pensions and other benefits, equal employment opportunity, and personnel management, each of which has a permanent status and function.

(b) When an enterprise has more than one establishment, the employee in charge of each establishment may be considered in charge of a recognized subdivision of the enterprise.

(c) A recognized department or subdivision need not be physically within the employer's establishment and may move from place to place. The mere fact that the employee works in more than one location does not invalidate the exemption if other factors show that the employee is actually in charge of a recognized unit with a continuing function in the organization.

(d) Continuity of the same subordinate personnel is not essential to the existence of a recognized unit with a continuing function. An otherwise exempt employee will not lose the exemption merely because the employee draws and supervises workers from a pool or supervises a team of workers drawn from other recognized units, if other factors are present that indicate that the employee is in charge of a recognized unit with a continuing function.

§ 541.104   Two or more other employees.

(a) To qualify as an exempt executive under § 541.100, the employee must customarily and regularly direct the work of two or more other employees. The phrase "two or more other employees" means two full-time employees or their equivalent. One full-time and two half-time employees, for example, are equivalent to two full-time employees. Four half-time employees are also equivalent.

(b) The supervision can be distributed among two, three or more employees, but each such employee must customarily and regularly direct the work of two or more other full-time employees or the equivalent. Thus, for example, a department with five full-time nonexempt workers may have up to two exempt supervisors if each such supervisor customarily and regularly directs the work of two of those workers.

(c) An employee who merely assists the manager of a particular department and supervises two or more employees only in the actual manager's absence does not meet this requirement.

(d) Hours worked by an employee cannot be credited more than once for different executives. Thus, a shared responsibility for the supervision of the same two employees in the same department does not satisfy this requirement. However, a full-time employee who works four hours for one supervisor and four hours for a different supervisor, for example, can be credited as a half-time employee for both supervisors.

§ 541.105   Particular weight.

To determine whether an employee's suggestions and recommendations are given "particular weight," factors to be considered include, but are not limited to, whether it is part of the employee's job duties to make such suggestions and recommendations; the frequency with which such suggestions and recommendations are made or requested; and the frequency with which the employee's suggestions and recommendations are relied upon. Generally, an executive's suggestions and recommendations must pertain to employees whom the executive customarily and regularly directs. It does not include an occasional suggestion with regard to the change in status of a co-worker. An employee's suggestions and recommendations may still be deemed to have "particular weight" even if a higher level manager's recommendation has more importance and even if the employee does not have authority to make the ultimate decision as to the employee's change in status.

§ 541.106   Concurrent duties.

(a) Concurrent performance of exempt and nonexempt work does not disqualify an employee from the executive exemption if the requirements of § 541.100 are otherwise met. Whether an employee meets the requirements of § 541.100 when the employee performs concurrent duties is determined on a case-by-case basis and based on the factors set forth in § 541.700. Generally, exempt executives make the decision regarding when to perform nonexempt duties and remain responsible for the success or failure of business operations under their management while performing the nonexempt work. In contrast, the nonexempt employee generally is directed by a supervisor to perform the exempt work or performs the exempt work for defined time periods. An employee whose primary duty is ordinary production work or routine, recurrent or repetitive tasks cannot qualify for exemption as an executive.

(b) For example, an assistant manager in a retail establishment may perform work such as serving customers, cooking food, stocking shelves and cleaning the establishment, but performance of such nonexempt work does not preclude the exemption if the assistant manager's primary duty is management. An assistant manager can supervise employees and serve customers at the same time without losing the exemption. An exempt employee can also simultaneously direct the work of other employees and stock shelves.

(c) In contrast, a relief supervisor or working supervisor whose primary duty is performing nonexempt work on the production line in a manufacturing plant does not become exempt merely because the nonexempt production line employee occasionally has some responsibility for directing the work of other nonexempt production line employees when, for example, the exempt supervisor is unavailable. Similarly, an employee whose primary duty is to work as an electrician is not an exempt executive even if the employee also directs the work of other employees on the job site, orders parts and materials for the job, and handles requests from the prime contractor.

SUBPART C—ADMINISTRATIVE EMPLOYEES

§ 541.200   General rule for administrative employees.

(a) The term "employee employed in a bona fide administrative capacity" in section 13(a)(1) of the Act shall mean any employee:

(1) Compensated on a salary or fee basis at a rate of not less than $455 per week (or $380 per week, if employed in American Samoa by employers other than the Federal Government), exclusive of board, lodging or other facilities;

(2) Whose primary duty is the performance of office or non-manual work directly related to the management or general business operations of the employer or the employer's customers; and

(3) Whose primary duty includes the exercise of discretion and independent judgment with respect to matters of significance.

(b) The term "salary basis" is defined at § 541.602; "fee basis" is defined at § 541.605; "board, lodging or other facilities" is defined at § 541.606; and "primary duty" is defined at § 541.700.

§ 541.201   Directly related to management or general business operations.

(a) To qualify for the administrative exemption, an employee's primary duty must be the performance of work directly related to the management or general business operations of the employer or the employer's customers. The phrase "directly related to the management or general business operations" refers to the type of work performed by the employee. To meet this requirement, an employee must perform work directly related to assisting with the running or servicing of the business, as distinguished, for example, from working on a manufacturing production line or selling a product in a retail or service establishment.

(b) Work directly related to management or general business operations includes, but is not limited to, work in functional areas such as tax; finance; accounting; budgeting; auditing; insurance; quality control; purchasing; procurement; advertising; marketing; research; safety and health; personnel management; human resources; employee benefits; labor relations; public relations, government relations; computer network, internet and database administration; legal and regulatory compliance; and similar activities. Some of these activities may be performed by employees who also would qualify for another exemption.

(c) An employee may qualify for the administrative exemption if the employee's primary duty is the performance of work directly related to the management or general business operations of the employer's customers. Thus, for example, employees acting as advisers or consultants to their employer's clients or customers (as tax experts or financial consultants, for example) may be exempt.

§ 541.202 Discretion and independent judgment.

(a) To qualify for the administrative exemption, an employee's primary duty must include the exercise of discretion and independent judgment with respect to matters of significance. In general, the exercise of discretion and independent judgment involves the comparison and the evaluation of possible courses of conduct, and acting or making a decision after the various possibilities have been considered. The term "matters of significance" refers to the level of importance or consequence of the work performed.

(b) The phrase "discretion and independent judgment" must be applied in the light of all the facts involved in the particular employment situation in which the question arises. Factors to consider when determining whether an employee exercises discretion and independent judgment with respect to matters of significance include, but are not limited to: whether the employee has authority to formulate, affect, interpret, or implement management policies or operating practices; whether the employee carries out major assignments in conducting the operations of the business; whether the employee performs work that affects business operations to a substantial degree, even if the employee's assignments are related to operation of a particular segment of the business; whether the employee has authority to commit the employer in matters that have significant financial impact; whether the employee has authority to waive or deviate from established policies and procedures without prior approval; whether the employee has authority to negotiate and bind the company on significant matters; whether the employee provides consultation or expert advice to management; whether the employee is involved in planning long-or short-term business objectives; whether the employee investigates and resolves matters of significance on behalf of management; and whether the employee represents the company in handling complaints, arbitrating disputes or resolving grievances.

(c) The exercise of discretion and independent judgment implies that the employee has authority to make an independent choice, free from immediate direction or supervision. However, employees can exercise discretion and independent judgment even if their decisions or recommendations are reviewed at a higher level. Thus, the term "discretion and independent judgment" does not require that the decisions made by an employee have a finality that goes with unlimited authority and a complete absence of review. The decisions made as a result of the exercise of discretion and independent judgment may consist of recommendations for action rather than the actual taking of action. The fact that an employee's decision may be subject to review and that upon occasion the decisions are revised or reversed after review does not mean that the employee is not exercising discretion and independent judgment. For example, the policies formulated by the credit manager of a large corporation may be subject to review by higher company officials who may approve or disapprove these policies. The management consultant who has made a study of the operations of a business and who has drawn a proposed change in organization may have the plan reviewed or revised by superiors before it is submitted to the client.

(d) An employer's volume of business may make it necessary to employ a number of employees to perform the same or similar work. The fact that many employees perform identical work or work of the same relative importance does not mean that the work of each such employee does not involve the exercise of discretion and independent judgment with respect to matters of significance.

(e) The exercise of discretion and independent judgment must be more than the use of skill in applying well-established techniques, procedures or specific standards described in manuals or other sources. See also § 541.704 regarding use of manuals. The exercise of discretion and independent judgment also does not include clerical or secretarial work, recording or tabulating data, or performing other mechanical, repetitive, recurrent or routine work. An employee who simply tabulates data is not exempt, even if labeled as a "statistician."

(f) An employee does not exercise discretion and independent judgment with respect to matters of significance merely because the employer will experience financial losses if the employee fails to perform the job properly. For example, a messenger who is entrusted with carrying large sums of money does not exercise discretion and independent judgment with respect to matters of significance even though serious consequences may flow from the employee's neglect. Similarly, an employee who operates very expensive equipment does not exercise discretion and independent judgment with respect to matters of significance merely because improper performance of the employee's duties may cause serious financial loss to the employer.

§ 541.203 Administrative exemption examples.

(a) Insurance claims adjusters generally meet the duties requirements for the administrative exemption, whether they work for an insurance company or other type of company, if their duties include activities such as interviewing insureds, witnesses and physicians; inspecting property damage; reviewing factual information to prepare damage estimates; evaluating and making recommendations regarding coverage of claims; determining liability and total value of a claim; negotiating settlements; and making recommendations regarding litigation.

(b) Employees in the financial services industry generally meet the duties requirements for the administrative exemption if their duties include work such as collecting and analyzing information regarding the customer's income, assets, investments or debts; determining which financial products best meet the customer's needs and financial circumstances; advising the customer regarding the advantages and disadvantages of different financial products; and marketing, servicing or promoting the employer's financial products. However, an employee whose primary duty is selling financial products does not qualify for the administrative exemption.

(c) An employee who leads a team of other employees assigned to complete major projects for the employer (such as purchasing, selling or closing all or part of the business, negotiating a real estate transaction or a collective bargaining agreement, or designing and implementing productivity improvements) generally meets the duties requirements for the administrative exemption, even if the employee does not have direct supervisory responsibility over the other employees on the team.

(d) An executive assistant or administrative assistant to a business owner or senior executive of a large business generally meets the duties requirements for the administrative exemption if such employee, without specific instructions or prescribed procedures, has been delegated authority regarding matters of significance.

(e) Human resources managers who formulate, interpret or implement employment policies and management consultants who study the operations of a business and propose changes in organization generally meet the duties requirements for the administrative exemption. However, personnel clerks who "screen" applicants to obtain data regarding their minimum qualifications and fitness for employment generally do not meet the duties requirements for the administrative exemption. Such personnel clerks typically will reject all applicants who do not meet minimum standards for the particular job or for employment by the company. The minimum standards are usually set by the exempt human resources manager or other company officials, and the decision to hire from the group of qualified applicants who do meet the minimum standards is similarly made by the exempt human resources manager or other company officials. Thus, when the interviewing and screening functions are performed by the human resources manager or personnel manager who makes the hiring decision or makes recommendations for hiring from the pool of qualified applicants, such duties constitute exempt work, even though routine, because this work is directly and closely related to the employee's exempt functions.

(f) Purchasing agents with authority to bind the company on significant purchases generally meet the duties requirements for the administrative exemption even if they must consult with top management officials when making a purchase commitment for raw materials in excess of the contemplated plant needs.

(g) Ordinary inspection work generally does not meet the duties requirements for the administrative exemption. Inspectors normally perform specialized work along standardized lines involving well-established techniques and procedures which may have been catalogued and described in manuals or other sources. Such inspectors rely on techniques and skills acquired by special training or experience. They have some leeway in the performance of their work but only within closely prescribed limits.

(h) Employees usually called examiners or graders, such as employees that grade lumber, generally do not meet the duties requirements for the administrative exemption. Such employees usually perform work involving the comparison of products with established standards which are frequently catalogued. Often, after continued reference to the written standards, or through experience, the employee acquires sufficient knowledge so that reference to written standards is unnecessary. The substitution of the employee's memory for a manual of standards does not convert the character of the work performed to exempt work requiring the exercise of discretion and independent judgment.

(i) Comparison shopping performed by an employee of a retail store who merely reports to the buyer the prices at a competitor's store does not qualify for the administrative exemption. However, the buyer who evaluates such reports on competitor prices to set the employer's prices generally meets the duties requirements for the administrative exemption.

(j) Public sector inspectors or investigators of various types, such as fire prevention or safety, building or construction, health or sanitation, environmental or soils specialists and similar employees, generally do not meet the duties requirements for the administrative exemption because their work typically does not involve work directly related to the management or general business operations of the employer. Such employees also do not qualify for the administrative exemption because their work involves the use of skills and technical abilities in gathering factual information, applying known standards or prescribed procedures, determining which procedure to follow, or determining whether prescribed standards or criteria are met.

§ 541.204 Educational establishments.

(a) The term "employee employed in a bona fide administrative capacity" in section 13(a)(1) of the Act also includes employees:

(1) Compensated for services on a salary or fee basis at a rate of not less than $455 per week (or $380 per week, if employed in American Samoa by employers other than the Federal Government) exclusive of board, lodging or other facilities, or on a salary basis which is at least equal to the entrance salary for teachers in the educational establishment by which employed; and

(2) Whose primary duty is performing administrative functions directly related to academic instruction or training in an educational establishment or department or subdivision thereof.

(b) The term "educational establishment" means an elementary or secondary school system, an institution of higher education or other educational institution. Sections 3(v) and 3(w) of the Act define elementary and secondary schools as those day or residential schools that provide elementary or secondary education, as determined under State law. Under the laws of most States, such education includes the curriculums in grades 1 through 12; under many it includes also the introductory programs in kindergarten. Such education in some States may also include nursery school programs in elementary education and junior college curriculums in secondary education. The term "other educational establishment" includes special schools for mentally or physically disabled or gifted children, regardless of any classification of such schools as elementary, secondary or higher. Factors relevant in determining whether post-secondary career programs are educational institutions include whether the school is licensed by a state agency responsible for the state's educational system or accredited by a nationally recognized accrediting organization for career schools. Also, for purposes of the exemption, no distinction is drawn between public and private schools, or between those operated for profit and those that are not for profit.

(c) The phrase "performing administrative functions directly related to academic instruction or training" means work related to the academic operations and functions in a school rather than to administration along the lines of general business operations. Such academic administrative functions include operations directly in the field of education. Jobs relating to areas outside the educational field are not within the definition of academic administration.

(1) Employees engaged in academic administrative functions include: the superintendent or other head of an elementary or secondary school system, and any assistants, responsible for administration of such matters as curriculum, quality and methods of instructing, measuring and testing the learning potential and achievement of students, establishing and maintaining academic and grading standards, and other aspects of the teaching program; the principal and any vice-principals responsible for the operation of an elementary or secondary school; department heads in institutions of higher education responsible for the administration of the mathematics department, the English department, the foreign language department, etc.; academic counselors who perform work such as

administering school testing programs, assisting students with academic problems and advising students concerning degree requirements; and other employees with similar responsibilities.

(2) Jobs relating to building management and maintenance, jobs relating to the health of the students, and academic staff such as social workers, psychologists, lunch room managers or dietitians do not perform academic administrative functions. Although such work is not considered academic administration, such employees may qualify for exemption under § 541.200 or under other sections of this part, provided the requirements for such exemptions are met.

Subpart D—Professional Employees

§ 541.300   General rule for professional employees.

(a) The term "employee employed in a bona fide professional capacity" in section 13(a)(1) of the Act shall mean any employee:

(1) Compensated on a salary or fee basis at a rate of not less than $455 per week (or $380 per week, if employed in American Samoa by employers other than the Federal Government), exclusive of board, lodging, or other facilities; and

(2) Whose primary duty is the performance of work:

(i) Requiring knowledge of an advanced type in a field of science or learning customarily acquired by a prolonged course of specialized intellectual instruction; or

(ii) Requiring invention, imagination, originality or talent in a recognized field of artistic or creative endeavor.

(b) The term "salary basis" is defined at § 541.602; "fee basis" is defined at § 541.605; "board, lodging or other facilities" is defined at § 541.606; and "primary duty" is defined at § 541.700.

§ 541.301   Learned professionals.

(a) To qualify for the learned professional exemption, an employee's primary duty must be the performance of work requiring advanced knowledge in a field of science or learning customarily acquired by a prolonged course of specialized intellectual instruction. This primary duty test includes three elements:

(1) The employee must perform work requiring advanced knowledge;

(2) The advanced knowledge must be in a field of science or learning; and

(3) The advanced knowledge must be customarily acquired by a prolonged course of specialized intellectual instruction.

(b) The phrase "work requiring advanced knowledge" means work which is predominantly intellectual in character, and which includes work requiring the consistent exercise of discretion and judgment, as distinguished from performance of routine mental, manual, mechanical or physical work. An employee who performs work requiring advanced knowledge generally uses the advanced knowledge to analyze, interpret or make deductions from varying facts or circumstances. Advanced knowledge cannot be attained at the high school level.

(c) The phrase "field of science or learning" includes the traditional professions of law, medicine, theology, accounting, actuarial computation, engineering, architecture, teaching, various types of physical, chemical and biological sciences, pharmacy and other similar occupations that have a recognized professional status as distinguished from the mechanical arts or skilled trades where in some instances the knowledge is of a fairly advanced type, but is not in a field of science or learning.

(d) The phrase "customarily acquired by a prolonged course of specialized intellectual instruction" restricts the exemption to professions where specialized academic training is a standard prerequisite for entrance into the profession. The best prima facie evidence that an employee meets this requirement is possession of the appropriate academic degree. However, the word "customarily" means that the exemption is also available to employees in such professions who have substantially the same knowledge level and perform substantially the same work as the degreed employees, but who attained the advanced knowledge through a combination of work experience and intellectual instruction. Thus, for example, the learned professional exemption is available to the occasional lawyer who has not gone to law school, or the occasional chemist who is not the possessor of a degree in chemistry. However, the learned professional exemption is not available for occupations that customarily may be performed with only the general knowledge acquired by an academic degree in any field, with knowledge acquired through an apprenticeship, or with training in the performance of routine mental, manual, mechanical or physical processes. The learned professional exemption also does not apply to occupations in which most employees have acquired their skill by experience rather than by advanced specialized intellectual instruction.

(e)(1) Registered or certified medical technologists. Registered or certified medical technologists who have successfully completed three academic years of pre-professional study in an accredited college or university plus a fourth year of professional course work in a school of medical technology approved by the Council of Medical Education of the American Medical Association generally meet the duties requirements for the learned professional exemption.

(2) Nurses. Registered nurses who are registered by the appropriate State examining board generally meet the duties requirements for the learned professional exemption. Licensed practical nurses and other similar health care employees, however, generally do not qualify as exempt learned professionals because possession of a specialized advanced academic degree is not a standard prerequisite for entry into such occupations.

(3) Dental hygienists. Dental hygienists who have successfully completed four academic years of pre-professional and professional study in an accredited college or university approved by the Commission on Accreditation of Dental and Dental Auxiliary Educational Programs of the American Dental Association generally meet the duties requirements for the learned professional exemption.

(4) Physician assistants. Physician assistants who have successfully completed four academic years of pre-professional and professional study, including graduation from a physician assistant program accredited by the Accreditation Review Commission on Education for the Physician Assistant, and who are certified by the National Commission on Certification of Physician Assistants generally meet the duties requirements for the learned professional exemption.

(5) Accountants. Certified public accountants generally meet the duties requirements for the learned professional exemption. In addition, many other accountants who are not certified public accountants but perform similar job duties may qualify as exempt learned professionals. However, accounting clerks, bookkeepers and other employees who normally perform a great deal of routine work generally will not qualify as exempt professionals.

(6) Chefs. Chefs, such as executive chefs and sous chefs, who have attained a four-year specialized academic degree in a culinary arts program, generally meet the duties requirements for the learned professional exemption. The learned professional exemption is not available to cooks who perform predominantly routine mental, manual, mechanical or physical work.

(7) Paralegals. Paralegals and legal assistants generally do not qualify as exempt learned professionals because an advanced specialized academic degree is not a standard prerequisite for entry into the field. Although many paralegals possess general four-year advanced degrees, most specialized paralegal programs are two-year associate degree programs from a community college or equivalent institution. However, the learned professional exemption is available for paralegals who possess advanced specialized degrees in other professional fields and apply advanced knowledge in that field in the performance of their duties. For example, if a law firm hires an engineer as a paralegal to provide expert advice on product liability cases or to assist on patent matters, that engineer would qualify for exemption.

(8) Athletic trainers. Athletic trainers who have successfully completed four academic years of pre-professional and professional study in a specialized curriculum accredited by the Commission on Accreditation of Allied Health Education Programs and who are certified by the Board of Certification of the National Athletic Trainers Association Board of Certification generally meet the duties requirements for the learned professional exemption.

(9) Funeral directors or embalmers. Licensed funeral directors and embalmers who are licensed by and working in a state that requires successful completion of four academic years of pre-professional and professional study, including graduation from a college of mortuary science accredited by the American Board of Funeral Service Education, generally meet the duties requirements for the learned professional exemption.

(f) The areas in which the professional exemption may be available are expanding. As knowledge is developed, academic training is broadened and specialized degrees are offered in new and diverse fields, thus creating new specialists in particular fields of science or learning. When an advanced specialized degree has become a standard requirement for a particular occupation, that occupation may have acquired the characteristics of a learned profession. Accrediting and certifying organizations similar to those listed in paragraphs (e)(1), (e)(3), (e)(4), (e)(8) and (e)(9) of this section also may be created in the future. Such organizations may develop similar specialized curriculums and certification programs which, if a standard requirement for a particular occupation, may indicate that the occupation has acquired the characteristics of a learned profession.

§ 541.302 Creative professionals.

(a) To qualify for the creative professional exemption, an employee's primary duty must be the performance of work requiring invention, imagination, originality or talent in a recognized field of artistic or creative endeavor as opposed to routine mental, manual, mechanical or physical work. The exemption does not apply to work which can be produced by a person with general manual or intellectual ability and training.

(b) To qualify for exemption as a creative professional, the work performed must be "in a recognized field of artistic or creative endeavor." This includes such fields as music, writing, acting and the graphic arts.

(c) The requirement of "invention, imagination, originality or talent" distinguishes the creative professions from work that primarily depends on intelligence, diligence and accuracy. The duties of employees vary widely, and exemption as a creative professional depends on the extent of the invention, imagination, originality or talent exercised by the employee. Determination of exempt creative professional status, therefore, must be made on a case-by-case basis. This requirement generally is met by actors, musicians, composers, conductors, and soloists; painters who at most are given the subject matter of their painting; cartoonists who are merely told the title or underlying concept of a cartoon and must rely on their own creative ability to express the concept; essayists, novelists, short-story writers and screen play writers who choose their own subjects and hand in a finished piece of work to their employers (the majority of such persons are, of course, not employees but self-employed); and persons holding the more responsible writing positions in advertising agencies. This requirement generally is not met by a person who is employed as a copyist, as an "animator" of motion-picture cartoons, or as a retoucher of photographs, since such work is not properly described as creative in character.

(d) Journalists may satisfy the duties requirements for the creative professional exemption if their primary duty is work requiring invention, imagination, originality or talent, as opposed to work which depends primarily on intelligence, diligence and accuracy. Employees of newspapers, magazines, television and other media are not exempt creative professionals if they only collect, organize and record information that is routine or already public, or if they do not contribute a unique interpretation or analysis to a news product. Thus, for example, newspaper reporters who merely rewrite press releases or who write standard recounts of public information by gathering facts on routine community events are not exempt creative professionals. Reporters also do not qualify as exempt creative professionals if their work product is subject to substantial control by the employer. However, journalists may qualify as exempt creative professionals if their primary duty is performing on the air in radio, television or other electronic media; conducting investigative interviews; analyzing or interpreting public events; writing editorials, opinion columns or other commentary; or acting as a narrator or commentator.

§ 541.303 Teachers.

(a) The term "employee employed in a bona fide professional capacity" in section 13(a)(1) of the Act also means any employee with a primary duty of teaching, tutoring, instructing or lecturing in the activity of imparting knowledge and who is employed and engaged in this activity as a teacher in an educational establishment by which the employee is employed. The term "educational establishment" is defined in § 541.204(b).

(b) Exempt teachers include, but are not limited to: regular academic teachers; teachers of kindergarten or nursery school pupils; teachers of gifted or disabled children; teachers of skilled and semiskilled trades and occupations; teachers engaged in automobile driving instruction; aircraft flight instructors; home economics teachers; and vocal or instrumental music instructors. Those faculty members who are engaged as teachers but also spend a considerable amount of their time in extracurricular activities such as coaching athletic teams or acting as moderators or advisors in such areas as drama, speech, debate or journalism are engaged in teaching. Such activities are a recognized part of the schools' responsibility in contributing to the educational development of the student.

(c) The possession of an elementary or secondary teacher's certificate provides a clear means of identifying the individuals contemplated as being within the scope of the exemption for teaching professionals.

Teachers who possess a teaching certificate qualify for the exemption regardless of the terminology (e.g., permanent, conditional, standard, provisional, temporary, emergency, or unlimited) used by the State to refer to different kinds of certificates. However, private schools and public schools are not uniform in requiring a certificate for employment as an elementary or secondary school teacher, and a teacher's certificate is not generally necessary for employment in institutions of higher education or other educational establishments. Therefore, a teacher who is not certified may be considered for exemption, provided that such individual is employed as a teacher by the employing school or school system.

(d) The requirements of § 541.300 and Subpart G (salary requirements) of this part do not apply to the teaching professionals described in this section.

§ 541.304   Practice of law or medicine.

(a) The term "employee employed in a bona fide professional capacity" in section 13(a)(1) of the Act also shall mean:

(1) Any employee who is the holder of a valid license or certificate permitting the practice of law or medicine or any of their branches and is actually engaged in the practice thereof; and

(2) Any employee who is the holder of the requisite academic degree for the general practice of medicine and is engaged in an internship or resident program pursuant to the practice of the profession.

(b) In the case of medicine, the exemption applies to physicians and other practitioners licensed and practicing in the field of medical science and healing or any of the medical specialties practiced by physicians or practitioners. The term "physicians" includes medical doctors including general practitioners and specialists, osteopathic physicians (doctors of osteopathy), podiatrists, dentists (doctors of dental medicine), and optometrists (doctors of optometry or bachelors of science in optometry).

(c) Employees engaged in internship or resident programs, whether or not licensed to practice prior to commencement of the program, qualify as exempt professionals if they enter such internship or resident programs after the earning of the appropriate degree required for the general practice of their profession.

(d) The requirements of § 541.300 and subpart G (salary requirements) of this part do not apply to the employees described in this section.

SUBPART E—COMPUTER EMPLOYEES

§ 541.400   General rule for computer employees.

(a) Computer systems analysts, computer programmers, software engineers or other similarly skilled workers in the computer field are eligible for exemption as professionals under section 13(a)(1) of the Act and under section 13(a)(17) of the Act. Because job titles vary widely and change quickly in the computer industry, job titles are not determinative of the applicability of this exemption.

(b) The section 13(a)(1) exemption applies to any computer employee compensated on a salary or fee basis at a rate of not less than $455 per week (or $380 per week, if employed in American Samoa by employers other than the Federal Government), exclusive of board, lodging or other facilities, and the section 13(a)(17) exemption applies to any computer employee compensated on an hourly basis at a rate not less than $27.63 an hour. In addition, under either section 13(a)(1) or section 13(a)(17) of the Act, the exemptions apply only to computer employees whose primary duty consists of:

(1) The application of systems analysis techniques and procedures, including consulting with users, to determine hardware, software or system functional specifications;

(2) The design, development, documentation, analysis, creation, testing or modification of computer systems or programs, including prototypes, based on and related to user or system design specifications;

(3) The design, documentation, testing, creation or modification of computer programs related to machine operating systems; or

(4) A combination of the aforementioned duties, the performance of which requires the same level of skills.

(c) The term "salary basis" is defined at § 541.602; "fee basis" is defined at § 541.605; "board, lodging or other facilities" is defined at § 541.606; and "primary duty" is defined at § 541.700.

§ 541.401   Computer manufacture and repair.

The exemption for employees in computer occupations does not include employees engaged in the manufacture or repair of computer hardware and related equipment. Employees whose work is highly dependent upon, or facilitated by, the use of computers and computer software programs (e.g., engineers, drafters and others skilled in computer-aided design software), but who are not primarily engaged in computer systems analysis and programming or other similarly skilled computer-related occupations identified in § 541.400(b), are also not exempt computer professionals.

§ 541.402   Executive and administrative computer employees.

Computer employees within the scope of this exemption, as well as those employees not within its scope, may also have executive and administrative duties which qualify the employees for exemption under subpart B or subpart C of this part. For example, systems analysts and computer programmers generally meet the duties requirements for the administrative exemption if their primary duty includes work such as planning, scheduling, and coordinating activities required to develop systems to solve complex business, scientific or engineering problems of the employer or the employer's customers. Similarly, a senior or lead computer programmer who manages the work of two or more other programmers in a customarily recognized department or subdivision of the employer, and whose recommendations as to the hiring, firing, advancement, promotion or other change of status of the other programmers are given particular weight, generally meets the duties requirements for the executive exemption.

SUBPART F—OUTSIDE SALES EMPLOYEES

§ 541.500 General rule for outside sales employees.

(a) The term "employee employed in the capacity of outside salesman" in section 13(a)(1) of the Act shall mean any employee:

    (1) Whose primary duty is:

        (i) making sales within the meaning of section 3(k) of the Act, or

        (ii) obtaining orders or contracts for services or for the use of facilities for which a consideration will be paid by the client or customer; and

    (2) Who is customarily and regularly engaged away from the employer's place or places of business in performing such primary duty.

(b) The term "primary duty" is defined at § 541.700. In determining the primary duty of an outside sales employee, work performed incidental to and in conjunction with the employee's own outside sales or solicitations, including incidental deliveries and collections, shall be regarded as exempt outside sales work. Other work that furthers the employee's sales efforts also shall be regarded as exempt work including, for example, writing sales reports, updating or revising the employee's sales or display catalogue, planning itineraries and attending sales conferences.

(c) The requirements of subpart G (salary requirements) of this part do not apply to the outside sales employees described in this section.

§ 541.501 Making sales or obtaining orders.

(a) Section 541.500 requires that the employee be engaged in:

    (1) Making sales within the meaning of section 3(k) of the Act, or

    (2) Obtaining orders or contracts for services or for the use of facilities.

(b) Sales within the meaning of section 3(k) of the Act include the transfer of title to tangible property, and in certain cases, of tangible and valuable evidences of intangible property. Section 3(k) of the Act states that "sale" or "sell" includes any sale, exchange, contract to sell, consignment for sale, shipment for sale, or other disposition.

(c) Exempt outside sales work includes not only the sales of commodities, but also "obtaining orders or contracts for services or for the use of facilities for which a consideration will be paid by the client or customer." Obtaining orders for "the use of facilities" includes the selling of time on radio or television, the solicitation of advertising for newspapers and other periodicals, and the solicitation of freight for railroads and other transportation agencies.

(d) The word "services" extends the outside sales exemption to employees who sell or take orders for a service, which may be performed for the customer by someone other than the person taking the order.

§ 541.502   Away from employer's place of business.

An outside sales employee must be customarily and regularly engaged "away from the employer's place or places of business." The outside sales employee is an employee who makes sales at the customer's place of business or, if selling door-to-door, at the customer's home. Outside sales does not include sales made by mail, telephone or the Internet unless such contact is used merely as an adjunct to personal calls. Thus, any fixed site, whether home or office, used by a salesperson as a headquarters or for telephonic solicitation of sales is considered one of the employer's places of business, even though the employer is not in any formal sense the owner or tenant of the property. However, an outside sales employee does not lose the exemption by displaying samples in hotel sample rooms during trips from city to city; these sample rooms should not be considered as the employer's places of business. Similarly, an outside sales employee does not lose the exemption by displaying the employer's products at a trade show. If selling actually occurs, rather than just sales promotion, trade shows of short duration (i.e., one or two weeks) should not be considered as the employer's place of business.

§ 541.503   Promotion work.

(a) Promotion work is one type of activity often performed by persons who make sales, which may or may not be exempt outside sales work, depending upon the circumstances under which it is performed. Promotional work that is actually performed incidental to and in conjunction with an employee's own outside sales or solicitations is exempt work. On the other hand, promotional work that is incidental to sales made, or to be made, by someone else is not exempt outside sales work. An employee who does not satisfy the requirements of this subpart may still qualify as an exempt employee under other subparts of this rule.

(b) A manufacturer's representative, for example, may perform various types of promotional activities such as putting up displays and posters, removing damaged or spoiled stock from the merchant's shelves or rearranging the merchandise. Such an employee can be considered an exempt outside sales employee if the employee's primary duty is making sales or contracts. Promotion activities directed toward consummation of the employee's own sales are exempt. Promotional activities designed to stimulate sales that will be made by someone else are not exempt outside sales work.

(c) Another example is a company representative who visits chain stores, arranges the merchandise on shelves, replenishes stock by replacing old with new merchandise, sets up displays and consults with the store manager when inventory runs low, but does not obtain a commitment for additional purchases. The arrangement of merchandise on the shelves or the replenishing of stock is not exempt work unless it is incidental to and in conjunction with the employee's own outside sales. Because the employee in this instance does not consummate the sale nor direct efforts toward the consummation of a sale, the work is not exempt outside sales work.

§ 541.504 Drivers who sell.

(a) Drivers who deliver products and also sell such products may qualify as exempt outside sales employees only if the employee has a primary duty of making sales. In determining the primary duty of drivers who sell, work performed incidental to and in conjunction with the employee's own outside sales or solicitations, including loading, driving or delivering products, shall be regarded as exempt outside sales work.

(b) Several factors should be considered in determining if a driver has a primary duty of making sales, including, but not limited to: a comparison of the driver's duties with those of other employees engaged as truck drivers and as salespersons; possession of a selling or solicitor's license when such license is required by law or ordinances; presence or absence of customary or contractual arrangements concerning amounts of products to be delivered; description of the employee's occupation in collective bargaining agreements; the employer's specifications as to qualifications for hiring; sales training; attendance at sales conferences; method of payment; and proportion of earnings directly attributable to sales.

(c) Drivers who may qualify as exempt outside sales employees include:

(1) A driver who provides the only sales contact between the employer and the customers visited, who calls on customers and takes orders for products, who delivers products from stock in the employee's vehicle or procures and delivers the product to the customer on a later trip, and who receives compensation commensurate with the volume of products sold.

(2) A driver who obtains or solicits orders for the employer's products from persons who have authority to commit the customer for purchases.

(3) A driver who calls on new prospects for customers along the employee's route and attempts to convince them of the desirability of accepting regular delivery of goods.

(4) A driver who calls on established customers along the route and persuades regular customers to accept delivery of increased amounts of goods or of new products, even though the initial sale or agreement for delivery was made by someone else.

(d) Drivers who generally would not qualify as exempt outside sales employees include:

(1) A route driver whose primary duty is to transport products sold by the employer through vending machines and to keep such machines stocked, in good operating condition, and in good locations.

(2) A driver who often calls on established customers day after day or week after week, delivering a quantity of the employer's products at each call when the sale was not significantly affected by solicitations of the customer by the delivering driver or the amount of the sale is determined by the volume of the customer's sales since the previous delivery.

(3) A driver primarily engaged in making deliveries to customers and performing activities intended to promote sales by customers (including placing point-of-sale and other advertising materials, price stamping commodities, arranging merchandise on shelves, in coolers or in cabinets, rotating stock according to date, and cleaning and otherwise servicing display cases), unless such work is in furtherance of the driver's own sales efforts.

Subpart G—Salary Requirements

§ 541.600   Amount of salary required.

(a) To qualify as an exempt executive, administrative or professional employee under section 13(a)(1) of the Act, an employee must be compensated on a salary basis at a rate of not less than $455 per week (or $380 per week, if employed in American Samoa by employers other than the Federal Government), exclusive of board, lodging or other facilities. Administrative and professional employees may also be paid on a fee basis, as defined in § 541.605.

(b) The $455 a week may be translated into equivalent amounts for periods longer than one week. The requirement will be met if the employee is compensated biweekly on a salary basis of $910, semimonthly on a salary basis of $985.83, or monthly on a salary basis of $1,971.66. However, the shortest period of payment that will meet this compensation requirement is one week.

(c) In the case of academic administrative employees, the compensation requirement also may be met by compensation on a salary basis at a rate at least equal to the entrance salary for teachers in the educational establishment by which the employee is employed, as provided in § 541.204(a)(1).

(d) In the case of computer employees, the compensation requirement also may be met by compensation on an hourly basis at a rate not less than $27.63 an hour, as provided in § 541.400(b).

(e) In the case of professional employees, the compensation requirements in this section shall not apply to employees engaged as teachers (see § 541.303); employees who hold a valid license or certificate permitting the practice of law or medicine or any of their branches and are actually engaged in the practice thereof (see § 541.304); or to employees who hold the requisite academic degree for the general practice of medicine and are engaged in an internship or resident program pursuant to the practice of the profession (see § 541.304). In the case of medical occupations, the exception from the salary or fee requirement does not apply to pharmacists, nurses, therapists, technologists, sanitarians, dietitians, social workers, psychologists, psychometrists, or other professions which service the medical profession.

§ 541.601 Highly compensated employees.

(a) An employee with total annual compensation of at least $100,000 is deemed exempt under section 13(a)(1) of the Act if the employee customarily and regularly performs any one or more of the exempt duties or responsibilities of an executive, administrative or professional employee identified in subparts B, C or D of this part.

(b)(1) "Total annual compensation" must include at least $455 per week paid on a salary or fee basis. Total annual compensation may also include commissions, nondiscretionary bonuses and other nondiscretionary compensation earned during a 52–week period. Total annual compensation does not include board, lodging and other facilities as defined in § 541.606, and does not include payments for medical insurance, payments for life insurance, contributions to retirement plans and the cost of other fringe benefits.

(2) If an employee's total annual compensation does not total at least the minimum amount established in paragraph (a) of this section by the last pay period of the 52–week period, the employer may, during the last pay period or within one month after the end of the 52–week period, make one final payment sufficient to achieve the required level. For example, an employee may earn $80,000 in base salary, and the employer may anticipate based upon past sales that the employee also will earn $20,000 in commissions. However, due to poor sales in the final quarter of the year, the employee actually only earns $10,000 in commissions. In this situation, the employer may within one month after the end of the year make a payment of at least $10,000 to the employee. Any such final payment made after the end of the 52–week period may count only toward the prior year's total annual compensation and not toward the total annual compensation in the year it was paid. If the

employer fails to make such a payment, the employee does not qualify as a highly compensated employee, but may still qualify as exempt under subparts B, C or D of this part.

(3) An employee who does not work a full year for the employer, either because the employee is newly hired after the beginning of the year or ends the employment before the end of the year, may qualify for exemption under this section if the employee receives a pro rata portion of the minimum amount established in paragraph (a) of this section, based upon the number of weeks that the employee will be or has been employed. An employer may make one final payment as under paragraph (b)(2) of this section within one month after the end of employment.

(4) The employer may utilize any 52–week period as the year, such as a calendar year, a fiscal year, or an anniversary of hire year. If the employer does not identify some other year period in advance, the calendar year will apply.

(c) A high level of compensation is a strong indicator of an employee's exempt status, thus eliminating the need for a detailed analysis of the employee's job duties. Thus, a highly compensated employee will qualify for exemption if the employee customarily and regularly performs any one or more of the exempt duties or responsibilities of an executive, administrative or professional employee identified in subparts B, C or D of this part. An employee may qualify as a highly compensated executive employee, for example, if the employee customarily and regularly directs the work of two or more other employees, even though the employee does not meet all of the other requirements for the executive exemption under § 541.100.

(d) This section applies only to employees whose primary duty includes performing office or non-manual work. Thus, for example, non-management production-line workers and non-management employees in maintenance, construction and similar occupations such as carpenters, electricians, mechanics, plumbers, iron workers, craftsmen, operating engineers, longshoremen, construction workers, laborers and other employees who perform work involving repetitive operations with their hands, physical skill and energy are not exempt under this section no matter how highly paid they might be.

§ 541.602   Salary basis.

(a) General rule. An employee will be considered to be paid on a "salary basis" within the meaning of these regulations if the employee regularly receives each pay period on a weekly, or less frequent basis, a predetermined amount constituting all or part of the employee's compensation, which amount is not subject to reduction because of variations in the quality or quantity of the work performed. Subject to the exceptions provided in paragraph (b) of this section, an exempt employee must receive the full salary for any week in which the employee performs any work without regard to the number of days or hours worked. Exempt employees need not be paid for any workweek in which they perform no work. An employee is not paid on a salary basis if deductions from the employee's predetermined compensation are made for absences occasioned by the employer or by the operating requirements of the business. If the employee is ready, willing and able to work, deductions may not be made for time when work is not available.

(b) Exceptions. The prohibition against deductions from pay in the salary basis requirement is subject to the following exceptions:

(1) Deductions from pay may be made when an exempt employee is absent from work for one or more full days for personal reasons, other than sickness or disability. Thus, if an employee is absent for two full days to handle personal affairs, the employee's salaried status will not be affected if deductions are made from the salary for two full-day absences. However, if an exempt employee is absent for one and a half days for personal reasons, the employer can deduct only for the one full-day absence.

(2) Deductions from pay may be made for absences of one or more full days occasioned by sickness or disability (including work-related accidents) if the deduction is made in accordance with a bona fide plan, policy or practice of providing compensation for loss of salary occasioned by such sickness or disability. The employer is not required to pay any portion of the employee's salary for full-day absences for which the employee receives compensation under the plan, policy or practice. Deductions for such full-day absences also may be made before the employee has qualified under the plan, policy or practice, and after the employee has exhausted the leave allowance thereunder. Thus, for example, if an employer maintains a short-term disability insurance plan providing salary replacement for 12 weeks starting on the fourth day of absence, the employer may make deductions from pay for the three days of absence before the employee qualifies for benefits under the plan; for the twelve weeks in which the employee receives salary replacement benefits under the plan; and for absences after the employee has exhausted the 12 weeks of salary replacement benefits. Similarly, an employer may make deductions from pay for absences of one or more full days if salary replacement benefits are provided under a State disability insurance law or under a State workers' compensation law.

(3) While an employer cannot make deductions from pay for absences of an exempt employee occasioned by jury duty, attendance as a witness or temporary military leave, the employer can offset any amounts received by an employee as jury fees, witness fees or military pay for a particular week against the salary due for that particular week without loss of the exemption.

(4) Deductions from pay of exempt employees may be made for penalties imposed in good faith for infractions of safety rules of major significance. Safety rules of major significance include those relating to the prevention of serious danger in the workplace or to

other employees, such as rules prohibiting smoking in explosive plants, oil refineries and coal mines.

(5) Deductions from pay of exempt employees may be made for unpaid disciplinary suspensions of one or more full days imposed in good faith for infractions of workplace conduct rules. Such suspensions must be imposed pursuant to a written policy applicable to all employees. Thus, for example, an employer may suspend an exempt employee without pay for three days for violating a generally applicable written policy prohibiting sexual harassment. Similarly, an employer may suspend an exempt employee without pay for twelve days for violating a generally applicable written policy prohibiting workplace violence.

(6) An employer is not required to pay the full salary in the initial or terminal week of employment. Rather, an employer may pay a proportionate part of an employee's full salary for the time actually worked in the first and last week of employment. In such weeks, the payment of an hourly or daily equivalent of the employee's full salary for the time actually worked will meet the requirement. However, employees are not paid on a salary basis within the meaning of these regulations if they are employed occasionally for a few days, and the employer pays them a proportionate part of the weekly salary when so employed.

(7) An employer is not required to pay the full salary for weeks in which an exempt employee takes unpaid leave under the Family and Medical Leave Act. Rather, when an exempt employee takes unpaid leave under the Family and Medical Leave Act, an employer may pay a proportionate part of the full salary for time actually worked. For example, if an employee who normally works 40 hours per week uses four hours of unpaid leave under the Family and Medical Leave Act, the employer could deduct 10 percent of the employee's normal salary that week.

(c) When calculating the amount of a deduction from pay allowed under paragraph (b) of this section, the employer may use the hourly or daily equivalent of the employee's full weekly salary or any other amount proportional to the time actually missed by the employee. A deduction from pay as a penalty for violations of major safety rules under paragraph (b)(4) of this section may be made in any amount.

§ 541.603   Effect of improper deductions from salary.

(a) An employer who makes improper deductions from salary shall lose the exemption if the facts demonstrate that the employer did not intend to pay employees on a salary basis. An actual practice of making improper deductions demonstrates that the employer did not intend to pay employees on a salary basis. The factors to consider when determining whether an employer has an actual practice of making improper deductions include, but are not limited to: the number of improper deductions, particularly as compared to the number of employee infractions warranting discipline; the time period during which the employer made improper deductions; the number and geographic location of employees whose salary was improperly reduced; the number and geographic location of managers responsible for taking the improper deductions; and whether the employer has a clearly communicated policy permitting or prohibiting improper deductions.

(b) If the facts demonstrate that the employer has an actual practice of making improper deductions, the exemption is lost during the time period in which the improper deductions were made for employees in the same job classification working for the same managers responsible for the actual improper deductions. Employees in different job classifications or who work for different managers do not lose their status as exempt employees. Thus, for example, if a manager at a company facility routinely docks the pay of engineers at that facility for partial-day personal absences, then all engineers at that facility whose pay could have been improperly docked by the manager would lose the exemption; engineers at other facilities or working for other managers, however, would remain exempt.

(c) Improper deductions that are either isolated or inadvertent will not result in loss of the exemption for any employees subject to such improper deductions, if the employer reimburses the employees for such improper deductions.

(d) If an employer has a clearly communicated policy that prohibits the improper pay deductions specified in § 541.602(a) and includes a complaint mechanism, reimburses employees for any improper deductions and makes a good faith commitment to comply in the future, such employer will not lose the exemption for any employees unless the employer willfully violates the policy by continuing to make improper deductions after receiving employee complaints. If an employer fails to reimburse employees for any improper deductions or continues to make improper deductions after receiving employee complaints, the exemption is lost during the time period in which the improper deductions were made for employees in the same job classification working for the same managers responsible for the actual improper deductions. The best evidence of a clearly communicated policy is a written policy that was distributed to employees prior to the improper pay deductions by, for example, providing a copy of the policy to employees at the time of hire, publishing the policy in an employee handbook or publishing the policy on the employer's Intranet.

(e) This section shall not be construed in an unduly technical manner so as to defeat the exemption.

§ 541.604 Minimum guarantee plus extras.

(a) An employer may provide an exempt employee with additional compensation without losing the exemption or violating the salary basis requirement, if the employment arrangement also includes a guarantee of at least the minimum weekly-required amount paid on a salary basis.

Thus, for example, an exempt employee guaranteed at least $455 each week paid on a salary basis may also receive additional compensation of a one percent commission on sales. An exempt employee also may receive a percentage of the sales or profits of the employer if the employment arrangement also includes a guarantee of at least $455 each week paid on a salary basis. Similarly, the exemption is not lost if an exempt employee who is guaranteed at least $455 each week paid on a salary basis also receives additional compensation based on hours worked for work beyond the normal workweek. Such additional compensation may be paid on any basis (e.g., flat sum, bonus payment, straight-time hourly amount, time and one-half or any other basis), and may include paid time off.

(b) An exempt employee's earnings may be computed on an hourly, a daily or a shift basis, without losing the exemption or violating the salary basis requirement, if the employment arrangement also includes a guarantee of at least the minimum weekly required amount paid on a salary basis regardless of the number of hours, days or shifts worked, and a reasonable relationship exists between the guaranteed amount and the amount actually earned. The reasonable relationship test will be met if the weekly guarantee is roughly equivalent to the employee's usual earnings at the assigned hourly, daily or shift rate for the employee's normal scheduled workweek. Thus, for example, an exempt employee guaranteed compensation of at least $500 for any week in which the employee performs any work, and who normally works four or five shifts each week, may be paid $150 per shift without violating the salary basis requirement. The reasonable relationship requirement applies only if the employee's pay is computed on an hourly, daily or shift basis. It does not apply, for example, to an exempt store manager paid a guaranteed salary of $650 per week who also receives a commission of one-half percent of all sales in the store or five percent of the store's profits, which in some weeks may total as much as, or even more than, the guaranteed salary.

§ 541.605   Fee basis.

(a) Administrative and professional employees may be paid on a fee basis, rather than on a salary basis. An employee will be considered to be paid on a "fee basis" within the meaning of these regulations if the employee is paid an agreed sum for a single job regardless of the time required for its completion. These payments resemble piecework payments with the important distinction that generally a "fee" is paid for the kind of job that is unique rather than for a series of jobs repeated an indefinite number of times and for which payment on an identical basis is made over and over again. Payments based on the number of hours or days worked and not on the accomplishment of a given single task are not considered payments on a fee basis.

(b) To determine whether the fee payment meets the minimum amount of salary required for exemption under these regulations, the amount paid to the employee will be tested by determining the time worked on the job and whether the fee payment is at a rate that would amount to at least $455 per week if the employee worked 40 hours. Thus, an artist paid $250 for a picture that took 20 hours to complete meets the minimum salary requirement for exemption since earnings at this rate would yield the artist $500 if 40 hours were worked.

§ 541.606   Board, lodging or other facilities.

(a) To qualify for exemption under section 13(a)(1) of the Act, an employee must earn the minimum salary amount set forth in § 541.600, "exclusive of board, lodging or other facilities." The phrase "exclusive of board, lodging or other facilities" means "free and clear" or independent of any claimed credit for non-cash items of value that an employer may provide to an employee. Thus, the costs incurred by an employer to provide an employee with board, lodging or other facilities may not count towards the minimum salary amount required for exemption under this part 541. Such separate transactions are not prohibited between employers and their exempt employees, but the costs to employers associated with such transactions may not be considered when determining if an employee has received the full required minimum salary payment.

(b) Regulations defining what constitutes "board, lodging, or other facilities" are contained in 29 CFR part 531. As described in 29 CFR 531.32, the term "other facilities" refers to items similar to board and lodging, such as meals furnished at company restaurants or cafeterias or by hospitals, hotels, or restaurants to their employees; meals, dormitory rooms, and tuition furnished by a college to its student employees; merchandise furnished at company stores or commissaries, including articles of food, clothing, and household effects; housing furnished for dwelling purposes; and transportation furnished to employees for ordinary commuting between their homes and work.

SUBPART H—DEFINITIONS AND MISCELLANEOUS PROVISIONS

§ 541.700   Primary duty.

(a) To qualify for exemption under this part, an employee's "primary duty" must be the performance of exempt work. The term "primary duty" means the principal, main, major or most important duty that the employee performs. Determination of an employee's primary duty must be based on all the facts in a particular case, with the major emphasis on the character of the employee's job as a whole. Factors to consider when determining the primary duty of an employee include, but are not limited to, the relative importance of the exempt duties as compared with other types of duties; the amount of time spent performing exempt work; the employee's relative freedom from direct supervision; and the relationship between the employee's salary and the wages paid to other employees for the kind of nonexempt work performed by the employee.

(b) The amount of time spent performing exempt work can be a useful guide in determining whether exempt work is the primary duty of an employee. Thus, employees who spend more than 50 percent of their time performing exempt work will generally satisfy the primary duty requirement. Time alone, however, is not the sole test, and nothing in this section requires that exempt employees spend more than 50 percent of their time performing exempt work. Employees who do not spend more than 50 percent of their time performing exempt duties may nonetheless meet the primary duty requirement if the other factors support such a conclusion.

(c) Thus, for example, assistant managers in a retail establishment who perform exempt executive work such as supervising and directing the work of other employees, ordering merchandise, managing the budget and authorizing payment of bills may have management as their primary duty even if the assistant managers spend more than 50 percent of the time performing nonexempt work such as running the cash register. However, if such assistant managers are closely supervised and earn little more than the nonexempt employees, the assistant managers generally would not satisfy the primary duty requirement.

§ 541.701   Customarily and regularly.

The phrase "customarily and regularly" means a frequency that must be greater than occasional but which, of course, may be less than constant. Tasks or work performed "customarily and regularly" includes work normally and recurrently performed every workweek; it does not include isolated or one-time tasks.

§ 541.702   Exempt and nonexempt work.

The term "exempt work" means all work described in §§ 541.100, 541.101, 541.200, 541.300, 541.301, 541.302, 541.303, 541.304, 541.400 and 541.500, and the activities directly and closely related to such work. All other work is considered "nonexempt."

§ 541.703   Directly and closely related.

(a) Work that is "directly and closely related" to the performance of exempt work is also considered exempt work. The phrase "directly and closely related" means tasks that are related to exempt duties and that contribute to or facilitate performance of exempt work. Thus, "directly and closely related" work may include physical tasks and menial tasks that arise out of exempt duties, and the routine work without which the exempt employee's exempt work cannot be performed properly. Work "directly and closely related" to the performance of exempt duties may also include recordkeeping; monitoring and adjusting machinery; taking notes; using the computer to create documents or presentations; opening the mail for the purpose of reading it and making decisions; and using a photocopier or fax machine. Work is not "directly and closely related" if the work is remotely related or completely unrelated to exempt duties.

(b) The following examples further illustrate the type of work that is and is not normally considered as directly and closely related to exempt work:

(1) Keeping time, production or sales records for subordinates is work directly and closely related to an exempt executive's function of managing a department and supervising employees.

(2) The distribution of materials, merchandise or supplies to maintain control of the flow of and expenditures for such items is directly and closely related to the performance of exempt duties.

(3) A supervisor who spot checks and examines the work of subordinates to determine whether they are performing their duties properly, and whether the product is satisfactory, is performing work which is directly and closely related to managerial and supervisory functions, so long as the checking is distinguishable from the work ordinarily performed by a nonexempt inspector.

(4) A supervisor who sets up a machine may be engaged in exempt work, depending upon the nature of the industry and the operation. In some cases the setup work, or adjustment of the machine for a particular job, is typically performed by the same employees who operate the machine. Such setup work is part of the production operation and is not exempt. In other cases, the setting up of the work is a highly skilled operation which the ordinary production worker or machine tender typically does not perform. In large plants, non-supervisors may perform such work. However, particularly in small plants, such work may be a regular duty of the executive and is directly and closely related to the executive's responsibility for the work performance of subordinates and for the adequacy of the final product. Under such circumstances, it is exempt work.

(5) A department manager in a retail or service establishment who walks about the sales floor observing the work of sales personnel under the employee's supervision to determine the effectiveness of their sales techniques, checks on the quality of customer service being given, or observes customer preferences is performing work which is directly and closely related to managerial and supervisory functions.

(6) A business consultant may take extensive notes recording the flow of work and materials through the office or plant of the client; after returning to the office of the employer, the consultant may personally use the computer to type a report and create a proposed table of organization. Standing alone, or separated from the primary duty, such note-taking and typing would be routine in nature. However, because this work is necessary for analyzing the data and making recommendations, the work is directly and closely related to exempt work. While it is possible to assign note-taking and typing to nonexempt employees, and in fact it is frequently the practice to do so, delegating such routine tasks is not required as a condition of exemption.

(7) A credit manager who makes and administers the credit policy of the employer, establishes credit limits for customers, au-

thorizes the shipment of orders on credit, and makes decisions on whether to exceed credit limits would be performing work exempt under § 541.200. Work that is directly and closely related to these exempt duties may include checking the status of accounts to determine whether the credit limit would be exceeded by the shipment of a new order, removing credit reports from the files for analysis, and writing letters giving credit data and experience to other employers or credit agencies.

(8) A traffic manager in charge of planning a company's transportation, including the most economical and quickest routes for shipping merchandise to and from the plant, contracting for common-carrier and other transportation facilities, negotiating with carriers for adjustments for damages to merchandise, and making the necessary rearrangements resulting from delays, damages or irregularities in transit, is performing exempt work. If the employee also spends part of the day taking telephone orders for local deliveries, such order-taking is a routine function and is not directly and closely related to the exempt work.

(9) An example of work directly and closely related to exempt professional duties is a chemist performing menial tasks such as cleaning a test tube in the middle of an original experiment, even though such menial tasks can be assigned to laboratory assistants.

(10) A teacher performs work directly and closely related to exempt duties when, while taking students on a field trip, the teacher drives a school van or monitors the students' behavior in a restaurant.

§ 541.704　Use of manuals.

The use of manuals, guidelines or other established procedures containing or relating to highly technical, scientific, legal, financial or other similarly complex matters that can be understood or interpreted only by those with advanced or specialized knowledge or skills does not preclude exemption under section 13(a)(1) of the Act or the regulations in this part. Such manuals and procedures provide guidance in addressing difficult or novel circumstances and thus use of such reference material would not affect an employee's exempt status. The section 13(a)(1) exemptions are not available, however, for employees who simply apply well-established techniques or procedures described in manuals or other sources within closely prescribed limits to determine the correct response to an inquiry or set of circumstances.

§ 541.705　Trainees.

The executive, administrative, professional, outside sales and computer employee exemptions do not apply to employees training for employment in an executive, administrative, professional, outside sales or computer employee capacity who are not actually performing the duties of an executive, administrative, professional, outside sales or computer employee.

§ 541.706   Emergencies.

(a) An exempt employee will not lose the exemption by performing work of a normally nonexempt nature because of the existence of an emergency. Thus, when emergencies arise that threaten the safety of employees, a cessation of operations or serious damage to the employer's property, any work performed in an effort to prevent such results is considered exempt work.

(b) An "emergency" does not include occurrences that are not beyond control or for which the employer can reasonably provide in the normal course of business. Emergencies generally occur only rarely, and are events that the employer cannot reasonably anticipate.

(c) The following examples illustrate the distinction between emergency work considered exempt work and routine work that is not exempt work:

(1) A mine superintendent who pitches in after an explosion and digs out workers who are trapped in the mine is still a bona fide executive.

(2) Assisting nonexempt employees with their work during periods of heavy workload or to handle rush orders is not exempt work.

(3) Replacing a nonexempt employee during the first day or partial day of an illness may be considered exempt emergency work depending on factors such as the size of the establishment and of the executive's department, the nature of the industry, the consequences that would flow from the failure to replace the ailing employee immediately, and the feasibility of filling the employee's place promptly.

(4) Regular repair and cleaning of equipment is not emergency work, even when necessary to prevent fire or explosion; however, repairing equipment may be emergency work if the breakdown of or damage to the equipment was caused by accident or carelessness that the employer could not reasonably anticipate.

§ 541.707   Occasional tasks.

Occasional, infrequently recurring tasks that cannot practicably be performed by nonexempt employees, but are the means for an exempt employee to properly carry out exempt functions and responsibilities, are considered exempt work. The following factors should be considered in determining whether such work is exempt work: whether the same work is performed by any of the exempt employee's subordinates; practicability of delegating the work to a nonexempt employee; whether the exempt employee performs the task frequently or occasionally; and existence of an industry practice for the exempt employee to perform the task.

§ 541.708   Combination exemptions.

Employees who perform a combination of exempt duties as set forth in the regulations in this part for executive, administrative, professional, outside sales and computer employees may qualify for exemption. Thus, for example, an employee whose primary duty involves a combination of exempt administrative and exempt executive work may qualify for exemption. In other words, work that is exempt under one section of this part will not defeat the exemption under any other section.

§ 541.709   Motion picture producing industry.

The requirement that the employee be paid "on a salary basis" does not apply to an employee in the motion picture producing industry who is compensated at a base rate of at least $695 a week (exclusive of board, lodging, or other facilities). Thus, an employee in this industry who is otherwise exempt under subparts B, C or D of this part, and who is employed at a base rate of at least $695 a week is exempt if paid a proportionate amount (based on a week of not more than 6 days) for any week in which the employee does not work a full workweek for any reason. Moreover, an otherwise exempt employee in this industry qualifies for exemption if the employee is employed at a daily rate under the following circumstances:

(a) The employee is in a job category for which a weekly base rate is not provided and the daily base rate would yield at least $695 if 6 days were worked; or

(b) The employee is in a job category having a weekly base rate of at least $695 and the daily base rate is at least one-sixth of such weekly base rate.

§ 541.710   Employees of public agencies.

(a) An employee of a public agency who otherwise meets the salary basis requirements of § 541.602 shall not be disqualified from exemption under §§ 541.100, 541.200, 541.300 or 541.400 on the basis that such employee is paid according to a pay system established by statute, ordinance or regulation, or by a policy or practice established pursuant to principles of public accountability, under which the employee accrues personal leave and sick leave and which requires the public agency employee's pay to be reduced or such employee to be placed on leave without pay for absences for personal reasons or because of illness or injury of less than one work-day when accrued leave is not used by an employee because:

(1) Permission for its use has not been sought or has been sought and denied;

(2) Accrued leave has been exhausted; or

(3) The employee chooses to use leave without pay.

(b) Deductions from the pay of an employee of a public agency for absences due to a budget-required furlough shall not disqualify the employee from being paid on a salary basis except in the workweek in which the furlough occurs and for which the employee's pay is accordingly reduced.

§ 221. Collection or receipt of wages previously paid

It shall be unlawful for any employer to collect or receive from an employee any part of wages theretofore paid by said employer to said employee.

NEW YORK LABOR LAW §§ 190–93, 197–98

§ 190. Definitions

As used in this article:

1. "Wages" means the earnings of an employee for labor or services rendered, regardless of whether the amount of earnings is determined on a time, piece, commission or other basis. The term "wages" also includes benefits or wage supplements as defined in section one hundred ninety-eight-c of this article, except for the purposes of sections one hundred ninety-one and one hundred ninety-two of this article.

2. "Employee" means any person employed for hire by an employer in any employment.

3. "Employer" includes any person, corporation, limited liability company, or association employing any individual in any occupation, industry, trade, business or service. The term "employer" shall not include a governmental agency.

4. "Manual worker" means a mechanic, workingman or laborer.

5. "Railroad worker" means any person employed by an employer who operates a steam, electric or diesel surface railroad or is engaged in the sleeping car business. The term "railroad worker" shall not include a person employed in an executive capacity.

6. "Commission salesman" means any employee whose principal activity is the selling of any goods, wares, merchandise, services, real estate, securities, insurance or any article or thing and whose earnings are based in whole or in part on commissions. The term "commission salesman" does not include an employee whose principal activity is of a supervisory, managerial, executive or administrative nature.

7. "Clerical and other worker" includes all employees not included in subdivisions four, five and six of this section, except any person employed in a bona fide executive, administrative or professional capacity whose earnings are in excess of * * * nine hundred dollars a week.

8. "Week" means a calendar week or a regularly established payroll week. "Month" means a calendar month or a regularly established fiscal month.

9. "Non-profitmaking organization" means a corporation, unincorporated association, community chest, fund or foundation organized and operated exclusively for religious, charitable or educational purposes, no part of the net earnings of which inure to the benefit of any private shareholder or individual.

§ 191. Frequency of payments [omitted]

§ 192. Cash payment of wages

1. No employer shall without the advance written consent of any employee directly pay or deposit the net wage or salary of such employee in a bank or other financial institution.

2. This section shall not apply to any person employed in a bona fide executive, administrative, or professional capacity whose earnings are in excess of nine hundred dollars a week, nor to employees working on a farm not connected with a factory.

§ 193. Deductions from wages

1. No employer shall make any deduction from the wages of an employee, except deductions which:

a. are made in accordance with the provisions of any law or any rule or regulation issued by any governmental agency; or

b. are expressly authorized in writing by the employee and are for the benefit of the employee; provided that such authorization is kept on file on the employer's premises. Such authorized deductions shall be limited to payments for insurance premiums, pension or health and welfare benefits, contributions to charitable organizations, payments for United States bonds, payments for dues or assessments to a labor organization, and similar payments for the benefit of the employee.

2. No employer shall make any charge against wages, or require an employee to make any payment by separate transaction unless such charge or payment is permitted as a deduction from wages under the provisions of subdivision one of this section.

3. Nothing in this section shall justify noncompliance with article three-A of the personal property law relating to assignment of earnings, nor with any other law applicable to deductions from wages.

§ 197. Civil penalty

Any employer who fails to pay the wages of his employees or shall differentiate in rate of pay because of sex, as provided in this article, shall forfeit to the people of the state the sum of five hundred dollars for each such failure, to be recovered by the commissioner in a civil action.

§ 198. Costs, remedies

1. In any action instituted upon a wage claim by an employee or the commissioner in which the employee prevails, the court may allow such employee in addition to ordinary costs, a reasonable sum, not exceeding fifty dollars for expenses which may be taxed as costs. No assignee of a wage claim, except the commissioner, shall be benefited by this provision.

1–a. In any action instituted upon a wage claim by an employee or the commissioner in which the employee prevails, the court shall allow such employee reasonable attorney's fees and, upon a finding that the employer's failure to pay the wage required by this article was willful, an additional amount as liquidated damages equal to twenty-five percent of the total amount of the wages found to be due.

2. The remedies provided by this article may be enforced simultaneously or consecutively so far as not inconsistent with each other.

3. Notwithstanding any other provision of law, an action to recover upon a liability imposed by this article must be commenced within six years. All employees shall have the right to recover full wages, benefits and wage supplements accrued during the six years previous to the commencing of such action, whether such action is instituted by the employee or by the commissioner.

Part E

ISSUES OF PROCEDURAL DESIGN

FEDERAL RULES OF CIVIL PROCEDURE
F.R.CIV.P. 23

Rule 23. Class Actions

(a) Prerequisites. One or more members of a class may sue or be sued as representative parties on behalf of all members only if:

(1) the class is so numerous that joinder of all members is impracticable;

(2) there are questions of law or fact common to the class;

(3) the claims or defenses of the representative parties are typical of the claims or defenses of the class; and

(4) the representative parties will fairly and adequately protect the interests of the class.

(b) Types of Class Actions. A class action may be maintained if Rule 23(a) is satisfied and if:

(1) prosecuting separate actions by or against individual class members would create a risk of:

(A) inconsistent or varying adjudications with respect to individual class members that would establish incompatible standards of conduct for the party opposing the class; or

(B) adjudications with respect to individual class members that, as a practical matter, would be dispositive of the interests of the other members not parties to the individual adjudications or would substantially impair or impede their ability to protect their interests;

(2) the party opposing the class has acted or refused to act on grounds that apply generally to the class, so that final injunctive relief or corresponding declaratory relief is appropriate respecting the class as a whole; or

(3) the court finds that the questions of law or fact common to class members predominate over any questions affecting only individual members, and that a class action is superior to other available methods for fairly and efficiently adjudicating the controversy. The matters pertinent to these findings include:

(A) the class members' interests in individually controlling the prosecution or defense of separate actions;

(B) the extent and nature of any litigation concerning the controversy already begun by or against class members;

(C) the desirability or undesirability of concentrating the litigation of the claims in the particular forum; and

(D) the likely difficulties in managing a class action.

(c) Certification Order; Notice to Class Members; Judgment; Issues Classes; Subclasses.

(1) *Certification Order.*

(A) Time to Issue. At an early practicable time after a person sues or is sued as a class representative, the court must determine by order whether to certify the action as a class action.

(B) Defining the Class; Appointing Class Counsel. An order that certifies a class action must define the class and the class claims, issues, or defenses, and must appoint class counsel under Rule 23(g).

(C) Altering or Amending the Order. An order that grants or denies class certification may be altered or amended before final judgment.

(2) *Notice.*

(A) For (b)(1) or (b)(2) Classes. For any class certified under Rule 23(b)(1) or (b)(2), the court may direct appropriate notice to the class.

(B) For (b)(3) Classes. For any class certified under Rule 23(b)(3), the court must direct to class members the best notice that is practicable under the circumstances, including individual notice to all members who can be identified through reasonable effort. The notice must clearly and concisely state in plain, easily understood language:

(i) the nature of the action;

(ii) the definition of the class certified;

(iii) the class claims, issues, or defenses;

(iv) that a class member may enter an appearance through an attorney if the member so desires;

(v) that the court will exclude from the class any member who requests exclusion;

(vi) the time and manner for requesting exclusion; and

(vii) the binding effect of a class judgment on members under Rule 23(c)(3).

(3) *Judgment.* Whether or not favorable to the class, the judgment in a class action must:

(A) for any class certified under Rule 23(b)(1) or (b)(2), include and describe those whom the court finds to be class members; and

(B) for any class certified under Rule 23(b)(3), include and specify or describe those to whom the Rule 23(c) (2) notice was directed, who have not requested exclusion, and whom the court finds to be class members.

(4) *Particular Issues.* When appropriate, an action may be maintained as a class action with respect to particular issues.

(5) *Subclasses.* When appropriate, a class may be divided into subclasses that are each treated as a class under this rule.

(d) Conducting the Action.

(1) *In General.* In conducting an action under this rule, the court may issue orders that:

    (A) determine the course of proceedings or prescribe measures to prevent undue repetition or complication in presenting evidence or argument;

    (B) require—to protect class members and fairly conduct the action—giving appropriate notice to some or all class members of:

        (i) any step in the action;

        (ii) the proposed extent of the judgment; or

        (iii) the members' opportunity to signify whether they consider the representation fair and adequate, to intervene and present claims or defenses, or to otherwise come into the action;

    (C) impose conditions on the representative parties or on intervenors;

    (D) require that the pleadings be amended to eliminate allegations about representation of absent persons and that the action proceed accordingly; or

    (E) deal with similar procedural matters.

(2) *Combining and Amending Orders.* An order under Rule 23(d)(1) may be altered or amended from time to time and may be combined with an order under Rule 16.

(e) Settlement, Voluntary Dismissal, or Compromise. The claims, issues, or defenses of a certified class may be settled, voluntarily dismissed, or compromised only with the court's approval. The following procedures apply to a proposed settlement, voluntary dismissal, or compromise:

(1) The court must direct notice in a reasonable manner to all class members who would be bound by the proposal.

(2) If the proposal would bind class members, the court may approve it only after a hearing and on finding that it is fair, reasonable, and adequate.

(3) The parties seeking approval must file a statement identifying any agreement made in connection with the proposal.

(4) If the class action was previously certified under Rule 23(b)(3), the court may refuse to approve a settlement unless it affords a new opportunity to request exclusion to individual class members who had an earlier opportunity to request exclusion but did not do so.

(5) Any class member may object to the proposal if it requires court approval under this subdivision (e); the objection may be withdrawn only with the court's approval.

(f) Appeals. A court of appeals may permit an appeal from an order granting or denying class-action certification under this rule if a petition for permission to appeal is filed with the circuit clerk within 10 days after the order is entered. An appeal does not stay proceedings in the district court unless the district judge or the court of appeals so orders.

(g) Class Counsel.

(1) *Appointing Class Counsel.* Unless a statute provides otherwise, a court that certifies a class must appoint class counsel. In appointing class counsel, the court:

(A) must consider:

(i) the work counsel has done in identifying or investigating potential claims in the action;

(ii) counsel's experience in handling class actions, other complex litigation, and the types of claims asserted in the action;

(iii) counsel's knowledge of the applicable law; and

(iv) the resources that counsel will commit to representing the class;

(B) may consider any other matter pertinent to counsel's ability to fairly and adequately represent the interests of the class;

(C) may order potential class counsel to provide information on any subject pertinent to the appointment and to propose terms for attorney's fees and nontaxable costs;

(D) may include in the appointing order provisions about the award of attorney's fees or nontaxable costs under Rule 23(h); and

(E) may make further orders in connection with the appointment.

(2) *Standard for Appointing Class Counsel.* When one applicant seeks appointment as class counsel, the court may appoint that applicant only if the applicant is adequate under Rule 23(g)(1) and (4). If more than one adequate applicant seeks appointment, the court must appoint the applicant best able to represent the interests of the class.

(3) *Interim Counsel.* The court may designate interim counsel to act on behalf of a putative class before determining whether to certify the action as a class action.

(4) *Duty of Class Counsel.* Class counsel must fairly and adequately represent the interests of the class.

(h) Attorney's Fees and Nontaxable Costs. In a certified class action, the court may award reasonable attorney's fees and nontaxable costs that are authorized by law or by the parties' agreement. The following procedures apply:

(1) A claim for an award must be made by motion under Rule 54(d)(2), subject to the provisions of this subdivision (h), at a time the court sets. Notice of the motion must be served on all parties and, for motions by class counsel, directed to class members in a reasonable manner.

(2) A class member, or a party from whom payment is sought, may object to the motion.

(3) The court may hold a hearing and must find the facts and state its legal conclusions under Rule 52(a).

(4) The court may refer issues related to the amount of the award to a special master or a magistrate judge, as provided in Rule 54(d)(2)(D).

FULL FAITH AND CREDIT ACT
28 U.S.C. § 1738

§ 1738. State and Territorial statutes and judicial proceedings; full faith and credit

The Acts of the legislature of any State, Territory, or Possession of the United States, or copies thereof, shall be authenticated by affixing the seal of such State, Territory or Possession thereto.

The records and judicial proceedings of any court of any such State, Territory or Possession, or copies thereof, shall be proved or admitted in other courts within the United States and its Territories and Possessions by the attestation of the clerk and seal of the court annexed, if a seal exists, together with a certificate of a judge of the court that the said attestation is in proper form.

Such Acts, records and judicial proceedings or copies thereof, so authenticated, shall have the same full faith and credit in every court within the United States and its Territories and Possessions as they have by law or usage in the courts of such State, Territory or Possession from which they are taken.

(June 25, 1948, c. 646, 62 Stat. 947.)

FEDERAL ARBITRATION ACT—
SELECTED PROVISIONS
9 U.S.C. §§ 1–5, 9–11, 16

§ 1. "Maritime transactions" and "Commerce" defined; exceptions to operation of title

"Maritime transactions", as herein defined, means charter parties, bills of lading of water carriers, agreements relating to wharfage, supplies furnished vessels or repairs to vessels, collisions, or any other matters in foreign commerce which, if the subject of controversy, would be embraced within admiralty jurisdiction; "commerce", as herein defined, means commerce among the several States or with foreign nations, or in any Territory of the United States or in the District of Columbia, or between any such Territory and another, or between any such Territory and any State or foreign nation, or between the District of Columbia and any State or Territory or foreign nation, but nothing herein contained shall apply to contracts of employment of seamen, railroad employees, or any other class of workers engaged in foreign or interstate commerce.

(July 30, 1947, c. 392, 61 Stat. 670.)

§ 2. Validity, irrevocability, and enforcement of agreements to arbitrate

A written provision in any maritime transaction or a contract evidencing a transaction involving commerce to settle by arbitration a controversy thereafter arising out of such contract or transaction, or the refusal to perform the whole or any part thereof, or an agreement in writing to submit to arbitration an existing controversy arising out of such a contract, transaction, or refusal, shall be valid, irrevocable, and enforceable, save upon such grounds as exist at law or in equity for the revocation of any contract.

(July 30, 1947, c. 392, 61 Stat. 670.)

§ 3. Stay of proceedings where issue therein referable to arbitration

If any suit or proceeding be brought in any of the courts of the United States upon any issue referable to arbitration under an agreement in writing for such arbitration, the court in which such suit is pending, upon being satisfied that the issue involved in such suit or proceeding is referable to arbitration under such an agreement, shall on application of one of the parties stay the trial of the action until such arbitration has been had in accordance with the terms of the agreement, providing the applicant for the stay is not in default in proceeding with such arbitration.

(July 30, 1947, c. 392, 61 Stat. 670.)

§ 4. Failure to arbitrate under agreement; petition to United States court having jurisdiction for order to compel arbitration; notice and service thereof; hearing and determination

A party aggrieved by the alleged failure, neglect, or refusal of another to arbitrate under a written agreement for arbitration may petition any United States district court which, save for such agreement, would have jurisdiction under title 28, in a civil action or in admiralty of the subject matter of a suit arising out of the controversy between the parties, for an order directing that such arbitration proceed in the manner provided for in such agreement. Five days' notice in writing of such application shall be served upon the party in default. Service thereof shall be made in the manner provided by the Federal Rules of Civil Procedure. The court shall hear the parties, and upon being satisfied that the making of the agreement for arbitration or the failure to comply therewith is not in issue, the court shall make an order directing the parties to proceed to arbitration in accordance with the terms of the agreement. The hearing and proceedings, under such agreement, shall be within the district in which the petition for an order directing such arbitration is filed. If the making of the arbitration agreement or the failure, neglect, or refusal to perform the same be in issue, the court shall proceed summarily to the trial thereof. If no jury trial be demanded by the party alleged to be in default, or if the matter in dispute is within admiralty jurisdiction, the court shall hear and determine such issue. Where such an issue is raised, the party alleged to be in default may, except in cases of admiralty, on or before the return day of the notice of application, demand a jury trial of such issue, and upon such demand the court shall make an order referring the issue or issues to a jury in the manner provided by the Federal Rules of Civil Procedure, or may specially call a jury for that purpose. If the jury find that no agreement in writing for arbitration was made or that there is no default in proceeding thereunder, the proceeding shall be dismissed. If the jury find that an agreement for arbitration was made in writing and that there is a default in proceeding thereunder, the court shall make an order summarily directing the parties to proceed with the arbitration in accordance with the terms thereof.

(July 30, 1947, ch. 392, 61 Stat. 671; Sept. 3, 1954, ch. 1263, at 19, 68 Stat. 1233.)

§ 5. Appointment of arbitrators or umpire

If in the agreement provision be made for a method of naming or appointing an arbitrator or arbitrators or an umpire, such method shall be followed; but if no method be provided therein, or if a method be provided and any party thereto shall fail to avail himself of such method, or if for any other reason there shall be a lapse in the naming of an arbitrator or arbitrators or umpire, or in filling a vacancy, then upon the application of either party to the controversy the court shall designate and appoint an arbitrator or arbitrators or umpire, as the case may require, who shall act under the said agreement with the same force and effect as if he or they had been specifically named therein; and unless otherwise provided in the agreement the arbitration shall be by a single arbitrator.

(July 30, 1947, c. 392, 61 Stat. 671.)

§ 9. Award of arbitrators; confirmation; jurisdiction; procedure

If the parties in their agreement have agreed that a judgment of the court shall be entered upon the award made pursuant to the arbitration, and shall specify the court, then at any time within one year after the award is made any party to the arbitration may apply to the court so specified for an order confirming the award, and thereupon the court must grant such an order unless the award is vacated, modified, or corrected as prescribed in sections 10 and 11 of this title. If no court is specified in the agreement of the parties, then such application may be made to the United States court in and for the district within which such award was made. Notice of the application shall be served upon the adverse party, and thereupon the court shall have jurisdiction of such party as though he had appeared generally in the proceeding. If the adverse party is a resident of the district within which the award was made, such service shall be made upon the adverse party or his attorney as prescribed by law for service of notice of motion in an action in the same court. If the adverse party shall be a non-resident, then the notice of the application shall be served by the marshal of any district within which the adverse party may be found in like manner as other process of the court.

(July 30, 1947, c. 392, 61 Stat. 672.)

§ 10. Same; vacation; grounds; rehearing

(a) In any of the following cases the United States court in and for the district wherein the award was made may make an order vacating the award upon the application of any party to the arbitration—

(1) where the award was procured by corruption, fraud, or undue means;

(2) where there was evident partiality or corruption in the arbitrators, or either of them;

(3) where the arbitrators were guilty of misconduct in refusing to postpone the hearing, upon sufficient cause shown, or in refusing to hear evidence pertinent and material to the controversy; or of any other misbehavior by which the rights of any party have been prejudiced; or

(4) where the arbitrators exceeded their powers, or so imperfectly executed them that a mutual, final, and definite award upon the subject matter submitted was not made.

(b) If an award is vacated and the time within which the agreement required the award to be made has not expired the court may, in its discretion, direct a rehearing by the arbitrators.

* * *

(July 30, 1947, c. 392, 61 Stat. 672; Nov. 15, 1990, P.L. 101–552, 104 Stat. 2745, Aug. 29, 1992, P.L. 102–334, 106 Stat. 946, P.L. 107–169, 116 Stat. 132.)

§ 11.   Same; modification or correction; grounds; order

In either of the following cases the United States court in and for the district wherein the award was made may make an order modifying or correcting the award upon the application of any party to the arbitration?

(a) Where there was an evident material miscalculation of figures or an evident material mistake in the description of any person, thing, or property referred to in the award.

(b) Where the arbitrators have awarded upon a matter not submitted to them, unless it is a matter not affecting the merits of the decision upon the matter submitted.

(c) Where the award is imperfect in matter of form not affecting the merits of the controversy.

The order may modify and correct the award, so as to effect the intent thereof and promote justice between the parties.

(July 30, 1947, c. 392, 61 Stat. 673.)

§ 16.   Appeals

(a) An appeal may be taken from—

(1) an order

(A) refusing a stay of any action under section 3 of this title,

(B) denying a petition under section 4 of this title to order arbitration to proceed,

(C) denying an application under section 206 of this title to compel arbitration,

(D) confirming or denying confirmation of an award or partial award, or

(E) modifying, correcting, or vacating an award;

(2) an interlocutory order granting, continuing, or modifying an injunction against an arbitration that is subject to this title; or

(3) a final decision with respect to an arbitration that is subject to this title.

(b) Except as otherwise provided in section 1292(b) of title 28, an appeal may not be taken from an interlocutory order—

(1) granting a stay of any action under section 3 of this title;

(2) directing arbitration to proceed under section 4 of this title;

(3) compelling arbitration under section 206 of this title; or

(4) refusing to enjoin an arbitration that is subject to this title.

(Added Nov. 19, 1988, P.L. 100–702, Title X, § 1019(a), 102 Stat. 4671; Dec. 1, 1990, P.L. 101–650, Title III, § 325(a)(1), 104 Stat. 5120.)

§ 201. Enforcement of Convention

The Convention on the Recognition and Enforcement of Foreign Arbitral Awards of June 10, 1958, shall be enforced in United States courts in accordance with this chapter [9 U.S.C. §§ 201 et seq.].

(Added July 31, 1970, P.L. 91–368, § 1, 84 Stat. 692.)

§ 202. Agreement or award falling under the Convention

An arbitration agreement or arbitral award arising out of a legal relationship, whether contractual or not, which is considered as commercial, including a transaction, contract, or agreement described in section 2 of this title [9 U.S.C. § 2], falls under the Convention. An agreement or award arising out of such a relationship which is entirely between citizens of the United States shall be deemed not to fall under the Convention unless that relationship involves property located abroad, envisages performance or enforcement abroad, or has some other reasonable relation with one or more foreign states. For the purpose of this section a corporation is a citizen of the United States if it is incorporated or has its principal place of business in the United States.

(Added July 31, 1970, P.L. 91–368, § 1, 84 Stat. 692.)

§ 203. Jurisdiction; amount in controversy

An action or proceeding falling under the Convention shall be deemed to arise under the laws and treaties of the United States. The district courts of the United States (including the courts enumerated in section 460 of title 28 [28 U.S.C. § 460]) shall have original jurisdiction over such an action or proceeding, regardless of the amount in controversy.

(Added July 31, 1970, P.L. 91–368, § 1, 84 Stat. 692.)

§ 204. Venue

An action or proceeding over which the district courts have jurisdiction pursuant to section 203 of this title [9 U.S.C. § 203] may be brought in any such court in which save for the arbitration agreement an action or proceeding with respect to the controversy between the parties could be brought, or in such court for the district and division which embraces the place designated in the agreement as the place of arbitration if such place is within the United States.

(Added July 31, 1970, P.L. 91–368, § 1, 84 Stat. 692.)

* * *

§ 206. Order to compel arbitration; appointment of arbitrators

A court having jurisdiction under this chapter [9 U.S.C. §§ 201 et seq.] may direct that arbitration be held in accordance with the agreement at any place therein provided for, whether that place is within or without the United States. Such court may also appoint arbitrators in accordance with the provisions of the agreement.

(Added July 31, 1970, P.L. 91–368, § 1, 84 Stat. 693.)

§ 207. Award of arbitrators; confirmation; jurisdiction; proceeding

Within three years after an arbitral award falling under the Convention is made, any party to the arbitration may apply to any court having jurisdiction under this chapter [9 U.S.C. §§ 201 et seq.] for an order confirming the award as against any other party to the arbitration. The court shall confirm the award unless it finds one of the grounds for refusal or deferral of recognition or enforcement of the award specified in the said Convention.

(Added July 31, 1970, P.L. 91–368, § 1, 84 Stat. 693.)

§ 208. Chapter 1; residual application

Chapter 1 [9 U.S.C. §§ 1 et seq.] applies to actions and proceedings brought under this chapter [9 U.S.C. §§ 201 et seq.] to the extent that chapter is not in conflict with this chapter [9 U.S.C. §§ 201 et seq.] or the Convention as ratified by the United States.

(Added July 31, 1970, P.L. 91–368, § 1, 84 Stat. 693.)

†